DISCIPLESHIP
IN THE NEW AGE

Volume Two

BOOKS BY ALICE A. BAILEY

DISCIPLESHIP IN THE NEW AGE

Volume Two

by

ALICE A. BAILEY

LUCIS PUBLISHING COMPANY
New York

LUCIS PRESS LTD.
London

First printing, 1955

Fifth Printing, 1979 (2nd Paperback Edition)

Sixth printing, 1980

The publication of this book is financed by the Tibetan Book Fund which is established for the perpetuation of the teachings of the Tibetan and Alice A. Bailey.

This Fund is controlled by the Lucis Trust, a tax-exempt, religious, educational corporation.

The Lucis Publishing Company is a non-profit organisation owned by the Lucis Trust. No royalties are paid on this book.

It has been translated into Dutch, Spanish, French, German, Italian and Greek. Translation into other languages is proceeding.

MANUFACTURED IN THE UNITED STATES OF AMERICA
By FORT ORANGE PRESS, INC., Albany, N. Y.

DEDICATED TO

THE MASTER DJWHAL KHUL

THE GREAT INVOCATION

From the point of Light within the Mind of God
Let light stream forth into the minds of men.
Let Light descend on Earth.

From the point of Love within the Heart of God
Let love stream forth into the hearts of men.
May Christ return to Earth.

From the centre where the Will of God is known
Let purpose guide the little wills of men—
The purpose which the Masters know and serve.

From the centre which we call the race of men
Let the Plan of Love and Light work out
And may it seal the door where evil dwells.

Let Light and Love and Power restore the Plan on Earth.

The above Invocation or Prayer does not belong to any person or group but to all Humanity. By using it and encouraging others to use it, no particular group or organization is being sponsored.

This Invocation appears frequently in newspapers and magazines in many countries, and is being broadcast by radio stations all over the world. Many thousands of people are using it every day, thus creating a world-wide spiritual public opinion which can become irresistible.

"The beauty and the strength of this Invocation lies in its simplicity, and in its expression of certain central truths which all men, innately and normally, accept—the truth of the existence of a basic Intelligence to Whom we vaguely give the name of God; the truth that behind all outer seeming, the motivating power of the universe is Love; the truth that a great Individuality came to earth, called by Christians the Christ, and embodied that love so that we could understand; the truth that both love and intelligence are effects of what is called the Will of God; and finally the self-evident truth that only through *humanity* itself can the divine Plan work out."—ALICE A. BAILEY.

EXTRACT FROM A STATEMENT BY THE TIBETAN

Suffice it to say, that I am a Tibetan disciple of a certain degree, and this tells you but little, for all are disciples from the humblest aspirant up to, and beyond, the Christ Himself. I live in a physical body like other men, on the borders of Tibet, and at times (from the exoteric standpoint) preside over a large group of Tibetan lamas, when my other duties permit. It is this fact that has caused it to be reported that I am an abbot of this particular lamasery. Those associated with me in the work of the Hierarchy (and all true disciples are associated in this work) know me by still another name and office. A.A.B. knows who I am and recognises me by two of my names.

I am a brother of yours, who has travelled a little longer upon the Path than has the average student, and has therefore incurred greater responsibilities. I am one who has wrestled and fought his way into a greater measure of light than has the aspirant who will read this article, and I must therefore act as a transmitter of the light, no matter what the cost. I am not an old man, as age counts among the teachers, yet I am not young or inexperienced. My work is to teach and spread the knowledge of the Ageless Wisdom wherever I can find a response, and I have been doing this for many years. I seek also to help the Master M. and the Master K.H. whenever opportunity offers, for I have been long connected with Them and with Their work. In all the above, I have told you much; yet at the same time I have told you nothing which would lead you to offer me that blind obedience and the foolish devotion which the emotional aspirant offers to the Guru and Master Whom he is as yet unable to contact. Nor will he make that desired contact until he has transmuted emotional devotion into unselfish service to humanity,—not to the Master.

The books that I have written are sent out with no claim for their acceptance. They may, or may not, be correct, true

vii

and useful. It is for you to ascertain their truth by right practice and by the exercise of the intuition. Neither I nor A.A.B. is the least interested in having them acclaimed as inspired writings, or in having anyone speak of them (with bated breath) as being the work of one of the Masters. If they present truth in such a way that it follows sequentially upon that already offered in the world teachings, if the information given raises the aspiration and the will-to-serve from the plane of the emotions to that of the mind (the plane whereon the Masters *can* be found) then they will have served their purpose. If the teaching conveyed calls forth a response from the illumined mind of the worker in the world, and brings a flashing forth of his intuition, then let that teaching be accepted. But not otherwise. If the statements meet with eventual corroboration, or are deemed true under the test of the Law of Correspondences, then that is well and good. But should this not be so, let not the student accept what is said.

AUGUST 1934

TABLE OF CONTENTS

INTRODUCTION

MRS. BAILEY asked me to write an introduction to the second volume of "Discipleship in the New Age" and I therefore now gladly comply. The introduction written by her in the first volume may be profitably reread in relation to both volumes.

The Master Djwhal Khul, known also as "The Tibetan," took advantage of the opportunity of the availability of A.A.B. as a trained collaborator and initiated an unique and pionecring experiment in new age training for group initiation. This involved the entry of those qualifying into His Ashram there to stay as they hastened their progress or to pass on to other Ashrams as the case might be.

For this purpose the Master selected some fifty people, most but not all of whom were known to A.A.B., to whom this unique and transcendent opportunity was offered. Almost everyone accepted but some did not stay very long. It was not easy. As was inevitable and very human, some as time went on reacted well, others not. It is hard to keep a right balance between the soul and the personality when the spiritual stimulant is relentlessly high. The rushing into the personal life of soul force is like sunshine in a garden. Weeds as well as flowers emerge.

It was a new age group forcing process, tested in operation by the use of this group of chelas all of whom had voluntarily accepted, and any one of whom was free to leave at any time without blame. The values achieved were much more than any obvious comment can display. Much of the deeper values are more subtle and slow to emerge. Individuals benefited greatly. As a group achievement it was not a success as is made abundantly clear in these pages, but the group is a living entity on the inner planes of possible great future usefulness.

Mrs. Bailey gave unsparingly of her life and strength to do this work which was to her an extra and a heavy burden. It was particularly distasteful to her to take the personal instructions. Indeed sometimes when certain individuals did not like what the Tibetan said to them about themselves they blamed her.

The training given to this group was not a part of Mrs. Bailey's system of training in the Arcane School. The Arcane School is not a training school for initiation and the goal is not to help the student to get into an ashram or to contact a Master. The purpose of the Arcane School is, and always has been, to help the student to move forward more quickly on the Path of Discipleship. It does not deal either with the problems incident to the Probationary Path nor of the Path of Initiation. The Master Djwhal Khul has stated that in the new age the field of training for the disciple is in the New Group of World Servers.

The decision to publish the record (or most of it) was an unexpected development to the Tibetan but welcomed by Him. He said that this act attracted the attention of other members of the Hierarchy. The appearance of the first volume has already proved a major addition to the entire esoteric field, especially in terms of what modern discipleship really is, and the practical realistic attitude that a Master has to his chela.

This second volume brings additional teaching both in the general text and in the remaining personal instructions which are amazingly frank and direct. A few personally assigned meditations are included to show the technique of the training in individual cases, but the individual training was always incidental to a planned special group achievement.

It should be remembered that these meditations are dangerous to use except as prescribed by a Master and used under His watchful eye, just as there are many medicines available to the public which are not safe except as directed by a physician.

An examination of the text will reveal many factors knowable only to a Master which made these meditations safe and the breathing exercises useful while He was watching the effects. For example: He knew not only the Ray qualities of all the vehicles but also the degree of response to Ray stimulant of any particular vehicle in relation to total, balanced progress. He knew also the conditioning Rays of the previous incarnation which may appear as a "hangover" not to be developed but to be transcended.

He knew the astrological characteristics of the soul, a factor as yet unknown to present day astrology but of much importance in advanced stages of discipleship.

He knew the exact condition and degree of unfoldment of all the force centres in the chela which in certain cases He stated in exact percentages. Even with this knowledge given us we could not know which centre to stimulate next nor how much. Moreover Djwhal Khul has said that given a consecrated active life of selfless service to one's fellow man the centres will unfold naturally and safely without attention to them.

The Master also knew the basic and planned purpose of the soul for the present incarnation, the hidden hindering karmic forces working out and the latent spiritual capacities previously achieved which could be wisely called upon.

Someday we shall have occult schools of meditation giving training for initiation. There are none such today. Those claiming to give such training are false teachers, often sincere but self-deluded. This also has been stated both by the Tibetan and by A.A.B.

FOSTER BAILEY

March 1955.

SECTION ONE

TALKS TO DISCIPLES

TALKS TO DISCIPLES

INTRODUCTORY REMARKS

January 1940

MY BROTHER:

May I say that when I am able to start my instruction to this New Seed Group with the words "My Brothers," you will then know that an adequate measure of group-integration has been achieved and that the real group work can begin. I have earlier stated the wider and more important objectives* which are, as you saw, entirely impersonal. I would commit this particular objective to your intelligent consideration. I would have you begin your new work with this objective and goal in your defined consciousness. I therefore stated the objective clearly, so that your minds may be tuned to mine—as far as that may be practically possible. Let your horizon be wide, my brother, and your humility great. I am here speaking individually to you, for you are as yet (the majority of you) *individually* polarised and the group polarisation lies ahead.

I have given much thought to what I have enjoined upon you in your personal instruction. I have attempted to gauge you and your need from the point of the next lesson you need to learn and the next step that you can take which will release you, each and all, for fuller and deeper spiritual service. I have not attempted to consider you from the point of your attainment upon the Path. I have attempted to aid you in the instructions *as a group* more than as individuals, and I will therefore ask you to read each other's instructions with great care, for you will find your name and perhaps some suggestions occurring in other papers than your own. It is as a group that you work and as a group you go forward.

---

*Discipleship in the New Age, Vol. I, Pages 80-81.

The sense of criticism and wrong reaction to each other's knowledge is rapidly disappearing from among you. That is good. The growth of impersonality must be steady and sure. The faults evidenced by each and all of you are on the surface of your lives, but the deep inner integration and the activity of the divine nature in each of you is more definitely vital than before. I do not say that it is as yet in full right outer expression. It can and does produce at times a surface turmoil, but this, if rightly handled, need cause no true disturbance.

Give to each other real love in the times that lie ahead, for it is the fusing and illuminating element in the life of the disciple. Let not your love remain theoretical, but give that true understanding which ignores mistakes, recognises no barriers, refuses all separating thoughts, and surrounds each other with that protecting wall of love that meets all need wherever possible—physical, emotional and mental. It is this which blends the group into one organised whole, which the Masters of the Wisdom can use in the service of the Plan. The pressure at this time is great upon Them and the urgency of humanity's cry grows stronger in Their ears. I have given you much time and thought, and earnestly I have sought to aid you on the Way. My love and strength are ever yours, but not always my time and attention. My earnest prayer is that the Light may enfold you and the Love of God transmute your lives.

For many years I have been looking ahead with definite planning and intent to the work which began in the late summer of 1936. I have sought—with the knowledge of some of you—to prepare you all as a group for an active participation in this future work. As I enter upon the task of preparing you for future increased usefulness and for closer co-operation, I must myself perforce take certain risks, and there must be established between us a trust which will be based — not on secrecy and reticences — but on truth and understanding.

This formation of the New Seed Group is my second attempt to be of hierarchical assistance in inaugurating the New Age methods and technique and to train groups (for it is a group age) which can express the New Age types of work. In my first attempt certain group limitations initiated difficulty and led to the closing of the several individual groups. You will have noted that I assigned the major failure to the inactivity of the heart centre in the majority of the members; this leads necessarily to inadequate integration. I mention this now because I would urge those members who have been selected to work in this new group to bear in mind that they may quite easily carry their earlier tendency into the new group. Only a fresh dedication and a renewed *aspiration towards inspiration* can prevent the recurrence of a certain static tendency; only a clear vision of the nature of glamour and of its effects in the individual and group life can eliminate the danger of infection from that tendency; only a humble spirit which is not occupied with the faults and failures of others can prevent the injection of an attitude of criticism and judging; and only an attentive watchfulness on the part of a certain few of the members can protect this new vehicle from disaster based on inexperienced self-confidence.

I have seriously considered what action I should rightly take. Various alternatives presented themselves—all of them concerned with the group work per se; none of them concerned you, as individuals. I could continue with the groups as they existed but, brother of mine, what more could I say, or do or teach them? The *constant* impartation of teaching and of information, the *constant* pointing out of failure, and the *constant* individual training are no part of the technique of the Hierarchy—certainly not as far as the individual aspirant is concerned. Where world values and where group consciousness are involved, the indication of needed change, the cyclic bringing about of the presentation to the soul of the Ageless Wisdom and the training of the world disciples—such is the definite and ordained technique of the Hierarchy. But this is *not* Their method of work with personalities and with those whose orientation is primarily in the three worlds of human endeavour.

Their method and procedure is to try out the personalities of Their intended and indicated disciples and—should these measure up with adequacy—then to proceed with the work of esoteric training. It is the same with groups; these are tested and tried in connection with the group personality, and upon the response depends the future activity of both the group and its Master and Teacher. But it is the *group,* as you see, which decides procedure.

I have endeavoured to remove out of this group those elements which might perchance have handicapped it, and which the group members—as they are at present constituted and motivated—are not capable of absorbing. *Group unity is not dependent upon personal sympathy, personal liking and understanding* as it may exist between the group members, *but upon capacity to absorb and assimilate, to lift, to change and to transmute those units which seem at first to be uncongenial* or even unsuitable—from the limited point of view of the group member. This is oft overlooked, but upon the capacity to do this depends much of group success. When a group cannot yet be depended upon to do this necessary absorption, the apparent rejection of certain people is not the fault of those people, but that of the group which is not yet integrated enough or unified enough to assimilate certain types of character and certain tendencies. The recognition of this should be fruitful in the preservation of much needed humility. You are being tendered another opportunity. I would ask you to remember this and to endeavour, in relation to this new experiment, to cultivate from the very start a humble spirit and the priceless gift of silence.

A group of disciples must be distinguished, as I already told you, by pure reason which will steadily supersede motive, merging eventually into the will aspect of the Monad, its major aspect. It is, technically speaking, Shamballa in direct relation with Humanity. What, therefore, is the group will in any ashram or Master's group? Is it present in any form vital enough to condition the group relations and to unite all into a band of brothers—moving forward into the light? Is the spiritual will of the individual personalities of such strength that it negates the personality relation and leads to spiritual recognition, spiritual interplay and spiritual relation? It is only in consideration of these fundamental effects of standing *as a group* in the "head's clear light" that it is permissible for a disciple to bring into the picture personal sensitivities of thought, and this only because of a group temporary limitation.

I have pointed out along what lines there has been failure, not because I seek to put the emphasis upon failure or to enlarge upon it, but because clarity of thought and of vision is necessary if the work is to go forward in a reorganised and more vital manner. If this New Seed Group measures up to requirements, then there may again arise correspondences to the original groups as planned. They will arise as the spiritual result of the esoteric manifestation of the potency of life to be found in the seed group.

The work to be done by us in joint cooperation (as regards your training) was organised by me into seven teaching units:

    I. *Definite planned Meditation.*
   II. *Teaching upon the subject of Initiation.*
  III. *Training in Telepathy.*
  IV. *Consideration of the Problems of Humanity.*
   V. *Teaching anent the Etheric Body.*
  VI. Added to the above, I seek to give each of you a measure of *Individual Help and Instruction.*
 VII. As time goes on, I will convey information anent the work of the *Masters' Ashrams and their planned Externalisation.*

I am going to ask you to give two relatively brief periods of time each day to definite and defined meditation. One period (the most important) must be given to the general group meditation, and the other to that meditation which I feel will enable you to function as an integrated personality, fused and blended in consciousness with the soul. This will lead the group as a whole to function correctly, because the individual group units are aligned and rightly adjusted.

Why is it necessary for the disciple to intensify his inner link with his teacher? Not because the teacher is his Master, not because the disciple is subjected to the imposition by the

Master of any subjective control, not because of any special privilege in the matter, but because if a student's mind is in true rapport with the teacher, then that student himself can become a source of inspiration to his fellow students; if he is thinking with clarity along the line of his chosen theme (note the word "chosen"), then he too can teach. A Master looks at each member of His group from the angle of their usefulness in the general group service. The contribution of each may differ; one disciple may have achieved much along the lines of clear thought and an impersonal attitude; his usefulness to the group can be that, and the Master will seek to train him still more along these two lines.

What is it therefore which prevents a disciple, as an individual, from having direct approach and direct contact with a Master without being dependent upon a senior disciple as an intermediary? What is it that prevents you from having such direct relation to myself? One or two in this group *have* direct approach, and another one of you has it but knows it not; several others are well-intentioned and hard-striving disciples but never for a second do they forget themselves; the problem of glamour and preoccupation with spiritual ambition condition some aspirants, a spiritual ambition which is working through a very small personality; some could make rapid progress but are prone to inertia— perhaps they just do not care enough. All desire to move forward, all possess a strong inner spiritual life, but the group antahkarana is usually still incomplete and the aspect of pure reason, which is of the heart, does not control. The evocative power of the Spiritual Triad is not, therefore, adequate to hold the personality steady and the invocative power of the personality is nonexistent—speaking from the angle of the group personalities which make up the personality aspect of the Ashram. This is a factor which can only become potent if certain personality relations are adjusted and inertia is overcome. Then, and only then, can the "group stand."

I propose to give you personality instructions only once a year, at the time of the Full Moon of May. I shall then indicate to you any needed changes in your individual meditation or in the group meditation. At this time I will give to this new seed group a meditation intended to produce coherent relations and a *conscious* group interplay. I will give each member also a meditation which will serve to integrate his personality more completely but will also serve, above all else, to fuse it with his soul. I shall enlarge later upon this when giving each of you his personal instructions. As I am to instruct you individually only once a year, I shall handle you with directness, and shall pay small attention to your personal reactions. Those are essentially your own business and not mine.

August 1940

Some of you have really studied my previous instructions; others have given them a definitely cursory and perfunctory reading and have, in the last analysis, given no real thought to what I have said. Hence the need of reminding you of my major points prior to continuing with the next phase of the teaching. I would have you demonstrate your grasp of the subject and also your response to the effort I am making to instruct you. The best paper turned in was by W.D.S. because it was the most esoteric and touched upon the spiritual techniques of approach, insight and vision.

Incidentally, the question arises in your minds as to the method whereby I ascertain the content of your papers. Do I read them? Does A.A.B. read them and convey to me her impressions? Do I psychometrise them? None of these expresses my method or conveys the true mode of ascertaining. I do not read them; candidly, my brother, they do not warrant my taking the time. Does A.A.B. read them and then convey their significance to me? No, because as they filter through her mind and brain they would take on the powerful colouring of her thought, and from this she has ever carefully protected the group and all work she does as an intermediary between you and me. I do not psychometrise them. Let me endeavour to explain.

All detailed, outer forms are expressions of some subjective significance which is the cause of their appearance and which can be discovered by those who can function in the world of meaning. These "foci of significance" carry a note, a vibration and a symbolic aspect which conveys to the trained mind of the esotericist far more than does the outer form of words convey meaning to the trained mind of the exoteric reader. One glance in the direction of the disciple with the thought in mind of ascertaining the value of his contribution in words, serves to bring into my line of vision the symbol which is the product of his written thought. This symbol may be and probably is distorted—a symbol without true balance; it will find its place upon some level of consciousness — astral, mental or spiritual — and its vibratory note will depend upon its "occult location." Forget not that the world of meaning and the world of outer forms express in essentiality the world in which multiplicity is reduced to simplicity, though this does not connote synthesis.

I wonder if any of you really grasp the extent of the effort which I have to make in order to reach your minds and teach you? When, for instance, I seek to send out these instructions I have to make the following preparation. First, I seek to ascertain the mental state and preparedness of the amanuensis, A.A.B., and whether the press of the other work upon which she is engaged in connection with the Plan of the spiritual Hierarchy permits of her right reception; for if the work is exerting extreme pressure and if she is occupied with urgent problems, it may be needful for me to wait until such time as circumstances give her the needed leeway both of time and strength, and of mental detachment. My own sphere of occult work must also come under consideration. Then, having established a rapport with her, I have three things to do.

First, I must gather the group of disciples as a whole into my aura and so gauge its general condition of receptivity— for that must determine the scope of the intended communication. Do you realise, my brothers, that as you extend your power to grasp the needed lessons and learn to train your minds to think in ever wider and more abstract terms, you draw from me a correspondingly adequate instruction?

The limitation to the imparted truth lies on your side and not on mine.

Second, I must isolate in my own consciousness the extent of the instruction, detaching myself from all other concerns and formulating the needed material into a thought-form which will be comprehensive, clear-cut, sequential in its relation to that which has already been imparted and which will lay the ground for the next instruction in due time.

Then third, I have to enter into that meditative condition, and that extraverted attitude which will enable me to pour out in a steady stream of constructive sentences which will express, to the mind of the amanuensis, the thoughtform as I see it and build it. Putting it otherwise, I become creative with deliberation and endeavour to convey to the vision, to the mind and to the intellectual perception of A.A.B. an ordered presentation of the thoughtform which embodies the lesson I desire the students to learn.

All this necessitates an expenditure of force and of time on my part which I feel is well warranted if the students—on their side—will prepare their minds, give the needed time, respond to the few requests I may make, and eventually cooperate with the work of bringing the edited instructions to the attention of aspirants and disciples everywhere and later to a wider public.

And let me here clarify also the question which is in your minds concerning the basis of the rapport between A.A.B. and myself. Earlier, I explained that a neophyte in an ashram is under the guidance of a more advanced chela and that "the Master is receiving regular reports (based on certain charts) from the senior disciple who has the neophyte in charge. It is in this way that many hierarchical relationships are established." (*Discipleship in the New Age,* Vol. I, page 723.) Several lives ago I was thus responsible for A.A.B. and hence the close link between us and the basic understanding and hence, therefore, the work we have been able to do together, even though I am not her Master. I explain this so that you can get some understanding of the interrelation in ashramic work. We both belong to the Ashram of the Master K.H. I should like to add a further point: Reception such as that by A.A.B. is very rare indeed, not only because of the subject matter, but also because of the delicate sequence of ideas and the good choice of words; through this, she has made my books unique. She provides a standard which has no competition.

I assured you that I would deal with directness when teaching this group, owing to the urgency of the time and the need for the intelligent work of the trained disciple. Will you bear this in mind, and apply my suggestions to yourself and not to your group brothers? One of the most needed things for all disciples is to apply the teaching I may give to the idea of promoting and increasing their world service, thus rendering practical and effective in the world the teaching received and the stimulation to which they have been subjected.

In your personal instructions I will give you information as to the nature of your prevailing glamour. You may ask, what do I really mean by that phrase? I mean that aspect of thought, that quality of feeling, or that innate predisposition, which stands between you and the light of life and truth. There is in the life of every aspirant some outstanding tendency which acts as a limitation. This should receive due attention, leading to its eventual eradication. Most disciples and aspirants are too general in their handling of themselves and of their respective characters. Less diffused attention to the multiplicity of inherited habits and a more concentrated attention to a main, or at least a major, issue would result in a more rapid progress. What I shall therefore reveal to you as needing correction, adjustment or eradication should occupy your attention and be consciously dealt with during the coming year. Small notice need be paid to less important faults and errors; so oft faults that seem to you of paramount importance are of no moment in the eyes of the Masters. So much of the thought life of a disciple is occupied with a ceaseless interrogation and consideration of himself. What I shall say may be very brief and very scant. I am only seeking to indicate and not to direct;

I intend to point out, but not dictate to you, modes of eradication.

The times are serious and the world disciples are hard pressed. The Hierarchy and its affiliated groups are seeking active help and cooperation in the work of salvage. All disciples and aspirants are needed, and all can give much if the desire, the loving heart and the consecrated mind are united in service. I ask aid in the task of reconstruction. I ask for your consecrated help. I ask you to discipline yourselves anew, to hold back nothing, either objective or subjective. I ask for your wholehearted cooperation in the work of world salvage.

Group Instruction

December 1941

My Brothers:

I would like to start off this instruction with the simple statement as to the task which all disciples of the Masters throughout the world are engaged in undertaking and which you also should consciously consider. It is the task of *confronting* the Dweller on the Threshold in your own life and also in the group life, and then—from that vantage point of strength—face that Dweller on behalf of humanity and thus aid humanity to vanquish this ancient evil. To do this presupposes crisis in your life and in the life of humanity. The handling of crises is the hallmark of the disciple, and every crisis met and rightly handled provides (once the difficulty is occultly "under the feet") the place from which an extended vision can be gained, fresh knowledge can flow in and the transmuting light can shine from the Angel of the Presence and thus produce results.

Each of you has passed through a cycle of real difficulty and strain. This is true of all disciples. The past eighteen months have been months of precipitation, producing a chemicalisation, an interior process of upheaval and probably outer behaviour which may have caused concern to the Observer within. This however is but the reaction of the

personality to undue pressure and strain, to world conditions
and clearer vision. Vision reveals both the light and the
dark, a thing which is oft forgotten. Disciples are fortunate
if the major results work out in the physical body. The reactions of the physical body are the least important and do
the least harm to others. Where they work out in an emotional or mental condition they are then apt to become a
problem of fellow disciples, adding to their strain and neces-
sitating an effort upon their part to carry the brother through
with the least damage to the group.

In this group work you need to remember that increasingly there will be no *individual* life. This is as it should
be. Increasingly disciples should be aware of each other and
tune in with ease on each other; increasingly the bonds of
illumined loyalty should control; increasingly you will participate in each other's attitudes and conditions and thus
learn the basic lesson of understanding. Understanding is the
secret behind all power to achieve identification with any
form of divine expression; understanding is one of the prime
factors in producing revelation, and this is one of the paradoxes of occultism. In the world of human thought, understanding follows the prescribed routine, it follows the presented fact. In the life of the spirit, understanding is a
necessary predisposing *cause of revelation*. I would ask you
to ponder on this, bracing yourself for revelation, through
a deep understanding of the initiator in yourself. Each of
you has to initiate your own individual crises; there is no
one else who is responsible. Each of you together initiates
the activity for which the group is responsible and for which
you have been brought together; each of you initiates himself into the Presence, through the medium of the Angel,
and into the shadow of the Dweller on the Threshold.
Through this process, full consciousness is achieved.

The work of this group, and of other groups similarly
motivated, is to achieve these undertakings together: Together to face the Dweller and triumph; together to arrive
at understanding; together to stand before the Presence because the Angel's light reveals "that which the eye has never
seen;" together to walk the Path of Revelation; together to

serve and together to aid the faltering steps of humanity, the world aspirant; together to stand with your backs to the light because you comprehend the ancient aphorism which states:

"He who faces the light and stands within its radiance is blinded to the issues of the world of men; he passes on the lighted way to the great Centre of Absorption. But he who feels the urge to pass that way, yet loves his brother on the darkened path, revolves upon the pedestal of light and turns the other way.

"He faces towards the dark and then the seven points of light within himself transmit the outward streaming light, and lo! the face of those upon the darkened way receives that light. For them, the way is not so dark. Behind the warriors—twixt the light and dark—blazes the light of Hierarchy."

I have been thinking of you all with tenderness and love. The struggle is so hard and oft you feel alone. There is strength in all of you or I would not have chosen you to serve your fellowmen *with* me; there is weakness in all of you which can evoke your brothers' strength and thus you will be strong; there is love in all of you but it needs expression, and for that the group exists; there is light in all of you and with that light you serve. As the Hierarchy stands as a centre of light and strength to humanity, so do your souls stand to you, and—as your Master—I blend my light with yours and thus increase the efficiency of your service; I blend my love with the love which pours forth from the soul towards each of you, and thus I deepen the relation of love between each and all of you. It is not often that I speak to you in this manner, but in the process of freeing you for increased service I have drawn nearer to you and my love surrounds you. Learn, my brothers, the meaning of words, their transmitting potency and their spiritual significance.

I am going to take the time and spare the needed energy to get in touch with the group during the coming full moons, prior to that of May. I ask you, at no matter what hour the full moon each month may fall, to endeavour to keep half an hour free so that you can attempt to enter into my consciousness. I realise that it may not always be possible for you in your busy Western lives to keep the exact minute free, but you can attempt to find some time, as near to the full moon period as is reasonably possible in your own particular circumstances. This, my brother, is to be a group effort, and not an individual one, and it is *as a group* that I shall seek to contact you. Therefore it is necessary for you to have this in your mind as you prepare for that moment. You must link up first with all the group members, pouring yourself out in love to each of them, and to all collectively, and associating yourself with them as a part with the whole. Then in united effort attempt the following procedure:

1. Having linked up with all your group brothers, and having raised your consciousness as high as you possibly can, endeavour then to hold steady, holding the mind unwaveringly "in the light," and letting the brain consciousness and its registration drop below the level of consciousness.

2. Then initiate a new effort. Realise that, on my side, I also stand steady, pouring out upon you my love and strength and endeavouring to lift you up into a higher state of consciousness.

3. Visualise ahead of you (if I may use so inadequate a word) a disk or sphere of indigo blue, a deep electric blue. In the centre of that disk *imagine* that I, your Tibetan brother, am standing. My appearance and personality matter not.

4. When you have visualised me thus standing waiting, then endeavour to see—stretching between yourself, the group and me—a band of golden light and know this to be the symbol of the Path which we are all treading. See this path gradually shortening, thus bringing us closer together, slowly and steadily, until you enter into the heart of the blue disk.

Whilst doing this, hold the mind positive and attentive, using simultaneously the faculties of imagination and of visualisation. This triple activity will test and tax your powers but will be good training in active esoteric work. Regard this always as a united group effort and remember that in doing it you aid each other, and may facilitate the work to be done at the time of the Wesak moon. I would like to add that the results of this work will not become apparent to you until the full moon of May, and even then you will only (through the synthesis of the two years' work) begin to comprehend the fusing and blending and awakening that your own souls are bringing about.

I would ask you also to make a careful record every full moon—from two days before until two days after the full moon—of all experiences and visions. Then in June turn in your full moon records along with your other work, for the helping and informing of the group members. Turn them in, my brother, even if there is naught to relate but failure to register anything.

I think that there is a certain vagueness in your minds as to the processes which I shall follow in dealing with this group of disciples and in the working out of the experiment hinted at earlier—the experiment of group initiation. I would like, therefore, to make the whole plan clearer and indicate anew the lines along which the training given will go. This might be called the exoteric aspect of the esoteric training, for much must and will transpire upon the inner planes in the inner Ashram about which nothing can be said and which will be individual as well as group expansion. I will outline the outer processes in the order of their *present* importance, and this in its turn is determined by the group condition—for which you are one and all responsible.

I. *Definite and planned Meditation.* The theme, if I might so call it, of the work will be threefold:

a. The interior interrelation of the seven centres in the body will be the objective of the meditation, basing the work upon the occult maxim that "energy follows thought." We have started upon one formula which relates the heart, the higher head centre, and the solar plexus.

    b. The subsequent relation of the centres in any one in-
dividual to the remainder of the group members, regarding the centres as radiating transmitters of energy
to the centres of the other group members. This will
result in the forming of seven great centres of energy
which will constitute the group centres, fed and enlightened by the energy transmitted by each individual.

    c. The fusion (consciously undertaken) of the individual
soul with the group soul and consequently a conscious
rapport with the Hierarchy, which is inherently the
kingdom of souls.

The first meditation affects the three centres in the individual disciple and also, and consequently, his astral body.
They can—when related, awakened and functioning, and
when the two points in the solar plexus are balanced and
"enlightened," a word which I shall frequently use in connection with the centres—evoke response from the love-
petals of the egoic lotus. This must happen automatically
and need not be regarded as a complicated technicality. Do
the required meditation faithfully and correctly and the results will follow spontaneously.

    II. Unfold to you and reveal the *techniques of work, pre-
paratory to initiation.* I referred to this earlier (in Vol. I,
Page 99): "As time goes on, I shall bridge between the old
techniques and the newer modes of training by using a part
of the ancient technique, now becoming somewhat obsolete,
and give you hints as to the nature and methods of educating
accepted disciples in the processes of initiation."

    You will note, therefore, that it is my intention to give
you such hints. This I shall do from the angle of initiation
and in preparation for the second or the third initiation.
Bear this in mind. Hitherto I have not taught you from that
particular angle, but I have instructed you as accepted
disciples *in training for preparation*—a much earlier stage.
These hints I will convey to you in the ancient symbolic
formulas which will require much deep reflection on your
part and an effort to evoke the intuition and thus arrive at

the three meanings which they hold for you, and for disciples like you. There are literally seven meanings, but I would advise you to confine yourself to the comprehension of the first three. There will be one meaning for your personality, indicating certain brain and mind realisations which are essential for the right transmission of force upon the physical plane—one of the first things an initiate has to master. There will be the soul meaning which will indicate relation to the Hierarchy, in the same way that the personality significance will indicate relationship to humanity. Then there will be a still higher meaning which will be exceedingly difficult for you to grasp, but for which you must strive and which will necessitate the consciously acquired use of the antahkarana. You will understand, therefore, why the study of the Science of the Antahkarana forms part of my instruction to this group. No major initiation can be taken until there is some measure of conscious use of the antahkarana.

The accepted disciple never receives any detailed information or instruction; he is given no list of rules which must govern his daily life and no minute instructions as to what he must do to "take initiation." He receives—at specific "points in time"—according to his success in expanding his consciousness, certain definite hints. These hints have, in the past, been given without calling attention to the fact that they are hints. The disciple either recognised them for what they were and profited thereby, or else he failed to sense their import and so delayed his moving forward. In this group experiment which I am undertaking, I propose to change this somewhat and I shall let you know which are the hints I give, so that *together* the group may profit by them, stimulated by each presented idea and thus evoke together the overshadowing soul. This will result, eventually, in an inflow of light from the Spiritual Triad via the group antahkarana, constructed of the "rainbow bridge" of each disciple.

III. *Develop in each of you some measure of telepathic rapport*—to each other, to me, your Master, and the hierarchical Plan. A Master can give no real teaching (by means of stimulation) to His group until there is established by the disciples—as individuals—a proper relation to each other,

free from all criticism (which always severs telepathic interplay) and based on loving understanding in which they—
again as individuals—ask nothing for the separated self but
only seek to give to each other and to the group.

The above concerns and applies to your relation to me,
to the Hierarchy (which is "entered" through the process of
initiation) and to each other. This relation, which indicates
ability to touch the sources of power, love and light, carries
with it the implications of service and work for humanity.

IV. I shall, therefore, endeavour to *interpret humanity
to you* (and to disciples everywhere) so that its present problems and its immediate opportunity may emerge clearly in
your minds, and you will be able consequently to work intelligently and understandingly. The Science of Service needs
elucidating and the Path of Man needs understanding. The
attitude of the initiate consciousness to human problems is
not identical with that of the ordinary human being. I do
not desire to deal with problems already considered by us in
the various pamphlets and in my books. It is the new world
which we shall start to study, the new opportunities and
the new complexities, as well as the new and coming sim-
plifications in life and being. They concern primarily the
service of the initiate; hitherto we have only considered the
service which disciples, aspirants and men of goodwill can
render.

V. I shall give you some clear and definite *instructions
anent the uses of the etheric body.* This vehicle of vitality or
energy is the ultimate conditioning factor in the activity of
the physical body. It is an initiator, for there is no physical
activity as we understand it unless impulsed by some energy
emanating from the etheric body. An understanding of some
of the processes of initiation will come from an understanding of the body of vitality. The etheric body is the organ
whereby personality or soul expression becomes evidenced
upon the physical plane. Its potency is that which evokes the
physical form. Most of the vehicles have a dual capacity—
invocation and evocation. They also have a third function:
they ground or focus energy, thus producing a point of tension, of crisis and an interlude, prior to a process of trans-

mission. Ponder on these words. The physical body can be evoked into manifestation and subsequent activity, but it has no power of invocation. Hence it is *not* a principle (as H.P.B. tells us in *The Secret Doctrine*) but is basically an automaton. The etheric body invokes and evokes; but it also, in relation to the physical plane, precipitates energy through a process of appropriation. A study of these things will bring to our attention the entire subject of the centres and this we will approach from the angle of invocation and evocation.

The teaching upon the etheric body naturally follows upon any instructions which I may give anent telepathic communication and the manipulation of energy by the initiate-disciple, via the centres, via the group centres and—when of very high development and initiate degree—via the planetary centres. I have not yet given you much on this theme but there is much that will later be said. I shall, however, have to deal with it only briefly and tentatively, as the majority of aspirants and disciples are not yet ready for this particular study.

VI. I shall, once a year, give to each of you a measure of *individual help, personal instruction and individual medita-tion.* The clue to your next step towards the door of initiation and towards the Presence will also be indicated by me. This I will do at the time of the Full Moon of May (Taurus) each year. This may involve at times an analysis of your group relation, of the effect that your national and racial thoughtforms have upon you, and also the assets and the liabilities of your personality and egoic rays. I shall endeavour to bring to your attention your personal point in evolution. I would remind you at this point that these seven rays are sharply different as to colouring and phenomenal effect and, at the same time, I would remark that—under the Law of Occult Paradox—the seven Lords of Being (the seven Rays) are widely different but remain non-separative.

VII. We are also trying *the experiment of externalising the Ashram.* This is an effort which, if successful, will be the prelude to the manifestations of the Hierarchy upon Earth. This is one of the next intended undertakings, if and when the Forces of Light have driven the forces of evil and of aggression back to their "dark habitation." As time goes on I will convey information anent the work of the Masters' Ashrams, their planned externalisation and, eventually, the externalisation of the Hierarchy.

Such, brother of mine, is our appointed task. Out of all that might be said or written by me will eventually emerge a Treatise on Discipleship which will be useful in the New Age. You are accustomed to the teaching of the Piscean Age upon this subject and also to the Piscean interpretation. It is part of my work to begin to indicate the methods and processes and the modes of instruction which will distinguish the Aquarian Age. This will only be possible to aspirants with an open mind. For this you must strive.

This programme is an ambitious one, my brothers; it will call forth your utmost capacity and staying power but, if persisted in, it will hasten your development; this will also entail obedience. We are basically occupied, little as you may realise it, in compiling an elementary manual for initiation. Ponder on this. Much antagonism will be evoked and an uprising of scepticism will be naturally aroused; those who see no need or possibility for any changing of hierarchical methods, and who are the fundamentalists of the theosophical movement and the narrow theologians among the esotericists, will make an outcry. They will be annoyed and bewildered, but they can make no further progress this life *unless* they widen their point of view; they must learn that the past methods and techniques were devoted to bringing the personality into relation with the soul, with character building, integration and alignment processes, as well as with laying the foundation for what could be given out when humanity reached its present stage.

Now the preparatory work has been done and has proved effective; it will be continued for those who need its aid, but the more advanced work can be made exoteric. This planned externalising of the teaching must go on all the time. It is the testimony of the Hierarchy that the points of crisis in the evolutionary process have accomplished their intent and have demonstrated success. These points of crisis are ever succeeded by "points of revelation" and it is with such points of revelation that we are at this time occupied.

August 1942

MY BROTHERS:

I would like first to remind you briefly of three points which I made in my last instruction.

1. This is my last effort to bring you each in this incarnation up to the point in your spiritual development which would be entirely possible, *if you so desired*. Success or failure in conforming to requirements is entirely your personal affair. Each of you can be active or inactive as it seems best to you, but I would remind you that whatever you do affects your group—either constructively or adversely.

2. There are outer processes at work which are effects of inner happenings in your own souls, in the Ashram and in the Hierarchy itself. My task is to aid you in fusing the inner and the outer events so as to bring about a true expression of the facts as they are in your life, in the Ashram life and in the Hierarchy. Your task is to develop sensitivity in these three classes of spiritual events.

3. The *group* is the factor of importance and, as I said, increasingly the individual life of the disciple lessens and his group awareness and sensitivity increases. Bear this in mind as you master the hard lesson of impersonality—an impersonality shown to you by me, by A.A.B. and (so difficult a thing to learn!) by your own souls. It is an impersonality which you yourselves must develop and apply, once you love enough. Love is the basis of impersonality.

This is, as I have repeatedly told you, an experiment in group initiation. This means that though each of you takes various steps in line with your particular point of development, there is also being developed by the Hierarchy a new technique which—when perfected and understood—will initiate entire group units into the Light and into the "Labour of the Plan." Such a group must itself be composed of people who have taken initiation. As one of your group members will only take the first initiation next life, it is obvious that the group initiation to which I refer will not be taken in this immediate cycle. The rest of the group have to wait for him.

In any case, they are not yet ready and there is much preparatory work to be done, much unfolding of awareness and developing of sensitivity before there can be a going forward *together* as the situation desired demands. The time equation is one of great difficulty to the average disciple. He is either working constantly under a sense of pressure and of haste or he is "strolling along the path of life," feeling that evolution is long and why, therefore, the need to make speed? Only a very few work from that point of balance which inhibits the spasmodic rushing activity of the intense devotee or the lazy moving forward of the awakened aspirant. I would ask you to study *time* in relation to your own souls, having in mind the peculiar opportunities of the present cycle and the outstanding need of humanity. Many are still too preoccupied with what *they* are attempting to do, with their own development and with their own capacity or noncapacity to help; but at the same time they are inadequately handling the problem of self-effacement and complete dedication to their fellowmen. "What can *I do?*" is of less importance to them than "What am I learning, and is the Master satisfied with me?" I shall be satisfied with you when you have forgotten both yourself and me in your strenuous service for mankind.

Service, I would remind you, is a scientific process, calling forth all the soul powers into full expression on the physical plane. It is service which causes a divine manifestation or what you call a divine incarnation. If a man is truly serving, he will perforce draw upon all the resources of spiritual strength and light and all the wisdom and directing power of his soul, because the task to be done is always too big for the personality. Some of the world's greatest servers are men and women who are very close to the spiritual Hierarchy and working under its direction, inspiration and impression, but who know naught of esotericism so-called, do not recognise the Hierarchy and (in their brain consciousness) remain unaware of its Personnel, the Masters of the Wisdom. One of the tragedies today of the esoteric world is the vast amount of facts in the possession of esoteric students, and the piling up of knowledge anent the Hierarchy and its Personnel. In the minds of disciples this knowledge and this aspiration obliterates the need of their fellowmen. This constitutes one of the problems with which the Hierarchy is faced. The problem of balance and of dual orientation is a very real one. As regards the impartation of spiritual knowledge, the Masters Who take pupils are faced with two problems:

1. The problem of the unawakened aspirant.
2. The problem of the learned disciple.

Ignorance and knowledge must both give place to understanding and wisdom.

I particularly wish to speak about the work that I desire you should do at the time of the full moon during the coming year. This aspect of your work should become increasingly potent and interesting. I regard it as of major importance in the group endeavour, and if I, your teacher and friend (under the pressure of the present world opportunity), can spare the time to aid the group in this particular way, it is surely not too much to ask that I receive reciprocal attention.

Perhaps some of you may get increased light upon the usefulness of the attempt if I tell you the interesting fact that —at the time of the full moon—it is almost as if a door suddenly opened wide, which at other times stands closed. Through that door, ingress is possible; through that door or opening, energies can be contacted which are otherwise shut off; and through that door approaches can be made to the planetary Hierarchy and to reality which are at other times not possible. In this statement, you have the rude outlines of a *Science of Approach* which has been little known up to the present time, even to advanced disciples, but which it is intended during the New Age to develop. It is a part of the true and emerging technique of the *Path*.

I would like somewhat to change your work in connection with your full moon contact. Two days before the time of the full moon, I will ask you to begin to cultivate that inner attitude of poised re-collectedness which will lay the right foundation for further work and which will help to shift the focus of the attention from the objective to the subjective work. It is an attitude more than an activity. Ponder on this phrase. It is a state of consciousness which can be carried forward, no matter what may be the outer activity or interests, and it involves no outer silence, or cessation of normal behaviour. It is part of the training which has for its goal the living (by the disciple) of a dual life—a life of active participation in world affairs and a life of intense mental and spiritual preoccupation.

Make a most definite effort during these two days to step up your consciousness a little higher at each of the three spiritual points in each day: at the early morning meditation, at the noonday recollection, and at the sunset hour of contact. This means—if you follow instructions correctly—that you subject your subtle bodies to six equal points of spiritual stimulation and that you do it consciously. Then at some hour in the day of the full moon, but prior to the exact hour if that hour is not possible, follow the procedure outlined below:

1. Centre the consciousness in the head.
2. Imagine yourself as retreating even more consciously within towards that point of contact where personality-soul and the teacher in the world of souls can meet and become as one.
3. Then hold yourself as poised and steady as possible, preserving that detached poise as fully as may be during the following process which is carried forward silently by the creative activity of the imagination.
   a. Imagine or visualise yourself as standing before a golden or ivory door.

b. See that door slowly open, revealing a long low room with three windows—one looking east, one looking west and one looking north. Seated before the eastern window on a low carved chair (but looking towards you, and therefore sitting with his back to the window) you may visualise your Tibetan brother, in deep meditation, seeking to contact you and all for whom he is, as a teacher, responsible.

c. Then picture yourself as advancing slowly up the long room (which is his study and work room) and then standing before him. See also your group brothers standing with you. Then each of you can constitute himself, in imagination, as spokesman for his group and offer the group in service and deep consecration to the service of the Plan.

d. When you have accomplished this, imagine that you see me rising from my chair. Then as a group we face the East and say together the Great Invocation. Endeavour consciously to follow my lead as we say the words, and listen with care, using the imagination. This will involve intense concentration.

Do this until the time of the full moon of May, for it is a preparatory exercise in order to train you all in esoteric participation.

Make a careful analysis each month of your success or failure to carry out this discipline, and note with exactitude all reactions, results and phenomena. Success will depend upon your ability to achieve a strong mental reorientation and focus, to keep detached from brain activity, and yet at the same time to preserve the waking brain attentiveness. The resultant effects, reactions, and the registering of any realisation must be noted for the two days succeeding the time of the full moon, for the seeping through of information and knowledge is often a slow process, owing to the inadequate alignment of the bodies. The May full moon will inaugurate the first real united effort to synthesise subjectively the present existing groups. This synthesis and corporate effort will become an annual endeavour as time goes on, and will take place regularly each Wesak Festival.

Of the original twenty-four members of the new (reorganised) seed group only eighteen now remain working on the physical plane. Two of them have passed into what we in Tibet call "the clear cold light"; they have gone over to the other side of the veil but are still actively cooperating with the group, and receiving the same instructions from me. I can, however, approach them more directly, as the limitations imposed by the physical brain no longer exist. P.D.W., though the latest to pass over, was held by the handicap of the astral body for an exceedingly brief time; he is now focussed and working in connection with my Ashram, upon the mental plane. C.D.P. is now in process of freeing herself from astral limitations, and by the time the sun moves northward she too will be working entirely mentally. They are both of them of real service to me at this time of world need, one owing to her understanding heart and utter selflessness, the other because of his outstanding wisdom.

Three of the original members (C.A.C., S.C.P., and W.O.I.) could not stand the spiritual pressure, and their personalities forced their withdrawal (probably for this incarnation) from the group work. The tests of discipleship are severe, as you well know, and only the pure heart, true love and mental activity can serve to pull the disciple through them; this is always possible, however, where these exist and where there is also a determined orientation towards the light. It is this determined orientation which has enabled W.D.S. to stand steady through his tests. There is a stage of discipleship which is described as that of "light fluctuation." *The Stanzas for Disciples*, which I have at times quoted to you, speak of this stage as follows:

"In and out of the light, as a moth around a candle, flicker the sparks. These sparks are men, awakened to the light, but men who know not that the greater Light puts out their little light and draws the sparks unto itself. They cannot face the light. They fear its utter truth.

They come; they go; again do they return, only again to leave."

Hold these brothers, who still remain your group brothers though temporarily in pralaya, warmly in your hearts. Hold them in love. Seek not to bring them aid or draw them back again within the circle of your service. They are at the point where their own souls alone and I, their Master, know the right timing of approach.

Finally, my brothers, one parting word as I close this instruction. The world tension increases and will increase; anxiety grows and there is no sign of its immediate lessening; the darkest hour of human life is upon us and it frequently brings to the earnest disciple the experience—terrible yet beautiful—to which has been given the name of the "dark night of the soul." This dark night takes different forms and different degrees of intensity, according to the ray, the type and the point in evolution of the disciple. From it you cannot escape. But one error emerges if careful thought is given to this dark night as pictured by the mystics down the ages. Their emphasis has, in the past, been laid upon the suffering which the personality experiences and the agony through which the personality goes. But in reality and from the angle of the facts, that is not the true dark night. The real "dark night" is that of the soul as it participates in the pain of humanity as a whole, in the agony of humanity's separation from God (a separation based upon illusion but not on actuality) and upon the desperation of humanity's reaching forth towards what appears to be an unresponsive God. Personality pain, agony and desperation are very different things and are not concerned with the totality of pain and suffering to which mankind is subjected.

I would therefore ask you to steel your souls to endurance, knowing that the *Hierarchy Stands;* I would ask you to love blindly and unchangingly in spite of all that may happen, knowing that *Love Stands* unmoved amid the wreckage of all around and eternally loves; I would ask you to put your hand into that of the Master and move forward with Him and in the strength of your group, irradiated by the life and light of the Hierarchy; I would ask you to be a strong hand in the dark to your fellowmen because you *are* affiliated with the Hierarchy and the love and strength of the Hierarchy can flow through you, if you so permit.

I would remind you in this time of trial that I, your Master, love and guard you, for your soul and my soul are one soul. Be not unduly disturbed. There is no light or dark to the soul but only existence and love. Rest back on that. There is no separation but only identification with the heart of all love; the more you love the more love can reach out through you to others. The chains of love unite the world of men and the world of forms and they constitute the great chain of *Hierarchy*. The spiritual effort you are asked to make is that of developing yourself into a vibrant and powerful centre of that fundamental, universal *Love*.

September 1943

MY BROTHERS:

The New Seed Group has now been in existence for several years. During this time, I have only been in communication with you annually. Those who are in preparation for initiation *must* inevitably work alone. I would have you remember this. There are, as you know, three sources of inspiration which indicate to the disciple—struggling on the physical plane—his goal:

1. His own soul...........through direct contact, as the result of alignment.
2. The Master............through impression, as a result of sensitivity.
3. The Ashram group.....through service, as a result of interplay.

Later, as the initiate-disciple makes progress and as he builds the antahkarana, the energy of the one Life, emanating from the Monad, brings in the fourth type of inspiration. To these spiritual sources of inspiration must be added lesser ones, such as mental impression, telepathically registered and coming from a multitude of thinkers and minds. These work both as individuals and as members of a group. There is also emotional inspiration to which—in its most easily recognisable appearance—we give the name of aspiration. All these are, esoterically considered, evocative of desire, to be transmuted into will if (and only if) "the energy of the will-to-good is the emanating principle and the actuating result of the inspired impulse; it must constitute the motivating impulse at the centre of the disciple's being." Thus spoke one of the Masters not long ago to a disciple who sought to grasp the synthetic effect of inspiration. It is the Will and its immediate evocation which is the major need of this particular group of my disciples. The hierarchical Plan is the objective of that will; the purpose of Sanat Kumara is the revelation which comes to those who demonstrate that will, and it is the strength of the divine Power which makes that will possible. Strength is to Power what desire is to aspiration, or what the personality is to the soul. It is the revelation of quality.

I have started this communication with this note of Will because the use of that will (under instruction) is the objective of your next year's work; as we proceed with the various phases of our study which I have earlier outlined, my use of this theme will emerge clearly in your consciousness.

It has seemed to me necessary to open this instruction with a brief resume of the past teaching. The pressure of life these days is very great; everybody is tired; you will therefore approach this fresh addition to the teaching with renewed zest if the past teaching is clearly apprehended and is clearly illumined in your minds.

What is the task which confronts you, both as individuals and as a group? It is a fivefold task:

1. To confront and deal adequately with your own personal Dweller on the Threshold.
2. To share—as a group—in humanity's effort to confront the *group* Dweller on the Threshold; this "Dweller" is constructed of the evil desires of all mankind, of humanity's mistakes and weaknesses, thoughts,

distorted strengths and perverse motives. This confronting is one of the objectives of the present world
war.

3. To arrive at that understanding which is the foundation of wisdom, which is the result of a developed intuition, and which is also an intelligent application
of the truths apprehended.

4. To stand — as a group — before the Angel of the
Presence.

5. To take initiation yourself, as an individual, and also
as a coherent unit in the group effort towards initiation.

Other goals will emerge as you strive, study and serve; the
simplicity, however, of the above statement will convey to
you your immediate objectives. These objectives must be
thought through together and their import must be grasped
as a group. The contribution which each of you can make to
the cause of clear thinking, ardent aspiration and determined
application may sound easy and quite familiar. The moment,
nevertheless, these goals become techniques and are expressed factually, their simplicity seems to vanish and the
proposition appears extremely hard.

Since my last communication to you, certain changes have
taken place in the personnel of the group. L.U.T. has been
dropped (temporarily and for this particular incarnation)
out of the group, and therefore out of my Ashram. The constant condition of irritation in which he lived was the result
of the ceaseless conflict between his aspiring soul nature and
his inert and essentially selfish personality; that is now over
and for the rest of this life it can be assumed that he has
reached his high water mark and is passing through a period
—definitely temporary—of retrogression or of recession.
Next life will see him pass triumphantly his present point of
attainment, leaving him stabilised upon the Way. He remains, therefore, tenuously linked with the New Seed Group
—a linking which is stronger upon the subjective side than
upon the outer.

Three of your comrades in the earlier groups have rejoined the group; the demand of their souls for reinstatement has been recognised by me and has evoked from me due response. Their linking with the group was not tenuous but was a strongly knit cable. H.S.D. has again taken her place among you, having learnt some measure of inner calm and mental poise. L.T.S-K., I felt, needed the protection of the group against his constantly recurring glamours and his innate glamour-making tendency; I, therefore, reinstated him for his own protection so that in a coming life he can start earlier, and move forward with greater precision. R.V.B., having learnt the lessons which an interlude of complete aloneness can give to the ardent disciple (who craves and rests back upon companionship) is now ready to prove what he essentially has ever been—a strength and a centre of poised peace to his group brothers. He is a definite asset in the group work and has reached a point in his unfoldment where it will not hurt him to know this.

So, my brothers, we face a new cycle of work and one in which C.D.P. and P.D.W.—working on the inner side of life —are definitely sharing. The latter has moved on into the Ashram of his Master, the Master Morya. He is now preoccupied with the work of breaking up—along with other trusted first ray disciples—the crystallisation which is the disastrous condition of France. His past incarnation in the French nation has well fitted him for this task; his heart of love and his very profound development will also enable him greatly to assist, thus offsetting the destructive tendencies of the first ray worker. He has never been destructive in his application of truth.

C.D.P. is working continuously with the children of the world (including those who died victims of the horrors of war), preserving inviolate her affiliation with my Ashram but working in a group composed of disciples upon all the rays and whose personalities—in their last incarnation—were upon all the many nationalities; they are doing what they can and must be done to salvage *the consciousness* of the children and to preserve them from complete disintegration.

K.E.S., who died prior to the reorganisation of the New Seed Group, is now subjectively affiliated with the group and must be regarded by you as a fellow worker. His work is very largely with those who pass over to the inner side from the British and American Armed Forces; for this he is eminently well equipped, being English by birth but having spent long years in the United States; he has also worked for many years in the spiritualistic movement.

I am giving you information anent your group brothers who are not in physical bodies because I seek to have you realise the unity of all life, the identity of purpose and the close sense of relationship which characterises an Ashram. A Master's Ashram has people working both on the outer and on the inner planes and in this work, the Master sees no difference, being released from the concepts of time and space. This has relation to the "double life pattern of the disciple" to which I referred when I last communicated with you.

At that time, I gave you no explicit instruction or individual meditations. I gave each of you six statements upon which to ponder. Through the close consideration of these statements you can create fresh aspiration and a renewed tendency to creative living. Statements such as these are formulations of truth and are also voiced concepts of spiritual import. They are potent in their transforming effect, if rightly used. I have not been too satisfied with the results of my past requests to you. The pressure of life has been great these days; to that pressure many of you have succumbed. You might have carried through and been more effective had you given careful attention to your thought life.

One of the problems confronting disciples in times of world stress is that of the preservation of a right sense of proportion. This leads to right paralleling activity—the activity of the inner disciple and the work of the outer man. A perfect balance is the goal and this is not at all easy of achievement. In all times of world agony and catastrophe (such as we are at this time experiencing) a third and paralleling aspect of life appears and complicates the problem with which the disciple is faced and which he already regards as most difficult and challenging. There is (within the man) the inner disciple, oriented consciously towards the Hier-

archy and the life of the Kingdom of God; there is the busy
outer man, preoccupied with various activities, playing the
part of the intelligent citizen and seeking always to shoulder
his share of national and group responsibility; there is also a
suffering emotional human being, bewildered oft by world
agony, reacting painfully to the sorrows and distresses of his
fellowmen, horrified by the appalling psychological results
of world war, by the psychological impacts and complexities,
aghast at the present and overwhelmed by fear of the future.
The greater his power to include, the greater his strain and
pain; the further on he is upon the Way, the more keen are
his reactions and the more he thinks and plans for the future,
and the greater also the clarity with which he can view the
imminent possibilities. I would not have it otherwise; this
threefold position which inevitably you have to take and
which you cannot avoid if you are true disciples, gives opportunity for planned integration and also proffers an invitation
for you to shoulder an individual share of hierarchical responsibility and comprehension.

The only thing that I would ask is that you accept the
implications of this triple situation and that you do not use
it as an alibi; this, some of you have definitely done; you
have regarded your complex problems as so strenuous and
difficult that it makes your work in the group (which is a
definite part of my Ashram) entirely out of the question.
You have—many of you—not done the work which I requested; only a few—a very few—endeavoured to fulfill requirements. Had you managed to carry them out, you might
have found your entire path in life more simple and easy and
your service more effective.

Certain things anent the group aura, or rather anent its
general characteristics, might prove of interest to you. A
Master, when studying a group considers, first of all, the
various lines of force which relate the individuals in the
group to Him, to the inner Ashram and to each other. He
looks for the constancy of the interplay, for the brilliance of
the group light, as a whole, and for its emanatory influence,
its radiation and its magnetic effect in the world. Changes
constantly occur. In the past, the lines of force between the

group and myself were strong, and the relationship between the group members was definitely weak. Today, the lines of energy, carried by thought and directed towards me, are steady but not so brilliantly fluctuating; the lines between the group members are strengthened by mental determination, but not by emotional or embryonic love. This indicates, on the whole, improvement, because the tide of devotion, poured out to me was not something which guaranteed to me that the group had staying power. There is a more wholesome attitude. The relation between you as an individual and your co-disciples is one of a relative indifference, but of a mental recognition of your joint group affiliation. The magnetic radiation of the group is the weakest point in the entire presentation which you make to the world. As yet, from the angle of service, you do not count, for the group is doing nothing *as a group*. That is serious, my brothers. As individuals, many of you are serving in some way or another, but it is a detached and personal service and has no relation to a fused group endeavour.

You might here ask: What can we as a group accomplish? What is it that we can do? You can, for one thing, begin to work as an Ashram works, using the power of thought, originating pressures, directing thought currents along specified lines out into the world, creating thoughtforms which will make clear-cut contact with other minds and which will bring about definite changes in the consciousness of humanity. This you do not as yet do, nor have you evidenced any desire so to work. I have waited to see if the initiating impulse would come from you without any prompting by me. I have waited in vain.

I told you elsewhere that "an Ashram is an emanating source of hierarchical impression upon the world. Its 'impulsive energies' and its inciting forces are directed towards the expansion of the human consciousness, through the magnetic lives of the group members as they carry on their duties, obligations and responsibilities in the outer world; it is aided also by the steady vibratory activity of the members of the Ashram who are not in physical incarnation and by the united clear thinking and convinced awareness of the entire Ashram."

I have thus explained the need because you require clear understanding as we consider our first point, meditation, and begin to plan the work to be done by you during the coming year. Will you accept my words that you need a reorientation and a greatly lessened preoccupation with the Ashram, its Master, its personnel and its life? If you will do this, and thus mentally free yourselves, you can and will go on to a fuller life of service, with your eyes on human need and not upon your co-disciples, their activities, my plans and the purpose at this time of your preparation for initiation.

I would like now to try an experiment. Continue with your group work with me at the time of the full moon, exactly as outlined in your group instructions, but to that work I want to add another activity.

Each month I will speak three words, forming one consecutive sentence. Will you see if you can, in the silence of intensity, record these words? To help you in your task, I am giving a list from which I will choose each month a phrase. Send in what you think you registered each month on your full moon report. I will signify to A.A.B. the correctness, or otherwise, of your choice, by letting her know what I said.

This is the list from which I will choose:

1. Go in peace.	2. Faith, hope and charity.
3. God keep you.	4. God bless you.
5. Enter within thyself.	6. Love thy brother.
7. Stand in light.	8. Om Tat Sat.
9. Where art thou?	10. Tread the Path.
11. God guard thee.	12. Enter into peace.
13. Lift up thine eyes.	14. Speak low, brother.
15. Give love always.	16. The open gate.

The work to be done is now outlined and you enter upon a fresh period of study, of effort, and of training. May I, in order to stir you to fresh decisive living, remind you that:

1. You are in training for initiation. Therefore, face the future with clearer vision.
2. You are pledged disciples, therefore take up your task and move forward.
3. You are members of the New Group of World Servers, and have therefore, no time to be idle.
4. You are not alone, but your group brothers stand with you, and I stand also by your side.
5. That there is no task which is insuperable, and no way that is too long for you to tread it. You are a soul with all the powers of the soul and—as you *are* linked with the Hierarchy—you are facing toward success.

As I earlier said, I at this time shall not deal with certain points connected with the growth of the human family and its stabilisation into a new civilisation. I shall begin to do so as soon as the war is over. When the needs of humanity are changed, and they will then be radically different to the conditions and demands prior to the war, then I will consider them. With the period of reconstruction, in which the New Group of World Servers will be active, we shall later deal in detail, and I will give two series of instructions which can act as a guide for all your reconstruction work. One instruction will be for my disciples, and through them for the New Group of World Servers, of which they are a part; another will be for the men and women of goodwill, and through them for the world of thinking men. However, I might state that the background or groundwork of all that you may be asked to do is *the Triangle work*. In the subjective work, the New Group of World Servers will be peculiarly active, creating the network of light; in the objective work, the men and women of goodwill will bestir themselves, creating the network of goodwill. The function of the New Group of World Servers is dynamically to "force" the energy of the will-to-good into the world; the average man and woman, responding unconsciously, will express goodwill. Disciples, such as you are, must perforce work in both fields, creating and building both types of network. This you can do now, and you can form thus the nucleus of that great interwoven pattern of light and of goodwill which must underlie or "sub-stand" all exoteric work of renovation, renewal, rehabilitation and reconstruction. I ask you and other disciples, therefore, again to work with renewed interest at the forming of triangles, reaching people who are already active, and seek to aid them in forming new triangles. This is a work of major importance and has the endorsement of the Hierarchy.

As regards our sixth subject, my personal instructions to each of you, you will find them as usual after this group instruction and after the teaching which I shall give you on the building of the antahkarana.* Your personal instructions are fuller this time and I would ask you to *accept them as instructions to be followed.* Constant reading and consciousness of instructions and teaching which are *not* carried through into action upon the outer plane, simply present a way of escape from reality. Unless a Master's instructions meet with an experimental response, they loosen the ashramic tie and eventually the disciple slips into an interlude (sometimes of great length and involving several lives) of drifting, of reading and thinking and not working, of the pleasure of attention without the pain of accomplishment. This has happened in the case of several who have been temporarily suspended from active work in my Ashram. See that it happens not to you.

May I remind you that your brothers' instructions may be interesting to you and should be read by you in an endeavour to understand him and work with him, but that they may convey to him a meaning which is not open to you at all and that, therefore, your conclusions may prove entirely erroneous. These personal instructions are, as you may realise, exoteric instructions within the field of esoteric relationships. They can be read and studied by all of you. However, I also deal with you in a purely esoteric and subjective manner, and this is a point upon which few of you, if any, ponder. Do you at any time register such teaching or recognise its source? You need to learn to make careful distinction between:

*Education in the New Age,
  A Treatise on the Seven Rays, Vol. V.*

1. Teaching which comes to you directly from your own soul, via your mind.
2. Instruction given by me to you in my inner Ashram, at which time you are also subjected to the stimulation of disciples senior to you.
3. Impression which comes to you from the great aggregate of all Ashrams, the Hierarchy.

Later I will give you some training on this matter, but you are not yet ready for it.

The final point, which concerns the externalising of the Ashrams, will be given to you when the Ashram of which you are a part is more real to you than it is at present.

I would have you remember that when the war ends two great conditions will emerge for which you must be prepared and for which you should now begin to prepare others. These are:

1. There will be a great settling back by mankind in an effort to find security, to obliterate the effects of war from their troubled minds, to forget that which has happened, to return to the familiar, and to re-establish the old ways of life. Human beings forget easily, and besides this ancient habit, humanity is very tired. Get ready to deal with this, for it must not happen if it can in any way be prevented.
2. There will also come the cessation of the "great sounds of the material aspects"—the sounds of war, the noise of explosion, and the cry of suffering humanity. This will create a curious false peace, but it will at the same time create a channel of approach for new spiritual forces and energies which—directed by the Hierarchy —will pour into the human family, causing spiritual stimulation, spiritual receptivity, spiritual aspiration and a great readiness for that which is new. You will therefore have two opposing conditions to consider, with which to deal, and you will need much wisdom. You will have to assist in the task of preventing the relapse of a tired humanity into the state of mind of

which inertia, a reverting to the old, and a demand for the ancient ways are characteristic. You will also have to aid in the directing of the registered spiritual energies into avenues and channels of usefulness where they can accomplish the greatest good. Ponder on this.

I have given you much in this instruction. I seek to make my Ashram useful at this time of crisis. We have had a great crisis of materialism and the powers of darkness have very nearly assumed control. But we *are* seeing the slow domination of the good. Humanity has been the battleground for a major conflict between the two great Lodges—the great White Lodge and the Black Lodge. The former is now gradually gaining control.

The withdrawal (quite imminent in time, my brothers) of the evil group will leave humanity relieved but bewildered, beaten to the ground, but with enough strength to rise to greater heights than ever before. For this withdrawal I ask you to prepare—with intelligence, wise understanding and deep love.

The work to be done by the world disciples, the world aspirants, the New Group of World Servers and the men and women of goodwill can be a determining factor in the New Age and can tip the scales between a static and retrogressive activity and a steadily planned moving forward into light. You can play your part in this determination, if you so will.

That you will do so, and that you will have the opened eye which will see the dawning light and the fading darkness is my earnest wish for you.

November 1944

TO MY GROUP OF AFFILIATED DISCIPLES:

It is more than a year since you received your last set of instructions from me — a year of momentous happenings upon earth and of significant changes in the hierarchical relation to humanity. There is, as a result of the war, a much closer rapport and spiritual confidence apparent between those pledged disciples who have been faithful to their as-

signments and Those of Us Who are seeking to use them in
the service of world betterment; there is a more definite recognition of emerging spiritual values among aspirants everywhere and a greater readiness to relinquish hindrances to
service; the plans of the Christ for humanity's release are
more matured for these had to wait until such time that the
trend of human aspiration became more clearly emphatic;
the new era, with its latent possibilities, can be seen upon
the horizon, stripped of the veils of glamour and wishful
thinking which obscured it ten years ago.

The significant spiritual effects of the war can now be
clearly seen, and I can begin to consider with you (earlier
than I had anticipated) some of the problems with which
you—as potential servers of the race and pledged disciples—
can now deal. I could wish, as far as the immediate present
is concerned, that you were all younger and had availed yourselves more definitely of the teaching I have sought to give
you these past years. *Above everything else, I wish you were
more courageous.* Does that word surprise you, my brothers?
In considering this year as a whole, I question not your devotion or your steadfastness; I have confidence in the depth
of your aspiration and your desire for the will-to-good; I
know that naught will turn you for any length of time from
the pursuit of your goal.

I do, however, question your courage. It takes courage to
make spiritual decisions and to abide by them; it takes
courage to adjust your lives—daily and in all relations—to
the need of the hour and to the service of mankind; it takes
courage to demonstrate to those around you that the present
world catastrophe is of more importance to you than the
petty affairs of your individual lives and your humdrum contacts; it takes courage to discard the alibis which have prevented you from participating to date in the all-out effort
which characterises today the activities of the Hierarchy; it
takes courage to make sacrifices, to refuse time to nonessential activities and to deal with the physical body as if it were
free from all impediments; it takes courage to ignore frailties
which may be present, the tiredness incident to a long life,
the physical tendencies which handicap and limit your

service, the sleeplessness which comes from world pressures or from a badly regulated life programme, and the nervousness and strain which are the common lot today; it takes courage to attack life on behalf of others, and to obliterate your own wishes in the emergency and need.

One of the points which disciples need to grasp more clearly is the well-recognised fact (and thus easily overlooked from very familiarity) that the assertion of one's determination to function as a server and as a disciple brings about a refocussing of all the forces of the personality and the soul (in unison); it is, symbolically speaking, a recurrence of the ancient event of individualisation upon a higher turn of the spiral, this time entered into with full conscious cooperation. This refocussing brings its own difficulties. It leads often to a distressing consciousness of one's own nature, one's aims, one's life theme, one's aspirations and one's handicaps, of one's equipment and experience, plus the various aspects and vehicles through which the soul has perforce to work. All this produces an intensification ofttimes of self-interest and of concentration upon one's self, always with the best of intentions and aspiration. One's limitations, physical or otherwise, look unduly large; one's faults are exaggerated in one's consciousness, though not so oft in expression; the extent of the service needed and demanded by the soul appears so great that the disciple at times refuses cooperation for fear of failure or from undue consciousness of himself; excuses for non-service or for only partial service are easily found and appropriated; postponement of all-out help today, plus complete dedication to human need, is easily condoned on the basis of health, time, home limitations, fear of one kind or another, age, or a belief that this life is preparatory to full service in the next; alibis are easy to discover, some of them even taking the form of believing that the demands of the Master and the programme of the Ashram with which the disciple is affiliated are unreasonable or—as is the case with two of you in this group—that the Oriental does not understand the demands upon the Occidental disciple.

I have for years endeavoured to arouse all of you, and through you the thousands you can as a group reach, to the urgency of the times, but hitherto with only partial or temporary results and as yet (for some of you, though not for all) the work to be done in response to the demands of the Ashram is secondary to your daily life pattern, to the requirements of your business or your home or to what you believe to be the physical limitations, the emotional liabilities and the mental handicaps of your equipment.

My brothers, let me repeat: The disciple has to take himself as he is at any given time, with any given equipment, and under any given circumstances; then he proceeds to subordinate himself, his affairs and his time to the need of the hour, particularly during a phase of group, national or world crisis. When he does this within his own consciousness, and is therefore thinking along lines of the true values, he will discover that his own private affairs are taken care of, his capacities are increased and his limitations are forgotten.

Until this is your experience, a closer relation to my Ashram will not be possible because the heavy and lethargic quality of your group life would entail undue effort on the part of the other disciples in the Ashram (and particularly in the inner Ashram) in order to offset it. I am putting this to you with frankness as we together face the end of the war, and a period of renewed and different opportunity opens before all world servers. It is for you to decide whether your contribution during the war period measured up to your opportunity; it is for you to decide what part you will play, as individuals and as a group, in the coming cycle—a cycle wherein the new ideas and ideals must be stressed, and for which a fight must be made, wherein the wider plans must be understood, endorsed and preached, the new and clearer vision for human living must be grasped and finally brought into being, and a cycle wherein the effort of all members of the New Group of World Servers (and surely you are that!) must be given to the lifting of humanity's heavy load.

No definite assignments were given in the last instruction, as I felt I would like to see whether the rhythm of the past—reporting on the meditation work and on the Full Moon Approach which has been carried on now for many years—was so strongly established that, for the sake of the group, it would be carried on, even if not specifically demanded. Only a few have kept the group meditation; the work of interpreting the Formula, as outlined earlier and not specifically discontinued by me, has received no attention, and the group is the loser thereby. I point out these factors because I would have you realise that this is *group* work, and that it is the *group* which is the teacher of the group, under inspiration from me, when you—as individuals —reach me, and under the inspiration of your own souls and of the Spiritual Triad when these contacts are made and utilised.

In my previous instruction I stressed three points to which I would like again to refer in the light of the emerging opportunity. My task is not to change you or to give you orders and commands. I have only one task, and that is to find and test out those who can serve the race under inspiration from the Ashrams of the Masters. I referred at that time to the *loneliness* which is one of the first things that indicates to a disciple that he is being prepared for initiation. It will be apparent, therefore, that the loneliness to which I refer is not that which is incident to those weaknesses of character which repel one's fellowmen, to an aloof or disagreeable nature, or to any form of self-interest which is so emphasised that it antagonises other people. There is much loneliness in a disciple's life which is entirely his own fault and which is subject to cure if he employs the right measure of self-discipline. With these he must deal himself, for they concern the personality, and with your personalities I have no affair. I refer to the loneliness which comes when the accepting disciple becomes the pledged disciple and steps out of a life of physical plane concentration, and of identification with the forms of existence in the three worlds, and finds himself in the midway place, between the world of outer affairs and the inner world of meaning. His first reaction then is that he is alone; he has broken with the past; he is hopeful but not sure of the future; the tangible world to which he is accustomed must, he knows, be superseded by the intangible world of values, involving a new sense of proportion, a new range of values and new responsibilities. This world he believes exists, and he steps forward bravely and theoretically, but it remains for a while wholly intangible; he finds few who think and feel as he does and the mechanism of sure contact only exists within him in embryo. He is breaking loose from the mass consciousness with which he has been merged hitherto, but has not yet found his group, into which he will eventually be consciously absorbed. Therefore, he is lonely and feels deserted and bereft. Some of you feel this loneliness; few of you have, for instance, reached the point where you feel yourselves to be a definite, integral part of the group; only two or three of you realise—briefly and fleetingly at times—the close link with the Ashram; your attitude is largely one of hope, coupled with the idea that it is your physical limitations which prevent your realising all that truly *is*, in connection with your inner affiliations. But, my brothers, such a sense of loneliness is only another form of self-consciousness, of undue self-interest, and (as you make progress upon the Path) you will find it disappearing. If you therefore feel lonely, you must learn to look upon it as a glamour or illusion and as a limitation which must be overcome. You must begin to act as if it were not. If only more disciples would learn the value of acting *"as if."* There is no time for any of you to be lonely these days, for there is no time for you to think about yourselves.

The second point I made was the need for you to emphasise and develop the *Will*. Presumably, you have all been working at the task of building the antahkarana, the channel of communication between the brain and the spiritual will, or the Monad, working through the medium of the Spiritual Triad. If you have been successful, it will be beginning to dawn upon you that there is a great distinction between goodwill which the masses can and often do grasp, and the will-to-good which is the goal of the disciple. Goodwill is relatively simple of expression and all of you know much about it and express much of it. For that, no commendation is required, for it is a human attribute lying very near the surface of expression in all men. But the will-to-good is far more difficult to express, for it involves the ability not only to use the spiritual will, but to know somewhat the nature of the "good." *The will-to-good is the basic quality of divine purpose, involving planned activity and a definite goal to be achieved.* It necessitates the ability to think in terms of the whole, an appreciation of the next step which humanity must take in the imminent Great Approach (for this must be a reciprocal Approach), an understanding of the lessons of the past and a vision, based—not on love or on soul-sight—but on a conviction as to the immediate purpose of Sanat Kumara, as He works it out through the Christ and the planetary Hierarchy. This conviction is based, as far as the Hierarchy is concerned, on pure reason; it is based, as far as humanity is concerned, through its disciples, on intuitive perception, implemented by love and expressed intelligently. Upon this I would ask you to ponder, and as you ponder, make the needed changes in your personal approach to the problem.

The third point grows out of the above. You are all pledged disciples, and as such your immediate personal problem (in which I may not and therefore cannot help you) is to overcome and destroy the hold which the Dweller on the Threshold may have upon you. We are back, therefore, to our starting point, and a question now arises in your minds: "How can I overcome this Dweller and yet at the same time refuse to concentrate upon myself and my problems? This I am told by you not to do, and yet the Dweller is the sum-total of all personality holds and defects, all potencies—emotional, mental and physical—which limit my expression as a soul. What can I therefore do?"

My answer would be: You must first of all accept the fact of the Dweller, and then relegate that Dweller to its rightful place as part of the Great Illusion, the great phantasmagoria of existence and as an integral part of the life of the three worlds. You must then proceed upon your planned life service (What definite plan or plans have you, my brother?) and act as if the Dweller existed not, thus freeing yourself from all personality influence in due time and leaving your mind free for the task in hand. I could perhaps word it another way. When your interest in hierarchical work and the programme of the Ashram with which you are connected is adequately strong, it will then dominate all your actions, and all your thoughts (waking or sleeping); you will then find that the grip of the Dweller will be broken, that its *life* has been destroyed by the force of attrition and its *form* destroyed in the fires of sacrifice. Such, briefly, is the story; I waste no time with elaborations, for there is much I seek to give you in this instruction.

I desire to give you the help you need for the coming year which faces you. Above all, however, I am endeavouring to make clear to future generations certain basic principles and certain aspects of hierarchical truth which must in the New Age govern those who seek to tread the Path of Discipleship and who are willing to be prepared for initiation. Changes in curriculum and in techniques are being made by the Hierarchy; the adaptation of old methods to modern needs and to more highly developed men is under way. I write not for you in reality. You have already had more than you have used. I write for the coming disciples and initiates of the next two generations.

It is essential that disciples in all Ashrams consider these days what humanity's problems are, what they mean and what their solution entails; they must know what the Masters of the Wisdom want done and then they must talk and write, act and live so that others too may understand.

Humanity has never really lived up to the teaching given to it. Spiritual impression, whether conveyed by the Christ, by Krishna or by Buddha (and passed on to the masses by Their disciples) has not yet been expressed as it was hoped. Men do not live up to what they already know; they fail to make practical their information; they short-circuit the light; they do not discipline themselves; greedy desire and unlawful ambition control and not the inner knowledge. To put it scientifically and from the esoteric angle: Spiritual impression has been interrupted and there has been interference with the divine circulatory flow. It is the task of the disciples of the world to restore this flow and to stop this interference. This is the major problem facing the Ashrams at this time.

This year, I will make clear to you what work is asked of the group in relation to the planned group work, the group meditation and the group thinking; the rules then laid down will hold good for all future years, though their fulfillment is necessarily optional, as you are free disciples, working under the new rules, and are adult aspirants.

Your full moon work remains unchanged and I will again send a phrase chosen out of the set of phrases already given. I will change my technique somewhat and in speaking the phrase each month at our full moon contact, I will do it the day before, on the day of the full moon, and on the following day, and will also lay the emphasis upon the leading word in the phrases. If this leading word is recorded by you, the effort can be regarded as successful.

I suggest that you continue with the work, as hitherto given and undertaken, but I will give you a fuller picture of the full moon activity and purpose with some of the implications which may enable you to work with greater interest and understanding.

The first time, my brothers, that I outlined for you the work I sought to have you do at the time of the full moon, I undertook to work with you along these lines for a preliminary period of three years, each year expanding the work somewhat until the full moon of May of the third year. This period of time is now nearly completed, and today I ask you two questions:

1. What has this work meant to you?
2. Have you grasped the importance of the work to be done?

There has been a purpose behind all this effort which I have made, and an experiment of importance has been carried forward in preparation for the coming New Age activity.

In some of the earlier instructions* I indicated that the coming world religion would be based upon a new Science of Approach and that this would, in time, supersede the present world religious formulas and ceremonials. Hence the importance of the efforts now being made by disciples in these new seed groups. They are in reality occupied with the

*A Treatise on the Seven Rays (Esoteric Psychology), Vol. II, page 701.

process of anchoring upon earth a new religious idea or concept, a seed thought or germ of a new activity which (at some later date) will bear fruit and inaugurate a new method of drawing nearer to God.

It might be of value to all disciples if I here analysed the three years' work intended to be done during the full moon periods as outlined to you by me. Each year saw an addition to or expansion of the work and an enlargement of the concept. I seek now to make it all clearer to you, thus laying the foundation for the work to be done during the coming years, if you desire to continue with the work. Let us get these instructions into tabular form for the sake of clarity.

I

1. The first thing which I emphasised to you was that this was a group endeavour, and that its success depended upon the group fusion, the group love and the group understanding. The success of the desired inner contact was based upon a realised group relation. It was intended to be an endeavour which would be the outgrowth of a love, stabilised in and accentuated by all the group members. Hence my constant reiteration of the need of love between the group members. Towards the establishing of this loving relationship, I have been working for years with all of you. You may perhaps have believed that I did so in order that your group work in relation to your individual endeavour might be successful. That was *not* the major intent. The forming of units for special service in organising the life forces, processes and forms for the new technique of Approach to God or to the Hierarchy (which is the intermediary between spiritual reality and human life) was and is the major objective. Upon this statement I would ask you to ponder with renewed interest. Your interpretations are so often motivated by an unrealised spiritual selfishness and an undue emphasis upon your specific group importance. The groups are simply the field for hierarchical expression, and we are not yet convinced that the expenditure of force on our part is warranted by the results achieved. The group members have been pri-

marily occupied with the registering of the more phenomenal results and with what they, as individuals, sensed, and have neglected to pay due attention to the inner group relation which is the only thing of major importance. It is the only thing which will release the stored up energy on the subjective side.

2. The second factor of importance is deep recognition of the subjective reality of the spiritual world. I, in myself, as you thought of me, am only the symbol of that world, as are other Masters, focussed—as channels of contact and service—in the Hierarchy. You, as a group, unitedly and together, were asked to approach me and to contact me just as, in the coming New Age, the churches of the future will (at the full moon period) make a definite approach to the Hierarchy in order to

    a. Intensify their spiritual life by the bringing in of spiritual force, with deliberation and consciously.
    b. Achieve spiritual illumination through contact with the powerhouse of light, the Hierarchy.
    c. Store up strength for increased dynamic activity for an ensuing period of service.
    d. Bring about a fusion between the objective and subjective life of humanity.

3. This leads to a Technique of Approach, based upon the realisation of the above objectives, to an effort to see me (as I symbolise for you the spiritual vision), and to the establishing of a pathway of Approach, symbolised in the ritual I gave you as a golden band of light. This you were to visualise as extending between yourselves, as a group, to your Tibetan brother. This pathway of Approach is the *Path* which it is planned should constitute a more familiar symbol than has hitherto been the case in the religious life of the race.

4. This pathway of light leads to the heart of a dark blue disk at the very centre of which you were told I could be contacted. Those of you who are in any way adept at meditation work know well that the light in the head—when seen and

recognised—passes usually through three stages of intensification:

    a. It is, first of all, a diffused light, surrounding the head, discovered later within the head and producing an inner radiance, which is the rudimentary halo.

    b. This diffused light then consolidates and becomes an inner radiant sun.

    c. Finally, at the centre of that sun, a point of dark blue, or a small indigo disk, appears. This is, in reality, the exit in the head through which the soul passes out of the world of phenomenal existence, and it is the symbol of the path or the door into the kingdom of God. This is the symbolical interpretation of the phenomena.

As the group approaches nearer and nearer to reality, the pathway or the band of light shortens (symbolically) and in time, when you are expert in this work and when your spiritual nature is truly intensified, you will enter almost immediately into, or through, the disk of blue and become aware of the higher consciousness, or divinity.

    5. Three things are, at this stage, essential to success:

    a. The mind must be "held steady in the light," and for this receptive experience all the previous work in meditation has been essential. Its positive, attentive activity has been an essential factor in producing the desired mind control.

    b. The creative imagination, involving as it does the power to visualise, has also to be developed and consciously used in obedience to instruction in the early stages. This obedience has to be rendered voluntarily, even though blindly, before the true objectives can be grasped.

    c. Results must be expected and an inner sensitivity developed which will eventually obviate surprise and lead to a conscious recognition of achievement. This sensitivity may differ according to ray and type, but the general indications will be in the field of similarity and of *group* value.

All this was the objective of the work I outlined. Much remained to be done, and each year I have expanded the concept and laid the foundation for future work to be carried forward with steadfastness over a long period of time. A beginning has been made.

II

In the second stage of the work outlined by me when you had worked for a year at this full moon activity, I began to widen the teaching and I added to the earlier technique. In the religion of the future, three years will always be given to training the youth of the period (from the ages of fifteen to eighteen) in a preparatory technique of Approach.

The stages in the second year's activity were as follows:

1. The recognition by the group members of the necessity for a closer group relation within the circle of the group and with me. This is symbolic of the recognition of the world need of love, as exemplified by an attitude of goodwill and understanding, and a closer approach by humanity to the Hierarchy. In the past, the religious emphasis upon the esoteric side of instruction has been the approach of the individual man to the God within, to his own higher self, the soul, the first Master. In the future, the emphasis will be upon the united approach of humanity (as represented by an increasing number of groups of aspirants and disciples) to the Hierarchy. According to the status of the groups and their awareness and condition of illumination, so will be the grade of hierarchical Worker with Whom they will be in touch.

2. The recognition that in this work, true occult obedience or the intelligent response to the urge of the group soul and to the "pull" of the Hierarchy, is the next major requirement. This will produce the right carrying out of the required assigned technique and a complete refraining from

any interest in phenomenal results or an analysis (at this stage) of any reactions experienced. Individual analysis hinders group recognition and true realisation. This is a point to be considered and remembered.

3. The next step which I indicated to you was that in which I pointed out that these Full Moon Approaches required one entire week of inner activity, divided as follows:

a. The three days prior to the full moon were to be dedicated to preparation. This preparation involved *confidence,* which swept the brain (the focus of the physical plane expression) into the right condition; *aspiration,* which held the astral body in the right attitude; and *dedication,* which was the intelligent process, motivated by free will and involving mental concentration, which enabled the confident aspirant to "hold the mind steady in the light."

b. Then, there were the twelve hours on the day of the full moon, wherein a consciously achieved contact (dependent upon the success of the previous three days' work *by the group*) became a definitely proven possibility. By training you in these early stages in the attempt to contact me, I was laying the ground for two eventualities: your future contact with your Master, prior to initiation, and a contact with the Hierarchy. This was intended to be symbolic of humanity's future contact.

c. The three days succeeding the full moon period then were considered. In these days, it was pointed out, the personality could become conscious of the success of the previous work done and the subsequent contact. That realisation would be facilitated by an inner attitude of *registration* (by the mind) of that which the soul has sought to impress upon it at the moment of attempted or achieved contact; by the *sense of expectancy* which the emotional nature would be trained to express and experience; and by the acknowledged attitude of the physical brain as it held to the *belief* of true success, when the requirements had been duly met.

It will be apparent to you, if you have followed the above in the right spirit, that from the very start I have been working towards objectives unrealised by you. I am trusting that the importance of this full moon work will become increasingly clear to you and make you more eager to work as requested by me.

III

The third stage, outlined by me during the past year's work, brought in a far more complicated activity than heretofore. I explained to you, if you will remember, that at the time of the full moon it was as if a door was opened between the Sun and Moon, making certain events of a spiritual nature possible. The band of golden light, extending between the Sun and the Moon, completely "irradiated the lunar surface" (to use the ancient formula) and made possible certain revelations. To students such as you, the symbolism should be apparent and can be seen as inviting a dual interpretation:

1. It concerns the relation of the Solar Angel to the lunar forces, of the Sun and the Moon and their work in synthesis.
2. It concerns the relation of the Hierarchy to humanity and consequently, of the subjective world to the objective worlds, of the realm of causes to the realm of effects. Ponder on this.

Individual approach must be merged into group approach, and the approach of groups will some day be superseded by the organised approach of humanity as a whole. This third stage can (like the two previous ones) be divided into the following activities, which require to be mentally grasped by the group:

1. That certain realisations become possible. These are two in number:

a. *Realisation one:* That entrance upon the Path of Approach is possible for individuals, for groups, and for humanity as a whole, as a unit.
b. *Realisation two:* That energies, not usually or normally contacted, can be touched, grasped and utilised at the time of these Approaches, *provided that they are contacted in group formation.* Thus the individual, the group and humanity are enriched and vitalised.

2. That the spiritual Hierarchy can, at these times, be approached, verified and known, thus leading to active conscious cooperation with the Plan which the Hierarchy serves. It must be remembered that, on the side of the Hierarchy, a Technique of Approach to humanity will also be employed, and thus we have an essential dual activity. The first stage of this dual activity took place millions of years ago at the time of *Individualisation,* and produced the emergence of the fourth kingdom in nature, the human family. The second stage is being rapidly worked out today, and will produce the emergence of *Initiation.* The intermediate stage is that of *Integration.* We have therefore the germ of a new scientific religion, called (as I have earlier pointed out) the Science of Approach. It is one in which humanity can now consciously share, for their stage in evolution warrants it. Men can today grasp the objective, share in the united aspiration, and carry out the needed requirements.

3. The time to be given, at this stage of the training, to the Full Moon Approach was shortened, but tremendously *intensified,* and the objective was to produce a far more *dynamic activity.* A state of tension had to be achieved, which would eventually release dynamic energy from—if possible —levels higher than that of the soul. Hence the need for group integration and work. This period was divided as follows:

a. There were two days of intensive preparation. This involved the achieving of a right attitude of a dual kind: The group member fused his outer activity and his inner orientation into one blended concentrated spiritual activity. He proceeded with his usual avocations, but at no time—whilst so occupied—was he to lose sight of the inner orientation and specific recollection. All the time he was outwardly busy, he was simultaneously occupied with a constant realisation of a retreat inward, a heightening of his vibration, and a raising of his consciousness.

b. On the day of the full moon, you were asked to go through a symbolic performance in the realm of the creative imagination, and through the medium of its agent, visualisation. This performance involved the following steps:

1. The recognition that in the blue disk, at the end of the golden pathway, was an ivory door which was slowly opening into a room with three windows.

2. The recognition that the group, as a unit, was advancing into that room and there, united in an act of solemn dedication, stands ready for revelation.

3. The recognition, by the group, of me, your teacher and Tibetan brother, and the saying by all of us together of the Great Invocation. This produces fusion and releases something from "that which lies above to that which lies below," speaking in the words of symbolism.

It will be obvious to you that in this symbolic ritual there is typified, first of all the Path, the goal, the kingdom of God, distinguished by spiritual mind, spiritual love and spiritual will (the three windows, atma-buddhi-manas, or the three aspects of the soul). Secondly, the focussing of the consciousness in that of the soul, followed by a group dedication; and, finally, that humanity (symbolised by the group) and the Hierarchy (symbolised by me) and the subsequent voicing by me of certain Words of Power were all intended to produce the fusion of the objective and subjective worlds, and the consequent emergence of the fifth kingdom in nature. Thus the skeleton structure of the new religious ceremonial can be dimly seen and inadquately sensed. This stage is followed by:

4. Two days of intensive recollection by the group in their *brain* consciousness. This involves:

a. The development of the power to recall the Words of Power which had been spoken by me, and later, the listening for a Word of Power. This recognition of the *Words* will be one of the major objectives of the new world religion, and hence our effort (not particularly successful hitherto) to do something symbolically analogous in our group activity.

b. A subsequent definite intensification of the life processes, and a spiritual demonstration upon the physical plane as a result.

The above elucidation should give you a new and more intelligent grasp of the symbolic significances of the work we are now attempting.

I am going to ask you to go over the whole process in these first three major stages, studying with care my interpretation.

1. During the months of January and February, please study what I have said, reading and rereading it until it is clear and fixed in your minds.
2. During March take the first stage and work faithfully at it.
3. During April take the second stage.
4. During May, take the third stage. Then for the remainder of the time, until October, work at this third stage. In October, if you have faithfully fulfilled requirement, I will outline the work next to be done. May I ask for your real interest, service and co-operation?

Your personal instructions I have placed at the end to indicate to you its relative importance and so impress upon you the necessity for your individual teaching taking a sec-

ondary place; it is of less importance than the group development and the service of humanity. You will all awaken some
day to the realisation that the Science of Service is of greater
importance than the Science of Meditation, because it is the
effort and the strenuous activity of the serving disciple which
evokes the soul powers, makes meditation an essential requirement, and is the mode—ahead of all others—which invokes the Spiritual Triad, brings about the intensification
of the spiritual life, forces the building of the antahkarana,
and leads in a graded series of renunciations to the Great
Renunciation, which sets the disciple free for all eternity.

I am giving you here certain needed hints and much
upon which to ponder. I give you of my time and of my love,
of my interest and my understanding. Let us together *serve*.

January 1946

To My Group of Affiliated Disciples:

Since I last communicated with you the outer aspects of
the world war, the carnage and the slaughter are over, except in a few sporadic instances. The struggle now being
waged is to reach a point of stabilisation in human thinking
and understanding from which a true and reliable peace can
emerge. On the emotional plane, there is as yet no peace. On
the mental plane, a great and deep-seated cleavage is going
on and the occult significance of certain words, enunciated
by the Christ when in Palestine, is being worked out. He
gave them as the keynote for the particular subjective happening which is taking place at this time. He said: "He that
is not with Me is against Me." This refers to the after effects
of the conflict between the Forces of Light and the Forces of
Evil. Great decisions have to be made all over the world, as
to whether humanity moves forward into a New Age of cooperation and of right human relations or whether the materialistic groups will reassert their control and succeed in
winning the day. This great cleavage is now in process of
settlement.

On the other hand, a deeply spiritual division is also taking place. In a peculiar sense, and speaking largely symbol-

ically, the first phase of the Great Judgment is asserting itself. The sheep and the goats are forming into two distinct groups. The judgment being given is not the generally assumed one of assigning penalties or rewards; it is *not* the negation of all effort as the result of decisive moves, nor will it result in the emergence of major dividing lines. Such interpretations are man-made and are not true interpretations of the parable or word picture which Christ gave to His disciples nearly two thousand years ago.

The judgment referred to has relation to a mysterious process which is going on in *the thinking* (if one dare use such a word for such a comprehensive process) of the planetary Logos. He is deciding at this time the mode by which a momentous event or happening within the Hierarchy shall take shape; He is timing the process of its externalisation; He is deciding which Ashrams shall be externalised and Who, within those Ashrams, should and must proceed with the purely inner and subjective work, and Who should be chosen to work—consciously and openly—in the outer world of men, thus duplicating in Their numbers what Christ experienced when He "descended into Hell." Many things have to be considered; the objectives in view of the Masters concerned, the rays in manifestation, and many astrological relationships.

In this deciding judgment Sanat Kumara is being aided by certain Members of the Great Council at Shamballa, by the Christ and by the seven Masters Who are responsible for the seven groups of Ashrams. He is also reaching certain conclusions as to the groups of disciples who have hitherto been under training during the final stages of the Path of Discipleship. This decision has to take under advisement *the rapidity* with which the entrance of men and women into the Ashrams can take place; it is also dependent upon the members of the Ashram moving forward according to their degree, and upon the power of the Ashrams to absorb and assimilate the much larger numbers, without upsetting ashramic stability. He has also to consider the ability of the neophyte under training to take and hold the far greater tension necessarily incident to true ashramic life in the New Age.

These points are all being most carefully considered, because a major expansion of the Hierarchy as a whole, and the consequent reaction upon humanity, again as a whole, is not a thing lightly to be undertaken. Expansion—if it is to be safely undertaken—must proceed hand in hand with consolidation. The expansion now contemplated in the highest quarters will greatly alter the potency of the relation of the Hierarchy to Humanity, and therefore of the second divine aspect to the third. Can Humanity take this increased potency correctly and safely? Will the aspirants of the world— if given opportunity to pass off the Probationary Path on to the Path of Discipleship—be stable enough to stand steady under the impact of hitherto undiscerned spiritual energy? Can the Masters, under the pressure of Their enormous task of world reconstruction, find the needed time to increase Their training of Their disciples? For They are still governed by the time equation where Their disciples are concerned. Can the senior members in any Ashram relieve to some extent the pressures upon the Masters as well as upon the incoming and junior, and therefore inexperienced, disciples? If, however, the relation between the Hierarchy and Humanity is thus strengthened and there is freer access in both directions, there will clearly emerge the invocational pull or the magnetic potency of these blending centres; the pull will be upon Shamballa, which is the highest centre of all.

Is the etheric web of the planet sufficiently stable and balanced so that it can adequately respond to the new and potent forces which could and will pour through it into objective expression? I would remind you that the release of atomic energy has had a far more potent effect in the etheric web than in the dense physical vehicle of the planet. Three times the atomic bomb was used, and that fact is itself significant. It was used twice in Japan, thereby disrupting the etheric web in what you erroneously call the Far East; it was used once in what is also universally called the Far West, and each time a great area of disruption was formed which will have future potent, and at present unsuspected, results.

The formation of the Triangles of Light and of Goodwill

—essentially the manipulation of energy into a desired thought pattern—has a definite relation to this area of disruption. It will in due time be found that the Japanese people, with their peculiar knowledge of thought power (used along wrong lines in the war period), will respond more intelligently to this type of work than many of the Western peoples. An effort should therefore be made to reach the Japanese along the lines of the Triangle work.

I would like to point out that the distinction between the "sheep and the goats" is mainly hierarchical. The term "goats" is esoterically applied to initiated disciples and to those who have climbed the mountain of initiation. The term "sheep" is applied to those who are following blindly the inner urge of their souls and who are groping their way (in relatively large numbers) toward the Hierarchy. For them still has to come the great revelation that the "kingdom of God is within you." Such is the word for them at this stage in humanity's history. Once they have realised that, they are already being absorbed into the Hierarchy. Life will now for them simplify. For the "goats" must come the impelling call from the highest aspect of the Spiritual Triad, "Seek the way of Ascension"—ascension out of even triadal life into that of pure Being and of monadic existence.

In this Great Judgment all decision lies in the conclusive thinking of Sanat Kumara. It is His judgment; neither the sheep nor the goats, nor the great mass of men from among whom they have emerged, can affect that decision in the slightest degree. Any moment or climax of decision on the part of the Lord of the World institutes new law and brings into play new energies. Laws are only the unalterable conditions brought about by the activity, the orientation and the emanated decisive thoughts of the One in Whom we live and move and have our being, just as the activities, the orientation and the thinking of a human being carry the cells and the atoms of his body *along the line* of his wishes. Energies are but the rhythm of His breathing and the results of the systolic and the diastolic action of His heart. From these energies we cannot escape, but—in a mysterious and peculiar

manner—the planetary Logos directs them or withholds
them to suit the recognised planetary needs of the period.

At this time the "eye of His direction" is turned towards
a needy and waiting world, and particularly towards the large
number of waiting people who hold within themselves the
potencies of discipleship. They are the hope of the world.
This outpouring of directed energy means a great stimulation of all sensitive and responsive aspirants; the result is not
an easy one for them. Everything in them is raised to the
surface of consciousness, and whilst they are faced with a
vital and beneficent opportunity, they are also faced with
the problem of absorbing more "punishment" (is not that
the word I want, my brother?) than they would normally
take. Will they break under the impact of self-discovery and
the opportunity to eliminate personality? Or will they rise
triumphant from the ashes of their dead selves into living
power and beauty?

Though Sanat Kumara is naturally unaware of the individual disciple or aspirant, He is not unaware of their massed
effect, quality or status. Contact and relationship are based
upon vibratory reaction, and the potency of the united vibration of the disciples and aspirants of the world is today—
for the first time in human history—strong enough to reach
Shamballa. This is a new and very interesting fact.

The Hierarchy therefore is:

1. In a position of extreme tension.
2. In a condition of quiescent waiting. It awaits:
   a. The decision which is on the verge of emanating
      from the judgment seat of Sanat Kumara.
   b. Notification as to the period and mode of the com-
      ing externalisation.
   c. The proposed influx into its ranks of disciples and
      aspirants.
   d. The reaction, later to be sensed by Them, of the
      massed use of the Great Invocation.
   e. The clear sounding of the invocative, though in-

choate, cry of the masses of those who are not yet even upon the Probationary Path.

3. Passing through a process of reorganisation. This involves the following:

   a. Senior disciples in the major Ashrams are now beginning to form subsidiary Ashrams, as I began to do in the year 1925.

   b. Owing to the war and the intensive efforts of the world disciples, more people along many and varied lines are being reached.

   c. The mode, methods and techniques of training (as I have earlier told you) are being remodeled and rearranged in order to suit the modern mind and needs.

   d. Senior disciples are undergoing a forcing process to enable them more rapidly to take the initiation immediately ahead of them. This necessarily brings added strains and risks, sometimes even to the point of death, but also greater spiritual light and life.

4. At the entrance to the Way of the Higher Evolution, which is now more easily to be found, owing to the rapid construction of the antahkarana by enlightened souls functioning upon the physical plane and working desperately to aid humanity. Their spiritual desperation is what is needed to provide the required "point of tension" from whence the antahkarana can be built. There is a basic distinction between desperation and pessimism. Desperation is related to the time element and to a correct and discriminative perception of the need. Pessimism is related more to an unjust appraisement of the quality of humanity.

All these things are at this time characteristic of the Hierarchy. I would remind you that when you think of the Hierarchy you think in terms of the Masters (as most people do) or of the higher initiates. This is *not* correct. Every accepted disciple is within the periphery of the Hierarchy and of its influence, and—as I have frequently pointed out—all have in some past life taken the first initiation. Every disciple has been to Bethlehem and has seen the Star in the East—that star which shines forth in fuller splendour each time another initiation is taken.

The difference between such disciples as you and the more advanced initiates is that your basic orientation is different to that of the Masters. They are oriented to Shamballa; They are relatively unaffected by affairs and happenings in the three worlds, even though that is the sphere wherein Their work lies; there is nothing within Them to react to these phases of planetary livingness. Disciples and all initiates below the third initiation are oriented to the Hierarchy. Not the Council Chamber at Shamballa or the Way to the Higher Evolution engrosses their attention, but the life of the Ashram with which they are affiliated and the Way of Initiation. This is a useful point to bear in mind. There is much in them which can and will react to qualities and events within the three worlds, and—from the angle of human consciousness—life for them is very difficult because the dualism of existence is apt to produce violent strain.

The extreme psychical tension affecting the Hierarchy puts an undue strain upon the emotions and the mental mechanism of the disciple because he is, as yet, unable to achieve that "quiescent waiting" which distinguishes the higher initiates. The Will of God is not yet adequately factual in his consciousness; he is preoccupied with the attempt to make his personal will synchronise with the spiritual will of the soul—a very different matter. The reorganisation being planned at this time by the Hierarchy and by the ashramic groups affects the personal lives of disciples and their efforts at accepting training; with the proposed changes and with the results of the outer ashramic work they *must* fall in line and they *must* accept the changing curriculum. Forget not that disciples in this particular period have to make adjustments which are not easy. They have been taught in terms of the old tradition, perpetuated and summarised by the Theosophical, Rosicrucian and other occult groups; they have had, since 1900, to accept and work with the newer modes of training and the changing forms of teaching applied by the Masters Who take pupils. This has created temporary difficulties which will not be present when the newer modes and methods are more generally established. The problem, therefore, of the modern disciple is peculiarly hard, and the Masters bear this ever in mind. Also the strain of the world cataclysm has increased these difficulties, and that strain is far more wide-reaching than is generally believed. Do you realise wherein the strain consists, apart from the physical disasters and chaos, with its agony, despair, anxiety, and its demand for a poised and efficient exterior to be presented to the world? Do you appreciate the keen ability of the trained disciple to react to the harrowing conditions of human suffering and to penetrate the controlled response which has to be given?

There are also other factors of a more subjective nature to which the disciple is sensitive, and among them are the following:

1. The astral or emotional vortex which humanity has inevitably set up as a result of registered pain and through which the observing disciple must move.

2. The glamour induced upon the astral plane as the result of three intermingling and inflowing streams of energy:

    a. The energies set in motion by the uprising cry of humanity itself, which inevitably shapes and moulds astral substance.

    b. The new inflowing spiritual energies which the planetary Logos is steadily bringing to bear upon human life and upon all forms of physical existence. These must traverse or cut across the astral realm in reaching the physical plane.

    c. The retreating forces of evil which are endeavouring to make a last desperate stand upon the astral plane.

These three types of force (when brought into relation with each other) are producing an unparalleled vortex of energy of which all disciples are necessarily aware, particularly those (and they are a large number) who are preparing for the second initiation. All disciples, working among their fellowmen, are brought into contact with this astral whirlpool. (I would call the attention of D.E.I. to this fact because it accounts for his reaction during the past two years and has led him to relinquish his position in my outer work and to retire into a phase of living which will provide him with no true scope for his pledged experience and his years of training; this present phase is in the nature of a cul-de-sac. Eventually he will have to retrace his steps and admit the reality of the time lost—lost in the moment of humanity's greatest need. Yet he will retrace his steps. I mention this as it is a typical instance of the effects of this glamour.)

3. The stimulation to which the lower vehicles of a disciple are unavoidably subjected. This evokes a full expression of all his inherent qualities, both good and bad. Everything in his nature is intensified, and the more mental he may be, the more he is *consciously* aware of these revelations. If his orientation is towards his life expression in the three worlds, a phase of depression, of self-accusation and frequently of doubt may have to be endured, thus handicapping his general usefulness.

4. The evocation of a strong sense of the soul within the personality. An emphasis upon the attitude of the soul to the personality life may also be induced and may prove very misleading. It would appear from the (apparently) voiced expression of soul comment, criticism, encouragement and planning that the main interest of the soul is with the dedicated personality. Such is *not* the case. The soul is very little aware of the personality nature, its disposition and ideas. The soul can be conscious of the limitations within the personality and of the barriers opposed to the inflow of soul energy, but the details are of no interest to the soul. The soul is occupied with *recognising* hierarchical planning, with *registering* world need, and with *responding* (faintly, very faintly at first) to the developing monadic inflow. These attitudes and reactions of the soul (upon its own plane of being) affect profoundly and fundamentally the personality life and produce those basic changes which evoke the vocation of the disciple. The disciple is occupied with vocation and not so much with evocation. (I would call this to the attention of

D.H.B. This type of evoked response is in the nature of illusion. He will know to what I am referring.)

5. The danger of "Imperil," as the Master Morya has
called it. This is somewhat erroneously interpreted as irritation by the neophyte, but it is not in fact irritation in the
ordinary connotation of the word. The surface ripples of
ordinary irritation and the evanescent angers to which all
disciples are prone are relatively of small importance. They
pass and, in the sumtotal of the soul's attitudes to the personality, evoke no response or registration whatsoever. What is
referred to is the reaction of the disciple to world evil. This
produces uncertainty as to the future, annoyance at what is
being done throughout the planet by non-disciples, criticism
of national and international planning and a general atmosphere of unhappiness, plus a sense of superior knowledge.
All this is expressed in a negative, unconstructive manner.
To this many disciples are today prone; they need to realise
that world affairs are not and cannot be moulded or determined by any hierarchical knowledge in the possession of
the disciple. World affairs and conditions have necessarily to
be based upon the demand and the point in evolution of the
mass of humanity, working through their representatives,
chosen or imposed, in every country. This demand can be
and is affected, modified and spiritualised by the attitude and
the teaching of disciples everywhere who are vocal and of
humanitarian instinct. If, however, the will and knowledge
of disciples in all nations were to condition world affairs and
control entirely the political, economic and social life of the
people, it would produce a far more serious cleavage than
now exists, for instance between the rich and the poor, or
between the classes and the castes. *It would produce a pronounced line of demarcation between the Kingdom of God
and the kingdom of men.* This would run counter to hierarchical intention, which is rapidly healing the existent
breach, and thus offset the work which Christ set out to do
on Earth. This point is often overlooked by well-intentioned
disciples. It is humanity which determines its own destiny.
Disciples point the way, indicate the vision, set a needed example and emphasise the ancient landmarks.

A realisation of these few points which I have chosen to enumerate out of many, will indicate to you the difficulties with which disciples are today confronted—each of you among the many who are also struggling to meet human need in a modern world.

As a group of ashramic affiliates, you (together with disciples everywhere) are all reacting to this inflow of energies, and with consequent conflict; with some of you it has produced a definite crisis and one that you have not yet resolved; with one or two of you in this group, it has led to a seething inner turmoil accompanied by an overemphasised introspection. This will be apt (if too protracted) to hinder your exoteric service. It is needless to remark that all of you need to become so sensitive to the quality of my Ashram, and so preoccupied with the opportunity to serve which confronts every disciple these days, that your own personal development, your unique problem (so regarded by you) and your reactions should be forgotten. You need to remember that you are not as interesting to your soul as you may think.

From the angle of the Master, it is the ability of the soul to control its instrument, the personality, and to work through it, that is of interest; it is for these types of ability that He looks, and not at the reaction of the personality. This is hard, if not humiliating, for the disciple to remember. The more engrossed he is with his personal responsiveness and capacities, the more impenetrable the barriers he is setting up between himself (upon the physical plane) and his soul; as a result of this, barriers are then being set up between the disciple and the life of the Ashram of which he is intended to form a part. Have this in mind and be, therefore, so occupied with the life of the soul that you have no time for personality introspection. The pure life of the soul will galvanise the centres above the diaphragm into activity, and your lives will become simple and uncomplicated expressions of the second aspect of divinity—of which all Ashrams are *focal* points.

As you know, it is not my intention to give you any more personal instructions; you no longer need them during the rest of this life, because if you carry out those already given there will be nothing to hinder your taking the initiation which is for you the next step forward. *Do you realise the import of what I am saying?* This initiation which confronts you can be taken either during the remaining years which are left to you; this, in the majority of cases is not probable, though a small minority—a very small minority—may achieve the goal. Or initiation may be taken in the interim period between incarnations, or else immediately upon return to physical plane life. This latter is the most probable for those who are not taking initiations higher than the third; and, at present, for that initiation I am not preparing disciples. It is usually regarded as essential that disciples who are taking the second or third initiations should register them in their brain consciousness. As I have often told you, the initiate consciousness is *not* the factor which requires to be thus recorded; it is seldom so. Recognition of it comes when the candidate is participating in the "esoteric installation" of a candidate into the ranks of the Great White Lodge. What the disciple undergoing initiation (and I choose the word "undergoing" with deliberation) must and eventually does record are the crises which brought about his fitness to take initiation, as it is erroneously called in theosophical circles. These, correctly handled and surmounted, will result in his being an initiate—a very different interpretation to the current theosophical one. As I often told you, a man *is* an initiate, prior to any initiation ceremony. The ceremony concerns hierarchical recognition of the disciple and does not concern the candidate's fitness. I find it needful to re-iterate this fact.

The planetary crises through which the planetary Logos is at this time passing should result in the emergence of many initiates; no true disciple is exempt from the effects of this planetary situation. Inevitably, changes are wrought by the soul in the personal life. When these changes are focussed through the lower centres and the lower bodies, the general result is purification and character building. The aspirant is then still upon the Probationary Path. When the disciple is in the position where he can pass through the first three initiations, then the inflowing energies work through the heart, the throat and the ajna centres; when the highest head centre and the lowest spinal centre are simultaneously involved, the disciple is then able to take the higher major initiations. Much of this has been given you in the earlier teaching you have received, but I repeat these statements, so that with clarity you may proceed.

One of you asked a question concerning divine intervention as a result of prayer, and I would point out that there is a distinction between Divine Intervention and Answered Prayer. One admits of reciprocal energies, the other predicates action from above only. The measure of success in either case is dependent upon humanity as a whole. Classically the body is not equipped to receive the fire, until consciousness is importuned to racial need. This is secondary to Divine Intervention which isolates the few and uses their organism to fuse and free the energies of dispersion. This is sudden death to the physical vehicle if unprepared. Think upon this and know the consequences of emotional fanaticism.

There are three ways whereby the inception may come:

1. Disciples aware of their charge, relinquish all personal ambition and are willing to meet the test and be used. For, be not surprised my brother, a disciple can meet the test if he *will*. Accepted discipleship is in itself a guarantee of a certain amount of preparedness administered through right devotion, pure purpose and rigid discipline.

2. The focussed intent of the hard pressed peoples of the world clamouring for peace, forms a nucleus of unregenerate energy which can and will be used. It is less potent in effect, but in these days of crisis everything must be used.

3. Every kingdom on earth is encumbered with *shock*— animal, vegetable, mineral, as well as human. This disturbance is a phase of promotion. There are crashed areas of released energy, causing forces to be freed which again can and will be used in the reconstruction.

The responsibility of this group is *purpose*. It is *will* fused and blended and dispersed. I charge you to waste no time in idle speculation, but to carry your responsibility as it should be carried, remembering that your only value is group determined. Placement determines effort (I suggest that you analyse this statement). Consequences are hierarchical. There is lowered vitality in the world today due to a fear psychosis.

Command your forces, stand in the Light, and the suspended mental link will recharge the magnetic field for which you, as a group, are responsible. The fusion exists in a small degree now, but *Purpose* is the magnetised line along which the fire may travel.

You have preserved your interest and effort for many years now. Can you continue with this enterprise? It is for you a task of perseverance and of faith. You may not in your various lifetimes see the *world* results. That I frankly tell you. You can undoubtedly realise and reap the benefit of the *group* results, for your fusion into one close bond of brotherhood and devotion, into one united band treading the Path together is adequate reward. It will offset the usual loneliness of the disciple's way and enable him to realise that he travels *not* alone.

Above and beyond your personal compensation (which some of you know already to be your group relation and its persistence) will be the building of an aspect of the mechanism of contact and of approach which can be known and seen by Us from the other side of life, but which has to be largely taken on faith by you. It might be regarded as the mechanism of inspiration, for—in the last analysis—it is individual and world inspiration which is the goal of all our work. This mechanism is a subjective fact, and is slowly built as disciples aspire and serve and obey. It is an individual mechanism, and a group mechanism, and will eventually form part of the mechanism of humanity, viewing it as a whole and as the fourth kingdom in nature. This kingdom is destined to act as a transmitter of force, of energy and life and of inspiration to the three subhuman kingdoms. It is this mechanism which will constitute the bridge between the fourth and fifth king-doms. It is the individual and the group antahkarana.

I am going to change your full moon work a little. Pro-ceed as heretofore, but as you stand with me before the "open window" and prior to the attempt to hear me speak the words which I may have for you, imagine yourselves as bathed in a vivid butter-coloured living light which is pouring through the open window and enveloping the group. Note, as this happens, which centre responds or registers the vibration and stimulation or any phenomena of any kind, and then record this upon your monthly reports. I am also going to change the words spoken and am choosing phrases which will con-vey a pictorial connotation to your minds; in this way the power of visualisation will be evoked and aid you in register-ing what I say. Here are the phrases among which I shall choose one for each full moon contact.

1. The golden lotus of the heart.
2. The burning ground of fiery red.
3. The mountain top, bathed in the morning sunrise.
4. The uplifted hand.
5. The equal four-armed cross.
6. The open door.
7. The triangle of fire.
8. The golden way to God.
9. The ocean and the rocky shore.
10. The silver torch.
11. The iridescent cube.
12. The burning bush.

I shall picture these to you and name them in your hear-ing. Note whether you can both see and hear.

My blessing rests upon you and together we go forward into the future.

June 1946

My Brothers:

The papers which I am at this time sending out to you are perhaps the most important which you have ever received. This is so—not from the teaching angle—but from the angle of the Ashram with which you are affiliated.

I would like to start by emphasising the *fact* of your affiliation, because it is a subjective relation with which nothing can permanently interfere. There may come these interludes (where neophytes are concerned) when the relationship seems severed, and others wherein the disciple appears to be making no progress at all and has nothing to contribute to the life of the Ashram. But—in the turning of the wheel of life—lessons *are* learnt, and usefulness returns.

I would like to ask you to read this with care, with detachment, with undimmed aspiration, and with the realisation that this present life is but a minute in the life of the soul. This life is, however, of *major* importance in the life of some of you; it is of *focussing* importance in the life of a few; it is of *testing* importance for some.

I have now definitely decided to disband the New Seed Group. My experiment in reorganising the earlier groups into one large group has not succeeded. I have told you frequently that the Hierarchy itself does not know what decisions humanity will make in world affairs, or if mankind will profit from proffered opportunity. Equally so, the Master of an Ashram does not know what "disciples on the periphery" of an Ashram will do, because their training and testing is only in process. He does know what the accepted disciple, admitted freely into ashramic intimacy, will do in any given circumstance, because he has been tested and tried and the Master knows that there are certain things which he will *not* do.

This experiment with the New Seed Group has lasted five years. The earlier experiment with the groups lasted ten years. These experiments were undertaken in the most difficult period of the world's history and during a particular time of stress and strain. Of this I am not unmindful.

I am disbanding this group *exoterically* on four counts:

1. (Deleted by A.A.B.)
2. In spite of many years of work with me, the group is not yet integrated and has produced no particular spir-

itual enterprise. I have indicated many spiritual enterprises which called for your full measure of enthusiasm, time, money and interest. Many of you in this group are doing less for the Triangle work, the Goodwill work and the distribution of the Invocation than the average School student, and it is you to whom I should look for aid in what I am attempting to do. Why not aid me where I have asked for aid? Why search for something unique and special and different from that of the rest of the students?

The spiritual enterprise into which I hoped to see you all throw yourselves was the work I have outlined, the distribution of the Problems of Humanity, the spread of the Invocation, the Triangles and the Goodwill work. I am *not* interested in some particularly occult work which you will evolve in meditation or in discussion. F.C.D. is entering upon his life work along the lines of my enterprises; it will be a hard one, growing out of the Problems, presented by me to you. Forget not that these Problems were part of your instructions released for the general public. I have no criticism of F.C.D., who has come through deep waters to heights from which he can do most effective work. I am happy to be associated with him and have asked the Master K.H. to leave him a little longer in my group. I have no criticism of J.W.K-P., who has handled a profoundly difficult task for me with beauty, understanding, judgment and courtesy.

3. My next reason for disbanding the group is the failure in occult obedience of many of you. Voluntarily and willingly you joined the groups for training, discipline and expansion. This involved the following of certain suggestions, meditations and instructions. For years, quite a number of you have done absolutely nothing about your personal instructions. I refer here not only to exoteric exactitude but (above all else) to esoteric understanding. When, my brothers, I assign meditation work and make suggestion over the years, I have a definite purpose in view and a plan worked out

which is adapted to the particular student. When the work is not done, I—owing to the freewill of the disciple—am helpless.

4. Another reason upon which I must very briefly touch, and which is a factor in my decision, is A.A.B.'s integrity in the work. Among some of you, if what I write is agreeable to you, expresses your own ideas and is in line with your group thinking, then it is I who write it. When what I dictate runs counter to the ideas of the disciples, or places a finger on a weakness, or makes a statement which runs counter to the lower mind, then it is written by A.A.B. This situation has existed for some time.

For these main reasons, and because I seek no further to burden A.A.B. with your personal instructions, I am closing this aspect of my work. A.A.B. has much to do for me in finishing the Instructions as outlined. Her own Master (and mine) also requests that she no longer do this work, and with Him I am in full agreement. A.A.B. has also to conclude the Ashram papers* and finish the papers on Healing.** Then her task for me will be accomplished.

D.E.I. is no longer in this group, and for this life and probably the next, he will be learning the lessons of adaptability, of impersonality and renunciation. He made one serious and irretrievable move prior to the outbreak of the war, and he did this against the advice of senior disciples and of his own inner monitor.

I would here again remind you that the inner link remains unbroken. *You are still members—each and all of you —on the periphery of my Ashram.* Nothing can alter this. Some of you warrant no criticism from me and are not responsible for what has happened.

Let me reiterate: The ashramic link remains unbroken, but the outer relation is ended for this incarnation. You can still reach me *individually,* if you fulfill the requirements and seek to serve the Plan outlined to you by me.

With this general letter I am sending very full personal

---
*A Treatise on the Seven Rays, Vol. V.
**A Treatise on the Seven Rays (Esoteric Healing), Vol. IV.

instructions—the last you will receive from me this life on the outer plane. I would ask you to read with extreme care what I have to say and suggest, because of the effect it may have on your outer life of service.

I use not words lightly. A.A.B. has taken me down with accuracy during these many years, including the past nine years of illness. She has never been too ill to take my dictation and send it out to you and to the world exactly as I gave it. Please read not only your own instructions but those given to the other members of the group, and you will then understand more clearly the reasons for the disbanding of this group. The personal instructions will be full and concise and will give you enough work, coupled with all your previous instructions over the years, to occupy your attention for the remainder of your lives and lead you into a closer association with the Ashram. You have the instructions, covering many years and given to each of you, preserved for you in *Discipleship in the New Age* (Vol. I). You have much intensified and concentrated individual teaching, much indication of opportunity and of the work which you are individually asked to do, a great deal of help in dealing with personality limitations, and much inspiration.

Read now my personal instructions to you in the light of our long personal relations. We have worked together for many years and I know you all well. I have told you that in the light of the Ashram there is naught concealed. These instructions are bridging instructions which will suffice until the day comes when you will step into a closer relation and will have overcome the personality to such an extent that there will be no fear of your making any serious mistakes; you can then be depended upon, as are all true accepted *serving* disciples.

The teaching—along special lines—of the New Age presentation of esoteric truth, necessary in preparation for initiation, will continue; it is essential that the second volume of *Discipleship in the New Age* should reach the public. This new teaching (or rather this new sequence of teaching) in its timed presentation consists, as you already know, of six themes or subjects:

Instruction on Meditation.
Teaching on Initiation.
Training in Telepathy.
Teaching anent the Etheric Body.
The Problems of Humanity.
The Externalisation of the Ashrams.

You will continue to receive these papers, *not* as an affiliated member of my Ashram, but only as an intelligent, trained aspirant who is privileged to be used in building up the needed thoughtforms anent the correct aspects of the teaching so that the seed or germ may be truly implanted in the human consciousness and thus truly grow and influence the coming age. Forget this not.

March 1947

MY BROTHERS:

You will by now have recovered from the shock of the cessation of our outer communication. As you may well realise (or do you?), my inner relation to you remains an entirely private and individual matter, known only to the aspiring disciple and myself. Such it must remain for this immediate life cycle. The strength of your radiance, your potential as a light bearer, and your ability to serve your fellowmen will demonstrate to your co-disciples in my Ashram or on its periphery the *fact* of that relationship; it will prove that you, the personality, the soul, and the Master of the Ashram, are in contact. The supreme Master, the Christ, said when last on Earth: "By their fruits ye shall know them." In so saying, He indicated a definite line of guidance for all of us.

A Master has to know and gauge the disciple by the work which he does in the furthering of the Plan, and not by the disciple's reaction to his aspiration. The attentive world has also to gauge the existent phase of divine expression in the disciple's daily life. By what else can the onlooker gauge it? The disciple is therefore under constant dual investigation; to this test, he must perforce himself add a third: his own position as the Observer. He is thus exposed to criticism and

judgment from three angles, and upon this fact I would ask
you carefully to ponder.

A review at night along these three lines would be of
value to all disciples, using the imagination as far as possible
as an instrument of spiritual perception; learn to "imagine,"
as far as you can, how a Master would view your day's endeavour, how your watching environment would have reacted to your life and words, and how you yourself regard
the day's accomplishments. I would recommend this to all
disciples and all of you in training for my Ashram; and what
I have here suggested might well be used also by the Arcane
School for the senior students.

March 1948

MY BROTHERS:

Another year has gone by and it is again time for me to
extend the teaching already given still a little further. You
are still functioning as a group with closely interrelated
links with the Ashram, with me and with each other. The
situation is not, however, the same as it was last year, and
there are certain differences and distinctions. These are due
to the reorganisation which has gone on within the Hierarchy itself, necessitated by the imminent reappearance of
the Christ. This has produced certain basic changes.

As you know, I have for years (with the assistance of
A.A.B.) been endeavouring to help and aid many disciples
who belong to other Ashrams than the second ray Ashram
of K.H. or my own. I have given to them the basic teaching
which they would have received from their own Masters and
—because my Ashram is a second ray Ashram—they have had
an imperative stimulus given to their love nature, and their
sense of universality has been developed, in order to fit them
for the work of the coming cycle. In the cycle now so near
at hand, the Lord of Love will seek to organise the new era
along the new or Aquarian lines. In the series of papers on
the externalisation of the Ashrams or of the Hierarchy,* we
are in reality considering the goal or supreme expression of

* *The Externalisation of the Hierarchy.*

the teaching given to many disciples anent that great event
—teaching intended to evoke their intelligent cooperation.

In your preceding series of instructions I dealt specifically
with the Return of the Christ, and that message was sent out
on a large scale to the general public. Since then I have
written two other papers, entitled: The Work of the Christ
and The Teaching of the Christ. These have been added to
the original instruction anent Christ's reappearance, so as
to reach a larger public than just this handful of disciples.
These instructions are now available to all of you in book
form, entitled. The Reappearance of the Christ.

The point which I am seeking to make is that this book
is primarily your contribution to the effort which the Hierarchy is making to reach and arouse men everywhere to the
imminence and the inevitability of Christ's emergence; it is
in the nature of a seal set upon your faithfulness and steadfast faith over the years in which we have worked together.
More important still, you have (as a group) provided the
pool of thought that could be stirred into activity, and thus
make possible the giving out of this terrific proclamation—
for that is what it is. Thus you have served and helped at
this critical time—critical not only among men and in connection with world affairs but critical also in the Hierarchy
itself.

In your thinking, reflection and activities carried on
henceforth, this major, presented hierarchical intention must
constitute the very groundwork of your life pattern. As members of an Ashram, you are part and parcel of the present
crisis within the Hierarchy, and you cannot avoid it.

One of the effects of the reorientation is that four or five
of you will be working more actively, and eventually more
consciously, in the Ashram of your own Master and less
actively in mine; you must remember, however, that the link
is by no means severed. Another effect is that several disciples
from other Ashrams will be working in my group, and one
of the Master K.H.'s disciples is now to function as senior
disciple in my Ashram, because A.A.B. is no longer available
in that capacity as she has been since 1932; she resumed her
own activities in the Ashram of the Master K.H. over three

years ago. The completion of my books is practically all that she is now doing for me.

This reorientation and this "outward movement" of the Hierarchy requires the assuming of a certain attitude on the part of all of us, and the development of certain mental habits, which I will proceed to discuss with you as part of the usual first theme in all these instructions, that of meditation.

January 1949

MY BROTHERS:

This new year of 1949 is a peculiarly momentous one from the angle of spiritual values. Last year was one of decision—as public affairs have demonstrated—decisions which were not always sound and which infringed the principle of right human relations. It was a year of decision for the Hierarchy as well as for many world leaders, both secular and spiritual. The disciples of the world were under great and peculiar strain, many of them working off and handling severe personal karma, and some of them descending into the very depths of realisation—depths where world iniquity and world sorrow confronted them and world issues were made very clear to them. It was therefore a year of peculiar testing and trial, and the more advanced the disciple the greater has been his problem, involving as it has done both personal and world problems. The load upon them has been heavy.

To this condition the members of the New Seed Group and those affiliated with them and with my Ashram have been no exception. This new year holds in it great potentialities for expansion and growth and for the progress of all movements, particularly those oriented to the work of the spiritual Hierarchy of our planet. The inflowing force is *beneficently* potent and the destructive forces which have prevailed during the last few years are not so dynamic. This should be a year of moving forward and of expansion (implemented and directed by the Hierarchy). The spiritual vortex of force which is moving nearer to manifestation will make possible certain moves and will clear away some (though not all) of those forces which have held back the proposed expansion and which have limited the work that disciples all over the world have sought to do. Every disciple has been tested; unsuspected weaknesses have emerged and characteristics which should be straightened out have come to the surface; a few—a very few—have fallen by the way, but a large majority have passed the test.

Weaknesses of motivation, of purpose, of technique and of personality faults have been exposed and recognised by truly earnest disciples; this has been necessary, for the incoming energies will render excessive the weaknesses (if they are recognised for what they are) and will enhance the contribution to world service of those disciples who can stand the strain and face themselves with truth and sincerity.

The call is going out from every Ashram to all workers to close their ranks and to stand together in the closest comradeship of loyalty and understanding; the challenge is for them to subject themselves (and by that I mean their personalities) to a drastically applied self-discipline, to a purifying process, and to effect those reforms within their own natures which will make them more effective instruments in service. I am impressing the minds of those members of my Ashram of whom you have never heard with these same ideas in connection with the work that they may be doing for the Hierarchy.

It was the knowledge of this coming inflow and opportunity for increased usefulness which prompted A.A.B. to put through the reorganisation of the Arcane School, to close its ranks and to deepen the proposed trend of the teaching and thus to take those steps which will make the work more effective and potent. She has also taken and will in the near future take the needed steps for the effective functioning of the Arcane School after she passes to the inner side of service.

The organising and work of the Arcane School is the spiritual project of A.A.B. and with it I have nothing whatsoever to do, nor shall I ever in the future guide or take any part in the affairs of the Arcane School. That is the task of those whom A.A.B. will choose to carry on. It is a living organism which will grow of its own inherent potentialities and under the spiritual inspiration of the energy coming from the Ashram of the Master K.H. in which A.A.B. is a worker and disciple.

I seek now to make a few comments anent the work for which A.A.B. has been responsible and for which F.B. will be responsible when she passes over.

During the years in which I have been in touch with all of you, much world work has been started, and the influence of the group of workers whom A.A.B. and F.B. have gathered around them has spread all over the world. I refer here to what they stand for internationally and—as a result of the spread of the teaching for which I am responsible—to the change which has been wrought in the general consciousness. That is far greater than you know. The world-wide spiritual ferment which has been consequently set up has been due to two main causes:

1. *The Arcane School* as members have adhered to it in every land and have each in turn become distributors of light.
2. *The publication and distribution of my books* everywhere; they are far more widely read than you have any idea.

Out of the apprehension of truth by many thousands in many lands and the need for it to be put to practical use in these days of dire world need, two other modes of work were initiated: the *Triangles* and the *Goodwill* work. There is here no need for me to go into details anent these two spiritual enterprises. You know them well, though only a few of you have been truly interested or thrown yourselves, heart and soul, into assisting.

The Arcane School is not one of my activities or enterprises, and has never been. In view of the condition of esoteric schools (so called) in the world, when A.A.B. organised the Arcane School she deliberately refused to let me have anything to do with it, and I fully concurred in her decision. The extent of my connection with the School lies in the fact that I outlined for her the degrees of the School, and once or twice—in my instructions used in the Disciples Degree—I appealed to the students for cooperation in some matter. Forget not that these instructions were not School instructions, but were the early form of my books and went out unchanged to the general public. Also, it has only been within the last five years that any correspondence course for the School has been arranged around one or other of my books.

The policy of the School, its principles, curriculum and techniques, have been entirely those of A.A.B., working in conjunction with F.B. and after consultation with one or two senior students living in or around New York or in Europe.

There has necessarily been questioning among senior students and in this group as to what will happen when A.A.B. passes on. The past record of this group in effective and steady work would not incite A.A.B. to have much confidence in your leadership. You have shown no organised group ability to take a piece of work embodying some one or other of my suggested spiritual enterprises and effectively work together for its furtherance. What have you done *as a group* to aid the Triangle work or the Goodwill work, or to throw yourselves successfully behind the work of the School? There are many outside the New Seed Group who have done a more consecrated and selfless task than have you, though there are a few exceptions. But, my brothers, out of fifty-one, how few!!

When A.A.B. passes on she will leave the Arcane School and, with my full approval, all the other activities in the hands of F.B. She will leave also, in the departments, dedicated men who will continue to assume, as far as in them lies, the direction of the work, in consultation with F.B.

There will be no need whatsoever for any reorganisation. Why should there be? A.A.B. has been interested in and has initiated, with F.B., all departments. She has never been a worker in any of them, which may be a new idea to you. When she finishes her job there is no gap in any department. So why reorganisation? The work will go on with the same workers, and new ones will be added as need arises. Young workers must be chosen who may not see things as all of you see them, and in that lies the hope of the work's persistence, for most of you are too old for the work of reconstruction and too crystallised; you can, however, form a strong foundation and give courage to the young ones. Most of you are too anxious to see the old methods and modes of work perpetuated. I and A.A.B. are more interested in seeing that the need of the youth of the world is met. The *principles* of the Ageless Wisdom must be preserved, but all outworn forms must go.

The success and growth of the work will depend upon the smooth transition which can be made between the past and the coming new world; it will be dependent upon the determination of the workers to continue with what they are doing, to renew their dedication and above all, their vision; to eliminate all desire for prominence in the work and all ambition, and with a will to meet the need in the new ways, with the expanded truths and with no dogmatism.

I am looking for no new "stenographers" to take the place of A.A.B. and shall dictate to none of you. You have masses of undigested material with which to work, and enough teaching to express and make available to the public for twenty-five years to come. You have enough information from me to enable you to make your individual contact with me if you follow the rules and live the outer life of a disciple.

It is the books which bring people into the various phases of the work; you can aid in keeping them in constant circulation, and you can also hold together subjectively so that the relation *of the group* to the Ashram is still preserved and externalisation later can still be possible. Those are the two major undertakings with which I present you; and these with your intensified individual approach and the work of the Triangles and Goodwill, will provide you with much to do.

Throw yourselves behind those who have made themselves responsible—under F.B.—for the Triangles and Goodwill work. Make their work possible and avoid interference; they will make mistakes, and these you will be prompt to note; your sole duty is to stand by. Mistakes do not matter if clarity of vision, spiritual persistence and love accompany them. Keep the personnel of the work as far as possible masculine and put no sixth ray people in positions of influence; they know not how to cooperate and are frequently points of dissension and dislike.

You see, my brothers, I am making no startling plans for handling the work in the event of the death of A.A.B. I suggest no changes. I would like to see the work left in the hands of those who are already doing it; I suggest the addition of young people to the group of workers as need arises and place occurs. I suggest that the work be kept fluid, as A.A.B. has always kept it.

Above all else, remember that the work of the Triangles, the Goodwill work and the Arcane School is that of an *organism* and not an organisation, and it will grow through its own inherent life and not through planning. If this is borne in mind, you will see where some of you have been in error, both in criticism and in planning the future of the various aspects of the work. The work will go on in the strength of its own inherent life; it will be damaged by planning, interference and organisation. Let the work alone, giving it assiduous attention and meeting its needs as they arise. The Triangle work and the Goodwill work are in the hands of young people who must be strengthened, trusted and encouraged. The Invocation work, tied in with the Goodwill work, the Triangles and the School, is moving steadily forward and is the responsibility of all three. If rightly handled, its distribution will be automatic, mechanical and momentous.

The various phases of the work will proceed as desired if all talk of executive heads, of assumed responsibility, and of the need for the New Seed Group is ended. The thought of reorganisation must be dropped; it would immediately disrupt the present smoothly working organism. A transition carried forward without any change or difficulty will greatly reassure all groups. Young people should be found and trained—*trained in the principles*. There should be no doctrinal teaching given. If it is, inevitably the School will die. The new truths are being fast recognised, but it is youth which is recognising them. Those who have for twenty years absorbed a system of thought are apt to be so absorbed by it that it is hard for them to recognise the new and vital incoming truth, and the sad part is that they are often sure they do. The new truths are overshadowing us today; if the Invocation means anything, it is what must be expected.

The principles to be emphasised are:

1. The Arcane School trains disciples. Its curriculum is therefore eliminative. Its standard cannot be lowered. It is not a school for probationers. It will consequently always remain relatively small.
2. It is a school for adults wherein occult obedience is developed. This is not obedience to man-made rules or school obediences, but involves soul obedience.
3. This is a school wherein belief in the Hierarchy is scientifically taught, not as a doctrine but as an existent and provable natural kingdom; the rules of the Ashram and the dual life of the disciple are emphasised.
4. This is a school wherein the student is taught that "the souls of men are one."
5. No claim for place or power is made, and the claim of being an initiate is never heard. The Headquarters Group and the workers in the School are there because of spiritual inclination.
6. The Arcane School is non-sectarian, non-political and international in its thinking. Service is its keynote. Its members can work in any sect and in any political party, provided they remember that all paths lead to God and that "the One Humanity" governs all their thinking.
7. The fundamental doctrines of the Ageless Wisdom, recognised all over the world and as expounded in my books, constitute the foundational teaching of the Arcane School. This is so, not because they are my books but because they are part of the continuity of the Ageless Wisdom and constitute the latest emanation of the Ageless Wisdom issued by the Hierarchy. They must not be permitted to become a Bible of a sect, as has been the case with *The Secret Doctrine* and the

Theosophical Society. This incidentally has been a profound disappointment to the Hierarchy. A.A.B. must not be turned into an occult authority. Those connected with the Great White Lodge favour no Bibles or authorities—only the freedom of the human soul. The teaching matters, not the source or the form.

Let me reiterate for the sake of clarity: None of you has any responsibility for the Arcane School or for the service activities though you can work helpfully, with humbleness and pure motive in any or all of them, under the direction of A.A.B. or of those into whose hands she has put responsibility. . . . It is in these relationships that you will develop the humility and pure motives which are the outstanding hallmarks of the disciple.

One thing I would however like you clearly to grasp and that is the *pattern* which underlies the various aspects of the work now in process of expansion. A brief diagram should make the relationship clear, and *these relationships are factual today:*

THE SPIRITUAL HIERARCHY OF THE PLANET
working through
/
THE NEW GROUP OF WORLD SERVERS
using many agencies, among them
/
THE ARCANE SCHOOL
working through
/
THE SERVICE ACTIVITIES
the Triangles, the Goodwill work, the Invocation work
allied with
/
THE LUCIS PUBLISHING COMPANY

The energy of the New Group of World Servers could be likened to the antahkarana which connects humanity with the Hierarchy and provides a channel of contact with the Ashrams of the Masters. The Arcane School can be consid-

ered as one of the results of the activity of the New Group of
World Servers. There are many others scattered all over the
world. The same holds true of the Service Activities. No esoteric group is soundly handled and correctly motivated unless the spiritual energies which are available to it and the
knowledge and the wisdom unfolded find expression in
definite service. The service activities are, therefore, an expression of the livingness of the Arcane School and that relationship must be valued and preserved.

As disciples, your place is in the senior ranks of the New
Group of World Servers and your responsibility, as a group,
is to aid a phase of the work to be done which is strictly the
project of the Hierarchy as a whole. I ask you to throw your
efforts into the work of preparation for the reappearance of
the Christ, to further in all possible ways the distribution
both of the pamphlet so entitled and the book which deals
with His reappearance. The world must be flooded with the
information and through the hope and expectancy thus engendered may move forward into greater light, better human
relations and a newer happiness. The results of your activities along this line should enhance the usefulness of the service activities of the Arcane School and swell the ranks of
those who are working on mental levels in the Triangles
and for right human relations through the medium of the
Goodwill work.

Begin, my brothers, to do your own work, leaving others
to shoulder their assigned responsibilities and waste no time
in interfering in any phase of work which does not call for
your attention. *You are in my Ashram.* The Arcane School
is not a project of my Ashram and is, therefore, no responsibility of yours. It has been the means of giving you a
greatly needed esoteric training and will continue to do so if
you so desire, but the work of the Christ (to which all Ashrams are pledged) calls for your cooperation; it is this responsibility which I lay upon your shoulders.

That the years may see developed in all of you a firmer
dedication, a self-sacrificing service and a deepened humility,
is the hope and prayer of your friend, collaborator and
Master.

March 1949

MY BROTHERS:

I have no group instructions for you now. Nor shall I have again. When the instructions on the designated themes are completed, I will write an instruction upon group work which will close all that I have to say on the subject in the two volumes of the book *Discipleship in the New Age.* The major intention of this book is to awaken the aspirational public to the opportunity for training which is theirs *if* they so choose; it should make them think with greater clarity of the Hierarchy and its functions; much good may come of sending forth its teachings and a new era in the field of spiritual instructions may result. My present objective is now to help A.A.B. conclude the important teaching which I have—with her aid—been giving to the group over a long period of years; it will then be available to the general public, after certain specific deletions, about which she knows and which are similar to those in the first volume. You have had more, much more, than you can assimilate; of the original group of students only a few are left; of the more than fifty original members who have been affiliated with my Ashram, only sixteen remain, and of these only eight are truly active; and of these eight, two are causing me some questioning.

You might at this point appropriately ask the following questions: Wherein lies the fault, and was there error in the choices I made? Where does the blame lie for what—on the surface—appears to be such an outstanding failure? It may perhaps interest you to have some of the reasons presented to you:

1. A Master, in choosing the personnel of His Ashram, is Himself governed by certain unavoidable factors:
    a. The fact that the aspiration and the development of a disciple (usually stimulated by some senior disciple) has enabled him in thought and consciousness to reach the periphery of the Ashram; sometimes the spiritual forcing process brings him to that

point prematurely. The disciple is, however, *there;* the next move is (as you say) up to the Master; He must then give the disciple the opportunity to move closer, if the capacity for such a step lies in him.

b. The fact of karmic relationship. Many of those who have been given the opportunity to work with me have had some relationship with me over past lives and—because of certain activities—have warranted the opportunity to work in a still closer relationship. This they prove by working off karma. Such were H.S.D. and S.S.P., neither of whom has completely failed.

c. The fact of the need—existent in the world today— for workers. The Masters are perforce driven to use people to carry out certain phases of the exoteric work of service for which they may be fitted but for which they, from other angles, are not ready. Such a one was W.D.B.

All these factors necessarily governed my choice, for I too (even though I may be a Master) am controlled by esoteric Law and must proffer opportunity. Among those chosen there has been much failure, but because consecration and devotion to either the Hierarchy or Humanity are still to be found in them, the affiliation with my Ashram still persists, even though in so few cases can permission to move closer be granted; they are *not* yet ready to reach a "more enlightened ashramic position," as it is called.

2. Affiliation with an Ashram subjects the aspirant to intensified stimulation; in many cases it proved impossible for some chelas to handle it. Spiritual energy pouring into the personality, via the aspirant's own soul, fostered the emergence of that which was good but also of that which could not be taken closer into the Ashram itself. The undesirable qualities had to be eliminated. (Such were S.C.P. and L.U.T.) This stimulation cannot be avoided and is one of the tests of an accepted disciple's fitness for "ashramic sharing." Per-

fection is not looked for or expected, but certain personality faults of pride, temper and an undisciplined nature must at least be controlled.

3. A dislike of criticism eliminated others from the group. They could not stand the exposure of their faults, either to themselves or to the group. They knew certain tendencies existed but not how serious they were; when I attempted to help them along these lines, resentment only was evoked. In many cases (as I have elsewhere told you) the position was taken that praise, commendation and interesting personal instructions were written by me, but should any criticism be involved—then A.A.B. was responsible. This was never once the case. In fact, several times I have modified my criticism (or analysis, as I prefer to call it), and once or twice eliminated it altogether at the request of A.A.B., who knows the Western mind better perhaps than I do. (Such members were I.S.G-L. and D.E.I.)

4. Several of the students did not spiritually appreciate the opportunity with which they were faced. It was in reality a case of nonrecognition, of which they were practically unconscious; they remain in this condition, awaiting another incarnation. (L.D.N-C. was a striking instance of this attitude; another was J.A.C. though he would greatly like to be reinstated. This is not possible; however, had the tenure of life by A.A.B. been better, it might have been accomplished. Another of these types was B.S.D.)

5. Certain other students regarded "occult obedience" as an infringement of their freewill, as did D.A.O. Quite a number of you simply suffered from inertia, and though pleased and excited over the material received from me, in the group or personal instructions, were too lazy to avail yourselves to the full of that which was given, and consistently failed to comply with my requests.

It is valuable to note a most significant point of interest: All those who passed through the gates of death passed to a definitely closer relationship; they had earned this reward and have availed themselves of that which I had taught them. They are, as you know, C.D.P., K.E.S., D.P.R. Two others are today rapidly fitting themselves to follow these three disciples into the Ashram. They are: B.S.W., who was temporarily sidetracked for a few years prior to his death, and G.S.S., whose personality vehicles could not carry the stimulation which reached her via the group. This sensitivity to undue stimulation is a matter easily rectified now; it does not constitute a fault, but only a karmic liability.

I have taken the time to say these things so as to make clear to you certain reasons for what may look to you as failure. I am greatly pleased with the work being done by some of the eight members who remain truly active. Two of you have fought through great tests and are today very much better servers. They are D.H.B. and R.S.U. One of you, R.S.W., is in danger of sidetracking her activities but will, I believe, come through the test; it will take her two more years to fight through to clarity of vision. To the other eight remaining of the original group I have no comment to make but that of encouragement. They are holding steady, but have enough teaching whereon to work and can take no more stimulation. The majority of them will not be kept waiting for admission to a definitely more positive penetrating in the Ashram when they pass through the gates of death. H.S.D. for the remainder of her life should work at the attainment of a quiet spirit, and she should also stand by A.A.B. as long as A.A.B. needs her. L.D.O. must attain to a broader point of view in place of her limited approach to humanity's problems; she must give up her assurance that the palliatives and solutions which she suggests are completely right. F.C.D. is doing well, but he is an old and trained disciple, and about him no anxiety has been needed. The same is true of J.W.K-P.

I have not, as you will note, covered the whole ground. I have, however, indicated enough to show my reasons why there is so poor an exoteric showing of a truly esoteric, inner movement—an inner movement which remains intact even though the outer form does not hold together, owing to the weaknesses of its members and the pressure of daily life upon the outer group. All of you—from the first admitted to the last who joined the group—are still within my aura or within the aura of the greater Ashram of the Master K.H., and will, I am confident, remain so. I would remind you also that there are many members of my Ashram of whom you know nothing and who came into my Ashram without the help of A.A.B. You are not the group of major importance. Forget not these other co-disciples. Some day, when you have established continuity of consciousness, you will know them, for you will consciously meet with them within the ring-pass-not of my Ashram. You will know also and discover the reasons for the experiment with these outer groups which is now being tried by the Hierarchy, if you will read with care the teaching upon the externalisation of the Ashram of Sanat Kumara, the Hierarchy.

August-September, 1949

BROTHERS, AS OF OLD:

The thought constantly enters my mind as to what I can say in order to make the group work, group relationships, group identification and group initiation a sound, active and factual reality in your minds and in the minds of other aspirants and disciples. I seek with profound earnestness to make this theme or subject true and vital, because it is an essentially new esoteric concept and a germ thought which the many aspirants of the world must grasp. At the same time the aspirant must realise that the ideas are of no real importance to him as an individual—to you, therefore, as an individual and pledged disciple. As long as your state of awareness lays emphasis upon the fact of your individuality, the group *idea* cannot take form as a group *ideal*. The sense of separativeness is still present. It is a sense which has been laboriously developed — under evolutionary law — from the moment when your soul decided to experiment, to experience, and to express divinity. Separative effort, separative emotional reactions and separative materialistic endeavour have been (if I may so unfortunately express it) the spiritual essentials which must perforce precede group effort and conscious group relations. The factor entailed, therefore, is a definite "break with the past," and the entering into a new state of awareness—an awareness which is fundamentally inclusive and not exclusive.

This is a primary platitude of which you are well aware. In most of you this platitude remains a mental proposition. You *hope* some day to arrive at this basic sense of inclusiveness which is characteristic of the Hierarchy. At present you do not feel fused, blended and incorporated into the mental, astral and etheric auras of those who form the group of which you know yourself to be a part. I would ask you to study what I have just said with care. Do you like, for instance, to penetrate into the mental atmosphere of a fellow member, or do you care to have him penetrate into yours and thus find out what is the content of your thought? A major test is here involved, and it is one which you will have some day to face. Do you, again, like to share your emotional reactions with a co-disciple? Are you interested in his? If so, why? Some day this responding interest must prove itself effective, and this must necessarily connote self-sacrifice in both directions. Do you want or deem it appropriate to have a fellow-worker come under the influence of your etheric body and, therefore, of the energies which flow through it? And do you want his energies to flow through you?

These are some of the implications of group work, and for these you must be prepared. The realisation of the inevitability of these necessities will lead you eventually to a careful scrutiny of your thinking, of your emotional reactions and of the energies to which you give entrance all the time *because* (for the first time in your soul's history) you feel the need to guard your brother from the results of your personality reactions; consequently, scientific service supersedes your hitherto thoughtless and undisciplined activity. I would here point out that at no time do you ever attempt to guard yourself from the personality reactions of a co-disciple; you welcome them and absorb them and—whilst dealing with them—you aid the cause of liberation in his life, as well as in your own.

The entire subject of group interplay is far deeper and

more significant than you suspect or appreciate; it can be summed up in the words of St. Paul: "No man liveth unto himself." Feeling, thinking and absorbing the many actuating and incentive energies constitute a vast process of many interrelations and this, most aspirants are apt to forget.

I suggest that during the coming year you go over your individual instructions and then—during the course of the year—answer six questions which I will dictate. The purpose of this task (shall I call it this?) is to clarify your minds as to your problems and opportunity and latent knowledge, gained as the result of years of work under my tuition; the replies will give to your group brothers a sense of relationship with you, a feeling of shared responsibility, a recognition of group assets and *group richness* (again using a peculiar word) and a realisation of possibility which may greatly strengthen each and all of you. This will close our cycle of instruction. If you avail yourselves of the opportunity for this personal research work, coincident with the post-war period, you may find a sudden spiritual deepening and strengthening of your life, your spiritual contacts and your group relation; you may also find yourselves in closer rapport with the Ashram, its programme and potency, and you may likewise discover yourselves being presented with the opportunity to learn in a new and subjective manner, of which I may not speak, until you have registered it yourselves. You will thus greatly increase your usefulness to humanity, to the Ashram, and to me.

The Science of Impression* is of major importance to the group. The time for close attention to yourselves and to your individual characters is past; group activity should take its place. By this I mean the activity of this particular group of disciples in relation to my Ashram and in relation to world service.

I would like you to do some further thinking upon the theme of our seventh point, the externalisation of the Masters' Ashrams, so that what I hope to say in the next instruction may mean more to you.

Take your group papers and the book *Discipleship in the*

Telepathy and the Etheric Vehicle, Pages 41-57.

New Age (Vol. I) and run quickly through these two sources of information and then write down:

1. Any definitions of an Ashram you may find. There are many.
2. A short, tabulated statement as to the *unique* work which every Ashram carries on in the outer world through its initiates and disciples and through affiliated disciples, such as the majority of you. Two or three of you are beyond the stage of affiliation.

This assignment need not take you long.

My brothers, I am spiritually ambitious for you. I have gathered you into my ashramic group and, therefore, into my aura for vitalising, for training and for protection. My love goes ever out to you and my unifying desire. Will you not aid me in my task? Will you stand with me in the hierarchical endeavour to which I am pledged and which I have undertaken in consort with the other Masters? There is much that you can do by speech, by pen and by example. Will you not do it—with a simple heart and a single eye for the helping of a deeply suffering and overburdened humanity.

The six questions are intended to summarise and make deeply personal and significant in your consciousness the instructions, given during the past few years to this group of affiliated disciples. They can be regarded as being put to the disciple by his own soul and will mark—if correctly and creatively used—the closing of a preliminary cycle and the beginning of a new cycle of spiritual usefulness and of fresh growth and development.

These questions should receive most careful consideration and much serious reflection, prior to answering. The answers should convey the *truth,* as the disciple sees it today and not in the light of his wishful thinking and of his aspiration; the answers should be written down (so as to focus that truth) with no thought or fear of what other members of the group may think. In an Ashram, my brothers, a man is known as he *is;* for this clear knowledge, the members of this group (affiliated with my Ashram) should prepare themselves.

One suggestion I will make: There are six questions, providing one question, therefore, for consideration each two months during the coming year. Give two months to careful consideration, reflection and interior investigation and then, at the end of the second month, formulate your reply.

Question 1. From a study of the instructions given by me on your five conditioning rays and from a study of yourself in connection with the information given:
a. Which of your five conditioning rays controls you or which is the most dominant?
b. Which ray should control you and how can you strengthen that control?
The answering of this question will require a truthful consideration of your good and bad qualities, of your assets as well as your limitations.

Question 2. Looking back over the years of instruction, do you feel that you have definitely advanced upon the Path? If so, upon what grounds do you base this belief? Could you have made more progress under the circumstances and if you have not, what was the reason or reasons?

Question 3. In what do you personally feel that your work in the future should consist in the following three relations:
a. With your personality, in its particular circumstances and environment, so as to make your daily life more spiritually effective?
b. In order to establish a closer contact with your soul, with the same objective of effective spiritual living?
c. In order to bring about soul and personality at-one-ment and clearly demonstrate the fact. What do you regard as the pres-

ent greatest hindrance to this accomplishment?

Question 4. Are you satisfied with the relationship you have established with your group brothers?
    a. Do you know them better and love them more than you earlier did? This means all of them, as a group.
    b. Along what lines do you feel that you have failed them, if you have, and what do you propose to do to rectify the situation?
    c. In what way do you feel that you have been an asset to the group?

These four questions concern largely your ability to live as a soul in your little outer world and have reference primarily to your *objective* expression. The next two questions concern your *subjective* relationships.

Question 5. What is your attitude towards your Master, Djwhal Khul, as a result of years of training under His instruction?
    a. Can you sense my vibration at any time? How do you know the difference between my vibration, that of your own soul or the group?
    b. What effect has the work of the full moon had upon you? Have there been any results of that attempted contact and, if so, what are they?
    c. What should now govern your efforts in relation to your work as my disciple during the coming remainder of your life?

Question 6. What part in my plans and in the task assigned to my Ashram are you prepared to take? This question concerns both your outer and your inner work of a practical nature.

> a. Have you any definite schedule of work
>   outlined in your mind as your contribu-
>   tion to the activity of my Ashram?
> b. If so, what is it and how do you propose
>   to implement it and make it effective?
> c. What is the main task of the Ashram at
>   this time? Do you know the type of as-
>   sistance—subjective or objective or both
>   —that you could give?

This last question goes deeply into your ability to react to *impression* from me and from the Ashram. I would have you answer it, to the best of your ability, from that angle.

Pass on, my disciples, into a closer relation to the Ashram of which I am the focal point; aim at a closer rapport with your fellow-workers and with me. I am the director of your work. That this relationship may prove the signal achievement of the coming year for each and all of you is my earnest wish.

November-December 1949

MY BROTHERS OF LONG ASSOCIATION:

In my last instruction to you I gave you only a very little teaching anent group work, though there were several signifi-cant hints if you had the intuition to grasp them. I have, however, given you much over the years; yet, when I look back over those years, I am forced to realise how relatively little you have profited by this teaching upon group work, though many of you have profited much by the personal in-structions I gave you. Only sixteen of you are left out of an original fifty aspirants to discipleship; I think you yourselves would be the first to admit that there is little group interplay and no group enterprise animating those few of you who remain steadfast.

Certain of you (F.C.D., J.W.K-P., R.V.B., P.G.C., R.S.U., and R.S.W.) are actively working in relation to my plans, though those plans are not in reality mine, but simply the required cooperation in hierarchical endeavour. The rest of you are engulfed in the processes of daily living or else too tired to be more active than you already are, and for that condition of the personality I have no criticism.

It is necessary for you to remember that this group effort which I initiated with the assistance of some of the older and more experienced Masters, is by no means completed; it may be (and probably is) an experiment in this particular life for you, but next life may evoke from you a new attitude and a deeper comprehension of what is subjectively going on. It has been your lack of comprehension and of understood opportunity which has distressed me and bewildered A.A.B. Like all disciples, she had at first to work in the dark; she knew nothing in her physical brain consciousness of the Masters or the Hierarchy when she started to serve, but she continued to serve for many years till discovery rewarded her or (should I perhaps say?) recovery of ancient links and knowledge clarified her vision and her position in regard to truth. Slowly she now withdraws into that service which will (within the Ashram) enable K.H. to do more deeply spiritual work in collaboration with the Christ. It was to train her and thus enable her to do this that she undertook, *alone and without my help,* to found and organise the Arcane School; it gave her much needed training and experience and enabled her to demonstrate the quality of the teaching and that esoteric psychology which is the major task in each Ashram and particularly in the second ray Ashram.

I would like to say at this point to all of you who have remained steadfast, even if perforce inactive, that I would ask you as life proceeds and you face eventually and inevitably the discarding of the vehicle, to hold increasingly on to your knowledge of the Hierarchy and thus to pass over to the other side with complete dedication to the hierarchical Plan. This is not simply a suggestion on my part; it is an attempt on my part to call to your attention the concept of a spiritual continuity of knowledge and of a rightly oriented attitude. Thus time will not be lost; you can—if you so choose, each and all of you—attain a true continuity of consciousness and it is one of the factors which will serve to hold this group of disciples together.

There are some things which I must say to you as this will be my last instruction on the theme of group work. It is not necessary for me to say much more upon the subject. I would start with some questions. Do you ever think with recognition of those who are no longer working with us? For instance, is D.A.O. ever in your minds? Do you ever think of S.C.P., of W.D.B., of J.A.C., or of that expert worker for the Hierarchy, L.D.N-C? I would guarantee that they seldom enter your mind. Yet they are still an integral part of this group which had the task and the responsibility of being one of the first groups (not by any means the only one, however) to attempt to make the first steps towards the externalisation of the Ashrams of the Hierarchy.

One of the major recognitions which is essential to the spiritual aspirant is that the Hierarchy is completely unable —under the law of the freedom of the human soul—to work in the world of men without those representative groups which can "step down" the hierarchical quality of energy so that the average man (with his average vibration and quality) can find in himself a point of response. It was for this specific reason that I engineered this experiment in group work with all of you in order to test out the human capacity in its higher brackets to respond to this much higher quality. It has not worked out as I had hoped, but owing to the fact that all of you are—from our point of view—of the same spiritual generation and that the difference in age was in no case more than twenty-five years at the outside (and believe me, my brother, I forget physical plane ages!) you will all return together to continue with this inevitable experience.

In the coming cycle of service, however, you will not have the association that you have had during this life with A.A.B. and F.B., who will then be working in the Ashrams of their own Masters, as will also F.C.D. and R.S.U. Do not infer from the above statement that contact and mutual interplay in world service will not then be present; it will. The union of all the Ashrams under the spiritual Plan is complete and the interlocking relationships will be increasingly present. But neither of these four people will be working in my Ashram and for this I would have you prepare. Remember nevertheless that personal karmas have been established and are based upon many unexpected relationships, and there is much personal karma in this group of over fifty people; this was necessarily so; otherwise little personal relationships would have been possible, which may present a difficult point for you to understand.

I would like to arrest any tendency to consider one Ashram as superior to another. The forty-nine Ashrams which constitute the Hierarchy in this planetary period are some of them fully active; some are in process of formation, and some are, as yet, in a totally embryonic condition, awaiting the "focussing ability" of some initiate who is today preparing for the fifth initiation. Essentially and potentially all the Ashrams are equal, and their quality is not competitive; all of them differ as to their planned activity—an activity which is all part of a carefully formulated hierarchical activity. This you need most carefully to remember. The devotion of a disciple to some particular Master is of no importance to that Master or to His ashramic group. It is not devotion or predilection or any personality choice which governs the formation of a Master's group. It is ancient relationships, the ability to demonstrate certain aspects of life to demanding humanity and a definite ray expression of quality which determines the hierarchical placement of aspirants in an Ashram. This will perhaps be a new thought to you and is responsible for the reason why A.A.B. has never emphasised concentration on some one of the known Masters. She has always been aware that each central Ashram has associated with it six other Ashrams which are steadily and constantly being organised to meet planetary need. You will note that I did not say "human need," for the needs of the planet which the Hierarchy has to meet embrace more than those of the fourth kingdom in nature. I would have you ponder on these points.

It would be of benefit to you also to consider the Masters' Ashrams as expressions of the highest type of constructively functioning groups. There exists amongst its personnel a complete unity of purpose and an utter dedication (without any reservations, as far as the disciple involved is concerned) to the furthering of the immediate ashramic enterprise. The

position of the Master at the centre of the group has no relation to that of a teacher at the centre of a group of learners
and devotees, such as we have learned to recognise in this
Piscean Age. He is the centre simply because through the
quality of His vibration, through karmic ancient relationship and through the invocative demand of disciples, initiates
and some aspirants, He has gathered them together in order
to further the ends of His ashramic enterprise; He has *not*
gathered them together in order to teach them or to prepare
them for initiation as has hitherto been taught. Aspirants and
disciples *prepare themselves* for the processes of initiation by
becoming initiated into the mysteries of divinity *through
discipline, meditation and service.* You need to bear in mind
that a Master of an Ashram may, for instance, attract to Him
other Masters of equal rank as His Own. I have five Masters
working with me in my Ashram. It would be of value to you
if you considered the factors which hold an Ashram together
and which establish its unity. The major ones, and those
which you can understand, are as follows:

1. The most important capacity of a Master of an Ashram is
   that He has earned the right to communicate directly with
   the Council at Shamballa and thus to ascertain at first
   hand the immediate evolutionary task which the Hierarchy is undertaking. He is not called Master by the
   initiates in His Ashram; He is regarded as the Custodian
   of the Plan, and this is based on His ability to "face the
   greater Light which shines in Shamballa." It is the Plan
   which gives the keynote to the activities of any Ashram
   at any particular time, during any particular cycle.
2. This unanimity of purpose produces a very close subjective relationship, and each member of the Ashram is occupied with making his fullest possible contribution to the
   task in hand. Personalities do not enter in. You will remember how some years ago I told you that the personality vehicles are ever left outside the Ashram—speaking
   symbolically. This means that the subtler bodies of the
   personality have perforce to follow the same rules as the
   physical body—they are left outside. Remember also that

the Ashrams exist upon the plane of buddhi or of the intuition. The joint undertaking and the united adhering to the desired and arranged cyclic technique binds all members of the Ashram into one synthetic whole; there is therefore no possible controversy or any emphasis upon individual ideas, because no personality vibratory quality can penetrate in the periphery or the aura of an Ashram.

3. The planning and the assignment of tasks connected with the enterprise in hand is carried forward through the medium of an ashramic, reflective meditation, initiated by the Custodian of the Plan. The Master of an Ashram does not say: "Do this" or "Do that." Together, in unison and in deep reflection the plans unfold, and each disciple and initiate *sees* occultly where he is needed and where—at any given moment—he must place his cooperative energy. Note my wording here. The members of an Ashram, however, do not sit down for a joint meditation. One of the qualities, developed through ashramic contact, is the ability to live always within the field of intuitive perception—a field which has been created, or a sphere of energy which has been generated, by the united purpose, the combined planning and the concentrated energy of the Hierarchy. An analogy (but only an analogy, however) would be to regard this field of reflecting, reflective and reflected energies as resembling the brain of a human being; this brain reflects the impacts of telepathic activity, the sensory perceptions and the knowledges gained in the three worlds; reflection then sets in in relation to the mental processes which are synchronised with the brain, and then follows the impartation of these reflections to the outside world. The ashramic reflective meditation is an integral part of the constantly developing perception of the disciple-initiate, and it (in its turn) is a part of the whole hierarchical reflective meditation. This latter is based upon inspiration (in the occult sense) from Shamballa. The moment a disciple can share in this constant unremitting meditation or reflection without its interfering with his service and his other lines of thought, he becomes what is called "a disciple who shall no more go out."

4. Another factor productive of group unity and synchronous precision in working is the complete freedom of the Ashram from any spirit of criticism. There is no tendency among its personnel to be critical and no interest whatsoever in the outer, personal lives of the members, should they be amongst those functioning in the three worlds. Criticism, as seen among men, simply is a mode of emphasising the lower self and deflects the attitude to the material aspects of a person's life. There is necessarily clear vision among the members of an Ashram; they know each other's capacities and limitations and they know, therefore, where they can complement each other and together create and present a perfect team in world service.

5. One other factor I will mention among the many possible: The members of an Ashram are all in the process of demonstrating love and pure reason, and they are—at the same time—focussing themselves in the Will aspect of divinity. This statement may mean little to you at present but it is fundamentally the factor which creates the higher antahkarana, uniting the Hierarchy and Shamballa. This makes the planetary purpose of so much importance.

These are the major factors which produce group unity; they have, as results, telepathic rapport and intuitive perception; but these are effects and not causes and are the product of the measure of the attained group unity.

You can see, therefore, the scientific reason I had when I urged you in past years to have a group enterprise, for it is a major unifying factor, and the inner Ashram with which you are affiliated stands to you (at your particular point of development) as Shamballa stands to the Hierarchy—from the angle of dynamic inspiration. Had you done this (which you did not) the group would not have fallen apart—as it has done. Had you eliminated criticism, the essential unity would have been strengthened. One of the reasons I had for the complete frankness and so-called exposure of your individual weakness and limitations to the group as a whole was to train you in the light of pure perception which knows the reason

why and sees with clarity the ends in view. Where true perception exists, criticism is automatically eliminated.

Modern groups (and groups form a large part of every
field of thought and activity) are usually composed of people
possessing some basic idea upon which they are all agreed
and which they are trying to express through the medium of
their clashing personalities and, frequently, in obedience to
some leader or person of more powerful mentality than that
of the majority, and in order to exploit and use the methods
which they regard as essential to success. There is therefore
little true unity, and often what there is is based on expediency or good manners.

Everywhere, however, the newer type of groups are slowly
being gathered together. Have you ever realised (I seek here
to make you think and reason) that a group composed entirely of people upon the same ray, and who were also at
exactly the same point in evolution, would be relatively
futile and useless? Such a group would lack dynamic—the
dynamic which comes into expression when many and different ray qualities meet and combine. When you speak of an
Ashram being a first or a second ray Ashram—to mention
only two out of the seven—it is essential that you bear in
mind that though its members may have the same basic soul
ray, they are apt to be found on one or other of the six subsidiary sub-rays; there is also a constant shifting of people
as they make true progress from a minor ray to a major ray or
(for service reasons) on to a different sub-ray of their own
ray; this is a point which is very apt to be forgotten. It is wise
to realise that an Ashram is composed of disciples and initiates of all degrees. It is this interplay of diverse elements
that enriches an Ashram and tends inevitably to successful
service in the three worlds.

I am anxious to see the group, with which I have been
undertaking an occult experiment for the Hierarchy, hold together. When I say this, I refer not only to the few of you
who are now active (and perhaps patting yourselves on the
back for your steadfastness!), but also to the inactive members, to those likewise who of their own freewill dropped out,
those whom perforce I myself had to drop, and those also

who are functioning upon the other side of the veil. I have asked A.A.B. to send each of you a complete list of all who were in the earlier groups as well as those who were or are in the reorganised group. The names will be sent to you without comment and without addresses. I would ask you on one day each month—the day of the full moon—to sit down and mention each of these names of your co-disciples in the light, sending out light and love to one and all. This will strengthen the relation of you all to each other and it will also create an energy body—an etheric body—for the entire subjective group and will integrate them closely as time goes on, restoring those who broke away and strengthening those who unfortunately proved themselves to be weak.

This entire problem of group integrity and personnel-synthesis (if I may coin such a phrase) is at this time presenting a major problem to the Hierarchy. It is based, as you see, on the point in evolution which humanity has reached. There are many millions today—and this may surprise you— who have already achieved a definite measure of permanent personality integration. They are *people* in the fullest sense of the term although they may yet be lacking any contact with the soul or any desire for such contact. This means that they are relatively dominant men and women in their own setting, environment or milieu; they therefore constitute a problem in this preparatory cyclic era because they refuse— usually quite unconsciously—to form part of any group; they seek ever the position of leader. This is true of spiritual aspirants just as much as it is true of workers and group leaders in any other phase of human thought and procedure.

Therefore we ask: How can we create extra-ashramic groups out of aspirants and disciples who primarily value spiritual status, kudos or an elevated position? We cannot. All we can do is to train aspirants in recognised group re-quirements. We must also point out to them the dangers of mental pride, detail to them their personality limitations and the difficulties of true spiritual leadership, and then plead with them to mind their own business where each other is concerned and ask them to serve the human race; this of course means, incidentally, serving the Hierarchy and thus demonstrate their ability to work within an Ashram. Disciples—in the earlier stages—are apt to be didactic; they like to express in words their profound understanding of occult truth and thereby, in reality, establish their superiority over non-esoteric students, and in so doing (again incidentally) antagonise those they otherwise could help. They like to show their unique familiarity with hierarchical principles but, as they are not yet living those principles, they hinder more than they can help; at the same time, through self-discovery, they learn much thereby. They believe that in expressing their knowledge of petty and unimportant details anent the lives and methods of the Masters, a high point of spiritual understanding and development is thereby indicated. This is not by any means the case. In the last analysis, it indicates a superficial sense of false values, and seventy per cent of their information is wrong and of no importance.

I feel it necessary to emphasise the unimportance of their claims to information because the work of the Masters and Their freedom to serve humanity as They desire have been greatly hindered by these foolish thoughtforms and by the preconceived ideas of well-intentioned aspirants. The Masters very seldom resemble the theories, the pictures and the information which is so frequently circulated by the average aspirant. This whole business of occult gossip and of misinformation governs the majority of the many little occult groups.

Until groups are formed which consist of disciples and senior aspirants who possess self-ascertained knowledge and who are capable of correct interpretation of the occult facts, and who are also endowed with the rare group virtue of silence, we shall not have the desired externalisation of the Ashrams. I would have you think on these matters and prepare yourselves for a better and sounder appreciation, plus a more adequate meeting of hierarchical requirements in your next incarnation.

And now, my brothers and co-workers, I leave you to work, serve and study; by that last word, I mean reflect and think. I would commend to your consideration (because you cannot as yet think truly constructively, but only imaginatively) the place in this hierarchical planning, adjusting and aligning that my Ashram should take and of your part in it, as an individual and as a group, above all. I ask your aid so that one of the newest Ashrams may play a good part in the group of Ashrams, gathered around that of the One Who was my Master, the Chohan K.H.

There has been much pressure on you this year; I have seen and noted it; the group—as a group—has done better this year than for some years past; and I have seen a deepening of devotion and a strengthening of conviction. Failures, where they may be found, need not persist, for the group love can offset them all; personality weaknesses, mistakes and faults are overlooked and forgotten in the urgency of human need; they do not even penetrate into the Ashram. I would ask you to remember this, and with humility in your hearts, persistence in your efforts and love to all men, pass on your way.

Let love play its part in all your lives and all your interrelations as it must and does in the Hierarchy; look upon the Ashram to which you are affiliated as a miniature Hierarchy and model your efforts upon what you have learned anent the Hierarchy; count all things but loss unless they are productive along the line of service to humanity, and become increasingly factual in your attitude to all disciples and to the Hierarchy. The coming cycle is momentous in its offering of opportunity, and I would have you—again as individuals and as a group—measure up to this chance. Fix your eyes on human need and your hand in mine (if I may speak thus to you in symbols) and go forward with me to greater influence and deeper usefulness.

SECTION TWO

TEACHINGS ON MEDITATION

TEACHINGS ON MEDITATION

Part I

In continuing the instructions on the Science of Meditation, I would remind you that we are building upon the same fundamental truths which have been earlier laid down (in *Discipleship in the New Age*, Vol. I), and that our goals and objectives likewise remain the same. Our immediate concern is the bringing about a group unity rooted in love, and this requires the awakening of the heart centre into greater potency. In this connection, let me repeat what I earlier said, for it makes a fitting preface to what I shall ask you to do:

> Only from the heart centre can stream, in reality, those lines of energy which link and bind together. For this reason, I shall give you for your *group meditation* a form which will stimulate the heart into action, linking the heart centre (between the shoulder blades) to the head centre through the medium of the heart centre which is found within the head centre (the thousand-petalled lotus). This heart centre, when adequately radiatory and magnetic will relate you afresh to each other and to all the world. This again—when connected by an act of the spiritual will to the solar plexus centre—will help to produce that telepathic interplay which is so much to be desired and which is so constructively useful to the spiritual Hierarchy — provided it is established within a group of pledged disciples, dedicated to the service of humanity. They can then be trusted. (Page 87.)

The activity of the heart centre *never* demonstrates in connection with individuals. This is a basic fact. What devastates most disciples is the solar plexus ability (when purified

113

and consecrated) to identify itself with individuals. The heart centre cannot react, except under group impetus, group happiness or unhappiness, and other group relations.

The following diagrammatic form illustrates the procedure which I suggest that you follow:

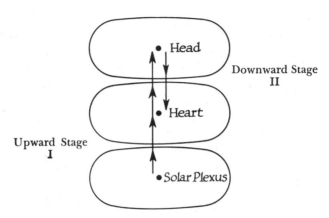

There are two points of vital light within the solar plexus centre, which makes this centre of dominant importance and a clearing house for the centres below the diaphragm to those above it. One of these points of light is connected with the lower psychic and astral life, and the other is brought into livingness by the inflow from the head centre. I would here remind you that the centres above the diaphragm have only one vital point of energy, whilst the centres below the solar plexus also have only one, but that the solar plexus itself has two points of dynamic energy—one most ancient and awakened, being expressive of the life of the astral or lower psychic body, and the other waiting to be brought into conscious activity by the soul. When this has happened, the awakening to the higher issues of life makes the disciple sensitive to the higher "psychic gift waves" (as the Tibetan occultists call them) of the spiritual world.

All this is a somewhat new concept for the average esotericist and theosophist, and is one of the new items of information which disciples (in preparation for initiation) are told. This truth lies behind the method of meditation which I shall seek to give you, and which is divided into two parts—one aspect or technique will cover approximately the first six months, and the other the second six months. This dual meditation is a group meditation and will have primarily a group effect. This fact must be most carefully recognised by each disciple.

I would have you ponder most earnestly upon this imparted information. The meditation which I wish to assign will be divided into two parts:

Stage I. A stage wherein there is a lifting of the energy of the heart centre to the head by means of directed, controlled aspiration — deliberately stimulated, mentally appreciated, and emotionally propelled. I am here choosing my words with care for their symbolic import.

Stage II. Next, the deliberate dispatch of spiritual energy to the solar plexus, through an act of the will; this will result in the awakening of the hitherto quiescent point of force which lies behind (or rather within) the active and awakened centre.

It will be apparent to you that the first stage is occupied with what is regarded esoterically as the "withdrawal to the centre of inspiration" and it is to this withdrawal that I call you all today, prior to the definite and detailed group work —later to be outlined. Under cyclic law there are periods of outgoing and of withdrawing, of progressing in service towards the periphery of activity and also of a conscious abstraction of the consciousness from the outer circle and its centering again at the very heart of life. It is to this retreating within that I summon you—a retreat which must be continued and consciously held until the next Full Moon of May. You might regard it as the *individual* phase of alignment and of preparation to which each of you is called, and called prior to participation in the group meditation with which you will be occupied for the remainder of the year, after May. Stage II and its successful issue will be largely dependent upon the success achieved during Stage I.

Stage I itself is divided into two parts, and to these I now call your attention. The first part of Stage I is a short dynamic meditation, carried out every morning with the greatest regularity. The second part is a reflective process or cultivated recognition which will serve to condition your day's activity. This conditioning attitude should be one of a constant recollection of purpose and objective, and a process of what has been called "intentional living." It connotes the effort to *live consciously* at the centre and then to work outward from there in radiatory, magnetic activity. I am not here speaking symbolically but literally for it is all a question of the focus of consciousness. If this attitude can be constantly held until the Full Moon of May, the individual seeds within the group periphery (could we symbolically call it the seed pod or sheath?) will become living and potent units of energy (spiritual energy) and the succeeding period of group interrelation and group activity will be correspondingly potent. In the furtherance of this process, leading to radiatory and magnetic living, the method suggested is as follows:

STAGE I

1. Reflective alignment of soul and personality, using the creative imagination in the process. This is a "feeling" or astral activity.
2. Assumed relation of solar plexus, heart and head, and the focus of the assuming consciousness to be in the region of the ajna centre. This is done mentally.
3. When this has been achieved and realised, there follows next the concentration of aspiration and of thought in the heart centre, imagining it to be just between the shoulder blades. It must be recognised that the concentration of thought energy is definitely there.
4. Then follows the conscious and pictorial (or imaginative) withdrawal of the heart's aspiration, life and

devotion into the centre above the head (the thousand-petalled lotus), and its conscious focussing there.

5. When this stage has been reached, and the conscious recognition of place and activity is being gently yet surely held, then sound the Sacred Word, O M, very softly three times, breathing out and towards:

    a. The Soul.
    b. The Hierarchy.
    c. Humanity.

These three recognised factors now constitute a definite and linked triangle of force.

6. Then say with *heartfelt intent* (consider the significance of those two words) the invocation which I gave you in my communication in September, 1939:

The sons of men are one and I am one with them.
I seek to love, not hate;
I seek to serve and not exact due service;
I seek to heal, not hurt.

Let pain bring due reward of light and love.
Let the soul control the outer form and life and all
    events,
And bring to light the love which underlies the
    happenings of the time.

Let vision come and insight.
Let the future stand revealed.
Let inner union demonstrate and outer cleavages be
    gone.
Let love prevail.
Let all men love.

7. Endeavour throughout the day to continue holding this recollection steady and work always in due remembrance of the morning's meditation.

This activity should take only a few minutes, but if it is carried out with a fully awakened consciousness and with the

most carefully focussed attention, the results may be most
potent and effective—far more so than you may think. The
meditation should take less than ten minutes, after you have
succeeded in familiarising yourself with the process; firm
foundations will thus be laid for the group work and the
group meditation, which I intend to give you in May, when
I will give you your personal and group instructions.

At the time of the Full Moon each month—dating from
the time that you receive these instructions and until further
notice—I would ask you to work as follows:

1. Group yourselves, all twenty-four of you, symbolically,
   pictorially and imaginatively around your Teacher,
   and—with Him—face the East, standing in a semi-
   circle slightly behind Him.
2. Then stretching out your hands in blessing, say together with solemn, voiced intent the formula or
   Mantram of Unification, beginning "The sons of men
   are one," which you have been using each morning in
   your personal meditation. Throw the power of your
   focussed thought and will into and behind the words.
3. Stand then together in the light which streams ever
   from the East and see it pouring through the Master
   to each of you, entering by the head centre, passing
   from thence to the heart centre, and then from the
   heart it is directed by an act of the focussed will—
   expressed and propelled forth consciously — to the
   quiescent point of dim light within the solar plexus.
4. Then, withdrawing again to the head centre, endeavour consciously to see the three centres (head, heart
   and solar plexus) linked together so that the heads of
   all the group members are thinking as one and the
   hearts of the group members are loving as one. Your
   aspiration also (through the spiritual awakening of
   the solar plexus) will then surge upwards as one spontaneous movement. This will in due time create a
   magnetic field of light and life, within which the New
   Group of World Servers will live, mature and come to
   fruition.

Keep the whole process, my brother, very simple and un-complicated in your mind. If you will follow the above instructions with the simplicity of a little child, you will bring about a situation wherein work will be possible. Look not for results. Yours is to do the outlined work and this, when rightly done, makes the due result inevitable. But as I told you before, "it is the inner life of reflection and the outer life of expressed love which will determine the success of the needed group relation and the potency of its future work" in the service of humanity.

PART II

In the last instruction, I started you on the first part of the new meditation. The completed meditation involves the process of relating heart and head and then—by an act of the will—linking up both with the quiescent point within the solar plexus—that point of which nothing has as yet been taught (though the necessity for such a point was obvious in the work of transferring energy) but which is of vital signifi-cance in all preparation for initiation.

That is as far as I took you in the last meditation but to it must be added the individual meditation which will aid in group integration and in the unfoldment of the individual disciple.

You will have noted, I am sure, that in the meditation assigned for daily use, I did not carry it forward to where the will is exerted and the energy in the head is driven to the quiescent centre in the solar plexus. You will have noted also that at the time of the Full Moon and in group forma-tion, plus direct contact with myself, you were permitted together to link heart, head and solar plexus. Once a month and then only through the protective magnetic field of the group life can you complete the meditation.

The Full Moon work will remain as already assigned for the remainder of the year, but we will complete the medita-tion and I will now outline for you Stage II in the group meditation. The first half should now be so familiar to you that it will be automatic in its doing and should take only a few minutes to complete. It is in the nature of a preface to the one I am now seeking to assign. It should leave each of you (if carrying it forward to a right conclusion) with the consciousness and heart energy focussed in the head. The activity of the true spiritual man has not been aroused, and when it is, the effect on the downflow of energy from the head centre will be threefold:

1. The awakened point in the solar plexus will become extremely active and—if the work is correctly done— it will make that point also exceedingly magnetic, gathering all the energies of all the centres below the diaphragm (except the one at the base of the spine), and this involves the sacral centre and other little focal points of energy, up into the solar plexus. There they must be held steady until such time as the man is ready to deal with them occultly.

2. The unawakened or quiescent point of light in the solar plexus comes slowly to life and to a state of new vibratory activity. Its magnetic field steadily increases and widens until it contacts the periphery of the magnetic field surrounding the heart centre.

3. When the two above stages are completed, then comes a lengthy process of transference. The solar plexus is the clearing house between the lower energies and the higher. This process is in itself dual:

   a. The two points within the solar plexus field of activity become definitely related to each other, and the lower sacral and material energies are transferred into the hitherto quiescent point of light, now awakened and intensifying in quality and potency.

   b. The concentrated energies in the new centre within the periphery of the solar plexus are then lifted by an act of the will into the heart centre and from thence to the head.

In this triple transference of the lower energies to the solar plexus, to the heart and finally to the head, we have a pictorial and symbolic presentation within the life experience of the disciple of the interrelation and eventual transference of energy from the personality (symbolised by the solar plexus) to the soul (symbolised by the heart centre) and from the soul to the Monad (symbolised by the head centre). These correspondences are of value as they are an argument for the factual nature of the process and they also enable the aspirant to grasp somewhat the nature of the undertaking to which he is committed. Certain aspects of relationship, therefore, emerge into the consciousness of the disciple and at this point in his training the following four relations are of major importance:

1. The relation of the energies, found below the diaphragm and corresponding to the personality life (motivated by desire), and the higher energies found above the diaphragm and motivated by the soul. These are as yet in the case of the average aspirant, practically entirely quiescent and only become a realised activity as the soul establishes increasing control over the disciple.

2. The relation between the two points within the solar plexus itself. These are symbolic also of the personality-soul relationship. One point is awakened, as to the lower life of man; the other point is awakening, as in the case of the aspirant, or is totally awakened as is the case of the pledged disciple, prior to the second initiation.

3. The relation between the solar plexus and the heart. This is of great importance and serves to clarify the mind of the aspirant because it is symbolic again of the immediate present problem of the personality and the soul.

4. The relation between the ajna centre (between the eyebrows) and the thousand-petalled lotus. When these two centres are correctly related to each other, then the man can take the third initiation at which time the potency of the Monad can begin to make its presence felt, linking heart and head and solar plexus.

There is an intermediate stage in which the heart and the ajna centre become aligned and related. This stage is omitted from the enumeration given above owing to the fact that it is of a sevenfold nature and the method of transition and of transference is dependent upon the ray quality. One new item of information comes naturally here. The throat centre is not included in these relationships between centres above the diaphragm as it is to them what the sacral centre is to the solar plexus—a point of pure creative activity, set in motion by the interplay of the other centres but particularly is the throat centre energised and actuated eventually by the sacral centre itself. It is an effect or result of relation more than anything else.

Three other items of interest might here be mentioned. First, the throat centre is brought into real activity by the direct action of the soul, via the head centre, in conjunction with the raising of the energy of the sacral centre simultaneously. This is analogous to the fact that the solar plexus is brought into real constructive usefulness by the direct action of the soul, via the heart centre. That is why people who work creatively usually have first ray personalities at the time that the throat centre becomes dynamically active for the first time. Secondly, the solar plexus centre is awakened by the inflow of energy of a dual nature—the energies of the heart and the head, working synchronously. This is a correspondence to the dual energy which constitutes the essential nature of the soul—atma-buddhi, or spiritual will and spiritual love. The third soul energy, manas or mental energy is related more directly to the throat centre. Thirdly, it might be stated that the awakening of the centre at the base of the spine is the result of an act of the will directed from the head and resulting in the elevation of all the energies to the head, just as the solar plexus was awakened and energy was carried to the heart—also by an act of the will. The energy of the solar plexus, that great clearing house for personality energy, must be carried always to the heart.

Here I would again caution you and call attention to my earlier statement that all stimulation of the solar plexus and all focus upon that centre carries with it definite danger, and disciples are enjoined to exercise wise control over the emotional nature. A decentralised attitude as regards personality reactions and a steadily deepening love of humanity will safeguard disciples at this stage—the stage of seeking to fit themselves for the first or the second initiation.

We will now continue with the second phase of the meditation. It was carried to the point wherein you were asked to say *as a soul* the great Mantram of Unification.

STAGE II

1. Repeat rapidly Stage I, taking not more than five minutes in so doing. Lift your consciousness and relate the head and the heart. Repeat thoughtfully the mantram which eventually leads to the realisation of unity.

2. With the focus of the consciousness then in the head, summon the Will to your aid and by an act of the will carry the energy focussed in the head to the solar plexus. To facilitate this process, you can use the following formula:

   a. I am the soul. And also love I am. Above all else I am both will and fixed design.

   b. My will is now to lift the lower self into the light divine. This light I am.

   c. Therefore, I must descend to where the lower self awaits my coming. That which desires to lift and that which cries aloud for lifting are now at-one. Such is my will.

   Whilst saying these mantric words (taken from a very ancient disciples' manual) vision pictorially the process of focussing—demanding—descending and at-one-ing.

3. Pause here and endeavour to *feel* and sense the initiatory vibration or embryonic interplay which is being established between the awakened and the awakening points within the solar plexus. This can be done, but it involves an act of slow concentration.

4. Then sound the O M twice from the head centre,

knowing yourself to be the soul which is breathing it forth. Believe this sound, carried on the breath of will and love, as capable of stimulating the solar plexus in the right way and able to transmute the lower energies so that they will be pure enough to be carried first of all to the awakening point and from that point eventually to the heart centre.

5. As you vision the energies of the solar plexus being carried *up the spine* to the heart centre (situated, as you know, between the shoulder blades) I would ask you to breathe out the O M again into the solar plexus but this time, having done so, draw the focussed energy up the spine towards the head. The vibration thus established will carry the energy to the heart, for it has to pass through that centre in the spine on its way to the head. In the early stages that is as far as it may go, but later it will pass through the heart, leaving its due quota of energy, and finally reach the head centre.

6. Then focus yourself in the heart, believing that a triangle of energy has been formed between the head, the heart and the solar plexus. Vision it then as composed of the energy of light, something resembling a triangle of neon light. The colour of this neon light so-called will be dependent upon the ray of the soul.

7. Then again repeat the Mantram of Unification, beginning "The sons of men are one . . ."

8. Standing, therefore, in the centre of the heart see the energy of your group brothers as the radiating spokes of a great wheel of light. This wheel has twenty-four spokes and at the centre of the wheel, like the hub of the wheel, can be found your Master (D.K.). Then slowly with love, mention aloud the names of each of your group brothers, not omitting yourself.

9. Then see this wheel as actively moving and scintillating, and thus serving humanity through its focussed radiation. This radiation is the radiation of love. All the above is purely symbolic but carried out as a

visualisation process for some months—consistently and consciously—it will create a state of mind and of awareness which will be enduring because "as a man thinketh, so is he."

10. Then close with the new Invocation and also with the Gayatri, with its emphasis upon one's duty.

O M   O M   O M

This meditation process is relatively simple if you familiarise yourself with its stages for a few weeks. Much of the above is explanatory in nature and can be dispensed with when you can follow the process automatically.

I will now proceed to give you each your personal instructions and individual meditation. This meditation should be done at some time of the day which is *not* the time chosen for the group meditation. I do not want the two meditations done together at the same time, for I do not want your personality problems and your possible glamours to be interjected into the group consciousness. Beware of doing this because the task of each of you is hard enough without being complicated by the personal problems of some distressed brother in the group. In giving you your personal instructions, I shall speak with complete frankness and shall not spare you either praise or blame. If you resent what I may say, then it will simply indicate the power of your personality to react unfavourably to the truth and will consequently point out to you an area of blindness and of weakness in your consciousness. You will be thereby the gainer and will be able to grasp somewhat more clearly the nature of the battle which you have to fight.

PART III

As individuals, many of you have used regularly (and profited thereby) the meditation which I gave you thus far in this series of instructions. But speaking generally, the group *as a whole* has not given as much attention and thought to the processes outlined in the two parts of the one meditation, as I had hoped and asked. I would ask you, there-fore, to renew your activity along this line from now until May, when—if you work with tension and achieve results—I can give you another meditation which will climax the work done and bring another centre into activity. There is little that I can do with you until this meditation work has been patiently and regularly done and produced effective results—from my point of view. I shall not be able to give you another meditation unless you strive afresh, and to-gether, at the daily process outlined by me.

This meditation is one of the most important of the steps I shall ever ask you to take in these early preparatory stages of your work. It must precede the more definite training which may be possible if you persevere in the work outlined. I would remind you that this is my last effort with you in this incarnation and on the physical plane. You have put your hand to the plow and there is no turning back for any of you, but the time factor is determined by each of you and not by me. There may be times in the process of training you and preparing you for initiation when you may tempo-rarily fail to understand the reasons for the requests I may make and for the requirements presented to you. Forget not that the aspirant to the Mysteries proceeds blindly in the early stages; only after the third initiation do the scales fall from his eyes. Therefore, follow obediently (though volun-tarily) my requests as I endeavour to teach you the ancient rules.

Will you also, at this point, study anew the teaching I gave in the earlier instructions on the theme of Visualisation and explained why it is the secret of all true meditation work in its earlier stages? I seek not to repeat, but that teaching is needed by you at this stage. (*Discipleship in the New Age,* Vol. I. Pages 89-91).

In connection with your Full Moon work, I seek to change the process which has been followed by you for so long—the process of entering my study and there contacting me. I will give you another symbolic process which will fol-low five stages:

1. At the time of the Full Moon (covering five days) picture to yourselves an ocean of blue and upon the horizon can be seen slowly rising a blazing sun.

2. Picture yourself as throwing yourself into the ocean, free of all encumbrances, worries, anxieties and cares, and as swimming towards a rowboat, lying midway between you and the rising Sun. As you swim, you become aware of your group brothers, also swimming in the same direction. You recognise, know and love each other.

3. Then visualise yourself as climbing into the boat. When all of the group are in, then see yourselves as each grasping an oar, and together, rhythmically and steadily, rowing towards the rising Sun. There is harmony of stroke, of purpose and of direction.

4. Then see—between you and the rising Sun—a figure moving toward you. It will be myself (the Master D.K.), coming from the light, in your direction. In the clear pathway of the light you can see me distinctly. You see me *together*.

5. Then say, inaudibly, yet as a group:
   "Into the light we move, beckoned thereto by thee. Out of the dark we come, driven thereto by the soul of all. Up from the earth we spring and into the ocean of light we plunge. Together we come. Together we move, guided and led by the soul we serve and by thee, the Master we know. The Master within and the Master without are *One*. That One are we. The One is all—my soul, thy soul, the Master and the soul of all."

If you will each of you do this on the five days of the Full Moon (as earlier detailed), you will produce a group fusion of purpose which is for you the next desired step. You have worked at a group fusion in love; some success is apparent. Now work at the united evocation of the will.

Each month send in your Full Moon report. I would ask you to do this each month, embodying your Full Moon report and your meditation report into one unit because the activity of reporting is of real service in centralising your thought and therefore your life within the group life. It is simply in the nature of a symbolic happening—a symbol of your progress, your purpose, your contribution and your cooperation, and all from the *group* angle. Therein lies its value. The so-called informative aspect of these reports is relatively negligible as such to groups like this. But the symbolic usefulness is great and has a definite group usefulness.

One suggestion I will make. At the time of your Full Moon Approach to me, endeavour to have in your consciousness the words from Formula One (given in Section Three): "Upon the stream, between the two extremes, there floats the eye of vision." You need to remember that from one point of view these symbols are related to the antahkarana, that line between two points, and that as you build the antahkarana in your own lives so will be the growth of your understanding of the formula. As you progress upon the "way of the chela," so will grow your power. Use the formula actively as far as you can and do not rest satisfied with just attempting to understand some of its significances. It has a magical import, and when understanding is coupled with the use of the will, this formula constitutes a Word of Power of magical service.

Part IV

As I have studied the meditation work of each of you (and both you and I know whether it has been faithfully followed or not), I have become aware of a basic need and that is the need for *Alignment*. You need a more direct contact between heart-head-soul. This, necessarily, in preparation for a still higher contact. The two parts of the exercise you have been following since the new seed group was organised have not done what was intended and only three of you have profited adequately from that work. I am, therefore, giving you a very simple alignment exercise which I would ask you to follow *together* until further notice. I emphasise the word *together* and shall continue so doing in the hope that the group will move forward with a uniform procedure for this will produce the greatest and most rapid results. It is good for you to have in mind that the better you do this exercise and the quicker and closer your alignment, the better will be the group alignment. The exercise is so short and simple that you may regard it as too elementary. I assure you that it will reward any constant effort. It had been my intention to give another meditation, involving another centre, but the results of the work done do not warrant this. Perhaps a better alignment may lead to a more constant application and a more direct and understanding occult obedience. I would ask you, therefore, to do this simple alignment exercise every day.

I. Start with the point of soul focus of which you know much theoretically and can know more practically. This falls into three stages:
    1. Raise the consciousness into the head.
    2. Carry the thought or consciousness upward through the astral body and the mind to the soul.
    3. Identify the personality consciousness with the soul consciousness, and realise that they are one.

II. From that point, definitely and consciously, assume the attitude of the Observer. This also involves three stages:
    1. Observe the personality and consider it from the angle of the etheric body.
    2. Consciously throw soul energy down into the centre at the base of the spine. Then raise it slowly, via the five centres and the two head centres (ajna and highest head centre), up into the soul body. This produces, when correctly done, a vivifying of the sutratma and links the personality and soul into one blended unit. It is what might be called the acme of alignment.
    3. Then endeavour to throw the attention of the united soul-personality toward the Spiritual Triad.

III. Reflect upon the antahkarana and its relation to soul-personality and the Monad.

In your personal instructions this year, I am not going to be explicit nor am I going to give you each an individual meditation. The time for that is past. You have had much along that line. I am going to revert to an aspect of the old system of training and give you hints and brief injunctions, leaving you to do your own interpreting, to make right application and to profit or fail to profit as seems best to you.

These injunctions will take the form of six statements, sentences or aphorisms which will contain for you a particular message at which you can arrive if you will take each of them into your daily meditation. You have a year in which to do this and can, therefore, make the six statements into six seed thoughts for meditation, or reflective brooding—one for each month for six months. Then repeat with the thought in view that during the second six months you will do what you can to make the effects of the previous period of reflection, a dynamic factor in your life. Thus you will externalise the results of the preceding cycle of spiritual and mental brooding. In this way, your subjective realisation can become an objective happening. Do this exercise each morning at the close of the alignment work, endeavouring to hold the mind steady in the light and to achieve as far as you can the brooding quality of the soul when in deep meditation. This will not be easy at first, but if you adhere faithfully to instructions, you will consciously realise sure gain. I suggest ten minutes' brooding each day (with pencil in hand if you so prefer) and then—during the day—keep the seed thought or statement in what is called "the back of the mind." There it can gestate. In this way you will not only arrive at the meaning of your personal injunctions, hints or instructions (for that is what they may prove to be when you arrive at their intended meaning), but you will at the same time learn to cultivate the "double life pattern" of the pledged disciple. He carries on with the lower mind and the higher mind simultaneously, and the stream of spiritual thought and activity consciously flows whilst the outer pattern of his life proceeds with increasing usefulness.

Here are the six statements* for each of you, and I will take you alphabetically as usual. One word I would add: Seek not to interpret and understand your brother's instructions. Telepathic interplay, unrealised, naturally exists among you and your thought and interpretations (based on insufficient knowledge) would undoubtedly impinge upon your brother's mind. This could not fail to have effects. You might interpret wrongly and in any case you know not my intentions where your brother is concerned. Your thought might emphasise a concrete meaning whereas I might have in view a totally different application. Keep your mind, therefore, off your brother's instructions. Your duty lies in the daily releasing of steady illumined love, free from all criticism. It is not your duty to aid your brother to become a better occultist and disciple. That is his concern, his soul's concern and mine.

Many of the hints given and the sentences in which they are embodied are taken from an old Book of Rules for disciples. Some are directly from me, your Master, and are applicable to your problems or your duty.

Part V

The meditation work assigned to you thus far falls into three parts:

a. The stage of raising the energy of the heart centre into the head centre.
b. The stage of sending energy from the head centre to the solar plexus centre.
c. A definite and planned process of alignment.

I found, as you know, that the great need of the group was to develop the relatively simple attitude of instantaneous relation to or contact with the soul, and through the soul

*Note: The "six statements" appear in the Personal Instructions dated August 1942.

with the Master and His Ashram. I therefore assigned an alignment exercise when I last communicated with you, and this I did in lieu of more abstruse meditation practices.

This meditation is intended to bring about three most definite results:

a. The interrelation of the seven centres, and therefore an uninterrupted flow of energy.

b. The interplay of energy between the members of this group in my Ashram, via the seven centres. The group thoughtform will have in it seven points of energetic life, the energies of which will be contributed by the group members. This etheric form of the group life will be an expression of the sumtotal of the seven types of energy as each individual member utilises them.

c. The fusion, consciously and deliberately engineered, of the individual soul with the group soul, and later with the Hierarchy—via my Ashram.

To do this work correctly, we will start with the premise that "*energy follows thought.*" This is the first and most fundamental, as well as the most ancient, premise of the esotericist. The second is related to the first and will have a place in our considerations. It states that "*the eye, opened by thought, directs the energy in motion.*"

Disciples, during the early stages of their training, are apt to regard energy as a pool or a reservoir upon which they can learn to draw, thus appropriating a quota of that energy for their need, their service and their use. But energy is fluid and in motion; we live in a veritable sea of moving forces, qualified in countless ways, conditioned by countless minds, misdirected oft, directed wisely sometimes, yet all of them perforce finding place in the mind content of the One in Whom we live and move and have our being, and outside Whose range of influence naught can be. Disciples have, for aeons, been using the energies and forces found in the three worlds for personality ends and for the furthering of their major interests, whatever those may be. They have learnt somewhat to lay hold and use a measure of soul energy, thereby enlightening their way, improving their spiritual expression in the three worlds and serving a little. They are also beginning to grasp the significance of intention and of purpose, whilst an inner programme is slowly conditioning their daily lives. There comes, however, a point—a point which it is now your duty and privilege to grasp—wherein another source of energy, of inspiration and of light can be made available to disciples and can be used for service. That is the energy of the Forces of Light, originating in the Ashram and emanating thence; you stand as yet upon the periphery of the Ashram but can avail yourselves of these energies.

The force of the Ashram must be "routed" through the soul (if such a word is permissible). The disciple has therefore to learn the esoteric significance of a most familiar symbol—that of the Triangle and the Square.

This has hitherto signified to him the threefold soul and the fourfold personality, or if he is advanced enough in knowledge, the Spiritual Triad △ and the fourfold □ personality. Now he must view it in another light and learn to know it as the triplicity of the Ashram, the soul and the disciple himself, with the square representing humanity, the fourth kingdom in nature. This is consequently a great decentralising symbol, and around it your new meditation will be built. This meditation, if carefully followed, can and will bring about basic changes in your lives. The symbol is capable of being arranged in several ways, and all of them have to be mastered factually by the disciple—theoretically, visually, practically, intuitionally and factually. Each of these words will convey a specific meaning, and rightly apprehended will bring about changes in the disciple's life, in his service, and therefore in his effect within the Ashram.

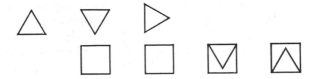

Let me now, brother of mine, outline for you the line of thinking which should be pursued by you as you seek to penetrate into the true significance of this symbol which is the theme of your meditation. It constitutes a normal development from the work already done. In the first two meditations given, you dealt with the centres of the etheric body, and were therefore dealing with the personality, the "city which stands foursquare." You were next enjoined to practice alignment, thereby arriving at the recognition, and in some cases the contact, with the spiritual triplicity, which is that which "hovers over the square and radiates the energy of light into this waiting field of active thought."

You will note that the entire process is therefore kept in the realm of the non-material and that the physical brain is not, at this stage, at all involved. You, as you seek to meditate, are thinking on planes of mental perception; you are focussed there, and the brain is held throughout this period in a state of waiting and attentive quiescence. The disciple has—as oft I have told you—to master the process of carrying on a dual thinking process, wherein he is preserving a continuity of mental impression and a constant activity connected with daily living and service. This is registered in due course by the brain. This is of major importance and one of the objectives which should provide you with ample opportunity for effort during the coming year's work.

This threefold spiritual reality (which is the "impressing agent") is the goal of the presented meditation work. It is *not* in this case the soul, whose impression upon the mind is that of love, its manifestation and its place in the Plan of the Hierarchy. The source of the impression to which you now seek to be sensitive is the Spiritual Triad, and the quality of the impression is the will, as it implements divine purpose. I am therefore indicating a far more advanced stage, and I do so for two reasons: One is that for years the effort of all of you has been towards the registering of soul contact and the expression of loving understanding; you are familiar with what the Hierarchy (of which my Ashram is a part) seeks to accomplish, and there is nothing to be gained by a constant reiteration of the familiar. I am, secondly, outlining procedures, meditations and objectives which will be of use to those who come after you and who will be the hierarchy of workers at the close of this century and during the first quarter of the coming century.

I stated that one significance of this symbol is that it stands for the triplicity of

1. The Ashram,
2. The soul on its own plane,
3. The disciple upon the physical plane,

whilst the square represents humanity; that this is frequently spoken of as the "city which stands foursquare," and is familiarly referred to in modern literature and discussions as the "city of man."

In considering the higher point of the triangle, which is the Ashram, I would remind you that radiation from Shamballa enters the triangle at that point and that, through the Ashram, will, purpose and strength can pour. This is a relatively new achievement within the Ashrams of the Masters. In the major group Ashram (which is the Hierarchy itself) this reaction to impression from Shamballa is arrived at as the energy pours in, via the two Great Lords, the Manu and the Christ. It is also registered by Their senior disciples, the Chohans and initiates of the sixth initiation, such as the Masters Morya and Koot Hoomi. Lately the Master R. has taken the position of Mahachohan, and that achievement has carried the entering force down into the ranks of those Masters Who have taken the fifth initiation thus enabling Them to step down this Shamballa force to Their individual Ashrams. This happening has produced a tremendous stimulation with all the attendant opportunities, manifestations, and dangers. Masters such as myself have had to learn to handle this great potency, and at the same time to make as much of it as we can (safely and wisely) available to our senior disciples.

It might be said symbolically that "the point of the triangle is based in the courts of Heaven (Shamballa) and from that point two streams of power pour forth into the realm of soul and into the heart of the disciple. Thus is the Triad formed; then are the energies related unto the world of men; thus can the will of God appear, and thus can the Great Lord Who guards the Council Chamber of this sphere of solar Life carry His purpose to the holy groups (the Ashrams. A.A.B.), and thence into the minds of men, and this because their hearts are safeguarded by the fire of love." Ponder upon this ancient writing: It refers to the cycle immediately confronting us, of which the work I am at this time seeking to do is but a tiny living part.

Therefore, as you prepare for the meditation process which you will undertake during this coming year, start by a consideration of the Ashram of the Hierarchy itself, of its relation to Shamballa, of its constitution, formed as it is of many Ashrams. Some of these are working under the Chohans; others are working under the Masters, and some are embryonic as yet, being gathered slowly together by Adepts of the fourth initiation. Will you endeavour to realise the factual nature of this great, living, spiritual organism? It constantly "substands" or underlies the world organisation. See it as a growing, vital reality, of such life and potency that it can break through or break up all limiting outer organisations and, by the very force of its interior life, eventually externalise itself.

This coming externalisation of the groups which constitute the Ashrams of the Masters (not yet of the Chohans, because they are still basically too potent) will be a gradual process, but it will in time restore the Mysteries, bring the first two initiations into a relative prominence as integral parts of the coming world religion, familiarise the whole of mankind with the fact of the subjective world, and finally bring the most developed of the sons of men into a faint glimmer of understanding of the essential Reality underlying all phenomena, and give some grasp of the purpose of Shamballa and the will of the Lord of the World. Humanity has now reached a point of development where there is a definite grasp of the Plan of the Hierarchy—call it brotherhood, sharing, internationalism, unity or what you will. This is a growing and factual apprehension and is a general recognition by the thinkers and esotericists of the world, by the religious people of enlightenment, by broad minded statesmen, and even today by the man in the street; divine purpose, however, implemented or engineered by the divine will, eludes as yet the most advanced.

The work of the next few centuries will bring about changes in this respect, and these changes will be brought about by the work done in the Ashrams of the Masters, guided by the Ashrams of the Chohans, welded together in the great Ashram of the Hierarchy itself, and moving ever into closer relation with the great Council Chamber of Sanat Kumara, the Lord of the World, in Shamballa. This has to be brought about on Earth by disciples, acting under instructions such as I now give you and by their prompt collaboration with their Masters. The doing of this will invoke the creative imagination of the disciple, and this, in its turn, will be conditioned and controlled by the illumined mind.

A second stage comes when the disciple, having considered the Ashram as outlined above, and having thereby imaginatively "fixed" the fact of Shamballa in his consciousness, turns his thoughts to the Hierarchy or to the soul. Remember always that *the Hierarchy is simply the world of souls,* that it is consciously aware of the Plan, sensitive to the purpose, and creatively and constantly impressing humanity with the aim in view of expanding the human consciousness. Of this your soul—in its pure nature—is a part. You will therefore think of the Hierarchy; you will attempt to vision its work, and you will endeavour to relate yourself to my Ashram by an act of faith and of will which is, in this case, the sublimation of the personal self-will; you will also take your position as a conscious, integral part of my Ashram, and consequently of the Hierarchy. Such is the duty of all disciples. You have had much instruction as to the Ashram and I need not further enlarge.

The third point of the triangle (as far as your work in this meditation is concerned) comes into the light of your reflective consideration. You will now turn your attention to yourself, the soul, the conscious disciple in preparation for that expansion of consciousness which is the next step in your spiritual unfoldment, leading eventually to initiation. This reflective consideration you do, *not* from the angle of the consciousness of your imperfections, qualifications or capacities, your failures or your successes, but entirely from the angle of cooperation with the Plan, with the divine Will and Purpose. It is with these highest aspects that the disciple is asked to cooperate.

It is not possible for the individual disciple in any Ashram to cooperate in all phases of the Master's work, and it is not possible for you, for instance, to cooperate in every phase of the work in my Ashram which I have outlined in my pamphlets (and which has been summarised in the one entitled *My Work*). But it is possible for you to choose some phase of that plan and give it your paramount attention. . . . These activities can—if adequately and strongly carried forward—aid in the esoteric work of the world and the exoteric rehabilitation of right human relations. . . .

The fourth stage of the meditation work is concerned with the square which—for the purposes of our work—we will simply regard as the field of service and of experience—experience in work and not individual life experience.

You will note that this description of the meditation work, which I am asking you to carry forward for a year at least, is based upon the three previous meditations; these sought to bring the etheric body with its various force centres into such a condition that it could become receptive to impression, and cooperate thereafter actively; through the alignment exercise you endeavoured to bring that organised instrument of service into contact with the source of inspiration and the source of impression, i.e., the Ashram and the soul. Now we are in a position (theoretically at least and dependent individually upon the successful action of all work previously done) to begin the task of bringing through the inspiration and impression consciously, by determined contact with their sources. I will therefore briefly outline the work, asking you to do it after close study of all that I have written above:

I. *The Stage of Recognition.*
   1. Recognition of your pledged discipleship.
   2. Recognition of your equipment, gratefully rendered.
   3. Recognition of your achieved alignment.
   4. Recognition of the soul, the source of love-wisdom.
   5. Recognition of the Hierarchy.
   All this should be done very rapidly, holding the consciousness steadily in the mind, and *not* in the head. It presupposes an immediate mental focussing of the disciple at the very beginning of his meditation work.

II. *The Stage of Consideration.*
   1. Of the Ashram as a whole, i.e., of the Hierarchy as the Ashram of Sanat Kumara. You will see, through the use of the creative imagination, all the Ashrams in close contact with Shamballa as:
      a. Responsive to the Purpose, implemented by the Ashrams of the Chohans.
      b. Impressed by the energy of Will as the great Ashram energises its component parts—the various Ashrams within its periphery of influence.
      c. Vitalising the initiates and disciples who are affiliated with the Masters and working in Their Ashrams.
      d. Reaching out, through the accepted and pledged disciples, into the world of men.
      Then you will say with purpose and determination:
      "I strive towards comprehension.
      Thy will, not mine, be done."
      All the above section of your meditation work concerns purpose, will and the "destiny" of Shamballa, to use an old occult phrase.
   2. Of the world of souls which is the Hierarchy in relation to this world of men, and not in relation

to Shamballa as in the first part. This involves:

    a. A study of the nature of the hierarchical effort, as it is expressed through love.

    b. A conscious identification with the Plan.

    c. Dedication to the work originating in the Ashram with which you know yourself to be in touch, seeing it all as an integral part of the hierarchical work.

Then you will say with love and aspiration:

"I strive towards understanding.

    Let wisdom take the place of knowledge in my life."

3. Of yourself as a unit in my Ashram. This will involve:

    a. Recognising which aspect of my planned work you are equipped to do.

    b. Determining how to do it.

    c. Considering the factor of preparation for eventual initiation, as a means of increasing your capacity for hierarchical cooperation.

    d. Energising by light, faith, love and power, the spiritual centre within which you serve and the ashramic projects for which you accept responsibility. In this instance it can be the Arcane School and the Service Activities. You will then say:

"I strive towards cooperation.

    Let the Master of my life, the soul, and likewise the One I seek to serve, throw light through me on others."

III. *The Stage of Fixed Determination.*

    1. A reflection upon the distinction between Purpose, Will and Intention.

    2. A period of complete focussed silence as you seek to present an unobstructed channel for the inflow of light, love and strength from the Hierarchy.

A statement made by you, the soul, the disciple, to the personality:

"In the centre of the will of God I stand.
Naught shall deflect my will from His.
I implement that will by love.
I turn towards the field of service.
I, the Triangle divine, work out that will
Within the square and serve my fellowmen."

If you can do this work correctly, you will not only greatly
increase your own realisation, service and understanding,
but you will definitely be cooperating in the task of externalising the Ashram and furthering the work of the Hierarchy
(from the foundation angle in relation to the New Age), and
so aid in bringing in the new civilisation, the new world attitudes and the new world religion.

PART VI

The meditation given you in your last instruction had
several objectives in view. It was a preliminary meditation
to a wide scheme for a particular kind of developing meditation, greatly needed by disciples, prior to unfolding a
unique kind of ashramic sensitivity.

It was intended, first of all, to give you (if you worked
with faithfulness) a growing sense of planetary relationship,
from the subjective angle, and above all, from the angle of
"intelligent supervision"—a phrase which will mean more
to you later. A true grasp of the implications and intentions
behind this meditation would develop in the disciple's
consciousness a realisation of a living world of Intelligences,
linked together from Sanat Kumara downwards until the
chain of Hierarchy reaches the individual disciple, leading
him to a later realisation that he too is but a link, and that
there are those whom he also must reach and relate to the
world of realities and awaken to their responsibilities. In
the training of all disciples, one of the goals is to make the
world of phenomena recede into the background of consciousness whilst the world of meaning becomes more vital
and real. This world, in its turn, is the antechamber to the
world of causes, where conscious relationship can be established with the Initiator.

The second purpose of the meditation was to bring to light the fact that the disciple (as an outpost of the Ashram as a functioning soul) must be oriented to humanity in a more definite manner; the purpose of such orientation is that the "life of the triangles may penetrate the area of the square and produce the inevitable consequence, the germinating of ideas and the flowering of the new civilisation and culture." So has one of the Masters expressed the purpose of certain phases of the ashramic work, particularly that connected with meditation. Another Master has explained the purpose of the hierarchical intent as the "merging of the higher with the lower triangle and their fusion in the square." The Masters view the work of Their disciples from this symbolic angle. The disciple who reaps the benefit of this last suggested meditation becomes—through an enlargement of his consciousness and the greater scope of his vision—"a sower of the seed within the world of men"; he distributes ideas, living and potential, in the field of the world, and these he receives from two sources:

1. His own soul, as his intuition awakens.
2. The Ashram, as he grasps more of its purposes and becomes accustomed to assimilating its teachings. This takes time.

Still another objective of this meditation was to bring the disciple to the point where his interest (evoked through the stages of recognition and consideration) would lead him to a realisation of the need for the evocation of the Will, the first faint indications of which I called that of "fixed determination." In the above statements you have the goals which I had in mind when assigning the meditation last year.

It is hard, I know, for the neophyte at any stage along the Path to grasp the necessity for engendering (to use an unusual word in this connection) a magnetised area of thought upon which the higher impressions can play, yet persistence in the daily recognition and consideration, accompanied by a fixed determination to bring the life and service into conformity with the revealing relations will (almost unexpectedly) produce great and transforming results. The Masters waste not Their time or yours in assigning needless exercises; the disciple who faithfully and with a definitely unbroken rhythm follows his instructions, can expect to see effects of a surprising and lasting nature within himself, and consequently within his environment. It is not upon the results, however, that you are asked to focus, but simply upon the themes presented for your use and consideration.

In the earlier stages of your training the emphasis was laid upon the form side, upon the achieving of alignment (still most necessary), upon the sounding of the O M, with its power to clarify the aura and the atmosphere, and upon the processes to be followed. In the meditation which you should now be doing, alignment should be instantaneous and easy and the following of a set form unnecessary, because you start as a centre of focussed thought, as the ready recipient of awaited impression, as the trained analyser of ideas, and finally as a transmitter of that which has been received from the higher sources of inspiration. This involves also the power to distinguish the sources from which the impression comes. It is these aspects of yourself in action which will form the basis of the suggested meditation to be followed by all of you during the coming twelve months.

The basic intention of the meditation is to train you to be intelligently aware of what Patanjali calls "the raincloud of knowable things," of the intentions, purposes and ideas which, at any given period, motivate the hierarchical work and condition the quality of the inspiration which can be received from the Ashram to which you may be attached. By "attached" I mean the sense of relationship and *not* devotion or affection. Attachment, in reality, is an expression of the freewill of the subject, choosing and recognising its relationships and adhering thereto. In the spiritual sense, the motivation will be loving responsibility; in the personality sense, it will be sentient emotion.

As an aid to your concentration and receptivity, I will give you twelve words which will be the theme for twelve months' work, and which could—as you gain the power to meditate, relate, receive and transmit—provide the seed thoughts for twelve years' work instead of twelve months. Words are living things, possessing form, soul and spirit or life; this you should ever bear in mind as you use them to open the door to a month's realisation and inspiration, plus the consequent service. Here are twelve words. Use one each month in your daily meditation.

1. Recipient	2. Impression
3. Recognition	4. Relationship
5. Source	6. Ashram
7. Transmitter	8. Expression
9. Determination	10. Seed
11. Idea	12. Attachment

You will notice how the meditation now to be outlined is a natural sequence to the one which presumably you followed all last year.

STAGE ONE . . . *Preliminary.*

Pass rapidly through the steps of recognition, consideration and fixed determination. These, if correctly followed, will bring you to the point at which this new meditation starts.

Then proceed as follows:

STAGE TWO . . . *The Centre of Focussed Thought.*

1. Polarise yourself consciously upon the mental plane, tuning out all lower vibrations and reactions.
2. Then orient yourself to the Spiritual Triad, through an act of the will and the imaginative use of the antahkarana.
3. Next, take your theme word under consideration and ponder deeply upon it for at least five minutes. Endeavour to extract its quality and life, thus lifting it and your thought to as high a plane as possible.
4. Then sound the O M, and wait silently, holding the mind steady. This is "the pause of reception."

STAGE THREE . . . *The Recipient of Impression.*

1. Assuming an attitude of the highest expectancy, you

will now express in your own words the highest truth
of the monthly word-theme that you have been able
to reach.

2. You then relate that theme to the present *world* opportunity, thus universalising the concept, seeing its
relationship to world affairs, its usefulness and spiritual value to humanity *as a whole.*

3. Holding the mind in the light, you will then write
down the first thought (no matter what it is) that enters into your waiting mind in connection with the
theme of your meditation. The ability to do this will
grow with practice, and will eventually evoke the intuition and thus fertilise your mind.

4. Again sound the O M, with the intent of refocussing
yourself upon the mental plane. If your work has
been successful, your original focus will have shifted
to intuitional levels or to the levels of the higher, abstract mind, via the antahkarana. This must happen,
in time, if your work has been faithfully followed.
But bear ever in your thought that you must work as
a *mind,* and not as an aspirant or from the angle of
memory. Think on this.

STAGE FOUR . . . *The Analyser of Ideas.*

1. You now analyse or think over with clarity the work
you have done, and the ideas now in your mind, seeing them in a true perspective in relation to the whole
problem of the day.

2. Then, choosing one of the ideas which your theme-
word has evoked, you think about it, analyse it and
relate it to life, getting all you can out of it. This
evoked idea may and should vary from day to day but
will always remain related to the monthly theme.

3. Then study the idea in connection with yourself, the
disciple, active in service and the Master's work, but
not in connection with the personality. This you will
find an interesting distinction. Make the idea practical, enabling it to "qualify" you or enrich you.

4. Again sound the O M, with the intent of making the
sensed idea a part of your very nature.

STAGE FIVE . . . *The Transmitter of Ideas.*

1. As the disciple, you have realised that a knowledge of truth and the reception of ideas lays on you the responsibility to be a transmitter to others. Ponder on this.

2. Now take the idea which the theme has engendered, or take the theme-word itself if no ideas have come to you, and in imagination formulate it in such a way that it can be presented to others, to your friends, to those you seek to help and to humanity—when opportunity offers. Think the idea through mentally, emotionally, and practically, thus precipitating it outwards into the world of thought.

3. Then (using the creative imagination and seeing yourself as a responsible transmitter, doing the work of the Ashram) breathe out the idea as a formulated, living thoughtform into the great stream of mental substance which is ever playing upon the human consciousness.

4. Sound the O M, thus "closing the episode."

Close the above meditation with a daily dedication of yourself to the service of humanity; renew your pledge to your Master and say the Mantram of Unification I gave you some years ago:

> The sons of men are one and I am one with them.
> I seek to love, not hate;
> I seek to serve not exact due service;
> I seek to heal, not hurt.
>
> Let pain bring due reward of light and love.
> Let the soul control the outer form, and life and all
>   events
> And bring to light the love that underlies the happenings of the time.
>
> Let vision come and insight.

Let the future stand revealed.
Let inner union demonstrate and outer cleavages be
 gone.
Let love prevail.
Let all men love.

I have given you this meditation in some detail, as I am
anxious to have you comprehend what it is you will be
doing. A shortened form of the meditation follows at the
close of this general instruction.

At the end of each month, go through the ideas you
have jotted down in your daily work and from them pick
three which seem to carry the most inspiration and which
you judge could be a seed for useful distribution or transmission. At the close of the year send in your thirty-six seed
thoughts. As you will all have been using the same theme-
words, much help can be accorded to the entire group by
each of you. You will find this work most interesting. It is,
in a way, a tiny reflection of the technique of the Hierarchy
and the way the Masters work (though on a much higher
turn of the spiral) in times of crisis, or when there is need
for all the groups or Ashrams—as there is today—to unite
in some endeavour, necessitated by the need of humanity or
by some planetary emergency. The Masters, starting Their
work on one of the planes of the Spiritual Triad, instead of
the mental plane as do Their disciples, concentrate on the
"theme" under Their consideration, during the period of
three Full Moons. They then meet in conclave and each
makes His contribution to the joint problem, as also does
the Christ and, at critical times, Members of the Council
Chamber of Sanat Kumara. On the basis of the proposals,
and after due analysis and discussion, the united decision is
transmitted by impression to the initiates and disciples in
the Ashrams, and from them to the world. If you study the
above statement you will see the importance of the meditation which I have outlined; it is to prepare you for closer
work—along correct hierarchical lines—in the Ashrams and
with the Master.

SHORT FORM

I. Preliminary stage of recognition, consideration and fixed determination.
II. The Centre of Focussed Thought:
   1. Polarisation.
   2. Orientation.
   3. Meditation on theme word.
   4. O M. Pause.
III. The Recipient of Impression:
   1. Statement of highest idea received.
   2. Relation of theme to present world opportunity.
   3. Write down first thought then received.
   4. O M. Refocus on mental plane.
IV. The Analyser of Ideas:
   1. Period of analytic thought.
   2. Summarise conclusions practically.
   3. Breathe out the idea into the world of thought.
   4. O M.
V. The Transmitter of Ideas:
   1. Dedication of yourself to service.
   2. Pledge yourself to the Master.
   3. Say the mantram: "The sons of men are one . . ."
VI. Intensive work at the time of the Full Moon along established lines.

PART VII

April 1945

MY BROTHERS:

As this world catastrophe draws to its inevitable close and the Forces of Light triumph over the forces of evil, the time of restoration opens up. For each of you this indicates a renewed time of service and of activity. I send you herewith the final stanza of the Great Invocation, as per my promise. I gave you the first about nine years ago and the second during the course of the war. I would ask you to use it daily and as many times a day as you can remember to do so; you will thus create a seed thought or a clear-cut thoughtform which will make the launching of this Invocation among the masses of men a successful venture when the right time comes. That time is not yet.

This Great Invocation can be expressed in the following words:

> From the point of Light within the Mind of God
>> Let light stream forth into the minds of men.
>> Let Light descend on Earth.
> From the point of Love within the Heart of God
>> Let love stream forth into the hearts of men.
>> May Christ return to Earth.
> From the centre where the Will of God is known
>> Let purpose guide the little wills of men—
>> The purpose which the Masters know and serve.
> From the centre which we call the race of men
>> Let the Plan of Love and Light work out
>> And may it seal the door where evil dwells.
> Let Light and Love and Power restore the Plan
>> on Earth.

It has been difficult to translate into understandable and adequate phrases the very ancient word-forms which the Christ will employ. These word-forms are only seven in number, and they will constitute His complete, new utterance. I have only been able to give their general significance. Nothing else was possible. But even in this longer form, they will be potent in their invocative appeal, *if* said with mental intensity and ardent purpose. The points of emphasis upon which I would ask you to dwell (once it is permissible to use the phrases) are two in number:

1. *May Christ return to Earth*. This return must *not* be understood in its usual connotation and its well-known mystical Christian sense. Christ has never left the Earth. What is referred to is the externalisation of the Hierarchy and its exoteric appearance on Earth. The Hierarchy will eventually, under its Head, the Christ, function openly and visibly on Earth. This will happen when the purpose of the divine Will, and the plan which will implement it, are better

understood and the period of adjustment, of world enlightenment and of reconstruction has made real headway. This period begins at the San Francisco Conference (hence its major importance), and will move very slowly at first. It will take time, but the Hierarchy thinks not in terms of years and of brief cycles (though long to humanity), but in terms of events and the expansion of consciousness.

2. *May it seal the door where evil dwells.* The sealing up of the evil forces, released during this war, will take place within the immediate future. It will be soon. The evil referred to has nothing to do with the evil inclinations, the selfish instincts and the separativeness found in the hearts and minds of human beings. These they must overcome and eliminate for themselves. But the reduction to impotency of the loosed forces of evil which took advantage of the world situation, which obsessed the German people and directed the Japanese people, and which worked through barbarity, murder, sadism, lying propaganda, and which prostituted science to achieve their ends, requires the imposition of a power beyond the human. This must be invoked, and the invocation will meet with speedy response. These evil potencies will be occultly "sealed" within their own place: what this exactly means has naught to do with humanity. Men today must learn the lessons of the past, profit from the discipline of the war, and deal—each in his own life and community—with the weaknesses and errors to which he may find himself prone.

I would here recall to you what I said last year to . . . anent this final stanza of the Invocation:

"I am preparing to present to you for wide distribution throughout the world, the last stanza of the Great Invocation. It is by no means easy to translate the words of this stanza in terms which will make it of general appeal and not simply of importance to convinced esotericists. . . . It can be so presented that the masses everywhere, the general public, will be prompted to take it up and will use it widely; they will do this on a relatively larger scale than the intuitional, the spiritually minded or even the men of goodwill. A far wider public will comprehend it. I will give A.A.B. this stanza at the earliest possible moment; this will be conditioned by world affairs and by my understanding of a certain esoteric appropriateness in the setting of a time cycle. If plans mature as desired by the Hierarchy, the new stanza can receive distribution at the time of the Full Moon of June 1945, as far as the Occident is concerned, and considerably later for the Orient. Prior to these set points in time, the stanza can be used by all esoteric school members, after being used for one clear month by my group, dating that month from the time that the most distant members of the group receive it."

I seek to have this Invocation go forth on the power generated by my Ashram and by all of you affiliated with my Ashram; the Ashrams of the Master K.H. and the Master M. are likewise deeply committed to participation in this work.

I would ask you also to read and reread the two Instructions—one dealing with the Cycle of Conferences,* and the other with the work of the Christ.** Master their contents and let the blueprint of the hierarchical plan take shape in your minds. Then you can do your share in implementing it and will be able to recognise those who, in other groups and in different lands, are also a vital part of hierarchical effort.

PART VIII

Before we proceed further with this subject of meditation, I would like to call your attention to the fact that the type of work I am now giving you is *formless* in comparison with the earlier meditations outlined. I have already given you five meditations which, as a group, you have been asked to follow. I would like to summarise their objectives for you so that (again) you may intelligently go forward.

The first meditation was concerned with the transfer of energy from the solar plexus centre to the heart centre, so

---

*The Externalisation of the Hierarchy.
**The Reappearance of the Christ.

that the great dividing barrier (of which the diaphragm is the exoteric symbol) could be bridged and the emotional personality be controlled by the heart. By this means, the selfish individuality of the average man could be transmuted into the group awareness of the dedicated disciple. I sought to help you set up a facility of transference which would be of primary importance to you in your daily lives.

The second meditation was concerned with the impartation of a major concept. I wonder if it was so registered by you? The idea behind that meditation was the free flow of directed energy. You need ever to bear in mind that the initiate is eternally occupied with energies and forces which he directs and manipulates in accordance with hierarchical intent. Before, however, he can do this, he must be in control to some extent of the seven types of energy to which the human mechanism responds. He must be able to direct the flow of energy to any particular centre, to focus certain types of force in certain centres—at will and with understanding —and to institute a free flow and interchange throughout his own little microcosm. The meditation given was not intended to bring this about; it had only one objective: the impartation of an idea and the presentation of a possibility.

The third meditation was closely allied to these two, even if this is not immediately apparent to you. It concerned alignment. You have been apt to think of alignment in terms of the process whereby the personality is brought into relation with the soul. This is entirely accurate, yet alignment is a term which in reality covers four processes:

1. The alignment of soul and personality, resulting in a conscious relation to the Kingdom of God.
2. The alignment of soul and personality with the Ashram, resulting in a conscious relation with the Master of the Ashram.
3. The alignment of the initiate of higher degree with the Spiritual Triad and the consequent result of a recognition of monadic energy.
4. The alignment of all the centres in the etheric body

of the disciple. This results in the ability of these centres to register and transfer energies which enter into the lower mechanism as a consequence of the three higher alignments—listed above.

I would ask you to study the above tabulation with care.

The fourth meditation was definitely directed towards bringing about a closer relation to the Hierarchy, via the Ashram and its life of pledged service. This statement is of importance to you at this time. This meditation was divided into three stages: Recognition, Consideration, Determination. Disciples need to build into their brain consciousness recognitions of relation and of attitude. These must eventually and automatically condition the personality, and this, not through a forced effort, but through a positive receptivity. This receptivity is brought about by a stabilised orientation. Disciples need constantly to reflect upon the life of the Ashram as it makes its impact upon their consciousness. What impact, my brother, are you individually aware of? Upon this reflection must succeed a planned determination to form a constructive part of the ashramic life to which their thinking and their service have admitted them. The first faint efforts of the emergence of the spiritual will can be seen in the working out of this determination.

This was followed by the *fifth meditation,* which has been the subject of your attention during this past year. You will have noted how the meditations have become increasingly abstract until—in this last one—you have been occupied with the consideration of ideas and with what those ideas can reveal when they are regarded as *seed ideas,* shielding or containing a flowering—as yet unseen and recorded.

I have been working, as you can now realise, upon a definite plan and (if you have done your work regularly and conscientiously) you are now ready for the next phase in this abstract work. I would like at this point to refer to two concepts which I have already presented to you; they are related to the fact that the initiate has two things to do:

1. Become sensitive to impressions coming to him from various levels of the divine consciousness and awareness.
2. Become aware of the "raincloud of knowable things" to which Patanjali refers.*

Both of these will become clearer to you as we proceed with our consideration of our third point in these instructions—the point which deals with telepathy.** Each of these possible registrations involves a certain and specific phase of alignment, a conscious use of the mind as a contact agent, and a receptive activity of the brain.

Putting the objective of all this into its highest possible terms, the disciple and the initiate are learning the technique (through meditation) whereby the Mind of God, the Universal Mind, or the thinking process of the planetary Logos, can be recorded and registered. For the majority, at present, the knowledge of the divine thought (as registered by disciples, as it works out in the emerging Plan, and as it gives livingness to life purpose) is reached through the Ashram. The Master imparts the nature of the Plan or the Purpose—according to the status of the initiate—and that is accepted by him under the Law of Free Occult Obedience. But the disciple or the initiate must not remain forever dependent upon the transmission of the divine thought to him by Those more advanced than he. He must learn to make his own contacts and to tap the "raincloud" for himself. He must—unaided—penetrate into the thinking processes (by permitted spiritual telepathy or impressibility) of Sanat Kumara. I have the responsibility at this time to give you those meditations which will enable you to take the first steps towards this knowledge; it is for me to give to you the A B C of the later greatly simplified, yet exceedingly abstruse, techniques. Have these thoughts in mind as you study this résumé of the meditations already given, and then go forward with that to be suggested in this series of instruc-

*The Light of the Soul, Pages 38, 424-426.
**Telepathy and the Etheric Vehicle.

tions. On the basis of what I have here said, I would ask
you also to write a clear statement:

1. Of your understanding of the progressive synthesis of
    the six meditations which you will have received and
    of their purpose in connection with your moving for-
    ward towards initiation.
    a. What have these meditations done to you?
    b. What were they supposed to do?
2. A clear definition of the phrases:
    a. The Science of Impression, referring here to the
       mechanism of impression and stating what you
       know about the technique of impression.
    b. The "raincloud of knowable things." What is
       the nature of these things? Why the symbol of
       the raincloud?

You will endeavour to bear in mind that the source of these
impressions shifts steadily higher or deeper, as the case may
be, and that for average disciples, such as you, the impressions to be recorded until such time as you have taken the
third initiation concern:

1. The ideas, purposes and intentions which motivate
    the Hierarchy and which are transmitted to you by
    the Master of your ray and therefore of the Ashram
    with which you are affiliated.
2. The quality of the inspiration which you can receive
    and register and which emanates from the Ashram in
    which you find yourself. This again will have the
    outstanding characteristics of your ray, though those
    of the other six rays will also be present, implied and
    inherent.
3. The nature of the hierarchical mode of work and
    the methods to be employed in any particular world
    period, such as the present difficult and transitional
    era.

You will see from the above how diverse, spiritually speaking, are the impressions to be received by the attentive disciple. The word "diverse" here employed is not of a separative connotation; it signifies the basic unity in diversity and the vastness of the inclusive thinking of the planetary Logos. Achievement, for the disciple, consists (along this line) in a sequential and growing capacity to include in his thinking more and more of the divine *conclusions*. I use this word in its esoteric significance.

It is my intention this year to have you concentrate upon the new Invocation from the point of view that it embodies the divine intent and summarises the conclusions of the thinking of the planetary Logos. It is the most abstract form of meditation with which you have yet been presented. The meaning of this Invocation has been expressed in terms which are understandable, in a measure, to the average person because of its familiar wording, based on many Scriptural terms. But the true inner implications and significances are of very deep import and are not superficially apparent. I challenge you to penetrate, through meditation, more deeply into the vital meaning of these words, these amazing words. They embody, as far as is possible in modern language, a formula which has been in possession of the Hierarchy ever since it was founded on Earth, but which is only now available for use, owing to the point in evolution reached by mankind. The wonder of these mantric stanzas is that they are comprehensible to members of the human family and to members of the Kingdom of God. They mean one thing to the ordinary man, and that meaning is good, powerful and useful; they mean another thing to the man upon the Probationary Path, for he attaches to the words a deeper and more esoteric meaning than is possible to the man who is entirely polarised in his lower nature; these words mean still another thing to the disciple affiliated with and functioning consciously in an Ashram; to initiates and to the senior Members of the Hierarchy, they convey a still higher and more inclusive significance.

I am anxious to ascertain your reaction to these words, and am asking you for one entire year to concentrate your

meditative thinking and your reflective power upon them.
At the same time, they provide, in an almost singular manner, the next developing stage in the series of meditations I
have planned for you; they should also (in a peculiar manner) enable you to move forward in your thinking and in
your ability to grasp abstractions. *Look for the underlying
abstract idea in this Invocation.* It is there. From your reaction to this Invocation, and your ability to use its phrases
as "stepping-stones" to certain levels of abstract thought not
hitherto attained, I shall be able to judge your readiness, as
individuals, for certain specific preparatory work for the initiation which you (again as an individual disciple) should
take.

The final stanza of the "Invocation for Power and Light,"
as it is called in the Archives of the Masters, is apparently
simple. It has, in these Archives, an indicatory symbol beside it which indicates the era or period in human history
during which it can and should be used. It is interesting to
us to note that the evolution of humanity is in line with the
indicated timing. This Invocation will have a potent appeal
to mankind. My considered advice is that in its presentation
to a definitely Christian public (as for instance to the ecclesiastics of all denominations) the third verse in the stanza
be changed and that its last line should read: "The Purpose
which the Master knows and serves," or perhaps "which
disciples know and serve." The word "disciple" is an inclusive word, in the hierarchical sense; it is, at the same time,
one easily recognised by the orthodox but offers no limitation to the esotericist. It covers every grade of human aspirant from the newly accepted disciple up to and inclusive
of the Christ Himself. Let me here quote the Invocation:

> From the point of Light within the Mind of God
>   Let light stream forth into the minds of men.
>   Let Light descend on Earth.
> From the point of Love within the Heart of God
>   Let love stream forth into the hearts of men.
>   May Christ return to Earth.
> From the centre where the Will of God is known

Let purpose guide the little wills of men—
The purpose which the Masters know and serve.
From the centre which we call the race of men
Let the Plan of Love and Light work out
And may it seal the door where evil dwells.
Let Light and Love and Power restore the Plan
on Earth.

Each of the four stanzas refers to one or other of the three aspects of divine energy, plus a reference to humanity itself in which the three meet, are potentiality in latency, and finally develop into the full flower of divinity, with all three lines perfectly expressed. Hence, my brothers, the intensity of the human conflict—a conflict unparalleled in any other differentiation of the divine Life. In humanity all lines and aspects meet. This is a fundamental of the occult teaching. The subhuman kingdoms find their consummation in humanity, and the superhuman kingdoms their opportunity, and through the human kingdom all superhuman lives have at some time passed. This you well know.

In the *first three lines* you have reference to the Mind of God as a focal point for the divine light. This refers to the soul of all things. The term "soul," with its major attribute of enlightenment, includes the anima mundi, the animal soul, the human soul, and that consummating point of light which we regard as the "overshadowing" soul of humanity. It is an aspect of the divine manifestation to which that great Son of God refers when (as Shri Krishna) He remarks, "Having pervaded this entire universe with a fragment of Myself, I remain." That fragment is the soul of all things. That soul brings light and spreads enlightenment.

In the *second three lines,* the Heart of God is evoked and the focal point of love is considered. This "heart" of the manifested world is the Hierarchy—that great transmitting agency of love to every form in the divine manifestation. Upon the essentially "loving nature" of the Hierarchy I need not dwell; too much has been written about it; too little understood; too much has been talked about love and not enough has been realised as to the task confronting the Hierarchy as it transmits love. Love is an energy which must reach the hearts of men and which must fecundate humanity with the quality of loving-understanding—*that* is what is expressed when love and intelligence are brought together.

In the *third three lines,* we find reference to Shamballa —"the Centre where the Will of God is known"—the centre from whence the Hierarchy draws its life, as it draws its impulse towards service from humanity. You well know that there is indication in these lines that humanity itself cannot as yet grasp the purpose of Sanat Kumara. Only advanced Members of the Hierarchy and initiates of at least the third degree (the first degree of the Lodge on Sirius) have any idea as to the nature of the purpose which underlies the Plan. Ponder on that phrasing.

Having invoked the three aspects or potencies of Mind, Love, and Will, in the *fourth three lines* we have indication of the anchoring of all these powers in humanity itself, in "the Centre which we call the race of men." Here and here alone lies the promise of the future and its hope and opportunity. Here and here alone can all the divine qualities—in time and space—express themselves and find fulfillment; here and here alone can love be truly born, intelligence correctly function, and the Will of God demonstrate its effective goodwill. Through humanity, alone and unaided (except by the divine Spirit in every human being), can the "door where evil dwells be sealed." It is not Sanat Kumara who seals that door; it is not the Hierarchy which forces evil back into the place from whence it comes. It is struggling, aspiring and suffering humanity to whom the task is committed and, my brother, humanity is adequate to the task.

This statement is borne ever in mind by Those most potent in using the Invocation; it serves to focus and anchor the invoked energies in the human kingdom. That is Their task. From that point, humanity takes over the undertaking.

This Invocation is also unique in the sense that it invokes all the three divine aspects. It is synthetic in its approach. This is the first time in human history that this has been done. Hitherto the development of mankind did not warrant such an utterance.

In *Lemurian* times, the third divine aspect, that of Intelligence, was invoked by the mass appeal of instinctual animal-man; he little knew what that almost inchoate appeal would invoke. Light appeared on Earth and true progressive enlightenment became possible. I am not here referring to physical light, but to the light of the intellect.

In *Atlantean* days, as a result of the strife between the Lords of Light or of the Shining Countenance and the Lords of the Dark Face (as they are called in the ancient Scriptures and in *The Secret Doctrine*) another "era of invocation" occurred and the second divine aspect of Love became a possible unfoldment, though still only an embryonic quality of mankind. The mass appeal was then more intelligently voiced, though the instinctual appeal still persisted. It was not intelligence, however, as we understand the term.

In our *Aryan* cycle, another great invocative cry is issuing forth. It is this time a threefold cry. It is the cry for light upon our way and for light to flow into the dark places of the Earth; it is also a cry for more love in the world as voiced by the men of goodwill and of humanitarian attitudes; it is, finally, the intuitive appeal of the aspirants and the disciples of the world for the full expression in time and space of the will-to-good—the Will of God. Average instinctual humanity, the men and women of goodwill, and the disciples of the world are all concerned in this invocation, bringing in the attributes of instinct, intelligence and intuition. All three are blended in this great Invocation. Have also constantly in mind this basic fusion, now finding voiced expression, and take courage from the massed approach to the Source of all Life, Love and Light. Nothing can withstand the united demand of men everywhere in their graded and their serried ranks.

This entire Invocation refers esoterically to the "rain-cloud of knowable things" to which Patanjali refers. It is that impending, overshadowing and revelatory storehouse of energy which is the immediate cause of all events on Earth and which indicates the emergence of that which is new and better and progressively *right*. The events and happenings thus precipitated demonstrate the moving onward into greater light of the human consciousness. These "knowable things" are the sources of all revelation and of all human realisations—cultural and leading to what we call civilisation. Their "condensation" (if I may use such a word) is brought about by the massed invocative appeal of the entire human family at any one period. This appeal has been, on the whole, projected unconsciously, but more and more it will be consciously voiced. Results, therefore, can be expected more rapidly and prove more effective. This raincloud is formed through the joint action of the Central Spiritual Sun, working through Shamballa, and humanity itself, working hitherto through appeal to the Hierarchy, but increasingly making its own direct appeal.

There is necessarily a subtle indirect appeal going forth continuously from the three subhuman kingdoms in nature, but that appeal focusses itself in the human kingdom, for that kingdom is the receiving and the transmitting agent for these kingdoms, just as the Hierarchy has been and is the receiving and the transmitting agent for every human appeal. Note here the beautiful interlocking and the fine interrelation which has been established by our planetary Logos. This new Invocation expresses this complete interdependence in an unique manner.

Precipitation of the new and long awaited energies is brought about in three ways:

1. By the direct action of the Hierarchy as its Members train Their disciples to tap this source of inspiration, to become sensitive to the awaited impression, and to bring down that which is needed for the enlightenment and restoration of mankind to its original high spiritual state. There is a higher condensation awaiting precipitation, but to humanity that will form a "raincloud of unknowable things" and necessitates not, therefore, your consideration.

2. By the disciples and aspirants of the world who provide a channel by means of which the energies and the fructifying forces can reach mankind. This they bring about by:

    a. The deepening of man's spiritual realisation through reflective meditation, aspiration and devotion. These in time give place to conviction and mental knowing.

    b. Receptiveness to spiritual impression. This entails the awakening of an intelligent use of the intuition, plus the capacity to hold the mind steady in the light whilst the brain is quiescently ready to record that "descending knowledge."

    c. Practical ability to relate the idea to the ideal and to take those steps which will create the form of that ideal upon the physical plane.

  3. By the steady progress of humanity, en masse, towards the light. This in time produces in humanity itself a quality and a vibration which make themselves felt. This quality and this vibration are essentially evocative.

Today this "raincloud of knowable things" has condensed or brought together energies which have been made available by the Spirits of Restoration, Reconstruction and Resurrection. These now available energies are—on a larger scale and of a higher nature—similar to those which the individual soul (parodoxical term) makes available to the personality when that personality is ready for the Path of Probation or of Discipleship. These energies are far more potent because they are, in their turn, a precipitation of energies which have been placed at the disposal of Shamballa, plus energies and forces generated by the Hierarchy. Extra-planetary forces can now be utilised on Earth, owing to the forward progress of our planet and its relation to the solar system as a whole.

There has never been a period in our planetary history in which opportunity has loomed so large or when so much spiritual light and force could be contacted and utilised by humanity.

The *first indication* of this massed and available energy produced coordination of the New Group of World Servers upon the physical plane.

The *second indication* produced a pronounced cleavage between the forces of evil and the Forces of Light; this cleavage resulted in the world war (1914-1945) and initiated the seething emotional and psychic turmoil in which humanity today finds itself.

The *third indication* was the release of atomic energy and the discovery of how to transmute energy into matter and matter into energy.

The spiritual energies have, therefore, impersonally and with a "vivid directive of pure intent," penetrated from the highest point of spiritual purpose to the lowest aspect of matter, the atom; they have thus proved the truth of the statement that matter is spirit at its lowest point and spirit is matter at its highest, and that the apparent duality is but an essential unity.

A concentration of spiritual forces in and through the New Group of World Servers, the production of a world conflict with its disrupting and at the same time its unifying result, and the release of certain impressive energies in matter itself *for the benefit* of all created things on Earth— these are the immediate results of the pressure of the overshadowing spiritual resources.

These forces have affected the spiritual and the humanitarian people of the world, blending them into one group upon the inner planes (even if this still remains outwardly unrealised), and have thus given a death blow to the great heresy of separateness. This will later make itself invincibly apparent. They brought pure evil to the surface in such a manner that the issues between good and evil became apparent in a clearer light and the causes of human misery received fresh and keener recognition; the knowledge and the responsibility of mankind everywhere cannot now be denied. They also made possible the use of energy locked up in substance itself; this, if rightly used, can and will completely alter and change man's attitude to life, his sense of values and his use of time.

All this has been brought about by what we might call with exactitude the first precipitation. Its effects have been mass effects to a very large extent. They have affected the spiritual workers and the men of goodwill, producing the purifying fires of pain and agony through the medium of war, and making available also the essence of the material world. I have endeavoured to express the majesty of the recent happenings in various ways in order to impress upon you all the stupendous nature of what has occurred.

The second precipitation must be more consciously brought about by humanity itself, and it is to facilitate this that the new Invocation has been given, and for this reason it must be widely distributed.

This precipitation is to be brought about by the gradual engendering of the divine idea in the human consciousness. Above everything else required at this time is a recognition of the world of meaning, a recognition of Those Who implement world affairs and Who engineer those steps which lead mankind onward towards its destined goal, plus a steadily increased recognition of the Plan on the part of the masses. These three recognitions must be evidenced by humanity and affect human thinking and action *if* the total destruction of mankind is to be averted. They must form the theme of all the propaganda work to be done during the next few decades—until the year 2025—a brief space of time indeed to produce fundamental changes in human thought, awareness, and direction, but—at the same time— a quite possible achievement, provided the New Group of World Servers and the men and women of goodwill perform a conscientious task. Evil is not yet sealed. The spread of the Christ consciousness and His *recognised* Presence with us is not yet attained. The Plan is not yet so developed that its structure is universally admitted. Evil has been driven back; there are enough people aware of the possibility of divine enlightenment and of the interdependence (which is the basis of love) to form a potent nucleus, provided again that the inertia so prevalent among spiritual people is overcome. There is divine indication of coming events and a planned progress towards them, and this is already arousing interest among thinkers in many lands. However, the necessary responsive planning is still lacking.

This new Invocation, if given widespread distribution,

can be to the new world religion what the Lord's Prayer has been to Christianity and the Twenty-Third Psalm has been to the spiritually minded Jew.

I would like to indicate to you three approaches to the subject of this Invocation. I will do so briefly, as time lacks. It is for you to arrive—according to your evolutionary status and the depth of your reflection—at what I may leave unsaid. These three approaches are:

1. That of the general public.
2. That of the esotericists, that is, of aspirants and disciples.
3. That of the more advanced disciple (as far as I can) and of the Hierarchy.

First, *the general public* will regard it as a prayer to God transcendent. They will not recognise Him yet as immanent in His creation; they will send it forth on the wings of hope —hope for light and love and peace, for which they ceaselessly long. They will also regard it as a prayer for enlightenment of all rulers and leaders in all groups who are handling world matters; as a prayer for the inflow of love and understanding among men so that they may live in peace with one another; as a demand for the working out of the will of God —a will of which they can know nothing (this is, after all, quite true for all except initiates) and which ever seems to them so inscrutable and so all-inclusive that their normal reaction should be patience and a willingness to refrain from questioning; as a prayer for the strengthening of human responsibility, in order that the recognised evils of today which so distress and trouble mankind may be done away with and some vague source of evil may be harnessed; they will regard it finally as a prayer that some equally vague primeval condition of blissful happiness may be restored and all unhappiness and pain disappear from the Earth. This is, for them, entirely good and helpful and all that is immediately possible. I have so worded and rendered the Invocation that the Christian world, through its churches, may not find it impossible to use.

Second, *esotericists and aspirants* of the world will have a deeper and more understanding approach. To them it will convey the recognition of the world of causes and of Those Who stand subjectively behind world affairs, the spiritual Directors of our life. They stand ready to strengthen those with true vision, ready to indicate not only the reason for events in the various departments of human living, but also to make those revelations which will enable humanity to move forward out of darkness into light. With this fundamental attitude, the necessity for widespread expression of these underlying facts will be apparent and an era of hierarchical propaganda, engineered by disciples and carried forward by esotericists, will mature. This era began in 1875 when H.P.B.'s proclamation of the *fact* of the existence of the Masters of the Wisdom was made. It has been carried forward in spite of misrepresentation, attack upon the concept and scorn; recognition of the substantial nature of the available evidence, and an appearance of an intuitive response by occult students and many of the intelligentsia throughout the world have been present.

A new type of mystic is coming to be recognised; he differs from the mystics of the past (except in a few outstanding instances) by his practical interest in current world affairs and not in religious and church matters only; he is distinguished by his lack of interest in his own personal development, by his ability to see God immanent in all faiths and not just in his own particular brand of religious belief, and also by his capacity to live his life in the light of the divine Presence. All mystics have been able to do this to a greater or less degree, but he differs from those in the past in that he is able clearly to indicate to others the techniques of the Path; he combines both head and heart, intelligence and feeling, plus an intuitive perception, hitherto lacking. The clear cold light of the Spiritual Triad now illumines the way of the modern mystic, and not simply the light of the soul, and this will be increasingly the case.

Both of these groups—the general public and the world aspirants in their varying degrees—have among them those who stand out from the general average as possessing a deeper insight and understanding; they occupy a no-man's-land, intermediate in the one case between the masses and the esotericists, and on the other between the esotericists and the Members of the Hierarchy. Forget not that They also use this great Invocation and that not a day goes by that the Christ Himself does not sound it forth. As you read the next few pages, you may find some clue to the attitudes and points of view of these spiritual Intelligences.

On the surface, the beauty and the strength of this Invocation lies in its simplicity, and in its expression of certain central truths which all men, innately and normally, accept—the truth of the existence of a basic Intelligence to Whom we vaguely give the name of *God;* the truth that, behind all outer seeming, the motivating power of the universe is *Love;* the truth that a great Individuality came to Earth, called by Christians the *Christ,* and embodied that love so that we could understand; the truth that both love and intelligence are effects of what is called the *Will* of God, and finally the self-evident truth that only through *Humanity* itself can the divine Plan work out.

This Plan calls mankind to the expression of Love and challenges men to "let their light shine." Then comes the final solemn demand that this Plan of Love and Light, working through mankind, may "seal the door where evil dwells." The final line then contains *the idea of restoration,* indicating the keynote for the future and that the day will come when God's original idea and His initial intention will no longer be frustrated by human freewill and evil—pure materialism and selfishness; the divine purpose will then, through the changed hearts and goals of humanity, be achieved.

This is the obvious and simple meaning and it ties in with the spiritual aspiration of all men everywhere.

There are deeper implications and upon them I will later touch, but the clarity of spiritual desire and aspiration is expressed in these words in such a form that its use offers no barrier to the different types of mind which may receive it. Only those who recognise no subjective or inner world, and who reject the concept of an inner world of causes being responsible for the outer world of effects, will deny its truth and usefulness; such people are fortunately few and far between.

It is apparent, therefore, that the first three stanzas or verses invoke, call for or appeal to the three aspects of divine life which are universally recognised—the mind of God, the love of God, and the will or purpose of God; the fourth stanza points out the relation of humanity to these three energies of intelligence, love and will, and mankind's deep responsibility to implement the spread of love and light on Earth.

Right here the work of the Triangles—so close to the heart of the Hierarchy at this time — becomes obvious. Through the network which the Triangles are creating, light or illumination is invoked by the daily work and attitude of the Triangle members; thus light can indeed "descend on earth" and goodwill, which is the love of God and basically, the will-to-good, can also stream forth in fuller livingness into the hearts of men; thus they are transformed in their lives and the era of right human relations cannot be stopped. This is an era hitherto only dimly sensed and which only the forward-thinking people of the world have desired. Thus through the "centre which we call the race of men" the Plan of love and light works out and strikes the death blow to evil, selfishness and separateness, sealing it into the tomb of death forever; thus also the purpose of the Creator of all things will be fulfilled.

No one can use this Invocation or prayer for illumination and for love without causing powerful changes in his own attitudes; his life intention, character and goals will be changed and his life will be altered and made spiritually useful. "As a man thinketh in his heart so is he" is a basic law in nature; the constant turning of the mind to the need for light and the prospect of illumination cannot and will not be ineffectual. Also, as the work of the Triangles grows and the network spreads all over the Earth, the idea of a downpouring of light and goodwill (which is the immediate aspect of love required today among men) can be looked for; nothing can prevent the appearance of the expected results, for the eternal law holds good. The illumination of men's minds, so that they can see things as they are, can apprehend right motives and the way to bring about right human relations, is now a major need; the motivating power of goodwill is an essential to right action; given these two—light and love—it will not be many decades before the idea of right human relations will have become the ideal of the masses and will be rapidly taking form in all national, public and community affairs. The history of humanity has been that of the apprehension and the use of ideas as applied to human living and as expressing forward moving concepts; today the two ideas needed are light upon our way and practical goodwill.

I would like now to touch upon some of the deeper meanings for you who are disciples or who are in training for discipleship. If I can do this, your meditation work may be useful in linking hierarchical intent with human aspiration; such should be the work of all disciples.

You will already have noted—as you have studied the Invocation—that the three major centres in our planet are linked up: Shamballa, "where the Will of God is known," the Hierarchy, where Christ rules and from whence He seeks closer contact among men, and the centre which we call Humanity. There is a close relation between the first stanza and the final one; humanity's destiny is, as you know, to be the exponent of the mind of God, thus expressing active intelligence, motivated by love and implemented by will. That time has not yet come, but if human timing is correct and right desire is potent enough, for the first time in human history this destiny can be publicly recognised and people can be swept increasingly and voluntarily into an activity which is particularly their own destiny. That again is one of the primary objectives of the Invocation; its steady use will bring about an inclusive view of spiritual development and impart a synthesis to human thinking which has hitherto been lacking. As "light streams forth into the minds of men" the divine plan will be more widely sensed and the will-to-good will be more widely desired and invoked.

It is necessary always to remember that light is active energy and that love is also an energy. It is useful also to bear in mind that light and matter are synonymous terms scientifically, and that the network of light is veritably substance, and therefore the carrier of goodwill. That is why, consequently, it is necessary to realise that *it is one network, composed of two types of energy.* For this reason, the work of creating Triangles falls into two categories; some people work more easily with one type of energy than another; it is interesting also to note that the Triangles of Light are basically more material than the Triangles of Goodwill because they are related to substance, to the energy which mankind wields familiarly, and to etheric matter. The Triangles of Goodwill are hierarchical in origin. I would ask you to ponder on this.

However, in this world crisis, the origin of the network in both its aspects is hierarchical; the Masters work in substance (i.e., light) though not with matter; the work to be done by Triangle members is consequently purely mental and hence exceedingly powerful — this of course when rightly done. "Energy follows thought" and the work of the Triangles is that of directing thought. The work therefore falls into two categories: that of invoking divine aid (to use Christian phraseology) and then—through faith and acceptance—directing the energies of light and love (which have been invoked) to all men everywhere. They will, from the popular attitude, be registered as illumination and goodwill. It is a deeply scientific work but fundamentally simple. Invocation, prayer or aspiration, meditation—it matters not what word you use—by means of these three methods spiritual energies are tapped and brought into activity. By clear thinking, directed thought and mental perception, they can be made objects of human desire. Ideas are simply channels for new and desired divine energies; ideals are these ideas changed or reduced into thoughtforms, and thus presented to the public. Ideas telepathically become ideals, which is another phrasing of the old law, "energy follows thought."

The work of the network of light and goodwill, focussed on the plane of mind, is the utilisation of this knowledge in order to affect the public consciousness. These are points which should be simplified and gradually taught, and in the clearest language, to all Triangle members. The work of the

Triangles is to work with the minds of men, and with a factor which is used and exploited by leaders everywhere; the
effort is to impress these minds with certain ideas which are
necessary to human progress. People recognise the present
darkness and misery, and consequently welcome light; men
are tired of hating and fighting, and therefore welcome
goodwill.

Let me touch for a moment upon another point of view.
Just as stanzas one and four are related, so stanza two and
the final line are also related. The Plan will be restored on
Earth through illumination and goodwill, and when that
takes place Christ *will* return to Earth. I would ask you not
to misunderstand this phrase. Christ has never left the Earth
and He said when bidding farewell to His disciples: "Lo, I
am with you always, even until the end of the days." His
Presence, however, is not recognised by the masses of men,
and is only sensed and dimly hoped for by the orthodox
religionist of all the world faiths.

As I have earlier pointed out, the return of Christ will be
expressed, in the first place, by an upsurging of the Christ
consciousness in the hearts of men everywhere; its first expression will be goodwill.

In the second place, disciples everywhere will find themselves increasingly sensitive to His quality, His voice and His
teaching; they will be "overshadowed" by Him in many
cases, just as before, He overshadowed His disciple Jesus;
through this overshadowing of disciples in all lands, He will
duplicate Himself repeatedly. The effectiveness and the potency of the overshadowed disciple will be amazing.

One of the first experiments He made as He prepared for
this form of activity was in connection with Krishnamurti.
It was only partially successful. The power used by Him was
distorted and misapplied by the devotee type of which the
Theosophical Society is largely composed, and the experiment was brought to an end; it served, however, a most
useful purpose. As a result of the war, mankind has been
disillusioned; devotion is no longer regarded as adequate or
necessary to the spiritual life or its effectiveness. The war
was won, not through devotion or the attachment of millions

of men to some prized ideal; it was won by the simple performance of duty, and the desire to safeguard human rights.
Few men were heroes, as the newspapers stupidly proclaim.
They were drafted and taught to fight and had to fight. It
was a group recognition of duty. When Christ again seeks to
overshadow His disciples, a different reaction will be looked
for. It is because of this that A.A.B. has so consistently be-
littled devotion and advocated spiritual independence. No
devotee is independent; he is a prisoner of an idea or a
person.

When Christ comes, there will be a flowering in great
activity of His type of consciousness among men; when
disciples are working under the recognition of the Christ,
there will then come the time when He can again move
among men in a public manner; He can be publicly recognised and thus do His work on the outer levels of living as
well as upon the inner. For these three events, which are
connected with the inherent divinity in man, the Hierarchy
is working and preparing, and it will essentially register
another of the results of the successful use of the new Invocation to aid in this task of preparation.

Those of you who are disciples will easily see the significance of the third stanza. Its meaning is that the Invocation
as used by the Hierarchy (note this) will help to bring about
the evocation of the spiritual will in humanity and the recognition of the divine will by the Hierarchy. There is little
that can be said to the general public anent this third stanza.
They will interpret it in all simplicity as a prayer that the
human will can be brought into conformity with the divine
will, even though that may not be understood. Even from the
angle of the Hierarchy, the divine will as it is essentially
remains the great mystery, but in spite of that They can and
do "know and serve" the purpose; the purpose is that aspect
of the divine will which seeks immediate expression on
Earth. The Hierarchy is the distributor of energy—the energy of love. Therefore, as the purpose of the will of God
(known and understood in the Council Chamber of Shamballa) seeks to influence human will, it is an expression in
hierarchical terms as the will-to-good and in human terms as

goodwill, as *loving determination* or as *a fixed intention to bring about right human relations.*

Even Christ Himself struggled with the problem of the divine will, and addressed Himself to the Monad at the moment when He first realised the extent and the complexity of His mission as World Saviour. He then cried aloud: "Father, not My will but Thine be done." Those words marked the relinquishing of the vehicles through which He had been attempting to salvage humanity; it indicated to Him what might at that time have appeared to be an apparent failure and that His mission was not accomplished. For nearly two thousand years He has waited to bring that mission to fruition; it has marked also for Him the entrance into a new cycle of activity; this cycle will culminate during the next three hundred years in success if this Invocation—as used by all of you and by the Hierarchy—proves its effectiveness. He cannot proceed with His assigned mission without reciprocal action by humanity.

This mantram is peculiarly and essentially Christ's Own mantram and its *"sound* has gone forth" to the entire world through the medium of His enunciation of it and through its use by the Hierarchy. Now its *words* must go out throughout the entire world by means of its enunciation by men everywhere, and its *meaning* must be expressed by the masses in due time. Then Christ can again "return to Earth" and "see of the travail of His soul and be satisfied."

The final line of the last stanza is also perhaps in need of explanation. It speaks of the task of the Plan as implemented by humanity to "seal the door where evil dwells." This is (needless to say) a symbolic way of expressing the idea of rendering evil purposes both inactive and ineffectual. There is no particular location where evil dwells; the New Testament in the Book of Revelations speaks of evil and of the destruction of the devil and of the rendering of Satan impotent. Those passages all refer to the same time cycle with which this Invocation deals and which it seeks to bring about.

The "door where evil dwells" is kept open by humanity through its selfish desire, its hatreds and its separateness, by its greed and its racial and national barriers, its low personal ambitions and its love of power and cruelty. As goodwill and light stream forth into the minds and hearts of men, these evil qualities and these directed energies which keep the door of evil open will give place to a longing for right human relations, to a determination to create a better and more peaceful world and to a worldwide expression of the will-to-good. As these qualities supersede the old and undesirable ones, the door where evil dwells will symbolically slowly close through the sheer weight of public opinion and through right human desire. Nothing can possibly stop it.

Thus the original Plan will be restored on Earth; this is symbolically referred to in the Bible as the Garden of Eden; the Angel with the Flaming Sword will no longer guard the Door of Initiation into the Kingdom of God, but will be transformed into the Angel of the Presence. Simultaneously, the door into the world of spiritual reality will open before mankind, and the door where evil dwells will be closed. These few thoughts may serve to make this Invocation live afresh in your minds and take on a new and vital livingness. It is uniquely related to all true and ancient beliefs; it holds out hope for the future, and it is of present import and of practical importance.

Your meditation work should be confined exclusively to a deep understanding of this stanza* of the Great Invocation, and of the production within yourself of the invocative spirit.

I am going to give you today a very ancient mantram which is called the *Affirmation of a Disciple*. It has been used by disciples in the Masters' Ashrams for thousands of years and is today given out by me to all true disciples; it can now be used by them upon the outer plane and incorporated daily in their meditation. During this coming year I would like you to follow a meditation procedure as outlined below, the intention of which is to strengthen your pledge through

*Here the Tibetan refers to this Invocation in its entirety as *one* stanza, the third and final of three "stanzas" or Invocations. He gave out the first one, beginning with the line, "Let the Forces of Light bring illumination to mankind," in 1935, and the second in 1940, beginning, "Let the Lords of Liberation issue forth."

affirmation, stabilise your orientation and give you intuitive insight into this new Invocation.

1. The *Stage of Alignment and Recollection*. This produces recognition of spiritual status and objectives. It involves recognition also of the Ashram and dedication to the Master, under two symbols: the soul and the central Point in the Ashram.

2. The *Stage of Affirmation*. Say with your whole heart as a soul the following ancient mantram:

> "I am a point of light within a greater Light.
> I am a strand of loving energy within the stream of Love divine.
> I am a point of sacrificial Fire, focussed within the fiery Will of God.
> And thus I stand.
> I am a way by which men may achieve.
> I am a source of strength, enabling them to stand.
> I am a beam of light, shining upon their way.
> And thus I stand.
> And standing thus revolve
> And tread this way the ways of men,
> And know the ways of God.
> And thus I stand."

This, brother of mine, is the best I can do with words and phrases as I attempt to transcribe into language words so ancient that they antedate both Sanskrit and Senza. But the meaning is clear and that is the point of importance.

3. The *Stage of Orientation*. This is a period of quiet thought upon the significance of the affirmation.

4. The *Stage of Meditation*. This is concerned with the four stanzas of the new Invocation. I am going to leave you free to consider this Invocation in your own way and to approach this most important and significant mantram from the highest possible point of your individual intuitive perception. I would ask you to medi-

tate on what appear to you to be the planetary implications, but would also remind you to consider the individual parallels. All that is invoked on behalf of humanity is also susceptible of interpretation in a personal sense, regarding the personality as the microcosm of the Macrocosm and as the field for the circulation of light and love, for the expression of the Christ Life and of the sacrificial Will, plus the instrument of service and an area in which evil is sealed, frustrated and rendered futile. At the end of the year, I would ask you to embody your understanding of the Invocation and your interpretation of it (both macrocosmically and microcosmically approached) in a paper. These papers, if truly the result of intuitive perception, could constitute a useful book, giving the general public a truer comprehension of words which will condition the thinking of spiritually-minded people for many decades.

5. The *Stage of Fixed Determination.*
   a. A reflection upon the distinction between Purpose, Will and Intention.
   b. A period of complete, focussed silence as you seek to present an unobstructed channel for the inflow of light, love and strength from the Hierarchy.
   c. A statement to the personality, made by you the soul, the disciple:

> "In the centre of the will of God I stand.
> Naught shall deflect my will from His.
> I implement that will by love.
> I turn towards the field of service.
> I, the Triangle divine, work out that will
> Within the square and serve my fellowmen."

Part IX

Six meditations have already been given to you, culminating in the meditation on the Great Invocation. How closely you have followed this last meditation I know not. My attention has been occupied with many vital matters and also with the effort to render futile a series of attacks upon the Hierarchy; these are being engineered in various parts of the world by spurious claimants to world discipleship. They were mainly aimed at A.A.B., and she could have absorbed them, as she has frequently done in the past, had it not been for the direct line of attack on my Ashram. . . . As I have told you, my Ashram, and to a lesser extent that of K.H., have felt some of the repercussions, and A.A.B. has been unable to deflect all of it. I have had, therefore, to do some protective work; that is now finished, and I am somewhat freer.

I plan to give you the seventh and last meditation, and with these seven outlined meditations you will have plenty of work to do for the remainder of this incarnation. The ones hitherto given are all planned and sequentially related to each other. The first one started with the heart, as must all divine expression and all true creative work. Next the factor of energy was considered and the seven points of energy reception were noted. Then followed an exercise on alignment, so that the structure or the "set-up" (if I may use such a word) of the inner spiritual man might be correctly oriented and aligned, and thus present no obstacle to the inflow of divine energy. These three meditations are of major importance, but quite elementary. They had, however, to precede any meditation (and its subsequent effects) that was in any way related to my Ashram as was the next. A meditation on certain theme words, as they embodied an idea, was then given; the meditation was totally different to the preceding three in its emphasis, which now has no relation to the disciple—as had the earlier three; they related almost entirely to preparatory work for ashramic service.

The first definite act of this type of service was embodied for you in the sixth meditation, in which the group was given the task (or rather the spiritual enterprise) of launching the Great Invocation. The magnitude of this task you have never realised and you have done little of a truly objective nature to bring this Invocation to the attention of the public. Three of you have done a great deal; the rest little or nothing at all.

Now I will outline for you a meditation which is not easy for you to do, but which symbolises both the *vertical* and the *horizontal* life of the disciple; this meditation is, again, built up around certain words esoterically understood.

1. Affirm earnestly your discipleship and endeavour to link up with me, as the Master of the Ashram.
2. Say the Great Invocation, emphasising one of the four stanzas during each of the four weeks of the month, and dwelling on its significance longer than the others.
3. Your meditation must then be built up around eight words which you can arrange within your consciousness in the following manner:

This Cross concerns your VERTICAL life

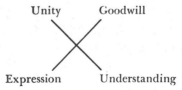

This Cross concerns your HORIZONTAL life

The mode of your application of all this must be related to your daily life expression, and at some point you (the incarnated soul) must realise the factual nature of your dual life as a disciple. This the superimposed Crosses show.

4. Give ten or fifteen minutes to the consideration of the Vertical-Horizontal life and note how one vertical line supports the other lines in many cases, but that no horizontal lines do this.

5. Taking your stand at the point where all the lines meet, endeavour to realise yourself as the *one* at the centre, radiating throughout your most definitely defined ring-pass-not.

6. Then sound the O M seven times inaudibly.

One of the formulas, brother of old, is related to this meditation. You would find it of value to contrast what is said.

Part X

In the last set of papers I gave you a group meditation; this completed a unit of seven meditations, all of which were sequential and all of which were intended to bring about creative results in your lives.

I would like to repeat at this time some of the ideas which I earlier gave you; I would like also to show you the synthesis of the entire seven meditations and demonstrate to you how they can lead the aspirant on, step by step, from knowledge into wisdom; I would like you to grasp the fact that if these meditations are carefully followed by you they can change you from a heart-focussed aspirant to an ashramic worker, implementing the Great Invocation. This Invocation, which I have lately given to you, is the group prayer of all humanity in the Aquarian Age; therefore it is essential that every disciple (aspiring to the service of humanity) should make its distribution as well as its daily use a major duty and obligation. This I have earlier impressed upon you and would ask you now if you are doing so?

Meditation I . . . Heart Control . . . Transference

You have here a technique whereby you create a line of related energy between the solar plexus centre and the heart centre. This is in reality a reflection or a symbolic activity (within the physical man, or rather, his etheric centres) of the building of the antahkarana. Bear in mind here, as always, that the etheric body is a physical mechanism.

It was this meditation which started the rhythm which made possible the presentation of the new Invocation to the world; I refer not solely to its use by you but to its use by many disciples in many Ashrams. The exhaustion of emotion and its transference—as a force—into the heart, there to be transmuted into the energy of love, was symbolically undertaken during the time that humanity was developing certain new recognitions. Humanity, through the exhaustion of emotional energy (incidental to the war agony) is today far more heart-conscious than at any other time in its history. Had you realised that and the opportunity with which you were presented?

The world of men has been subjected to such strain and suffering that hundreds of thousands in nearly every land—either factually or imaginatively—could "feel" no more; the solar plexus centre could take or absorb no more. Nothing was left to the sufferer but the realisation that all men everywhere were in a similar plight and that this community of shared agony brought all men together, irrespective of nation, religion or class.

Therefore, for the first time in their history, humanity began to recognise a definite phase of universality; mankind as a whole began to "share in the heart's reaction." This happened so generally and so acutely that the heart—as a motivating radiance—became a point of human focus. One of the first fruits of suffering, as universally shared, has appeared on Earth, and in its appearing all future suffering will be greatly lessened.

I seek to give this first meditation an added importance in your eyes. Much that I have given you has significance far beyond your crediting; these significances will appear if you follow instructions and do these meditations carefully, regularly and sincerely. It would profit you much in the years to come if you followed this meditation formula each day for two months, doing so with intensity. You should also endeavour to realise not only your individual reaction, but to recognise also the symbolic import of what you are doing. Those of you also who know with certainty that you are being specifically prepared for the second initiation would do well to follow this meditation for one week in each month of the year.

Meditation II . . . Directed Energy . . . Circulation

This meditation constitutes the second stage of the first one given. That first meditation was in the nature of a foundational exercise, related to the control and the direction of energy; it was so planned that it could enable you to enter into the field of energies and from there — choosing the needed energy—direct a particular type of energy through some particular centre to a particular point. I gave you only the preliminary idea, for all physical plane demonstrations are founded on an ideal. Do not forget that "as a man thinketh in his heart, so is he." There is therefore a direct relation between Meditation I and Meditation II; the first makes the second possible and eventually effective.

This meditation, when practised, understood and perfected, prepares the disciple for the work which he will later do as a Master or an initiate. He will manipulate energies in line with the Plan; he will then direct such energies from his own place within the Ashram, using his own etheric body as the implementing factor. He has consequently to begin with the energies working through his own centres before he can proceed to direct ashramic force through them from what is referred to as the heart centre of the Hierarchy. There is, symbolically speaking, a heart centre in every major and every secondary Ashram, and these heart centres pour their energy through the central centre in the Hierarchy; it is used as a reservoir of energy. Disciples have to learn to work with this pure energy of love as it blends with the forces of the disciple's own ray; that, in turn, colours somewhat the Ashram with which he is affiliated.

It is necessary, therefore, for you to extend your thinking about the meditation, as given above, so that it may become Ashramic in nature and effect. Thereby you are trained to

use the heart and to work with and through heart centres
wherever they are found in manifestation. I have here given
you a most valuable hint and item of information. In this
connection it is valuable to bear in mind that the first meditation has relation to the heart centre in the spine, and that
this second meditation is only effective when the disciple can
work with the heart centre in the head. As soon as this becomes possible, the disciple realises three things:

1. The relation of the heart centre to the twelve-petalled
   lotus in the head.
2. The necessity of directing the energy of love (the product of the activity of the heart centre) to the service of
   humanity via the ajna centre.
3. The establishing of a triangle in the etheric body,
   composed of a line of energy between:
   a. The twelve-petalled lotus in the head.
   b. This lotus and the ajna centre.
   c. The ajna centre and the heart centre. This creates
      a peculiar triangle:

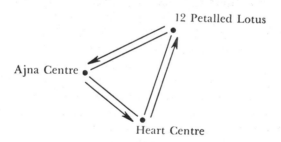

This is in reality more in the nature of a funnel of
reception than a triangle.

This is also the first esoteric triangle of energy which
the disciple creates. Later comes the creation of a
spiritual triangle in the head between:

   a. The ajna centre and the thousand-petalled lotus.
      This becomes effective physically through the
      medium of the pineal gland and the pituitary
      body.

b. The thousand-petalled lotus and that focal point or junction of energies to be found in the medulla oblongata, and which is called the alta major centre. This centre becomes physically effective through the carotid gland.

c. The alta major centre and the ajna centre.

You have, therefore, another triangle, of the following nature:

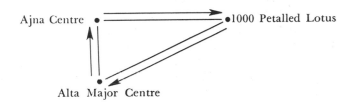

Ajna Centre

1000 Petalled Lotus

Alta Major Centre

Here you have, therefore, some of the concepts which are implicit in this second meditation; they indicate a free, flexible and fluid interplay between all the centres involved.

Meditation III . . . Alignment . . . Mode of Contact

This deeply esoteric alignment exercise is preparatory for a state of more occult and general alignment; of this alignment, the effective use of the new Great Invocation will be an expression. In this third meditation you have man, the spiritual man, grounded in the soul, entering into a close contact (leading eventually to fusion) with the Spiritual Triad, the reflection of the Monad. This is done through the alignment of heart, mind and will. Thus is a world server created. This alignment exercise (when correctly and persistently followed) will find expression as a Master upon the physical plane. It must inevitably produce the initiate. It "seals to him the door where evil dwells," in the personality sense. The Invocation, when rightly used by humanity and when it becomes a world prayer, will enable humanity—as a whole—to express Light and Love and Power and also to seal the door where evil dwells, using the word "evil" here in a very much wider and larger sense than when individually used. All these results—individual and general—are brought about by right alignment.

Nine is, as you know, my brother, the number of initiation. It presupposes the alignment of three different triplicities:

1. The threefold Personality.
2. The three aspects of the Soul.
3. The Spiritual Triad.

When these have been correctly aligned and the resultant integrity has been stabilised and fully accepted, the disciple then becomes a Master; He is now ready to tread the Way of the Higher Evolution. There is then a direct channel of contact—whenever needed and desired for service—with the physical brain and also an alignment or unimpeded relation between:

1. The disciple and Humanity.....The throat or creative centre in the planetary sense.
2. The disciple and the Hierarchy...The heart centre of the planetary Logos.
3. The disciple and Shamballa.....The head centre of the planetary Logos.

These are great and abstruse esoteric facts. The use of the Invocation will likewise relate human beings within the ring-pass-not of humanity itself; it will bring the human centre en rapport with the Hierarchy, creating a free interplay between the two of them and thus making possible the appearance of the Kingdom of God on Earth.

Meditation IV ... Spiritual Livingness ... Ashramic Relation

In assigning this meditation I made a remark of major importance. I said that this meditation was the first one given by me which carries the disciple into the true world of esotericism. It concerns his relation to that vortex of special energies which we call an Ashram. It is therefore intended to teach the disciple how to absorb energy and what to contribute of energy to the whole; it does this not by indicating the modes and acceptances of transference, but by establishing a constant habit of *spiritual livingness*. One sentence was particularly a key to my comments: "Disciples need to build into their brain consciousness a stable recognition of relationship and of attitude." So much of the life of a disciple, even when he has been admitted into an Ashram as an earned right, remains esoteric, below the surface and almost entirely subjective. Of this the iceberg is by far the best symbol. His knowledge and capacities and his spiritual abilities do not become a practical demonstration in daily life, as they should. Esoteric knowledge is not intended to drive your spiritual life into greater and increasing subjectivity; the goal is not a more inward life and a training which will make of you a true introspective and consequently a pure mystic. Exactly the reverse is intended; all that the disciple essentially is upon the inner planes has to become objective; thus his spiritual livingness becomes an everyday affair.

It is here that the dual life of discipleship starts and at the same time demonstrates its essential unity. The disciple becomes outwardly effective. His Ashramic consciousness and his power to function as a disciple or an initiate must be blended with his transformed personality life, until gradually "the two become the One." In the last analysis, discipleship is the recognition by the Master of a certain stage (elementary, at first) of fusion, and then a training given and a process instituted which create a still greater fusion. It is this that the meditation here given is intended to facilitate.

Meditation V . . . Precipitation . . . Reception

Each of these meditations carries the practising disciple on to greater insight, or should do so, if properly approached and correctly employed. One of the principal tasks of the combined Hierarchy is the presentation to humanity of the basic divine ideas; in this manner They mould human ideals and consequently in time create its current civilisation, thus providing a field for its culture. The culture approximates the ideal closer than does its civilisation.

Disciples must be taught this work of presentation and the relation of time and the event. A right sense of timing is something that every worker for the Hierarchy must cultivate. Before, however, he can do this, he has to recognise and work with ideas himself, learn the mode of approach and the consequent use of that "raincloud of knowable things" (to which Patanjali refers) and later how to translate these contacted ideas into practical ideals. As time proceeds, this "raincloud" will become more generally recognised; scientists will begin to realise that it is the true source or fount of all ideas and of the inspiration which makes their work possible; they will develop a technique of directed concentration which will enable them to attain that source of ideas and to profit by its existence.

Such ideas are contacted usually at first in the form of vague perceptions or remote prophecies; when contacted by churchmen of any of the world religions, these ideas normally receive a far too literal, and therefore misleading, interpretation. This has been responsible for much misery in the world. The scientific method safeguards the scientist from this type of error.

Part of my task within my Ashram is to train disciples to recognise the new, emerging ideas and translate them into the concepts which will condition human thinking in the cycle just ahead. The second stage of this training involves the cultivation of a *correct sense of timing*. This will prevent the disciple from taking precipitate or premature action; it will give him the key to the real meaning of the Eternal *Now*—the synthesis of Past, Present and Future. He will next be taught the art of precipitation, or the mode of conveying these ideas to the minds of the intellectuals in the world. Through these concrete and receptive minds the presented ideas are transformed into ideals and then are brought to the attention of humanity. The place and the responsibility of the intelligentsia is not yet fully appreciated, nor have they truly shouldered their task or recognised its defined importance. Their work and their presentation of the ideal to the masses of men everywhere does not concern the disciple. His work lies primarily with the advanced, pioneering thinker and not with the demanding masses. I would ask you to remember this.

Therefore, when I gave you the fifth meditation I gave you also twelve words for consideration in meditation. They were intended to evoke your abstract mind and their obvious meaning and significance was not intended to form a part of your thinking. As you later review these words, I would have you consider them:

1. As embodying the viewpoint of the Spiritual Triad.
2. As part of the work assigned to you in leading humanity forward. These words have new and prophetic meanings and you must discover for yourselves what they are.

This you have not yet done, and in neither of these two ways have you truly meditated on the given words. It is essential that there be a reorganisation of your meditation technique in these two directions. Your entire meditation work is too concrete. There are the twelve words which I earlier gave you (Page 144). Please use one each month in your meditation work.

Meditation VI . . . The New Invocation . . . Spiritual Inflow

I wonder, brother of mine, if you have grasped the momentous significance of this presentation of a cosmic, planetary and individual alignment exercise, prayer or invocation? It provides, as a result of its correct use, a spiritual inflow— right to the very heart of humanity and from the highest sources. For the reception of this last part or final stanza of the great hierarchical "Invocation for Power and Light," all previous teaching you have received and all your earlier meditation work was simply an elementary prelude. In receiving this Invocation, in its use and distribution, you have been participating in a cosmic event of tremendous importance. The intention—connected with this Invocation—is as follows:

1. To focus the inchoate mass demand of humanity on to the highest possible level.
2. To initiate a great invocative cycle wherein invocation will unify, blend and bring together the two methods (hitherto in use) of prayer and meditation.
3. To give to the world a new prayer.

This meditation or invocation is essentially a prayer. It can, however, be used with profound effectiveness, primarily by those who know something of meditation; they have a special and peculiar advantage over the average man who is accustomed to pray, because the technique of meditation brings in the factor of mental concentration and an intense focussing. The trained disciple can therefore use this Invocation on several levels simultaneously.

This Invocation is *not,* however, a meditation exercise; it is essentially a prayer, synthesising the highest desire, aspiration and spiritual demand of the very soul of humanity itself. It must be used in that way. When the trained disciple or the aspirant in training uses it, he will assume the attitude of meditation—that is, an attitude of concentration, spiritual direction and receptivity. *Then he will pray.* The attitude of the occult student who has thrown over in disgust all old religious practices, and believes that he has no further need or use for prayer, or that he has passed to a higher phase, that of meditation, is not a correct one. The true position is that he uses both at will and at need. In connection with the Invocation he assumes the attitude of meditation (an inner mental attitude and firm assumption), but employs the method of prayer which—when divorced from all relation to the separated self—is a potent means of establishing and maintaining right spiritual and human relations. When in the attitude of meditation and using the implement of prayer (by means of the Invocation), he attains a relationship with the mass of humanity not otherwise possible, he can implement their recognised though unvoiced need, and he also allies himself with the Hierarchy, Who work from the cosmic astral plane but—through the use of the planetary antahkarana—work also on buddhic-mental levels and are evoked by the desire of the mass of men.

I do not intend to deal further here with the Invocation, because I did so fully in the earlier meditation instructions. I earnestly beg you, however, to reread what I there wrote.

Meditation VII . . . The Cross . . . Spiritual Position

It is an occult truism to say that the disciple is crucified upon the Fixed Cross of the Heavens. This he is prepared always to accept, for he knows from bitter experience how true it is; he lives in the recognition that the life of the disciple is hard and its exigencies are inescapable. Curiously enough, a good deal of this recognition is based upon an unconscious and unrealised self-pity. To offset this unrecognised habit of thought, this meditation is intended to teach the disciple to create—with deliberate intention—his own cross, and in this manner do away with his idea (again unrealised) that the cross is the result of his point in evolution, that it is imposed upon him by astrological conditions, and that through it the Lords of Karma work, exacting from him the full price for all past misdeeds. This, in reality, is not so.

By the time a man is admitted into an Ashram he has already worked off a very great deal of his karma, both good and bad, and is now ready to build his own cross upon which he takes his stand—with his hands *stretched out in blessing.* That is the idea underlying this seventh meditation on the vertical and the horizontal position of the practising disciple. In this meditation you therefore have:

The Vertical Life
1. *God,* or the divine Reality, veiled by all forms.
2. The polar opposite to this, i.e., the *matter* in which this divine nature is expressed.
3. The *method,* based on ray tendencies, of this revelation.

4. The polar opposite, i.e., *achievement.* The trained disciple works always from the angle of achievement, of attained success. This attitude he assumes as regards himself, the serving disciple, and the work to be done.

The Horizontal Life

1. *Unity.* As a result of his successful vertical life, the disciple feels himself at-one with all life in all forms and with humanity in particular.
2. This works out naturally in *understanding.* Because there are absolutely no barriers present, and there is also no realisation of difference, the disciple can "tune in" on the life in all forms, and therefore enter into a full measure of inclusiveness, with all that that word implies.
3. His motivation is that of *goodwill,* which is a growing potency as the will-to-good (which he contacts indirectly in the Ashramic life) begins to affect him. Ponder on this statement. The goodwill of the masses is based on innate divine tendency; that of the disciple is based on knowledge and receptivity to certain energies from Shamballa.
4. This goodwill—as it is released—produces a normal *expression* upon the physical plane.

You have, consequently, the crosses (+ ✕) which—when superimposed, provide a most interesting chart for the disciple's life. This meditation, therefore, provides a complete and rounded-out form for the disciple to follow; it will suffice him for many years to come. I have given you only a few hints in the above analysis, but you can arrive at much greater light on the matter if you will definitely realise that your daily life is based on a vertical attitude and a horizontal effectiveness.

In these seven meditations, my brothers, you have all you need in order to make progress in your own life and also in the group life—functioning subjectively at present. If you follow these meditations with care in the years to come, you will find that they will lead to an extension of your service, which (as far as the majority of you are concerned) has not been of great importance.

These seven meditations make a perfect synthesis of recognitions, of unfoldment and of spiritual direction; if they are followed with care, they will eliminate selfishness and build in ashramic quality.

PART XI

In our last series of instructions I summed up or summarised all the meditations (seven in number) which I have given to the group. I tried to show you the sequence of critical points in the life of the man in training for initiation. The last of these meditations was called *The Cross as the Expression of the Vertical and the Horizontal Life*. This was portrayed by the two crosses:

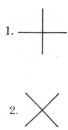

To these two symbols of the life of the disciple I seek at this time to add another one, which is a symbol of the attitude you should hold during the cycle into which you are now entering.

You will see that I have combined the two crosses of the vertical and the horizontal life with the cross of Humanity

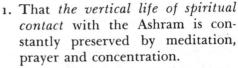

and have also added a circle at the summit of all three. What, my brother, does this mean? It signifies the following:

1. That *the vertical life of spiritual contact* with the Ashram is constantly preserved by meditation, prayer and concentration.

2. That *the horizontal life of service* is preserved with equal care and that there is a constant stream of planned energy going out to all those who need help.

3. The long limb of the triple cross symbolises to the disciple that he must go down into the very depths of human life in order to prepare the masses for the reappearance of the Christ and for the externalisation of the Hierarchy.

4. The sphere at the summit of the cross portrays the "place of the disciple's consciousness." His life of reflection, of constant awareness, and the steady focus of his attention is higher than the vertical life of the aspirant, than his horizontal life of service, and indicates the measure of his conscious activity in the Ashram. Forget not that an Ashram in the Hierarchy is on a higher plane than that of the soul.

He is therefore alive and active on three levels of activity simultaneously, and is in the process of demonstrating—as far as in him lies and his degree of discipleship permits—the three divine aspects: the *Will* aspect, governing his work within the Hierarchy in relation to the coming great movement; the *Love* aspect, governing his vertical life and producing spiritual steadfastness in form; the *Intelligence* aspect, governing his horizontal life and making him a wise server of his fellowmen. Finally, the long line from the point of radiant spiritual focus symbolises the *Path* from the highest point attained by the disciple to the lowest point of service.

You will notice also, in this symbol, that the secondary point of focus appears where all the lines meet and cross each other. This point represents the disciple's personality, into which the higher radiance must pour and from which spiritual energy reaches out on all sides. Also, if you will study and think for a while, it will be apparent to you that this cross is only correctly appropriated by (or is symbolic of) the man who has built (or is in process of building) the antahkarana. Where that bridge is not created the consciousness of the aspirant cannot focus in the Ashram or upon the intuitional levels of consciousness.

You can see, therefore, why I have given out the teaching upon the Antahkarana. It was done in order that the completion of the antahkarana could be systematically and scientifically carried out by you. I shall not, therefore, repeat the instructions here; you have them and should follow them carefully, bearing in mind that you have at least bridged the gap between the personality and the Spiritual Triad to a certain extent, and that for you the need is to complete and strengthen the Rainbow Bridge and then to use it with facility.

The symbology of the antahkarana tends badly to complicate the grasp of its real nature. May I remind you that, just as the soul is *not* a twelve-petalled lotus floating around in mental substance, but is in reality a vortex of force or twelve energies held together by *the will* of the spiritual entity (the Monad on its own plane), so the antahkarana is not a series of energy threads, slowly woven by the soul-infused personality, and met by corresponding threads projected by the Spiritual Triad, but is in reality a state of awareness. These symbols are true and living forms, created through the power of thought by the disciple, but—in time and space—they have no true existence. The only true existence is the Monad on its own plane, active, expressive Will in emergence, and in turn, active Love in establishing relationships and equally active Intelligence in the use of the two higher energies. It must not be forgotten that the energy of intelligence, focussed in the mind, is the instrument or implementing agency of the other two monadic energies.

H.P.B. taught that the antahkarana was primarily the channel of energy relating forms and their forces to their originating sources and that across the mental plane (with its three aspects of mind) the life thread necessarily passed, linking Monad, soul and personality into one living whole. Technically speaking, therefore, there is no need for the so-called bridge, except for one important factor: there is, on the part of the soul-infused personality, a definite break *in consciousness* between the lower mind and the abstract mind. The higher mind (being the lowest aspect of the Spiritual Triad) can be regarded as a door admitting the consciousness of the soul-infused personality into a higher realm of contact and awareness. But again—as you can well see—there is nothing here but symbolism; there is no door, but simply a symbol indicating means of access.

In the total evolution of the spiritual man through physical incarnation during untold hundreds of lives, the entire process is simply one of expanding consciousness and of attaining—sequentially and stage by stage—an ever more inclusive awareness. This is good to bear in mind, for eventually all this symbolic picturing will give place to reality. The task—and it is a real one—of building the antahkarana and creating that which will bridge the gap is in truth the planned and conscious effort to project the focussed thought of the spiritual man from the lower mental plane into areas of awareness which have been *sensed but not contacted;* it entails using the totality of the awareness already developed and already "enlightened" by the soul, and (with deliberation) making it increasingly sensitive to the focussed activity of the world of the higher spiritual realities; it is directing the stream of conscious thought towards the sensed and theoretically recognised world of the Masters, of the Spiritual Triad and, finally, of Shamballa. Disciples should remember that the Higher Way of Evolution is far simpler than the lower way, and that therefore the teaching on the significance and the meaning of the antahkarana—which is the first creation of the soul-infused personality acting as a unitary being—is far simpler than that relating to the personality in the three worlds of human evolution.

I would ask you to ponder on these matters, because out of the practice of group meditation should grow that conscious, focussed attitude which can be regarded as *reflection* —an act of reflection which, because the consciousness is held steady in the light, because the antahkarana is a realisation to the disciple, and because the mind is oriented towards the Spiritual Triad, is a definite factual experience.

It is a reflection carried on throughout all the vicissitudes of life and automatically registers these events; it therefore builds or creates that stream of ascending energy which is tinctured by the life qualities and the developed ray characteristics. Along that stream, the life qualities and the developed ray characteristics can pass at will; the disciple will increasingly register the "things of the spirit," as it is called in the New Testament; he will consequently acquire the facility to penetrate into the world of the Hierarchy, and to reach eventually the door to the Way of the Higher Evolution. He will at the same time function in the three worlds as a serving disciple.

With this simple presentation of the antahkarana, you may find it easier to work during the coming year. As this thought-projection process or exercise becomes a part of your normal state of mind, it will serve also to focus you upon the mental plane, thus withdrawing your attention from the world of the emotions and of desire or aspiration and placing you "upon the lighted point upon the lighted way, where light may shine and show a star which shines above the brow of the Initiator."

I suggest to you that you take the seven meditations and work regularly with them. I suggested this to you a year ago. Few of you took my advice or have adhered to the process or followed the rhythm set up by the sequence of meditations. I suggest that you give two months to each of the meditations, thus covering a period of fourteen months; then, I suggest that you make Meditation VII your major meditation, to be followed for one year. If this is done by you as directed and with no questioning as to effectiveness, you will understand far more clearly the projection—realistic and energising—which the personal consciousness will register.

I shall give you no more meditation outlines. The careful following of those given will do much for you during the remainder of your lives. You need no more.

Part XII

I would like today to extend the teaching given in the preceding instruction anent the antahkarana and expound to you—from the *group angle*—a paragraph there given; I will here rephrase it.

It is a reflection—a conscious focussed attitude—carried forward in all life circumstances, which automatically registers the events conditioning the life of humanity. It therefore creates a stream of ascending energy which is tinctured by the life quality and the ray characteristics of the group personnel. Along this stream both *the ascending* and *the descending* life quality and ray characteristics *can pass at will,* and the disciple will increasingly register the "things of the spirit"; he will consequently acquire the facility to penetrate into the world of the Hierarchy and reach eventually the door to the Way of the Higher Evolution. He will, again consequently, function efficiently in the three worlds *as the serving disciple.*

In this paragraph you have indicated the spiritual, meditative way of life of the individual disciple in relation to his own soul, and later to the Ashram; you have the group way of life, as it penetrates into the Hierarchy, and you have also the hierarchical technique which enables that great Group to penetrate into a still higher spiritual centre and bring down from Shamballa that understanding of divine Purpose which will precipitate as the hierarchical Plan; this will enable the Hierarchy to form a great serving group. No matter how high you may go in the scale of Being, you will find —from the fourth kingdom of nature onward—that *the technique of meditation governs all expansions of consciousness,* all registration of Plan or Purpose and, in fact, the entire process of evolutionary unfoldment. It is a technique of spiritual apprehension, of focussing attention on some level of consciousness or other, and also of originating modes of contact.

The entire Science of Invocation and Evocation is contained in the word "meditation"; this science ranges from the subjective, unconscious appeal of the inchoate, voiceless masses, through many phases, until it attains that high mode of scientific invocation which governs the contact made in the Council Chamber of Shamballa with extra-planetary sources of spiritual inflow. It is through meditation in some form or another that contact is made; this again is progressive in nature. The formulated idea of the unspiritual man to make a contact with that which will later condition his life and lead to a betterment of his daily life in a *material* sense, or which will make living possible, is perhaps the lowest aspect; the brooding, experimental thinking of the scientist or artist is another form of meditation and higher in purpose and in intention, and this meditative process is better formulated and has (if you think correctly) definite group implications. The mode whereby the Members of Hierarchy and the personnel of Their Ashrams arrive at an intense spiritual perception, and arrive also at a selfless formulation of the divine Plan which will implement divine Purpose in the world, is likewise an expansion of all previous meditations; whilst the concentrated clear and dynamic invocation of the spiritual Beings Who have created—or more accurately—have formed Shamballa, is the highest form of meditation possible upon our planet.

It might also be stated that it is meditation which is responsible for transforming the desire of the ordinary human being upon our planet into the spiritual will, which is ever the agent of the Purpose. It is therefore meditation which produces individual, group and planetary alignment, and this alignment is always the first stage of the meditation objective and the final or permanent stage attained. Think on this.

Meditation is also eliminative in its effects and (if I may use such a term) *ejects* out of the individual and out of the group that which is undesirable—from the angle of the immediate spiritual goal.

Meditation is essentially the highest instrument and the perfected consummation of the third divine aspect, that of intelligent activity, and—as I have earlier pointed out—is from every possible angle carried on within the ring-pass-not of the Universal Mind. It is the essential, divine Prompter, the predominant creative agent, and the factor which fuses and blends every aspect in the great Hierarchy of Being which is related to the basic spiritual nature of our planet; this was our major inheritance from the previous solar system—the Mind or Active Intellect.

Meditation brings into creative alignment instinct, intellect and the intuition, as well as conscious Identification. It relates (in an indissoluble unity) the so-called lower or concrete mind, the group mind, the hierarchical mind and the universal Mind; it leads to a conscious alignment of the disciple's centres and also of the three planetary Centres; it is invocative, demanding, fusing, receptive and distributory in nature. In the disciple it is the agent which creates or builds the antahkarana, controls—via the soul or the Spiritual Triad—the head centre, which is the point of focus, of spiritual appeal and of spiritual reception; it controls also the ajna centre (the centre between the eyebrows) which, in the disciple, is the prime agent for the distribution of spiritual energy.

In the group, meditation leads to the fusion of the group personnel, to their united invocative appeal, and—when invocation has evoked response—it leads to group receptivity to that which has been spiritually demanded, and thus to the spiritual service of the group.

In the Hierarchy, meditation takes two major forms, and

(you must remember) in that great spiritual Centre meditation is an instinctual habit and needs no forced process:

1. Meditation is that which sets in motion hierarchical response to the invocative appeal rising from the three worlds, and mainly to the invocative appeal carried forward consciously by all who pray, all who make mystical appeal and all who employ the method of occult meditation and direct invocation.

2. Meditation is the instinctual mode whereby the Hierarchy—in response to the invocation from the three worlds — approaches the higher Centre, Shamballa; then the Hierarchy evokes the energies, the Beings and the spiritual inflow which hierarchical service in the immediate future requires. It is also—in a unique sense—the technique whereby the Masters Themselves prepare for the sixth initiation, thus conditioning the Path of Life upon which They will eventually find Themselves and pass thence to higher cosmic undertakings.

You can see, therefore, why I have laid such emphasis upon your individual meditation, but have also laid a still greater emphasis upon group meditation. Nevertheless, I have only been endeavouring to turn your instinct towards spiritual expression into scientific lines; I have sought also to initiate you into a planetary technique which all planetary beings must and do master. Meditation, in its most rudimentary form, is the instinct which leads to recognition of the physical Sun and governs, for instance, the turning of planetary vegetable life towards the Sun as its dominant source of life. In its intermediate form, it is that which reveals to the aspirant and to the Hierarchy the Heart of the Sun, and—in its highest form—it is the mode of contact which relates the highest Beings on our planet to the Central Spiritual Sun. In every case, I would like to point out that this capacity to meditate (the spiritual expression of the mental processes) focusses itself in certain group formations which it would profit us briefly to consider.

It might be said that, intermediate between the great planetary centres, a group of those who can meditate creatively can be found; they are chosen out of each of the larger centres and from among those who are already accustomed to meditation. I would like to pause at this point and ask you to remember that I refer not here to religious meditation, strictly understood, or to those invocative appeals for help and aid which are so closely associated in the mind of the western Christian thinker. I refer to all who—in quiet reflection, focussed appeal and with a true background of knowledge—are able to "think through" into a higher state of consciousness than the one of which they are normally aware; in that higher state they arrive at those intuitional and spiritual "discoveries" which can produce the seed of a new creation, or which can open up (for those unable thus to meditate) a new field of *possible* awareness. The motive of all such group meditation must be selfless service; the keynote of all such groups is creativity; they are all of them demonstrations of the perfected third aspect of active intelligence, plus other developing aspects; all of them are in direct relation or alignment with one of the Buddhas of Activity, Who embody within Themselves the essence of the third Ray of Active Intelligence, through which the third aspect can successfully project and express itself. It is these three Buddhas Who were instrumental in the amazing and occult process of implementing the mental principle upon our planet, and Who — through Their creative meditation — brought our planet, the Earth, and the planet Venus into direct alignment. This made possible the coming of the Sons of Mind and the formation of the fourth kingdom in nature, Humanity. They are Embodiments of the intuition, and control the inflow of intuitional energy into the minds of men.

The point which I would have you bear in mind is that these intermediate groups of Workers Who know the power of meditation are primarily creative, and that the efficacy of Their work is demonstrated in the larger group whose behests They are carrying out and in the group which is creatively influenced by the meditation work accomplished.

Curiously enough, in view of the fact that the principle of Mind is the fifth principle, there are five major groups who function primarily through "creative and sustaining" meditation. These are:

1. The New Group of World Servers.
2. The Ashram, with which disciples in the New Group of World Servers may be affiliated.
3. The Hierarchy itself, the Ashram of Sanat Kumara.
4. The Nirmanakayas or the "inspired Contemplatives."
5. The higher correspondence of the Nirmanakayas Who find Their place in relation to Shamballa; this is analogous to that of the Nirmanakayas to the Hierarchy.

The personnel of these groups is supplied from the larger groups to which they are intermediate:

1. The New Group of World Servers gathers its personnel out of the great planetary centre called Humanity.
   a. The more advanced members of the group are affiliated with some Ashram within the ring-pass-not of the Hierarchy.
   b. The greater Ashram, composed of many Ashrams, is the fulfilled production of the New Group of World Servers, down the ages. This is a statement full of important implications.
2. The Nirmanakayas gather Their personnel out of the Hierarchy, the second great planetary centre. Their relation to Shamballa is not one of affiliation, nor is it the same as that of the New Group of World Servers to the Hierarchy. Their major relationship is with the Triangle of the Buddhas of Activity, and it is under Their creative inspiration that They work. This stream of inspiration or of "energy flooded with creative light" is made available to the Hierarchy at all

times and when needed for Their creative work; it is
a part of that dynamic, galvanising energy which feeds
the enthusiasm of the New Group of World Servers,
binds them together in the One Work, and enables
them to work intelligently and with creative ability.

3. A mysterious body of what have been called "Reflecting Lights"; the Members of this group are to a certain extent extra-planetary. They are affiliated with
Shamballa and focus cosmic creative energy, thus making it available (on demand) to the Members of the
Council Chamber at Shamballa. There is little that we
need consider about Them; They are the "Helpers of
the Lord of the World," and implement His purposes
as they are formulated by Him on the cosmic mental
plane.

The point which I seek to emphasise, and which I hope will
remain in your minds, is that this technique of *meditation
is the outstanding creative agent on our planet.* When you,
as an individual, are endeavouring to "build the new man in
Christ" which will be an expression of your true spiritual
self, meditation is, as you well know, your best agent; but
the meditation process must be accompanied by creative
work, or else it is purely mystical, and though not futile, is
nevertheless negative in creative results.

Members of the New Group of World Servers are gathered from all branches of human enterprise, of which organised religion is only one. There are scientists who, repudiating violently the unproven, yet are giving all they have of
scientific ability and knowledge to the service of humanity—
each in his chosen scientific field; there are men of financial
stature who regard money as a responsibility to be dispensed
wisely in the service of others, yet the mystical or occult
terminology may mean nothing whatsoever to them; there
are educators, preoccupied with wise formulations of knowledge and with an encyclopedic understanding of the garnered
wisdom of the ages, which they seek to utilise in fitting the
younger generation to live beautifully, constructively and
creatively; there are churchmen and religious leaders (in

some one or other of the world religions) who are not tied or handicapped by the form; the spirit of light is in them and they intelligently love their fellowmen. All of these people, if they are members of the New Group of World Servers, must inevitably be reflecting thinkers, must have creative objectives, must be truly intelligent, and must have added *expanding* love to their intelligence.

These men and women have a dual relationship: to the rest of humanity whom they seek to serve, and also to the Hierarchy, via some Ashram—an Ashram which is the source of their inspiration and of their creative efforts to think and to work.

The accepted disciple in this group work is in conscious rapport with both planetary centres (that of Humanity and that of the Hierarchy) and their creative thinking largely conditions the group. Many, however, in this group are conscious of their relation to humanity and of their planned service, but are totally unaware of the unseen source of their inspiration. This matters not, for—if their motive is pure, their intelligence keen and their meditational capacity adequate—they receive the inspiration and develop the intuition in any case. It is those in the New Group of World Servers who can and do meditate who are the real agents of the relation existing between the Hierarchy and Humanity. Such a relation has, of course, always existed, and always there have been many mystics and a few occultists who have served as channels of relationship; today, the group is newly organised and the task of invocation and evocation is for the first time in history evenly balanced, or is upon what you might call a fifty-fifty basis.

Again, the New Group of World Servers is composed of widely diverse men and women, gathered out of all nations, holding many different points of view and following the many different professions and ideologies; it is therefore more truly representative of humanity and more truly potent than ever before.

When the work of the Invocation reaches a high stage of development and the climaxing year of 1952 is over, it will then be wise to bring to the attention of the general public,

and on a worldwide scale, the factual nature of the New
Group of World Servers.

This New Group of World Servers is an aspect of the
world antahkarana and it gives students of the antahkarana
a sound example of the intent and purpose of the Rainbow
Bridge which each disciple is endeavouring consciously to
build. It is composed of those who have penetrated in consciousness *upward* to such an extent and height that their
ascension has become invocative and has produced a descent
from the Hierarchy which meets and merges with the energies of the ascending group reflection. Words here are apt to
hinder, but the visualisation indicated will prove helpful. In
the case of the New Group of World Servers, it is not simply
ascending energy which must be considered; there is also a
focussing of consciousness and a receptivity which can develop into fixed intention; this can be followed later by a
recognition *in the physical brain consciousness* of what has
transpired. Forget not that—in detail—the New Group of
World Servers is composed of the following groups:

1. Initiates and disciples who are consciously a part of
   the Great White Lodge.
2. Aspirants and lesser disciples who are affiliated with
   the Hierarchy, but who do not usually possess that continuity of consciousness which will come later.
3. Those upon the Probationary Path who are not yet
   affiliated with the Hierarchy; they are, however, subject to hierarchical impression and are determined to
   serve their fellowmen.
4. An increasing number of people who respond to the
   idealism and the purpose of the New Group of World
   Servers and who will rapidly join the group.

The main requirement is *Meditation* but—as you know—it
is not necessarily the set meditation of occult schools and
churches; membership in the group, however, requires the
development of the reflective spirit along some line of human understanding; it requires also the power to focus atten-

tion upon that which can serve humanity and a compassionate recognition of human need. The unthinking man or woman, or those engrossed entirely in business, political and family ties, cannot form a part of the New Group of World Servers, because the group demands a definite measure of decentralisation; to this, habits of meditation rapidly contribute.

As the members of this group meditate and serve, they will gradually find that they are becoming aware of an inner group—the Ashram of the Master on Whose ray the individual server is to be found. This will necessarily vary according to the ray; the ray—it must be remembered—determines the quality and the nature of the service to be rendered. Gradually the neophyte swings into the rhythm of the Ashram, and gradually his meditation changes and falls into line with the instinctual and constant ashramic meditation. It must be remembered that ashramic meditation is entirely devoid of personality elements. *It is in the nature of a constant and uninterrupted group meditation* upon the Plan, and particularly upon that aspect of the Plan which must immediately be put into operation; this is the apportioned duty of the Ashram or the Ashrams in question. This constant attitude of reflective meditation in no way impairs the efficiency of the Ashram or of the individual disciple, because two or more lines of thought and several lines of activity are simultaneously possible. This is another lesson which the disciple learns.

Later again, the disciple in the Ashram becomes aware of the meditation proceeding all the time within the greater Ashram, the Hierarchy. This is the Ashram (if I might repeat the statement) of Sanat Kumara, the Lord of the World. This great Ashram is headed and controlled by the Christ. The aspiring disciple becomes conscious of a vast meditational rhythm which is like the action of the human heart in its beat; it is both receiving and distributing, invocative and evocative; as he becomes habituated in this meditation rhythm, he learns to swing his own individual meditation into the set rhythm of the Hierarchy; this is a definite step forward, for the hierarchical rhythm is one of tremendous potency—a potency so great that it penetrates beyond the hierarchical ring-pass-not.

The effect of that reflective vibration is both vertical and horizontal, and this wide diffusion has led to the formation of that major group of contemplatives, the Nirmanakayas; They focus the hierarchical invocative appeal and (to quote the *Old Commentary*) "put it into the musical form which will please the ear of the One Who dwells in the highest plane." They then transfer the focussed received energies—after due reflection and contemplation—to Shamballa. One of Their functions is to relate the invocative appeal of the Hierarchy to karmic law, and thus determine "in the deep silence of Their united work" what can be possible because it does not infringe upon karmic intention, and what is not yet possible in time and space—those two major factors which are governed by karmic law. They have to bear in mind that the time has not yet come and "the karmic era cannot yet demand that demanded good become accomplished good."

The members of this group are also transmitters to the Hierarchy of the response evoked from Shamballa. They are constantly in touch with the Council Chamber at Shamballa. Just as the Hierarchy—in this present cycle of world endeavour—is working through the New Group of World Servers, so Shamballa is carrying out its intentions (as far as humanity is concerned) through this group of Nirmanakayas. This all connotes a great centralisation of the work in connection with the reappearance of the Christ.

You can see, therefore, that a gigantic group meditation is going on in many differing phases upon our planet. All the meditating units and the reflective groups are related to each other through unity of spiritual motive; they are seeking closer cooperation and endeavouring to bring their meditation work—consciously or unconsciously—into a state of positive universal quiet, so that the formulation of spiritual desire can be carried successfully forward, and the reception of spiritual energy can be *a united reception*.

Therefore, brother of mine, a great effort towards alignment is going on, and when the individual aspirant can so meditate that his voice can reach the New Group of World Servers, that group can then impress the individual; through him humanity can be reached. It can also impress the Hierarchy; then the Contemplatives Who are in touch with Shamballa can contact the Hierarchy, and through the Hierarchy can impress the New Group of World Servers; then, and only then, the moment will arrive when the Christ will come.

Already upon the mountains of initiation the sound of His feet can be heard. He works now with His initiates within the Hierarchy; Their united meditation is hastening the preparatory work and is also leading to the initiation of countless disciples, thus rendering them far more useful than would otherwise be the case.

The united meditation of these disciples is collaborating with that of the Christ and of the Masters, and senior initiates will impress the members of the New Group of World Servers; those in this latter group who are, as disciples, members of the Hierarchy, become the agents of this impression. The meditation of the New Group of World Servers, in conjunction with the hierarchical meditation, will inevitably impress the sons of men who are seeking and longing for liberation; thus a great channel or Path of Light is created by cooperative meditation, and along that Path—speaking symbolically—the Christ will come.

PART XIII

In my last instruction I made the statement that meditation was the major creative agent in the universe. There are other universes that are ahead of us in development and, in them, the emphasis may not be upon creation by use of mental energies; others may not be so advanced and, in them, mental energy may be in process of unfolding or expressing itself—in the evolutionary sense. There are also universes and solar systems where the quality and the conditions of the manifesting universe, solar system or planet are unknown to us. It must be borne in mind that though in all manifestations the three aspects (of purpose or will, attraction, magnetic love or plan, and appearance as manifestation of both of these) are necessarily present, the manifesting Entity (responsible for these expressions of divinity) may work through and "occultly declare" conditions and qualities of which we have no experience or knowledge. We may possess utterly no idea in the highest flights of our abstract thinking (and this includes the most advanced thinkers upon our planet) of the nature of the impulses and concepts which animate certain universal Creators. Ponder on this.

I also pointed out to you that there are three major groups of meditating agents who act as intermediaries between the three groups of Self-conscious Lives upon our planet, and also between our planet and that which lies behind and beyond it and with which our planetary Logos has intimate and intensive relation. I am not, however, going to deal today with that which is extra-planetary; it would be, for you, sheer waste of time. I will deal with the theme of meditation as the agent of the creative process *Now,* and with the part meditation must play in the preparation for the coming of the Christ and the inauguration of the new civilisation which is so definitely on its way.

There are, as you may surmise (if you have read my instructions intelligently), seven phases of the creative meditative process; all of them are productive of the required results. All that at present exists in the three worlds and in the higher spheres is the result of some form of meditative activity. These seven sources are:

1. *The planetary Logos Himself,* Who formed and informed the world by His thought, and Who holds all together within His Mind for the many, many aeons of manifested existence. As I have before said, the occult truism that "God thought, God visualised, God spoke and the world was made and is sustained" remains eternally true.

2. *The Group which is the higher correspondence of the Nirmanakayas.* This group sustains and cooperates with the planetary Logos in His concentrated creative thought; its Members are the agents for attracting—through the potency of Their meditation—those extra-planetary ener-

gies which He needs to *carry forward* His vehicle of expression, the planet, and thus to bind all together into one great created Whole, tending ceaselessly to the greater glory of God. They wield the Law of Synthesis and hold steadfastly (in the universal Mind of the Logos) the ultimate result of the divine Will-to-Good.

3. *Shamballa,* with its life and intention focussed in the Council Chamber of the great Lord, Sanat Kumara. Here is known and embodied *the Purpose* of the planetary Logos under the meditative impression of the group which knows His will and which wields the Law of Synthesis. In the hands of this august Council, the Law of Karma finds adequate planetary guidance; this does not refer to the law as it affects the individual human being because of such individuals the Council Members have no knowledge, for the reason that They think and meditate only in terms of the Whole; but They know the nature of planetary karma and of its delayed or rapid application, according to transient planetary indications. The great Wheel of Life, with its passing manifestations and its recurring civilisations, is directed by Them; the manifesting kingdoms in nature, great cyclic expressions of life, are controlled by Them, and all this is produced through the potency of Their creative meditation which impresses the needed inspiration (another phrase for the breath of life itself) upon the Nirmanakayas and through Them upon the spiritual Hierarchy. Their link with all these planetary groups (and it is real and vital) can be grasped in the key statement that "all Lives upon or within the aura of the planetary Logos and of His manifested Body, the Earth, have been, are or will be in the future human beings, thereby establishing and demonstrating their past, present or future identity with humanity, the fourth kingdom in nature." This kingdom is the planetary group or centre which expresses in time and space all the divine aspects—sometimes in latency and sometimes in potency. Here lies the clue to the entire mystery of divine guidance, and here is also to be found the guarantee of the divine Will-to-Good.

4. *The Nirmanakayas, the divine Contemplatives.* This is the receptive group which receives impression from Shamballa in relation to the planetary creative purpose. Then They, on Their own level of atmic activity, build—through contemplative meditation—a vast reservoir of potent energies which are impregnated with the qualities of the seven energies of the seven planetary Rays. They are the Custodians of life, under the direct inspiration of the Buddhas of Activity, and They spend the aeons of Their planetary service:

    a. In active contemplation of the divine Purpose.

    b. In a developed receptivity to that aspect of the Purpose which must be expressed through the medium of the divine Plan, and thus presented to the Hierarchy.

    c. In developing that spirit of sevenfold receptivity which will make Them a channel for the inflow of ray energies from Shamballa into the Hierarchy. Their united aura or area of influence and the extent of Their magnetic and dynamic radiation correspond roughly to the aura of the planet itself; They contain (within Their ranks) Members Who are identified with the Lords of the seven Rays.

They are, in a peculiar sense, the creative agents of life as it streams forth from Shamballa into all the aspects, areas, kingdoms and fields of manifestation. This They are enabled to do through sustained, concentrated, intensive and dynamic meditation. They are necessarily a second ray group (as the second ray is the ray at present of the planetary Logos) but They focus Their meditation largely along first ray lines (which is a subray of the second ray in this solar system, as you know) because They are the creative agents of life itself and the knowers and the custodians of the will of the planetary Logos, as it works itself out in manifestation. They are the source in reality of planetary invocation and evocation. Again, ponder on this.

5. *The Hierarchy of Masters*, the Masters of the Wisdom and the Lords of Compassion. This group, which stands midway between Shamballa and Humanity, is subject to impression from Shamballa, via the Nirmanakayas, and its Members are Themselves the agents for the impression of Humanity. They embody and express the love aspect of the divine purpose; They wield, direct and control the Law of Attraction—the motivating energy which swings the Law of Evolution into activity in the three worlds. Much is known by you anent this group of divine and spiritual Workers, and I will not enlarge upon it here. Basically, They work through directed meditation and each Ashram is a centre of meditation to which every disciple, initiate and Master contributes. I would have you bear this in mind and endeavour to realise, as disciples, that your meditation—both individual and group meditation—if it is of an adequate nature and quality— will be absorbed into and become part of the ashramic meditation. The theme of the hierarchical meditation is the Plan, as it embodies the divine Purpose.

6. *The New Group of World Servers* is fast becoming a major centre of planetary meditation. Much of this meditation is far from being of an occult nature but that is of no importance; it is largely based upon deep reflection upon the problems of humanity, backed and aided by the deep aspiration of the mystics found within its ranks, and aided also by the meditation of those few esotericists (technically speaking) who are working there also. This group is a reflection of the invocative and evocative capacity of the Nirmanakayas, but this aspect of their activity is only in process of being learnt and applied. The entire activity of the New Group of World Servers along the invocative line was stepped up and greatly hastened by the giving to the world of the three Invocations during the past few years. What was actually a vague demand and a fluid nebulous receptivity became (by the use of the Invo-

cations) a powerful invocative plea, and resulted in the evocation of energies from the Hierarchy which were transmitted by the New Group of World Servers to Humanity and which are responsible for much of the constructive work now going forward in many parts of the world. I have told you much about this group and will not enlarge upon it here; your understanding of the work to be done should be instinctual for you all belong to it, if you are in any way dedicated to the service of humanity, under inspiration of the Hierarchy; your instinctual reaction to hierarchical impression as a member of this group should develop rapidly into an habitual life tendency. Thus is a Master created. The creative meditation of the New Group of World Servers has for its objectives the creation of the new civilisation and of the new world order.

This group itself works through another group: the intelligent men and women upon the mental plane, those who, added to the intelligence, possess a love of their fellowmen; these, in their turn, work through the idealists who seek a better world and those who respond to the inspiration of goodwill. This last group, in its turn, works with all who are emotionally implicated in the desire to help humanity change its living conditions for the better. These people are not open to direct spiritual impression, but the intellectual approach and the presentation of ideas appeal to them, and they constitute the active creative group who act as the dynamic inspiration to the seventh group, which is

7. *Humanity itself*. Men everywhere are, if they only knew it, always in a state of unconscious meditation, dreaming of better things, fighting for desired material benefits, longing for that which lies beyond their present possession and their present attainment and, in many cases, even their vision. All these desires, longings, wishes, visions and dreams are the "ingredients" of the focussed meditation which they will some day know; they are the first results which produce success in the three worlds, and which lead

eventually to an integrated personality, ready to appreciate the higher aspects of meditation when concentration upon worldly material success and benefits has proved no longer appealing. That which they have, through meditative concentration, succeeded in creating (and all men, under the Law of Karma, create their own world) no longer satisfies; their meditation then shifts into the creation of higher things, into the world of spiritual values and of that which we cover by the unsuccessful and inadequate term of "heaven."

See you, therefore, how all that is, is created by meditation, by desire merging into transient thought, and transient thought becoming clear thinking and, eventually, abstract and transcendent thought. Prolonged concentration upon some form or another eventually becomes meditation upon that which is *not* of the nature of form; from thence it passes into that contemplation which is the source of inspiration and of illumination.

Trace these concepts which you, who have studied the Science of Meditation, know to constitute its recognised stages, and note how each stage is creative in nature, each stage produces creative changes and that (as far as humanity is concerned) the Christ spoke scientifically and also in a planetary sense when He said: "As a man thinketh in his heart, so is he."

You have, therefore, three major groups of thinkers and three other groups of intensive, creative thinkers, all of them responsible for and also dedicated to the comprehension of the divine Purpose as it works out through the spiritual hierarchical Plan; this is applied under the Law of Evolution to humanity and, through humanity, to the subhuman kingdoms in nature. From the human family, all divine Lives and Beings have come; in humanity the creative process is constantly working; and into humanity all subhuman lives must eventually proceed. As regards the meditative creative process, the diagram on the following page may serve somewhat to clear your minds:

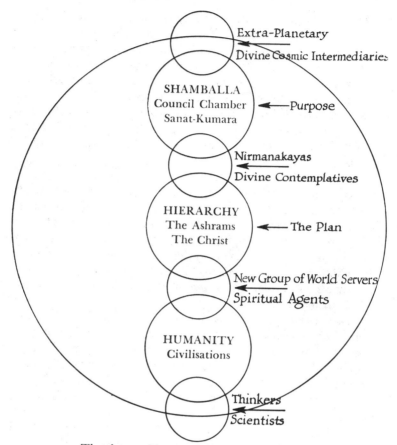

Extra-Planetary

Divine Cosmic Intermediaries

SHAMBALLA
Council Chamber
Sanat-Kumara   ←——Purpose

Nirmanakayas

Divine Contemplatives

HIERARCHY
The Ashrams   ←—— The Plan
The Christ

New Group of World Servers

Spiritual Agents

HUMANITY
Civilisations

Thinkers

Scientists

The three subhuman Kingdoms in Nature.
Esoterically, the reflection of the three major groups, listed above.

We need not deal here with the higher groups of spiritual Intermediaries and Their techniques of creative work, because Their meditation lies on too high a level for your consideration. But the meditation work done by the Hierarchy and by the New Group of World Servers lies within your range of understanding; many disciples will read what I am here saying and, in time, many of the lesser workers and aspirants in the ranks of the group will come to an understanding of my meaning. It might profit us if I briefly stated the grades of meditative work, leading to creative result of an effective nature, upon which you might reflect. For our purposes we will divide them into seven grades, of which four might be regarded as individual and the other three types as representative of their group nature:

1. *Desire,* leading to the attainment in the three worlds of that which the lower man desires and wants; this will include the desires of the lowest types of human beings through all intermediate types up to and inclusive of the aspirational mystic.

2. *Prayer;* this is the stage wherein the aspirant, the mystic or the spiritually inclined man blends personality desire with aspiration for soul relation and contact; he, through the proved efficacy of prayer, discovers the subtler powers and the fact of the essential dualism of life; he finds that he himself is both a lower self and a higher Self.

3. *Mental reflection* or concentrated thinking. This in time produces integration and definite personality achievement in the three worlds, leading eventually to controlled reflection and scientific or concentrated thought; this type of thinking has produced all the creative wonders of our modern civilisation and it culminates in the concentration achieved in occult meditation. This meditation finally brings about the reorientation of the personality and soul fusion.

4. *Straight meditation.* This is a focussed, concentrated mental attitude and fixed reflection; it is creative in nature, for it creates the "new man in Christ" or produces the soul-infused personality; this personality then proceeds to recreate his environment and to co-operate consciously with the creative work of the Hierarchy.

Little as you may realise it, all these expressions of human meditation or concentrated thought—whether it is concentrated desire for physical or emotional objectives or the higher aspects of spiritual, concentrated aspiration—do defi-

nitely create that which is desired. This is equally true of
the other three stages, for they are intelligently and effectively creative and these four stages are responsible for all
that is seen, possessed, utilised and known as existent in the
three worlds. Men have inherited from previous civilisations
much of value and much which is disastrous in nature; in
their turn, modern men have created this present civilisation. This civilisation is unique, because it is the result of all
the combined factors, and these factors have succeeded in
bringing humanity to the point where there is recognition of
failure, and in proving that religion and science together
have reoriented men to the world of subtler and of higher
values than the strictly material.

The other three stages of human meditation are as
follows:

5. *Worship.* This is the united recognition and the subsequent reflection of humanity upon the fact of divine
   Transcendence and divine Immanence. It is implemented by the world religions and it created that path
   of return to the centre or source of divine life to which
   the world religions and the heart of man bear equal
   testimony.

6. *Invocation and Evocation.* This form of spiritual, dynamic meditation is largely in the hands of the New
   Group of World Servers and of the men and women
   of goodwill in every land. These will be generally unknown to each other, but they are all creatively striving and creatively thinking towards the worldwide-
   uplift of mankind; they are earnestly working at the
   creation of a new world order and for the manifestation of a more definitely spiritual civilisation.

7. *Ashramic Meditation.* This is based upon the evocation of human response to the higher spiritual values;
   it concerns itself with the creation of those conditions
   wherein these new values can, under the divine Plan,
   flourish; it is focussed on that immediate aspect of the
   Path which humanity needs to tread, and its intent is
   to swing into creative activity the desires, aspirations,

reflections and concentrated meditation of men, at
whatever may be their particular point in evolution,
so that a mighty, coherent and invincible movement
will be instituted which must and will result in the
creation of the new heavens and the new earth. This
is one way of expressing the significance of the coming
of the Kingdom of God on Earth, and the creation of
a new order and way of life.

There are crisis points at times of superlative tension in the meditative work of all hierarchical Ashrams. At the times of the new moon and of the full
moon, all members of all the Ashrams meditate deeply
in an invocative and evocative manner; their meditation, therefore, falls into two parts: the first part is
evocative of inspiration from the Nirmanakayas with
Whom they deliberately get in touch; the second part
is invocative of the New Group of World Servers and
enables them responsively to come under hierarchical
impression. Three times a year—at the April, May
and June Festivals*—there is a united hierarchical
meditation led by the Christ; these Festivals are invocative of Shamballa or of that which lies beyond the
Nirmanakayas and can only be safely carried forward
in united meditation, under directed guidance and
the highest possible inspiration. Each Ashram can approach the Nirmanakayas *as a group* at stated periods
for which due preparation is made; only the entire
group of Ashrams, the Hierarchy as a whole, can approach Shamballa. The New Group is invocative to
the Hierarchy for purposes of impression and can be
impressed by any Ashram through its disciples in that
group; thus the great chain of contact and the great
channel for the inflow of spiritual energy reaches from
Shamballa to humanity and then, through humanity,
to the three subhuman kingdoms; in this way, these
lower kingdoms are "enlightened and raised." All this
is accomplished through meditation, through invoca-

---

*The full moon of Aries or Easter, of Taurus or Wesak, and of Gemini or of
the Spirit of Goodwill.

tion and evocation, carried forward in the spirit of
worship, which is the fundamental method of spiritual
recognition. Thus, creatively, the glory which is hidden in every form is evoked and slowly brought to
exoteric manifestation.

In the destruction of the old world order and in the chaos of
these modern times, the work of the new creation is going
forward; the task of reconstruction, leading to a complete
reorganisation of human living and to a fresh reorientation
of human thinking, is taking place.

What, therefore, is the creative work confronting the
Ashrams in the Hierarchy and the members of the New
Group of World Servers, working creatively under the inspiration and the impression of the Hierarchy? It falls into
two parts:

1. The work of bringing order out of chaos.
2. The task of preparing the way for the reappearance of
   the Christ.

There is much that must be done to change conditions,
institute new values and produce the bringing in of an entirely new civilisation—a civilisation which will permit the
externalisation of the Ashrams, or of the Hierarchy, and a
restitution, therefore, of hierarchical or spiritual control as it
was known in old Atlantean days, only this time on a much
higher turn of the spiral and with the intelligent cooperation also and the wise assistance of humanity, which was a
factor lacking in the earlier civilisation. Once this has been
dealt with in the reflective, concentrated meditation of the
individual aspirant, in the united reflection and meditation
of the many spiritually inclined groups in the world today,
and once the New Group of World Servers and the Hierarchy are working in the closest kind of cooperation, then
the visualisation and the projection of the *intended* civilisation will have reached a definite and a most important *point
of precipitation.* Then, the invocative appeal of the united
Hierarchy and of the New Group of World Servers will be

so potent that it will evoke a response from humanity and a cycle of organisation, of planning and of effective expression will follow. Reflection, meditation and visualisation will give place to scientific *thinking* (which is essentially meditation) and to the needed physical plane activity.

This will take place, esoterically speaking, under the impression of the Masters upon the three major rays. The first Ray of Will or Power (the Ray of the divine Destroyer) is already actively working, destroying the old and outworn conditions and bringing about the wreckage of the old civilisation so that the new order can be effectively brought into expression. As the Christ said, when He instituted the Christian civilisation of the past two thousand years (which has gone so sadly far from His original intention), you "cannot put new wine in old bottles." The war (1914-1945) started the needed process of destruction, and the post-war period is carrying forward the planned undertaking. It is nearing its desired finish, if men work towards the freedom for which all their souls long.

The second Ray of Love-Wisdom, through the many extant educational processes and through the modern *conflict of ideas* (producing thus a borderland between the areas of influence of the first and second rays) is opening the minds of thousands of people. The pronounced contrast in ideas— as, for instance, the contrast between totalitarianism and the democratic freedom of thought (does such democratic freedom really exist, my brother?)—is forcing men to think, to reflect, to question and to meditate. The world is thereby greatly enriched, and the whole human family is transiting out of a pronounced cycle of karma yoga into the required cycle of raja yoga, from unthinking activity into a period of illumined mind control. It is a mental illumination which is brought about by the meditative and the reflective activity of humanity as a whole, and this is carried forward under the guidance of the New Group of World Servers, working under hierarchical impression.

Members of all the ray types are to be found in the New Group of World Servers, either through the activity of the personality ray or of the soul ray; therefore, the energies of all the rays are being brought to bear upon this creative period in modern human history. It is interesting to have in mind the fact that through the medium of all the fighting forces of the world (naval, military and air) much needed hierarchical work is being accomplished; the energy of the fourth Ray of Harmony through Conflict is making itself phenomenally felt—this time in conjunction with the unusual activity of the first ray. Therefore, through the Forces of Light, liberation into freedom will come and it will mean the freedom of all mankind. I make here no defense of war or of fighting, brother of mine. I simply deal with world conditions as they exist today, and with the processes and the methods which are characteristic of the civilisations which have already disappeared and of the civilisation out of which we are today emerging. As man leaves the animal, the strictly physical and the highly emotional and inflammable stages behind him and *learns to think,* then (and only then) will war cease. Fortunately for humanity, this is happening most rapidly.

For the first time in human history, the lines of demarcation between that which is right from the angle of the spiritual values (the essential freedom of the human spirit) and that which is wrong (the imprisonment of the human spirit by materialistic conditions) are clearly perceived by the majority of the nations of the planet. Within the United Nations is the germ and the seed of a great international and meditating, reflective group—a group of thinking and informed men and women in whose hands lies the destiny of humanity. This is largely under the control of many fourth ray disciples, if you could but realise it, and their point of meditative focus is the intuitional or buddhic plane —the plane upon which all hierarchical activity is today to be found.

The fifth Ray of Concrete Knowledge is also expressing itself powerfully in the meditation and the reflection of the world scientists in all fields of human interest; in their hands the form of the new civilisation is being constructed. I would remind you that when I use the word "scientist," I refer to all who are working in the social sciences and the economic sciences as well as the large group of chemists, biologists, physicists, etc., who are usually covered by that term. The organising, defining power of the mental plane is being brought to bear upon all phases of human life by the scientists of all the many schools of thought; out of this meditative and creative thought which they all so admirably demonstrate will come the structure of the new civilisation.

The sixth ray disciple is active also in organising the mystical aspiration of the masses of men everywhere which is in itself a most potent energy; these aspirational men (no matter what may be their immediate aspiration) are necessarily polarised upon the astral plane but are not yet capable of the clear mental perception of the massed intelligentsia or susceptible to the influence of the accurate, esoteric approach. Their guided, mystical orientation will be one of the most powerful factors in the destruction of the old values and in the massed recognition of the spiritual truth which underlies all life; it is with this reorientation that sixth ray disciples, wielding sixth ray energy, are occupied at this time. You need to remember that the one-pointed attitude of the mystic, functioning in group formation, will be a powerful factor in the creative work being done by the Hierarchy and by the New Group of World Servers, because theirs will be a massed effect, and usually wielded unconsciously.

Under the influence of disciples on the seventh Ray of Organisation or of Ceremonial Order, that powerful physical concretisation of energy which we call "money" is proving a topic of the most definite concentration; it is being most carefully considered, and the minds of thinking financiers and of wealthy humanitarian persons and philanthropists will be gradually led forward from a strictly philanthropic activity to an activity which is impulsed and brought into expression by spiritual insight, and by *a recognition of the claims of Christ* (no matter by what name He may be called in the East or in the West) upon the financial reservoir of the world. This is a hard thing to bring about, for the subtle energies of the inner worlds take much time in producing their effects upon the objective, tangible plane of divine manifestation. Money is not yet used divinely, but it will be.

Nevertheless, the task is well in hand and is engaging the attention of disciples upon all the rays, under the guidance and the impression of the powerful seventh ray Ashram— now already in process of externalisation.

The effect of human meditation at this time is to change conditions, to invoke the higher, spiritual potencies, to work with concentration — both vertically and horizontally — within the world of men and within the Kingdom of God. *This vertical and horizontal activity holds the secret of creative meditation.* It is invocative of the higher energies, and creates a channel of contact between soul and spirit. This is brought about by what I have called "vertical meditation." It is also evocative and creates a ferment or dynamic movement in that level of being which must be affected or changed, and this is the horizontal aspect. Both the vertical and the horizontal activities are descriptive of the method of invocation and of evocation, as employed by all the linking groups between the various planetary centres; a reference to the chart (page 214) should help make this clear.

But all these processes and the entire scheme of manifestation are brought about through organised and conscious meditative methods; planetary, group and individual meditation is creative in results, and it is this aspect of it with which I am dealing in this instruction.

Therefore I shall give—for your constructive use if you care to use them—two meditation forms or outlines for reflection. Shall I call them two presented rings-pass-not for your controlled reflective thinking? One is a meditation for workers in the New Group of World Servers who are interested in preparing the way for the reappearance of the Christ, and the other is a meditation of a simple nature (combining the aspects of prayer, meditation and invocation) which has for its objective the deflecting of money from material ends into the work which the Hierarchy seeks to have accomplished.

To sum up:

The Lord of the World, through meditation, is carrying forward processes which He instituted in His original, creative meditation—back in the darkest night of the time when

He decided to create this planet of ours for strictly redemptive purposes. The whole creation is the result of His directed and controlled thought—a process of sustained thinking which sweeps all the creative energies into evolutionary and cyclic activity, in conformity to the pattern which He eternally visualises. He has organised a group which is responsive to His meditative intention; these Beings aid Him by Their *concentrated and realised Purpose* to bring into our planetary livingness certain extra-planetary energies which are needed to carry forward the planned work of the planetary Logos. Shamballa itself is also permeated with His thought and conscious (if I may speak symbolically) of that which the Logos has visualised. They are the Custodians of His Purpose, as it is revealed to Them, cycle by cycle. The length of these cycles is one of the mysteries which is strictly guarded in the Council Chamber of the Lord of the World; these cycles have reference only to manifestation in the three worlds wherein the concepts of time and space control.

The Hierarchy is the Custodian of that aspect of the cyclic, planetary Purpose which is called the *Plan;* this covers such relatively brief periods as civilisations—where humanity is concerned. In relation to Shamballa, the intermediate group of meditating, creative Workers is called into activity in order to receive impression of the immediate, desired hierarchical activity, to transmit the needed energies from Shamballa to the united Ashrams and thus, esoterically, "inform" the Hierarchy of that which merits immediate attention.

Again, upon a lower level of the evolutionary spiral, the Hierarchy in its turn impresses the New Group of World Servers with the Plan to be at once applied to the helping of humanity. This group is the major creative agent in the three worlds for the remainder of this cycle of planetary experience. This has not always been the case. Humanity can now intelligently work with the presented Plan, and this for the first time in human history. I would have you note this. Men can now do their little share in bringing the divine Purpose into manifestation, because they have now unfolded the needed mental capacity. The control and the creative development of the three lower kingdoms in nature is slowly being taken out of the hands of the deva evolution (hitherto responsible) and placed under the supervision of mankind; as it is said in the ancient Archives of the Masters:

"Eventually, the solar Lords, through manas (the mind) will control the lunar lords of elemental substance, and not alone their own but that which looks to them for aid. Thus will redemption come to all through man, and thus the glory of the Lord of Life be seen."

Focussed intention, concentrated meditation, visualisation, directed invocation (producing evocation) and leading to responsive results, are the major processes of creation upon all levels and by all beings. Prayer, focussed desire, meditation and focussed intention are the graded and sequential lessons which mankind has to learn. Worship, or recognition of divine Transcendence and divine Immanence underlies all the mass recognition of spiritual potency. Thus the meditation of the planet penetrates into that which lies beyond the planet and is fused and blended in a solar sense with the Voice of Him Who has brought all into being, and with the Will of Him Who is carrying all forms of His livingness towards the perfection which He purposes; in so doing, the great processes of *Redemption* are furthered, to which all World Saviours (in relation to humanity) are the symbol, the guarantee and the eternal testimony.

In giving you these two meditations, I would remind all who undertake to use these meditative forms that they will not prove effective and of the needed vital potency *unless* the one who thus meditates identifies himself with the purpose and objective of the meditation, dedicates himself to cooperation with this objective and *redeems* all aspects of his own life in conformity with the focussed desire expressed in this spiritual appeal. It is useless, my brothers, to meditate along lines which will aid in preparing the world for the coming of the Hierarchy and for the reappearance of the Christ *unless*, again, that preparation is an integral part of your own constant daily endeavour, and is not just simply wishful thinking and the formulation of a hopeful theory anent the future of humanity. It is useless for you to meditate in order to reorient money, for instance, towards spiritual work (and by "spiritual work" I do not here refer to the work of the churches and of the world religions) unless all the monies which *you* individually have to handle are dedicated to right usage, the fulfilment of your right obligations and the covering of your karmic responsibilities, plus the constant recognition of the relation of all money to the spiritual future of the race and the requirements of the hierarchical Plan. There must always be, in your consciousness, a recognition of the needs of all men, and this must be true of all spiritually-minded people, of all true esotericists and of the religiously inclined man whose heart and understanding are more divinely inclusive than are the hearts of the average followers of any religious doctrine, enunciated by the theologians of any faith.

It *must* be realised that money is the energy which can set in motion and make possible the activities of the New Group of World Servers—no matter what their colour, caste or church. Money does not yet lie in their hands. Their need for it is great. Millions are needed to spread the required knowledge of the hierarchical Plan; millions are needed to further the work of men of goodwill; millions are needed to educate the masses in the fact that He for Whom all men wait is on His way back to ordinary visibility. The billions which are spent at present on luxuries, on expensive and unnecessary objects of desire, the billions (and, my brother, it is billions, as world statistics show) which go towards the purchase of candy, liquor, tobacco, jewelry and expensive furs, the millions which go in the violent search for excitement and for ceaseless nightly pleasure and, finally, the billions which go the way of armed conflict in all nations *must* be deflected towards those expenditures which will make the plans of the Hierarchy possible, which will aid humanity in its search for the new, spiritual and free way, and which will therefore bring into being the new civilisation. Billions are required to overcome the materialism which has domi-

nated mankind for untold aeons; billions are also needed to
bring about the reconstruction of human affairs and thus
purify and beautify our modern world to such an extent that
the Christ can appear among men; through the wise expenditure of the financial resources of the world in the many fields
of human betterment and uplift, the Christ will be enabled
to "see of the travail of His soul and be satisfied."

I ask you, therefore, to follow these two meditations at
least once a week and upon different days. These two forms
of invocative appeal can be used by all who are willing to
participate in the indicated service.

REFLECTIVE MEDITATION UPON
PREPARATION FOR THE REAPPEARANCE OF THE CHRIST

Stage I.

After achieving a positive and intended personality quietness, formulate clearly to yourself in your own words, the
answers to the following questions:

1. As a member of the New Group of World Servers,
   what is my specific, fixed intention at this moment of
   dedicated contact with my soul?

2. Is my concentrated and expressed personality purpose
   in line with hierarchical intention—as far as I am permitted to know it?

3. Have I—in my own personal daily life—earned the
   right (because of definite effort and not so much because of success) to stand with those Servers Who are
   now undertaking the work of Preparation?

This is the one time in the meditation where you think
of yourself, and it is here because it is a method of personality, focussed attention and aligns your personality
upon the mental plane.

Stage II.

Having answered these three questions in the light of the
soul, then say with emphasis:

> "Forgetting the things which lie behind, I will
> strive towards my higher spiritual possibilities. I
> dedicate myself anew to the service of the Coming

One and will do all I can to prepare men's minds
and hearts for that event. *I have no other life
intention.*"

PAUSE

Stage III.

1. Visualise the world situation as best you can and in
terms of your major world interest and with what
knowledge of world affairs you may possess. See the
mass of men everywhere glowing with a dim light and,
here and there, points of brighter light where members of the New Group of World Servers and men of
spiritual intention and of loving hearts are working
for their fellowmen.

2. Then visualise (through the creative imagination) the
vivid light of the Hierarchy, streaming towards humanity and slowly merging with the light which is
already in men. Then say the first stanza of the
Invocation:

"From the point of Light within the Mind of God
Let Light stream forth into the minds of men.
Let Light descend on Earth."

3. Then ponder upon the reappearance of the Christ;
realise that no matter by what name He may be called
in the many world religions, He is still the same great
Identity; reflect and speculate upon the possible results
of His appearance. Then say the second stanza of the
Invocation:

"From the point of Love within the Heart of God
Let Love stream forth into the hearts of men.
May Christ return to Earth."

4. Endeavour to concentrate your fixed intention to
serve and to spread love in your surroundings and
realise that *in so far as you can do these things* you are
attempting to blend your personal will with the divine
Will. Then say stanza three of the Invocation:

> "From the Centre where the Will of God is known
> Let Purpose guide the little wills of men—
> The Purpose which the Masters know and
> serve."

5. Consider practically what you can do in the coming week to further the preparations for the coming of the Christ.

PAUSE

Then sound the O M three times, dedicating the threefold personality to the work of preparation.

Suggestions:

1. It is suggested that you do this meditation once every week, each *Thursday,* in the place of your usual meditation; endeavour to assume an attitude of aspiration, devotion, prayer and fixed intention (in this order), prior to following the outline. Esoteric students need the heart approach, as well as the mental approach, in order to make this meditation the powerful instrument which it can be.

2. Between Thursdays endeavour to carry out the results of the reflection expressed in this meditation. Lay practical plans and then review each week the planned activities when you sit down to this meditation, in the light of your expressed *Intention.*

3. Make this meditation brief and dynamic. After doing it a few times, this should be easily possible; forget the various stages and be impelled by the sequence and the synthesis of the form.

REFLECTIVE MEDITATION ON
ATTRACTING MONEY FOR HIERARCHICAL PURPOSES

Stage I.

After achieving a positive and intended personality quietness, formulate clearly to yourself and in your own words, the answers to the following questions:

1. If money is one of the most important things needed
   today for spiritual work, what is the factor which is at
   present deflecting it away from the work of the Hierarchy?
2. What is my personal attitude towards money? Do I
   regard it as a great and possible spiritual asset, or do I
   think of it in material terms?
3. What is my personal responsibility in regard to money
   which passes through my hands? Am I handling it as
   a disciple of the Masters should handle it?

PAUSE

Stage II.

1. Ponder on the redemption of humanity through the
   right use of money. Visualise the money in the world
   today as
   a. Concretised energy, at present largely used for
      purely material purposes and for the satisfaction
      (where the individual is concerned) of purely per-
      sonal desires.
   b. Visualise money as a great stream of flowing
      golden substance, passing out of the control of
      the Forces of Materialism into the control of the
      Forces of Light.
2. Then say the following invocative prayer, with focussed mental concentration and from a *heartfelt*
   desire to meet spiritual demands:

> "O Thou in Whom we live and move and
> have our being, the Power that can make all
> things new, turn to spiritual purposes the money
> in the world; touch the hearts of men everywhere
> so that they may give to the work of the Hier-
> archy that which has hitherto been given to
> material satisfaction. The New Group of World
> Servers needs money in large quantities. I ask
> that the needed vast sums may be made available.
> May this potent energy of Thine be in the hands
> of the Forces of Light."

3. Then visualise the work to be done by those groups which claim your present allegiance (i.e., the Arcane School and the Service Activities, or any other group which you know is attempting to carry out the hierarchical Plan). Then, through the creative imagination and by an act of the will, see untold and unlimited sums of money pouring into the hands of those who seek to do the Masters' work.

4. Then say aloud, with conviction and emphasis:

> "He for Whom the whole world waits has said that whatsoever shall be asked in His Name and with faith in the response will see it accomplished."

Remember at the same time that "faith is *the substance* of things hoped for and *the evidence* of things not seen." Then add:

> "I ask for the needed money for . . . . . . and can demand it because

> 'From the Centre which we call the race of men
> Let the Plan of Love and Light work out.
> And may it seal the door where evil
> dwells.' "

5. Close with a careful consideration of your own responsibility to the Plan, and each week plan your financial cooperation with the Hierarchy. Be practical and realistic and know that if you do not give, you may not ask, for you have no right to evoke that which you do not share.

Suggestions:

1. This meditation is so simple that many of you may regard it as innocuous and perhaps futile. Used by many simultaneously, it may shatter the impasse which

at present prevents adequate funds pouring into the work which the Hierarchy seeks to accomplish.

2. Do this meditation every *Sunday* morning. Take what you have saved during the previous week and dedicate it to the work and present it in meditation to the Christ and His Hierarchy. Whether the sum is large or small, it can become an attractive and magnetic unit in the Masters' plans.

3. Realise the occult Law that "to those who give shall be given" so that they can give again.

4. Attempt to feel true love sweeping through you, and have the fixed intention to express this love to all you contact. It is the great attractive and selfless agent in world affairs.

Part XIV

In my last series of instructions I gave you a group meditation which was based upon the furthering of the work of the New Group of World Servers, as they sought to prepare humanity for the reappearance of the Christ. That preparatory work is the major incentive lying back of all that I do, and was the prime reason for the formation of the group in the early part of this century. Pioneers of this group appeared in the nineteenth century but the organisation, as it now exists, is of relatively modern days.

In this instruction we will consider the relation of group meditation to the work of the New Group of World Servers, and the necessity of establishing in the world a united world group, given to unanimous and simultaneous meditation upon the work of preparing the world for the new order and for the jurisdiction of the Christ (if I may use such a phrase).

It is necessary for you all to get a wider vision of the enterprise which this group has undertaken, or else the meditation work which you will do will hinder and not help. The task of the group of World Servers is *not* the spreading of esoteric or occult information. In preparing the world of men for the reappearance of the Christ, the needs of all the many grades in the social order must be met; world groups of every description have to be contacted. Much of the work to be done, therefore, will be purely economic and will concern the right feeding and the development of a true security for millions who—for many lives—will not be interested in matters esoteric. The reform of the churches of the many world religions is another aspect of the same work, requiring no occult information but the introduction of commonsense and progressive ideas into theology, and the shift of the ecclesiastical emphasis from material values to the spiritual. The political regimes of the world need orienting to each other; it has never been the divine plan that all nations and races should conform to some standard political ideology or be reduced to a uniform general form of government. Nations differ; they have different cultures and traditions; they can function adequately under varying and distinctive governments; nevertheless, they can at the same time attain a unity of purpose, based upon a genuine desire for the true welfare and progress of all men everywhere.

In all these spheres of human thought and activity, the New Group of World Servers are playing a prominent part. At the very heart of that worldwide group are those who are in the Ashrams of the Masters—as are some of you—or on the periphery or within the sphere of influence of these Ashrams. Their task is largely a meditative one, carried on in order to influence the minds of those members of the group who are not yet in touch with any Ashram; they work thus from humanitarian, interested and basically ray reasons, and all such members are more or less under the control of their soul ray; this affects most definitely the varying fields of service. These are the areas of thought within the human family wherein the preparation for the coming of the Christ must be carried forward; but this activity is not, as a rule, associated with the esoteric angle or approach to truth but strictly with the angle of the betterment of human relationships. The Christ Himself (two thousand years ago) tried to demonstrate this mode of helpful activity; He kept the esoteric teaching for the few, the very few, who could approach understanding, but He dealt with the masses from the angle of commonsense and physical plane helpfulness. Have this ever in mind.

I have been for some time seeking to impress upon you the eternal fact that the entire universe has been created and its evolution processed through the power of thought, which is only another word for controlled meditation. This covers the combined meditation of numerous subjective, spiritual and mental groups; the laws of this meditative work are the result of certain mental determinations, which embody the will of the planetary Logos and are imposed upon all lesser groups of lives by Those Whose task it is to wield the divine laws and enforce them. Freedom of the will is here to be noted in relation to the *Time* concept but not in relation to the final and inevitable divine results at the end of the immense world period. The major thoughtform of the spiritual Hierarchy, created by joint ashramic meditation, is called by us the *Plan*. The basic purpose of Sanat Kumara is revealed from cycle to cycle by His Agents in Shamballa, and is by Them impressed upon the minds of the senior Members of the Hierarchy. They, in Their turn, make this impression the subject of Their ashramic meditation, adapting its various concepts and the outlined purpose to a most carefully formulated Plan, presenting—as far as humanity is concerned —seven aspects or phases of evolutionary development and endeavour, according to the work desired of any Ray Ashram implicated at any particular time. Each Ashram thus undertakes meditation upon the general Plan and thus (if you could but realise it) each initiate and disciple finds his place and sphere of activity and service—from the very highest initiate to the least important disciple.

You might here ask: What is the value of the meditation and contribution of a new disciple, unaccustomed to ashramic patterns of thought and unable to carry much weight in the general group meditation? That is a questioning worth answering and of great encouragement to the neophyte. The various grades and ranks of initiates and disciples are so constituted that the result of their meditation upon the Plan is that the many needs of the varying masses of humanity (from

those of the advanced intelligentsia down to those of the un-
skilled labourer) can be adequately met and the great mass
of men swung accurately into line with evolutionary purpose.

Have you ever stopped to think that the meditation of a
Master upon the Plan of which He is custodian, and His
formulation of what He can do along the line of effective
cooperation, is of no service or usefulness to the illiterate
inhabitants of our great cities and agricultural areas? The
need of these unthinking masses must be met by disciples of
less spiritual development, and probably their greatest appeal is through the application of economic help; the task of
these lesser disciples is to prove to the ignorant masses that—
as the centuries slip away—spiritual living and true spiritual
understanding include every aspect of physical plane expression and not simply the religious or the philosophic modes of
thought. The meditation, therefore, of every grade of disciple
and initiate has its use, for by their meditation (carried forward on their own level) they can adapt the Plan to the
widely differing masses and thus the hierarchical Plan can
reach from the Masters of the Hierarchy, through the Ashrams to the New Group of World Servers, and thus to the
whole of the human family. I would like you to grasp the
true simplicity of this picture, if you can, for you can have a
share also in this great meditative task.

One of the things which I set myself to achieve when I
undertook this work of making the Plan clearer to the minds
of men, and thus preparing the way for the Master of all the
Masters, was to prove not only that the Plan was based upon
planetary meditation but that, in its progress towards expression, it met the need of all possible groups and grades of
human beings; and that—more important still—it could be
proved that the word "spiritual" covered every phase of living experience. Ponder on this statement. That is spiritual
which lies beyond the point of present achievement; it is that
which embodies the vision and which urges the man on
towards a goal higher than the one attained. The ecclesiastics
of the world have made a great line of demarcation between
what is human and what is spiritual, between what is material and what is not; in so doing they have created sin and

greatly complicated human living and understanding. They
have given a selfish import to human aspiration; they have
not taught mankind that meditation and prayer were simply
phases of cooperation with the divine Plan. Individualism
was fostered and group understanding was lost. Maybe—
owing to the work of the Brothers of Darkness—there was no
way to avoid this dangerous sidetracking of human intent
and truth. But the time has now come when the great
rhythm of meditation, ranging from desire through prayer to
worship, and from thence to meditation and invocation, can
be imposed by men upon their own thinking.

This is the immediate task of the New Group of World
Servers, cooperating everywhere with the men of goodwill;
each member of the New Group has to ascertain for himself
where he stands, where his meditative responsibility lies and
in what field destiny indicates his service to the race of men
must be found. This is no easy task, brother of mine. Men
are frequently so spiritually ambitious and waste their time
in doing that which is not their destined task because in so
doing they satisfy their spiritual pride.

You must learn to give a wider connotation to the word
"meditation" than you have hitherto given. Concentrated
thought is part of the planetary meditation; planning with
care for the helping of the needy and pursuing all avenues
of thinking to make that plan useful and effective is meditation; laying oneself open to spiritual impression and thus to
cooperation with the Hierarchy is meditation; in this enumeration of meditative possibilities I have not touched upon
the major creative meditation which is responsible for the
evolutionary process and the controlled moving forward of
all the world of forms into greater glory and light.

The work hitherto done in such occult groups as the
Arcane School and others, as they teach meditation, has been
nothing but the learning of a needed concentration. Only in
the meditation work of the fourth degree has some of the
creative work become possible and that in its most elementary stages; yet the Arcane School leads the aspirants of
the world in meditation of an occult nature, though not in
any way a mystical nature. The mystical type of meditation

is of ancient formulation and its use indicates the next step for the masses of men; the practice of mystical meditation is not that which should be followed by aspirants and disciples who seek to work in an Ashram in cooperation with the Plan and under the guidance of a Master.

Meditation only becomes effective creatively and on all the three planes in the three worlds when the antahkarana is in process of construction. The worlds of the personality are the worlds of the third divine aspect and the creation of thoughtforms therein (as usually carried forward by the concrete mind) is related to form, to the acquisition of that which is desired and dedicated largely to the material values. But when a man is beginning to function as a soul-infused personality and is occupied with the task of rendering himself sensitive to the higher spiritual impression, then the creative work of the Spiritual Triad can be developed and a higher form of creative meditation can be employed. It is a form which each person has to find and discover for himself, because it must be the expression of his own spiritual understanding, initiated by a conscious construction or creation of the antahkarana and subject to impression from the Ashram with which he may be affiliated.

Earlier in this instruction I used the words: "An united world group given to unanimous and simultaneous meditation . . . for the jurisdiction of the Christ." I particularly want to call your attention to this last phrase which introduces a new concept into the preparatory work to be done by the New Group of World Servers. The task is, through meditation, to establish the knowledge of and the functioning of those laws and principles which will control the coming era, the new civilisation and the future world culture. Until the foundation for the coming "jurisdiction" is at least laid, the Christ cannot reappear; if He came without this due preparation, much time, effort and spiritual energy would be lost. Therefore, we must assume (if these premises are accepted) that there must be organised—in the near future—a group of men and women in every country who, under due and proper organisation, will "simultaneously and unanimously" meditate upon those juridical measures and those basic laws upon which the rule of Christ will be founded and which are essentially the laws of the Kingdom of God, the fifth kingdom in the evolutionary and natural processes of planetary unfoldment.

So much has been discussed in relation to these laws from the mystical and strictly Christian angle that the terms used are essentially meaningless; the whole subject requires revitalising; it needs to be endowed with a fresh and new presentation and a new terminology, more suited to the growing mental grasp of the scientific and modern mind. There has been endless talk about Brotherhood and the establishing of the principle that we are all the children of God, and this has done little to change men's approach to each other and to the shared human problems.

The New Group of World Servers will talk in other terms and their emphasis will be upon:

1. The Law of Right Human Relations.
2. The Principle of Goodwill.
3. The Law of Group Endeavour.
4. The Principle of Unanimity.
5. The Law of Spiritual Approach.
6. The Principle of Essential Divinity.

If you will study the many books which I have written, you will discover that they have been basically occupied with the rules which govern the ability to do group work—which is the work to which the Hierarchy is eternally committed. I have given you the Rules for Disciples in *A Treatise on White Magic,* the Rules for Aspirants in *Initiation, Human and Solar,* the Rules for Disciples and Initiates in *A Treatise on the Seven Rays, Volume V.* In other volumes you will find the Rules for Group Work; all these rules are, in essence, modes of conduct which, when imposed upon, impressed upon and followed up by an aspirant, will enable him to reach an understanding of spiritual law and of the nature of the Kingdom of God. All these are preparatory to the establishing of the new dispensation on Earth.

I would also call your attention to the words "unanimous

and simultaneous" meditation; they are not idly chosen. A situation which is unanimous is not one which is—from the spiritual angle—imposed. It is in the nature of a spontaneous mutual reaction—a reaction which is evoked by the immediate response of a soul, in touch with its personality, to a spiritual truth or intuition, and from this there is no lower mind escape. The concept of unanimity which has been presented by Soviet Russia runs completely counter to the truth. Their idea is that the concept, the idea, the decision and the interpretation of a group of powerful men establishes the truth, and to this truth the docile masses render prompt allegiance. This is a basic misconception and to it no member of the New Group of World Servers will render homage; they will fight this imprisonment of the human soul to the last gasp. True unanimity is free decision in response to a presentation of truth which is as near the achieved reality as possible. Therefore, *it is in the enunciation of truth that security for all men lies.* This necessarily involves a deeply spiritual presentation of essential facts. The principle of simultaneity is allied to this, for a mutual recognition of an identical approach to truth renders inevitably activity in unison.

The whole point, brother of mine, is that in both connections the incentive towards activity lies with the individual and there is *no* imposing authority. The only authority recognised is the truth as it emerges in the human consciousness, in any world or historical cycle. Today more truth is being recognised (and incidentally, repudiated) than at any other time in human history. Men have attained the point in evolution where they are able to know the truth *if* and *when* presented, because the concrete human mind is now more highly responsive to abstract truth, and therefore to the next evolutionary presentation. It is this which the Totalitarian Powers, the unconscious (and I mean that, brother of mine) agents of the Black Lodge are fighting; they will not win; in the long run they cannot, for the human spirit is eternally sound and sane.

I would have you consider these suggestions with care and thus prepare yourselves for an elucidation of the spiritual laws and principles, as themes for meditation. I herein present to you six themes for group meditation; this is essentially your next consideration if the "unanimous and simultaneous" meditation which can be immediately effective is organised and developed.

SECTION THREE

TEACHINGS ON INITIATION

TEACHINGS ON INITIATION

PART I

Prior to profiting by more information and thus piling up increased responsibility, there is a vital need for the majority of aspirants and disciples to assume a different attitude towards the opportunity to prepare for initiation with which they are all faced. The more advanced among them are conscious of impending possibilities. The significance of the proffered training has made its just appeal. Others are so immersed in the tests and difficulties incidental to the clarification of the vision prior to the processes of initiation, that they have neither the time nor the strength to do more than live through the time of trial and, at the same time, to serve as best they can. Both the vision and their service suffer from their failure to develop that *divine indifference which is the hallmark of the true initiate.* Added to all this is the world situation with its inevitable all-enveloping psychic atmosphere, its attendant strains and its constant wearing anxiety, plus the hold which war sufferers have on all hearts and sympathies. Most aspirants and disciples believe that they are bearing enough and are tried to the limit of their capacity. This is not the case. The deeper sources of strength in them have not yet been evoked, and the tension under which they should act and live from day to day is only as yet a feeble one—it is not all-exacting. Ponder on this last phrase.

The objective demands being made upon all disciples and therefore upon all of you, are not simply to enable you to live through the present period as successfully—emotionally, mentally and spiritually—as possible. It goes far deeper than that, or should. Apart from the demands upon your spiritual resources (incident to the particular initiation which it is desired that you take) there is also the demand upon all disciples to participate in the effort of humanity, as a whole, to take the first initiation with all the physical relinquishments, and the agony that ever precedes the birth of the Christ in the heart of the individual—only this time it is the hearts of all humanity. Preparatory to this first initiation, there has always to be—individually and now collectively for the first time—the denial of the lower self and the fervid acceptance by the personality of the loss of all the material factors which have held the soul a prisoner in the womb of time.

Hence, my brothers, the wide extent of the material destruction to be seen on every hand, the depths of physical poverty into which all men have been and are being plunged, the detachment from *the priority of things* which is being enforced, and the necessity for rebuilding human life on sounder values than the physical. In all this disciples and initiates are today sharing and (when understanding is present and right orientation) the help which those can give who have already undergone the first initiation, is great. To this you are called, and upon your understanding response to the collective need will depend the rapidity with which you will be enabled to achieve the next expansion of consciousness or initiation which may be, for you as an individual, possible. You have, therefore, to consider your individual response to the demands of your own soul and your collective response to the collective need. It is the initiate in you, the Christ in you, which is now called to this collective service and the radiation today of the Christ spirit, actively present in the hearts of all disciples is the one thing which can salvage mankind, enable humanity to move forward on to the Path of Discipleship and thus evoke that new spirit which can and will build the new world.

I would like to deal somewhat with the theme anent the attitude of the accepted disciple towards his Master and towards the general subject of initiation, and then consider the immediate steps ahead which the disciple must take, where he is and with what equipment he has. This is the first and necessary step. Disciples must clarify their position and must continue to learn from their Master, in spite of the crises of initiation. Unless they act upon the proffered instruction and have confidence in His occult intention, all that the Master may say or do is of small usefulness. It serves only to increase grave responsibility with its attendant liabilities; knowledge and the pressure of spiritual energy become a danger if not used. This is a basic and important statement.

There are, my brothers, two major prerequisites which are needed by all of you in connection with group integration, and they follow upon what you have had earlier when I sought to help you to integrate with your brothers. I gave you, as you will recall, as part of your group meditation the following simple integrating formula:

"I am one with my group brothers, and all that I have is theirs. May the love which is in my soul pour forth to them. May the strength which is in me lift and aid them. May the thoughts which my soul creates reach and encourage them."

Of the two prerequisites to which I now allude as needed by all of you, one of them refers to your integration into my group of "practicing chelas," and the other relates to your capacity to contact me at will—a thing as yet only permitted to three of you at this time, and this because they seldom avail themselves of the privilege. Our first task is therefore to attend to these requirements which call for a right attitude on your part and the use of the first of the ancient formulas which it is my intention to give for deep consideration and eventual experimental use. Before I give this formula, however, I would like to deal with a question which is bound to arise in the minds of those of you who are senior in this group.

The question might be voiced thus: "If I am in preparation for the second or the third initiation, I must have been in a group of disciples—presumably the Tibetan's—for some lives at least. Why then the need for an integrating formula?" Because, my chela, though you have been in a group of disciples prior to this, it was not my group but the group of either the Master M. or the Master K.H. Owing to the fact of world urgency and the immensity of the work to be done by Them and owing also to the fact that They are preparing to pass through one of the highest initiations, these two Masters have handed all but a few of Their senior disciples to me and to two other of Their initiate disciples, themselves Adepts or Masters. They have also retained in Their groups of disciples those who have started specific work under Their direction in some previous life, and a few disciples who came into incarnation in this world period having the brain and the mind awakened to their relationship to these Masters. These conditions do not exist in this group in relation to me—the Master chosen to lead you forward. Yet (though you remember it not) all of you knew me well when working with the two Chohans, and hence the decision for you to work under my instruction and guidance. It has worked happily and with no delay so far.

Another reason for the use of this formula of integration by those who have had experience of group work is that there are some in the group who are as yet far from true integration, and the experience of the older chelas can be of inestimable help if they will thus to serve the group and me. Much of what I said in the earlier instructions (Vol. I) on the relation of chelas to their Master could well be applied here and with profit.

THE FORMULAS

There are six ancient formulas or symbolic forms which are to be found in the archives for disciples. They concern the six fundamental prerequisites for initiation. They are used prior to all the major initiations, and have therefore five significances or meanings which will become apparent only as each of these initiations is undergone. They are in the form sometimes of symbols and sometimes of words, and are amongst the oldest formulas in the world. They have been used down the ages by all disciples and initiates of the Great White Lodge. They concern what are called "the six relations." Each of these relations must find expression in attitude, in service, and in some deeper expansion of consciousness, to which I may not refer but which must be self-ascertained. It is essential that the would-be initiate discover for himself the esoteric, inner and subjective value of the formula under his consideration. Just one hint however in this latter connection I may give.

The disciple, when he becomes an accepted disciple (and this through the Lodge's recognition of his pledge to his own soul), arrives at a definite and factual recognition of the Hierarchy. His suppositions, his desires, his aspirational wish-life, his theories, or whatever you may choose to call his reaching out and up towards divinity, give place to clear knowledge of the liberated group of souls. This happens not through the occurrence of convincing phenomena, but through an inflow of the intuition. He undergoes, therefore, an expansion of consciousness which may or may not be registered in the brain. Every step of the way from that point of recognition onward has to be consciously achieved and must involve a conscious recognition of a series of expansions. These expansions are not initiation. Have that clearly in your mind. The initiation lying immediately ahead is simply the effect of the recognition. They might be called "stabilising points of crisis," in which the "occasional becomes the constant and the intended becomes the intentional." Ponder on these words. The Hierarchy is now a fact in your life and your awareness. What is the next fact or point of integration or consciously achieved inclusiveness? A study of the formulas and their correct use will reveal this to you. I have laid the emphasis upon visualisation and given you some hints connected both with initiation and the creative work of the imagination, because these teachings and the development of these faculties will require calling into play your understanding, if the formulas connected with initiation are to be given. These six formulas are therefore formulas of integration, and one or two hints may here be imparted.

Formula One concerns, as I have told you, integration into a Master's group, and it has two uses—if I might so express it from your particular point of view. One produces a group inclusiveness, which integrates you with your group brothers into my group and brings a revelation of the hidden side of a chela's life. When I say this I refer to his new astral *conditioning*. This is given the name of the *Revelation of Group Feeling*. This subject is vaster in its implications than you might surmise, for it concerns united group sensitivity or response, outwards to the world of men, inwards to the Hierarchy, and upwards to the Monad. It does not concern the sumtotal of the petty moods and feelings of the personalities of the group members. Its second use is to bring about contact with the Master of your group—in this case myself, the Master D.K. This is a process which I have already done my best to help you to achieve through my instructions re the Full Moon contact—something you have most inadequately understood and attempted. Perhaps now you will work harder at the production of "contact relationship" as it is esoterically called. It is with Formula One that you must now work.

Formula Two deals with alignment; not alignment as it is understood in the very necessary preparatory work of the Arcane School. That form of alignment is the production of effective and direct contact with the soul. The alignment to which this formula refers is connected with the antahkarana. This will be our next consideration when Formula One has brought about certain changes in consciousness. I shall not consider these formulas at present. I will only point out their major implications which will be seldom what you think, conditioned as you are by the terms and interpretations of the lower mind.

Formula Three is related to certain changes in the egoic lotus. These changes might be inadequately expressed in the terms of the *Old Commentary:*

"There is that which transmutes knowledge into wisdom within a flash of *time;* there is that which changes sensitivity into love within an area of *space;* there is that which alters sacrifice into bliss where neither time nor space exists."

Formula Four has a specific effect upon the "jewel in the lotus," awakening it to life; this it does (through effects produced) upon the three planes of the three worlds, thus bringing about changes in the seven wheels (centres) so that the "dynamic point at the centre of each wheel obliterates the lesser points of force, and thus the wheel begins to turn upon itself."

Formula Five awakens the *Will*, but any interpretation of this awakening would prove meaningless to you until the previous four formulas have established an effect upon you and the needed interior changes have taken place.

Formula Six is sometimes called "the word of death." It negates the destructive effect of the death process which is going on all the time within the mechanism of the disciple or initiate. The death proceeds with its needed work, but it is *not* destructive in effect. This formula has never been given out before to disciples, but can now be known because the Piscean Age is one in which at last the power of physical death is definitely broken and the signature of the Resurrection is revealed. In this esoteric negation of death are the deeply hidden and *impressive* causes of the two stages of the world war (1914-1945), and in this formula lies the significance lying behind the "fight for freedom" of the peoples of the world. It is sometimes called "the formula of liberation."

If you were a disciple who had access to the archives wherein instructions for disciples are contained, you would be confronted (in relation to the six formulas referred to above) by six large sheets of some unknown metal. These look as if made of silver and are in reality composed of that metal which is the allotrope of silver and which is therefore to silver what the diamond is to carbon. Upon these sheets are words, symbols, and symbolic forms. These, when related to each other, contain the formulas which the disciple has to interpret and integrate into his waking consciousness. This must be done through the medium of living processes.

As I cannot show you these formulas upon the physical plane, the best that I can do is to describe them to you, and in this Instruction I will seek to describe Formula One. The comprehension of the words and symbols produces two reactions in the consciousness of the disciple—and when a group of disciples are working with the same formula (as is the case in this group) this is intensified and of still greater value.

The first reaction is called the "Formula of Revelation" and is related to the united sensitivity of the group. As, together, the group members brood upon and come to an understanding of the formula, they will swing into a responsiveness to the feeling and sensitive reactions of the individuals in the group, and these, together, constitute and form the astral body of the group.

When this reaction has been established (and a spirit of non-criticism and of love will greatly aid in the process), the group together can arrive at the second purpose of the formula, which is called "the discovery of the point within the circle." This signifies—as far as the group is involved—the revelation of the central coherent force of the group itself. This is—at the same time and until after the higher initiation which we call the fourth initiation—the Master at the centre of the group. This is, consequently, the correspondence to the "jewel in the lotus," where the individual is concerned, to the Hierarchy, where humanity is concerned, and to the central point of life in all forms. Of form and of consciousness, the circle and the point are the natural symbols. This applies equally to the atom, to man, to the planet and to the solar system. The concept must constitute the foundational idea in all reflection upon this formula.

Now for the formula itself:

"A line of fire between two blazing points. A stream of water blue—again a line—emerging from the earth—and ending in the ocean. A tree with root above and flowers below.

"Out of the fire, and always at the midway point, appears the eye of God (Shiva). Upon the stream, between the two extremes, there floats the eye of vision—a thread of light unites the two.

"Deep in the tree, between the root and flowers, the eye again is seen. The eye that knows, the eye that sees, the directing eye—one made of fire, one fluid as the sea, and two which look from here to there. Fire, water and the earth—all need the vital air. The air is life. The air is God."

The significance of this formula is not difficult for the advanced student to grasp in connection with himself. The eye of knowledge, the eye of vision and the directing eye of Deity are familiar to him. But it is the great and major esoteric implications which I ask you to consider. An extension of these concepts to a Master and His ashram or His group of practising disciples, is of value to you in your reflective consciousness. The first and obvious interpretation concerns the eye of knowledge. But what of the eye of vision *when duality is being overcome,* and what of the "purpose for which the worlds were made"—the little world of the individual (once individuality is achieved) and the greater world of an organised group, integrated and functioning as a unit, and the distant subtle world of divine intent?

I say no more in this connection. I commend to your brooding reflection these subtle implications. I would ask you to ponder on them and—prior to the Wesak Full Moon —I would ask you to write your understanding of the formula from two angles. About these two angles you definitely should have ideas.

1. The angle of the individual.
2. The angle of a group of chelas.

Both these unities utilise the eye of knowledge and the eye of vision.

Part II

POINTS OF REVELATION

I have dealt considerably in my earlier writings with the theme, Points of Crisis. We can now approach and prove the livingness of our progress from the angle of *Points of Revelation*. The entire objective of the initiation prepara tory process is to bring about revelation. You must ever bear in mind that that which is revealed is eternally present. There is, therefore, occult truth in the statement that there is "nothing new under the sun." All that is revealed upon the Path of Discipleship and of Initiation is forever there, but that which can perceive, reach out and include has developed with the ages. Upon the Path of Discipleship, in the earlier stages, the eye of vision is the illumined mind. Upon the Path of Initiation it is that of which the eye of the mind is the exteriorisation—the intuitional perception of the soul itself. But as evolution proceeds, that which is brought to the point of perceiving the existing verities differs vastly as the centuries slip away. E'en the adept of the present is pronouncedly more perceptive and more accurately interpretive and his vision more penetrative than was the adept in Atlantean days, and the initiate who will achieve initiate-perception during the coming Aquarian Age will be greatly in advance of those who now function as the adepts of today.

I have warned you that discipleship is becoming increasingly difficult. This is owing to the increased sensitivity to the esoteric values and realities which the modern disciple manifests. He can and does perceive that which was the goal of initiation in earlier aeons and perceives these things normally and as an established fact in a developed awareness. It is the spiritual parallel of the development during material evolution of the five senses. His goal and his "pointed direction" lie far ahead and his inclusiveness opens for him doors which in earlier times only opened to the initiate knock. I consequently hold out to you no easy way but only one of difficulty and adjustment.

In all forward stages upon the Path of Initiation, there are three phases which concern the initiate-aspirant's reactions. There is first of all the vision of the soul, but whereas in the past there was the vision and the starting point, now the modern disciple perceives likewise many of the intermediate stages, the opposing forces, the obstructions and the rapidly arousing handicaps and hindrances. The words I here use are chosen with deliberation. He is not now totally blind nor does he move forward entirely in the dark. There is enough light in him to bring to him what is called the "little revelation," and, in that light, will he see the greater light and arrive at a truer perception. He sees himself, and that—for aeons—the disciple has ever been able to do. But now he also perceives and recognises his brother in the light, and this evokes personality reactions and he has to adjust himself not only to himself as he discovers himself to be, but likewise to what he finds his brother also to be. This is no easy adjustment to make, and this the earlier imparted *Rules of the Road** will have indicated to you.

I would like here, my brother, to list for you the most important of the statements made by me in the previous instruction, indicating those which embody important hints and showing you, this one time, with what care I prepare that which I seek to impart and how, therefore, I expect from you a careful study of my words. Here are these key thoughts:

1. Only that which you know for yourself and *consciously* experience is of importance. This refers especially to the following:
    a. Your perception of the vision.
    b. Your contact with me, your Master.
    c. Your recognition of the initiatory process.

I told you, therefore, that you must have (for the goal) the demonstrating of the initiate-consciousness through both mind and brain and consequently upon the physical plane.

*Discipleship in the New Age, Vol. I, page 583-584.

2. Initiation is, as far as you are at present concerned, a "moment of crisis wherein the consciousness hovers upon the border line of revelation." This involves consequently:
   a. A tremendous pull between the pairs of opposites.
   b. The existence, as a result, of a field of tension.
   c. The effort to stand firm at the midway point.

I would remind you that this does not refer to the man upon the path of life, pulled as he is between the pairs of opposites upon the plane of desire, but to the soul standing at the midway point between the monad and the personality and preparing to make the Great Renunciation—a renunciation which the personality makes possible—and to disappear, leaving the two (personality and monad) perfectly at-one. It is the man, as the soul, in full waking consciousness who takes initiation. Hence the emphasis upon soul contact when a man is upon the Probationary Path and passing through the early stages of discipleship. This leads, later, to the emphasis placed upon the need for two major activities—before the man can take the higher initiations:

   a. Upon alignment.
   b. Upon the scientific building of the antahkarana.

3. The revelation, given to the initiate, is not a vision of possibilities, but a factual experience, leading to:
   a. The evocation of new powers.
   b. The recognition of new modes and fields of service.
   c. Freedom of movement within the bounds of the Hierarchy.
   d. New hierarchical contacts and new responsibilities which face the initiate.

He, therefore, realises what St. Paul meant when—talking in hierarchical terms—he said "All things are become new." It is not simply a question of vision and contacts but of vital interrelation and of recognition which bring with them *insight into the Mind of God.*

4. Four lines of teaching were emphasised in past centuries and up until the year 1875:
   a. Hints as to the changing of personality character as preparatory to initiation.
   b. Teaching as to the oneness of Deity and of the universal order.
   c. Instruction as to the creative process.
   d. Laya yoga or the yoga of energy, working through force centres.

Two things must now happen: the imparted theories which have guided the disciple's thinking hitherto must become practical experiences, and there must be such a shift in consciousness that the present vision must become the past experience and a new and deeper and entirely different recognition must take the place of the old goals. Here comes, consequently, a complete test-out of past hierarchical methods and modes of work. Has what the past has given proved an adequate preparation for that which will be the methods and propositions of the future? Have the foundations of truth been so securely settled that the coming superstructure will be based on such a sound reality that it can stand the impact of the new incoming solar and cosmic forces? Will the past work of the Hierarchy stand? Such are the problems with which the initiate-teachers are today faced.

Just as the attitudes of the disciple to daily living and to world happenings are totally unlike that of the average man because he is living increasingly in the world of meaning, so the *initiate*-disciple develops an attitude to living processes and to world events which is based on character (necessarily), interpreted in the world of meaning but to them he brings a different light to bear and a motivation—based on newly acquired knowledge and understanding—which is entirely different to the two previous conditions. The four lines of teaching are taken for granted; the initiate is supposed to have grasped and mastered all of it in some experimental and experiential measure. Now the new formulas of life must control; they are life formulas, not soul formulas. New knowledge must supersede the old and it will not concern that which has hitherto been regarded as the ultimate goal.

An illustration of this is the fact that to the esotericist of the past little was known of the seven Rays and the seven ray types, and naught had been given out anent Shamballa. Now the world of instructed disciples is slowly awakening to these newer values and truths and to the sevenfold source of life expression; the Will of God is going to take shape consciously in the minds of men in the future in such a manner that the old truths will condition and control as never before, but will drop automatically below the threshold of consciousness and the new emerging values and recognitions will take their place in the surface consciousness of all disciples—and their name will be Legion.

5. The astral body provides no hindrance to the initiate-disciple, but provides a medium of facile contact with the Hierarchy. This is due to the fact that the link between the astral body and the buddhic consciousness becomes at this stage increasingly close. They constitute essentially a pair of opposites which will eventually fuse; then the astral body will disappear as does the soul body at a later stage of development.

6. Every disciple has to discover for himself and alone for which initiation he is being prepared; the Master never gives this information. Light on the subject comes through the recognition of tests and the types of experience which come his way. "It is a matter," I have elsewhere told you, "of interior orientation and not of outside information." Recognition and orientation are the keynotes of this phase.

7. Always there exists the need for humility. This involves:
   a. An adjusted sense of right proportion.
   b. A balanced point of view.
   c. A dispassionate attitude.
   d. Truthful recognition of *assets* as well as debits.

Here also I gave you a hint in stating that true humility is based on fact, on vision and on time pressures.

8. Two immediate objectives face the disciples, plus the need for one quality:
    a. To integrate into the inner Ashram as "practicing chelas."
    b. To contact the Master at will.
    c. To develop divine indifference.
9. In connection with the formulas, two reactions are automatically evoked in the true disciple and in the true group within the Ashram:
    a. The reaction which is called the "formula of revelation." This designates sensitive response to the ancient formulas which are given to those being prepared for initiation. One of these I have already given to you.
    b. The reaction called the "discovery of the point within the circle."

Have you ever thought, my brother, that one reason why you have not as yet contacted me freely in your waking consciousness and talked with me face to face may be due to the fact that the "circle" is for you only as yet a theory? Until the circle of your brothers is a fact in your everyday awareness and of prime importance in your daily life, it is not possible for you to arrive at contact with the "Point." The disciple starts on the periphery of the Master's circle and works towards the centre; he is apt, however, to reverse this procedure in his consciousness.

I have stated that initiation is essentially a process of revelation. For the disciple who is being prepared to take an initiation the emphasis is necessarily laid upon *recognition*—the intelligent recognition of what is to be revealed. This requires on his part a definite emergence from the world of glamour so that there can be a clear perception of the new vision; a new light is thrown upon old and well-known truths so that their significance is extraordinarily changed, and in that changing the plan or purpose of Deity takes on an entirely fresh meaning. The inexperienced neophyte is constantly receiving revelations and recording what he regards as most unusual intuitions. All that is really happening, however, is that he is becoming aware of soul knowledge, whereas for the initiate the intuition is ever the revelation of the purpose of Shamballa and the working out, both from the short range and the long range angle, of the divine Plan. The revelation which is accorded at initiation is given to the soul, recorded by the "mind held steady in the light" and then later—with greater or less rapidity—transferred to the brain. You can see, therefore, the true intention of the system of Raja Yoga as it trains the mind to be *receptive eventually to the Spiritual Triad.* You can also see why for centuries the emphasis of the Teachers of the Ageless Wisdom has been upon the necessity for discrimination, particularly where the probationary disciple is concerned.

I am at this time carrying the current teaching upon initiation a step forward and am seeking to show that it is not essentially a process of soul-personality fusion (though that has to be a preliminary step) but of monad-personality integration, carried forward because of an attained alignment with the soul. Initiation is in fact the essential and inevitable process of transferring the primary triplicity of manifestation into the basic duality of spirit-matter. It is the "dissolution of the intermediary," and to this the crucifixion and death of the Christ was dedicated and intended to be the revelation, to the initiates of the past 2000 years, of the transmutation of the trinity of manifestation into the duality of purpose. I cannot word this in any other way but the enlightened will comprehend my meaning. The interpreters of the Gospel and many disciples of the Christian dispensation have singularly failed to grasp this revelation; they have laid the emphasis upon the death of the personality, whereas when Christ experienced the "great void of darkness" and chanted aloud the occult mantram "My God, My God, why hast Thou forsaken Me," he was recognising simultaneously the distinction between His "robe of glory" (symbolised by the partition of His garment by the Roman soldiery) and also calling the attention of all future disciples and initiates to the disappearance of the "middle principle," the soul; He was projecting (into the world consciousness) the recognition which must come of relation to the Father or the Monad. This great dissolution is culminated for us at the time of the third initiation when the Light of the Monad obliterates the light of the soul and the material atomic light of the threefold personality. But—and here is the point—the recognition of this death and its effects is only symbolically enacted and recognised at the time of the fourth initiation, the Crucifixion. All lesser dissolutions, deaths, renunciations and disappearances of that to which the lower nature holds and is held are enacted in relation to the accustomed aspects of form-life, and of conscious sensitivity and awareness; they are simply preparatory to and symbolic of the final great dissolution of the causal body, consummated at the Crucifixion. This leads to the resurrection or uprising of the personality-soul consciousness (duly fused and blended) into that of the monad. This is finally carried to the point of solar perfection at the Ascension initiation.

I have given you this teaching in terms of the Christian presentation as it may be simpler for you to grasp, but there are many other formulations and approaches to these truths and the newer they are the more difficult necessarily are they to present. Only those who are on the immediate verge of initiation will understand; the others will prefer to interpret these truths to themselves in the easier and well-known formulas of the preparatory stage of the at-one-ing of soul and personality.

The stage of recognising the revelation which is accorded to the initiate of the major Mysteries is itself divided into lesser phases. These might be described as three in number though much is dependent upon the initiation to be taken and the ray of the prepared disciple. These are:

1. *The Stage of Penetration.* This refers to the piercing through the world glamour and thereby effecting two objectives:

a. The Light of the Spiritual Triad streams into the consciousness of the initiate, via the antahkarana, so that the Plan for humanity and the divine Purpose in relation to the planet become increasingly clear. This initiates relation to Shamballa.

b. Part of the world glamour is thus dissipated and thus a clarifying of the astral plane takes place and humanity is consequently served. Every disciple who arrives at a recognition of the initiate-revelation releases light and dissipates a part of the glamour which blinds the mass of men. The sixth ray disciple takes far longer over this stage of penetration than do disciples on the other rays but only in this world cycle.

2. *The Stage of Polarisation.* This is the stage wherein the initiate, having let in the light and penetrated through the dense fogs and mists of the world of glamour, suddenly realises just what he has done and takes a firm stand, correctly oriented towards the vision (or to word it otherwise towards Shamballa). One of the things which must be grasped is that as the initiate is a point of hierarchical life (either on the periphery of the Hierarchy, or within the circle or at the centre) he is a definite part of the hierarchical effort. That effort is directed towards an orientation to the greater centre of life—*Shamballa.* Students are apt to believe that the orientation of the Hierarchy is towards humanity. That is not so. They respond to human need when the demand is effective, and are custodians of the Plan; but the orientation of the entire hierarchical group is towards the first aspect, as it expresses the Will of the Logos and manifests through Shamballa. Just as the disciple has to do two things: polarise his position by establishing right human relations and at the same time become a conscious, practising member of the Kingdom of God, the Hierarchy, so the initiate— upon a higher turn of the spiral—has to establish right relations with the Hierarchy and become simultaneously conscious of Shamballa.

All I can impart here is the desired point of attainment but the phraseology is relatively meaningless, except to those who are experienced in the processes of initiation to a greater or less degree, according to the initiations already taken. This polarisation, this point of focussed effort and this attained orientation is the basic idea lying behind the phrase "the Mountain of Initiation." The initiate "plants his feet upon the mountain top and from that point of altitude perceives the thought of God, visions the dream within the Mind of God, follows God's eye from central point to outer goal and sees himself as all that is and yet within the whole."

3. *The Stage of Precipitation.* Having thus identified himself through penetration and polarisation with the Plan and with the Will of God (which is the key to Shamballa), he then proceeds—as a result of this triple recognition—to do his share in materialising the Plan and in bringing through into outer manifestation and expression as much of that Plan as he can. He thus becomes first of all an outpost of the Hierarchy (which of necessity means sensitivity to the Shamballa energy), and then increasingly an Agent of Light—the Light universal, or the Light of the Monad.

I have no more to say today anent initiation. Ponder upon that which I have given and grasp as far as you *imaginatively* can the magnificence of the initiatory process—so vastly more inclusive than has been indicated by any of the teaching given hitherto. After the war is over and the new world, with its coming civilisation and culture begins to take shape, an increasing emphasis will be laid upon the *purpose* of the Controlling Deity or basic Life or Energy as it is working out through humanity. This will be done by those who are trained esotericists. Much that is now being said by world leaders and serving workers in every nation is an indication of an unconscious response to the Shamballa energy. Towards the end of the century and during the first few decades of the twenty-first century, teaching anent Shamballa will be given forth. The effort of the abstract mind of man will be towards the comprehension of this, just as the goal of hierarchical contact marks the present effort of the disciple. Glamour is disappearing; illusions are being dissipated; the stage of penetration into a new dimension, into a new phase of effort and of attainment is rapidly being promulgated. This is being done in spite of all the horror and agony and will be one of the first results of respite from war. The war itself is shattering illusions, revealing the need for change and producing a demand for a future new world and a coming beauty in living which will be revolutionary and a material response to an intensive initiation process in which all disciples can share and for which advanced aspirants can prepare themselves.

THE FORMULAS

Now that you have, presumably, brooded for some months on my instructions on the Formulas, I will seek to impart to you some of the deeper implications.

Formula One.   "A line of fire between two blazing points. A stream of water blue, again a line, emerging from the earth and ending in the ocean. A tree with root above and flowers below.

"Out of the fire and always at the midway point appears the eye of God (Shiva). Upon the stream, between the two extremes, there floats the eye of vision; a thread of light unites the two.

"Deep in the tree, between the root and flowers, the eye again is seen. The eye that knows, the eye that sees, the directing eye— one made of fire, one fluid as the sea, and two which look from here to there. Fire, water and the earth—all need the vital air. The air is life. The air is God."

These formulas and their implications have caused some of you concern because of their extreme difficulty of interpretation. I would ask you to bear in mind that you are individually quite unable to grasp the extent of your own comprehension because *the mind* (the major conditioning factor in a disciple's life in the early stages of his training) knows far more than the brain is capable of recording. Later, in the life of the initiate, the soul registers consciously for the disciple who can identify himself with the soul, far more than the concrete mind is able to register. I would ask you, therefore, to cease gauging your capacity to understand and instead simply to brood and reflect.

Let me briefly summarise for you some of the things I indicated anent these formulas in my previous instructions:

1. They are concerned with the six relationships, as the disciple succeeds in establishing them.
2. These six relationships are *not* six initiations but six intermediate expansions of consciousness, occurring between the major initiations.
3. They are definitely formulas of integration:
   a. They concern integration progressively into a Master's group.
   b. They also concern integration into some state of group sensitivity, on some one plane, for consciousness of sensitive response is the keynote of all the planes throughout the solar system.
4. They are also formulas of revelation. This is peculiarly so in connection with Formula One. They bring about, when rightly used:
   a. The revelation of group feeling.
   b. The revelation of the Master as He is, the centre of light and power within the circle.
   c. The revelation of the point of life at the centre of all forms.

These effects, resulting from right comprehension of the formulas, might be regarded as reactions—automatic and inevitable; I used this word "reaction" in my last instruction. These reactions are frequently, and I might say usually, unconscious and it is only gradually that the disciple wakes up to the fact that by quiet reflection upon the formula, certain expansions of consciousness, a greater sensitivity and an intuitive recognition of the hitherto unseen and unrealised have wrought definite changes in his subjective nature. He does the required work and the results naturally and simply happen.

Here is a hint as to the need for occult obedience. I have the responsibility of indicating to you the work I want done and the steps to be taken. You subsequently have to do the work. Most of you, living normally as you do in the world of effects and not in the world of causes, are preoccupied with the possible results and the phenomenal differences (if I might call them so) which are expected by you to eventuate from the work. Therefore, instead of concentrating upon exactitude of work and meticulous obedience, your energy goes into the thought of what will happen, into the consideration of the difficulties of the work, and into your belief that no results are demonstrating in your particular case. Primarily what I am doing in giving you these formulas is to aid you to work in the world of causes and so draw you consciously out of the world of effects. Therefore, I would ask you to do the indicated work, to concentrate your minds upon these formulas of power—"working without attachment," as the Gita expresses it—and refrain from looking for results, knowing that they will be there, e'en though unrecognised by you, until your focus is more definitely subjective. I did not say "introspective," my brother, but "subjective." To be an introvert really means that you, as a thinking personality, are always looking in to your inner feeling and thought life. That is not living subjectively; it is living as an outer observer who looks within. To live subjectively means that the focus of your consciousness is within and that from that point you look in two directions: outward at the personality upon the physical plane and inward at the soul. Ponder on this. The distinction is very real and one that you should grasp. The man who knows the difference between living an introspective life and a subjective life is well on the way to being a true esotericist.

Let us look for a minute at Formula One and seek its

simplest interpretation, and yet an advanced one from the angle of the neophyte (which you should not be). I will take one or two general ideas which emerge from an analysis of the whole and then a few sentences which—when interpreted —may throw light upon certain basic and practical significances.

I would first have you note the emphasis upon the *"eye"* in this formula. It is a keynote and appears in various guises. Behind all the ideas lies the concept of seeing, of a Seeing One, looking on at the created Whole. This same concept is to be found in the fundamental Masonic symbol of the Eye of God which dominates everything within the Temple. In this formula we have:

1. *The Eye of God.* Shiva is the first Person of the Trinity, the Destroyer, but at the same time the Final Absorber, the Whole and yet the part. This is the organ of the divine Will or Power, the Eye, through Whose directed gaze the power flows outward to its created Whole. In the case of the human spirit, it is the Monad.
2. *The Eye of Vision,* indicating this time not the directing energy, but the conscious Observer, the Soul, whether cosmic, solar or human.
3. *The Eye that Knows.* This is the disciple who, from stage to stage, reacts increasingly to the direction of the spiritual will and to the growth of sensitive response, and in both his brain and his mind consciousness in the three worlds *knows.* That knowledge is limited in the neophyte, deepening in the disciple and profound in the Master, but it is all related to vision.
4. At the same time this formula tells us that there are four eyes:
    a. "One made of fire" . . . the eye of God.
    b. "One fluid as the sea" . . . the eye of vision.
    c. "And two which look from here to there, the eye that knows." These are the eye of the disciple and the eye of the personality. There is a clue to this in a statement in *The Secret Doctrine* that the right eye

is the eye of buddhi and the left eye the eye of manas —these are the eyes of the high grade integrated personality, en rapport with the soul.

d. "Fire, water and the earth all need the vital air. The air is life." The clue again to this is to be found in *The Secret Doctrine,* I.80, where we find the words "Matter is the Vehicle for the manifestation of Soul on this plane of existence, and Soul is the Vehicle on a higher plane for the manifestation of Spirit and these three are a Trinity, synthesised by Life, which pervades them all."

You can see, therefore, upon careful reflection how simple this matter is, exoterically considered, and how the key to understanding lies in conscious identification with all three, both sequentially through growth and simultaneously through initiation. I have here given you an occult hint.

Secondly, I would have you note how this formula refers to the antahkarana:

1. "A line of fire between two blazing points"—the monad and the soul.

2. "A line, emerging from the earth and ending in the ocean"—referring to the sutratma which, when the antahkarana is completed, blends all types of consciousness, spirit and matter, into one living whole, the ultimate Reality.

These are some of the more obvious significances; deeper ones will emerge when these are realities and not speculative theories in your life. It will be apparent to you consequently the need for definite work upon the instructions given you upon the antahkarana. In connection with the above, I would call your attention to some words I wrote in my last instruction to you in reference to Formula Two. I there said that alignment "will be our next consideration when Formula One has brought about certain changes in consciousness. I shall not consider these formulas at present. I will only point out their major implications which will be seldom what you think, conditioned as you are by the terms and the interpretations of the lower concrete mind."

Part III

In past instructions we have seen that teaching upon the subject of initiation is given by me (as by all the Masters) in three ways:

1. By *Hints*. These—if seen and followed—will evoke the intuition. Initiation is never taken unless the intuition is becoming active. Spiritual instinct, the lowest aspect of the intuition, indicates readiness for the first initiation; an illumined mind and spiritual intelligence are the definite sign that a man can take the second initiation, whilst spiritual perception or intuitive instinct signifies preparedness for the Transfiguration, the third initiation.

2. By the use of certain great *Formulas* (one of which has already been given to you) certain definite revelations become possible. These formulas are six in number; they contain the six prerequisites for initiation, and they are sometimes in the form of words and sometimes in the form of symbols. These serve to develop the "initiate hearing" and the "initiate sight." They deal with the six relationships:

Formula One . . .Deals with integration into an Ashram and is concerned with the revelation of group *feeling*. It is related to the astral nature.

Formula Two . . .Deals with alignment. It concerns the revelation of the group antahkarana and is related to the mind nature, in which the antahkarana is anchored.

Formula Three . .Deals with certain changes in the soul nature. It is concerned with the relation of time and space, and is therefore related to the Eternal Now.

Formula Four . . .Deals with the Life aspect. It is concerned with the revelation of the nature of life, and is therefore related to the circulation and interplay of energy.

Formula Five ...Deals with the Will aspect. It is con-
cerned with the revelation of divine
Purpose, and is therefore related to
Shamballa.

Formula Six ....Deals with the nature of death. It is
concerned with the revelation of the
constructive work of the Destroyer aspect. It is therefore related to the passing Piscean Age and with all processes
of "abstraction."

These Formulas have seven interpretations; only three of
them are, however, possible of discovery by the disciple in
training at this particular time, because only the light
from the Spiritual Triad can convey this type of revelation and interpretation.

3. Through the presentation of *Points of Revelation:*

a. The present vision must become the past experience.
Its light of revelation will fade out as the experience
becomes a habit, and therefore falls below the
threshold of consciousness.

b. A new and totally different recognition must assume
control; this will express the initiate-understanding.

c. These points of revelation appear when the disciple
realises that initiation is not a process of soul-personality fusion but of Monad-personality integration.

d. These points of revelation assume three stages of
recognition:

The stage of Penetration.
The stage of Polarisation.
The stage of Precipitation.

The approach of the disciple to the entire subject of
initiation differs today from that of earlier times—even so
short a time ago as fifty years. It is essential that you grasp
the fact that his approach is now mental, and not as heretofore, devotional and emotional and aspirational. It has hitherto been kama-manasic, which connotes a blend of lofty
aspiration, of lower mind attention and focussing, and of
attention to the purely physical disciplines. Today, the true

disciple who is ready for this great step is in control of his emotional apparatus; his lower mind is keenly alert and focussed, and his higher mind is definitely en rapport with the lower, via the antahkarana. Perhaps clarity of perception will come to you if you realise that the conditional demands of the Initiator (until the period of the year 1400 A.D.) were for conscious soul contact; today, it is for a measure of established relation to the Spiritual Triad, via the antahkarana. This is a very different matter; soul contact is necessarily present, but is not deemed to give all that the initiate of the New Age must have. Love is of course needed; wisdom must be present, but the sense of universality is also required and indicates, when present, a measure of monadic inflow. This inflow comes naturally via the antahkarana or across the "rainbow bridge." Hence, you will see the reason for the emphasis which I have lately been giving to the building of this bridge. A great change in the human consciousness made it possible—in the year 1425 A.D.—to inaugurate changes in the requirements for initiation and definitely to lift the standard. Five hundred years have gone by since then, and the purpose of these changes in discipline and training have proved well warranted. In spite of all signs to the contrary, in spite of the world war with its attendant horrors and in spite of the apparent unawakened attitude of the masses, a very real measure of monadic energy is present. Humanity will increasingly demonstrate this as the insistent demand for unity and the growth of internationalism will demonstrate. The objectives, goals, theories, aims and determinations of the bulk of mankind already testify to this.

These expressions of the evolutionary development of humanity are related to the first manifesting qualities of the Will aspect. When I say this I give you a hint, reminding you that the candidate for initiation grows by the recognition and the interpretation of hints, and by extracting from a hint its true significance. The will is not, as so many believe, a forceful expression of intention; it is not a fixed determination to do thus and so or to make certain things to be. It is fundamentally an expression of the Law of Sacrifice; under this law, the unit recognises responsibility, identifies itself with

the whole, and learns the esoteric significance of the words:
"Having nothing (sacrifice) and yet possessing all things (universality)." I would ask you to reflect upon these words of
the great initiate, St. Paul. The full expression of these highest spiritual qualities (from the angle of modern man) comes
after the fourth initiation, that of the Great Renunciation.
Everything is then relinquished in order that everything may
be held in trust and used for the good of all; the will-to-good
then dominates. Hence the necessity for the scientific construction of the rainbow bridge; hence the emphasis upon
the Monad, the Father aspect which can now be revealed and
known, because the work of aeons is culminating in a general
soul contact, where humanity as a whole is concerned. This is
testified to by the fact that so very many thousands have (as
I have several times told you) taken the first initiation. The
Christ Child is present in truth, and the human heart and
mind are becoming aware of that fact; the goal for thousands
everywhere is the demonstration of the Christ spirit, and the
exemplification of a life conditioned by love and modelled
upon that of Christ or Shri Krishna, His earlier incarnation.

This makes possible, therefore, the next great human
unfoldment which grows out of the Christ consciousness and
"brings to light" (I know no other way in which to express
this concept) the will of God, and points also to the basic
distinction between goodwill and the will-to-good. Again I
would ask you to reflect upon this distinction, for it connotes
the difference between a life ruled and conditioned by the
soul and one which is ruled and conditioned by the Spiritual
Triad. This distinction is very real, for one quality grows out
of love, and the other out of the recognition of the universality of life; one is an expression of the Christ consciousness
and life, and the other is a responsiveness to monadic inflow,
and yet the two are one. More anent this will be indicated
as you study the teaching upon the antahkarana.

One of the tasks which I have undertaken is to awaken
the aspirants and the disciples of the world to the new possibilities and to the new incoming potencies which can become
available for use, if they will pass on to a fuller grasp of the
developments since 1425 A.D. Much that I am giving and

shall in the future give anent initiation, its methods, processes and application will appear entirely new. The New Age will bring in eventually a civilisation and a culture which will be utterly different to anything hitherto known. I would remind you here that all civilisations and cultures are externalisations — modified, qualified and adapted to racial and national needs—of the potent, vibrating and planned activity of the world initiates and disciples who constitute the Hierarchy of the time. Their plans, Their thinking and Their living potency pour out ceaselessly and affect the consciousness of Their disciples; these latter step down the inflowing energies so that the thinkers and idealists can grasp these new emerging truths more accurately. Eventually the truths thus grasped change the consciousness of humanity as a whole and raise it—if you like that phrase; thus modes of daily living, civilised methods of conduct and cultural developments eventuate. All this is traceable to the group of initiates upon the inner side who thus serve their fellowmen and carry forward, consciously and with intent, the Law of Evolution. Whilst doing this, They Themselves are preparing to tread the "Way of the Higher Evolution." What that Way is I cannot tell you, for you would be unable to grasp its meaning; it is related to the spiritual condition and purpose of the Monad whose goal is *not* expansion of consciousness, but of that which such expansions of consciousness will reveal—a very different matter and one which is as yet entirely meaningless to anyone who has not taken the third initiation. Forget not, the Christ and His great Brothers, and all of an even higher initiate-rank than They possess, have a definite goal, but it is one which will only define itself clearly in the third solar system, the system in which the Will of God is the dominant idea, as the Love of God conditions this system in which we now function. But this is not consciousness or awareness; it is a stage of Being which is connected with the Law of Sacrifice—the law which governs those states of being which grow out of the establishment of right human relations.

Purpose can only be revealed and understood when such right relations are the firmly fixed habits of all "points of divine expression." You can see, therefore, why it is not possible for those in process of grasping the need for right human relations to understand more than that a great possibility lies ahead. Of the nature of this possibility only the higher ranks of initiates are aware, and towards it they strive.

THE FORMULAS

We now come to the second of the great Formulas which give the initiate the key to the next stage of his work. These curious and ancient sets of phrases or symbols are endowed with power, owing to the potency of the minds which have reflected upon them, which have constructed thoughtforms anent them, and which have used them as modes or methods of focussing triadal light upon the personality. I would call your attention to the form of words just used. These formulas do not release the light of the soul into the attentive waiting mind. They release the light of electric fire (and therefore not solar fire) into the integrated personality, so that the entire man—now become the oriented mechanism of the Monad—is flooded with this higher form of energy—an aspect of the energy of will and related to the carrying forward of divine purpose. You can appreciate, consequently, how relatively impossible it is for any of you to do more than register the more obvious significances of these formulas and then await the time when your inner growth warrants a fresh approach to their interpretation.

This formula is seen by the disciple inscribed upon the plates of the unknown metal, described by me on page 249. It is formed of a series of lines which meet at a circle within a square, such as that depicted below:

 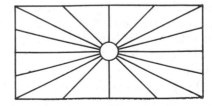

Curiously enough, it is this ancient symbol, with its indicated reference to the emotional nature, and therefore to the
Atlantean consciousness, which points to a basis for progress,
which is the subtle force behind the "flags of all nations."
Flags are symbols of the devotion of a people to their national soil and to their national spiritual objectives. They
have of course been prostituted to signify national separativeness and selfishness and national patriotism, but behind
the flag is a point of power which is the point of inspiration
to the soul of the people. Not yet, equally of course, is the
"point moving forward into the circle of the people's life";
as yet, you have only the square of the personality reactions
of the people and the lines of their evolutionary approach
to a deeper consciousness; this developing consciousness we
call the "soul of the people." Some day, the point will take
its place in the centre of the square and all the lines will converge upon that point; we shall then have a nation, galvan-
ised into activity by interior spiritual energy, and the lines
which have hitherto converged inwards towards the centre
will become channels or pathways along which spiritual
energy will flow into every phase of a nation's civilisation and
culture; the nation will then be linked up—through the
point at the centre—with the source of divine inspiration,
which is one for all types, all nations and all races in time
and space.

I have used the exoteric symbol of the flag to convey to
you a hint as to the esoteric meaning of this very simple but
most potent form. Four words, or rather phrases, are found
written, deep in the metal, around each side of the square:

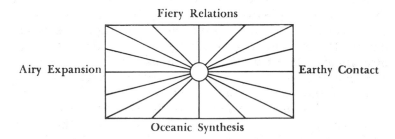

Fiery Relations

Airy Expansion

Earthy Contact

Oceanic Synthesis

These words convey the highly inadequate and even unsuitable translation of certain phrases in the ancient Sensa which are intended to convey the essential union, the related synthesis and the cooperative understanding which will some day distinguish a humanity, composed of many aspects which are nevertheless expressions of the One Life. They are, however, related to or expressions of monadic groupings or universal recognitions, and not of soul consciousness. My difficulty in explaining the higher meaning of the external simplicity of these phrases is great; you can only arrive at them yourself as you ponder the only three interpretations possible to you at this time: the individual application of the symbol, its national application, and its human application, remembering always that the clue to comprehension lies in the recognition of a "higher Way," of the existence of the "higher evolution," of the light which is distinctive of Shamballa, and of the use of the antahkarana, as it by-passes (if I may use such a term) the soul and so carries the human, yet spiritualised consciousness into the realms of hierarchical experience in relation to Shamballa.

POINTS OF REVELATION

This almost brings us automatically to the third aspect of preparation for initiation which I called in an earlier instruction the "presentation of points of revelation." These formulas, when rightly studied and eventually somewhat apprehended, at least intellectually, carry the disciple to the point where that which is new, hitherto unrealised and for which no words exist, is suddenly contacted. St. Paul had reached such a point when he referred to "the third heaven as it veiled the seventh" (which was the original wording, deleted by the recipients of his message at that time as utterly meaningless). Eye has not seen nor has ear heard the inexpressible revelation which comes to the initiate who can penetrate into certain high places where the nature of the divine Will suddenly assumes a different and amazing significance, where the purposes being worked out in the Council Chamber of Shamballa are visioned—not in detail but as a suddenly contacted inspiration; then for the first time the initiate becomes consciously receptive to the energy pouring into the Hierarchy from the Great White Lodge on Sirius.

It is at this point of revelation and in relation to this symbol that the initiate eventually stands. Then the "many lines of force within the square become the seven paths of light which claim His choice, leading Him on to the seven-fold Path of initiate evolution." This is the Way of the Higher Evolution of which man knows nothing. The words refer to the seven paths which the Master has to consider and from which He has to choose His future Way. Then the symbol takes on the following form:

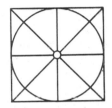

"All paths meet at the centre. The many become the seven and the eight. From point to point the lines converge. They stretch from point to point. The outer square, the circle of the One and the point of unity are seen as one, and the Master passes on His way."

He has *penetrated* to the centre by passing along the antahkarana which He has Himself constructed. There He *polarises* Himself and takes His stand, and from thence—at the centre of the circle and within the square of service—He *precipitates* the energies and forces which that service demands. From these few hints you can grasp the nature of this symbol and the quality of its meaning, plus the potency of the force which (through its correct apprehension) can carry the initiate-disciple from "the unreal to the Real."

The first formula was basically concerned with the monadic significance of the words "from darkness to Light," leading to vision and illumined purpose; the second formula gives the higher significance to the words "from the unreal to the Real," whilst the third we shall find expresses the true meaning of the words "from death to Immortality." Thus this prayer of the ancient past becomes the present effort of the distant future. Can you understand this statement, brother of mine? Into that light, that reality and that life the initiate penetrates. In that light of reality and life, he polarises himself, and from that point of universal life, reality and light he works.

PART IV

As you together study this subject of initiation, I would ask you to keep an open mind. I have told you that changes are imminent in the training of the initiates of the future, and that the techniques of developing a disciple's consciousness will be different to those used in the past. They will not be the same as those hitherto employed in the East. These have motivated the teaching along this line which has gone out in the West. This does not mean that the earlier methods were not correct and right. It means that the intelligent grasp of the disciple and the initiate is now so advanced (relatively speaking) that the old methods would no more apply than do the simple sums in arithmetic, set in grammar school, aid the progress of the college graduate. They were necessary in the early stages; the power or the ability to divide, subtract, multiply and add were conferred, but it is *the power* and *the ability* which are now used, and not the exercises.

ON HINTS

The hints a Master earlier gave were concerned largely with the building or changing of character and with the awakening of the chela. These no longer constitute hints to the modern disciple; he knows enough by himself to work on his own character, and he has penetrated to the fringe of the inner world by his own effort and on his own power. Such is the rule for the majority of aspirants today. The hints such as I will give you are superficially easy to understand and have an apparently obvious meaning; but they are concerned with service and with human and planetary affairs, and are capable of several interpretations—according to the point of unfoldment and the ray type.

In my last instruction I gave you three hints, and it might be useful if we briefly considered them. I will indicate to you the line along which light might come to you, as a group, at your particular point of development.

The first hint dealt with the changes wrought by the work done in the Ashrams which are enfolded in the one great Ashram of the Hierarchy. I said that the results of this would be that a closer relationship would be established with Sanat Kumara and His Council Chamber. This will be the result of the work done by the disciples of the world—in or out of incarnation. I wonder how many of you pondered on the significance of the statement that the changes were brought about by the activity of the disciples; by this I mean not the senior initiates, but what you mean when you speak of a disciple. You might naturally have assumed that the needed changes would be instituted by the Masters, or by the Christ, or even by Sanat Kumara. But it is not so. Why is this? What idea lies behind my flat statement? The disciples of the world are the intermediaries between the Hierarchy and Humanity. They are the product of *immediate* human endeavour; they set the pace for human unfoldment; they are therefore closely en rapport with the consciousness of the race of men. It is the quality of the new disciples, the rapidity with which men find their way into the ranks of the disciples, and the demand which the working disciples in the world make on behalf of humanity (which they *know*) that brings about the needed changes. The Masters are trained in the art of recognition, which is the consummation of the practice of observation; They stand ever ready to make the needed changes in the techniques or curriculum whenever human nature outgrows the old presentations of the ever-needed truths. The need is indicated to Them by Their disciples, and They then initiate the required changes. When these occur at a time of crisis and are far-reaching in effect and are determining of conditions for several thousand years to come, then the entire Hierarchy meets in conclave. Upon the basis of the light in this hint, you can for yourselves infer much.

The second hint I gave indicated that mankind had evolved so well that today the goals and theories, the aims and determinations now expressed in human thinking and writing showed that the will aspect of divinity, in its first embryonic manifestation, was beginning to make its presence felt. Have you followed this hint? Have you realised that the uprisings of the masses and their determination to overcome handicaps and all hindrances to a better world state are indicative of this? Do you grasp the fact that the revolutions of the past two hundred years are signs of the striving of the spirit aspect? That spirit is life and will; the world today is showing signs of new life. Think this out in its modern and immediate implications and see the way that the world is going under the inspiration of the spiritual Will.

The third hint I gave you was intended to suggest that it was the duty and the responsibility of the disciple, working under the inspiration of the Ashram, to "modify, qualify and adapt" the proposed plan of Shamballa (for which the Ashrams are responsible) in connection with the coming civilisation and culture. There is an "art of spiritual compromise" which must be learnt and which it is difficult to master, because it negates fanaticism, requires a trained and intelligent understanding of applied measures and truth, and also negates evasion of responsibility; it involves also a comprehension of the time equation, of differing points in evolution, plus experience in the process of discarding the outgrown and unnecessary—no matter how good it may appear to be.

In these three hints lie much scope for individual education and expansion of consciousness, and it is in the right use of these hints that the disciple learns to serve with adequacy and precision and to render satisfactory service to the Hierarchy. I shall ever indicate to you when I give you a hint, and upon these hints I would ask you to concentrate. I shall not always elaborate as I have done today, for you must grow by solving your own problems.

One of the difficulties which is associated with inaugurating a new and more advanced attitude towards initiation is the offsetting of the idea that the initiate always *knows* all there is to know. You need to remember that knowledge is associated with the *factual* world; it concerns the accumulated information of the ages; it is closely connected with memory and its subjective counterpart—recovery of past knowledge. This means regaining again, consciously, all that the Ego has stored up as the result of many incarnations and many different experiences; it is related to the "knowledge petals" in the egoic lotus and to the concrete lower mind. Knowledge is that which brings about an effective working relation between this outer tier of petals, the concrete mind and the brain. It embodies the "intelligence equipment" of a soul in incarnation during any one life, dealing largely with the ephemeral, the transitory and the passing. The factor which is enduring in knowledge is simply its power to relate the past and the present, and thus produce effective, phenomenal living today.

Wisdom is the hallmark of the initiate, and this he possesses even if his practical knowledge of mundane details— historical, geographical, economic, and cultural—may leave much to be desired. The disciples within a Master's Ashram can provide Him with what knowledge He may require, for they are drawn from different cultures and civilisations and among them can summarise the sumtotal of human knowledge at any one given time. This must not be forgotten. A Master of the Wisdom always knows where to go for knowledge. Knowledge and intelligence or mental polarisation must not be confounded in your minds. I might add to the above that knowledge deals with the ascertained and the effectual on the physical plane and in the three worlds; wisdom deals with inherent capacities and possibilities of spiritual expression. Knowledge can be expressed in concepts and precepts; wisdom is revealed through ideas against which (very frequently) much mundane knowledge powerfully militates. The concrete mind often inhibits, as you well know, the free flow of ideas intuitively impulsed; it is with this free flow of the new ideas that the initiate is basically concerned, because it is ideas, their right application and interpretation, which determine the future of humanity and of the planetary life.

The first thing, therefore, that the disciple in preparation for initiation has to learn is the nature of ideas and their distinction from contacted thoughtforms—to express it simply, and therefore, from the complexity of the subject, inadequately. The primary task of the Master is to aid the disciple to develop the intuition, and at the same time, keep the mental perception in an active and wholesome state. This is done, first of all, by enabling him to arrive at a right relation and correct evaluation between the abstract and the concrete realms of thought—those higher and lower aspects of the mind which are to the soul what the lower mind and the brain are to the personality. Think this out. A true recognition of this distinction produces a new focussing of the life force within the soul which will, in the earlier stages of discipleship, work through the abstract mind and the concrete mind. But the abstractions with which the disciple in training is then dealing are not in the nature of intuitions, and here is a point where confusion oft arises. They are merely the broad, general and universal perceptions and world inclusions which the gradually developing intelligence of mankind has registered and recognised and which the foremost thinkers of the race grasp with facility, but which seem so amazing to the neophyte. They appear to him of such magnitude and importance (as objects of his enhanced vision) that he confounds them with ideas and their intuitive perception. He has not learned to discriminate between abstract thoughts and intuitive ideas. Here lies the crux of his problem.

Ideas are other than this, as far as the initiate is concerned; they deal primarily with that which will eventually be, and are those formative new spiritual and creative impulses which will supersede the old and build the "new house" in which humanity will live; cycle after cycle and civilisation after civilisation, the fresh stream of inflowing ideas have conditioned the dwelling places of man and his mode of life and expression; through the medium of these ever-living and ever-appearing ideas, humanity passes on to something better and greater and more appropriate to the life of the slowly manifesting divinity.

Ideas, when intuitively contacted by the disciple or initiate, via the antahkarana, must be brought consciously down to abstract levels of thinking where (expressing it symbolically) they form the blueprints, prior to the institution of the creative process which will give them phenomenal existence and being. I would have you, therefore, remember the three factors:

1. The Intuition . . . . which contacts and reveals new ideas.
2. The Abstract World . . in which they are given form and substance and which is to the thoughtform eventually created what the etheric body is to the dense physical vehicle.
3. Concrete Thought . . . . producing the concretising of the thoughtform and thus making the idea available to mankind.

Here, in this simple summation, is expressed for you the process which the disciple will be able to follow when he is initiate; as each initiation is taken, the scope of the idea steadily increases, and its potency also, so that it might be said that the initiate—as he progresses upon the Path of Initiation—works first with the idea, then with ideas, then with the hierarchical Plan in a wide and general sense, and finally reaches the point where he comes under the influence of the purpose of Sanat Kumara. Then the will of the Lord of the World will stand revealed to him.

The work of the initiate is carried forward within the ring-pass-not of the Universal Mind; this is only a phrase expressive of the range of thought, planning and purpose which is that of a planetary or solar Logos. *The quality* of the approach which the initiate brings to the work is drawn, as pure energy, from the heart centre of the planetary Logos; it is pure love with its inevitable corollaries, wisdom and understanding. These give him insight into the plan. *The power* which he can bring to the task is drawn from his comprehension of the purpose of the planetary Logos and this expansive and all-inclusive work is entered into in graded sequences and carried forward under the influence of the initiate's expanding awareness and his growing sensitivity to impression.

I am seeking here to divorce your minds from the *idée fixe* that the initiate works because he knows. I would reverse the statement and say he knows because he works. There is no point of attainment at which the Initiator says to the initiate: Now you know, and therefore you can work. Rather it is: Now you serve and work, and in so doing you are embarked upon a new and difficult voyage of discovery; you will discover reality progressively and arrive at whole areas of expression, because serve. Resulting from this service, certain powers and energies will manifest, and your ability to use them will indicate to you, to your fellow initiates and to the world that you are a worker, fully conscious upon the inner side of life.

The initiate works from his place upon that inner side. During the early stages of the initiatory process he works in the *world of meaning*. After the third initiation he works consciously in the *world of causes*, until such time as he is advanced enough to work in the *world of being*. The aspirant is endeavouring to grasp the purpose of the world of meaning and to apply the knowledge gained to his daily life with understanding. The disciple is endeavouring to comprehend the significance of the world of causes and to relate cause and effect in a practical manner. The initiate of higher degree utilises the potencies of these three worlds of meaning, cause and being to implement the purpose of Sanat Kumara.

These differences are not hard and fast, with clear lines of demarcation; life is fluid and moving and the points of attainment are myriad in number and progressing forward all the time, but the general picture will serve to carry your thoughts away from the "trappings of initiation," from the colouring and the unimportant, so-called facts (actual and imagined) which have been so much emphasised by the occult groups and leaders and which have been held out as inducements to would-be disciples. I would have this group which I am training forget the details about initiation as presented so oft by the mystery monger and the emotional person, and concentrate upon the far more factual realities of meaning, cause and being. The old and outworn presentations were the product of the concrete mind, and are therefore crystallising in their effects and distorting in their results; they are also evocative of spiritual selfishness and isolation, as well as of astral curiosity. The new approach which I seek to indicate makes its appeal to the abstract mind and to the soul, whose values are sound, and eventually to the intuition; it is not so colourful an appeal as far as the personality is concerned, but it will produce more creative results and lead the neophyte along a safer road, with fewer disappointments and failures.

THE FORMULAS

The idea of meaning, cause and being underlies the symbology or the significance of the formula with which we are concerned in this instruction. I have pointed out to you before the difficulty of putting these ancient symbols or symbolic writings into such form that they can convey meaning through language. This difficulty is wellnigh insurmountable in connection with this third formula. The reason for this is that this formula has been preserved as *sounds* or (if I may use so ambiguous a phrase) as *trumpeted words*. It has not been committed to inscription as have the two previous symbolic formulas which you have already received. All that I can do is to give you a meaning (as far as I myself can understand and you can grasp) of these great sounds or chords, massed together and interspersed with certain very ancient phrases. You know yourselves how difficult it is to express the significance of the sound O M. This is a still more difficult task; little human thinking has been applied as yet to this Formula but much has been given to the Sacred Word. Until some thought has been applied to what I shall now attempt to give you, it is no easy matter to find the words to express the underlying idea—the idea you can contact at your present point of development.

This third formula concerns Time and the consciousness of the spiritual man who is unaware of separation, of divisions in time and space or of the spell of the Great Illusion. It deals with the fact of immortality and with the unshatterable continuity of consciousness and life. It is this formula which—at the third initiation—produces the transfiguration which comes when the Eternal Now is realised and when the continuity of awareness and of identity is seen as an aspect of Being. This formula has been called by one of the Masters "the seed of all philosophies," and in that phrase you may find light on the subject—provided you know what philosophy is!

To the initiate who uses this formula, creating the necessary sounds and enunciating the ancient words in due place (and these I may not give you), the following six thoughts are emphasised in his consciousness; these six thoughts will give you the intent of the formula as clearly as is possible. It is not possible to convey to you the true beauty of the concepts, but if you will have in mind the thought of meaning as light on life, of cause as the breath of experience, and of Being as the initiator of all that is, then some vision may come, some dream arise in your consciousness, and some power of accomplishment pour in. The Masters use this formula when faced with death in some form or another (and these words must be used literally). I refer not to death as it may affect Them, but to death as it affects God's created universe, producing release or finality, or opening the door to new life and closing the door on a cycle of manifestation, a civilisation, or a race or nation.

Here, therefore, are the six conditioning thoughts which the initiate holds in his consciousness *when using the formula*—a formula which is older than the Stanzas of Dzyan:

1. God *IS*. The Lord for aye stands firm. Being exists alone. Naught else is.
2. Time *IS*. Being descends to manifest. Creation is.

Time then and form agree. Being and time do not agree.

3. Unity *IS*. The One between comes forth and knows both time and God. But time destroys that middle One and only Being *IS*.

4. Space *IS*. Time and space reverberate and veil the One who stands behind. Pure Being *IS*—unknown and un-afraid, untouched, for aye unchanged.

5. God *IS*. Time, space, the middle One (with form and process) go, and yet for aye remain. Pure reason then suffices.

6. Being cries forth and says: . . . (untranslatable). Death crumbles all. Existence disappears, yet all for aye remains—untouched, immutably the same. God *IS*.

Each phrase out of the six has its own symbol at the close of each unit of thought, if I may call it that. These I may not give you or the chords upon which the phrases go forth. I have tried to indicate one of the meanings of the formula, but have not given a translation or a paraphrase. Bear this in mind and as you ponder these six sentences, try to give them an interpretation which will come to you from the *world of meaning*, producing a practical application, from the *world of causes*, producing an enlightened understanding, and (if you are far enough along) from the *world of being*, produc-ing inclusiveness. These formulas have naught to do with personalities or with souls in deep incarnation, identified with form in the three worlds; they concern world move-ment, great and universal developments, and human prog-ress (as a whole) towards the divine. You cannot yet think in those terms, but you can at least attempt to do so and grow thereby.

POINTS OF REVELATION

In the earlier part of your last instruction, I pointed out two most necessary requirements which the disciple in train-ing for initiation must grasp. As they are closely connected with this third point (referring to the revelations which the initiate can expect), I would like to touch upon them here. The first statement I made was to the effect that the will is fundamentally an expression of the Law of Sacrifice; the second was an attempt to emphasise the necessity for grasping and accepting two initial premises:

> First, that energy follows thought.
> Second, that the eye, opened by thought, directs that energy.

Why, I would ask you, is the will an aspect or an expression of the Law of Sacrifice? Because the will, as considered and understood by the initiate, is essentially that monadic essence, qualified by "fixed determination," which is identified with the Will or Purpose of the planetary Logos. It is the highest divine aspect which the initiate finally manifests, prior to entering upon the Way of the Higher Evolution. In this connection it is useful to remember that one of the appellations of Sanat Kumara is that of "the Great Sacrifice," and also to attempt to recognise some of the factors which have earned Him that name. These might be stated to be as follows, among others which you could not grasp if there was the language available to express them:

a. The basic sacrifice which the planetary Logos made was when He decided to incarnate or enter into the form of this planet. This was from pure choice, motivated by His "fixed determination" to function as the Saviour of the planet, in the same sense as the world Saviours come forth for the salvaging of humanity. Sanat Kumara is the prototype of all world saviours.

The initiate, on his tiny scale, must learn to function also as a saviour, and thus express the Law of Sacrifice through the medium of the developed, pure, reasoning will, and not simply from that of impulsive love and its activity. Here lies a basic distinction. Sacrifice must not be regarded as a "giving-up," but rather as a "taking-over." It has a mysterious relation to the Law of Karma, but on such high levels that only the advanced initiate can grasp it.

b. This sacrifice was imperative in the fullest sense, owing to the ability of the planetary Logos to identify Himself in full consciousness with the soul in all forms of life, latent within the planetary substance. When He "took over" this task, He, esoterically, had no choice, because the decision was inherent in His own nature. Because of this identification, He could not refuse the invocative appeal of the "seeds of life, striving within the substance of the form, and seeking added life and light," as the *Old Commentary* puts it. This striving and reaching forth evoked His response and the going out of His divinity, as expressed in will, activated by "fixed determination" to meet the deeply hidden divinity within these seeds. What He initiated then still persists and—under the Law of Sacrifice—He will complete the task, no matter how many aeons it may take.

The initiate, on his tiny scale, has to learn to work as a nourisher and saviour of the seeds of life within all forms with which he may achieve a measure of identification. His will must go out in response to the invocative demand of humanity, and his "fixed determination" must motivate his ensuing activity.

c. Under this Law of Sacrifice, Sanat Kumara (to express the idea in occult terms) "must turn His back upon the Central Spiritual Sun, and with the light of His Countenance irradiate the path of the prisoners of the planet." He sentences Himself to stay for as long as may be needed, "acting as the Sun and light of the planet until the Day be with us and the night of pralaya descends upon His finished task." Thus and only thus can the light of the Central Spiritual Sun begin to penetrate the dark places of the Earth; when this happens all "shadows disappear"—an occult reference to the all-embracing radiance of the Monad as it absorbs both its reflection, the soul, and its shadow, the personality.

The initiate, on his tiny scale, achieves a paralleling

expression of the Law of Sacrifice; he eventually turns his back upon the courts of Shamballa and upon the Way of the Higher Evolution as he retains his contact with the Earth and works as a Member of the Hierarchy for the extension of the will-to-good among men, and therefore among all the lesser evolutions.

d. Under the Law of Sacrifice, the Lord of the World remains ever behind the scenes, unknown and unrealised by all the "seeds" He came to save, until such time as they have reached the stage of flowering forth as perfect men and, in their turn, become the saviours of humanity. Then they know Him to exist. From the standpoint of the forms of life in the four kingdoms of nature, Sanat Kumara is non-existent. In developed humanity, prior to moving on to the Probationary Path, He is sensed and dimly sought under the vague word "God." Later, as the life which the "seeds" have manifested reaches the higher layers or brackets in the human hierarchy, there emerges in the consciousness of the disciple, the assurance that behind the phenomenal world is a world of "saving Lives" of which he may eventually form a part; he begins to sense that behind these Lives there stand great Beings of power, wisdom and love Who, in Their turn, are under the supremacy of Sanat Kumara, the Eternal Youth, the Creator, the Lord of the World.

The initiate, on his tiny scale, likewise has to learn to work behind the scenes, unknown and unrecognised and unacclaimed; he must sacrifice his identity in the identity of the Ashram and its workers, and later in the identity of his working disciples out in the world of daily life. He institutes the needed activities and brings about the required changes, but he receives no reward, save the reward of souls salvaged, lives rebuilt and humanity led onward upon the Path of Return.

These few thoughts upon the significance of sacrifice or upon the "taking over," through identification, of the task of salvage, of revitalising and of presenting opportunity, are important to all disciples, as a goal and a vision.

The second point made, based upon the occult platitude that "energy follows thought," should carry inspiring implications to the earnest disciple, if he truly considers the statements made and regards them of practical application.

Two things, I told you, are the result of thought, and though these may be mentally grasped by the intelligent disciple, they are very seldom understood. They are:

1. Thought generates energy commensurate with the potency of the thinking, and qualified by the theme of the thinking. You will see from this, therefore, some of the implications contained in the meditation I have assigned you. "As a man thinketh in his heart, so is he" is a statement of the Christ. From that demonstrating personal centre of thought, energy will stream down into the physical brain, via the etheric body. It will then condition the type of living, the expression and the influence of the man upon the physical plane.

2. As a result of focussed thinking "in the heart" the spiritual eye opens and becomes the directing agent, employed consciously by the initiate whilst doing his work under the Law of Sacrifice. What is meant here by the words, "in the heart"? The soul is the heart of the system of the spiritual man; it is the seat of the life and consciousness which animate the personality, and it is the motivating potency in every incarnation, according to the experience conditioning the expression of the spiritual man in any particular rebirth. In the early stages of experience, this "eye" remains closed; there is present no capacity for thought and no ability to think in the heart; i.e., from soul levels. As the intellect develops and the power to focus upon the mental plane grows, the fact of the soul's existence becomes known and the goal of attention changes. There follows the ability to focus in the soul-consciousness and so to fuse the soul and the mind that an at-one-ment takes place and a man can then begin to think "in his heart." Then also the "eye of the soul" opens and energy from soul levels, intelligently utilised, becomes directed from those levels and pours into what is now

ambiguously called "the third eye." Immediately the personality in the three worlds begins to express itself as the soul upon the physical plane, and will, purpose and love begin to control.

These two paragraphs are of importance to the disciple and warrant careful attention. As these developments take place, the spiritual will steadily grows into the directing agent, using the right eye as the distributing agent for the energy of love, animated with will. This is why the right eye has been called, in the esoteric teaching, "the eye of buddhi." This directing agent uses the left eye as the instrument for the distribution of the mental energy of the personality—now illumined and sublimated.

Having these thoughts in mind, I would call your attention to the entire theme of vision, which necessarily underlies our consideration of the points of revelation. It is simple to recognise that in the head of the developing aspirant there is a mechanism of great potency, capable of controlling the life of the personality. There is:

1. The third eye, *not* the pineal gland but its etheric correspondence. This is the responsive mechanism to the directing eye of the soul.
2. The right eye and the left eye, which take the incoming energy, *symbolically speaking,* and divide it into two streams which are the correspondence in etheric matter of buddhi-manas.
   a. Right eye . . . spiritual energy. Buddhi. Pure reason. Understanding.
   b. Left eye . . . mental energy. Manas. Thought substance.

It is the conscious use of these energies and the intelligent utilisation of this triple mechanism which is the goal of the initiate up to the third initiation. He learns consciously to direct force in the correct manner through the needed organ, doing so as the soul working in full consciousness on its own level, but so fully identified with the personality that the mechanism (now developed within the personality) can be used in the work of the Hierarchy.

Let me now expand the concept further, reminding you of the phrase so oft employed, "the All-seeing Eye." This refers to the power of the planetary Logos to see into all parts, aspects and phases (in time and space) of His planetary vehicle, which is His physical body and to identify Himself with all the reactions and sensitivities of His created world and to participate with full knowledge in all events and happenings. Through what medium does He, on His own high levels, do this? Through what mechanism does He thus "see"? What is His organ of vision? What is the nature of the sight whereby He contacts the seven planes of His manifested universe? What is the organ, employed by Him, which corresponds to the third eye in man? The answer is as follows: the Monad is to the planetary Logos what the third eye is to man; this will become clearer to you if you will bear in mind that our seven planes are only the seven subplanes of the *cosmic physical plane*. The monadic world—so-called— is His organ of vision; it is also His directing agent for the life and light which must be poured into the phenomenal world. In the same way, the Monad is to the personality in the three worlds, also the source of its life and light.

There are, therefore, three organs of revelation, as far as the spiritual man is concerned:

1. The human eye, giving "in-sight" into the phenomenal world, letting in the light, and bringing revelation of the environment.

2. The eye of the soul, bringing revelation of the nature of the interior worlds, of the kingdom of God and of the divine plan.

3. The centre within the One Life which we call by the unmeaning word "Monad," the spark within the one Flame. In the final stages of initiation, the Monad becomes the revealer of the purpose of God, of the will of the planetary Logos and of the door which opens on to the Way of the Higher Evolution. This Way leads a man *off* the cosmic physical plane on to the cosmic

astral plane, and therefore into the world of divine
sentiency, of which we can have no possible understanding, but for which the development of consciousness has given us the initial steps.

Man has learnt to use the physical eye and to find his way, by
its means, around and through his environment. The stage
in human evolution wherein he learnt first to "see" lies far
behind, but when man saw and could focus and direct his
course *by sight,* it marked a stupendous unfoldment and his
first real entrance upon the Path of Light. Ponder on this. It
has also interior repercussions and was indeed the result of
an invocative interplay between inner centres of power and
the groping creature in the phenomenal world.

Man is now learning to use the eye of the soul, and as
he does so he brings its correspondence in the head also into
functioning activity; this produces fusion and identification,
and brings the pineal gland into action. The major result,
however, is to enable the disciple to become aware, whilst
in the physical body, of a new range of contacts and perceptions. This marks a crisis in his unfoldment of as drastic and
important a nature as the attaining of physical sight and the
use of the physical eye was in the unfoldment of the curious
creature which antedated the most primitive animal man.
Things unknown can now be sensed, searched for and finally
seen; a new world of being stands apparent, which has always
been present though never before known; the life, nature,
quality and the phenomena of the kingdom of souls, or of the
Hierarchy, become as patent to his vision and as real as is the
world of the five physical senses.

Then later, upon the Path of Initiation, the initiate
develops his tiny correspondence to the planetary "All-seeing
Eye." He unfolds the powers of the Monad. These are related
to divine purpose and to the world in which Sanat Kumara
moves and which we call Shamballa. I have impressed upon
you elsewhere that the state of being of the Monad has
naught to do with what we call consciousness; in the same
way, there is naught in the world of Shamballa which is of
the same nature as the phenomenal world of man in the

three worlds, or even of the soul world. It is a world of pure energy, of light and of directed force; it can be seen as streams and centres of force, all forming a pattern of consummate beauty, all potently invocative of the world of the soul and of the world of phenomena; it therefore constitutes in a very real sense the world of causes and of initiation.

As man the human being, man the disciple, and man the initiate gradually move onward on the stream of life, revelation comes step by step, moving from one great point of focus to another until naught more remains to be revealed.

In all these spiritual points of crisis or of opportunity for vision, for fresh spiritual in-sight and for revelation (for that is what they are in reality), the thought of struggle is the first one to warrant attention. I used, in this connection, the words "stage of penetration"; the thought which this conveys to the initiate understanding signifies an extension of the struggle which the neophyte makes in order to achieve inner control, and then to use the mind as a searchlight so as to penetrate into new fields of awareness and of recognition. Forget not that recognition involves right interpretation and right relation to that which is seen and contacted. Into all revelation enters the concept of "whole vision" or a synthesis of perception, and then comes recognition of that which is visioned and perceived. It is the mind (the common sense, as it used to be called) which utilises the physical senses of perception, and through their united contribution gets a "whole vision" and a synthesis of perception of the phenomenal world, according to man's point of development, his mental capacity to recognise, rightly interpret and rightly relate that which has been conveyed to him by the activity of the five senses. This is what is meant when we use the phrase "the mind's eye," and this ability is the common possession of humanity in varying degrees of availability.

Later, man uses the "eye of the soul," as we have noted above; it reveals to him a world of subtler phenomena, the kingdom of God or the world of souls. Then the light of the intuition pours in, bringing the power to recognise and rightly interpret and relate.

As the disciple and the initiate progress from stage to

stage of revelation, it becomes increasingly difficult to make
clear not only what is revealed, but also the processes of
revelation, and the methods used to bring the stage of revelation about. The vast mass of mankind throughout the world
have no clear idea as to the function of the mind as an organ
of vision illumined by the soul; still fewer, only the disciples
and initiates, are able to glimpse the purpose of the spiritual
eye and its functioning in the light of the intuition. When
we come, therefore, to the great organ of universal revelation, the monadic principle, functioning through the medium of an extra-planetary light, we enter realms which are
indefinable and for which no terminology has been created,
and which only initiates above the third degree are able to
consider.

With the sequential stages of polarisation and precipitation I will not today deal; I am desirous that you grasp as far
as may be, the idea of penetration, of the struggle involved
and the instrument available in the struggle to see, to perceive and to register impression.

What I have given you at this time will provide much
ground for thought. Further instruction along this line
would be unprofitable until such time as the inner mechanism of progressive revelation is more clearly defined in your
consciousness and is at least theoretically understood and
hypothetically accepted. If you will think with clarity and
with spiritual brooding upon this subject during the coming
year, it may be possible for me greatly to enlarge upon the
matter in my next instruction.

PART V

I would like in this instruction, my brothers, to make
certain suggestions to you anent the approach to discipleship
that humanity is making and the approach to initiation
which disciples in every country and of all schools of thought
and of religious persuasion are today making. I have told
you in many places that the techniques for training disciples
are changing in order to conform to the rapid progress being
made in mass orientation, and that a new light upon the en-

tire theme of initiation is imminent. I would like, if possible, to be somewhat more explicit. You, at least, after these years of training by me, should be susceptible to some increased realisation along these lines.

Humanity—as has oft been said—is now the world disciple. Why is this? Primarily for two reasons:

1. Men are rapidly awakening mentally. The whole world is thinking, primarily along political lines and along lines of current ideologies. Even peoples long dormant are now convulsed by mental processes. This shift in human consciousness involves a rapid focussing of human intention on mental levels. This mental polarisation is essential to discipleship. It is as yet a general trend, but much progress has been made as a result of the tension of war.

2. Men are rapidly developing an understanding goodwill. The world is full of movements for relief and for the amelioration of human distress, and this from the point of small and large communities and also nationally and internationally. To this the Red Cross, UNRRA and many analogous and well-intentioned affiliations of men everywhere bear witness. This indicates not only a mental polarisation but responsiveness to the love nature of God; these together indicate a fusion and a sensitivity which is new in human history and which is most encouraging, testifying as it does to the success, at last, of the evolutionary process.

The time, therefore, when the Hierarchy had to deal almost entirely with the emotional devotee is past, and this has come about far more rapidly than had been anticipated. The task of the Masters before the eighteenth century was to take emotional aspirants and train them in the technique of mental polarisation, prior to permitting them to enter Their Ashrams. This was the best that could be expected, and in the last analysis was all that was required, because mentally polarised aspirants to accepted discipleship would have been of little use in the work of lifting mankind nearer to the light; the Ashrams exist primarily for that purpose. But the mentally focussed humanity of today cannot be reached by emotional workers alone. The mental approach is called for and a higher type of disciple is needed.

The training to be given aspirants (and this must be begun in our educational centres) will concern the dual use of the mind, the nature of energy, the indication of an evolutionary plan which includes more than the physical forms, and later of a definite and clear purpose for humanity as well as modes and methods of developing the subjective and subtle powers of the human being. This will involve a study of the constitution of man and the relation of its lower and higher threefold nature to the three aspects of divinity. You will note how increasingly, with all of you, I am emphasising man's essential duality and not his temporary triplicity. I would have you try to ascertain and understand my reasons. As this curriculum is firmly established it will revolutionise modern educational systems upon a planetary scale, and then man the reorienting aspirant, will become man the accepted disciple.

I wonder whether you have ever considered the widespread effect of all the reflective thinking, the aspirational prayers and the meditation work—untrained or as the result of training—done by people in their millions down the ages through the entire planet? Its quality is altering; its strength is increasing; its livingness is producing changes in the human organism. The tide of spiritual life is today so strong and striving that the next one hundred and fifty years will demonstrate the factual nature of the Kingdom of Souls or of God. This, as you can surely appreciate, will produce fundamental changes also in the immediate objectives before human progress, and in the Masters' plans, in the teaching given, and in the training presented.

This brings me to the objectives which are *now* before disciples in training for initiation. Instead of the past objectives—contact with the soul and entrance into an Ashram— the following might be listed, but must be understood esoterically and not literally:

1. A *sense of planetary relationships.* Instead of the emphasis

being laid upon the relation of the individual to his soul, to his Master and to the Ashram, his consciousness is consciously expanded (if I may use such an apparently redundant phrase) in order to bring about a realisation *upwards* into kingdoms hitherto unseen and unknown, *downwards* into kingdoms which we call subhuman, *outwards* into the human environment and into the human kingdom, and *inwards* (a meaningless word, my brother) toward divinity itself. This means towards synthesis, towards wholeness, towards the sense of the entire, towards totality. For all these four directions (of which north, south, east and west are symbols) there are specific techniques, but today I may only indicate direction.

2. A *sense of "intelligent supervision."* This must be esoterically understood. What does this mean? One of the most deeply spiritual qualities which would-be initiates must unfold is the constant recognition of a focussed control upon daily life, circumstance, the future and fate. This is as yet an embryonic sense or entirely new avenue of perception and relatively close to and an aspect of the will aspect of divinity. It makes man conscious of his destiny, develops in him predictive power and gives him initiate insight into purpose and its unfolding plan. It is a faculty which you would do well to consider and try to imagine as a step towards development.

3. The *sense of orientation to humanity.* I presume you will recognise the truth of what I say when I express the opinion that your individual or personal love of humanity and the focus of your attention upon human need is very largely theoretical. It is transitory and experimental in practice. Your intentions are good and fine but you have not yet the *habit* of correct orientation and much that you do is the result of imposed sacrifice and at a cost; it is not natural to you; it is still the result of hopeful endeavour; you are still bewildered over the problem of how to be oriented to the Hierarchy and your soul, and at the same time to be oriented to humanity and your fellowmen. But the time will come when you are personally so decentralised that automatically the sense of "others" is

far stronger in you than the sense of personality or of the lower self. Let your imagination run wild for a moment, picturing the condition of the world when the majority of human beings are occupied with the good of others and not with their own selfish goals. Such a play of imaginative thought is good and constructive and will aid in bringing out into manifestation that new world and that new type of humanity which the future will inevitably demonstrate. On this I shall not enlarge; the practice of goodwill will lay the foundation for this new type of sensitivity.

4. The *sense of registered impression*. With this new feeling out towards the unknown and towards that which requires a sensitive expansion of consciousness I shall not deal at this moment. It concerns the theme of training in telepathy; I shall deal with it as we consider that Science of Impression* which will eventually be the major objective of the educational systems which will be functioning at the close of the New Age, so rapidly approaching. Only now have those forces been permitted entrance into our planetary life which will present the new subjective environment which has ever been there though unrealised. The reason for this new sensitivity being the objective of hierarchical cultural training is that it is realised by the Hierarchy that man is now adequately intelligent to be trained in right interpretation.

5. The *evocation of the will*. This is, for disciples particularly, the new and most necessary development. As I oft have told you, the average aspirant confounds will with determination, with fixed intention, with self-will and one-pointed attention. He does not realise that the will is that divine aspect in man that puts him en rapport with and then controlled by divine purpose, intelligently understood in time and space and implemented by the soul as the expression of loving application. The mode par excellence by which the will can be developed is the cultivation of the recognition of the divine Plan down the ages. This produces a sense of synthesis and this sense of

* *Telepathy and the Etheric Vehicle*, Pages 41-57.

synthesis ties the man into the plan through recognition of:

    a. Its inevitability, therefore demanding cooperation.

    b. Its success, therefore evoking wise activity.

    c. Its immediate objective—to which all the past has led.

    d. Its rightness—to which the intuition testifies.

It is not easy for the disciple in training to associate the sense of synthesis and the use of the will together and to realise that a cultivation of this first ray perception is a potent mode by which the highest aspects of the spiritual will (as yet embryonic within him) can be unfolded. Elsewhere I deal in greater detail with the will, its nature and what it is.

6. The *sense of that which is imminent.* This concerns the "raincloud of knowable things." I would call your attention to the word *knowable.* It is not the recognition of that which is imminent in man, in nature, or latent in manifestation. Speculation along this line might be and frequently is of no true importance. It is what is spiritually imminent which concerns the true disciple, if I may be permitted this play on words. One of the first lessons in the esoteric field is the sense of timing, with which that which is imminent or impending is connected; the disciple has to awaken to that which is on the very verge of precipitation into human thinking, life and circumstance; he has to take those occult steps which will enable him to recognise not only that which is hovering over humanity on the point of revelation or of karmic usefulness (note the phrase), but also enable him to handle himself so correctly and wisely that he becomes a cooperator, step by step, in the process of aiding in this task of revelation. More light on this subject will come as we study the Science of Impression. The point, however, I seek to make here is that sensitivity to the overshadowing cloud presupposed the subjective existence of a power or divine faculty hitherto not consciously used by disciples but which can now be intelligently developed, producing more rapid vision and a more acute revelatory perception.

That power has always been present; it is an aspect of the force of evolution and has led man on from one point of revelation to another, from one power to another, one sense to another, and from point to point of understanding. It first of all produced the physical senses; it led man on to emotional expression and to mental development; it is the secret behind spiritual understanding, but *it has never yet* been consciously employed. It is to the mind what the mind, as the common-sense, has been to all the five senses. Think that out.

This raincloud is hovering, heavy with portent and knowledge, over a world today in process of reorganisation and regeneration. The Masters are seeking to hasten in Their disciples this recognition of that which is imminent, so that they can be the intelligent agents whereby the needed precipitations can be brought about. There is a definite technique for producing this peculiar form of cooperation, but it will not be possible to work with it or apply it for another twenty-five years.

Here I have very briefly outlined for you the new developments which are possible if the disciple is rightly focussed and oriented. These are within latent possibilities. If you will pause and consider, you will realise that the task of the Master in the past, as He sought to prepare the disciple for initiation, was largely concerned with awakening him to the need for occult obedience, for right orientation, for persistence, and for devotion to his objective. But all that lies far behind the true modern disciple. Today, the Master indicates to him the overshadowing cloud of knowable things; He assures him that he has within him undreamt of powers which will, when brought to the surface of consciousness, demonstrate to him his own essential adeptship and enable him to share in the great hierarchical task of illumining, precipitating, and lifting. Today the Master—having done the above—leaves the disciple to work through to knowledge and cooperative usefulness; He neither pushes him into premature action nor constantly supervises him; He surrounds him with the aura of His presence and the protection and stimulation of His Ashram; He gives him occasional hints, and as the disciple acts and works upon the hinted suggestions, the hint becomes a clear direction and a luminous area of enlightenment.

ON HINTS

I have been working with all of you in this manner for more than ten years now; I have sought to bring about a definite awakening to latent possibilities and to those capacities for cooperation which must be eventually realised by the disciple. I am *not* discouraged, because apart from my realisation of the inevitable limitations which encompass each of you individually, I am also aware that you have placed yourselves in my Ashram for training in the most difficult period in the entire history of humanity—a period in which the whole of humanity is passing through the reorientation required by the time cycle and through an entirely new adjustment to a higher rhythm and area of expression. This has greatly enhanced all your difficulties, and mine also, as I work with you. However, the next one hundred years will see great developments in my Ashram. It is, as I have told you, one of the newest of the Ashrams and is only now finding its own format, enunciating its own note, and taking on its own quality. This situation has also greatly increased your problem, for you are helping me to form something new.

Up to the present time, I have given you four hints which might be summarised as follows:

1. That the great changes being brought about in the Hierarchy, and in order to make the work of the New Age adequate and to establish a closer rapport with Shamballa, have been the result of the work done by the working disciples of the world. Why the working disciples, brother of mine, and not by the Masters? A hint ever evokes a question, and it is in the answering of these questions that the disciples learn and eventually become Masters.

2. That human planning and thinking, as the future is faced, are the first indications in the history of mankind of the emergence of the will aspect. Can you answer the question: Why is this indicated?

3. That disciples in all Ashrams have the task of "modifying, qualifying, and adapting the divine plan." Why has this to be so? This is a most significant and useful question. Why, brother of mine, is the plan not imposed? What are the distinctions between quality, modifications, and adaptations—for there is a distinction in each and every one of them.

4. That the initiate knows because he works. Christ gave the same hint to His disciples when He told them that if they wanted to know the doctrine they must carry out God's will. Do these words convey any true meaning to you?

You will note that all of these four hints or seed ideas (for much expanded thinking, leading to renewed activity) have to do with humanity and not with the individual man. This is a point of importance to bear in mind, for it again indicates the distinction between the training being given now and that which was given in the past. I, for instance, am not (in these group instructions) giving you individual hints as to your own lives. This I have done in the past, as have all Ashrams today, as they make their transition between the old and the new, emerging techniques; they have to employ compromise and adapt to that which is coming; the future will see, therefore, a gradual cessation of personality hints. In the future, the true method will be to develop in the disciple the sense of synthesis and of "place" in the One World, and thus decentralise him. The theme of *direction* underlies the system of instructing by means of hints. It is apparently a slow technique, but there is a point which esotericists would do well to remember. If information as to the nature of the microcosm and the macrocosm, as to divine Purpose and the spiritual Plan, as to occult events in time and space, and as to future or immediate possibilities were given out in plain terms (even if the needed language were available) there would be little understanding. I could, for instance, tell you much that would be as useful to you as the following statement might have been to unevolved prehistoric man: "There is naught in the world but energy. The Atom of atoms is only energy and God Himself is naught but energy." The phrases would have conveyed to their slow-moving brains absolutely nothing. Primitive man had not the mechanism whereby comprehension would have been possible. A key to the correct interpretation of a hint lies in its association with the idea of direction in time and space. And, my brother, in the above sentence I give you the hint which I have in mind for your consideration this year. The word "direction" is the key to the evolutionary process, to the concept of light, to the secret of Masonry, and to the motivating power behind manifestation. More I will not indicate, but I seek your intelligent assent to that word.

It will become increasingly apparent to you that the entire life of a disciple becomes one of reflective meditation. Meditation forms may at some point of unfoldment drop away, but the habit of meditation will become a permanent and considered habit and will know finally no termination; when that point is reached, the idea of direction will take on divine significance. Here is a second hint on the same theme. You will recollect that in my last Instruction the whole subject of meditation was summarised for you as follows:

1. A preliminary stage wherein the theme of meditation was recognised.
2. Receptivity in attitude, so that the possible and esoteric teaching may be recognised and absorbed.
3. The transmission of ideas in some form or another to the brain after they have been registered by the mind in the form of seed thoughts, hints or presented themes and concepts.
4. The deliberate focussing of thought upon these ideas.
5. As these ideas are considered and developed, they are subjected to analysis and take shape eventually as created thoughtforms.
6. They are then subjected to a process of unification through the conscious and constant use of a mantram.

If this outline for thinking is carefully considered, it will be apparent to you that it is suitable for all true thought processes, all mental moods, and all analysis and application of occult hints. I wanted you to realise the essential simplicity of all divine processes and to note the ultimate fact that such processes culminate in a spiritual identification, proving past all controversy that separateness is fundamentally nonexistent. This is true also of the formulas which we have been considering.

THE FORMULAS

As I told you in my last Instruction, the meaning and even the format of these formulas are so difficult to convey in words that I have hesitated several times in proceeding even with so brief an attempted elucidation on the subject. But even if I can convey but little of their significance, I can at least build in your minds the concept of these formulas. They are second ray presentations of soul ideas. We are told that God geometrises, when referring to the activity of the second aspect, and that a subtle geometrical form lies behind the exoteric manifestation. These forms convey to the occult student the symbolism of the world of meaning. Behind the mathematics and the geometrical designs, and behind the numerology which attempts (hitherto quite unsuccessfully) to convey the truth, but which in a mysterious manner conditions the creative work, are certain formulas which—as I have pointed out—express significance, intention, meaning. With three of the formulas we have spent a short time in consideration. Broadly speaking, these three condition the evolutionary process through the forms which are the result of the correct use of these formulas in such a way that a *directive is given*. I know not how else to express it. The three directives, therefore, already dealt with, embody and express the oldest invocative appeal in the world and (because of the age of this appeal) these three formulas have given a direction that naught can offset; the resultant conditions are inevitable:

Formula I ....Lead us from darkness to Light.
Formula II ....Lead us from the unreal to the Real.
Formula III.......Lead us from death to Immortality.

This brings us to a statement of the next formula and a consideration of its meaning:

Formula IV.......Lead us from chaos to Beauty.

This formula is presented in the form of a symbol—one which is in such constant movement that it is most difficult to describe or to make it live before you.

There lies before the investigator a square or oblong, composed of a kaleidoscopic mass of inchoate colours, moving, pulsating and in constant indescribable confusion. Superimposed upon this square is a radiant sun with a penumbra composed of the seven prismatic colours; these radiate from the sun in regular rhythmic bands and produce a marvellous blaze of colour. The background of the square appears to have its confusion of colours shown of a heavy, brilliant kind and quality; the scheme of beauty emerging (even if it appears as superimposed) is translucent and delicate and radiantly living in hue. The heavier background can be distinctly seen through the translucence. This formula differs according to the polarisation of the one who visions it and who studies it. If he is focussed in the personality, and is therefore conditioned by his personality ray, one type of energy will impinge upon his consciousness; if he is soul conscious and soul focussed, another type of energy will have its effect. Thus two different pictures will emerge. Both will be correct, but the interpreting agent will be different.

This formula, if carefully considered and studied for a number of years, will become a key form by means of which aspects of the creative process will come to the attention of the student, plus revelation as to some of the divine objectives which are wider and of greater and richer implication than has yet been realised. I would here remind you that these formulas are not symbols of what already *is*, but are indicatory key forms of what may or shall be—a very different matter and one which you should bear in mind. They are symbols of the future and not of the past; they are predictive and not consummating; they reveal what is on the way as the result of the divine thought and are not pictorial presentations of what already is.

Therefore, they are not easy to grasp and interpret, because it is only the activity of the intuition which will enable you to understand and move forward into the new impulsive causal area. Difficult though this task may be (and, my brother, is), it is of major importance to disciples in training for initiation, because it will steadily tend to facilitate their entry into the world of causes and their emergence from the world of effects. You can see also from this that this formula is related to the Law of Karma; in fact, in the ancient records from which these formulas are taken, Formula IV has the symbol of one of the four Lords of Karma at the four corners of this square or oblong design. This formula is sometimes called that of "the Sun upon the Square." I have no more to say anent this theme at this time or about this formula in this Instruction. All that I am giving you is intended to be suggestive and to develop in you the power to use the interpretive sense—one of the new senses as far as experience and experiment are concerned, but which is latent in every man.

POINTS OF REVELATION

Little as you may realise it, these words "Points of Revelation" summarise a most definite technique in the training of disciples for initiation. All life is intended to take the form of a progressive series of awakenings. Progress, movement, awakening, expansion, enlightenment, evolution, growth—these words are but a few of those applied to the effects, both within and without, of the creative process. What is this creative process but the working out into progressive demonstration of the divine intention as it assumes form? This intention is a fully comprehended scheme in the Universal Mind; we call it Purpose when considering the grasp by Shamballa of the synthesis of this comprehensive intention, and we call it the Plan when considering the work of the Hierarchy in bringing this Purpose as fully as possible into expression.

In our studies over the years and in the books which I have put before the public with the help of A.A.B. and of F.B. and of all of you who have cooperated with them, we have primarily considered the effect of this divine Intention, Purpose and Plan upon Humanity, and this because the Plan —emanating from the Hierarchy—has to be implemented by mankind. Hence the importance of their grasp and their understanding of the entire proposed programme. What, therefore, will be the quality of their reaction to what their developed understanding will reveal? What can they expect and what aspects or forms can the revelation be expected to take? Are they to look for a sudden blaze of light, or should they expect a gradual and progressive series of lesser lights? What is the relation of these revelations to the life of the occultist, and must he first of all register and accept what is conveyed to him as inexplicable but to be admitted, and to be viewed as incontrovertible though beyond comprehension? Or what?

Let me reiterate to you the well-known truth that no man is an initiate apart from understanding, that the life of the initiate is one of constant registration of new knowledge which must be transmuted into practical wisdom, of occult facts which must take intelligent place in the life-service of the initiate, and of new inclusions of areas of consciousness; these latter must become the normal field of experience and of expression; they then become the ground for further expansion. Every revelation has to be mastered from four angles:

1. The mental, occult, spiritual, hierarchical and triadal *facts* it embodies. Every revelation has its own format, for all our planes—so steadily being revealed—are the subplanes of the cosmic physical plane.
2. The meaning which the facts and the format veil and hide and for which the one who is being enlightened must search.

3. The effect which the revelation is intended to make in the daily life and service and the ashramic relationships of the disciple or initiate.

4. The germ, seed thought, key form and invocative potency of that which has been revealed. Every revelation has its place in a great series of revelations and enlightenments; the disciple has to find, within the form of the revelation, that which he must use in order to achieve the next destined point of attained revelation.

I have here given you, in a very brief form, one of the new techniques for disciples in the New Age and one of the modes of meditation whereby the processes of revelation can be hastened. Hitherto in the past, revelation has come unexpectedly, as it did to Saul of Tarsus in the Biblical narrative. In sincerity, the disciple struggles and works and serves; blindly he goes forward, and oft in much bewilderment he seeks knowledge and receives it at unexpected moments, and these frequently increase, at least temporarily, his bewilderment. But during the coming New Age, disciples will be taught how to work consciously and knowingly for light; they will be shown how to realise what will happen to them before they take the needed steps and follow initiation. This will save much time and "focus the light in the desired place" far more rapidly than hitherto.

You will see, therefore, why I have included this teaching upon the Points of Revelation in what I have to give you anent the processes of preparing for initiation. It is essential that the modern disciple no longer goes forward blindly but that he cooperates intelligently in the new systems of training. You will note the relation (if you call it no more than that) between the two phrases "points of revelation" and "mountain of initiation." In the *Old Commentary*, these are brought together in a very illumined statement—illuminating if duly reflected upon:

"The disciple climbs the mountain, its five peaks illumined by the Sun and hiding the other two.

From point to point he goes and the Way moves upward all the time—out of the dark into the light, from the jungle to the open space, from night to dawn.

From point to point he moves and at each point he gets new revelation. Five are the mountain peaks, and as he mounts towards each peak he receives five times the light. Five to the five and so from five to five till five fives have brought him light. Ten lie ahead, but these concern him not as yet."

What is meant here (to bring it down to the bare factual outline) is that there are five initiations ahead of the disciple, with two more ahead of the Master, making in all seven initiations, and that prior to each initiation—symbolically or factually speaking—there are five great revelations, making a total of twenty-five, with ten later to be registered by the Master.

I have indicated to you in my past instructions three of these revelations. They are, if you will remember:

1. Energy follows thought and the eye directs that energy. This has been an occult platitude ever since the days of H.P.B., during whose time it was decided that this was the first of the points of revelation which could safely be given to the general public. The assertion of this revealed fact was an essential piece of knowledge in the world, prior to the externalisation of the Ashrams—or, my brother, of the Hierarchy. The thought that all is energy has already been accepted by modern science, and the concept of vision (the first step towards understanding the use of the spiritual eye) is already part of the teaching of modern philosophy and of many of the metaphysical schools.

2. The Will is fundamentally an expression of the Law of Sacrifice. Paradoxically we found that when the spiritual will was—even in a small measure—expressing itself, there was no such thing as sacrifice. Incidentally, we considered the great exponents and the great field of sacrifice, considering the Great Life in which we all, as well as all other forms, live and move and have our being.

I would like here to quote something I said to you in connection with this subject: "These few thoughts upon the significance of sacrifice, or upon the 'taking over,' through identification, of the task of salvage, of revitalising and of presenting opportunity, are important to all disciples, as a goal and as a vision." (Page 288.)

3. The Monad is to the planetary Logos what the third eye is to man, esoterically understood. This is a most abstruse statement for all of you and will require much concentrated reflection and serene meditation. The vision of the solar Logos and of the planetary Logos is closely related to intention and purpose, and is the cause of the Plan. It is, however, beyond and different to the Plan. I leave this thought for your consideration and meditation, but can assure you that you will come to no easy or early comprehension.

Later on, as the years slip away and as students come and go, a clearer grasp of the techniques of comprehension—these emerging Points of Revelation—will form themes for prolonged meditation and doors of entrance to the new occultism. The foundations for this new occultism are well and soundly laid; the superstructure can be erected now, slowly and with due care, in conformity with the divine blueprints and in response to a sensitive reaction to spiritual impression.

I have also told you that, in connection with these Points of Revelation, there are three stages of activity which, when properly carried forward, will make that which is revealed of service to the disciple in his contribution to the salvaging of humanity. These three are Penetration, Polarisation and Precipitation. Let us now consider these three for a short reflective period.

You should realise that all phases of training—those that are associated with life itself and that specialised training which is given to initiates—are interlocking and interdependent. It is *training*, brother of mine, not strictly education. Educational processes, concerning knowledge as they do, may be specialised, and teaching can be taken in such isolated fields as conchology, biology or history. But in initiate training, where the objective is wisdom and (above all else) the development of spiritual sensitivity, every phase of approach to the divine unfoldment, and all expansions of consciousness, develop so that divinity is embraced, and every unfoldment of the understanding reveals to the initiate one major Reality—the *fact* of Being. Therefore, this consideration of our Points of Revelation is closely related to another of our themes: Training in Telepathy or the Science of Impression. Certain aspects of these two activities are the same, particularly the three points which we are considering here. The difficulty consists in this, that in relation to the Points of Revelation the initiate is presumed to work from a more advanced standpoint of comprehension than does the man who is taking the training which makes him sensitive to Impression. He knows the technique of Penetration, comprehends the process of Polarisation at the point penetrated, and —after due acceptance—understands how to utilise it and precipitate it into the human field of service; he consciously employs that which he has learnt, grasped and appropriated. It matters not, in this case, what word you use.

It should therefore be borne in mind that in this connection we are considering the point of experience where light pours in, bringing revelation, conveying information, evoking the intuition and drawing into the waiting consciousness of the initiate those spiritual laws, those rules of the creative process, those ray conditions and those new energies and forces for which the humanity of any particular period waits, and which are fundamentally needed if the race of men is to move forward into greater spiritual culture and out of the relative darkness in which it at present moves.

What we are dealing with here, in connection with initiate training, is the impending realisation for which any opening cycle attests its waiting, and for the new truths and the expanded spiritual presentations which it is the destiny of the initiate to bring to the people. You will note that I choose the word "destiny" in preference to the word "karma" because in this type of work the initiate is working and practicing and progressing under a Law of Destiny. This law affects the Ashram and the Hierarchy as a whole, and neither

is under the Law of Karma, as usually understood. This Law
of Destiny has been brought into being since the foundation
of the Hierarchy on Earth; it is the result of the pledged and
united dedication to service which is the outstanding note of
the united Ashrams. It is therefore a sevenfold law, for it
takes on the seven colours of the seven rays, the seven qualities, modes and methods, techniques and energy expressions
of all the seven rays. It is therefore, as far as humanity is concerned, free from all evil, because it is selflessly motivated
and is—in a measure—a difficult law for you to comprehend.
Pure destiny, devoid of all evil intent, is an enigma to the
average disciple. It appears to contravene other laws with
which he is familiar. As the race of men achieves increasing
purity in the three worlds, this pure destiny will become
correspondingly effective. This is an important point upon
which to reflect.

　　This penetration makes an event in the life of the initiate. It is indicative of success and of contact and present̃
the opening up of a new opportunity. The two succeeding
words indicate effects of this penetration; they are then
inevitable and cannot be arrested. By that you may infer
that once the initiate has penetrated to the point where revelation becomes possible he automatically attains the needed
fixation, concentration, poise, polarisation and focus which
will enable him to translate what has been revealed to him in
terms and symbols which will convey significance to the intelligentsia with whom all initiates principally work. I wanted
to make this clear because students almost inevitably think
in *terms of sequence*. The effects of penetration (in this case
two in number) are simultaneous and not sequential. The
polarisation of the consciousness of the initiate, and the consequent condensation of truth, produce an unavoidable precipitation which occurs in a flash of time; it results in an instantaneous intuitive perception, and this is one of the early
aspects of this dual process. Think this out and remember in
this connection that the initiate—in process of receiving
revelation—is working outside of time and space, as you
understand it.

　　His consciousness is free, as compared with that of the

average man, and the most urgent and the most difficult part of his task is correctly to apprehend the precipitating truth, information or revelation, and then to give it an equally correct *format* so that it can meet the immediate human need. You will see, consequently, that the initiate learns to penetrate into the realm of pure reason from the realm of mind, and there he polarises himself, and truth precipitates. He has learnt thus to penetrate, and the three stages preceding penetration have been necessarily sequential, until he has gained such facility that they can instantaneously be transcended. He has learnt through life in the three worlds, to penetrate into the world of mind and the lower concrete mind has become his instrument, integrating his personality, opening up to him the world of thought, and putting into his power the processes of thoughtform creation; he has learnt through meditation to make contact with the soul, the Son of Mind, Who is himself, and has in time identified himself with that soul; he becomes the soul in fact, and can create in the world of thought those living forms which bring light and help and truth to others; thus he serves; he learns also, through unfolding perception, to penetrate into the levels of abstract thought, the antechamber to the world of pure reason, and through these three aspects of mind he discovers that he possesses the "three keys" which will permit him to delve into the knowledge, wisdom and reason of the Universal Mind. This is what is revealed to him as he penetrates deeper into what is called the Arcana of Wisdom, the Mind of God, the third divine Aspect. This is essentially what is covered by the symbolic and pictorial phrase "the raincloud of knowable things." The raincloud is a symbol of that area of the as yet unrevealed purposes of God which can be immediately revealed if the world disciples and initiates care to "penetrate to the point of precipitation."

This idea should in the future lie behind all you do in your meditation work. Your meditation should now be regarded by you as a process of penetration, carried forward as an act of service, with the intent to bring enlightenment to others. I have been dealing with these Points of Revelation today from the angle of vision of the initiate. Process and techniques do their work, and these are followed by the recognition which the disciple accords within himself to that which has been accomplished.

Part VI

In my last instruction to you I dealt with some aspects of the new approach to discipleship and to initiation; it is essential that the old concepts—profoundly useful in their day—should be forgotten and the newer methods and techniques should be substituted. This is now necessary on account of the surprising unfoldment of the human consciousness during the past twenty-five years. The steps taken at the Conclave in Shamballa in 1925 (based on tentative conclusion at the previous centennial Conclave) and the pressures exerted by the Hierarchy have proved most successful, and out of the chaos of the world war (precipitated by humanity itself) there is developing a structure of truth and a paralleling responsiveness of the human mechanism which guarantees the perpetuation and the rapid unfoldment of the next stage of the teaching of the Ageless Wisdom.

I used a phrase in my last instruction to which I would like to call your attention. I spoke of the coming ability of mankind to "share in the great hierarchical task of *illuminating, precipitating and lifting.*" These words signify far more than their obvious meaning, and I would like somewhat to elucidate.

Men are apt to think that the entire objective of the work of the Hierarchy is to find and admit men into hierarchical contact. It is that minor phase of hierarchical activity which appears paramount in your consciousness; is it not so? Your main hope is that as you unfold your latent possibilities, you will be able to help others to do the same. This is indeed a worthy thought, but is nevertheless based entirely on misapprehension. Let me, therefore, throw light upon the matter by quoting the *Old Commentary:*

"When light illuminates the minds of men and stirs

the secret light within all other forms, then the One in Whom we live reveals His hidden, secret lighted Will.

"When the purpose of the Lords of Karma can find no more to do, and all the weaving and close-related plans are all worked out, then the One in Whom we live can say: 'Well done! Naught but the beautiful remains.'

"When the lowest of the low, the densest of the dense, and the highest of the high have all been lifted through the little wills of men, then can the One in Whom we live raise into radiating light the vivid lighted ball of Earth, and then another greater Voice can say to Him: 'Well done! Move on. Light shines.' "

You will note that the emphasis in these words is placed upon human accomplishment and not upon what the Hierarchy does for man. When men achieve illumination, intelligently precipitate the karmic quota of their time, and lift the subhuman kingdoms (with its reflex activity of lifting the Highest simultaneously), then they can and then they do share in the work of the Hierarchy.

That cycle of sharing has seemed for aeons too far away to be considered; when, however, humanity precipitated the war, they automatically and somewhat surprisingly brought the final achievement much nearer. The illumination of men's minds will rapidly follow. The process of lifting the subhuman kingdoms has been amazingly forwarded by science—the crowning accomplishment of which was the fission of the atom and the penetration of the "spiritual interfering" aspect of the human spirit into the very depths of the mineral world. Ponder on this.

Therefore, if you could see things as they truly exist in the world of today and view them in their true perspective (and this—as far as you are concerned—is from the angle of the Master), you would *know* that a great step has been taken towards:

1. The institution of more rapid initiation, and that in group form.

2. The possession of a much closer and a more widespread contact between the Hierarchy and humanity.
3. The revelation of the true significance of initiation.

This true significance lies still behind the curtain of that which veils the ultimate truth. The great secrets of Sanat Kumara are there to be found in due time, and the truth anent initiation is one of them.

When the Hierarchy withdrew behind the separating curtain in Atlantean times, it marked the beginning of an interlude of darkness, of aridity and a cycle of "blank abstraction," which persisted in its crudest form until 1425 A.D., and since then has sensibly lightened until we reached the year 1925. It became possible for the Hierarchy itself to regard the necessity for reorientation and the imminence of the revelation of the first secret—the secret of initiation. Note well what I say here. Humanity had reached a stage where it could do the "abstracting" itself, and could eventually and by sheer force of the spiritual will wrest the secrets from the custody of the Guardians behind the veil. This presented the Hierarchy with another problem. How could this be permitted with safety so that, in its avidity for pure truth, humanity could be simultaneously trusted? Revelation brings responsibility, and ofttimes danger. Men, as individuals, can grasp certain of these truths of initiation and use them for themselves with impunity, but their revelation to the unready might involve serious risks.

It was therefore decided that a truer picture of the nature of discipleship should be imparted to the waiting aspirant, the misunderstood principle of occult obedience should be "soft-pedaled" (if I may use such a word), and men should be set "free for penetration"—as it is called—and be taught the needed reticence through testing and experience.

It is interesting to note that the cycle now being inaugurated in the world is that of "Growth through Sharing," and that advanced humanity can now share the work, the responsibility and the trained reticence of the Hierarchy, whilst paralleling this and simultaneously, the mass of men are learning the lessons of economic sharing; and, my brothers, in this lies the sole hope of the world.

Every initiation to which disciples are admitted permits this closer occult sharing in the hierarchical life. This involves, for advanced humanity, a noticeable increase in vitality and in vital tension and potency. Its reflection among the masses is shewn in the constant demand for speed and in the enormous speeding up of the life of mankind in every department of living. This speeding up synchronises with the increasing readiness of disciples everywhere for initiation—according to their status and developed ability.

The difference, brother of mine, between the past and the present readiness lies in the fact that in the past this readiness was a purely individual matter; today it is something which is closely related to a man's group, and the individual aspect is of secondary importance. As time and speed increase in importance for the masses of men, the disciple (ready for initiation) regards his personal advancement upon the Path as of less importance than his developed capacity to serve his fellowmen, serving them through the group with which he may be affiliated and to which he may be drawn. For the disciple facing the first two initiations, this group will be some exoteric body of men who claim his allegiance and in which he learns group cooperation and methods of working; for the more advanced disciple, it is the Ashram and direct service under the instigation of some Master.

I have in the above paragraphs given you a number of ideas which, though not new in their stating, are *new in their reference*. This is of importance for you to remember—or discover? The significance of sharing and the relation of spiritual development to speed are points of importance to emphasise. Much that I have said above has a close connection with the hint given on pages 302-3. I suggest that you look it up.

ON HINTS

I have continually laid the emphasis upon the need of

disciples to *think esoterically,* and this is perhaps the most difficult demand that I can make upon you. A consideration of these hints should teach you much, for they are not what they seem upon superficial reading, and the effort to understand and to interpret should lead you far on your way towards "occult thinking." The Masters do not convey teaching through the medium of hints which could be safely given in a more open form. They have no intention at any time to be mysterious or to hold back teaching from the enquirer. Their method is, in reality, threefold:

1. The presentation of those truths which obviously grow out of a recognition of truths already presented. There is here usually a close adherence to the esoteric teaching of the time, and this method is essentially a *linking* presentation.
2. Occasionally (usually once in a century after Their Conclave at the close of the first quarter) there is the imparting of a more advanced body of teaching. This teaching will only be recognised by a few of the foremost disciples in the world; it will, however, prove to be the ordinary form of occult teaching during the next developing cycle. It is this type of work which I have been endeavouring to do with the aid of A.A.B.
3. There is also the teaching which is definitely given within the Ashram, and which is not, at the time when the other two forms are prevalent, reduced to writing; it will find its way out into expression as need arises and as opportunity is offered to the disciples who are its custodians. Its presentation is dependent upon the unfoldment—rapid or slow—of the lesser disciples of the world.

All these three methods are in use at this present time.

As a man progresses nearer and nearer to his goal, he finds himself beginning to realise that the entire technique of this unfoldment consists of a sequence of revelations which are induced by his recognition of subjective significances which are of a nature entirely different to the usual and apparent meanings. In the olden days, as you well know, the Master would say to a disciple: "Here is a hint" and, having stated it, He would proceed to enjoin upon His disciple the necessity to withdraw and search for the true meaning until he found it; then, and only then, could he return for a *consequent* new hint.

Today, this method is no longer being used, and this change constitutes one of the modes of training the disciples of the New Age. The modern disciple has to recognise the hint which is related to his point in consciousness and which is to be found in the mass of instruction made available for his use. He has to seek for the—to him—most deeply esoteric statement he encounters in the current teaching; from this isolated hint he has to abstract the significance, after removing it from its context; later, he must learn and profit from its meaning.

The hints given at this stage are related to the theme of revelation, or they concern themselves with the techniques which make revelation possible. The hint, for instance, with which you can work until you receive the next sequence of teaching is contained in this paragraph and the one above; you can discover it if you take each phrase, release your intuition and seek for meaning and significance related to the possibility of revelation. My one effort today is to indicate the relation between initiation and revelation. The revelation—induced by right orientation and right thinking—is a part of the training of the initiate, and many thus in training delay their progress by not recognising the revelation when it tops the line of their spiritual horizon.

Five hints have already been given to you, and I would like you to get their sequence, for it may prove valuable to you and to other disciples:

1. That the changes brought about in the Hierarchy have been the work of the disciples of the world. Have you asked yourself (in studying this hint), *Why* the disciples?
2. That human world planning is today the first indication of the emergence of the will aspect. *Why* is this rightly so?

3. That disciples in all the Ashrams have the task simultaneously of "modifying, qualifying and adapting the divine Plan." Why is this so? Why is the Plan not imposed?
4. That the initiate knows because he works. What does this hint mean to you?
5. A key to the correct interpretation of a hint lies in its association with the idea of direction in time and space.

Study these and see what is their relationship and what you feel is the inner meaning which they are intended to convey.

The Formulas

It might sometimes be remarked that these formulas are attempts by advanced aspirants to confine within due limits some of these escaped revelations. They express a past, indicate a revelation, and ground the thinking aspirant in the world of meaning because it is in that world that he must learn to work and live; it is from that world that he must begin now to work in two directions in time and space, for the world of meaning is the antechamber to the "Circle of Liberation." This "Circle of Liberation" is ever entered by the individual initiate, and has been down the ages, but now, for the first time, it is being entered by humanity itself and as a whole. This is the result of the experience of the war, 1914-1945. Humanity, entering this circle, will be confronted by the first major lesson: the Unity of the One Life. This form of presentation will be more easily recognised by the masses than such phrases as Brotherhood, Relationship, Fraternity. Life and its balancing partner, Death, are old and familiar aspects of general livingness to the masses, and their starting point in all revelation is life, and the result of all revelation is death or the disappearance of veils.

The formula with which I present you today consists of three closely related words, and the theme with which the student must concern himself is the nature of the relationship which is indicated—not by the words but by the very nature of that which relates them. This is *not* an obvious relation but the esoteric and subtle meaning which the intuition will reveal and that the outer words hide.

THE SUN . . . BLACK . . . ANTAHKARANA

These words constitute, and when placed in their correct order create, a most potent magical and mantric formula. It has a tenuous yet definite connection with the third initiation, but it is not this angle with which you are asked to concern yourselves but with the triangle created and the lines of force set in motion when the right word finds itself at the apex of the triangle.

The clue to rightly orienting your thinking lies in the realisation of the threefold aspect of the Sun, the unity of the reality and the dual nature of the antahkarana. More I must not say; it is for you to wrestle with the formula and unearth or bring to the surface its hidden significance. In line with the hints given in connection with the other four formulas, the keynote of this one would be:

Lead us from the individual to the Universal.

Points of Revelation

I would like at this point to call more directly to your attention the three stages of revelation; you have been dealing with them and considering them, if you have succeeded in following this work closely, and may already have achieved something of the automatic and the essential in their activity.

Revelation seldom breaks in all its completed beauty into the consciousness of the disciple; it is a gradual and steadily unfolding process. The three words I have given you as descriptive of the stages concern the individual disciple or initiate and express the stages of the impact of the revelation upon his mind. There are paralleling inner causes which are responsible for the outer stages of Penetration, Polarisation and Precipitation. These are:

1. The stage of the "advancing point of light."
2. The stage of right direction or the focussing of the "advancing" potency.
3. The stage of spiritual impact.

Again here (if you could but see it) you have an illustration of the processes and interaction of Invocation and Evocation and of the establishing of a triple relation between an inner reality and the outer man, the disciple on his own plane; you have an evocative activity of so potent a nature that it produces corresponding exoteric attitudes and expressions. In reality, you have here a phase of the working of the Law of Cause and Effect, demonstrated in a most illustrative manner. As the Law of Karma makes its presence felt upon the outer physical plane, you have the evidence before your eyes of the three stages of Penetration, Polarisation and Precipitation. At the same time, on the inner planes, and because of the existence of the inner reality, you have the three corresponding stages of Advancing Light, Right Direction, Impact. You have here also an indication of the close interrelation of the outer and the inner, producing a condition wherein the disciple creates a situation analogous to the phase—the long phase—of his creation of karma and its final precipitation in (so-called) "critical" disaster in his physical plane life.

A study of the three revelations indicated in the earlier instruction will reveal the accuracy of the above statement. I enumerated them for you in my previous instruction and wonder if you have read them often. You will find it of value to take these three points of revelation and apply to them the three outer and the three inner stages through which all revelations pass. You may also have noted how one point of revelation leads normally to another. You will (having studied the three revelations indicated on pages 309-10) note how all of them concern the first divine aspect, starting with the initial energy set in motion by God's thinking; leading to the expression of the Will, which is the great first ray in action, and then focussing itself through the Monad.

Curiously enough, in these three you have—symbolically and factually given you—expression of the three exoteric stages:

1. Penetration, the descending and circulatory nature of energy.
2. Polarisation, the effect upon this energy of the polarised will.
3. Precipitation, through the focussed intent and the directed impulse of the Monad.

The next sequential revelation will be that of creativity, the world of thoughtforms and the desire which each human being and humanity as a whole have created, and (note this well) the setting in motion by humanity and in relation to its own destiny, the Law of Cause and Effect, or of Karma.

I have here condensed into a relatively few short paragraphs much important teaching anent revelation and its processes and have emphasised a phase of human activity (needed to produce revelation) which has hitherto received little, if any, attention. Revelation is apt to be regarded as apart from all laws, as an extra-planetary activity, as something that occasionally happens to the well-intentioned aspirant, and as relatively unpredictable and unexpected. I have sought here to correct this erroneous impression.

PART VII

It would present a very real problem to would-be initiates if they had to answer certain questions, among them the following: Into what are you being initiated? Are disciples being initiated into the Hierarchy? Are there certain secret contacts that the initiation makes possible? Is the acquiring of certain mysterious and hitherto unknown knowledge the reward of initiation? There is much vague and loose thinking on these matters.

Over the years I have given you many definitions of initiation; all of them have been useful and true. Today I seek greatly to widen your conception of these matters and to give you an entirely new slant on this engrossing and assertive work. What I have to say grows out of certain hints I gave you in the preceding pages. These hints are good illustrations of that method of teaching which is profoundly rooted in hierarchical technique. I said:

1. That more rapid processes of initiation are now being instituted.
2. That initiation veiled a secret and that its revelation was imminent.
3. That every initiation permits a closer *sharing* within the hierarchical life and that this sharing is closely related to vitality and to vital tension.
4. That initiation is concerned at this time with group life and not with the individual.
5. That initiation concerns the future and involves prevision.
6. That time is one of the major underlying themes or secrets of initiation.

In this particular instruction I seek to deal with these six points.

1. When I say that *more rapid initiation is being instituted,* it must not be inferred that a certain slackness is to be permitted or that the requirements are not so drastic or that the disciple will be allowed to take initiation before he is truly ready or that he can pass on before he has proved his capacity to move forward upon the path. Such is not in any single point the situation. Three factors are responsible for this change in the hierarchical requirements:

a. The mental development of disciples everywhere is today of such a calibre that it does not take as long for them to make the needed adjustments or to change their attitudes and conditions of life as it did formerly; it does not take as long for them to assimilate a presented truth or to respond to an intuitive perception. Their grasp of the Law of Cause and Effect and their appreciation of the subsidiary Law of Consequences is far more prompt than in the past. These facts therefore necessitate a recognition upon the part of the Masters of the more advanced condition and a pronounced saving of time as the consequence. This you should note as of very real importance; its true significance is that the period required for a truth, a contact, or a spiritual apprehension to be registered by a physical brain has been greatly—almost phenomenally reduced. Disciples can now in a few months (if sincere and honest in their endeavour) master ideas and develop responses which it took them years to master in earlier cycles of hierarchical effort. This is true, on a lower turn of the spiral, of the masses of men everywhere. The *mind* factor is today alert, trained and controlling. These are facts which the Hierarchy cannot ignore, nor do the Masters desire to do so, because it is that mental alertness which has for ages engrossed Their attention and it is this for which They have worked for aeons.

b. Another factor is that many disciples are taking incarnation at this time who are already prepared and ready for initiation; they have done the needed work in previous lives. No time, therefore, need be lost, and there is today a constant series of initiations taking place. This must perforce produce certain important hierarchical changes; new situations come about in initiate circles and many fit candidates are supplied for hierarchical vacancies; this produces a shifting of the hierarchical personnel on a scale hitherto unknown. Needless to say, this shifting and changing presents its own peculiar difficulties and opportunities. One of the most important of the latter is that candidates for the Initiation of Decision are far more numerous than at any previous time in our planetary history.

c. Again: Initiation can now be taken in group form; this is something entirely new in the work of the Hierarchy. Not one by one do candidates stand before the Initiator, but many so stand simultaneously. Together they can think in complete accord; together they are tested, and together they reach the "point of triumph" which supersedes the "point of tension"; together they see the "Star shine forth," and together the energy emanating from the Rod of Initiation fits them for the reception of specialised energy, to be later used in their future world service. This group approach, this group intention, this "group silent reticence and vocal recognition," and this group dedication and vision are no longer in the experimental stage. This group achievement (I refer not here to your particular group which has not been outstandingly successful) marks the point where there can be the inauguration of a new phase of activity in Shamballa. This will enable the Lord of the World to become the Ruler of a Sacred Planet, which, up to date, has not been the case. Our Earth can now become a Sacred Planet, if all right conditions are fulfilled. A new divine quality (as yet unrevealed and which we would not at this time recognise if presented with it) is slowly crystallising into expression, through the medium of this hastened initiation process. Disciples are today witnessing the emergence of a solar characteristic, through the medium of their planetary Logos, just as the "Lives of similar Intention"—as it is esoterically called—witnessed it many aeons ago. It is to this unknown and mysterious quality that the "shining forth" of the Star refers.

More than this I cannot say, for you would not understand; what I have said above you can accept as a possible hypothesis without outraging your commonsense or violating your intention, that I do ask you to do—just accept.

A great opportunity is presented to you, and the success of the system of Raja-Yoga, the Kingly Science of the Mind (started by the great initiate, Patanjali, eleven thousand years ago) is being demonstrated and his techniques are being vindicated. What he issued on behalf of the Great White Lodge has now been satisfactorily launched and much of the original purpose justified. For the next seven thousand years his system will be used to train disciples in mind control. They will, through this system, achieve the stage of "isolated unity," and in that recorded unity—alone and yet with many others—take the initiation which will enable them to release energy into a waiting and demanding world of men.

2. We come now to our second point, that *initiation veils a secret and that the revelation of that secret is imminent.* Just what this secret is, I may not reveal, but it is concerned with a peculiar type of energy which can be induced at a moment of supreme tension. The only possible hint I can give you in connection with this mysterious matter is that it is closely related to the "Blinding Light" which Saul of Tarsus saw on the road to Damascus and the "blinding light" which accompanied the discharge of energy from the atomic bomb. The "Blinding Light" which ever accompanies true conversion (a rare and sudden happening always when true and real) and which is an attendant demonstration of all Lives Who have passed the human stage of consciousness— according to Their degree—and the light which is released by the fission of the atom are one and the same expression on different levels of consciousness, and are definitely related to the processes and effects of initiation. This will not even make sense to you until certain initiate-experiences have been undergone by you. It is not easy for the average aspirant to realise that progressive stages upon the Path indicate a progressive ability to "take the Light." When the aspirant prays in the new Invocation: "Let Light descend on Earth" he is invoking something which humanity will have to learn to handle; this is one of the things for which the disciples of the world must begin to prepare the race of men.

All these planetary developments are attended by risks, and none more so than that of the absorption of light—on a world-wide scale—by humanity, with a subsequent reflex action on the three subhuman kingdoms. Nothing which affects humanity or which stimulates it to a forward-moving activity is without its inevitable effect upon the three lower kingdoms in nature. Forget not! Mankind is the macrocosm to this threefold lower microcosm.

This as you may well surmise, can be among the secrets

of the initiatory process. The "principle of absorption" emerges as one of the subjects to be studied, understood and mastered between initiations, for each initiation carries the subject another step forward. At present, the physical effects of the fission of the atom and its subsequent *constructive* use is the immediate problem before modern science, and (I would remind you) it is now an *exoteric* problem. Its use, or corresponding use on esoteric levels, still remains one of the secrets of initiation.

3. I stated as our third point that *every initiation indicated a closer sharing in all forms of the hierarchical life.* Do you realise in any measure what that statement means or what the implications are? I am dealing with a point not only of profound significance but of major testing. There is a spiritual counterpart or higher correspondence of the economic life of our planet to be found in the Hierarchy. Sharing is associated with that which is of value, which should be shared if justice is to be demonstrated, and basically, with those values which are life-giving. The sharing to which I am here referring is the sharing in all reactions, of all attitudes, of all types of wisdom, of all problems and difficulties and limitations, so that they become constructive in the group sense and cease to be destructive. Nothing destructive has place in any Ashram, but disciples can and do use ashramic force in their work in a destructive manner, and in the three worlds. This is not easy to understand. Perhaps I can make it clearer to you if I point out that this sharing involves complete knowledge of all the personality reactions of all the members of the Ashram, i.e., of all preparing for the lesser initiations, and therefore of all below a certain degree. There is nothing secret which will not be known, and you can understand that the discovery of the factual nature of this constitutes a major test for all disciples. There is nothing in the mind of a disciple which cannot be telepathically known to all the other members of the Ashram who are at the same degree of development or to all of a higher degree, for it is a law that the greater can always include the lesser.

I wish students would consider this fact with great intelligence and closer attention; they would then arrive at the knowledge that their limitations definitely provide a problem for those less limited. The time has to come wherein candidates for admission into an Ashram, and later, for initiation, must realise that their limitations, their relatively petty points of view and their circumscribed attitudes are a hindrance to ashramic progressive events. If the principle of sharing has any significance whatsoever, these are points of great importance and are supremely worthy of consideration. An illustration of this can be seen in the response of this group to the work which I have asked you to undertake over the years. A tiny handful of you have responded and have made sacrifices and worked hard to further the Triangle work, to spread the Invocation and to help in the Goodwill work, but it is a very tiny minority. The rest have either been interested intellectually but could not make the needed sacrifices, or they refused to put first things first, and secondary issues occupied their lives. This limitation, as you may realise, has handicapped the ashramic plans, and those who wholeheartedly have worked (and they know I know who they are) have had to share—with pain and distress—in the limitation. I have frequently stated that on entrance into an Ashram the disciple leaves behind him his personality life and enters as a soul. What I have stated in the above paragraph in no way contradicts this fact. It must, however, be remembered that a disciple has become what he is as a result of his personality aspiration, his struggles in the three worlds, and an attained point of spiritual unfoldment. Therefore, though he may leave behind his personality with its faults and problems, he indicates clearly to his co-disciples and to those more advanced than he is, exactly what is lacking in his equipment, what is his point in evolution, and what stage of discipleship he has achieved. In this connection, I recommend the rereading of all that is said anent the six stages of discipleship in *Discipleship in the New Age* (Vol. I); the material given there is of great importance here.

At first the disciple may have little to share, and instead presents a great deal for senior disciples to record, for which they must make allowance and which they have to offset. They have also to regulate the energy which plays upon the entering disciple so that it is adjusted to his point of development and to his ray and nature. The group of disciples within the Ashram who are of equal development with the new disciple, act as a safeguarding group, and this is true, no matter what the degree, where *higher incoming energy is concerned*. When a disciple is temporarily bewildered, this safeguarding becomes a major necessity, and where glamour is present in a disciple's life, it places a real strain upon his co-disciples. They have to share the charge and shoulder unitedly the protection; it is not the task of the Master, but is carried forward under His interested and wise instruction.

This ashramic sharing is one of the great compensations of discipleship. By means of it added light can be "occultly endured." I would like to have you ponder on that phrase. Great united strength can be brought to the service of the Plan, and the occult significance of the words: "My strength is as the strength of ten, because my heart is pure" can be grasped. The perfected strength of the Ashram (symbolised by the number 10) becomes available to the disciple whose purity of heart has enabled him to penetrate into the Ashram; his knowledge becomes more rapidly transmuted into wisdom as his mind is subjected to the play of the higher understanding of Those with Whom he is associated; gradually he begins to contribute his own quota of light and of understanding to those just entering and to those who are his equals.

The strength, availability and usefulness of an Ashram is that of the sumtotal of all that its members can contribute, plus that which Those above the third degree of initiation can "import" from still higher sources or the Masters of the Ashrams can make available at need. Students are apt to think that an Ashram has only one initiate of the fifth degree (that of Master) within it. Such is seldom the case. There are usually three "cooperating Masters" in every Ashram, with one at the apex of the triangle; He acts as the Master of the Ashram and is responsible for the preparation of disciples for initiation; frequently there are also "associated Masters," particularly during cycles of rapid initiation, as is the case today. There are also Masters Who are preparing for the sixth initiation.

This "sharing" process does not involve what is usually understood as the "sharing of trouble." Personality difficulties and personality problems are not permitted entrance into an Ashram; only evolutionary limitations and lack of perfection (limitations in soul expression, indicating the grade or stage of discipleship) are recognised. If, however, disciples act or react in a way that brings attack upon the Ashram, that is naturally recognised, but these issues are fortunately very rare; they may become more common as the spiritual inspiration to which humanity is now subjected and reacting brings far greater numbers of disciples into relation with the Hierarchy. In the case where a disciple has opened a door of attack upon an Ashram—and this has happened, as you know, in the case of my Ashram—the work of the united disciples is to "seal the door" against the menacing evil, to withdraw themselves from the usual confidence shown to an erring disciple, but to stand at the same time in steadfast love beside him until such time as he has learned the error of his ways and has himself taken the needed steps to arrest the evil which he was responsible in starting.

It must be remembered that none of this is a personality or an individual attack upon an Ashram. The relatively feeble efforts of a person are unavailing and make no real impact upon the conscious life of the Ashram. The evil released must emanate from a group, though it is released through the agency of an individual disciple. That is a totally different matter. A disciple may do this through misuse of the lower mind and its rationalising capacity, which can make black to appear white and prove that good intention is responsible for evil-distributed energy; or the disciple can let in evil under the influence of glamour, provided again that it is group evil. In these ways, the disciple simply turns the key, and group evil enters. For instance, the harm done to the Ashram of the Master Morya by H.P.B. in his earlier incarnation as Cagliostro,* is only now fading out, and its

*Cagliostro, W.R.H. Trowbridge.

repercussions affected the whole Hierarchy. The harm attempted on my Ashram has been more easily offset, and the source of hate which it represented failed in its attempt because of its general ill repute. It has been offset by love and understanding which is not so easily the case in a first ray attack.

In an Ashram, therefore, the sharing takes place along the following lines:

a. The sharing in individual limitation but not in individual problems or personality difficulties.
b. The sharing in the "art of occult protection." This involves two activities: the protection of limited disciples and the protection of the Ashram from attempted attacks or intrusions.
c. The sharing in the service of the Plan, resulting in action in the three worlds.
d. The sharing in the Ashramic life, with all that that signifies, and in the opportunities which are thus presented.
e. The sharing in the stimulation which comes from the Master's Presence and in the instructions which He occasionally gives.
f. The sharing in the accession of power or love or insight which comes during any cycle of initiation. These cycles (for our purposes) fall into three categories:
  1. The initiation of members of the Ashram, either before the Christ or before the One Initiator.
  2. Initiations taking place within affiliated Ashrams and having a specific ray effect.
  3. Initiations into those degrees which are higher than the fifth degree; these create vacancies, and at the same time cause a tremendous influx of power.
  At the period of these cycles, all within the Ashram react in some way or another; no one moves forward upon the Path without creating a new relationship and becoming a better transmitter of power.
g. The sharing in the results of special spiritual events, such as:

1. The directed attention of Shamballa.
2. An inflow of extra-planetary force.
3. The "nearing" or the directed power of an Avatar of some degree.
4. The merging of all hierarchical thought and activity into some one directed event, such as the Wesak Festival and, increasingly, the Full Moon or Festival of the Christ.

There are other events which have a definite effect upon every Ashram, the effect being determined by the ray or by the "unfoldment of the ashramic Lotus."

Every great act of sharing results automatically in the production of two reactions:

a. The creation of a point of tension.
b. The emergence of a point of crisis.

On these I shall not here enlarge, for I have given you much along these lines in other and earlier writings. The bringing together of "two points of energy" (as, for instance, two disciples) creates inevitably a point of tension which can release energy in the service of the Plan. It produces also a point of crisis, according to the development of the disciples involved. There is not the same point of crisis where initiates of the higher degree are involved. The point of tension in these cases results in a "crisis of projection and direction" which is in no way related to the disciple's life or condition or to his aspiration and understanding.

4. *Initiation is today concerned with the group and not with the individual.* This is not an easy matter to elucidate to a group of people who are still so polarised in their personalities that it is the personality aspect of their fellow members which engrosses their attention at all times. I say this with emphasis. Aspiring disciples are far more conscious of the failings and the personality attributes of others than are the more advanced disciples in the Ashrams. The advanced disciple may be—and is—well aware of the failings, failures and undesirable qualities of others with whom he is

associated, but his critical mind is not the determining factor, as it is with most of the less developed. He is far more conditioned by the aspirations, the effort and the fixed intention than by the personality angle. He gauges the soul's grip upon the lower self, primarily from the angle of the stability of its hold; his treatment of the aspirant is therefore based upon that recognition, and not upon any analysis of the aspirant's lack of development. This is a point of immense importance, for it is this type of consideration which governs the Masters when They are choosing and training a group for initiation. The Master is not occupied with the temporary faults but with the soul grip and intention, and with the aspirant's *habitual* response to soul energy, when that energy is applied. Given a firm hold by the soul, an attentive ear by the personality, and consistent and enduring effort from both directions—soul and personality (and this is an instance of invocation and evocation)—and the Master can begin to train a group.

This is necessarily a slow process, from the standpoint of the physical plane, but upon the inner planes—where the time factor does not rule—this does not matter in the least. The Masters think in terms of cycles and not in terms of an individual life; as you cannot yet do that, except theoretically, it is not possible for you to understand. The experience, the failures and the achievements of the disciples in my Ashram are seen by me, for instance, in terms of one thousand year cycles. What you may have done in this life, unless of outstanding significance, is in all probability quite unknown to me; if I choose to know, I can do so, and I do so in those cases where the results of some activity have repercussions upon my Ashram or upon a large proportion of the group of disciples.

Let me put it this way: the petty selfishness and the silly little vanities and the irritations which disturb you, the unkind words you may speak of or to others, and the withholding of love or the fact of wrong emphasis in your daily life are *not* noted by me or by any Master. They are the affair of your own soul; the results affect your family, friend, or communal group, and are none of Our business. Yet those are the things which you notice in others and which affect your judgment, evoking like or dislike, praise or blame, but inevitably putting you—as an individual—upon the judgment seat. There no Master sits. When Christ said: "Judge not and ye shall not be judged," He indicated a state of mind where understanding so controls that the aspirant no longer praises or blames; because of this general attitude within his mental approach to people, he is then free to become a full member of an Ashram.

If you consider the many apparent failures in my experiment in forming an external group affiliated with my Ashram, and as demonstrated in the book *Discipleship in the New Age*, you may well wonder why on earth I chose such a group of people or why I chose to make myself aware of their thinking, faults and failures. I will tell you.

From a survey of one thousand years which I have been enabled to make (as are all the Masters), everyone of these people shows a definite soul intention, all are definitely oriented in their personality life to the spiritual world, and react to soul control correctly—if at times quite feebly. The soul has them in a true grip, and that grip has become a stable and persistent hold. Therefore, in spite of serious faults, and in spite of pronounced personality qualities of undesirable nature, and in spite of wrong emphases, these people were and are ready for training. Their failings and faults will disappear more rapidly than you imagine under the influence of the soul—as the dew disappears under the morning sun. The enterprise of the Masters to substitute group initiation in place of the laborious process of individual initiation is proving successful, even though it is still in the experimental stage.

The "cycles of interest," or those periods in which the Masters pay close attention to *the quality aspect* of mankind, are also being speeded up; the "gauging" process will take place now every three hundred years, instead of every one thousand years, as has been the case until 1575 A.D. This change can be attributed to the greater sensitivity of man's response to spiritual stimulation and to the rapidity with which he deals with his personality. This is, of course, not apparent to you, on account of your day by day consideration of each other; it is, however, apparent to Those Who view humanity with greater disinterestedness, deeper understanding and over much more extended cycles of time.

The result of this more frequent watchfulness on the part of the Hierarchy has been shown in the confidence with which the Masters have undertaken to prepare people for initiation.

This decision to do so, and permission having been granted from Shamballa, certain matters came up for consideration. Most of them would naturally be too abstruse for your comprehension—which is seated in the mind and brain instead of in the soul and heart. It is obvious that if initiation is a physical plane affair, requiring recognition in the brain consciousness, the disciples must be in physical incarnation together (and by this I mean within the ring-pass-not of the three worlds which are the dense physical planes of the cosmic physical plane) for a sufficiently long period of time to test their reactions, as a group, to the concept of group initiation and to each other as participants. For a great part of this time there must also be a physical plane life, shared by all in the group; this need not involve similarity or identity of location, but must involve similarity of world affairs and civilisation. This physical plane necessity is—as you will perceive—a test of individual integration, with a view to group integration later on.

It is this test which I have been applying in my work with all of you in this special group; the related state persists also on the inner plane after death, and in the consciousness of those (at present non-affiliated) who are still part of the group chosen for the experiment, on my part, of group preparation for initiation. Other Masters are doing the same as I am doing. We hope during the next five hundred years to present several such groups to the One Initiator. All who are in these groups have taken the first initiation, as have so many thousands of people in the world today. Many have taken the second initiation, particularly those who are working in fifth ray Ashrams and in third ray Ashrams, for such disciples are distinguished by a lack of emotional emphasis.

Group initiation has been forced upon the Hierarchy by the rapid unfoldment of the spiritual consciousness in humanity, an unfoldment which demonstrates—no matter what the ray—as goodwill. This goodwill is not to be interpreted as the sentimental sixth or second ray untrained aspirant is prone to interpret it. It can take many forms: it can show itself as sacrifice on the part of science and a dedication of the fruits of scientific research to human welfare; it may take shape in the third ray aptitude to dedicate great wealth to philanthropic or educational enterprises. In neither of these cases is the disciple apparently distinguished by a so-called loving nature. Yet the results of their application to science or their accumulation of the crystallised prana of the financial world are turned to the helping of mankind. This will be a hard saying for some of you who rate an irritable remark by a co-disciple as something disgraceful and belittle the efforts of the money-maker, and do both with a sense of self-righteous congratulation.

The old saying that "the evil which men do lives after them; the good is oft interred with their bones" is not occultly true. Evil may follow after a man in his next incarnation until he has learnt to eliminate it, but the good men do (even with mixed motives) is not forgotten but is entered upon the calendar of the Hierarchy.

Before the end of this century, thousands will stand before the Initiator and take initiation in group form; they will pass through the door of initiation *together* and *together* take their vows. This statement applies to the second and the third initiations. The higher initiations will still be taken individually or in groups of three, but not more. When the Masters take the sixth initiation, They perforce take it alone at the "midway point" between Shamballa and the Hierarchy, apparently deserted by both attentive groups. There, in complete silence and in a condition of "isolated unity," They will make Their great decision. Then and only then will They become aware of the vast attentive spiritual audience which has awaited Their will.

5. *Initiation concerns the future and involves prevision.* Again I must repeat myself and say that this theme or motif

of initiation is one most difficult to explain. Why should the fact of being initiated involve prevision? That is the immediate question which arises to your lips. I will counter this question with another one. What do you understand by vision? I refer, of course, to vision which is true, and which therefore presages events. In all mystical and occult writings the idea of vision, of seeing a vision or of materialising a vision, runs like a golden thread through the thinking of the aspirant. It is connected in his mind with spiritual achievement, with the attainment of his goal and with the recognition of that which lies at the heart of all high spiritual adventure. The mystical writings refer to visions and always in terms of that which lies ahead, of that which is deeply desired; the concept is often prostituted to an excessive emotionalism or to a sublimated sex expression. The occult writings frequently refer to vision as a moving point, advancing towards a progressive revelation of divinity. The whole concept is, however, relatively very simple.

Every initiation, and every stage preparatory to initiation, involves the seeing of the remote yet the attainable; all vision leads up to the momentous event of the sixth initiation, when the Master faces what is for Him the final vision within this planetary ring-pass-not. He makes His great decision on the basis of the seen opportunity, and through His response to the seven phases of that cosmic vision, He treads one or other of the seven Paths. For this great "crisis of vision" all the lesser visions have prepared the Master; after His decision is made there is no longer any vision as we comprehend the term. There is a factual perception of such a nature that the element of time—as evidenced by remoteness, by the distance between this and that, between here and there—forever disappears. This is, necessarily, a somewhat meaningless statement to the majority of people.

For the aspirant, whether his goal is the Path of Discipleship or one of the seven Paths leading away from known planetary experience, there is persistently that which conveys to consciousness two factors:

a. A dualistic perception of that which has been attained and of that which lies ahead to be attained.

b. A recognition of the events which will, if experienced, merge the two into one major happening; time, therefore, enters in. However, it is not time as it is conditioned by the receptivity of the human brain, but time as it represents evolutionary movements, resulting in an achieved though constantly relative perfection.

Oft I have said to you that time is the sequence of the states of consciousness, as registered by the human brain. It is therefore a physical event. Behind this definition, however, lies a real or true time of which the initiate becomes increasingly aware. The great Law of Karma has received little attention from the standpoint of time; yet it is that which determines the sequence of evolution, of evolutionary progress, the period of karmic recognitions, and the conclusion of a karmic cycle.

The ordinary teaching on Karma (particularly as to the time element) has been terribly prostituted by the purely selfish rendering given to it by those early theosophical teachers who misunderstood and misinterpreted what H.P.B. said. They had little chance to do much else than relate it to individual affairs, if they were going to familiarise the public with the concept, but they nevertheless did much harm with their puerile setting of times and seasons, and their attempt to take to themselves the mysterious functions of a Lord of Karma. It is always difficult to convey any true concept of Karma, because it predominantly concerns cycles and the sequence of world events. There is much to be done in relating time and conscious recognition together.

In this connection, initiation might be defined as embodying three recognitions:

a. A recognition of the end of a cycle of happenings, i.e., retrospection.

b. The recognition of the appearance of an eventual yet imminent cycle, i.e., prevision.

c. An acceptance of initiation or a recognition of its occurrence, i.e., the present attitude.

Here you have, in relation to the initiate, a situation which includes past, present and future, and—in this presentation of the Eternal Now to the attentive eyes and heart of the initiate—you have what is, for him, at his particular point of initiatory unfoldment, the consummation of all vision or visions. This tends to definite progress; it obliterates what is usually understood by Karma; it initiates new and spiritual causes which—in their turn—magnetically project the initiate onward until (at the sixth initiation) he "no longer needs incentive, for vision is incentive and the pull of the spiritual magnetism upon our planetary life." Thus it may be occultly expressed.

For the initiate (at this great stage of experience), Karma ends. By this I mean that Karma—as the ordinary student understands it—is no longer effective. Neither good Karma, resulting in a sense of bliss, nor bad Karma, resulting in a sense of penalty and related to a conviction of sin (as the Christian theology so dreadfully miscalls it), has any longer the slightest hold upon him. Manifestation and the Law of Cause and Effect are related; where manifestation exists, there this great Law—governing substance and innate in matter—must control and must condition form. The Master, however, stands free, endowed with the Christ-consciousness. He then wields this Law, but is not wielded by it. Such is the reward of following the vision: first of all, the mystical vision; then later, the vision of predetermined choice, of Plan and of cosmic opportunity.

This latter threefold vision is a very different thing to the self-centred and dualistic vision of the mystic. That vision is a part of the evolutionary spiritual development of all of us and lies behind most occult aspirants. More about this higher vision I may not say; the theme is too abstruse. It involves experiment and experience. Through both of these phases the initiate passes and learns the smallness and the inaccuracy of his past opinion and interpretation of experience.

6. *Time is one of the major underlying secrets of initiation.* You will note from this, the great emphasis on time as event, and as being of true importance in the career of the initiate. The time here referred to is time as the initiate understands it—free as he now is from the control of form or of material substance. It is time as it conditions speed; as it establishes rhythm; as it directs relationships; as it determines choice and fixes decision: activity, rhythm, relationship, decision! The decisions arrived at are *not* related to life in the three worlds, but embody the reactions of the Spiritual Triad. This is a point most difficult for you to grasp, because you have not yet truly built or employed the antahkarana; it is *time* as the opener of the door to extra-planetary existence and as it releases the initiate, not only from the cosmic physical plane but from the cosmic astral plane also. It is with these thoughts that I must stop my present exegesis, because language has not yet the capacity to indicate the truth, even if such indications were fruitful and of use even to the advanced aspirant.

On Hints

There is one mistake which esoteric students are prone to make; they are apt to believe that a hint is so carefully veiled and so cautiously concealed that it is only discoverable after most persistent search. Such is not the case. A hint is usually quite obvious, and should be; however, its meaning, as it concerns the life, work and activities of the disciple, is the factor which presents difficulty and calls for careful reflection. Take, for instance, the obviousness of the hint (on page 319) in which even the paragraphs where it was to be found were indicated. The hint which you were intended to take as a guide is to be found in the words that the disciple must "... recognise the hint which is related to his point in consciousness ... my one effort is to indicate the relation between initiation and revelation."

Four ideas emerge for the disciple as he studies this hint:

1. Recognition .... Of what?
2. His own point in consciousness .... What is it?

3. Initiation .... Which?
4. Revelation .... Again, of what?

One thing you are all apt to forget as you hunt feverishly for the hint, and that is: it is *a hint for the searching disciple.* It is not of general application as far as my intention is concerned, but must contain something each of you needs in order to take the next needed step forward during the year following your receipt of the instruction. Had you considered it in that light?

You now have six hints which can be summed up for you in the form of questions, addressed personally to you and to no one else; they require your personal application, understanding and reply:

1. How have I, as a disciple of D.K., contributed to the work of inducing the Hierarchy to make certain needed changes where the task of influencing humanity is concerned?

   This would involve a high-powered livingness.

2. Is the Will aspect in my life beginning to create situations which are related to the hierarchical Plan which I—as a disciple—must follow?

   This would involve a careful construction of the antahkarana.

3. In what way have I cooperated with the Plan in order to have "modified, qualified and adapted it" to meet the need I see?

   This would involve careful soul-personality cooperation.

4. As I work, do I see an increasing vision of divine intention, and do I know practically more than I did?

   This would involve occult obedience in its true sense.

5. Do I work with an inner programme, and are my thoughts and activities rightly directed?

   This would involve the dual life of the disciple and correct orientation.

6. Do I recognise in the life-training which I am receiving preparatory steps for initiation, and the possibility of impending revelation?

This would involve constant ashramic contact.

These *hints* are therefore intended for the guidance of the disciple in training; the *formulas* are of wider connotation and concern the group, the Ashram, the Hierarchy and the workers with the Plan upon the inner and the outer sides of life. The synthesis of the teaching or of the training given is something which you should not overlook. The unit, the individual and the part are always viewed in relation to an expanding and inclusive whole. One of the marks of readiness for initiation is the ability to see this inclusive entity and to note the law which is transcended when the part becomes the whole; the disciple must be able also to register and respond practically to the greater spiritual laws which take the place of those which have been transcended. In this last sentence I have given you the seventh hint.

It is through the medium of a hint that the Master in any particular group conveys to a disciple His desire for the disciple. In past times, the hint given was obvious and clearly stated by the Master. Today, owing to man's greater intellectual perception, the hint is still obvious, but it is contained in group instructions, given not to the individual but to the members of an Ashram at some particular stage of development—as is the case with all of you who receive these teachings.

You now have seven hints which are capable of a dual interpretation, of individual reception, and of group conditioning. It is with the aspect of individual receptivity that you should be concerned, for the effort to apply these seven hints to your daily life of service will train you in the techniques of my Ashram.

THE FORMULAS

I do not intend to give you a formula in this instruction. The five which you have already received still remain unexplored and unexplained by any of you. You have—with only one or two exceptions—omitted to give much thought or study to these important creative processes. To grasp the meaning of these mysterious presentations, the creative imagination must be brought into play; it must be remembered that these words, symbols and forms have relation (a progressive relation) to the initiation for which the disciple is being prepared. They are in the nature of keys to a door and—when properly grasped, understood and used—they render the disciple capable of demanding entrance on the basis of demonstrated, effective, creative work. They show also (and I would like you to note this with care) that each initiation is the evidence in the disciple's life that he has succeeded in grasping *some great divine idea.*

In the five formulas with which you were presented, five divine ideas were given to you. They were apparently familiar on the surface, but each of them veiled a deep and hidden significance. Each of these five ideas controls one or other of the five initiations, but they have not been given to you by me in their right order. That order is for you to determine. I have no intention to give it to you, and you have no need to receive any more of these formulas. I will however, in later instructions, take up each of these supreme, governing ideas and endeavour to give you initiatory insight into their esoteric significance.

You will have noticed that the formulas, as given to you by me, have been arranged into two different groupings. I mention this because these groupings emerge out of the general text and may not have been discriminately seen by you. In one group, you have five formulas indicated, each of them dealing with a major governing concept. These concepts are divine ideas, brought down into human thought-forms, and each of them conditions the work of our planetary Logos. They are so all-inclusive that there is little that the disciple can do about them, except *feel* himself as an integral part of them—from which he may not and cannot differentiate himself.

The second grouping is of not nearly so great importance, but it is probably of greater practical usefulness; it will, if subjected to deep meditation and concentrated thought, prepare the disciple for a deeper understanding of the first grouping of divine ideas. These five formulas hold within themselves a sixth, which I am not going to give you though I am here referring to it. The second grouping of the formulas is as follows:

Formula I ...Concerns integration into an Ashram. Group feeling. Dissipation of glamour through light.

Formula II ...Deals with alignment. Revelation of the group antahkarana. Reality revealed by an aspect of the mind.

Formula III ..Deals with changes in the soul nature. Time and space. The Eternal Now or immortality.

Formula IV ..Deals with the Life aspect. Concerns the circulation of energy, and therefore the mode of the creative process.

Formula V ...Deals with the first aspect, with the Will. Relates to divine Purpose. Shamballa.

Formula VI ..Concerns Death. The constructive work of the Destroyer aspect. The "passing" of zodiacal and other cycles.

This sixth Formula is a deduction from the other five. I have been dealing in these instructions with the larger formulations. The lesser might be regarded as the subjecting of the formulas to the first and third methods of interpretation, whilst the larger group of ideas concerns the second and the fourth interpretive methods. This is something which it is important for you to bear in mind.

POINTS OF REVELATION

It must not be forgotten that all that is here communicated is strictly in relation to initiation. The revelations accorded (of which three have already been indicated) concern the initiate and his work as it is impulsed from the moment that an initiation has been passed. Life for all men everywhere is full of revelation, recognised or unrecognised; it might be said that there is little else, though the majority of them are of small importance except in their *combined sequence.* They might rather be regarded as creating or constituting a "field of revelation" or an area of consciousness wherein five major points of revelation will some day be seen, grasped and understood; they are the substance which has within it that living something which is invocative of light; it is that material substratum which is capable of evoking that "lighted response" which the initiate demonstrates when he himself has learnt to generate the five points of revelation. These five points (which I shall indicate) must not be confused with the five initiations. They are indeed related to them, but the right order in itself constitutes a revelation, and none of them can be specifically applied by you to any particular initiation. In fact, it might be said that all five of them apply to each initiation, giving—as the initiate can receive and bear it—five aspects of divine activity; these are in the nature of five modes or techniques of the future work to be done by the initiate between initiations. The quotation from the *Old Commentary* as given on page 308 can be regarded as a key to the entire technique.

It is, however, a technique which is formulated by the initiate himself and is not one imposed upon him within an Ashram or by the watching Master. All these points of revelation also concern the techniques of creation, and indicate to the Master what will be the nature of the creative work with which He—under law, according to ray, and in relation to one of the seven Paths—will eventually work.

The entire theme is too complex for anything more than hinted concepts at this time. The general theme has been covered by me to date under four groups of thoughts or four groups of presented ideas. Even though I realise that I am repeating what has been earlier given, I must—for the sake of clarity—call your attention to them anew:

    1. *The Five Points of Revelation.* Of these, three have already been given:

      a. Energy .. Thought ...... Directive Energy.
      b. Will .... Expression .... Immolation. Sacrifice.
      c. Monad .. Universality ... Extra-planetary Light.

2. *Modes of Interpreting* the Points of Revelation:
      a. The mental, occult, spiritual, hierarchical and triadal approach, revealing facts.
      b. This fivefold significance as it is conditioned by the particular initiation being undergone.
      c. The consequent reactions by the initiate, affecting his daily life, service and ashramic activity.
      d. The germ, seed, key or inherent, invocative potency which will appear when the three previous groups of approaches have been taken. This potency will later be exploited.

3. *The Inner Subjective Techniques:*
      a. The stage of the "advancing Point of Light."
      b. The stage of right direction of the light potency.
      c. The stage of spiritual impact.

4. *The Outer Objective Technique:*
      a. Penetration.
      b. Polarisation.
      c. Precipitation.

You can see, therefore, how definitely all the above processes involve a planned creative activity. These ideas are not those, however, which can be used by the uninitiated aspirant. The use, through understanding, of these techniques is confined entirely to creative work, carried on in accordance with the Purpose of Shamballa and not in accordance with the hierarchical Plan. The above various stages of the fourfold process mark eventually the recognition by the Master of divine Purpose; it is also shown how that purpose is revealed in five stages, requiring in addition two final revelations of major importance.

One of the lines of thinking which it is most necessary to impress on advancing and advanced disciples is that of "initiated thinking." This means thought carried forward on purely abstract levels, and embodying, therefore, thought which is free from soul conditioning or from the crystallisations of the lower mind. It is essentially triadal thinking and is only registered by the brain when the antahkarana is somewhat constructed and there is some direct communication from the Spiritual Triad to the brain of the personality.

I am emphasising this point here because *the fourth point of revelation* concerns the sudden recognition by the initiate of the potency of Purpose, as it is expressed in creation, plus a paralleling recognition that creativity is—for the Master— the expression of all for which He has been trained; it is at the same time the lowest of the three possible recognitions anent divine Purpose. The others have nothing to do with creation within the planetary ring-pass-not, but concern the implementing factors of the divine thinking. I know not how else to express these deep and abstruse realities—abstruse because the adequate mechanism for their comprehension has not yet been created by the disciple. We might therefore word this fourth point of revelation as follows: Purpose itself is but an energy, released within the confines of the Council Chamber; there it must take shape. Behind it looms that which has brought it into being.

I would ask you to ponder deeply upon this section which we have called the Points of Revelation; they are aspects of the training given to the initiate. They are also—on a higher turn of the spiral—the esoteric correspondence or higher meaning of the words: "As a man thinketh in his heart, so is he." In the case of the initiate however, the heart is only one of the conditioning points of contact through which the "advancing point of light" can come.

It is perhaps a somewhat new thought to you as aspiring occult students that there is a major revelation—something entirely new and unforeseen—which is inherent in the situation when a candidate for initiation stands before the Initiator.

A consideration of the three points of revelation already given may show you how deep may be the present mystery where each of these points is concerned. The mystery of the eye and its relation to light (esoterically understood) is very great, and as yet no student, no matter how diligent, knows anything about it. For instance, brother of mine, when the third eye, the inner eye, and the Monad are brought into direct alignment with "the Eye of God Himself," so that what the planetary Logos sees can be partially (at least) revealed to the initiate, who can tell what that revelation will bring of results and enlightenment? When the true nature of the will is comprehended and the self-will of the personality (of a very high order, necessarily), the will of the soul (as demonstrated by the activity of the highest tier or circle of the egoic petals), atma, expressing itself as the spiritual will, and Sanat Kumara are also brought, through initiation, into direct alignment, who, again, can predict what the revelation will be? When, again (as hinted on page 313), the myriad thoughtforms of the concrete or lower mind are seen as illusion, and the lower mind, the knowledge petals of the egoic lotus, the abstract mind and buddhi or pure reason are all brought into alignment with the Lords of Karma in a direct relationship and as signifying the ending of karma in the three worlds, who can foretell the nature of the ensuing revelation? It is alignment that holds the clue or the key to all these deeply spiritual events.

It is these ideas which must arise as the true occult student faces up to the recognition of opportunity and prepares definitely and consciously for revelation. It will be apparent to you that the revelations with which I am dealing take place as a result or a consequence of standing before the One Initiator, and only when the initiate is presented by the Christ. The earlier initiations may have their corresponding revelations, under the great Law of Analogy, but they are themselves of a very high type of illusion; they have the quality of illusion and require the recognition (by the initiate) that they simply veil an ultimate possibility for which he must work and wait.

PART VIII

I feel it necessary again to reiterate that initiation is concerned with the consciousness aspect of the disciple or of the group that is to undergo the process. The emphasis has been laid in the past on contact with the Hierarchy and—as we have seen—with the use of devoted, emotional zeal as the medium of that contact. Again, as we have seen, the period of time which has passed since H.P.B. brought this teaching to the modern world has changed all that, and the emphasis is now on the initiation of the consciousness of the disciple or group into areas of divine expression, hitherto unrealised. Initiates, in the past, were admitted into the world of ideas, of intuitional perception or of buddhic awareness; their task was to transform these ideas into ideals; thus, they presented spiritual goals and hierarchical objectives to the race, this being their major form of service. Today, owing to the pronounced development of mankind, the accepted disciples of the world, those who have undergone the first initiation (and their name is Legion), and the initiates of higher degree, have objectives which their mental unfoldment has made possible; they can be admitted into divine areas of consciousness which are conditioned and brought into being, not by divine ideas but by the divine Will (their perception of that Will will be according to the degree of the initiatory control). Their task is therefore to perceive the Plan which is the hierarchical mode of implementing the divine Will, plus the Purpose which is perceived by the Heads of the Hierarchy. They have also to undertake to see that that Plan becomes a factual expression upon the physical plane and a part of the recognised consciousness of humanity as a whole. This, being a relatively new unfoldment, has not yet made the necessary headway, largely owing to the planetary Karma and the appalling situation with which humanity has confronted itself. I would have you here note my phrasing.

Evidence, however, of the growth of the human intellect along the needed receptive lines can be seen in the "planning" of the various nations, and in the efforts of the United Nations to formulate a world plan which will eventuate in peace, security and right human relations. It is interesting to note that, from the very start of this unfoldment, three occult factors have governed the development of all these plans: its clearcut significance, unperceived as yet by you, in the setting of a time boundary by the nations who formulate these plans, within whose announced limits certain objectives are presumed to be possible of attainment.

It will be obvious to you therefore that, owing to the changed polarisation of the disciples of the world, the entire quality, processes and modes of activity of the Hierarchy have undergone and are undergoing change. The nature or quality of the disciples being admitted into hierarchical participation necessarily condition the rhythm and the keynote of the Hierarchy at any given time. At the same time, nothing hitherto developed or gained is ever lost, and the quality of devotion is still potently present; enrichment proceeds and, if I may use such an inadequate phrase, *the perception of all within the Hierarchy* is tremendously enhanced; areas of the divine perception, clothing divine purpose, are steadily being revealed.

Revelation is not only the prerogative and reward of *the attaining initiate*, but it is increasingly taking on new forms and fresh outlines for the Masters Who *have attained*—a process made possible by the higher mental perception of the incoming disciples. Group work, group reaction and group possibilities are carried to their highest point of expression within the Hierarchy. I want you to consider this with care, and not regard the Hierarchy as a static point of love and mediatory activity, as is so often the attitude of the disciple. The evolutionary process conditions the Hierarchy as it conditions humanity and all else in the manifesting universe. There is, however, an evolutionary interplay which —in this era and at this time of crisis—is producing effects in relationship.

Approaching this subject from another angle, the mental polarisation of the disciple seeking entry into the hierarchical sphere of work is producing a unification of initiatory effort which is new in the spiritual history of the planet and which is the first step being taken at this time upon inner and subtle planes to bring about certain great "Crises of Initiation," involving simultaneously all the three major planetary centres—a thing hitherto unknown. Up to 1875, initiation was a sequential process as well as largely an individual process. This is slowly being changed; *groups* are being admitted to initiation because of a recognised and sensed relationship which is not that of disciple and Master (as heretofore), but which is based on initiate-relationship in group form, and which is present between Humanity, the Hierarchy and Shamballa. It is this spiritual and subtly sensed relationship which is today finding physical plane expression in the world-wide effort to establish right human relations.

Initiation is no longer regarded essentially as the moving of a human being who has accepted certain disciplines and made certain self-determined progressive advancement in consciousness into closer contact with the Hierarchy and a group within the Hierarchy; that angle of it will rapidly become a thing of the past. It is the moving forward of an entire group of spiritually-minded disciples and initiates into new areas of the divine consciousness and into a closer rapport with the Mind of the Lord of the World. This the disciples and initiates will do *together*, according to their degree and their point in spiritual evolution. I refer not here to the evolution of the form. Three things will thereby be brought about:

1. A closer linking of the three divine centres (Shamballa, the Hierarchy and Humanity) so that the flow of divine energy will be increasingly unimpeded, and Purpose, Plan and their Precipitation upon the physical plane will be facilitated.

2. A far more powerful Hierarchy and one much more closely linked to Humanity by the principle of intelligence — implementing the love principle — and far more en rapport with the Purpose, which is the dynamic focus of all planetary energising, development and evolutionary growth.

3. A fusion or establishing of relationship within humanity itself, producing right human relations and a consequent integration into the Hierarchy. This will be in the nature of a mass initiation and will be made possible by the relatively new process of group initiation, growing out of the slow method of individual initiation.

These are difficult matters to make clear, my brothers, but I may perhaps have succeeded in conveying to you some general idea as a basis for your further thinking.

The individual disciple, seeking initiation, is with deliberation and with his full and free consent merged into the group; he achieves this fusion by his own individual effort and is (throughout the entire process) an absolutely free agent, moving forward and becoming mentally inclusive, as rapidly or as slowly as he chooses. He determines the time and the event himself without interference or obstruction from any outside force.

This is the relatively new spiritual technique, and it is a technique accepted by initiates and disciples of all degrees in all three divine centres. Like everything else that happens upon the subjective plane of human living, a major distortion of the process and of the new technique will appear in some form or other in human affairs and constitute a great obstruction (apparently and temporarily) to human progress. It will be in the nature of a sidetrack and a glamour, brought into impelling and compelling use by the enemies of humanity and by those who work constantly against the Forces of Light. Today, this distortion can be seen demonstrating in all totalitarian countries; the individual is *not* free and his fusion with the state and his progress as a state-absorbed entity—deprived of the right of free choice and forced through fear and penalty to relinquish his own self-directed life—is a growing menace to mankind.

It is the right use of this same energy which makes fusion with the Hierarchy possible. These are points worth considering, and will convey to you some understanding of present world conditions. The underlying Principle of Fusion and of group endeavour is right and part of the divine plan; its implementation by grasping, greedy and ambitious men, or by deluded disciples, is terribly wrong and will lead to disaster. This disaster the Hierarchy is seeking to avert, but the Masters are handicapped (as usual) by the relatively few upon whom They can depend, and by the lack of understanding amongst the masses of well-intentioned people.

These, through their ignorance rather than through their planned ill-doing, know not how to stem the tide of evil.

ON HINTS

Thus far I have given you—for your searching consideration—seven hints. I intend to give you *no more than these seven*, because what you now have will prove adequate for many years of study. Each of them, in fact, could provide the theme of a book, and the search for their meaning will take all that you have of mental and intuitive perception. The significance which is immediately apparent is the one which probationary disciples can well see, grasp and appreciate. Disciples can, however, arrive at much deeper significances, and it is to these that the group attention is now called.

Let me point out that the apparent significance is applicable to the training and the unfoldment of the individual aspirants, and is therefore in line with the ancient use of hints by the Masters of the Wisdom. But the deeper meaning (for which you must search) is not so easily seen and is concerned with hierarchical impression, involving necessarily ashramic intention and its precipitation in service. It is here that the Points of Revelation are to be found of prime importance, and the reason why I am laying much emphasis upon this little-understood theme of revelation.

As you already know, a hint is susceptible of many interpretations, according to the point in evolution and the grade of the disciple. A Master can gauge a disciple's ability to pass onward and arrive at his attained status by his mode of handling a hint. In the preceding instruction I posited for you a series of questions relating to the subject of hints, but I did not tell you that they were in the nature of a test. They were framed in words that appeared to make them of general and personal application. Did you deal with them as such? There was no need to do so and (if you have truly understood what I have indicated re hints) you must have wondered why the questions were drafted in that particular form; you would then have proceeded to consider their themes and the answers required from the standpoint of the

Ashram, which is not the standpoint of the individual. I know not what you did. I can only hope for your right approach. If—to illustrate—you interpret the sixth hint, which states among other things that "my one effort is to indicate relationship between initiation and revelation," by pondering upon the initiation which *you* believe lies ahead of *you* as an individual, and the consequent revelation which will then be made to *you*, then you will be functioning as an aspirant and *not* as a disciple. If, however, you sensed, no matter how dimly, that each initiate-group enriches the Ashram with its invoked revelation, you will then be arriving closer to the desired consciousness.

For your instruction, I propose to take these seven hints and—in this instruction and the next—I will "open up" the hint for you and try to show you a little (not all) that a hint, rightly approached, can convey. As I do so, it will become apparent to you that you must always have in mind three things:

1. A hint today will concern the group—its interrelation, its fusion, its initiation and its service.
2. A hint is intended to teach you something *new in your experience*, even if—as a theory—it may seem quite familiar to you.
3. A hint, like all else in the occult teaching, is capable of seven interpretations which can roughly be divided into three. These three are that of the probationary disciple or aspirant, that of the accepted disciple and that of the Master or the higher initiate. That interpretation which I will indicate to you will concern the meaning which it has for the accepted disciple, and therefore its meaning for those of you who read these words.

The probationary disciple can arrive at the significance of a hint as it can be understood in terms of the three worlds, i.e., its physical application, its emotional or devotional expression, and its mental formulation; the disciple must interpret and apply it in terms of the Plan, of directed energy and

of the Ashram, as it exists as the servant of humanity. If you
will endeavour to arrive at this attitude and also at a spirit
of true self-forgetfulness, you will assuredly learn much. I
shall not be able to give you full and adequate interpretations or write you at length upon each hint, but I will give
you enough to enable you to go deeper into significances
than would otherwise be possible. Because we are considering the seven rays, do not waste your time attempting to
assign the seven hints to the seven ray influences or to the
seven principles. Disciples on all the rays can work with
these hints in terms of the seven rays, if they so choose; but
these seven terms of ray interpretation have to be used on
each hint, a task which is too great for our present endeavour.

These seven hints are used in all Ashrams as teaching
measures, and when I first gave them to you (scattered
through the papers during the past few years, beginning in
1941 and more definitely isolated for your reflection since
1945) I did not mention this fact. You can see, however, the
richness of the contribution of the disciples since the inauguration of the new technique. Since that time, disciples in all
the Ashrams, and therefore on all the rays, *delved into meaning and arrived at revelation.* I have given you these seven
hints in their simple modern rendering. I will try and give
them to you in their more esoteric presentation, as they are
thus preserved in the Archives of the Hierarchy.

> *Hint One.* As I have given this hint to you, the wording is
> as follows: *"The changes brought about in the Hierarchy
> have been the result of the work of the disciples of the
> world."*

Here you have a very simple statement but one which is
distinctly bewildering in its implications. Its ancient formulation in the Archives consists of an injunction to the Master and runs as follows:

> *"Regard and recognise the changes in the hearts of men,
> and change the rules as men in time and cyclic change*

approach the Ashram. The Ashram stands not still. New life pours in from either side."

This will perhaps throw light upon the interpretation which I originally gave to you. One of the most difficult tasks which confronts the Master is to teach the disciple to think of the Ashram and to act and serve, think and invoke, as a member of the Ashram would normally do. Two thoughts, therefore, emerge from a study of the two versions of this hint:

1. That the Law of Change governs the Hierarchy just as it governs Humanity.
2. That the disciple who functions under this law has the following things to do:
   a. Deal with the constantly transforming changes in his own personality.
   b. Adapt himself to the rapidly developing and changing events which are taking place within the Hierarchy.
   c. Contribute to the wise circulation and direction of the new energies which are pouring into and through the Ashram. This he does by realising himself as a centre of changing energies. This is the way the Hierarchy works.

You who read and study the ways of the Ashrams at this time are witnessing a period of extreme change and adjustment and of a far-reaching reorganisation. For ever the occult law holds good: "as above, so below," and the reorganisation of planetary affairs which is taking place at this time is partially the effect of the changes produced in the Hierarchy by two major factors, to both of which I have frequently referred:

1. The higher and more intelligent type of disciple who is now affiliating with the Ashram and his instinctive demand for *group* work and recognition.
2. The new energies pouring through Shamballa into the Hierarchy; these are of an extra-planetary nature

and have their source largely in the Aquarian quality of the present cycle; these energies are steadily eliminating the energies of the Piscean Age.

Therefore, my brother, from the angle of the searching disciple, this first hint (in one of its deeper meanings) provides you with three lines of thought or of meditative reflection: Evolutionary Change, Reorganisation, Group Responsibility.

The concept of service rendered by the Hierarchy is consistently present. The way to world change is also given. The Hierarchy as a meeting-place of energies is emphasised and — in the disciple's consciousness — these factors begin to emerge as a vital vortex of force, receiving, distributing and under order—that order being the directed focussed will of the many Ashrams within the one Ashram. In those Ashrams, groups of disciples are working, blindly and ignorantly at first, but with a growing sense of responsibility, of relation and of direction. As they work for the Plan on the physical plane, they carry with them to the Ashram the registered sense and the acute realisation of the basic changes in the human consciousness which are the immediate results of world affairs; from their reaction, from the quality of their recognition of immediate need, and from their efforts to present the truth in terms of the "newest mind"—as it is occultly called—the Master in the Ashram can change His techniques, use new ideas upon receptive minds, and thus keep pace with the rapidly developing humanity with which He has to deal.

One of the ideas which a disciple should learn from his reflection upon this problem is that he *is* already a part of the Hierarchy whilst at the same time he is a part of struggling, unhappy humanity. Therefore, he is not alone or isolated; he is a part of the Hierarchy because he has "entered with his group"; this is a fact, even if he fails to comprehend the full implications of that phrase. At the same time, he learns that only in so far as he has developed group consciousness and is beginning to function as "one absorbed within the group" can he truly pass into a closer and more vitally contributory relation to the Ashram to which he belongs.

Hint Two. "Human planning today is one of the first indications of the emergence of the Will aspect."

So this second hint runs. This sounds relatively simple and to be a rather trite statement, and that is because it gives in reality only a general idea and synopsis of the ancient formula. These formulas, which reach the candidate for initiation as hints, are fundamentally in the nature of instructions to the Master, and provide in their entirety a sequence of teaching and of progressive unfoldment of truth. This fact emerges more clearly in the original wording, as nearly as I can translate it for you, or rather, transfer into words what were originally word symbols or ideographs:

"When the stream of direction is noted by the one who seeks the inner side, then let the Master indicate the pattern and then await results. This may take time. Results come not through the action of but one; they appear when the many respond on Earth to that which comes from the higher Centre through the One. This they do blindly, when at stage the first; later they move with care and right direction. Thus affairs are changed on Earth."

To the aspirant, the statement re planning fixes his attention upon the physical plane; he then begins to see what are termed "indications of direction"; he sees them in terms of humanity's immediate purpose and becomes aware of the tiny part which he can play by cooperation with this planning—or, perhaps, by repudiating it. Decision in both cases is dependent upon his background, training, circumstances and prejudices, plus his ability to make choices. This is as far as he can go, and he usually is quite satisfied with the part he has played in the various processes, and regards his choices and decisions as aspects of his mental determination.

But in reality he is at fault, and the case as he visions it is not so. He must learn to function entirely differently. This hint is not concerned with a part which an aspirant must play as an individual, nor does it include the factor of mental appreciation of the qualities of his own nature. Where the true disciple is concerned, three things are involved and condition his whole approach to this problem of human planning:

1. Its relation to the Plan, as it has been communicated to him within the precincts of the Ashram.
2. His ability to use a measure of the true divine Will as it pours through the Ashram from Shamballa for the implementation of the Plan, and as constituting its directing agent.
3. The sequence of the planning as it materialises on Earth in relation to the *time* factor. Three things emerge in his thinking at this time:
   a. The immediate steps to be taken in order to carry the Plan forward, logically, practically and with the least expenditure of the destroying aspect of the will.
   b. The probable duration of the cycle in which the Plan can progress from its inception until its fulfilment.
   c. An appreciation of *the unfolding pattern* of which the material planning is an expression. He needs to discover how far human planning conforms to that pattern. He must sense where nonconformity originates and what steps—as far as his particular point in evolution permits—the Ashram should take to offset the distortion of the Plan. Only in this way will he learn himself to plan.

You can see from the above what a different approach is here involved when a disciple deals with a hint, how wide are the vistas which are opened up, how subjective his predominating attitude must be, and how inevitably the group relationship to the planning becomes apparent and important to him as an individual as well as to the group as a whole.

It is for this reason that disciples in an Ashram are of no political persuasion and own to no nationalistic bias. This is not an easy thing for them to achieve at once, but the group consciousness gradually assumes control, and with it the disciple's ability to think and work with the group in terms of the Plan. He grasps eventually that in relation to humanity, the planning of the Hierarchy falls into certain definite phases of activity—all of them related and all of them tending towards the externalisation of the Plan in any particular century, cycle or world period. These phases are:

1. The phase of *Purpose,* originating in Shamballa and registered by the senior Members of the Hierarchy.
2. The stage of hierarchical *Planning.* This is the formulation of the Purpose in terms of possibility, immediacy, appropriateness and the availability of the disciples, plus the energies to implement the Plan.
3. Next comes *Programme,* wherein the Plan is taken up by the particular ashram involved in its implementation and is then reduced to the formative stages of human impression and direction, the conditions necessary to bring about its emergence, and the two phases of this conditioning. These are usually in two parts; i.e., the destruction of all hindrances and the presentation of the Plan.
4. The emergence of the hierarchical *Pattern* (based upon the recognition of purpose, careful planning and a detailed and carefully thought-out program), both in the minds of the disciples in the Ashram who are involved in the implementation of the Plan, and among the intelligentsia on Earth. These two groups have the task—the first group consciously and the other unconsciously—of bringing the pattern of things to be into the mass consciousness, by no means an easy task, as the present state of world affairs demonstrates.
5. Then comes the final phase of *Precipitation,* when all the subjective work has been done on the basis of possibility, and when the pattern and a part of the programme are recognised by the world thinkers in every nation, either

favorably or with antagonism. The planning, having reached this final stage, then proceeds under its own momentum.

These are some of the ideas which lie behind the particular hint which I have given to you, as far as the disciple is concerned. According to his development and his point in evolution, so will be his emphasis; some disciples can aid the Master in the planning process because they are becoming sensitive to impression by Shamballa; others are engrossed in the formulation of the programme and in imparting some of its features to more limited disciples, thus setting them to work. A group of carefully chosen disciples are always held in the Hierarchy to work solely with the pattern; this is a most important phase of the work, requiring a spirit of synthesis and an ability to hold streams of hierarchical energy under control. Disciples who are not so advanced, and who are therefore closer to human thinking at the particular moment in history, undertake to supervise the precipitation of the Plan. Their work is necessarily far more exoteric, but is most responsible, because it is when the Plan has reached the stage of human implementation that error is apt to arise and mistakes can occur.

In every ashram are to be found those disciples whose task it is to make the needed readjustments of the pattern and the demanded changes in the programme as the process of precipitation goes forward. It is a law that human freedom may not be infringed. The staging of the Plan and its working out is, in the last analysis, an entirely human affair, once it has reached the stage of precipitation. It is dependent upon the responsiveness of human brains, and their recognition of need and its sources. This is a point which should be remembered.

The above short explanation of the implications of a hint, and particularly of Hint Two should show you how rich is the area or the atmosphere of a hint—if I may use such peculiar phrasing; it will show you also how hints are largely concerned with ashramic duty.

THE FORMULAS

All that I have done hitherto in connection with the presented formulas has been to give you five of them and to indicate the nature of the sixth, which is not to be given. It is all that I can at this time do. I would, however, like to summarise here what I have already given, because of the major importance of the theme.

I gave you certain definitions of a formula which it is necessary to repeat. They are not many, but they indicate a phase of hierarchical working and of training in a certain definite esoteric technique which is essential for every worker in an Ashram to grasp. This, therefore, concerns you.

I also covered their description and significance in two ways: the first concerned their application to the disciple and to his ashramic life and service, and the second had reference to the more universal and general meaning. We can therefore sum up what has been given in a threefold manner and provide a closely integrated yet widely useful approach to these fundamental formulas. I am thus provided with the background of what I feel the need of saying to you on these formulas:

I. *The Formulas Defined.*
  1. They are second ray presentations of soul ideas. Essentially, they are geometrical forms, lying behind all exoteric manifestations; even when presented as words or phrases they are susceptible of being reduced to definite forms. *They are building patterns.*
  2. They express significance and intention. To the disciple and the initiate who employs them correctly and with understanding, they indicate energy direction as a definite part of the creative work which emanates constantly from the world of souls, from the Kingdom of God and from the Hierarchy. *They are rightly oriented energy patterns.*
  3. They are related to the world of meaning and are the esoteric symbols to be found behind all exoteric

forms. They veil that which is in process of being
revealed. *They are revealing patterns.*

4. They contain or veil the six prerequisites for initiation, and are therefore six in number. They indicate
   the six relationships or the six intermediate stages
   of consciousness to be found between initiations.
   *They have unique reference to the pattern of the
   initiate-consciousness.*

5. They are definitely formulas of integration, both universal and individual. *They present certain great
   creative patterns* connected with the integration of
   lesser forms into a greater whole.

6. They are related to the entire process of death. Death
   —from the angle of the formulas—is the integration
   of the essential being in all forms with the pattern
   which produced its exoteric manifestation. *They concern the discovery of the pattern.*

II. *The Formulas from the angle of Discipleship.*

Formula 1 . . Concerns integration into the Ashram; it
concerns the "revelation of group feeling."
It is related to sensitivity and conditions the
life of the Ashram.

Formula 2 . . Concerns alignment in the three worlds
with the soul. It is related primarily to the
higher alignment between the Personality
and the Spiritual Triad, via the antahkarana. It conditions the whole spiritual
man.

Formula 3 . . Concerns the soul and the egoic lotus. It is
related to the transfer of soul energy into
the antahkarana, producing conscious
awareness of time and space in terms of the
Eternal Now. Right interpretation of this
formula gives insight into the past and into
the Law of Cause and Effect; it also gives
intelligent appreciation of present opportunity as well as an intuitive perception of

the future possibilities which confront the Hierarchy.

Formula 4...Concerns dynamic energy and is the basis of the true Laya-Yoga; this yoga deals ever with the point within the circle and its relation to other points which condition the evolutionary process.

Formula 5...Concerns the Will and is related to divine purpose. It conditions the establishing of all correct relationships.

Formula 6...Concerns the processes of death which have a most definite effect upon already established relationships. It concerns life-transference and has relation to the presentation of opportunity.

III. *The Formulas from the universal creative Aspect.*

Formula 1...The transition from darkness to Light. Creation in the Light.

Formula 2...Transition from the unreal to the Real. The nature of reality. Creation in time and space as understood in the three worlds.

Formula 3...Transition from death to Immortality. The nature of Life. The creative process and life energy.

Formula 4...Transition from chaos to ordered Beauty. Relation of the world of effects and the world of meaning. Then relation to the world of causes. The nature of karma. Progressive evolutionary creation.

Formula 5...Transition from the individual consciousness to the universal. Evolutionary processes from divine Purpose into plan and then into manifestation. The nature of individual renunciation. The one Life.

Formula 6...Transition from cyclic living into life itself. The Purpose of cycles. Control of time-space consciousness.

Two major ideas emerge from a careful study of these three tabulations: Pattern and Transition. It is upon these two that I would ask you to reflect constantly. In past years, I have frequently called your attention to the necessity of a vital and active programme, formulated by you and self-initiated by you, and therefore, in these tabulations, you have much that can throw light upon that necessity and upon the lines along which the programme should go; you must remember ever that the programme of a disciple and of an ordinary aspirant are not in any way identical.

Programme will—if followed with spiritual exactitude—reveal your soul-intended life *pattern* and this will be an expression of a life *purpose*. This summation of a disciple's life is also the summation of the life of the Lord of the World, Whose self-initiated programme, implemented by evolutionary energy and steadily revealing the "pattern of things to come" is increasingly known as an expression of the divine initial purpose.

The section upon formulas is perhaps the most exacting in the series of instructions I am now giving you, for it involves creative thinking, intuitive insight, and the use of the spiritual will; these three activities are relatively new to the aspirant and present as yet great difficulties. These you will have to think out for yourselves, and thus acquire the training which will enable you to see life in the process of producing great formulas of living which, in their turn, will produce the essential creative patterns.

There is nothing more that I need to say on this subject. Later teaching on the matter will be available next century. I have already given you more than you can understand, but not more than you can begin slowly to study and eventually to comprehend by direct programme-forming in your own life, and making it at the same time an essential part of the programme of the Ashram with which you find yourself affiliated. This you will have to do through self-devised formulas, thus producing a life-pattern which will be indicative to the watching Masters as to the point in evolution attained by the disciples.

POINTS OF REVELATION

It might here be noted by you, as we consider this entire subject of revelation from the angle of the initiate, that (in the initiatory process where the disciple is concerned) revelation is simply one way of expressing the constantly recurring effects of pressure forward and of vision. Throughout the entire evolutionary process there is essentially nothing but a growing revelation. The two terms, Evolution and Revelation, go together. Any distinction lies within the field of revelation or—to word it otherwise—within the various planes of consciousness, and particularly that in which the revelation is taking place. Earlier I said that "the next sequential revelation will be that of creativity, of the world of thoughtforms which humanity as a whole has created and the setting in motion—by humanity and in relation to its own destiny—of the Law of Cause and Effect or Karma. This will take us back into the very night of time and demonstrate the hope of the present era."

Revelation is both formless and also within form, and the closer to realisation, the more subtle and devoid of form will be the revelation. This is, of course, a platitude of which you are well aware but it needs renewed recognition. Again, there is necessarily, in revelation, always the concept of *Light* and that which it reveals. Light on the physical plane produces the organ of vision, the eye through which revelation of physical areas of consciousness becomes possible; the same theme of light runs through the analogous process by means of synchronising instruments upon all planes; nevertheless the physical concept of instrument falls increasingly into the background, and other words take its place as we deal with higher areas of consciousness: Recognising Perception. Interpreting Perception. Spiritual Perception. Decisive Perception. These terms will suffice to convey to the disciple the nature of the recognitions which he renders to the revelation that unfolds before him, once he is an initiate within the Ashram and is changing his apparatus of perception from the tangible one of the three worlds (tangible because within the world of forms) to the higher correspondences which he must use in the future.

It is at the sixth Initiation of Decision that Perception and Recognition of the revelation reach their heights for the initiate. After this, the subtler correspondences to the tangible senses of taste and smell begin definitely to demonstrate, but with them we shall not deal, for they are effects of revelation so far removed from the possible achievement of the majority of the Masters that they concern us not; they are more properly related to the unfolding consciousness of Those Who function in the Council Chamber of Shamballa. Human evolution or the human evolutionary process is entirely concentrated around the sense of sight, with its consequent effects and results of vision, recognition and perception—all of them constituting what we mean when we speak of revelation.

This revelation can be—as I said—either in form or formless; it can be a pictorial symbol or a subtle demonstration; it can be expressed only in words, or it can take the form of wordless recognition; it can be a goal or a future sensed possibility, but it can also be an incentive and the dynamic impulse of the initiate's life because it is not distant but is a real aspect of his divine equipment—I know not how else to express these possibilities to you, my brothers. It is with these aspects of revelation that we are here dealing, because they are strictly aspirational developments and are available as a result of ashramic training and of hierarchical initiation.

I would remind you that in all that I am giving you in this series of instructions I am dealing with hierarchical initiations and not with those advanced stages of unfoldment which are referred to when the subject of the Christ arises or of those times when He is spoken of as the Teacher of the Angels. Let us keep our thinking and its resultant aspiration in the realm of human possibilities. I would have you note the distinction that can be made between the aspiration which precedes thought and which presupposes an emotional orientation to light and revelation, and that which is the consequence of thought and which is the seed of an oriented perception of that which lies permanently within the consciousness of the Hierarchy.

As we consider these revelations, I would like to take them up with you from a somewhat new angle; I would ask you to remember that the concept of Light must always be established by you *mentally*, alongside that of the revelation itself. I would ask you also to remember that I am dealing with revelations which are no longer true revelations, because they have been formulated by the initiates of today and made visible in words. Revelation is therefore, as far as you are concerned, of two kinds:

1. Those that have been recognised and perceived in the past and (consequently) have been "reduced to words" —using the phrase in its occult and limiting significance.

2. Those that are as yet unrevealed to any except those who have taken the fourth initiation. The three points of revelation (indicated by me) can usefully be related by you to the first three initiations, though they necessarily have an interpretation appropriate to all the initiations.

Let me express for you here—in their briefest form—the four points of Revelation already indicated, and then "in the Light" let us consider them as suggested earlier.

1. Energy follows thought and the eye directs the energy.
   Involves the physical plane.
      Relates to the first initiation.
         Concerns the ajna centre and the so-called third eye.

2. The will is an expression of the Law of Sacrifice.
   Involves the astral plane.
      Relates to the second initiation.
         Concerns the heart centre, the "advancing point of Light."

3. The Monad is to the planetary Logos what the third eye is to man.

> Involves the mental plane.
> Relates to the third initiation.
> Concerns the head centre, the light of Purpose.
4. Purpose itself is only an energy, released within the confines of the Council Chamber. There it must take shape.
> Involves the buddhic or intuitional plane.
> Relates to the fourth initiation.
> Concerns the throat centre. Light upon the Path.

There follows next the fifth revelation, which is as follows:

5. When the light of the seven Rays is blended with that of the seventh Ray, then light supernal can be known.
> Involves the atmic plane.
> Relates to the fifth and sixth initiations.
> Concerns the alta major centre. Extra-planetary light.

You will see therefore, brother of mine, how very abstruse these apparently simple statements anent revelation can be. As I have formulated them above, they indicate the revelation in its primary and initiatory individual recognition; the meaning is, however, far greater than appears, and is in reality related to the unfolding purpose of the planetary Logos, involving the planetary Council. All that I have here given you in connection with the seven centres (if brought into relation with all that I have given you in *A Treatise on Cosmic Fire)* will afford you some general idea of the various planetary significances. This I have personally no time to do, even if it were desirable, but it will be obvious that what I have indicated along the line of correspondences *must* be true, for the ancient truism "as above, so below" holds eternally good, and it is the task of the Hierarchy to demonstrate this. The relation of the microcosm to the macrocosm can never be broken, and that relationship is deeply involved in these five points of revelation.

It has been occultly stated that:

"The five points of the five-pointed star are pyramids of ascension and, at the summit of each point—hidden within the emanating rays—lies a point of revelation, offsetting the radiation but preserving the deeply seated magnetism. Thus is there symbolised the going forth, the coming back and the point of peace, surrounded by activity."

I will endeavour (as we consider these points of revelation) to express as far as may be this relationship of the smaller to the great, of the part to the whole, and of the five points of spiritual contact upon the physical plane (outlets for the energy generated in the planetary centres) with the sumtotal of the means of expression. These centres are brought into expression—as far as the points of revelation are concerned— at their respective initiations:

1. The ajna centre.
2. The heart centre.
3. The head centre.
4. The throat centre.
5. The alta major centre.

I say not that these five exits for planetary energy are the planetary centres, for they are not; I say that they are the points through which the energy of a planetary centre is directed in the service of humanity at this particular time. The centres of the planetary Logos are necessarily directed in their inflow and outflow from Shamballa; they are expressions of the Purpose underlying the creative evolutionary process. The five corresponding exits are those which, in this cycle, disperse the energy—generated by the Hierarchy, under the inspiration of the divine Purpose and directed towards the carrying out of the Plan.

It is wise to remember that the Plan is as much of the divine Purpose as can be brought into expression upon the planet—under the Law of Evolution and the tension of this

planetary crisis through which we are passing at this time—
or at any one time or particular epoch in time and space. Let
us now consider these points of revelation so as to gain from
them some real understanding:

The First Point of Revelation: Energy follows thought and
the eye directs the energy.

We are not dealing here with the simple statement that
thought power is an energy and that the process of thinking
generates automatically an energy which produces objective
forms, induces related action, and is the source therefore of
all that appears or manifests. That is a platitude today, and
humanity is increasingly aware of the subjective power of
thought and of its consequences—objective realisation. We
are to concern ourselves with that which lies behind the
mental perception of the ordinary man and with the revelation which comes to the initiate disciple as he stands within
the ashram and perceives—as a result of the initiatory process—the nature of the divine Plan, as it can be seen working
out on various planes of our planetary existence. There are
three things which the initiate notes as the new panorama
unfolds in flashing light before him:

1. The *point of tension* which precedes revelation. There
   is much to be considered in relation to tension as the
   forerunner of initiation and its subsequent revelation.
2. The *stillness* by which the revealing vision is surrounded, if I may so inadequately express the idea.
   The revelation is given to the initiate as if there was
   nothing in all the world but himself (a point of tension) and a vortex of force which takes form before his
   eyes, revealing to him an inevitable but future activity.
3. The *level* upon which the revelation (apprehended at
   the highest possible point of consciousness for the
   initiate) must eventually be materialised or brought
   into being.

Initiation is always taken on levels of consciousness higher than the mental, and the initiate must not only realise the significance of the revelation but must also know the sphere of activity of which it will be the inspiration. I would have you ponder on the wording of this last sentence.

Each of the five points of revelation indicates to the initiate: procedure, location and objective. Each is therefore susceptible of many and varied interpretations; these are dependent upon the initiatory status of the disciple. With these we cannot deal, because it would entail the writing of another complete treatise and this would also be largely incomprehensible to the uninitiated reader. I can, however, give you some ideas anent the five points of revelation which I have indicated, leaving your intuition to wrestle with their import—or leaving it to your imagination if the intuition is not yet creatively active; it must always be remembered that the imagination is the seed of the intuition, because that which is not existent somewhere within our apparently complex planetary system cannot be imagined.

In connection with the aphorism that energy follows thought, I would have you relate this concept to the Science of Impression, bearing ever in mind that the Masters of the Wisdom work in three ways as They endeavour to implement the divine Plan:

1. They formulate, deliberately and in line with Their fixed intention, those thoughtforms which must be "impressed" upon the substance of the level of consciousness desired.
2. These living forms of thought are then occultly energised and become centres of energy or reservoirs of energy, with the original thoughtform as the creative source at the centre. These thoughtforms and this generated energy are held steady within the aura of the Master or of a group of Masters.
3. The energy is then projected on to a particular plane or into the mind consciousness of those disciples who are en rapport with the Master, or of those groups of disciples or aspirants who are working in close association with some hierarchical group. If I say to you that the initiated disciple uses the ajna centre, I am only stating a partial

truth; many of the Masters work through no physical or etheric mechanism whatsoever, but utilise what might be termed "a point of projection" within the ashram; this is a point of sevenfold contact, available at all times for the use of all those initiates who have taken the third initiation. They work consequently from that high place within the Hierarchy and do not need to employ the ajna centre or any other centre within the etheric body. Writing as I am, for disciples and initiates who have not yet taken the third initiation and who are still "confined" within physical vehicles, the information that the "eye directs the energy" is sure and far more easily understood.

From the angle of our studies, the revelation accorded to the initiate relates to the carrying forward of the divine Plan upon the physical plane and to the implementation of the will of Shamballa, through the medium of disciples and aspirants and of advanced humanity, working—consciously or unconsciously—in our modern world.

Down upon the level of daily living, disciples are today learning three things: the Technique of Impression, the generating of energy, and the use of the ajna centre. Many are responsive to impression, but fail to recognise or use the energy of which the impression is simply the forerunner; others respond to the energy, but fail to register the Plan which it is intended to implement, and the energy then leads to great but fruitless activity. Still others are learning to use the centre between the eyebrows, standing as silent and poised recipients controlling the third eye, the directing agent of the received energy. It must be carefully borne in mind that the energy to be used is not the energy which the disciple himself generates or his own life force, but is something different, something which he has received from the Hierarchy and of which he is simply the agent or channel. He has therefore to learn to distinguish between the various energies he contacts. The initiate has to master the techniques of differentiating between:

1. His own energy or energies, which have been generated

as the result of his life experiences down the ages or centuries.

2. His ray energy which, rightly used, conditions his work with and for the Hierarchy.

3. The energy of the ashram of which he may avail himself in the process of carrying out activities—initiated by impression. In the early stages he calls this the energy of his Master, but learns later that it is—in reality—the energy generated by his Master's group, the ashram.

4. Hierarchical energy or the energy of certain associated ashrams or of the entire group of Ashrams, the Hierarchy itself. The use of this highly qualified and most potent energy can only be employed when the disciple has earned the right to certain privileges and can be trusted to use the potencies correctly.

5. The energy of the Head of the Hierarchy, or the Christ force, as it is sometimes called. This force imports into the usually available energies certain conditioning qualities which emanate from Shamballa, and are therefore related to the Will aspect. This type of force has not hitherto been available to working disciples but is now available, having been released at the Wesak Festival of this year (1948). Even now it can be used only by highly trusted disciples, and usually by those only whose rays are the first Ray of Power or Will or the second Ray of Love-Wisdom. These will be the rays of one or other of the two major vehicles—that of the soul and that of the personality. There are naturally exceptions to this rule, and these exceptions will be increasingly numerous as time speeds by; but in the present time, first and second ray vehicles provide the line of least resistance.

The first Point of Revelation has necessarily an unique relation to the physical plane, to the hierarchical workers in physical bodies, and to those who consciously use the ajna centre. The number of those who can work with the energy of thought is now very great, because so many hundreds of thousands have taken the first initiation. This becomes clear when you realise the untold numbers of those who are defi-

nitely oriented towards the light, who are spiritually motivated and are consciously trying to tread the Path or—to
express the idea in Christian phraseology—to follow the foot-
steps of Christ. They may know nothing of the occult teaching or of esoteric techniques, but the discipline of their lives
and their realised fixed intention and service bring them
inevitably, eventually, on to the occult way. They are learning to think; they earnestly seek to know the right way for
humanity, and desire to ascertain the will of God; they are
therefore building thoughtforms and are developing the
power to be impressed. At present, they appear to be putting
the cart before the horse, and they need to learn to think
after impression; but this the spread of the various meditative processes will eventually correct. Later, the directing
potency of the ajna centre (the centre between the eyebrows) will attract their attention and the triple process of
impression, thoughtform construction, and energy direction
will be mastered by them, and the first point of revelation
will no longer be a revelation; they will be committed to an
intelligent implementing of the Plan upon the physical
plane.

*The Second Point of Revelation: The Will is an expression
of the Law of Sacrifice.*

The second Point of Revelation is of peculiar interest. It
concerns the first contact of the initiated disciple with the
energy emanating from Shamballa and transmitted to him
via the Master of the Ashram with which he is at this time
associated. He has not yet reached the stage wherein direct
contact is permitted, but still needs the ashramic protection
which the Master provides. At the indicated second initiation he receives a quality of stimulation which enables him
to "see" the astral plane *as it essentially is;* with this revelation comes also the recognition of the basic human necessity to "make it holy" or to "render whole" that which provides the most disturbing element in the existence of mankind.

I cannot here deal with psychic construction, with astral impulses or glamours, nor can I spend time referring to the usual astral conditions—so well known and so carefully followed by the mass of men. Each human being has eventually to make his own definite decision anent the astral plane and his release from its control, and has then to follow (for several lives) a policy of non-association with its phenomena. But the initiate-disciple receives an unique revelation and an applied conditioning which enable him to recognise it as a man-created whole or world or state of consciousness (whichever term you may care to employ) and therefore as something which must be transformed. Two things consequently emerge in his consciousness:

1. That the astral plane is not God-created, or divinely "inspired," but is the product of human desire, evinced at the very dawn of human intelligence; this desire has built thoughtforms which are in tune or allied to every phase of human desire from the lowest type of physical desire up to the spiritual aspiration of the man who is seeking liberation. What can the disciple, therefore, do to make the astral plane "holy" or "set apart" and segregated from the sumtotal which the Divine Thinker, Sanat Kumara, *has* created, and with which the desires of mankind— through the medium of the astral world—have, fortunately for the individual man, become entangled? At this point, he knows that he must, inevitably and eventually, contribute something. He realises that he must intelligently work towards the separation of the astral plane from the six planes of divine creation. I would ask you to remember, brother of mine, that the star of creation is the six-pointed star and not a seven-pointed star.

2. As the needed service which must be rendered takes possession of the heart and mind of the initiate, the method is simultaneously revealed to him. This method is the use of an "advancing point of light"; it is, however, a form of light which can only be implemented *by the will;* this will can only fully complete its task when all three

aspects of the will—as exemplified in the three points of the Spiritual Triad—have all been sequentially employed.

You can see, therefore, how different is the revelation which comes to the initiate than are those which the average aspirant and disciple regard as astounding revelations. Their sense of values is in error. There is a group service quality to the revelation with which we are dealing, and also about these five stages of revelation, which is unknown until the antahkarana has been created, thus linking the Spiritual Triad and the Personality. The energy then to be used is entirely related to the Will aspect of divinity. This does not demonstrate as it does with average advanced humanity, as applied goodwill, but it expresses itself as a dynamic destructive spiritual Will; it adds its quota of destroying energy to the task of destruction with which the Hierarchy is confronted in connection with the astral plane.

This Point of Revelation brings with it certain revelations of an unexpected nature and imparts to the initiate certain new and significant results which register as truths to the initiate-consciousness. He discovers that he must learn the divine nature of the destroying aspect of the Will; he learns that it is not related, when demonstrating as this particular aspect, to determination or fixed intention, but is a fluid energy which can be directed toward the plane of desire wherever and whenever contacted; he finds out also that, in order to combat this vast and vibrant astral world, an aspect of light must be employed, and that therefore he is being given his first opportunity to work with Light under the inspiration of the Will—as do all the Members of the Hierarchy; he realises, consequently, that he *must* employ this aspect of light under the action—definitely directed—of the Will, in order to bring about the disappearance of that world as a sentient conscious entity; he knows that he must primarily destroy the astral phenomena for which he is creatively responsible, and that (having done this) he must demonstrate his complete freedom from the phenomenal contact of the astral plane at the second, the third and the fourth initiations. This he must do through the "advancing light" of lower mental substance, and the activity of the buddhic level of activity; then to this he adds the destroying power of the atmic level of activity. He has to take note, in this process, of a certain level of responsibility. Thus he can finally destroy (with the means of the advancing light of the atmic plane) a certain proportion of astral substance for which he is not individually responsible but which is nevertheless related to the group or to the nation with which he is by birth or inclination affiliated. It is the united and synthetic use of the three triadal expressions of energy which makes the work of the world servers effective.

You can see from this short resumé which I have given you about the results of the second point of revelation, how widely comprehensive is the entire theme of revelation as it implements, impulses and motivates hierarchical activity. Through those revelations the initiate-disciple becomes aware of the task which he must fulfill and the next immediate step which humanity must take—through one or other of its grouped masses. These revelations concern the use of the Will in implementing the evolutionary aspect of the divine purpose. In all these points of revelation the Spiritual Triad is involved, and every one of the revelations is—in a steady crescendo of illumination—the result of initiation.

All the five points of revelation are conveyed or make their impression at each initiation, but differ greatly according to the initiation taken. The use of the Will aspect in "making holy" or in "setting apart," is active not only at the second initiation, but in all of them and—in a peculiar sense —at the sixth Initiation of Decision; of this initiation the six-pointed star is the symbol. The decision there involved tests the initiate as to how free he is from all desire—a factor which impregnates the entire creative world. Freedom from that control indicates the recognition of the Will as an expression of the Law of Sacrifice.

The Christian interpretation of the Will of God and of the significance of sacrifice is based, in reality, on human revolt and on human refusal to see anything in the spiritual life but an unintelligent acceptance of the inscrutable divine

Will; it posits also the need for pain and the suffering of sacrifice in the sense of complete abnegation of all that might be regarded as good and useful, as desirable and joyful. This revolt has coloured the entire presentation of what Christian theologians regard as God's Will; this presentation involves the unavoidable imposition of the will of a transcendental Deity, and leads inevitably (though totally inconclusively) to the dreadful and symbolic death of the Christ upon the Cross and to the painful and sacrificial life of the spiritual man. There is much teaching given out by the church upon the necessity of the submission of the human will to the divine Will; however, little or no teaching is given of the joyous use of the Will of Christ, immanent in every form, and peculiarly active in the form of humanity, and therefore capable of *joyous* and *understanding* use. The idea that sacrifice signifies happiness and a joyful process of making desire "holy" is absent; theologians refuse to recognise that the releasing of the energy confined and imprisoned upon the astral plane, into "enlightened" service upon other planes, is neither comprehended nor in any way understood.

The concept of *substance* runs through all that is here given; the atrophying of the substance of the astral plane, the merging of "lightened" substance with that of other planes, the use of the substance of light as a medium of spiritual destruction, and the bringing in of the three types and qualities of the substance of the Spiritual Triad (in order to liberate humanity) is never noted. Nevertheless, these three types of substance (mental, buddhic and atmic) are all symbolised for us upon the Mount of Crucifixion. There are also far deeper meanings to the well-known Gospel symbolism than those which have been recognised or studied.

I have here, however, thrown some light upon this second point of revelation, and much upon which you could well ponder and reflect.

Part IX

You will find it of value, brother of mine, to summarise the mass of information which I have given anent Initiation;

I refer not only to that which is contained within these particular instructions but to that which is to be found within
all the many books which I have written. Isolated statements
and interesting details are really of no major importance. It
is the entire general picture and the recognition of the place
of initiation in the evolutionary scheme which should engage
your attention. Earlier in these instructions I pointed out to
you that meditation was a planetary technique; in the same
way, *initiation may be regarded as indicative of successive
planetary consummations* marking, for instance, the birth
of each of the kingdoms in nature; initiation is, par excellence, a series of graded steps or awakenings which enable
the human being to become eventually a member, or a point
of light, in the Kingdom of God. When an adequate number
of members of the fourth kingdom have undergone the
process of initiation (technically understood), *then* the fifth
kingdom will come into exoteric manifestation. The method
of making this hitherto subjective kingdom a factual entity
is rapidly nearing, and the proof of this is—for the first time
in history—*group initiation*. This can now be undertaken,
and it is for this that the Hierarchy is working today, where
aspirants and disciples are concerned.

The problem of group initiation must be, I know, one of
difficulty for you to consider. Many questions must naturally
arise. Can, for instance, the faults of a disciple keep the
group back from initiation? The answer is no. The result
of the dominant shortcomings of the members of the group
being prepared for initiation only serves to eliminate them
from the group *temporarily*, but it does not thereby hold
back the group. The group moves forward through the door
when all the necessary eliminations have taken place, and also
when the group has developed certain capacities—as a whole
and mutually. Let me specify some of these capacities, but
without going into detail:

1. The capacity to be outward looking and interested in
   the reactions of life and of events *upon humanity*.
2. The steady tendency towards decentralisation, so that
   the personal self is handled with a just sense of propor-

tion but is not regarded as the dominant factor in the daily life.

3. As a result of this decentralisation the aspirant grows increasingly towards a more complete fusion with the group. He knows himself to be an integral part of the group and with all that such a relationship involves.

4. He is becoming every day more integrated. This integration is a fourfold one:

   a. His personality, in its various aspects, is integrated into one functioning whole.

   b. He is achieving a pronounced relationship with the soul, and for this reason is becoming a soul-infused personality.

   c. As a worker for humanity, he is blending always more closely with the group in training, and is becoming an integral part of it through similarity of aims, spiritual aspiration and trained techniques.

   d. He is slowly being integrated into the very heart of humanity; this puts him in touch with the Heart of the Hierarchy and—through the Hierarchy—energies from the Heart of the Sun can reach him.

5. He indicates a growing sensitivity to all that is spiritually esoteric (forget not that there is an esotericism which is not spiritual, but which is strictly related to black magic); his inner hearing and his eye of vision are rapidly being brought into an occult focus.

These are simply some of the capacities unfolded by the individual aspirant and—if you study them with care—you will realise that they are of fundamental importance. It is the fusion of all these capacities in group work which enables the group to seek initiation and to be welcomed through the slowly opening door by Those Who are to be found upon the other side.

Another question which might well be asked is: Do all the members of the group have to be at the same point upon the Path of Discipleship, or can they be at many differing

stages of discipleship or initiation? What you really mean
when you ask this question is: Is the group—composed as it
is of individuals—taking the same initiation? Are all its
members at exactly the same point in evolution? By no
means. A group should be (and is) composed of individuals
at varying points of development; some may be preparing for
the second initiation; others may be in training for the third
initiation, and a few may be ready for the fourth or the fifth
initiation. The nature of the initiation to be undergone is
known *only* to the disciple and his Master; it is of no interest
to the group itself; the diversity of the initiations for which
preparation is being made tends to enrich the group content;
the more ray types which are found functioning in the group,
the more valuable will be its service. It is the bringing together of groups in preparation for initiation which has led
to the present basic change in the methods of the Hierarchy.
A would-be-initiate does not, at first, work solely under the
care of the Master of a particular Ashram. Certain of the
Masters (usually Masters like myself who have only lately
passed through the fifth initiation) have been chosen to train
and instruct aspirants on all the rays until after the third
Initiation of Transfiguration.

Then and only then does the disciple-initiate pass into
the Ashram of the Master of his ray—one of the senior Masters in connection with the seven major Ashrams. If he is a
disciple in the Ashram of a Master Who is on one of the
Rays of Attribute, the task of that Master is to prepare him
for transition on to one of the major Rays of Aspect. This
shifting and interchange is taking place all the time. When,
for instance, the Master R. assumed the task of Mahachohan
or Lord of Civilisation, His Ashram was shifted from the
seventh Ray of Ceremonial Order to the third Ray of Active
Intelligence; the majority of those who have taken the second and the third initiations were transferred with Him
under what might be called a "special dispensation"; the rest
of the members of His Ashram remained for tuition and
training in service under that Master Who took His place as
the central point of the seventh ray Ashram.

Still another question could well be asked: What is the

attitude of the group during initiation *if* the individual members are undergoing different initiations? Is the group integrity imperiled? During the period of initiation, their attitude is one of focussed, concentrated and deep meditation in which *the inner attitude is given solely to the concept of Hierarchy.* The disciple is not, at this time, occupied with the Ashram of which he is a part or with any questionings as to the nature of the Ashram into which he is now entering as an initiate—either as an initiate of the Earth initiations or, in the senior grades, as an initiate of the Sirian regime. He is —during the first four initiations—entirely centred in consciousness upon the larger Whole wherein the Ashram to which he belongs is a part; he is attentive to the Christ, the Head of the Hierarchy, because He is the Initiator of the first two initiations which always seem to the neophyte of major importance. After the third initiation he is attentive to that "veiled Presence of awful Power Who tests his fitness for working in the will of God." I would ask you to note the peculiar phrasing "working *in* the will of God," and to remember that that Will, centred or focussed in Shamballa, is one of the great basic energies; the initiate has to learn to work in and through that Will. If, therefore, each initiate in the group is conscious of the initiation next to be taken, then subconsciously he eliminates all awareness of outer contacts and stands alone, and yet in group formation, before one or other of the two Initiators. The inflow of dynamic energy which comes to him through the application of the Rod of Initiation becomes a group inheritance and serves to galvanise, integrate and fuse the group into renewed actiity and a deeper subjective union.

There is one point which is oft overlooked, but which I gave to you earlier, and that is *the mental approach to initiation.* So much emphasis has been laid upon the love quality of the Hierarchy, on its being the expression of the second divine aspect, that the hierarchical mentality (if I may use such a phrase) is frequently forgotten; yet it is a law—closely related to initiation—that "the work of the initiate is carried forward *within* the ring-pass-not of the Universal Mind." I would have you give these words calm and mature consideration.

The planetary Logos works—as far as His manifestation, the Earth, is concerned—from cosmic mental levels; all that is manifested through His Creative Word is His focussed thought and His fixed mental intention. In order to create a material world, He directs His thought from what can be regarded as the concrete levels of the cosmic mental plane; the whole process is one of precipitation, consolidation and irradiation.

All the initiatory processes through which the disciple must pass are primarily concerned with the thought of the supreme, incarnating Deity; that thought demonstrates as the will-to-good. The disciple's progress from one initiation to another imparts a gradual unveiling of the divine Purpose, as it expresses itself through the hierarchical Plan and manifests that quality of love (the will-to-good) which gives to the Purpose and the Plan warmth, its magnetic appeal, and the major attribute of healing. It might be said that the Purpose of the planetary Logos, as it emanates from His high place *under the impact of His will-to-good,* is redemptive in nature.

This theme of redemption (which underlies all the initiatory processes) is hidden in the karmic responsibilities of Sanat Kumara; stage by stage, initiation by initiation, the disciple arrives at an understanding of redemption. First of all, he learns to bring about the redemption of his threefold personality; then the concept enlarges along paralleling lines as he seeks the redemption of his fellowmen; later, he shares the redemptive work connected with all true hierarchical endeavour and becomes an "active part of a redeeming Ashram." At the later initiations, and after the fifth Initiation of Revelation, he sees with a new clarity some of the karmic liabilities which have led the planetary Logos to create this planet of suffering, sorrow, pain and struggle; he realises then (and with joy) that this little planet is essentially unique in its purpose and its techniques, and that on it and within it (if you could but penetrate below the surface) a great redemptive experiment is going forward; its prime implementing factors and its scientific agents are the "sons of mind who choose to be the sons of men and yet for all eternity remain the Sons of God." These "sons of mind" were chosen, in that far distant time when the fourth kingdom in nature came into being, to carry forward the science of redemption. There is a true historical and spiritually esoteric significance in the words in *The New Testament* that the "whole creation groaneth and travaileth together in pain until now, waiting for the manifestation of the Sons of God." St. Paul is there referring to planetary purpose and to the determined insistence of the Sons of God that eventually— as they brought about the redemption of substance, of matter and form, and thus proved the possibility of that redemption through their own transfigured personalities—their reward should be their eventual manifestation as expressions of divinity. For this purpose and with this goal in view, they instituted the great evolutionary process of initiation, thus producing a continuity of revelation and of enlightenment. In reality, the period of time at which the final initiation is undergone is simply a climaxing, triumphant demonstration of the realisation and purpose of all past experiences; it is fulfilment (by the One Initiator) of the first promise ever made to the "sons of mind" when they originally started their redemptive work, and is "a sudden blazing forth of the individual glory and its merging at initiation with the glory of the whole."

These ideas may give you a fresh viewpoint anent initiation, and if you can ponder and think correctly, they will aid you in entering somewhat into the Mind of God, thus permitting you to penetrate at least into that "area of promise" upon which all spiritual hope, all expectancy and the dynamic intention behind the evolutionary process depend. The "halls of initiation" (to speak again in symbols) in which the initiate demonstrates his redemptive quality are the true "promised land." The whole story of the Jewish people is based upon a recognition of this fundamental truth; it is, however, distorted by them into a form of individual and racial possessiveness, owing to the profound materialistic selfishness of the race. They give to the entire, eternal hope (which is the hope of all the sons of mind) a material and racial distortion and a purely material objective—the objective of territory. All this is, in its turn, founded upon the arrogance, the aggressive nature and the lack of true perspective which are basic characteristics of the Jewish people, *in spite of many exceptions.*

The "area of promise" wherein the divine thought is projected, directed and held true to the originating impulse of the planetary Logos is to be found on cosmic levels and remains there unchangeably. It is that which holds **Sanat Kumara,** in His Council Chamber at Shamballa, standing steadfastly by all those lives which are undergoing redemption and by all those who are the agents of the redemptive process until "the last weary pilgrim has found his way home." These agents are the sons of men who will—each and all—demonstrate eventually "within the courts of Heaven" and at the place of initiation, the nature of their high calling; they will prove to all who can grasp the significance of the demonstration that they have only "become again in full expression what they have always been." Now the removal of the veils of matter permits the inner glory to shine forth and—the redemptive work now being finished—"they can walk with glory in creative undertakings." I am quoting some words which the Christ used (at an initiation held not so long ago) when addressing a group of new initiates.

ON HINTS

We will now proceed to a consideration of the hints which I have already given to you. They are seven in number. With two of them I have already dealt. They were:

Hint I.   The changes brought about in the Hierarchy have been the result of the work of the disciples of the world.

Hint II.   Human planning today is one of the first indications of the emergence of the will aspect.

Five hints remain to be considered, and I list them here, not in the question form as given earlier, but in their original wording. I would ask you to read them several times straight through with concentrated thought and to note how closely they are related to each other, and how they cast a light upon the initiatory process which is unique, synthetic in value and enlightening. As I have told you, they are each of them subject to seven interpretations, but for our purposes we will confine ourselves to the study of them from the angle of accepted discipleship, i.e., of the disciples working in an Ashram and preparing for service and for initiation.

Hint III. Disciples in all Ashrams have a task of "modifying, qualifying and adapting the divine Plan" simultaneously. Why is this so? Why is the Plan not *imposed?*

Hint IV. The initiate knows because he works. What does this hint mean to you?

Hint V. The key to the correct interpretation of a hint lies in its association with the idea of direction in time and space.

Hint VI. The disciple must recognise the hint which is related to *his* point in consciousness. . . . My one effort is to indicate the relation between initiation and revelation.

Hint VII. One of the marks of readiness for initiation is the ability to see the expanding and inclusive Whole, and to note the law which is transcended when the part becomes the Whole.

In connection with the sixth hint, I pointed out that revelation—induced by right orientation and right thinking—is part of the training of the initiate. Many thus in training delay their progress by not recognising the revelation when it arises above the line of their spiritual horizon.

You will note that the hints themselves frequently deal with the nature of a hint, because a hint is in reality and when properly considered, *the seed or germ of an intended revelation.* The Master knows well what is the next revelation which will be in order for the disciple in training; through hints He sows the seed of revelation, but it remains for the disciple to discover that which the hint is intended to produce, and to nurture the seed until it flowers forth in the beauty of revelation.

In seeking to elucidate these hints for you I am not doing work which you should do. I am, in fact, only marshalling for your benefit the ideas, information and concepts which are already to be found in your subconscious mind—placed there through meditation, study and experimental critical living. Having done that, I leave it to you to proceed alone and unaided towards the moment of revelation. You talk of a series of initiations, but the Masters talk in terms of *a series of revelations,* and Their work with Their disciples is to prepare them for revelation. Bear in mind, brother of mine, that revelation is hard to take and to hold—a point oft overlooked. It is exhausting to the personality of the disciple, but it is of no service unless the personality recognises it; it is excessively stimulating and the initiate passes through three stages where a revelation is concerned: First comes the stage of ecstasy and of supreme recognition; then darkness follows and almost despair when the revelation fades and the disciple finds that he must walk again in the ordinary light of the world; he knows now what *is,* but it is at this point that his test lies, for he must proceed on that inner knowledge but dispense with the stimulation of revelation. Finally, he becomes so engrossed with his service, with aiding his fellowmen and with leading them towards *their* next revelation that the excitement and the reaction are forgotten. He then discovers to his surprise that at any time and at will—if it serves his selfless interests—the revelation is forever his. Ponder on this.

Let us now study the remaining hints:

Hint Three. "Disciples in all the Ashrams have the task of 'modifying, qualifying and adapting the divine Plan' simultaneously. Why is this so? Why is the Plan not imposed?"

You will note immediately the relation of this hint to the first one given. The concept of responsibility underlies the significance of this hint, and in connection with it I would remind you that—from the angle of the esoteric science—the sense of responsibility is *the first* and the outstanding characteristic of the soul. In so far, therefore, as a disciple is in contact with the soul and is becoming a soul-infused personality, and is consequently under soul direction, so far will he undertake the task presented to him in this third hint. The "modifying, qualifying and adapting" process is carried on through the medium of an intellectually focussed personality and is aided by the comprehension of which the concrete mind is capable. It is a result of the activity of the soul upon its own level and is related entirely to the hierarchical group intention and to the furthering of the divine Plan.

The apprehension of this Plan by the disciple will necessarily vary according to the disciple's point in evolution. In the very early stages of discipleship, his capacity to "modify, qualify and adapt" is small indeed, but each expansion of consciousness fits him increasingly to do this. You would find it of interest to study again the stages of discipleship as outlined in Volume I of *Discipleship in the New Age.* You would note how each stage (when it is a factual experience) enables the disciple to see the Plan from the angle of the Ashram and of the Master with increasing clarity; finally, there comes the time when the disciple arrives at the very heart of things and is so close to the heart of the Master that the hierarchical planning becomes something in which he shares and to which he contributes.

There are two thoughts which should be here considered. First of all it should be realised that the disciple, under the Law, has to master the technique of spiritual compromise, and secondly that the three words: modify, qualify and adapt, have definite reference to the three worlds wherein the Plan must manifest. There are two kinds of compromise, brother of mine. There is the compromise in which the balance is attained for the sake of expediency, and this is usually on the side of the least desirable, the more material and the easiest. There is also the compromise which swings decision (and decision is always involved in the furthering of the Plan) over towards that which concerns the spiritual values, and which will eventually bring about the greatest good for the greatest number. It is this art of compromise which the disciple has to learn, for little is gained by the imposition of the spiritual values. The compromise to be established by the disciple lies between the recognition of the stage reached by average humanity and the immediate aspects of the Plan which the Masters feel should be presented to, and recognised by, everybody.

The value to the ashram of a trained and functioning disciple lies in his ability to "see with the Ashram" that activity which is required, and the technique and mode of bringing about still another development within the eternal Plan; to this must be added the disciple's understanding of the civilisation and the culture of which he is a part and a comprehension of the field in which his endeavour must lie. Being a functioning human being and a part of the great panorama of life, he can interpret to the Ashram what he sees of extended evil, what he notes of humanity's striving towards the good, and the "revealing voice" of the speechless masses; his suggestions as to the immediate mode of turning the hierarchical ideas into ordinary human ideals are of importance to the Master of his Ashram. His value in this aspect of the hierarchical work is that he is *not* a Master, that he is necessarily closer in touch with the daily life of ordinary human beings, and that the field of his activities is with personalities, whereas the Masters and the senior initiates work with souls. When a disciple is a truly soul-infused personality, he can give to the Master most valuable assistance. There are, it should be pointed out, three types of hierarchical workers:

1. Souls; i.e., those initiates who have taken the fourth Initiation of Renunciation and in whom the soul body, the causal body, has been destroyed. They are the Custodians of the Plan.
2. Soul-infused personalities; these are the disciples and the initiates of the first three initiations, through

whom the "souls" work in the carrying out of the
Plan.

3. Intelligent aspirants who are not yet soul-infused personalities but who recognise the necessity of the Plan
and who seek the welfare of their fellowmen.

The highest group formulates the Plan; the second group
"modifies, qualifies and adapts" the Plan to contemporary
human requirements and thus ensures the gradual and
steady continuity of the Plan; the third group are the agents
who carry this Plan to mankind and seek to make it work-
able, guided by spiritual compromise—the compromise evidenced by the second group.

Disciples, as they grasp the Plan and are spiritually informed as to the steps to be taken to modify the Plan upon
the mental plane so that its acceptance by humanity is intelligently progressive and is not dynamically imposed with consequent disastrous effects, are the primary agents. They
accept the responsibility for the needed compromise, for it is
their responsibility and not the responsibility of the Masters.
The various aspects of the Plan—as presented to them in the
Ashram—are then modified and rearranged so that the Plan
becomes a series of sequential steps and is not the violent
impact of an unrealised idea. It might be said that the spiritual compromise of the disciple (working with the Plan)
transforms the basic idea (through mental modification) into
an acceptable ideal.

When the process of modification is completed, the idea—
in the form of an ideal—descends to the astral plane, the
plane of the emotions. There it becomes tinctured with the
quality which the working disciple believes will make the
best appeal to the masses of men with whom he may be
working, and particularly to the aspiring intelligentsia.

Today two qualities are "tincturing" the ideal of the
coming civilisation for which all disciples are working: Freedom and spiritual security. This is true even if the man who
talks in terms of security omits the word "spiritual." It is
that for which they nevertheless seek. Then later, the ideal,
"duly modified and qualified" is presented to the world of

men upon the physical plane, is there *adapted* to the differing fields of thought, to the diverse types of consciousness, and to the nations and groups with which the New Group of World Servers is working. This triangle of workers is enfolded on all sides by the world of souls and of men; its apex reaches to the highest levels of the Hierarchy; its second point is anchored in the New Group of World Servers; its lowest point penetrates into the masses of men. You have, therefore:

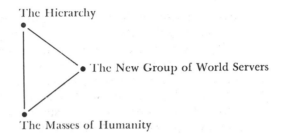

There is a straight line of spiritual descent from the Masters into the ranks of men, and—in the New Group of World Servers—the task of "modifying, qualifying and adapting" is carried forward. Mistakes are often made, because this triple work is dependent upon clear vision and a balanced judgment, but in spite of everything, the work goes on and (in the long last) that which is the divine idea does emerge as an accepted ideal and, in due time, is the means of carrying the entire human family onward along the Path of Evolution.

Hint Four. "The initiate knows, because he works. What does this hint mean to you?"

The entire story of evolution is covered in these few words. The Christ put it in other words when He said "If any man shall do His will, he shall know"; under the occult law, doing ever precedes knowledge because knowledge is gained through experiment and experience. The disciple or aspirant works always in the dark, particularly in the early stages of his unfoldment, following a deep and hidden instinct towards right activity. By that hard and persistent performance of duty, under the pressure of conscience at first, under the impulse of his awakening soul, and under the influences of the Master, he moves forward from darkness to light; he discovers that obedience to his spiritual instincts leads him inevitably into the realm of knowledge, and that knowledge—when acquired—is transformed eventually into wisdom. He then becomes a Master and walks no longer in the dark.

Aspirants usually bitterly resent the many cycles of darkness through which they seem to go; they complain of the difficulty of working in the dark and of seeing no light anywhere; they forget that the ability to work in the dark or in the light is all one inherent capacity. The reason for this is that the soul knows nothing but *being*, and light and dark are—to the soul—one and the same thing. Above everything else, knowledge comes through conscious experiment, and where there is no experimental activity no experience can be gained. Knowledge is the reward of both these factors—a knowledge which is not theoretical but which is proven, factual, and the intelligent result of hard work; it is also the result of frequent distress (rightly handled) and of spiritual anticipation.

The above is true of the life and work of the individual aspirant as he tackles the problem of his own lower nature and prepares for the stage of becoming a soul-infused personality; it is true also of the working disciple, seeking knowledge and wisdom as he works out the hierarchical Plan as best he can. He must perforce experiment and gain practical experience; he must learn the meaning of both success and failure, and the knowledge which can be gained thereby. Knowledge comes at first through the struggle to move forward into greater and clearer light; then it comes as the aspirant (seeking soul expression) learns to forget himself in the need of others as they demand whatever light and knowledge he may possess; wisdom takes the place of knowledge when, in the transmuting fires of struggle, pain and hard work, the aspirant transforms himself into the working disciple and is gradually absorbed into the ranks of the Hierarchy.

There are other and deeper meanings than the above, but I have here indicated to you the way to fuller knowledge; the latent significance will inevitably reveal itself, as you work through experiment and experience and from experience into a manifesting expression of divinity.

Hint Five. "The key to the correct interpretation of a hint lies in its association with the idea of direction in time and space."

I wonder, brother of mine, if you can realise that a hint is not a hint as long as it fails to give you *direction* and the power to move forward. A hint is not a static point of information. Correctly approached, it becomes the dynamic, underlying next step forward upon the Path of Return. It is *there* that the words "in time and space" come to have significance. One of the first things which a disciple has to learn is correct timing, both as regards his own experimental spiritual life and in relation to the work which he may be doing under hierarchical impression in the world of everyday affairs. It is one of the hardest lessons to learn, particularly during the stage wherein the disciple can be easily swayed by impulsive, emotional enthusiasm; it is a peculiarly hard thing for people upon the sixth Ray of Idealism or Devotion to grasp.

Disciples, in their novitiate, make more mistakes as regards *time* than any other; that would naturally be expected, because time is only a word for daily, *eventual* living. I would have you note the word "eventual" in its connotation with *current events.* Time is naught but a succession of events, as registered by the physical brain consciousness; these events are apt to have undue and too powerful an effect upon the disciple. Once, however, he can think of events as aspects of time, he not only begins to develop a needed continuity of consciousness, but he develops also a sense of proportion which has a stabilising and sound effect. Students would do well to take the words "direction in time and space" and use them as a seed thought in meditation. The reward would be great.

It is wise to remember that "space is an entity"—as H.P.B. expressed it. When he so defined space, he gave humanity one of the most important hints it has ever received. The realisation of the existence of this entity leads to a practical recognition of the aphorism that "in Him we live and move and have our being." It explains the necessity for the esoteric teaching anent planetary centres and the planes as states of consciousness. The disciple then begins to study himself in relation to this "all-enveloping Entity," to ascertain the "direction" from which the various energies (which empower his life and motivate his actions) come, and to familiarise himself gradually in "the location of these power stations and of those radiant centres of light which—founded by the divine Creator—are the sources of life and the origin of light and knowledge." Thus is it expressed in the ancient archives which, at times, I attempt to translate for you.

Direction. Time. Space. With these concepts in mind, occult information begins to assume a new and deeply esoteric importance. They can be studied in two ways by the disciple (and it is for disciples I write):

1. As indicating the direction in time and space from whence motivating energy and illumining love can make an impact upon the receptive disciple.
2. As indicating (again in time and space) the direction in which the energies, manipulated by the disciple, must go as he learns to cooperate with, and work out, the hierarchical Plan. This is the positive and not the negative aspect of these words.

The disciple moves always in a world of energies; they make an impact upon him from many and varying directions. He has to learn which energies should be rejected and those to which he should be receptive; all these energies are moving in space and are in reality the life-aspect of the space-entity; all are determined by the time factor with which the disciple must familiarise himself. On the other hand, the process is reversed at times. The disciple learns to use energies—located and found by him in space—within a set time and then to direct them accurately (via the ajna centre) into the work and into the group which is under hierarchical influence, through his own immediate efforts. Ponder on this, for in these words lies hid much illumination.

The remaining two hints will be covered in my next communication, and then the teaching upon the Hints will be concluded. The teaching upon the Formulas was concluded in the earlier instruction because enough had been given anent these abstruse forms to serve the purposes of instruction during the coming cycle.

POINTS OF REVELATION

We have already dealt with two of the points of revelation and have therefore considered the two which have reference to the first two initiations; these are taken upon the physical and the astral planes respectively. At the second initiation, the initiate begins for the first time (though in the most elementary form) to employ the will aspect and—in the revelation accorded—he takes a major step toward the third Initiation of the Transfiguration. This connotes the transfiguration of the personality and its liberation from the alluring imprisonment of the three worlds. Now he faces that great transitional initiation and is confronted with the revelation which has been expressed for us in the following words:

The Monad is to the planetary Logos what the third eye is to man.

These are mysterious words and can only be understood if brought into relation with the previous revelation, involving the Will and the Law of Sacrifice. It should be remembered that the Law of Sacrifice (in its destroying aspect) is dominant during the second, the third and the fourth initiations.

1. At the second Initiation of the Baptism, the control of

the astral body is broken; it is sacrificed in order that the intuition, the higher counterpart of the "propelling aspiration" (as it is sometimes called) may assume control.

2. At the third Initiation of Transfiguration, the control of the personality in the three worlds is broken in order that the Son of Mind, the soul, may be substituted finally for the concrete and hitherto directing lower mind. Again, through the Law of Sacrifice, the personality is liberated and becomes simply an agent of the soul.

3. At the fourth Initiation of Renunciation, the destroying aspect of the Law of Sacrifice brings about the destruction of the causal body, the soul body, in order that the unified soul-infused personality may function directly under the inspiration of the Spiritual Triad—the triple expression or instrument of the Monad.

The significance of these "destructive episodes which produce the freeing of the prisoner of the planet" (i.e., the divine, spiritual man) lies in the fact that, after the fourth initiation, the light of purpose is the sole controlling factor in the career of the initiate; he enters then upon a stage wherein he steadily approaches closer to the "centre where the will of God is known." It is an elementary revelation of the divine Purpose which is given at the third initiation; only the first stage of that mysterious all-embracing Purpose is at that time revealed; the remaining six initiations progressively reveal (to the Master) the all-enfolding Purpose.

Earlier I told you that three words should be considered in relation to the Points of Revelation: Procedure. Location, Objective. All three of them are of use here in considering the nature of the impending revelation.

The recognition of these Points of Revelation falls automatically into two main procedures or planned processes:

1. The procedure carried forward under the impulse of the Law of Sacrifice which "destroys all hindrances, breaks down all impediments and removes all indi-

vidual obstacles, thus releasing the initiate into that vortex of force in which he learns the method of handling the planetary correspondence of that which he has individually overcome." These words should be carefully studied in relation to the second, the third and the fourth initiations.

2. The procedure carried forward at the remaining five initiations; in these initiatory processes there is a "spiritual absorption of the initiate into the circle and into the cycle of the Universal Mind"; the initiate is then "caught up and liberated into planetary fields of endeavour wherein the will must be employed as the Monad may direct."

You can see from the above how abstruse all this advanced teaching must necessarily remain—veiled and protected in order to protect and guard the initiate. This dual procedure in relation to the crucial moment in each of the initiations is always most scrupulously guarded. The moment "wherein the initiate, standing upon the point within the triangle and not upon the square," sees (in a flash of time) the great aligning procedure which will carry him from the immediate point of revelation on to the final glory, must and will be forever protected.

The *location* of this particular point of revelation is on the mental plane; through the alignment of the concrete, lower mind, the Son of Mind and the abstract mind, a direct channel for vision is created. The medium of revelation at this initiation is the antahkarana, which is rapidly being constructed and can thus prove the connecting link and the esoteric mode of vision. The instrument of reception is the third eye which—for a moment—is temporarily suspended from its task of directing energy upon the physical plane and then becomes a stationary, receptive organ, turned inward toward the higher light. The head centre is therefore involved, and a secondary alignment takes place between the ajna centre, the head centre and the soul body. All this takes place at a high point during the third initiation; for the first time in his personal history the initiate is completely aligned and can function straight through from the head centre to the highest point of the Spiritual Triad. You have, therefore, the reason for the sudden inflow of transfiguring glory.

This is the *objective* of the initiation, and the triangle of procedure, location and objective is created, flashes into being, and then—at the close of the initiatory process—fades out, leaving however a permanent, new, spiritual and instinctual trend towards monadic perception and livingness.

You will note, therefore, how this information—by pointing out the attitude of the third eye during this initiatory process and its new function in relation to the Monad— throws fresh light upon the work of the Monad. This third eye is now receptive to light from the highest source, is arresting in its outward-going activity and functions like a lens for the reflection of light and for the attaining of the highest possible inner vision for the particular point in evolution reached. All this embodies an activity which (except in the case of the highest initiates) remains very mysterious. However, a study of the use of the third eye at the third initiation will bring illumination of the teaching that the Monad is to the planetary Logos what the third eye (in its initiatory function) is to the disciple of the third degree of initiation.

The Monad is the source of light, not only to the human family, but *it is the receiver of light from the threefold Sun;* it is the lens through which the light of the solar Logos can flow to the planetary Logos, preserving and holding steady in that light the vision, the purpose, the will and the creative intention of the planetary Logos.

More along this line I may not convey to you. I can only give veiled suggestions and formulate for you certain phrases or seed thoughts which (if duly considered and reflected upon) will begin to train your perception and develop the third eye, enabling it to reorient itself and change its function when the right time and the correct emergency come.

I have told you that these points of revelation are the germ or seed of a certain invocative potency; this is especially true and correct where the teaching anent the third eye is concerned. Initiation is not an abstract, mystical process to which the disciple is subjected upon some one or other of the subtler planes, the knowledge of which must gradually seep through into his consciousness. This may be partially true of the first two initiations (the Sirian initiations of the threshold), but all the remaining initiations involve the whole man and "three periodical vehicles," producing a steady fusion of these three, an increasing reaction to the Light of the World, and an ability to register in the physical brain (if the initiate is functioning through karma, decision or service in the physical body) that which is undergone; in this registration process the third eye is acutely involved. From the time of the third initiation this third eye is subjected to training and begins to function in the two following ways:

1. It is (in a measure) a correspondence to the concrete mind, with its capacity to interpret environment and experience.
2. It can also act as a lens or a light-gatherer from the inner and higher worlds.

You will note, therefore, the fresh significance that these ideas give to the three stages which accompany the points of revelation: the Stage of Penetration, the Stage of Polarisation, and the Stage of Precipitation. The inferences to be drawn I shall leave you to work out for yourselves after due study of the teaching.

Passing on to the fourth Point of Revelation, we find it covered in the following words:

"*Purpose itself is only an energy, released within the Council Chamber at Shamballa. There it must take shape.*"

This point of revelation carries the initiate to one of the highest points of contemplation; we are here concerned with his sudden apprehension—at the fourth Initiation of Renunciation—of another phase of the divine, conditioning Will. He has begun to recognise and to interpret—even though in an elementary fashion compared to what he will recognise at the ninth initiation—the destroying aspect of the Will as it expresses itself through the Law of Sacrifice. Now, for the first time (as a result of destruction), he can begin to grasp the essential building aspect of this same Will and to appreciate his future function as a creative Builder. The building here to be carried forward, I would remind you, is not the building which is distinctive of the second divine aspect— that of Love-Wisdom. It is strictly connected with that of the first aspect of Purpose, Power or Will; it deals with the processes which precede the actual creative building, the drawing up of the blueprints (if I may use such a term) "within the confines of Shamballa," where high spiritual Beings must lay Their plans. This is a different process to the creative building process, and is related to a mysterious undertaking which is carried forward under the "Law of Assembly."

The energy which is employed and with which the initiate at this time makes his first and very temporary contact is that which the planetary Logos employs as He gathers into His ring-pass-not that extra-planetary substance which must progressively be used, as the world of being and of forms makes progress under the Law of Evolution. It must be remembered, for instance, that the planetary forms are now composed of a much higher substance than in primeval days. It must also be remembered that a great process of elimination is forever going on, accompanied by a paralleling *process of substitution*. That which is rejected and which is occultly thrown out as no longer serving the purpose of the planetary Logos is replaced by that which "will measure up to the purpose of the Father." It is this concept which has been travestied and distorted by the Christian teaching anent the "vicarious atonement." This grew out of a basic confusion between the Law of Sacrifice and the Law of Assembly, and took place when any understanding of the nature of the Father remained a supreme mystery; the whole process was then interpreted in terms of the first and highest Aspect of the essential Trinity, of which man knew nothing, instead of in terms of the second Aspect, the building, magnetic aspect of Love. We are—if it could be but realised—in process of re-interpreting and re-arranging what can be called "the doctrinal structure underlying the relation between knowledge and wisdom." This involves the destruction of old concepts such as the trinity of manifestation, and the assembly of those new and more correct ideas which must inevitably be substituted for the old, as the unfoldment of the first aspect is presented to the initiate upon the Path. This, through certain later activities, will gradually seep downwards into the consciousness of humanity, and the new world religion will be founded upon a deeper spiritual perception of the Father or Life Aspect, in place of the rapidly crystallising vision of the Son or consciousness aspect.

You get a clue here to the teaching which I have oft given to you, that the higher processes of spiritual unfoldment must consciously give way to a much higher phase of perception, for which we have, as yet, no word. In relation to consciousness, we speak constantly of initiation; in relation to this new process of simultaneous perception and interpretation, we employ the rather vague word "identification."

The process in which the initiate is now permitted to share during and after the fourth Initiation of Renunciation (which is presented to him in a successive series of points of revelation) is made possible by his submission to the Law of Sacrifice. This, in its turn, brings his consciousness under the influence—in developing stages—of the Law of Assembly. This is a law to which I have not yet made reference in any of my previous instructions. The initiate can now—through appreciated and comprehended revelation—add to his work with the Plan and its building technique, a capacity to work with divine Purpose and with those substances (etheric in nature) and those energies which permeate the cosmic etheric body (the four higher planes of our cosmic physical plane) under a law which is set in motion by the Father, but which makes the building activity of the Son possible, so that it is utterly in line with divine Purpose.

Another angle of this process, revealed by the point of revelation attained in the fourth initiation, is that there is then indicated the very highest point of the process of redemption, because the energies *released* within the Council Chamber of Shamballa are "the living substance which is substitutory in nature and which is made available to the progressing point of light." That point in the divine consciousness which can be called (for our purposes) the Unit, Man, redeems sequentially the substance of which all forms are made and brings into manifestation the higher counterpart of that substance, released—for man's use—at Shamballa. This is a deep mystery and I fear it is not possible for me to express these ideas with greater clarity. However, under the Law of Correspondence or Analogy, the initiate can gradually come to a true perception of the significances involved. These points of revelation emanate from the world of significances, and not from the world of meaning; they cast light, if truly interpreted and in due time, upon that world of meaning, thereby redeeming and liberating the forms in the world of appearances.

You have therefore, in this suggested point of revelation, the same three sequential methods of apprehension of truth as is to be found in all such revelations. What are these methods?

There is, first of all, the recognition of *a great procedure* which must, under the Law of Assembly, be responsible for the bringing in of extra-planetary energies as the redemption of the worlds of being and of form is carried forward by the second divine aspect. Of this procedure I can tell you naught. The place or *the location* of the procedure of assembly is made clear. It is in the Council Chamber of Shamballa. I would, however, brother of mine, call your attention to the fact that Shamballa is simply a word conveying the idea of a vast focal point of energies which are assembled and brought together by the planetary Logos in order to create a manifestation adequate to His unfolding intention and planetary service. *The objective* is equally clear; it is the assembly of that which has in it energies of redemption. Just as the Science of Redemption, under the hierarchical Plan, is the technique employed to redeem the world of appearances, so—on a much higher level—the Law of Assembly produces the Science of Energy which is the redemptive process (in a sense which you cannot possibly understand) influencing the work of those who labour for redemption in the world of meaning.

Again you see how all this comes under the three stages of Penetration, Polarisation and Precipitation, for it is related to the assembling of the redemptive energies brought into our ring-pass-not through the activity of Beings at Shamballa Who can penetrate into extra-planetary spheres and then focus (within the Council Chamber at Shamballa) the energies thus assembled. They can then precipitate them into the ring-pass-not of the Hierarchy, and consequently hasten the redemptive work and carry the energies from the highest levels of the cosmic physical plane down to the lowest level of outer, dense physical manifestation.

The agent of this process is the energy of the intuition or the energy of pure reason. This is the mental quality "within the ring-pass-not of the Universal Mind" which is increasingly employed by the higher initiates in the work of assembling energies. This energy is perceptive of the stage of redemption attained in the world of appearances as the Hierarchy applies the redemptive energies; it is also perceptive of the quality and the stage of activity which the new energies to be assembled must possess.

I would call your attention to the fact that this point of revelation is related to the plane of pure reason or to the buddhic plane; this is the lowest of the cosmic etheric levels; it is therefore a plane of "transitional ejection"—a level from which the new and assembled energies are "let loose upon the world of outer forms." This process has been greatly facilitated since the entire Hierarchy shifted its location (since 1925 A.D.) from the higher mental levels to the buddhic plane, thereby making direct and unimpeded etheric reception possible. This is one of the significances of the words which we read in *The New Testament* that "the veil of the Temple was rent in twain from the top to the bottom" —a symbolic way of expressing the unveiling of an unimpeded channel. This was made possible by the Christ as the

Avatar, working in cooperation with the Master Jesus, and also by the point of evolution reached by the humanity of that time.

We will leave the fifth point of revelation at this time and consider it in our next instruction. It is one of tremendous importance, for it concerns the highest aspect of the Will and covers the synthesis of the energies of the five planes of human and superhuman evolution. This synthesis precedes the work done on the two highest planes of divine unfoldment, and comes to its focus and its full expression at the time of the sixth Initiation of Decision.

Part X

For years we have talked about group initiation, and it remains as yet, for you, an unsolved problem. The phrase, "group initiation" is only used by the Members of the Hierarchy in reference to the first two initiations—initiations of the threshold, from the angle of the Lodge on Sirius. After these two preparatory events, the initiate—at and after the third initiation—reaches the point wherein he "undergoes initiation" in his own right (as the phrase runs), for he can now be trusted to ask nothing for the separated self; his personality is tempered and adjusted to group conditions; increasingly he is manifesting as a soul-infused personality, and the antahkarana is being rapidly created and effectively used. To phrase it otherwise: as the number and expressions of soul-infused personalities grow and initiates of the third degree increase numerically on Earth, what will be the result? Three great happenings will take place with spiritual and focussed intention; they are today taking place, which is the point I wish to bring to your attention; it is this *conscious intention* which confers potency in the life of each disciple and initiate.

1. The Kingdom of God or of Souls, distinguished by the potency and therefore by the aura and radiatory emanation of love, is definitely anchored on Earth, and is pene-

trating ever more fully and successfully into the three
worlds of strictly human endeavour. There have always
been outposts of this kingdom among men; there have
ever been individuals in all parts of the world—in the
world religions or in other constructive groups—who
were linked consciously to their souls, and consequently
linked to the Hierarchy. There have always been those
in every land who developed and expressed the Christ consciousness; this is loving understanding and intelligent,
living service, no matter by what words or terminology
they expressed the tremendous spiritual event of which
they were aware. But—from the standpoint of the world
populations—the fourth kingdom in nature dominates in
every field of thought and of activity, and not the Kingdom of God or of Souls.

Today, as a result of a spiritual awakening which dates
from 1625 A.D., and which laid the emphasis upon a
wider, general education and upon a revolt from the imposition of clerical authority, the radiation from the world
of souls has greatly intensified and the Kingdom of God
is becoming a corporate part of the outer world expression, and this for the first time in the long, long history
of humanity.

The effect of this radiation or magnetic aura is now
so extensive that we need no longer talk in terms of bringing in the kingdom or of its manifestation on Earth. *It is
already manifesting,* and its aura is co-mingled with the
mental, astral and etheric auras of mankind. Recognition
only is required, but (and this is a factor to be noted)
recognition is being withheld until the kingdom of souls
can be safeguarded from the narrow claims of any church,
religion or organisation; many will claim (as they have
ever done) that admittance into the Kingdom of God is to
be found through their particular separative group. The
Kingdom of God is *not* Christian, or Buddhist, or to be
found focussed in any world religion or esoteric organisation. It is simply and solely what it claims to be: a vast
and integrated group of soul-infused persons, radiating

love and spiritual intention, motivated by goodwill, and rooted in the human kingdom, as the kingdom of men is rooted in and is a break-away from the animal kingdom.

2. The antahkarana is now being built by all soul-infused personalities (or constructed unconsciously by all struggling to attain spiritual orientation and stature), and is rapidly becoming a strong cable, composed of all the many threads of living light, of consciousness and of life; these threads are blended and fused so that no one can truly say: "my thread, or my bridge, or my antahkarana." This, in ignorance, they ofttimes do. All soul-infused personalities are creating *the* human antahkarana which will unite, in an indissoluble unity, the three aspects or energies of the Spiritual Triad and the three aspects of the soul-infused personality in the three worlds. In time to come, the phrase "life in the three worlds" will be discontinued; men will talk in terms of "life in the five worlds of the manifested Kingdom of God." Think in these terms today if you can, and begin to grasp somewhat the significance of the truth therein embodied. In the beautiful Eastern symbology, "The Bridge of Sighs" which links the animal world with the human world and leads all men into the vale of tears, of woe, of discipline and of loneliness, is rapidly being replaced by the radiant Rainbow Bridge, constructed by the sons of men who seek pure light. "They pass across the bridge into the Light serene which there awaits them, and bring the radiant light down to the world of men, revealing the new kingdom of the soul; souls disappear, and only the soul is seen."

3. Then follows that stupendous event for which all soul-infused persons prepare—the externalisation of the Hierarchy and the reappearance of the Master of that Hierarchy, with the Personnel of which it is composed; this group of liberated and functioning souls will appear on earth as part of the manifested phenomena of the outer plane. This I have been dealing with in another section* and will not enlarge upon it here. The outposts of that

*The Externalisation of the Hierarchy.

Kingdom and the vanguard of disciples and initiates is already here.

The work or the radiatory activity of the Hierarchy is today more potent than at any time in human history. The Masters and Their disciples (under the guidance of the World Teacher of that period) were physically present on earth in early Atlantean times, and the radiation emanating from Them was protective, guarding and nurturing. Later, the Hierarchy withdrew into a subjective expression and humanity was—under the Law of Evolution —left to its own devices thus to learn the Way and tread the Path of Return through individual experiment and experience. The Masters (in this long interim) have not come forth to contact humanity on any large or group scale; many of Their senior disciples have, however, emerged at varying intervals and when needed; the World Teacher has also come forth to sound the key or note for each new civilisation and to express the results of the passing civilisation. Men have had, therefore, to find their way alone to the Hierarchy; in silence that Hierarchy has waited, until the number of "enlightened souls" was so great that their invocative appeal and their magnetic radiation reached a potency which could not be denied; the balance of equilibrium, attained between the Kingdom of God on Earth and the Kingdom of God in Heaven (to use Christian phraseology) became such that the "Gates of Return" could be opened and free intercourse established between the fourth and the fifth kingdoms in nature. The gates (and I am still speaking in symbols) are already opening and soon will stand wide open to admit the passing of the "Son of Man, the perfected Son of God," back to the place—our Earth—where He earlier demonstrated perfect love and service. But— as you know—this time He will not come alone, but will bring with Him the Heads of certain of the Ashrams, as well as a trained group of initiates and disciples.

These happenings are taking place *today* before the eyes of all men, even though much that is going on remains totally unrecognised over vast areas of the world of thought and by many millions of men. However, brother of mine, there are enough initiates and disciples working upon the physical plane at this time to ensure a recognition so extensive that the steady, consistent arousing of human expectation is guaranteed. Ponder on this and learn to recognise on every side the signs of human anticipation, and the pronounced indication of the approach of the Hierarchy.

These three happenings will also indicate to you that, as far as the masses of men are concerned and the first two initiations are likewise involved, there is today and will increasingly be need for group initiation. It must be remembered that if these two earliest initiations are to be administered upon the physical plane by the Christ in His function as Initiator, that then the time factor must necessarily be involved, and that it will not be possible, therefore, to admit disciples one by one to initiation. Administration of the initiatory formula will have to be in group formation, and that—as you know—has necessitated drastic changes in the presentation of the training to be given to aspirants and disciples. People everywhere are joining groups of all kinds and working steadily in group formation; these can be regarded as preparatory classes in group fusion and group work. Among those in these many groups—functioning in every land—will be found those who form part of the subjective groups which the Hierarchy is everywhere forming upon all rays, on every plane and under many varying astrological aspects. Such a group is the one with which you are affiliated, objectively and subjectively; groups like the one to which you belong are far more common than you realise. The Masters are all working in a similar manner, where groups in preparation for initiation are concerned.

It is not easy to induce aspirants and disciples to function in this preparatory group formation and to make it the major interest in their lives, for they *must* at the same time fulfill as perfectly as may be their family and social responsibilities and their business obligations. None of you would have been offered this opportunity had you not been capable of this dual life. I would ask you to study carefully the background of this present hierarchical undertaking (I had almost said, adventure) and fulfill your part in the preparatory work which is demanded. This work falls into two parts:

1. Your own preparation, as a soul-infused personality, for initiation; this will embody personality life disciplines.
2. Preparation for the reappearance of the Christ; this will embody your life service to humanity and to the Hierarchy.

With these ideas on group initiation, I leave the subject and will now proceed with the subsidiary themes of our study.

ON HINTS

Two hints remain now for our consideration and both appear to be very simple when read for the first time; they must, however, be regarded as being given utterance in the "Halls of Initiation" and as, therefore, containing much that is not immediately apparent. Hints given by a Master are never obvious in their significance; any apparent simplicity is the veil of deeply hidden truth, and it is for this that the disciple must search. This is, curiously enough, a part of the content of the sixth hint which is earlier given as follows:

> *Hint Six. "The modern disciple must recognise the hint which is related to his point in consciousness. . . . My one effort is to indicate the relation between Initiation and Revelation."*

In the past, it was the Master Who succinctly gave the disciple the hint which He deemed appropriate to the immediate need. Decisions as to the need of a disciple are based on his soul-fusion and upon the world need at the time, which may be calling imperatively for the disciple's service. The hint given was usually removed from all context; the disciple had to recognise it for what it was, and had then to proceed to discover its meaning and to find the significance of its indications. Owing to the point attained in the evolution of humanity, the hint was practically and invariably of a mental nature, and stimulated the intelligence, and intensified the strength of the mind, the mental search light, or the soul. Such hints are now constantly given by senior disciples to aspirants upon the Probationary Path. They serve to clarify thought; they remove glamour and illusory veils; they reveal the mental approach of the personality to the problem of soul contact and are an integral part of the process which enables the aspirant to establish a rapport which will bring the soul and the personality together and lead to soul fusion with its instrument.

But, as the race has unfolded the principle or aspect of intelligence and has reached its present relatively high stage of mental understanding and perception, the older process has proved too simple and elementary; the modern disciple did not profit by the single mental statement presented to him by his Master; it proved no real challenge and became a point upon which discrimination of an interior activity must be made, and not a factor calling for the needed higher illumination. The older position was that of understanding and following a hint, and this brought the aspirant closer to acceptance in a Master's Ashram; it developed the mental apparatus, providing a better instrument for soul contact, and later, for service. The major emphasis was, however, soul contact, and the hint was usually of a purely personal nature, and was concerned with those inhibitions, wrong interpretations and negations which interfere with true soul contact and present a barrier to progress into an Ashram.

The Hierarchy was faced with the fact that thousands of aspirants have been coming into incarnation with much of this primary mental work well accomplished and with a substantial measure of soul contact already satisfactorily established; the ancient method, therefore, began to prove futile. The entire process was too easy and did not constitute a test of the disciple's intuition. When this was grasped, the whole subject was shifted, within hierarchical circles, from the mental plane to that of buddhi or of pure reason. This led to the discarding of a hint as a means of mental unfoldment and to the development of a new process whereby the presented hint was invocative of the intuition. The standard of requirements was consequently raised. The minds of men met this new challenge, and the consciousness of those who stood on the periphery of the Hierarchy, and in line, therefore, for ashramic training, was recognised as being now basically mental, with a growing sensitivity to intuitional understanding. It was realised in hierarchical Ashrams that the light of the soul was, speaking generally, beginning to flood the aura of the fourth kingdom in nature, and that there were many thousands of aspirants who were developing responsiveness to the light of the Spiritual Triad. The Masters, therefore, withdrew Their attention from aspirants upon the Probationary Path, and left them to be trained by disciples in some one or other Ashram, and gave Their attention primarily to those upon the mental plane who could be attracted by triadal expression and energy, and who were not entirely interested in the task of soul contact.

The problem confronting the Hierarchy was interesting. This new type of aspirant was responsive to three types of light:

1. The light of substance, or the innate light of the personality.
2. The light of the soul, attuned to the light of love, which dominates the Hierarchy.
3. The light of the Triad, which is an aspect of the spiritual Will, and which streams from Shamballa.

The first thing, therefore, which the aspirant must be taught is to know, past all *interior* controversy, where he stands upon that part of the Path of Evolution which stretches across the mental plane into the plane of buddhi, and thus is on the Way of the Higher Evolution. I am here using words symbolically. He must know which of the lights (to which he · finds himself responsive) is the light which he must use to make further progress. Is the light of the personality to be trained upon the point of soul contact, so that the lower mind becomes the searchlight of revelation? Or has the point been reached where the light of the soul, which is the pure energy of love, can be turned upon all life and circumstances in the three worlds, thus enabling the disciple to become a soul-infused personality and thus permitted entrance into the appropriate Ashram? Or has a still higher point been reached, and the light of the Spiritual Triad can begin to be directed upon the soul-infused personality, via the antah-karana?

These are the problems which the modern aspirant has to face, and therefore he must himself discover the hint which is related to his highest point in consciousness. I would ask you here to bear in mind that the point in consciousness is not necessarily identical with the point in evolution. A high point in evolution can be reached unconsciously and the disciple is frequently not truly aware of what he *IS*. He has to become consciously aware of his exact point of attainment *before* he can really know what the next step is which he must consciously take. He is presented at this stage with a vast body or structure of truth; his mental appreciation of these stages and principles can be very real, but there is apt to be much confusion when the concrete mind is unduly dominant (as it so often is); the abstract mind is likewise active, and faint indications of the functioning of the intuition and of the higher modes of knowledge and of realisation are given. The disciple then passes through the stage wherein he appropriates everything that comes his way; he seeks to use everything he knows or even senses in his effort to advance, to develop usefulness and to pass through the door of initiation.

It is at this point that the new training in this new era of hierarchical activity is applied to the modern disciple. Being naturally a mental type, he is unfolding rapidly a correct sense of proportion, and is therefore urged by ashramic activity and by the aura of the Ashram in which he is now permitted to work, to discover for himself that hint or veiled information which will clarify his way. He begins to understand that the lower mind, with its multiplicity of differentiations and its tabulating, analysing and complicated approach to truth, is only a foundation upon which he can take a firm stand, but that *he is faced with a profound simplicity;*

he realises that he must find out for himself that hint (which his own ray equipment hides but also reveals) which will enable him to substitute the pure reason for the many complexities of the lower mind. He has to wrestle with the problem of this simplicity, with its penetrating potency, and with its swift comprehension of the basic truth underlying the many truths; he learns, finally, to substitute the intuition—with its swiftness and its infallibility—for the slow and laborious work of the mind, with its deviousness, its illusions, its errors, its dogmatisms and its separative thinking and cultures. He finds out—as a preliminary step—the nature of his rays; he begins to discriminate between intelligence, love and what he believes, theoretically, the will may be, but he knows that he has as yet no real experience of this highest divine aspect. His developing intelligence is the result and the reward of experience; his understanding of love, the second divine aspect, is also in the experimental stage and his knowledge is not reliable; the fused expression of intelligence and love (of personality and soul, to be specific) can only be possible when the will aspect in some measure is beginning to function.

He has, therefore, to find a truth which is for him an immediate necessity. The Master will not tell him what it is; he must now formulate his own hint, based upon attained knowledge and recognised vision. He must then take action upon the basis of the hint, gauging the accuracy of his formulations by the measure of light, of intuitive perception and of revelation which appears to him to be present in his mind content. These factors should manifest *if* his formulation of the "hint of truth" is in line with his next delineated step. Certain factors must, therefore, be borne in mind if the disciple is to be sure of the ground upon which he stands, and if he is to know that the hint which he has forced to emerge out of the welter of unassimilated and heterogeneous knowledge is correct, and therefore vital for him. These factors are:

1. The hint upon which he is working will be, for him,
     a. A summation or anchored thoughtform of any wisdom which he may have attained. I did not say sum-

mation of knowledge, brother of mine, for wisdom and knowledge are two very different things.

b. Peculiarly distinguished by his ray quality, and therefore in line with his normal ray development. A hint, for instance, formulated by a first ray aspirant may have no meaning or instruction for an aspirant upon the third ray, and vice versa.

2. The hint upon which he is working will tend always towards the simplification of knowledge, of motive, and consequently of activity.

a. It will be distinguished by synthesis.

b. It will be recognised as calling for the exercise of the intuition or of the pure reason; this is what Patanjali describes as "straight knowledge," uncomplicated and, at the same time, profoundly inclusive.

c. It will be more easily interpreted by symbols than by words or by formulated sentences.

3. The hint upon which he is working will lead inevitably to revelation or into the light which will reveal the next step ahead, divorced from questionings and bewilderments. Such hints fall into various categories, indicative of progress and of attainment, i.e.,

a. Certain preliminary hints, concerning preparation for ashramic relationships.

b. Others concern the service to which the pledged disciple is committed by his soul and which his personality must ascertain and recognise as involving responsibility.

c. Others again will deal with the building of the antahkarana which will link the Spiritual Triad and the soul-infused personality. Such a hint was once given by a Master to one of His disciples, by way of illustration. He said: "Learn that all Ashrams are found upon the Antahkarana." It took the disciple a full two years to arrive at the hidden significance of this trite statement. Can you arrive at it in any quicker time?

d. Still other formulated hints deal with the particular initiatory process with which the disciple is faced. It is for that reason that I earlier remarked that my one effort at this time, as far as you as a group are concerned, is to indicate the relation between Initiation and Revelation. There is no initiation possible without a preceding revelation, and yet each initiation leads to a subsequent revelation. The objective of all initiation is a conferred revelation, yet no initiation is attained without an earlier self-engendered and not conferred revelation.

Let me here give you certain esoteric "hints" which may give you some idea of the nature of the concepts which you—as a soul-infused personality—must learn to formulate. We will start with the one given above by the Master:

1. All Ashrams are found upon the Antahkarana.
2. In that light shall we see light.
3. The Way of the Higher Evolution is ever preceded by the destruction of all other ways.
4. The Will of God destroys the wills of men, but both are needed to complete the whole.
5. Radiation and magnetism, invocation and evocation, are four aspects of a dual whole and all must be unfolded by the Server.
6. The seven, the forty-nine and the one are only ONE and this the initiate must know within himself, discarding all but one.
7. Loyalty must give place to identification, and the light is ever merged in darkness.

These seven hints are all hints of which you can make use, if you care to do so. They all lie within your range of capacity and would contribute much to your unfoldment. You would find it of value to apply what I have here explained anent the sixth hint to the understanding of all the others, and note what progress you could make towards the needed revelation.

Let us now consider the seventh hint which runs as follows:

Hint Seven. "One of the marks of readiness for initiation is the ability to see the expanding and inclusive Whole, and to note the law which is transcended when the part becomes the Whole."

This sentence, with its many implications, is more than a hint, though two deeply significant hints are contained therein. It is a statement of individual, group, planetary and cosmic import and is the one hint out of the many which I have given to you in my various books and in these more particularised instructions which has a definite application for every single and isolated initiation. It is capable of indicating to the initiate—no matter what initiation he may be taking (from the lowest to the highest)—his readiness to undergo the expansion of consciousness which each initiation involves, the nature of the expanding vision with which he will then be confronted, and the higher reflection of the Law or Laws which initiation enables the initiate to grasp and thereby relinquish the laws which have hitherto governed his conduct and which have conditioned his realised life experience. Those laws he perforce continues to obey, as a member of the human kingdom, but *his consciousness* is not conditioned by them but is rapidly becoming subservient to a higher and a much more deeply spiritual law.

Some of the more obvious meanings of this seventh hint it might profit us to consider. Its significance is, however, something which will be revealed as a result of initiation; you can see, therefore, that a close study and a vital comprehension of Hint VI must normally precede any true understanding of this final hint which I have here given you. There are—needless to say—nine esoteric interpretations of this hint, corresponding to the nine initiations. This sentence both in its individual, tonic and orchestral sounding forth, carries information and illumination even to the planetary Logos when it is uttered during any cosmic initiation that the planetary Logos may be taking—and which He is *Now* doing.

This hint is working out today in the consciousness of humanity as a whole: the reason for this is that the perfected

Personality of Sanat Kumara— focussed at present in His creative throat centre, Humanity—is reverberating to the orchestral effect of the formula which embodies this hint from the cosmic angle. To this I need not further refer, for you could not understand. Nor do I to any great extent, brother of mine, being but an initiate of the fifth degree. The reason lying behind all this is that the planetary Logos in this particular world cycle is undergoing an initiation which will shift His focus into the hierarchical centre, into that centre of energy which we call the Hierarchy; from that point of attained focus He will submit to the cosmic initiation for which His planetary work—creative and magnetic—has prepared Him. As He, in His Own essential nature, makes progress, every phase of His manifesting body, His expressive Personality, is involved, with the emphasis of the conditioning energies working out through the two centres at this time pre-eminently active; i.e., the centre which we call the race of men, Humanity, in which the energy of intelligence is focussed and critically active, and the centre where the love of God is demonstrated, the Hierarchy. In these two centres a great activity is on the move and a vital expansion or moving outward is taking place.

Remember, brother of mine, initiation ever connotes activity, intelligent understanding, focussed attitude, deliberated movement, conditioning new rapports and the attainment of a new and greater ring-pass-not in consciousness.

Let me list the leading and quite obvious inferences contained in this seventh hint, reminding you that each separated phrase, statement or concept is only the basis or foundation for a new and further understanding. Each grasped inference is like a seed thought in an ordered, concentrated and successful meditation. It is well to remember that the initiate, prior to and during any initiation, has attained a mental attitude of the utmost concentration; this point of tension is something of which you know, as yet, little, and yet you glibly use the words: Meditation and Concentration. *Temporarily*, and in order *to move forward* and at the same time *to leave behind,* the initiate becomes a "static point of concentrated contemplation." He then *stands* before the

Initiator in an intense interior preoccupation with the world of significances. He only moves forward again, dropping then the static attitude, *after* the application of the Rod of Initiation. His ability to contemplate significances rests upon his trained capacity to move with ease in the world of meaning (the major task which confronts all of you at this time). The objective of the first two initiations is to enable the initiate to live in the world of meaning; the objective of the next four initiations—up to and including the sixth Initiation of Decision—is to enable him to live in the world of significances. This must be carefully borne in mind when pondering upon the temporary static condition of the initiate as he stands in the hall of initiation.

Here are the points which must be consciously noted in the hint under consideration; each of them veils a deeper meaning and can convey a vital esoteric significance. Let me quote this hint again in full:

> "*One of the marks of readiness for initiation is the ability to see this expanding and inclusive Entity, and to note the law which is transcended when the part becomes the Whole.*"

I prefaced this statement by the words that "the unit, the individual and the part are always viewed in relation to an expanding and inclusive whole." Let us consider this statement in detail:

1. *The marks of readiness for initiation:* What, my brother, are these marks? For what signs does the Master look before He presents His disciple to the Initiator? Are these marks to be seen present in the three bodies in the three worlds? Or are these marks only to be seen in the body which will be primarily affected by the initiation to be undergone? Initiation affects both the consciousness and the form—each in a different manner; the difference is brought about by the effect of the inflowing spiritual life and the divine will upon the two differing types of substance. Forget not, that in this solar system all that we

know—even of the very highest aspects—are substantial, because our seven planes (if I may reiterate this basic fact) are the seven subplanes of the cosmic physical plane—a fact which is often forgotten in the loose use of the word "spiritual." Again, can the initiate himself recognise and register the marks of fitness? These are all questions which you must answer before you can pass on to a deeper meaning and significance.

2. *Ability to see the expanding Whole.* This leads naturally to the inference that, from a point of limitation, the initiate becomes aware of more than he ever before realised was in existence, and this he grasps up to another point of limitation. You have, therefore:

a. Recognition of past attainment, leading to a point of temporary static expectancy.

b. Recognition of a capacity, hitherto unrealised, to see that which has hitherto escaped conscious registration.

c. Recognition of a movement of an expanding nature which increases the range of the initiate's vision and which indicates a new area, both of future conquest (from the conscious control angle) and of service. This recognition will end the moment of acquiescent waiting, and inaugurate a new cycle of deepened hierarchical activity.

d. *Recognition of the limit of the permitted expansion of consciousness,* with a simultaneous recognition that the widened periphery of consciousness and of activity of which the initiate has suddenly become aware indicates the borderline of a still further expansion. This, when later undergone, will enable the initiate to grasp the true significance of the words "the Whole." Area after area of the Body of Him "in Whom we live and move and have our being" is steadily revealed to the progressing initiate until some day he will know, even as he is known. He will then be granted a vision—dim and distant though it well may be—of that which expansion means to the planetary Logos—those fields of divine activity which lie outside our planetary ring-pass-not. For their understanding, and for freedom of movement within those areas, all the past has prepared the initiate, and in the unfoldment of the three divine aspects of intelligence, love and will, the disciple or initiate has been creating the instrument and developing the faculties which will enable him to move out into solar or cosmic spheres of action, via one or other of the seven Paths; with these I have dealt as far as now is possible in the last volume of *A Treatise on the Seven Rays, Vol. V.*

e. *Ability to see the ... inclusive Whole.* This is the practical angle of the above mentioned reality. The initiate *consciously* includes in his thinking this new area of the divine Life to which any particular initiation can introduce him. Seeing, recognising and registering the vision and recording the expansion in his consciousness is not enough. The initiate grasps the fact that he is presented with a widened and widening field of service for which he has the equipment, or at least the latent capacity; he begins to establish those conditions which will enable him to make his magnetic aura adequately inclusive and competent within the new field of revelation.

3. *He notes the law which is transcended.* The simple illustration of this can be given here in terms of the teaching to be found in *A Treatise on Cosmic Fire.* As a human being, the disciple was ruled and conditioned by the cosmic Law of Economy, along with its various subsidiary laws which were active and conditioning in the three worlds of human evolution. This law is the basic law of nature and of the natural evolving man. After the first initiation, he comes under the Law of Attraction which carries and wields the energy of love and—though the Law of Economy is then abrogated—it preserves an habitual control over the habitual process of the form vehicles which are now used under the Law of Attraction; this law works within the consciousness of man and also within the forms in the service of the Hierarchy. This Law of Attraction is a major soul law.

Later, after the fourth initiation, the disciple comes

increasingly under the Law of Synthesis, which is the major Law of the Spirit in the universe. His capacity then to include rapidly develops and his sense of awareness can (after the sixth Initiation of Decision) begin to range in an extra-planetary fashion. The meaning of all this may be only theoretical, as far as your understanding may be concerned; its significance must be carefully sought and this will not, by any means, prove an easy matter. Revelation will, however, come if you study what is said about these three major laws in *A Treatise on Cosmic Fire*.

4. *The part becomes the Whole.* This phrase marks a consummation, and all initiate-consummations are unexpected and even staggering in their import. Upon these words I do not care to enlarge. Their familiarity is such that they are necessarily meaningless to the average esoteric student. We say the words glibly and they voice a vague objective. Nevertheless, they veil and signify the most tremendous experience of which the human consciousness is capable, and one which looms with increasing magnificence during each successive initiation. They infer—to sum it all up—participation, consciousness and cooperation in the thinking and the planning of the planetary Logos. Ponder upon the importance of these words and upon what they signify in relation to the human being.

You will see, therefore, from this brief exegesis how each of these hints carries in it more than you might imagine or anticipate; each of them hides in its heart and at the very centre of its meaning the germ of an expanding realisation. Keep this thought ever in your minds as you seek to learn the significance of an esoteric hint and begin to draw correct inferences from the veiling symbology.

POINTS OF REVELATION

You will have noted from the previous instructions that these points of revelation are essentially planetary in nature, even if they may have—at first reading and consideration—an individual connotation. These points of revelation concern the Hierarchy and its intelligent appreciation of the second or love aspect; they embody the fundamental realisations which the united group of Masters of the Wisdom bring definitely and consciously into the radius of Their awareness. As this phase of Their great work is carried forward, it frequently coincides with the initiatory processes which are being applied to initiates and disciples; they then become— if they are capable of the necessary understanding—participators in this great hierarchical activity. You will also note that each of these points of revelation can be phrased in such a manner that awareness of basic and fundamental law is conveyed to the student.

We have, therefore, in these five points of revelation, the expression of five hierarchical laws; it is interesting to realise that only the first point of revelation has been formulated into a law capable of ordinary human comprehension; this is the law that "energy follows thought" and that "the eye directs that energy." Mankind has reached the stage where comprehension of this first point of revelation is becoming possible and two factors have made this possible:

1. The formulation of this law related to energy coincided with modern scientific discovery, for today it is recognised that everything that exists is essentially energy in some form or another.
2. The enormous number of aspirants who have taken or who were in process of taking the first initiation.

Again, if you pause to think, you can see the processes of invocation and evocation in action.

The second, third and fourth points of revelation are (symbolically speaking) still retained within the Halls of Initiation, and their expression upon the physical plane—as an understandable law—still lies ahead and is subject to future elucidation. The second point will soon be capable of expression in the three worlds, because men are slowly coming to the realisation of the nature of the will and the right place and proper reality of sacrifice in the divine scheme of revelation.

The fifth point of revelation is worded as follows:

> *"When the light of the seven Rays is blended with that of the seventh Ray, then light supernal can be known."*

The implications attendant upon this fifth point are amazing at the first glance, and they demand an immediate recognition of the two factors of *time* and *space*. The significances which are implicit in this point may be clearer if I paraphrase the statement and thus give you a sense of significance which will give you understanding. When the energy of the light of all the rays can express themselves through the medium of the seventh ray, then the highest aspect of the divine light can penetrate down into the physical plane. This must be obviously a most difficult statement for you to grasp, but it is also a statement of fundamental truth.

In an earlier instruction I pointed out that three ideas were involved in grasping the significance of these points of revelation and—once you have grasped them—they are beautifully clear and simple. The *Procedure* required for the manifestation of "light supernal" takes place when a transitory point of synthesis is reached and the seven energies are blended into one great energetic Light. These seven energies have ever, unitedly, created the "light supernal" upon the highest levels of divine expression, but that revealing light only finds *Location* when the seventh Ray of Ceremonial Order is active and in process of manifestation in the three worlds, and necessarily, therefore, upon the seventh plane, the physical plane. Such a manifestation inevitably takes place in moments of planetary crisis, when the seventh ray is active and when the Sun is in Aquarius. Such a combination of relationships is being established now, for the seventh ray is rapidly coming into manifestation and the Sun *is* in Aquarius, for the Aquarian Age is just beginning. The *Objective* of this combination (which has occurred six times during the period of the fifth root-race) is to bring about illumination and the establishment of order upon the Earth. The first indication of the possibility of the effectiveness of these divine proposals was the giving out of the New Invocation; its potency was so great that right conditions *had* to be considered before its enunciation was possible. That was the first step in the planned precipitation of the "light supernal"; the second step will be the reappearance of the Great Lord, Who will act as the lens through which the light can be focussed and adapted to human need. Conditions are rapidly being brought about whereby this great event of light distribution will be possible. The Christ can and does function *now* upon the atmic plane and embodies within Himself the great Point of Revelation which has been expressed by me in the words: "The Will is an expression of the Law of Sacrifice." The invocation now mounting from humanity to that high Place where dwells the Christ is, at this time, focussed in or originates upon the plane of the emotions; because of this, we find the words in the Scriptures that at the end of the age "the *Desire* of all Nations" will come forth. The movement to bring Him—from the angle of the masses—emanates, therefore, from the astral plane. The plans for His coming are being laid in the higher correspondence of that plane, the buddhic plane, or the plane of pure reason.

The motivating power for His coming is being provided by all disciples and initiates; it is therefore a joint movement, qualified by the desire and the motivation of the united Hierarchy and Humanity; this Invocation cannot consequently be denied. Astrologically, the time is propitious; from the planetary angle, great and momentous events are imminent, as the planetary Logos is taking a cosmic initiation; the energy which produces order and which magically brings spirit and matter together (the energy of the seventh ray) is already organising human affairs and these three great coinciding events in time and space make it possible for the seventh ray energies to reach a high point of fused activity and of blended cooperation.

The result will be the creation of a direct channel for the precipitation of "light supernal" into the three worlds and its dominant focussing upon the physical plane. Thus will be brought about the new civilisation and the new world order, and the new approach to divinity will be rendered possible; the initial steps will then be taken to create the "new heavens and the new earth." You will need here to discriminate carefully between symbols and facts; more, I need not here indicate.

In our consideration of this fifth point of revelation, a most complete picture is given of the three stages of the process, which I mentioned earlier: Penetration, Polarisation, Precipitation.

In this particular revelation, all the planes (of the cosmic physical plane) are involved; this, in itself, is unusual; the entire proceeding concerns *the penetration* of the blended seven rays throughout all the states of consciousness as indicated by the seven substantial planes. This must be remembered, because the concept of "planes" is almost irretrievably (and I use this word advisedly) associated with the idea of matter or of substance. This is basically correct, and yet the emphasis *must* be upon the aspect of consciousness as it informs substance. The effect of the penetration with which we are now dealing is upon the many varied types of consciousness which express themselves through the seven types of substance. The blended energies penetrate through the medium of stage after stage of conscious awareness; nevertheless, they only affect those forms of life which react instinctively to their influence. The importance of the present penetration lies in its completeness and in the fact that response to these blended energies is definitely more rapid and inclusive than ever before in planetary history.

There are, therefore, three stages in the penetrating process at this particular time:

1. The initial act of penetration which takes place "within the area guarded by the Spirits of the seven Rays." This connotes extreme activity in Shamballa and also necessitates the cooperation of the Lord of the World and of the entire Council over which He presides.
2. The achievement of a point of polarisation. The preced-

ing penetration of the energies reaches a point of focus upon the mental plane and there—for a brief time—an unique process of consolidation and of consequently greater fusion is brought about. In this unique moment in the history of humanity, this moment of potency is appropriated by mankind.

I wonder if you realise the gravity and the importance of this statement. *Because* humanity has passed through a great cleansing process and *because* in the world today there are many aspirants and disciples, the effect of these penetrating energies is such that they inevitably evoke response. They become polarised or focussed upon the mental plane. Because of this also, everybody who is mentally centred and controlled, as well as aspirationally motivated, is faced with an imperative opportunity. This opportunity is unprecedented in human history and is also based upon certain astrological relationships which I have also touched upon in this series.

3. Because of the evolutionary preparedness, evident in the consciousness of humanity, the penetration of energies which have already reached a point of polarisation upon the mental plane is now being continued, and the result is a *definite precipitation* of all these energies upon the physical plane, in dense physical substance; the precipitation is also evident in the ordinary consciousness of ordinary mankind. This statement, you will have to accept on faith. The evidence for the truth of the statement will be found in increased human receptivity to the will-to-good which the activity of all the seven rays (custodians of the divine purpose) promotes.

We are therefore, my brothers, living in a time of spiritual crisis. When a human crisis and a spiritual crisis coincide, there comes one of the major periods of opportunity and decision in general human affairs; hence the extreme gravity of the present moment. All I can do is to call it to your attention; it is for you to watch and interpret current events, and it is for you to note the expression of the precipitating and penetrating energies, in order to cooperate as far as your insight permits, and thus further the right production of the required effects.

PART XI

One of the factors (and I believe I have earlier pointed this out) which has warred against a true understanding of initiation has been the puerile and feeble interpretations of it which the various occult groups have promulgated. Often have I wished that H.P.B. (my first and earliest amanuensis) and the many previous teachers of occult truth had given out nothing whatsoever about initiation, the Masters and the occult Hierarchy. Humanity was not ready, and the Hierarchy is *not* as it has been portrayed by earnest Theosophists and Rosicrucians. The Hierarchy has been pictured as a group of eager men, anxious to establish happy relations with humanity. In this, the Members of the Hierarchy are not primarily interested. The prime objective set before every Master of or in an Ashram is to see the purposes of Sanat Kumara working out successfully through the medium of hierarchical endeavour. Their work lies with the advanced thinkers in the human family who are capable of grasping the Plan and of penetrating to the periphery of hierarchical influence. The Masters seek disciples among the world intelligentsia, but They do *not* seek for them among those who *constitutionally* join occult groups and the ranks of the glamoured devotees who seek association with some Master. They seek for them among those who intelligently love their fellowmen and who are free from spiritual ambition and self-seeking. They never look for them among those who love the idea of being the sought and the beloved of the Masters. A man may have no practical knowledge of academic initiatory teaching but—if he loves his fellowmen and is dedicated to their service and can use his mind on their behalf—he is probably nearer to initiation than the devotees of the occult schools.

These schools have, however, done one vital and important task: they have familiarised mankind with the general concept of initiation; they have therefore posited an impelling goal, and they have consequently served. This must not be forgotten. It is really not the fault of the individual that he warps and distorts a presented truth. It is his point in the evolutionary cycle which makes that inevitable. The moment that such a point in the evolutionary presentation is twisted and distorted so that it is not progressive in its appeal, but serves only to feed individual pride and the sense of personality achievement, it is necessarily *not* spiritual.

In our approach to the entire theme of initiation I would ask you ever to have this in your minds; I would ask you to seek for the different and not the usual approach to this much discussed theme; I would ask you to question all that makes you personally feel adequate to the initiatory demands, and to look for that which will lead you to exert all that you have of intuition and spiritual perception. I would beg you to repudiate all that makes you feel a devoted follower of the individuality of any Master and which leads you to feel that you are in the vanguard of the evolutionary wave. I would like, in this instruction, to give you a new slant on the initiatory processes and thus to present to you a fresh incentive to constructive endeavour and towards a commonsense approach to this subject. My reason for so doing was given you in our last instruction, when I said: "When the human crisis and the spiritual crisis coincide, there comes one of the major periods of opportunity and of decision. Hence the extreme gravity of the present moment." I would suggest therefore that we study this problem of the initiatory process from the angle of *Penetration*, of *Polarisation*, and of *Precipitation*. These are words which have a practical usefulness if correctly understood; I would ask you to consider them from the angle of your individual approach to the Initiator. There are consequently two angles to this needed consideration: that of yourself, the individual disciple, and that of the group of which you should be (are you?) an integral part. Let us therefore take up these points and see what we can learn from them. What penetrates? Or into what do you, as a disciple, seek to penetrate? Where are you polarised? And what do you really mean when you use that word? What is precipitated when you have succeeded in the processes of penetration? or when you have arrived at a measure of polarisation? These are aspects of the teaching which are of importance; otherwise you are working with no intelligent perception and are using words without meaning.

Initiation is essentially *a penetration* into areas of the divine consciousness which are not within the normal field of consciousness of a human being. This initiatory penetration is achieved by the disciple through reflective meditation, the development of an interpretive spiritual understanding, plus the use of the trained discriminative mind. This leads eventually to the stabilisation of his consciousness in the new field of awareness, so that he becomes *polarised* there and can work intelligently from the attained point of awareness and of conscious vision. Once he can do this and is aware of the new energies with which he may now work, he enters the stage wherein he may *precipitate* these energies into the three worlds of human service and thus employ them for the furthering of the hierarchical Plan. These three stages of conscious activity—penetration, polarisation and precipitation—are definite and recognised stages in every initiation, with the exception of the first initiation. The disciple (as the Scriptures put it) "takes the Kingdom of Heaven by violence" and thus penetrates into the arena of activity of the Initiator; within that area of spiritual and dynamic influence he becomes polarised, with results which are conditioned by the particular initiation being undergone. From this point he carries forward the task of precipitating the contacted energies and learns how to make them available in his work for humanity.

At the same time, the Initiator "polarises" the energies of the "penetrating" disciple and "precipitates" them through his vehicle according to the Will or Purpose of divinity. The stage wherein the disciple is demonstrating the subjective *fact* that he is initiate is called the stage of penetration. That in which he stands face to face with

1. The Angel of the Presence,

2. The Initiator,
3. The Initiating Masters,

is termed the stage of polarisation. Then when the initiatory process is completed and "he returns from whence he came to carry out the Plan," the stage of precipitation takes place. Therefore, there are two processes of activity going forward simultaneously; i.e., that which is implemented by the Initiator, and one for which the advancing initiate is responsible.

The moment, therefore, that a disciple enters upon the Path of Initiation, he is—from the second to the ninth initiation—to be found functioning at one or other of these stages. He is either penetrating into new areas of divine awareness and penetrating deeply into the Mind of God, or he is learning to live and function from a point therein attained to which we give the name of polarisation, or else he is serving to the utmost of his ability in the precipitation of the energies which will make possible the manifestation of the Kingdom of God upon the physical plane.

Every initiate is himself a polarised point of precipitated energy; every initiate works from a known point of polarisation, and his main task is the precipitation of energy in order to energise, stimulate and create that which is needed in any immediate field of divine activity. Occult obedience is in reality the ability to work with these energies in relation to the Plan, even if only a tiny part of that Plan is known to the initiate. He becomes a part of a great energy distributing group. You will realise, therefore, from the above, that these three words which we have been considering are major key words in the hierarchical programme. One of the tasks of a Master, in connection with His disciples, is to aid them in bringing about effective polarisation and a consequent spiritual stability. The disciple has to effect the stage of penetration alone and unaided; during the process of polarisation, the Master of his Ashram is permitted to help. The stage of precipitation falls into three parts:

1. That in which a relation is set up between the initiate-

disciple and the Initiator. The Initiator focusses the new and probably unrecognised energies within Himself and by their means sets up a spiritual rapport with the new initiate.

2. That in which the energies, transferred by the Initiator into the aura of the initiate, are precipitated by him. This is preceded by a short primary phase in which the initiate polarised the energies of which he is the recipient into whichever centre is active in any particular initiation. For the second and third initiations he polarises them or focusses them in the heart centre. After the third initiation they are focussed in the head centre, but are precipitated and distributed through the medium of the centre between the eyes, the ajna centre. This latter centre is, as you know, the directing agency of the soul within the soul-infused personality.

3. Later, he finds that he can use any centre as the point of precipitation, according to the needs of the work to be done or the service to be rendered. An advanced initiate, however, works from a point of polarisation within the Hierarchy itself, distributing and precipitating the energies via any appropriate centre. In working with the subhuman kingdoms, initiates use the centres below the diaphragm more than initiates working in the human family.

The first Initiator is, as you know, the Soul, the Angel of the Presence, and the stage of penetration covers the long evolutionary cycle wherein the Soul is seeking to establish contact with and control of the personality. The stage of polarisation covers the cycle in which Soul control is stabilised and consciously imposed upon the threefold lower man. The stage of precipitation is only known for what it essentially is when the energies of the Spiritual Triad can be passed through the antahkarana into the soul-infused personality. We have, therefore:

1. The Path of Evolution . . The stage of Penetration.

  2. The Path of Discipleship . The stage of Polarisation.
  3. The Path of Initiation . . The stage of Precipitation.

These stages are presented in dramatic form during the process or the recognition of initiation. As you have oft been
told, it all concerns the use of energy, and covers the entire
period of training for energy distribution.

Initiation is in fact a process wherein the initiate is taught
how to work with energy, how to use the creative, attractive
and dynamic energies in accordance with the hierarchical
Plan in order to bring about the precipitation of the planetary Purpose into the outer field of manifestation. You may
say that there is little new in these things which I am telling
you and that is somewhat true, but not entirely so.

The use of the three words which I have been attempting
to elucidate for you brings in, however, an exceedingly deep
occult apprehension of the hidden Mysteries and of the
spiritual Realities: the conception of a goal to which penetration must be made; of a fresh area of consciousness in
which the initiate must be stabilised and polarised; and the
result—the dynamic use of hitherto unknown energies. These
are made available to the initiate *because* he is initiate and
must proceed to carry out what has been revealed to him of
the hierarchical Plan, from the attained *Point of Revelation*. All this is implicit in these words, and in their brevity
they convey the greatest spiritual truths. They convey an
increasing sense of eternal livingness, activity and movement;
the initiate discovers himself to be a point of energy in an
ocean of energies—energies which are being directed by
groups of Living Beings Who work from the angle of a
proved immortality, and Who—because of Their livingness
—can be precipitating centres of energy under the divine
Plan and in accordance with the divine Purpose.

The word "revelation" is one that has been greatly mis-
used by the mystics of the Church and of the great world
religions; by them, its use is usually of a selfish nature and
the concept implied is that revelation is the due reward,
conceded to the mystic because of his struggles and his deep
search for God. Then, suddenly, God is revealed to him;

suddenly the Angel speaks; suddenly his search seems ended and reward in the form of revelation is accorded him. This procedure and sequence of events has been the ordinary form for centuries and all the time the idea of God Transcendent dominated religious thought. But the revelation accorded is, in reality, related (until the sixth Initiation) to God Immanent, to God in form, to God in the human heart, and to that veiled and hidden supreme Reality which motivates all existence and which is for ever consciousness aware of itself. Revelation is a progress of penetration: first into the Mind, then into the Heart, and lastly into the Purpose of the One in Whom we live and move and have our being.

The agent of revelation is, for the first two initiations, the Soul and—for that reason—the first initiation is said to be (and with truth) the expression of the man's own inner divinity. This is the reason why these first two initiations are regarded as "initiations of the threshold." It is here that the work of the Christ or Whoever is the cyclic Head of the Hierarchy should be considered, working in cooperation with the Soul of the initiate upon the plane of the Soul, the mental plane; the Son of Mind is set free and then the higher initiations become possible. After that, the One Initiator can be faced or confronted step by step and revelation is accorded of the world soul, of the planetary consciousness—that of which the Soul or the individual consciousness is an integral part.

After the sixth Initiation of Decision, the revelation begins to shift on to cosmic levels and off the cosmic physical plane. A developed wisdom then grows in relation to God Transcendent. The initiate now has knowledge of God Immanent within the planetary sphere and can now add, to knowledge, wisdom and can learn to give correct and understanding interpretation to that which is being revealed to him, stage by stage, as he demonstrates that he is initiate. After the sixth initiation the initiate begins to penetrate, through his projected spiritual awareness, on to cosmic levels where he contacts unimagined revelations. The fact that I want you to understand can perhaps be best expressed by the following words out of the *Old Commentary:*

"The light that shines within the heart of man discovers light and, in these blended lights, comes revelation.
The light that shines within the sacred Hierarchy of
Souls discovers these two lights revealed and they reveal
a third—the revelation of the higher states of Being
which hide and veil a *Light* which is not of planetary
creation. These are four lights which reveal a Light Supreme, a Light which comes from distances beyond the
ken of man. Yet all these lights have been revealed because a light has burned—immovable, secure—within the
human heart."

The whole theme of revelation is the revelation of light,
and that implies many different interpretations of the word
"light"; it concerns the discovery of the lighted areas of being which otherwise remain unknown, and therefore hidden.
We create light; we employ light; we discover greater lights
which serve to reveal to us the Unknown God. It is the guiding light within us which eventually reveals those brighter
lights which usher in the process of revelation. I am, my
brother, speaking symbolically as you can well understand.
So much of human thought anent religion is concerned
with the light of knowledge; the reason for this is that the
first "great lighted area" which the initiate can grasp is the
"circle of the Mind of God," as it expresses itself in the living, active state of the planetary consciousness. There is a
point in the initiate process when the initiate becomes aware
—in a manner which I cannot or may not explain to you—
of the light as it blazed forth at the consummation of the
previous solar system; to it we give the inadequate name of the
"light of the intelligence." It is really the light of what we call
the light of the anima mundi; in this initiate experience the
light of the Kingdom of Souls is added to that light. At a later
initiation there comes a point of revelation where the initiate
perceives and records as a definite revelation the "light of
the divine Purpose," and this happens in such a way that the
light of the divine Mind or the divine Intelligence becomes
available for this increased enlightenment and informing.
When this takes place, a point is reached wherein the intelli-

gence and its various phases as known to him hitherto, drops below the threshold of consciousness and becomes instinctual, irrevocable habit, but is no longer a major preoccupation. The "light of love" which flows from the Heart of God (and —from the angle of the solar system—from the Heart of the Sun) supersedes the light which has hitherto enlightened his way. At that point of revelation (again speaking symbolically), he realises for the first time a threefold "lighted relation": a triangle composed of the light of the Spiritual Triad, of a light which is streaming forth from the "Heart of the Sun," and of a steadily burning light which glows from the cosmic physical plane. As he has penetrated into the higher stages of the Path of Initiation, he has moved forward into a light which has been revealed to him by the use of the triple light of his personality and the threefold light of his soul which (when blended) represent two great lights; as he moves forward again, he now blends with these lights the triple light of the Spiritual Triad; and the union of all these lights reveals a light and lights which are extra-planetary.

The above elucidation is of a deeply instructive, though symbolic, nature and can only be correctly understood if the basic premise is grasped that "light is substance" and that "substance is energy." I have here attempted to reduce to words which you could understand some pages out of the *Rules for Disciples* to which access is granted as the initiate proceeds on the Way and comes to the critical stage where "he recognises revelation." I would ask you to think carefully about these three words because they involve the perception of some truths which are apt to be forgotten. For instance, the truth that revelation is the revelation of *that which is ever present;* it is not in reality the revelation of something new and hitherto unknown. To put this in its simplest terms: the initiate discovers he can perceive more than he ever knew was existent or perceptible but that he is only perceiving something that has always been there. The limitation, he discovers, is in himself, and the Way of Revelation is through the discovery and the discarding of his own personal, or rather, individual limitations.

The next point to be remembered is that these limitations have been rejected by him under the applied stimulation of the Rod of Initiation, wielded by the Initiator. I would ask you to remember that this Rod is the Rod of Stimulating Light which is projected by the Initiator with all its Lighted energy on to the centre which is receiving attention during any specific initiation.

There is another point of revelation on the Way of Initiation to which I would like to refer. It occurs when the light which the initiate has generated or received is projected into the *Past* and the subconscious mind (as the psychologists inadequately call it) is revealed to him; this subconscious mind relates him to all the four kingdoms in nature. This is one of the earliest phases and precedes the shifting of the penetrating, focussed light in extra-planetary areas of consciousness. It constitutes a fundamental revelation and is in the nature of a "summarising point of penetration."

I endeavour, my brothers, to give you—as far as I can—some teaching on the points of revelation which the Christ will make possible for mankind to grasp, and try to give you some understanding of the quality of the light of knowledge which is inherent in the planet, and the quality of the light of love which is of solar origin; this is one of the teachings which He will make somewhat clearer to mankind.

More along these lines I cannot tell you. It was necessary for me, however, to speak of these matters, even if they sound to you to be but symbols and parables; they will aid you to gain a more just appreciation of initiation.

In the planetary and cosmic processes, the fate, the attainment and the progress of the individual initiate are of small importance in the vast scheme of the divine life. Can you grasp anything of what I mean when I say that initiation is a planetary activity, based on the life of the planetary Logos and the point of spiritual attainment of Sanat Kumara? This attainment sweeps or carries the initiate into ever widening spheres of "lighted consciousness," and this makes him not only welcome the revelations of light but also to become one of the Agents of the Light.

These are deep mysteries and you cannot expect or anticipate full comprehension. Many lives of struggle, service and progress lie ahead, but the reward of revelation is adequate compensation for all that must be endured as the initiate discards limitation. The goal of all this process has been summed up, as far as planetary humanity is concerned, in the words of the fifth Point of Revelation: "When the light of the seven Rays is blended with the seventh Ray, then Light Supernal can be known."

SECTION FOUR

PERSONAL INSTRUCTIONS TO DISCIPLES
BY THE TIBETAN

PERSONAL INSTRUCTIONS TO DISCIPLES

To L. D. O.

One of the things, my brother, which is being developed in your consciousness is the basic spiritual fact that "whether in the body or out of the body" (as the initiate Paul expressed it), the life of the disciple does not stand still but inevitably—if he is sincere and earnest—proceeds from revelation to revelation. But for the pledged disciple, such as you are, this revelation is not confined to mystical depths and heights but becomes increasingly part of the recognisable brain consciousness. This is a lesson which you are learning rapidly and on that fact I congratulate you. Continue so to do and in the coming period of reconstruction you will be of effective service.

But, brother of mine, to be truly effective in the manner desired, you must cultivate the attitude of being only a clear unobstructed channel, and you must not block that channel with *your* ideas, *your* plans and *your* physical plane activities. I would not have you cease planning and working actively but I would have you more discriminating and cautious. I would have you ponder on the relative usefulness of inspiring many to active work in the service of humanity, or sponsoring your own activities and focussing all your efforts upon organisation work. Such organisation work has ever faintly glamoured you. The arousing of the desire to serve and the kindling of the flame of intelligent love for mankind in the hearts of your fellowmen could provide for you an adequate field of service. It would enlist both your personality and your soul in active cooperation and is something you can do unusually well. The gift of divine inspiration, as it can be used to affect and galvanise others into activity, is rare, but is for you a natural result of your spiritual polarisation. This you know, and of this faculty you should increasingly avail yourself. Seek, as I have earlier told you, to *be;* aim at being a conduit for spiritual force; cultivate the power of identification with those you seek to inspire, for this leads to direct transference of energy; develop divine indifference as to your form of service and ponder deeply on the thought of "service by radiation."

As you already know, the five rays governing your monadic expression as soul and personality are not particularly well balanced. There is in this incarnation too much of the second ray line of approach to divinity; you are primarily 2-4 where your rays are concerned. Where the personality ray, the mental ray and the astral ray are closely allied there is always found an easy problem of inner contact, relation and integration. When, however, the aggregate of inner energy comes to outer expression upon the physical plane, there appears what I might call a lack of stiffening and a too fluid response to spiritual impulses and ideals. There is a correct and undeviating life tendency towards the realm of spiritual reality, but in the field of manifestation and of creative activity there is frequently a changeableness and a developed habit of experimentation. The very versatility of the second ray (twice repeated in your life expression) tends to confuse the issue of service and its correct rendering in your mind. You do so many things, my brother; if you look back over your life, you will find that it is composed of short periods wherein you were intensely preoccupied with what you sincerely believed was the purpose of the moment. The time has now come when the purpose of the soul, in time and space, must become a pronounced conviction governing all future activity and all expression upon the physical plane, subordinating your entire lower nature (the three bodies) with fixed intent to the directed will of the soul.

For you, I would repeat, *service by radiation is the way.* To bring this about, it will be necessary for you to evoke the latent will which must be developed and controlling in you by the time the third initiation comes; at that time the monadic influence is predominantly that of the divine, purposeful will. The expression of this higher aspect of the will, in relation to the three rays of aspect on which all initiates are eventually to be found, is likewise threefold:

1. There is the *dynamic will,* as it is expressed by first ray egos.
2. There is the *inclusive radiatory will* of second ray souls. This is the kind of will-expression and recognised life purpose with which you must learn to put yourself in direct contact.
3. There is the *magnetic will* of the third ray ego which draws, attracts, manipulates and arranges in accordance with divine purpose. This is not the same kind of magnetism as that of love.

In the meditation, therefore, which I seek to give you, we will have this inclusive, radiatory will primarily in mind, and for the next few months I would have you follow these instructions . . .

Life is difficult these days but you lack not courage, and the sense of inner reality will hold you true to the goal and steady in expression. My attention turns towards you when you need it. I can be reached.

August 1942

1. Stand at the centre of dispassion with heart aflame, yet still.
2. Be not the centre of the work you undertake, the service rendered, but be its fluid life.
3. Transmute devotion to a cause, to me, to your brothers or your group into a flaming love for all that breathes.
4. Learn that your causes are effects. Leave them behind and seek the world of causes.
5. Three in this group stand close to you. Discover who they are and know the reason why.
6. Ask your soul the question: Why is D.K. the Master Who has sought me out?

September 1943

MY BROTHER:

Since I last communicated with you, more than a year ago, life has brought you certain radical changes—some of them as a result of the war and your personality reaction to that war, and a few of them as a consequence of soul impulse. These changes and their resultant readjustments have been so many and have been brought about with such relative suddenness that you have not yet had time to know with clarity (within yourself) the distinctiveness of each change or its emanating source. Every change in a life condition upon the physical plane is *the result of some inner cause*. I hinted at this when I gave you the six statements which were intended to aid in the direction of your life. I said to you: "Learn that your causes are effects. Leave them behind and seek the world of causes."

These words embody one of the first lessons which a disciple has to master, as you well know. The initiate lives in the world of causes, for this is obviously the world of initiation. He deals therefore with those basic happenings which act as life-impulses, and initiates only those activities which are formulated by him as a soul and (bear this in mind) as a soul whose personality is initiate. Because of this personality capacity of seeing "eye to eye" with the soul, his activities are results of deliberate spiritual intention.

This is, therefore, one of the first lessons which it is my duty (as it is the duty of every Master) to teach all those who have just been accepted into my Ashram. Such people are not beginners in the world of occult life as far as the average man is concerned, but from the angle of an Ashram most of you indisputably are. I have therefore to teach each of you something as to the nature of that world of causes, and how to discover whether you are not functioning as a personality seeking, as far as may be, to be sensitive to soul incentive, or whether you are literally functioning as a soul. These are two very different matters, my brother. How can you, as a disciple, decide what you are doing and know your reasons? All that I, as your Master, can do is to indicate an approach to reality, and then leave you to arrive at right decision, via direct or intuitive knowledge, alone and unaided.

Decisions which a disciple has to make are based upon various urges, impulses and desires; they differ from those made by the average man because they are ever accompanied by *questionings* and by the practice of a constant and oft bewildering inner scrutiny of motive and purpose. You have faced many such periods of questioning in the past year, my brother, and your answers have definitely affected your personality life, your service to the Plan, your various group affiliations and your general attitude to the spiritual realm. This you know. One aspect of your nature is profoundly satisfied; the other is full of doubt and enquiry; your soul is on its way to a fuller and richer experience of life, and this involves difficulty.

In some ways, the war has not really touched you very profoundly, even if you retaliate by saying that it has touched you astrally and emotionally. Emotions are, however, ephemeral. Personality enterprises have offset greatly your reactions, and changes in your personality life, in your environment and in your established habits have offset much reaction. This is, perhaps, just as well. Then, too, your attempted world service has intensely preoccupied you, and you have tried to be what I suggested in my statement to you, "the fluid life" of all that you seek to do. In connection with that work I have only this to say: Your service will be best rendered if you refrain from regarding your planned organisation as unique and if you do not attempt to live up so entirely to the *world* concept. Your work is inspired from my Ashram; it is an integral part of much larger plans and is largely modelled upon those ashramic plans (which are part of still greater hierarchical endeavours) and has little in it that is original. It is a small part of a much larger whole and has a very needed part to play. I would remind you that very large trees can grow from very small seeds. Your seed is one of many in a large pod (to use a botanical symbol). This pod contains many similar seeds which will bear many similar trees.

You have a fluid mind and can do much if your emphasis

is placed where I suggest—a fluid *life*. Otherwise your fluid mind will incite you to so many useful activities that many of them will amount to very little. One of your major needs is a planned concentration and an ability to make discriminating choice as to activity and technique. You cannot possibly do everything that you see needs to be done; therefore, do that which will bring about the greatest amount of good to the greatest number of seeking souls. This is always a difficult matter for the creative worker to grasp. The doing of the thing which he plans is to him oft the satisfactory reward of effort, and his focussed activity and attention is founded upon what he creates. Yet the created thing is only an effect—an effect of what, my brother?

Again we come back to the subtle question which your soul seeks to have you answer this life, because in answering it you will find a release which will give you a definite opportunity in your next life. *What motives are impelling you to action* in your personality life, in your group relation, and in your service to humanity? A general answer will not suffice, for you will find that several widely different motives condition each field of expression, and when you know what they are, you will be able to bring all the three phases of your life into one rightly oriented functioning whole. Is your creative work the result of a desire to create, or is it impelled by love of humanity and, therefore, an automatic intelligent response to human appeal? Are you nurturing a small and healthy seed or are you endeavouring to transplant a tree? This last question has far more significance than perhaps you guess. It holds in its correct answering the secret of your success. Are you cooperating with the Plan, or in reality with your plans? Again a question of importance.

A rich life of service lies ahead for you in the coming period of reconstruction, but its full expression is dependent upon your achieving a point of focus, leading to a point of tension which will, in its turn, inevitably lead to a point of crisis. When these—focus, tension, and crisis—condition all your living, then your work will move ahead towards a most desirable fruition.

Like all creative workers, my brother and my friend, you

resent all forms which you do not yourself initiate. I am not, therefore, giving you a set form for meditation, but I am giving you a loose structure of thought which I would like to see govern your approach to life, to work and to all you do as a disciple coming forth from my Ashram. This will constitute your cooperative contribution to the group need and to humanity.

Take the three words which I have given you and seek to weave the energies which they represent into your life pattern, welcoming the changes which they may bring and knowing that they are, for you, the correct procedure because these three concepts govern the needed evolutionary process for you at this time—as they do for the bulk of disciples and, to a certain degree, all lesser developing nature.

I. Focus

Seek to ascertain in a wide and general sense where your major life focus is established. Is it emotional, mental, or on soul levels? Is it focussed consciously in the Hierarchy, in my Ashram, or where? What is your daily focus as you watch yourself each day of living? Where, each day, has your attention been, having in mind that a disciple's focus is frequently in one place whilst his attention is in another? Do you know what I mean when I say this?

II. Tension

Study for the next year whether you know the true significance of tension. For you, it should mean (speaking in a symbolism which you ought to understand) that moment of exquisite sensitivity which appears just as the life within reaches the point of "breaking forth" into the light. It is that moment of alert conscious anticipatory direction which distinguishes the runner in the Olympic games as he stands poised for his supreme effort and test. It should be, for you, the moment when you switch your identification with that which you do, away from that act of doing (which is in reality only an effect of an initiating cause or motive) into the world of origins, of motives and causes. In that supreme moment of tension you relate life and form, the fluid and the concrete; then an organism, and not an organisation, takes shape before your eyes.

III. Crisis

The comprehension and the system of right reflection which the two above processes will generate must inevitably eventuate in a point of crisis. About such a crisis I can say little. It will take place in conformity with your ability to focus, in line with your attainment of the right tension, and the precipitation of the crisis will, therefore, give you release, freedom, clarity of vision and entrance into light.

In closing let me say: Preserve your essential and innate integrity, my brother. Be like the sapling which bears up against the storms of wind and rain, holding its life in form intact and gaining added beauty as strength develops.

My blessing rests ever upon you, and my cooperation and my help when need arises. On that you may count. Meet happiness and distress alike with equilibrium, and be a strong hand in the dark to all you meet.

November 1944

BROTHER OF MINE:

I believe that when this reaches you and you scan the interval between these instructions and the previous one, you will realise the significance of your life events in a new way. They have been many, and they have been varied. Do you appreciate what they mean? The past year brought you crisis after crisis; it involved periods of quiescence and of enforced activity; it also brought periods of a definite recognition of growth wherein you registered expansion and arrived at certain inner decisions by which you must and will abide, because they marked a certain high water mark of your soul's development.

Your problem is now concerned with this point of attainment. Is the high water mark reached a temporary one, preliminary to a still higher attainment, or have you—for this life—set your pace and can proceed no faster? Disciples, such as you, need to learn that this type of decision indicates no choice between right and wrong, or between progress or non-progress. It is simply a decision, specifically related to *timing*. Such a decision calls for assessment, for recognition of pre-sented opportunity in both karma and service, and for dis-creet decisions in relation to your activities upon the Path.

It is easy to overestimate the importance of any particu-lar incarnation upon the path of life; it is easy to foster the consciousness of the personality in time and space, and thus fail to register the "insight" of the soul, regulating timeless-ness and knowing no past or future, but only a sense of *Being* (faintly and dimly, because this sense is a monadic pre-rogative) and of relationship (strongly and urgently).

Some souls in incarnation need constantly to spur their personalities on to action; they require to urge them to achievement and towards freedom from inertia. That is *not* a problem which confronts you, my disciple. For you, the *"lesson of the interludes" is of major importance.* I use this word in its most technical sense and as the Masters use it when attempting to incline any life within the Ashram into ways which are, for that unit of life, the essential process for the immediate moment.

In all breathing exercises, there are, as you know, the processes of inhalation and of exhalation, with two points intermediate between these two—that of the interludes. Be-ginners in the mechanics of right breathing seem inevitably engrossed with the processes involved, with the amount of air to be indrawn or out-breathed and with the consequent physiological effects and their etheric correspondence. Know-ers and disciples pay small attention to this dual activity. They are preoccupied with what is proceeding within their consciousness during the interludes between the fixed inhala-tions and exhalations. These phases of registered conscious-ness are in reality points of detachment. They mark the cycles of tension and should be carefully studied and employed by you. This is a point in your future development to which I earnestly call your attention.

In my last instruction to you I gave you three words upon which to meditate and which were intended to constitute the theme of your meditation work throughout the year. By the means of these words you could be enabled to gauge your life processes and determine activity. By means of them also (rightly used) you can arrive at a real understanding of the Law of Cycles—in your own life, in the life of any related group, and in the life of humanity itself. They are also closely related, as you can well imagine, to the rhythm of breathing. It might be regarded in the following way, holding the suggested relations in mind:

1. Inhalation ....Focus ....Life centralisation.
2. *Interlude* .....Point of Tension..Initiation of causes.
3. Exhalation ....Crisis ....Production of effects.
4. *Interlude* .....Recognition .....Prelude to refocussing.

These phases of activity—both positive and negative—can be applied in all aspects of life and in all activities. You can experience them and institute them as a personality, and the entire effect of these phases will then be contained within the personality life of the three worlds; you are meanwhile in process of learning them as a soul and as a disciple, and for the remainder of your life they should establish the rhythm of your effort; later, upon the Path of Initiation, you will re-learn this same process on the highest possible turn of the spiral within the planetary rhythm—but that time is not yet.

As I give you this individual instruction, my brother, I would enjoin upon you the need to establish this rhythmic, cyclic "breath of consciousness." Ponder on this phrase and make this objective a matter of real importance to you until the time comes when you will work upon inner levels, free of the physical body; you will find the effort both interesting and also practical.

Let these four stages condition the pattern of your daily meditation. Let them also mark the pattern of your daily life, indicating the gathering in of the sources of supply for that life of service which is your aspiration (I refer at this point to the meditation process, practiced daily). Let them mark also the carefully planned and silently implemented allocation of such energies to the arranged duties of the day, and to the active outer task of breathing forth into the world of men that which it is your duty to contribute. Then let there be the final interlude of recognition.

The point I seek to emphasise to you is the *need*—imperative and permanent where the remainder of your life is concerned—for the *interludes*. These interludes are, for you, the growing times; they are essentially the "epochs for storage" (if I may use such an arresting and unusual phrase), and they are the "seed of samadhi." What is samadhi, from the initiate point of view and esoterically comprehended? Simply those interludes in the initiate's life of service wherein he withdraws all his forces into a "well of silence"—a well, full of the water of life. In this state of consciousness two definite activities transpire: Tension and Recognition. Without these interludes of abstraction, his work would slowly weaken as the tension, earlier initiated, weakened; his ability to attract and to hold others true to the vision would likewise slowly disappear, as his power to recognise became myopic. The initiate, therefore, as he works within the Ashram, withdraws at the needed times. As he inhales the life of the Hierarchy, and increasingly that of the Monad (which he gradually learns to do), and as he exhales the living essence into the "world of serving lives," he becomes steadily more and more dependent upon the "interludes" wherein both these phases of activity cease and he becomes immersed in Being and in Consciousness—the intrinsic parts of the animating Whole. I use this phrase "animating Whole" advisedly to indicate that the points of interlude are *not* related to form life at all, but to the life of Life itself.

Am I being too abstract with you, my brother? I believe not. As I look ahead into your future and sense the quality of your life, I *know* that the keynote of your inner programme should be ever the recognition of the *essential* demand of your soul for rhythmic interludes; your personality emphasis should be, therefore, upon this withdrawing. I refer not to the withdrawing from outer service but to an inner, constant, cyclic attitude of determined and planned abstraction.

If you will study your ray combinations, you will note that you have only one of your ray energies along the line of the first ray—that is the ray of the seventh type of energy. All your other rays are related to the great Second Ray of Love-Wisdom. This necessarily constitutes a problem until you remember that the seventh ray is the ray of interlude—an interlude and a ray which becomes active when the attractive, magnetic work of the building rays is ready to precipitate into the phenomenal world and bring about—under the Law of Ritual and of Divine Ceremonial—new phases of work. These are initiated in the silence of the process of abstraction, released when the interlude of tension has completed its work, and become effective when the interlude of recognition has made a new refocussing possible.

I am not going to indicate to you the lines along which your service, as a disciple in my Ashram, should proceed. You have already initiated certain activities, both in your personality life through your marriage and in the world through the order which you have attempted to establish. With that which you have started you must proceed; and you can regard these words either as a statement of fact, as a predictory announcement, or as a command from your own soul. But your success in both these departments of life will depend upon your effective use of "interludes." Only you can determine their timing, and this—to be successful—will require the application and the recognition of need, but also the recognition of unfolding spiritual opportunity.

As a beginning, and in order to help you to find the length of your cycles of inhalation and exhalation, I would suggest that you attempt to place one of the interludes at the time of the full moon each month, and the second interlude might come at the close of every three months of work, at the time of the third new moon. You will have to work this out for yourself, but in doing so you could establish a basic rhythm in your life which you would never regret. You could work along the following lines of rhythmic abstraction:

1. Twelve brief, abstract monthly interludes at the time of the twelve yearly full moons.

2. Four brief quarterly abstractions at the time of the four new moons, dependent upon the date of the initial, major interlude.
3. Two longer periods of interludes or of abstraction at the time of May and June full moons.

These points of inner abstraction, of interludes in your subjective life, can be carried on without interfering with your objective life of service, of obligation and of duty. I commend these three words to you also as three themes for meditation.

Last year I gave you the three words: Focus, Tension, Crisis. For this coming year I give you another three: Obligation, Service, Duty. For the year beginning September, I give you: Emotion, Intuition, Wisdom. You have, therefore, themes for three years' work in the meditation field and "as a man thinketh in his heart, so is he." When you have covered these nine themes for reflection, I would suggest that you start again, thus establishing a three year cycle in your process of rhythmic mental building.

Keep close to your group brothers. Seek to establish a contact—subjective and real—with F.C.D. who is so close to you in nature, though with more first ray strength. Whether you ever work for and with him on the outer plane is of no great matter. The need is for you to work with him on the inner planes, giving him what support you can, and receiving from him the strength that you need. Some time, during each morning meditation, I would request you to call him by name three times, and then to send out your heart's thoughts to him. A link would thereby be established which you would never regret.

And as for your relation to me, my brother—naught can change that. You are integrated into my Ashram; you have my confidence and trust; the love of your brothers in the outer group of the Ashram surrounds you at all times. Seek to get in touch with me every Full Moon period, and expect results.

My love and blessing rest upon you, and the service of my Ashram holds you.

August 1946

My Brother:

I have for you today naught but a happy recognition. You have proceeded with your life task with patience, serenity and foresight. The dual life of a disciple (covering personality obligations and the chosen field of soul service) is being successfully attempted by you. Where the word "success" is used, I would remind you that the Master neither sees nor notices the small failures, the moments of distress or disturbance or the personality frictions which (from the angle of the observing disciple) seem to mar the picture. At intervals—rare at first but more frequent when the service rendered attains greater importance—the Master makes Himself aware of the general progress, the growth of the general structure of service which the disciple is creating and the extension of his light in the world. It amuses us at times to note that some disciples (particularly those trained in the earlier, personality-tainted groups) believe the Masters pry into their daily lives, know their petty faults and silly little failures and are fully aware of all they think and do. We wonder sometimes where they think the Masters find the time, and why They should be so interested in habits of thought and action and speech which the disciple is rapidly overcoming.

We are only interested in the good which any individual may be demonstrating; only the good reaches us, except in the case of an entire group where the group interplay, the group action and the group effect *does* affect the Ashram. The quality of the vibration which is felt when contacting you is of the nature of harmlessness and of goodwill to all men.

I am pleased that you are following along the line of your second ray energy, and are occupied with seventh ray activity; that means that, inspired by the sense of unity which is inherent in the soul, you are working on the physical plane (the point of expression for the seventh ray) and bringing spirit and matter together. Remember always that this ray which is again coming into cyclic manifestation is the one that relates the new and incoming spiritual energy and the substance or matter aspect which will respond to it, utilise it and eventually give it due form. Know therefore clearly what it is you are attempting to do.

The main hierarchical need today (apart from its need for workers) is the forming everywhere of such groups as yours, the relating of group with group within the range of influence of that super group, the Hierarchy. Such groups are forming now in their thousands and are to be found in every land, and they will eventually blend and fuse together into one great movement of goodwill, which is spirit in actual expression. Aspirants everywhere, Arcane School students the world over, and my group of special workers such as yourself, must contact these groups, bringing them together on one point only, and that is *Goodwill*. Each group must necessarily be left free to proceed with its own destiny and mode of work. Unity is a necessary ideal and is the reverse side of Goodwill. Unitedly, when the right time comes, these groups must issue a great manifesto to the world—identical manifestos being issued in each country by all the groups who stand for world unity and goodwill. Thus they will make the word "goodwill" carry power throughout the planet, whilst the disciples and aspirants will, through their thought, make the word "unity" carry hidden power. Thus a vast band of men of goodwill will be working unitedly, yet independently, and there will be made available—in moments of world crisis —an organised, ready and world-wide public opinion of such strength and organisation that it cannot be ignored.

Your life pattern, my brother, is now established; seek not unduly to change it, but seek to make your home a centre of spiritual light, and seek to make your order so vibrant, so alive, that other groups may gain stimulation from it. You have therefore a full life's work, and in that all aspects of your nature will find full mode of expression. For disciples, only those tasks which call forth the full quota of innate effectiveness are of real value.

Should you find it possible, I would ask you to aid (to the utmost of your ability) your brother disciple, F.C.D., whose rays are closely allied with yours. He has thrown himself into a supremely difficult task . . . and his future work will not be easy. Help him; he is one of our agents who is worthy of all aid, and though temporarily in my Ashram, is a powerful worker in the Ashram of K.H.—his Master and mine. You can work also with power with J.W.K-P. whose rays, with one difference, are the same as yours.

In twenty-five years' time enough work will have been done by groups such as yours so that the pattern of unity in the world will be distinctly seen. The theory will be comprehended and much straight application will be made. Unity will become a definite world goal in a sense different to the present one. The words "The souls of men are one" will be recognised doctrine of every world faith. So go on with the work of unifying, my brother—in rain or shine.

I have asked myself what I could suggest to you for meditation. The vision you have, and I believe will never lose it. Definitely planned meditation is not so easy for you, and yet —in order to make the vision factual—meditation is a basic essential, for just as it remains eternally true that "as a man meditateth in his heart so is he," it is also equally true that as a man meditateth in his head so will his vision appear on Earth. A great safeguard for you exists in the elimination of all personality problems—yours or those of anyone else— from your current meditation project; that project you will have to set for yourself each year, and adhere to it. Its theme must grow out of the work of unifying—out of the work you have set yourself.

My brother, link humility with that task; seek not to link groups with your group, but recognise your group and all other similar groups as parts of a *worldwide spiritual movement* which (when it reaches momentum) results in unity for all. A super-organisation which emphasises unity is the last thing to be desired; a multiplicity of living organisms held loosely together by cooperation, constant communication and possessing identity of goal and of purpose is what the world needs today. . . .

I assign you no specific meditation. Work out your own, but let it adhere to the general concept with which I have constantly presented all of you. You can (on your own and as an accepted disciple) seek entrance into the life of the Ashram and thus contact me. This may take time, but the link is strong and elastic (ponder on that term) and adherence to the rules will ensure success.

My blessing rests upon you and on your aspiration.

To F. C. D.

August 1940

MY BROTHER:

The past few months have been extremely difficult for you, have they not. Twice I have myself felt the necessity to envelop you with shielding care and stand as a wall between you and circumstance. Are you conscious of these two contacts? They came at moments of extreme fatigue and tension. The future also holds for you much anxiety and of this I warn you, for to be prepared is—in the case of sensitive, imaginative disciples—a great deal of help. It is conditions more than circumstances which will cause the anxiety. Can you understand the distinction? Racial, national, and personal conditions meet in your life and create a perfect whirlpool of difficulty and a mixture of glamour and reality. Disciples work hard (as you have ever done) to render their relation to humanity inclusive and they struggle to bring about those conditions which will produce this desirable expanded consciousness. But they oft forget that this expansion of consciousness will not make them susceptible only to superhuman influences and inclusive of soul conditions, but must necessarily include also all intermediate stages of awareness as well as the power to include the reactions, mental and emotional conditions and the pain and suffering of bewildered and sorely tried humanity. It includes also its joys and aspirations.

The glamour of an extreme sensitivity is your major handicap, my brother, and definitely limits your usefulness. The solar plexus is wide open to all impressions. But you, as a soul, are quite indifferent and—as a soul—you suffer not at all. Of this I believe you are conscious. Spring free, therefore, upon the physical plane from all psychic impressions, via the solar plexus, and seek instead to register only those impressions and contacts which concern your service and deal with man's next definite step forward. Watch this process with care in your life. Your extreme psychic sensitivity and impressionability (of a very high order, I must admit, but nevertheless of a personality nature) *must* be overcome by a paralleling extreme spiritual sensitivity. This again I think you realise, and you know also that this spiritual tendency is accompanied in you by a corresponding powerful, physical and mental inertia. The potency of your astral activity depletes the other two points of the personality triangle. Your spiritual knowledge is so real that you will apprehend my meaning without further extended elucidation.

You are, my brother, upon the path of the Christ, and in preparation for treading this path of aiding and salvaging humanity, you have to learn (through intense feeling) the futility of emotion and feeling as a means of salvaging your brothers. You need to acquire that divine indifference which leaves the soul free to serve—untrammelled by personality reactions, for that is what all solar plexus conditions basically are.

Above, I gave you one important hint or imparted fact, as the case may be, when I said that the "potency of your astral activity depletes the other two points of the personality triangle." Your problem this life has been the same as that of A.A.B.—the transfer of energy from the solar plexus to the heart. The first stage of that process is, esoterically speaking, the discovery of how potent is the astral polarisation of all your personality forces; the entire focus of your life is upon the highest level of the astral plane. This in your case (not in that of A.A.B.) has led to the withdrawal of energy from the physical body (the etheric body), leading to physical debility and fatigue and also to a pronounced inability to "ground" yourself upon the physical plane. It has also brought about a considerable depletion or enervation of the *Will* aspect. I refer here specifically to the will aspect as it produces physical plane expression of directed soul activity as the intelligence (focussed in the mind) must condition it. I do not refer to the will in the sense of any fluctuation of your spiritual aspiration or failure to progress undeviatingly towards your goal. But it must surely be apparent to you that if the focus of all your energies inherent in the personality life and also those inpouring from the soul is the astral body, then there must certainly be a condition of attrition or of semistarvation of the etheric body (determining the physical condition) and also of the mental body. This militates against the full manifestation of a very fine mental equipment. I am putting the problem quite clearly to you, because you are a tried and trusty disciple. Before you can take the initiation for which you are being prepared, there must be a change of life focus and a transfer of energy from the astral body into the mental body, and consequently from the solar plexus to the heart.

In this process, the group meditation should materially help and I advise you to follow it with real care. I advise also that you endeavour in the different circumstances of your life to insulate yourself (for selfless purpose) from too close a contact with those in distress. Aid them; love them; but do not identify yourself with them. I speak of an astral insulation and not of a refusal to meet and contact suffering humanity upon the physical plane. I refer to an attitude assumed and held by the soul and mind in regard to the astral body which enables you to express that divine indifference to feeling and to personal suffering as a result of that compassion which is the hallmark of the salvaging Elder Brothers of Humanity. Such is your basic problem.

Because of this, you will have to watch the earlier effects of this group meditation with care so that the solar plexus is not unduly stimulated, and thus your difficulty increased.

I wish also to give you a personal meditation which will, I believe, prove useful. It is more in the nature of an exercise and its results are based upon your ability to focus yourself in the soul consciousness and to hold that position undeviatingly. It is dependent also upon the power of *sustained imagination* which you may possess and is a good exercise in constructive creative work. It is also rendered more effective if aided by the will and as your mental body is on the first ray and as this work is largely the steady withdrawal of energy to the mental body, you should find it relatively easy and possible to get the desired results.

1. Focus yourself in the head. Sound the OM as the soul and believe that contact has been made between soul-mind-brain.

2. Then see yourself as focussed esoterically upon the mental plane and (from the angle of the soul) exoterically in the brain.

3. Then inhale deeply, drawing the breath up from the solar plexus in the spine and seeing that upward moving breath carrying the solar plexus energy up the spine into the head, after passing it through the heart. Believe that this takes place.

4. In the interlude between inhalation and exhalation dedicate the energy thus withdrawn by the soul, believing in its consequent and subsequent transmutation. (I would remind you that transmutation is the changing of one vibration and one vibratory activity into another and higher one.)

5. During exhalation—in which the breath is carried on the OM sounded inaudibly—breathe the solar plexus energy, now focussed in the head, to the throat centre. This should produce increased creative output for humanity.

6. In the following interlude, after exhalation, go over in your mind (pictorially) as a sort of recapitulation, what you have done.

OM.   OM.   OM.

Repeat this exercise three times and do this transference exercise three times a day. *Do not look for results.* A year's steady work with a detached attitude as to these results will be needed before you yourself will recognise difference of reaction and lessened emotional activities.

This exercise, coupled to the group meditation, will (as you will have undoubtedly noted) produce in the long run the linking up of the three centres above the diaphragm—the heart, the head and the throat. The exercise just given must be *done before* the group meditation as it is the nature of a clearing exercise. If done properly, it will hasten the results of the group meditation for it will clear the solar plexus of undesirable emotional force and leave "room for reception," as the process is sometimes technically called. True love will then take the place of emotion, and compassion will be substituted for pity; understanding will take the place of apprehension of suffering.

Disciples are apt often to think that the injunction to identify themselves with other people must involve complete identification with all their experiences, moods and reactions. It does not. It should not. It involves identification (through the intuition) with underlying soul purpose and a consequent ability to interpret and explain the present. Ponder on this, my beloved brother.

August 1942

1. You have given all you had to give. Now take it back enriched. Then give again.
2. Peace is to you the clearest light of all. The lessons of the dark have likewise been revealed. Pass out between the two.
3. The best is yet to be. Hold thou to Me.
4. The bridge of light is firmly built and on it you can move this way or that, but always on the Way.
5. The sorrows of the Cross of Man have weighted thee down but not submerged or blotted out the light. The joy of resurrection lies ahead.
6. Love is thy note and wisdom is thy guide. You need naught else but fire.

September 1943

MY BROTHER AND MY CO-WORKER:

I am not telling your co-disciples whether you are on this side of the separating veil or not. I am not informing them whether you have crossed the "bridge of light," to which I referred in my last communication to you. You need their protective love, no matter whether you are here or there; the turmoil on the other side is so great—as great as the turmoil on the physical plane. Whether you are in the body or out of the body, you are therefore peculiarly vulnerable, because, my brother (as I have told you oft during the past years), your intense sensitivity has complicated your life problem. Your karma . . . holds you back from that complete freedom and liberation which you deeply desire. Only those who have achieved freedom can return to that group with immunity and helpfulness in their hands—the group from which they have been freed.

I have for you a suggestion. I will not call it an order, for no Master ever gives commands, and in any case you belong to the Ashram of K.H. and will have received your instructions direct from Him. He feels as I do, that in the pressure and anxiety and in your psychic participation in the fate of your country and in your sensitive reaction to racial strain, the import of His conversation with you a year ago may not have registered adequately. It has been difficult for you and well-nigh impossible to concentrate on planning. I am therefore going to summarise for you what He then said. The group protection accorded you (greater than perhaps you realise) enables me to reach you more easily at this time than can any other member of the Hierarchy. I can find and reach you with a minimum expenditure of force.

Your Master, K.H., asked you at that time if you were ready to begin work in preparation for a definite assignment upon the Path of World Saviours. Assignment after assignment in connection with groups, nations, races and increasingly large units is ever the mode of developing a world Saviour until the time comes when he can make a world impact and achieve a measure of world salvaging. Many times in the past, I have pointed out to you that you were on that most difficult path of service. K.H. desired to find out if you were prepared to accept your first major assignment upon that Way. When you assented and told Him that you would do what you could but that you had no inner confidence in yourself, owing to the pressures of the time which appeared to you to have a definitely disintegrating effect upon your vehicles, He reassured you and told you that the potent inner unfoldment of your love nature and your complete decentralisation were a vital protection. He also informed you that —at the stage of spiritual development which you had attained—the aura of His Ashram and the aura of mine would act as a shield, and that the resources of both Ashrams were behind you. This, my brother, you know well, and to this fused efficiency you can testify. . . .

I have said enough here to enable you again to resume your active position as a pledged initiate-disciple (a position which your co-disciples have ever recognised as yours), and I have shown you definitely how valuable has been to you the past immediate experience. . . . Though you are a trained disciple of K.H., you are still working in my Ashram, as I remain in close touch with world affairs in relation to their immediate working out, whilst K.H., being a Chohan, is more active in the handling of the deeper incentives and purposes, and of those matters which will not materialise until such time as the work done by me, and others associated with the Great White Lodge and of like rank and of lesser rank, is completed or at least well on the way to fruition.

The work assigned to you, my beloved brother, will be work of profoundest difficulty. You will meet with rebuff from those you seek to help and . . . find very little understanding; you will meet with encouragement and assistance from the enlightened among the New Group of World Servers, and this will make your work possible but it will also greatly handicap you. . . .

Are you big enough for this inadequately outlined task, my brother? Is your stamina, your inner spiritual orientation and your fixed psychic determination adequate to the undertaking? Can you do it with your present psychic equipment, or must you build new bodies for integration, use and service? The decision rests with you, for those who tread the Way of a World Saviour are left peculiarly free (owing to certain difficulties in time and space within the planetary life) and must work as they will, with what they choose to offer and with a trained understanding of their task.

Such was the gist of your interview with your Master.

You can now go forth from where you are with the endorsement of your Master, with the aid and backing of myself and of A.A.B. and, at all times, the protective aura of K.H.; and —with reverence I would call your attention to this—an aspect of the aura of the Christ is incorporated in that lesser aura.

In my last communication to you I stated that "love is thy note and wisdom is thy guide. You need naught else but fire." That fire, my brother, is the residue of the pure fire which is left when you have trodden upon and passed the burning ground, through the Portal into the *Presence*. That you have done. The fire is there, and on it you can count if you seek to destroy opposition, to burn down barriers (inherent in yourself or presented by others), and also to blaze a trail straight from your heart into the heart of others. . . .

I stand by you, my brother, unalterably and at all times, and on this you can count. Such is also the wish of K.H., my Brother and also my Master, and on that you can also count. I am giving you no set form of meditation. Reflection and deep, considered concentration upon the work which I have outlined to you, and which your Master wants to see you do, is for you adequate spiritual focussing. The deep love of all your group brothers is yours, and many, many people are today sending love to you and many, many minds are thinking of you with thoughts of gratitude, of strength, of faith and hope. On this too you must count. The path of a world Saviour is, as you know, a hard one, but of compensations which far outweigh the difficulty. My blessing is yours and my hand is ever stretched out to you in helping.

November 1944

It is not my intention, my beloved brother, to give you any personal instructions at this time. Those given you during the past three years still need consideration, assimilation and factual demonstration. I simply take, at this time, those needed inner steps which are permitted to the Master of any Ashram in order to draw you into a very close relation to myself and to the group. Such a definite and close relation produces healing and strengthening; it also permits of such a clear vision that the picture unfolds as a unity and the past is seen freed from karma. This sentence may mean much to you, if subjected to the inner insight, or it may mean little. It is, however, of major significance to you personally, and to no one else in this group.

In your question, my brother (about the nature and the function of the counterparts in the head of the various chakras, and how to bring about a better adjustment between the heart centre and its counterpart in the head), you have voiced an exceedingly esoteric inquiry, and one that will warrant the most careful consideration and phrasing on my part. The reason for this is that as yet little is known (even in the esoterically instructed East) in regard to the head centre. This profound ignorance has not been realised, even by advanced students. The thousand-petalled lotus remains a secret, or closed mystery. Though much has been given out in connection with the heart centre, little has been communicated in connection with the head centre. The reason that more is known about the heart centre is due to its being the centre awakened by the highest initiation in Atlantean times. In our Aryan race the head centre is the objective of all stimulation—even the stimulation of the other centres being noted in relation to the effect upon the head centre. The race as a whole, however, is only just beginning to be ready for this awakening. Hence the complete silence hitherto held upon this subject.

Adeptship was achieved in the Atlantean race when the heart centre was alive and its twelve petals unfolded. The fourth initiation, which confers the status of adeptship, produced the mystic realisation, the unfoldment of the lotus of the heart and the deep conviction of the pairs of opposites, yet at the same time the *knowledge* that the phenomenal reality and the spiritual reality were one and the same reality. Thus the Atlantean attainment established in the consciousness of its adepts, through initiation, the duality of all creation.

The Aryan unfoldment will produce occult identification, the development of the head centre, and the realisation of unity. "I and the Father are One." This constituted the real achievement of the Christ, Who was the first of our humanity to achieve the *complete* realisation. This point is of vital interest. Our present Masters of the Wisdom have also entered into this same recognition. The distinction between Them and the Christ is that He added to this realisation the capacity to be a channel, pure and undefiled by any form of self identification, for a cosmic principle—that of Love. Only those Masters, however, Who reached adeptship in Atlantean times are dowered with this occult unfoldment. Disciples are apt to forget that the Masters Themselves are at various stages upon the path of Their peculiar evolution.

You will see, therefore, that the establishing of the significance of the counterparts in the head to the heart centre, for instance, involves one of the great mysteries to be revealed at a certain high initiation. In the next great race, which succeeds upon this one, the goal will be—above everything else—a dual one. It will be:

1. The *conscious* unity of the lower centres by means of a great awakening of the solar plexus centre. This next race will be buddhic or intuitional, and therefore will embody, as a higher expression upon the turning spiral, the higher mystery of the astral unfoldment in ancient Atlantis. It will vision forth the higher correspondence of that achievement. This consummating development will mark its fourth initiation, and will demonstrate the transmutation of the astral life into the buddhic consciousness.

2. The carrying of all this mobilised energy to the heart centre at the fifth initiation for group purposes, and the achieving of this in full waking consciousness.

In the final race the process will be repeated on a still higher spiral, and all that concerns the higher centre will be unfolded and occultly consummated, again through the medium of two stages:

1. Wherein the massed energies of the solar plexus (the

great clearing house) and the heart and throat will be carried—at the third initiation—to the ajna centre, and the complete racial "transfiguration" will take place.

2. The process will then be carried forward and at the fourth initiation the energies will be centralised in the head centre.

This will lead to a happening of such esoteric significance that I cannot express even its dimmest meaning to you because *I myself do not know.* It lies too far ahead, even for all Who are the Masters of the Wisdom at this time. Only the Christ and the Buddha begin dimly to sense its meaning.

Therefore I cannot answer your question because until the head centre is somewhat more awakened my explanation would be meaningless. All I dare say is that by the use of creative imagination, by a constant application to the way of the head, and constant group activity, with an increasing capacity to be detached, and therefore not so potently identified with the individual consciousness, you yourself can perhaps get a faint glimmer of light as to that vibrant reality of which the heart is the reflection.

One thing I can add. As I told you before, the activity of the heart centre never demonstrates in connection with individuals. This is a basic fact. What devastates most disciples is the solar plexus ability (when purified and consecrated) to identify itself with individuals. The heart centre cannot react, except under group impetus, group happiness or unhappiness, and other group relations. This may give you a needed hint. It is a subject which you will do well deeply to consider, and to discuss with A.A.B. who—like yourself—is also on the difficult path of teaching and of world salvage.

August 1946

MY BELOVED BROTHER:

You will have, by now, read and absorbed the papers and communications which have been held for you until the close of the war and the attainment of physical safety for you. There has been no great need for me to express myself on the situation which has existed, for the closeness of the link between the Master K.H., myself and you ensures understanding and precludes waste of time.

You have come through a period of great difficulty and danger with no loss of your spiritual grip upon essential reality or of your spiritual vision; your strength has been such that you have lifted your family with you and safeguarded them also all the time. Having achieved one pinnacle of spiritual success, another can be glimpsed, and between the two pinnacles lies a field of service, a sphere of danger, a land of glamour and deep morasses through which you must struggle, until the point of attainment planned by your soul for this life is yours. You can achieve, and for your aiding, I and A.A.B. stand ready.

A debate arose between your Master (K.H.) and myself. You had been sent (or *loaned* if I might call it so) to aid in my Ashram. We discussed the subject as to whether the sufferings of the past few years did not warrant your return to the Ashram of K.H.; the work there would be hard but not of the same kind, and there would not be so much need for contact work on the physical plane. I claimed that you were strong enough for the dual test; K.H. felt that you probably were, but that there was no need to ask a disciple always to drink the cup of sacrifice to its very last drop—not at least until the crucifixion initiation is your right. The task today proffered you, and its incidental strain and suffering, will be of another kind and the pain endured will be largely mental, but "you can take it," as the saying is. It was decided to let you attempt the task demanded for three years or for seven (according to your own choice) and then, if you decide to do no more along the indicated lines, you can relinquish the task . . . with no sense of failure. This work can be undertaken only by people who, like yourself, repudiate without any difficulty all separative attitudes and who ever act and think in terms of the one humanity and with inclusive love. You, my brother, meet all these requirements. . . . This work is most definitely part of my work . . . and I shall be in touch with you at frequent intervals. On that statement you can emphatically rely.

Your meditation work must keep pace with your vision. I suggest that you follow the simple outline which I call "The Pinnacles," and give much time for quiet thought and for *impression*. Know that guidance will be given—given step by step as needed. My love enfolds you, and the way into my Ashram stands open wide for you.

November 1948

MY BROTHER AND MY FRIEND:

It is two years since I last communicated with you, via A.A.B., and they have been years of great stress and strain for you. Every disciple in these troubled times carries three kinds of stress; no, my brother, I would say the major stresses are of four kinds:

1. There are the stresses and the strains incident to the disciple's family life or his immediate daily relationships, and of these you have had your full share.
2. There are stresses and strains due to the deep interior life of soul relation; these bring with them their own unique difficulties which can be shared with no one (except the Master, when the disciple has reached the point of unfoldment which you have now reached), and yet which bring about a life of inner tension which can lead inevitably to the next point of revelation.
3. There are the problems and circumstances which arise out of the period in which our modern humanity lives; these today are unique and of disturbing importance; they involve the balancing of values which is going on in every department of human living and which evokes in the disciple an almost unendurable pain and anxiety.
4. There are also peculiar complications and tests which have their origin in ashramic relationships which the disciple realises through his contact with the Ashram.

These are the result of his attempt to lift the burden of humanity and the measure of his understanding of the Plan, in unison with the entire Hierarchy. This produces an inevitable crisis and constitutes a load which—when added to the other three spheres of difficulty—often make the disciple feel that his cross (his vertical and his horizontal life) is more than he can bear. The Fixed Cross becomes a reality, and he begins to learn its true meaning.

All these four types of difficulties are further enhanced when you consider the fact that they are felt in all three aspects of the disciple's personality simultaneously. There is a reaction in his etheric body, in his emotional vehicle and in his mind. This makes what is sometimes called the "seven divine sorrows"; these are symbolically and most inaccurately depicted in the Christian discipline as the seven stations of the Cross. As I told you elsewhere* "from the standpoint of Christian symbolism (even though the interpretation is as yet inadequate) these seven crises correspond to the seven stations of the Cross which mark the way of an advancing world Saviour." Here again you have the four and the three brought together in a synthesis of service, of discipline and of unfoldment.

All these factors have been active in your life, my brother and co-disciple. I would like to commend you on one point. You have proceeded with your Ashram work, your thinking and your service in spite of all that has been going on. This has been noted by us and it is for this quality of spiritual stability that we watch. The field of your work remains the same; it is part of your karmic obligation which may not be avoided, but the mode of work and the nature of the work which should be done *will have to be altered* for reasons which I am confident you will understand. . . .

I have, as you will have noted, said little to you about yourself and your own spiritual development. The war taught many disciples that it is in serving and in thinking through that true wisdom comes; they came to realise that in

*A Treatise on the Seven Rays (Esoteric Astrology), Vol. III, Page 476.

enlightening others the radiance of the glory of God can be revealed. *This you have learned and from henceforth you enter in a new stage of discipleship* and can be regarded as one who can teach himself.

The work outlined for you will require only one discipline for you and that is a hard one. It is the drastic organising of your time, irrespective of personality claims, or the hindrances of an etheric body which is too loosely knit, and a sensitivity which makes life very hard for you. The great need of the service which you can render and the desperate task involved in the reorganisation of your time and plans will do much to offset the above difficulties and—*in time*—to cure them. You do not, my brother, belong to your family any more. You belong to humanity—a lesson which A.A.B. had much difficulty in learning.

I give you no meditation to follow. You may feel it necessary to make certain changes in the one you are now doing; feel free to change where you deem it desirable and seek constantly and daily a closer contact with your Master and with mine—the Master K.H.

Daily I look towards you, brother of mine, and that is no idle statement on my part. Rest back on my understanding and call on me at need. Develop telepathic sensitivity to my voice—as I have developed it to yours.

To R. A. J.

August 1940

MY BROTHER AND MY FRIEND:

For you, as for all disciples at this time of world crisis, life has been exceedingly difficult. This is not a platitudinous truism—in spite of A.A.B. remarking sub rosa that it was. She knows me so well that for years her comments have proved a source of amusement to me and sometimes have proved most helpful in aiding me to understand the occidental mind. I am an Oriental of the fourth root race and although I have had two European incarnations I still at times fail to grasp or understand the occidental reaction. But the remark above is not simply fatuous, but contains in it the clue to your future. Your difficulties at this time stem largely from others more than from yourself; they are instructive more than karmic.

You have led a useful and fruitful life; there is still much for you to do which will enable you to lay the finger of love upon the hearts and lives of others; as you do so, you relate them to yourself and bring them under "the eye's direction." The larger, wider work of a disciple has not, however, been yours this life. Your task has been preparatory to this, and—if you will carry this realisation in mind for the remainder of this incarnation—you will pass on into a life cycle which will reveal to you the path which, as an initiate, you are choosing to tread.

In this connection, forget not, brother of mine, that the teaching ray conditions you and that there is a major difference between teaching as a human being, no matter how good, and teaching as an initiate; it is as a pledged disciple that you will learn this basic distinction. It will also have a definite effect upon your life.

This thought gives me the chance to point out to you (and incidentally to your group brothers) that many disciples today—who, like yourself, are not engaged in any spectacular world work—are engaged in establishing those contacts, here, there and everywhere, which will form the nucleus of that group of aspirants and of younger disciples which every senior disciple and initiate automatically gathers around him. He does not, in any particular incarnation, go out into the world and say: "I will gather a group which will form my future ashram." If he does this, he will fail; if, however, he seeks to aid spiritually and to stimulate divinely those whom he meets in his daily round of duty, that tells a different tale. No one is then unimportant. Deliberately, he gathers people to him because he steadily loves and helps. Some of these may be just passing by to other goals, and with them he has no permanent link; others send out to him a responsive thread of understanding and request and—as his intuition develops—he recognises them as his own; he esoterically "intertwines the thread of his life with theirs," thereby assuming responsibility and forming a more permanent link, both in response and in karmic relationship. Both become indissolubly linked.

You have touched many lives in your lifework as teacher, and you know and understand in some measure those who have responded to you—to you as an individual and as someone to whom they can look for some measure of understanding. For the remainder of your life, I would ask you to have these thoughts in mind and begin to lay a planned foundation for the future. This is my definite *work* instruction for you at this time. It will entail a task of watchful observation, of a determined going out to help wherever that help may be needed. You have, in many ways, what I have referred to in my own mind as I have watched you, as a very well-managed inferiority complex—so well managed that you do not permit it to be a real hindrance; it is one which nevertheless exists and at times presents to you a problem. I would also ask you to ignore it increasingly, and in the decisions which you will have to make during the next twelve months please act with a positive belief in yourself and, without questioning, choose the field of largest opportunity.

August 1942

1. The note sounds clear for you today, my chela and my friend. It is the hidden note of sacrifice. But sacrifice is not the thing you think it is.
2. The wisdom of the eye is yours. Let the radiation of your heart follow the eye's direction.
3. Live not upon the surface of events; you dwell deep at the centre and the springs of life.
4. The next ten years will hold for you three crises. Make them opportunities for expansive work.
5. The diadem, the robe of rose, the sandals on your feet and staff in hand—these are your proud possession.
6. Draw near to me in closer personal touch, devoid of personality. This paradox is clear.

September 1943

My Brother:

I wonder if you drew out of the six statements what they were intended to convey to you of direction and instruction? To the fifth statement I seek to draw your attention. Reference is there made to the "diadem, the robe of rose, the sandals on your feet." What did these symbolic words convey to you? I mention them because I want to build your meditation for the next few months around the concepts hidden by these word forms. The first three statements were fairly simple for you to comprehend. The fourth conveyed a prophecy. The fifth contained some Words of Power and were intended to instruct you as to the nature of your life-orientation and the desired quality of your service during the coming ten years. They intimate that which you at this time possess but which needs increasing appreciation by you. Let me give you some idea as to their significances:

1. *The Diadem.* This is a dual symbol. It signifies accomplishment or the crowning period of your life (and this you now face, if you so choose), and it also conveys the idea of a more definite and steady use of the head centre. You are, of course, a "heart" person. The task ahead of you in your meditation work is to lift the energy of the heart centre into its correspondence in the head and begin to live more in the head than in the heart; you should begin also to fuse and blend the energy of this higher heart centre with that of the ajna centre, thus bringing the "directing eye" into greater service, prominence and usefulness. It is toward this objective that the meditation here suggested by me is planned.

2. *The Robe of Rose.* The symbolism here, my brother, is obvious. Rose is the colour of devotion, and of that quality you have a full supply. It is however to its magnetic attractive quality, as it affects others rather than yourself, that I seek to draw your attention. People of pledged devotion are those who have reached a point where that devotion is in no way a hindrance; it is seemingly a safe-

guard, simplifying their lives. Because of that fixed devotion, they can walk undeviatingly upon the Way. But they are apt to forget that—equally because of that devotion—they ray forth a quality which stimulates its correspondence in others. That is why sixth ray people can easily form a group around themselves. But they seldom succeed in holding those thus attracted for very long, because they do not understand the reason for this facility and ascribe it ever to wrong causes. Only your astral body is upon the sixth ray of devotion, but that makes it potent indeed and, in your case, produces that sense of inferiority to which I referred above. I would ask you to change your point of view and to regard your sixth ray astral body as a powerful piece of equipment to be used in service.

In these two symbolic phrases we have related the heart centre to the head centre, and likewise the heart centre to the astral body.

3. *The Sandals on the Feet.* Here, in other words, you have a simple reminder of the underlying and motivating power of your entire life. This can be summed up in the flat statement of three truths—unalterable and fixed because imposed upon your personality by your soul:

a. You are treading the Path of Discipleship.
b. You have arrived at a certain Ashram or centre of power upon that Path.
c. You are intelligently aware of these facts and they are the major conditioning factors in your life.

You have consequently established a thought rhythm which naught can change and which will be a powerful incentive in deciding the time of your return when this incarnation comes to an end, the type of vehicle which you will, as a soul, construct, and the nature of the race, nation and type of service to which the overshadowing soul will commit the personality. Energy follows thought. A definition of the personality might be expressed as follows: The personality of a disciple is a focal point of energy, established by the soul.

The "eye of direction," therefore, referred to in Statement 2, relates primarily to the long-distance view the soul is taking of you and your preparation for fuller service in the next life. A study of these three phrases will carry you into the realm of quality, and not simply of symbolism; the concept of heart radiation, attractive power, and the responsibility of preparation emerge clearly in the three ideas underlying the meditation suggested below. My proposal to you is that you do this meditation only twice a week—on Sundays and on one day in the middle of the week. On the other days you will simply carry forward the group reflective assignment with your group brothers. In this way the days of your personal orientation in meditation will be gladly anticipated events. Will you try out this plan, my brother?

Stage I. The Diadem.
1. The establishing of relation between:
   a. The heart centre and the head centre.
   b. The heart centre in the head and the ajna centre.

   Thus a lesser triangle of energy or of "lighted, living relation" is established: heart, head and ajna centres.
   c. The waiting, dedicated, devoted personality and the soul.

   Thus a greater triangle is established: soul, head and heart.

   Visualise these triangles as relating and focussing your consciousness as far as may be in the head, midway between the soul and the heart centre up the spine—and therefore using as that midway point the heart centre in the head. Avoid concentrating upon location. Just imagine the point of attainment as that of the Diadem.

2. Then reflect quietly upon the directive power of the soul:
   a. Working within the symbolic "diadem of attainment."
   b. Using the impelling "eye of the soul" as a directing agent; i.e., the ajna centre, or the centre between the eyebrows.

    c. Then say the following words with full intent:
"May that soul of mine whose nature is love
and wisdom direct events, impel to action,
and guide my every word and deed."

Stage II. The Robe of Rose.

  1. The next undertaking is a conscious establishing of
relation with others through:

    a. The focussing of the power or energy of devo-
tion within yourself so that it becomes:

      1. A radiation affecting others.

      2. An attractive force relating them to you as
their temporary source of spiritual light.

      3. A magnetic influence, stimulating a new activ-
ity of their soul in connection with their
personalities.

    b. An act of service, wherein you flood the person-
alities of those you are seeking to help, with the
pure rose colour (most carefully visualised by
you) of spiritual devotion. This stream of warm
rose and radiating light will esoterically drive
them in devotion to their own souls and will not
attract them to you — a thing which is never
desirable.

  2. Then say with all the outpouring love of which you
will increasingly find yourself capable:

"Let the love of the soul attract and the light of the
soul direct all whom I seek to help. Thus will humanity be saved by me and all affiliated with the
Hierarchy."

Stage III. The Sandals on the Feet.

  1. Reflect more now in relation to yourself, and ponder
upon the Path in three ways:

    a. The Path which you have travelled to my Ash-
ram. This will involve *the Past.*

    b. The Path of Service which you seek to travel
now, moving freely in and out of my Ashram.
This involves *the Present.*

    c. The Path of Initiation for which you are being

prepared. This involves *the Future*—your future and its goal. You begin to realise yourself as a pledged, devoted servant.

2. Then in your own words, and aloud, you will dedicate yourself in a threefold manner to an increased conscious activity as an accepted disciple.

3. Seek now—definitely and quietly and with a spirit of waiting anticipation—to contact me, your Master and your friend. Expect results, though not at the time you anticipate.

4. Sound the O M softly seven times.

May peace and courage abide with you, my brother.

November 1944

As I give you this personal instruction (one which can suffice you for this life) I ask myself: What is the thing of greatest moment that I can say which will indicate the point of future emphasis, which will convey strength and positive assurance, and which will enable you to prepare for the next great step which immediately confronts you? Disciples seldom realise the responsibility that a Master shoulders as He seeks to prepare a group of people for world service; seldom do they understand the problem with which He is faced, even when dealing with the least advanced or dynamic among His neophytes. What are the factors which He has to consider and which are potent enough to negate much of His effort (as has been the case in this group), and which frequently condition a disciple to such an extent that he takes no definite steps to meet ashramic requirements, even when, technically and theoretically, he admits responsibility? Let me tell you one or two of these for your guidance and the guidance of the group:

1. *The karma of the disciple.* Of this, the disciple knows little and the Master much; with that karma He may not interfere, because growth and development eventuate as the disciple meets the inevitability of events,

accepts his karma and works to offset it, actuated by right motive. Let me illustrate. The Master knows that it is the destiny of, and within the capacity of, a disciple to carry out a certain piece of work and thus to serve humanity in a particular manner. He knows also that it is His duty to bring the disciple to the point of comprehension and to aid him in the accurate performance of this duty. But as He considers the disciple's karma, He finds that mortal disease will, in a few years' time, lay the mechanism of accomplishment low and prevent both effort and accomplishment. He therefore refrains from an educational process which would otherwise be obligatory upon Him.

2. *Faulty equipment.* Oft a disciple, in a particular incarnation, lacks some needed characteristic, or some desirable quality, either in his emotional nature or in one or other of the bodies. He may, for instance, have a fine physical vehicle, great devotion and a brilliant intellect, but along with these, the quality of persistence is not present; the Master knows, therefore, that a steady cooperation and continous effort is not yet possible. He dare not, consequently, incorporate the disciple (along with other members of His Ashram) in some designated piece of work and of service, because He knows that he will imperil the success of the joint endeavour. The group has therefore to proceed without the help which the disciple is otherwise competent to give.

3. *A blind spot.* This is one of the most frequent deterrents which confront a Master as He seeks to lead His disciples along the Way of Service. The disciple has some one great outstanding weakness of which he is entirely oblivious and completely unaware. If told of its existence, he flatly, conscientiously and sincerely denies its presence. He violently affirms the opposite virtue or strength. Yet all the time, this affirmation simply indicates the effort of his soul to build in a quality which, when adequately strong, will result in the expulsion of the deterring fault. As long as this

condition exists, it is not possible for the disciple to be fully integrated into the Ashram, nor is it possible to convince him that—in this specific connection—he is totally blind. Vision will eventually and inevitably come, but it will come as a result of the disciple's own effort and his self-initiated awakening; once awakened, never again will blindness be possible.

4. *An overenthusiastic nature.* This induces the disciple to rush wildly forward in an effort to accomplish the indicated task, to prove to the Master his staunch determination, and to his fellow members in the Ashram his great usefulness. This enthusiasm can wreck designated projects, shorten the life of the disciple, and thus interfere with his karma and make him a source of amusement and concern to his group.

All these factors, and several others still more subtle, have to be taken into account by a Master, as well as the age, the background and the time cycles of the disciple.

I would point out to you, therefore, that it lies entirely in your own hands to increase your usefulness in the Ashram. If I were asked by you today what phase of your development should receive your attention, I would reply: Seek consciously and strenuously to overcome negativity. For you, a cultivated and conscious negativity has been an escape mechanism from the executive and administrative nature of your life. Your soul has forced you for decades into the position of an executive, superintending and administering agent. Basically, this ran counter to your natural inclination. Yet it was supremely necessary and educational. Once however you had fulfilled the duties and obligations entailed, and had successfully and adequately carried out your task (which you always did), your personality—shrinking and sensitive—took refuge in a negative attitude to people as a whole; you developed an insulation which made it difficult for you to set up any major relation with other people.

Yet, my brother, little as you may realise it, those relationships with others, and a positive interplay with those you contacted, were ever desired by the people you met; people have always wanted to get closer to you; they have longed to know you better and to be of service and of moment to you. As an executive, you were ever available; as a soul, within a personality, you have lived your own life apart from others; you have not been easy to contact or to know; you were never responsive to approach, and your reactions to those who desired contact have been negative, and this at times when you yourself wanted closer rapport. Herein lies your task and your problem for the remaining years of your life. Learn, please, my brother, to be individually outgoing towards the people you meet and with whom life and circumstance bring you into association. Break loose—hard though it may be—from the thoughtforms which so powerfully condition you, based frequently upon an inferiority complex; refuse to permit the factors which so powerfully condition the trained, cultured person and the man who is the product of tradition, of good heritage and generations of civilised forbears to control you.

Your work with children has also tended to set you apart and make you the victim of an enforced loneliness. You could ever be free and magnetic with them but they intruded not upon the entrenched and enforced fortress of your being. You must now fit yourself to teach adults in your next incarnation, and this will necessitate a different approach and one which will invoke and involve every aspect of your being. The disciple teaches principally by what he *is* and by giving all of himself to all whom he meets. He moves outward spontaneously when someone comes within range of his possibility of contact. This is almost unknown to you. The lesson, therefore, which the trained disciple has to master is one of discernment. He needs to learn discrimination in contact if he is to avoid a useless, if well intentioned, promiscuity.

The stage of the world is so set at this time that there is full opportunity for you to find a wide sphere of contact, to work in full cooperation with other people and with co-disciples, and thus to force yourself to release *the magnetic power of your soul-infused personality*. Your inner development is greater by far than your outer expression; you need not, consequently, work with perseverance at interior unfoldment;

you need to strain after outer ability to contact, to influence and to evoke response from all and sundry with whom your lot may be cast. Rebuffs, misunderstandings and lack of response will be natural at first until your "technique of contact" is discovered by you and established in action. Each disciple develops his own technique. You have yet to discover yours.

As with some others, I give you three words upon which I would ask you to reflect as time elapses, and from which you can expect definite results *if* there is any truth in the aphorism that "as a man thinketh in his heart, so is he."

The first word which I would suggest is *Contact*. Much soul contact and contact also with your group brothers on interior levels is easy for you and presents no difficulties, even if you believe it not. You have a well established contact along these lines, but your physical brain does not yet register it adequately. That is due entirely to conditions of insensitivity, inherent in your brain cells, and is of no great moment. From the standpoint of your daily meditation, I would ask you to go forth to each day's work with the intention of magnetically attracting (in order to help and serve) at least three people—either known to you or unknown. You might find it useful (at least for a time) to keep a diary of contacts; you should enter into it a conversation by means of which you got close to someone, a contact with some stranger which seemed fruitful and interesting, or a joint piece of work which you carried out in full comprehension with someone else. This will develop in you an outgoing spirit and an interest in the whole process of contact. It is through contacts and the development of a resultant mechanism, plus a habit of magnetic rapport, which is the secret of all expansions of relationships, and this is preliminary to initiation. Think on this, for it has its major importance to you.

The second word which I want to give you is *Impression*. This word gives you much scope for reflection, invoking as it does the entire problem of sensitive response to inner contacts and outer relations. It is the key to the development of a trained psychologist and is a branch of that aspect of the universal mind which we call *truth*. The power of correctly registered impression, the ability rightly to interpret it and then to draw from it correct deduction, is the secret of all diagnosis where psychology is concerned. When this is taken into consideration by a disciple in relation to people contacted, it is of enormous usefulness; impression—when analysed and the results of analysis are employed—presents a most useful study, particularly to people like you.

Finally, I would ask you to reflect upon the word *Relationship*. I would have you do this with the specialised objective of understanding how you, as a disciple in training, can set up those relationships which will bring aid and strength to others and thus sustain the work of the Ashram. I do not intend to enlarge upon this as I want you to arrive at your own conclusions and knowledges.

What I am really doing, my brother, is indicating to you the field of your future training—a training which will engross the remainder of your life. This training must be self-initiated and it must ever be undertaken in order to fit you to work in the Ashram, as a branch of the great Ashram of the Hierarchy. You are peculiarly fitted for this work; you need only to release the magnetic quality of your already developed nature and thus break down the barriers which may exist; thus you will find your field of service tremendously extended and your potency brought into the field of a realised inclusiveness.

August 1946

MY BROTHER:

It is in no way your fault that this group on the physical plane is being disbanded until the next life cycle of the majority of the members has arrived. It is distressing that the work on the physical plane has to end, but a close and honest analysis on the part of the group itself would probably show that the major reaction is a blend of two reactions: first of all, that they could not integrate and, secondly, a sense of loss because my communications with all of you have exoterically ended. Both of these are personality reactions. From the standpoint of a Master Who knows the unimportance of years, both of these reactions are of small importance. Few of you are really young; some of you are quite old, though none of you are as old as I am; in a relatively short time all of you will drop the outer handicap of the physical body and be ready for a fresh spiritual enterprise. Esoterically (if any of you so wish it), the situation remains unaltered, provided you keep it so yourselves. The inner contact is still there, exactly as it was before; the goal ahead for each of you is just the same and the door into my Ashram stands wide open to those who fulfill the requirements.

What, my brother, is basically your goal? Taking into consideration your ray and type, it is to infuse your personality with soul energy. This is in the nature of a platitude and you may well respond that this is true of all aspirants. This is assuredly so, but *your* particular soul-objective in this life was to bring this soul energy down from the subtler bodies into the three worlds so that they can charge the brain. This charging will result in a hastened development of soul quality as it can be demonstrated upon the physical plane.

As I have told you before, you are well developed on the inner planes, but your esoteric expression of this inner unfoldment is not adequately dynamic; it does not make adequate impress on the outer conditions of living. This you know. You have, I feel sure, pondered and studied the three words—Contact, Impression and Relationship—I gave you in my last instruction. I am equally confident that your approach was along the line of strengthening your *contact* with me, the Ashram and the group; to render yourself sensitive to spiritual *impression,* and also to see that your *relationship* was right in two directions: towards the Ashram and towards your fellowmen. That is all to the good but—for the sake of your own development and increased usefulness—I would have you take those same three words and (for the remainder of your life) direct your thinking towards *contact* with your fellowmen, towards the type of impression which you can establish—an *impression* which will enable them to impress others with the desire to discover truth and to persevere until the end. It will also involve your establishing with them an educational *relationship* evoked by the quality of your approach to them and the "satisfying tincture" of your life, as one of the Masters has expressed it.

Therefore for you, until I see you on the other side of the separating veil, there must be the expression of the three types of work—expressed in two directions: the stabilising of that expression towards the Ashram (and that, with you, is well-nigh a habit and need not, therefore, form a drive), and also an intensified effort to work out the meaning of these words with your fellowmen. That will be very much harder. There is so much dammed up spiritual power in you; if you released it whenever possible and in all directions, you would be surprised at the result. You could then make the last years of your life fruitful and rewarding, far more than they have ever been in the past. Your life has been a life of loveliness, though somewhat dimmed by negativity.

You are in process of stepping over the periphery of the Ashram towards its centre. It needs only a little dynamic effort on your part to give you the unquestioning assurance that you are within the ring-pass-not of the Ashram and are functioning as a conscious disciple. Most of the group are not yet at that stage. The Ashram enfolds you all, but the next move is for each and all of you—without aid or help—to step over the mental barrier which keeps you from conscious knowledge and which (when accomplished) will enable the Ashram to give you "the freedom of the city."

One of the ideas which disciples would find it helpful to grasp is that the process of passing over to the other side involves no discontinuance of the three processes of Contact, Impression and Relationship. These being the three words with which I earlier impressed you and which seem to me today to be of major importance in your life, I would have you grasp, if possible, somewhat the permanence of their importance. With the mass of ordinary humanity, focussed in all their activities and their thinking upon the physical plane, the period after death is one of semi-consciousness, of a failure to recognise location, and of emotional and mental bewilderment. With disciples there is still contact with people (usually those with whom they have been associated) in the hours of sleep; there is still the reception of impression from environment and associates, and there is still the recognition of relation with (as on earth) the assumption of responsibilty.

One of the students in this group asked me a question some time ago which I have been long in answering. As it has a bearing on the subject we are considering, I shall answer it here. After a few subsidiary comments the student said: "I can still the outer shells or bodies, but have not dared to let go the connecting cord. Is it safe? Can you see my condition and can you tell me?" My reply is quite simple and I know he will understand:

Were you twenty years younger, my brother, with perfect safety you could break the connecting link, but owing to your age it is not, at this time, right so to do. There are some you have yet to help and one or two threads as yet to gather up. Undue strain upon the physical vehicle—no matter whether one is young or old—is never necessary and often of a harmful nature. Many aspirants in this group, in the Arcane School and elsewhere, are in training for work in the New Age and in the next life cycle, and their realisation is often bigger than the present equipment of brain cells warrants. Therefore, knowledge and registered expansion of consciousness is temporarily withheld until a better physical vehicle is available. I mention this because some suffer from discouragement when, after years of work and the achievement of old age, they find themselves registering a static condition, or what they deem to be static. There is no need for such a feeling, but there is need for care and the progression of the interior work, e'en when the external recording is apparently lacking.

To resume with your own instruction, if you would care to increase the capacity of the three activities—contact, impression, relationship—you might follow a simple exercise when going to sleep at night.

After achieving complete comfort, as far as may be possible, attempt to assume an inner attitude of planned, quiet discarding of the physical body, keeping the whole concept upon the mental plane, yet realising it to be a simple brain activity. The heart is in no way to be involved. Your objective is to preserve consciousness as you withdraw it from the brain and pass out on the subtler levels of awareness. You are *not* discarding the physical body permanently, therefore the life thread anchored in the heart is not involved. The aim is, for a few hours and whilst clothed in the astral and mental vehicles, to be *consciously* aware elsewhere. With determination you become a focussed, interested point of consciousness, intent on emerging from the casing of the physical body. That point you hold, refusing to look backward at the physical vehicle, or at the worries, interests and circumstances of daily life, fixedly waiting for the moment when your negative attitude to the physical plane and your positive attitude to the inner planes will bring a moment of release, perhaps a flash of light, the perception of an aperture of escape, or the recognition of your surroundings, plus the elimination of all surprise or the expectation of any phenomena.

You are (as you practice this exercise of withdrawal) only going through an ordinary everyday process. If facility in doing this exercise is achieved, the hour of death will find you automatically and easily—because the physical body is making no resistance but remains quiescent and negative—able to make the Great Transition without concern or fear of the unknown. This is an exercise I would like to see all the group undertake. It involves only the steady preservation of an attitude, a fixed determination to hold on to the point of consciousness which is your persistent Self, plus a live expectancy. I have chosen these words with care and would ask you to study them with equal care.

I would like also to formulate your meditation along these three concepts of Contact, Impression and Relationship. The length of the meditation is entirely dependent upon your own choice or temporary need; it is susceptible of application to all or any circumstances and you could use it for the remainder of your life (many years or few) without exhausting its possibilities or usefulness. The outline is not a rigid form, as are so many which I have given to the group. It is intended simply to be suggestive. You can make your life a rich experience by the use of these suggestions:

1. Poise yourself at the "door of exit" in the head. Realise that that point is one from which you can look *outward* upon the world of physical living, *inward* upon the world of the emotions or of mental perception, or *upward* towards the soul. These three directions form a triangle of projected sensitivity.

    Then sound the O M three times, bearing these directions in mind.

2. Take then the word Contact into your consciousness and ponder upon these three fields of contact in which it is possible for you to move—the physical plane, the kama-manasic plane, and the kingdom of the soul. Study these planes of possible and unavoidable contact (for the aspiring disciple) and study them from the angle of things as they are. When you have somewhat exhausted this work of familiarising yourself with the possible contacts, remembering that this particular work will make your life fruitful in all three directions:

    Then again sound the O M and attempt to withdraw to a point of silent contemplation upon the mental plane. Again sound the O M.

3. The fact of the possibility of Impression now must engross your attention. You begin to study the general tenor and the outstanding lessons which physical, astral or mental contact makes on you, what they have done for you during this life cycle or during the past week or day; then definitely and with full concentrated interest and attention—*you orient yourself to the soul;* you stand *consciously* ready for impression. What that impression will convey, what thought will come to you or what call to service will sound forth, you know not. Your attitude is one of a radiant, silent, poised expectancy, and nothing else is permitted. This you must work to attain. Note (if it comes) the emergence of some clear thought, the clarification of some bewilderment, the expansion of some mental perception into an intuition, with its consequent expansion of

consciousness. You can give as long or as short a time to this as you choose, but never less than ten minutes.

Then *orient yourself to me,* your Master and friend for many years, and again wait. Perchance there may be something I may have to say to you. You will note that I have used the word "orient" in both cases; I have not said "achieve contact." The task of receiving impression is not an easy one, and you may have to work some time on these different levels before you register any definite response from an achieved contact, for that is what it then will be.

Then sound the O M twice.

4. Having reached as high a point of contact as you can, at any given time, you then begin to reorient yourself to the physical plane and the life of daily experience through a systematised process of Relationships. You assume—as a disciple on the physical plane—responsibility for those relationships (to the Ashram and to me) through service planned and rendered; to the soul through fusion, rendered expressive on the mental plane; to the group emotional expression, and to your fellowmen. Grasp these recognitions of relationships, both as they affect your daily life expression and in relation to others with whom you live and work, down on the physical plane. Again, you bring this concept of essential relationships to the effect you have, as a human being on the Path, to all you meet and seek to aid. Couple ever with this thought the idea of responsibility.

Then sound the O M.

5. Next say the Invocation beginning with the stanza
"From the point of Light within the Mind of God
Let Light stream forth into the minds of men.
Let Light descend on Earth,"
and sound the O M three times. Please note that the O M in this meditation is to be sounded inaudibly.

If you will follow these suggestions, my brother, you will make rapid progress into spiritual objectivity, and your light will shine forth more radiantly. I, your Master, know your inner radiance. Permit the world of outer things to know it too. The wishes, coming from my heart for you, surround you.

To I. A. P.

August 1940

BROTHER OF OLD:

In the present world upheaval and with its steady approach to the western hemisphere, it is not easy for world disciples—with their unusual sensitivity—to detach themselves from the general psychic condition. Yet the aim of each pledged and obligated disciple (such as you are, my brother, by your own proving—which is the only sure testimony) must be to hold a subjective attitude of detached contact—an occult paradox!—and at the same time to carry forward the life of active service upon the physical plane. This is your problem and one which you will have increasingly to face in the future. The present situation must and will touch all nations and every disciple will be tested and will have to express the utmost that is in him in service. I point this out so that you can comprehend the present and be prepared for the future.

I write to you as a soul and not as a personality and would ask you to study the implications of that attitude which I hold towards you. For the remainder of your life there should be a close application to the establishing of the gained soul contact and the training of the inner attentive man to catch the communications of the soul, plus the dedicated will to forget all personality applications in the meeting of surrounding need—as far as you can in your own country and allied nations. This may come to you as a surprising statement but at the close of the war, the period of rebuilding and the establishing of right human relations may (I do not say it will, for the constant element of freewill must enter in) force each disciple to work in those places where earlier effort, the ties of karma and national heritage, and inclination determine his personal allegiance. This will be true for you too but only time will indicate whether you work with close relationship or from a distance—the first being preferable, if possible. I ask you simply to hold these possibilities in mind, to avoid fanatical conclusions, and to be prepared to work where the opportunity confronts you.

The glamour to which I referred in my first communication to you this year (Vol. I, Page 188) is being handled by you with right attitude and common sense. For this I commend you, reminding you always that soul contact is universal and inclusive in its effects but that the separative mind (even at soul levels) can still differentiate and place imparted truths under categories and sources. It is the imparted truths, the teaching and the inspiration which is of moment and this fact I believe that you are learning. I, the Master D.K., am a member of the Hierarchy and am teaching you through your own soul on mental levels, in the world of glamour at times also, and exoterically upon the physical plane through a much older disciple, A.A.B., who transmits to you my ideas. Through me, however, and through your contact with me (which is based on the recognition and unfoldment of your soul) you are en rapport with a world of spiritual inspiration and awareness which you can appreciate. Appropriate it, my brother, and transmit the teaching to those you serve but be not occupied or interested in the sources or origins of this teaching. *They matter not.* Nevertheless, the responsibility of the teacher rests upon you. The teacher should be so occupied with the need of the taught and with the clarification of the truth, as it is given to him, in terms that they can comprehend that he cannot be sidetracked through undue interest in the origin of the revelation.

A.A.B. here reminds me that I have not given you the rays which control your personality. Your major rays—I and II—are identical with those of J.W.K-P. and C.A.C., and should lead to a satisfactory understanding between you. This combination of the first and the second rays—governing either the soul or the personality—is the dominating influence in this work which I am attempting at this time to do. They are to be found quite often in this group and this is to be expected owing to the fact that the Masters M. and K.H. are the overshadowing influences behind my efforts. Seven of the group members are conditioned by these energies and most of the others have the second ray present either in their personality or egoic expressions. This should be noted as definitely colouring the group and creating (if I might so express it) the group note. Of these potencies the whole group can, therefore, avail itself for it means that the inflow of understanding, light and love is thereby greatly facilitated.

The rays of your personality are as follows:

> Mental body—The fourth Ray of Harmony through Conflict.
> Astral body—The first Ray of Power.
> Physical body—The third Ray of Active Intelligence.

This constitutes an interesting combination and produces a close relation and a line of least resistance in connection with the soul ray, through the medium of the brain (embodying the third ray force) and the astral body. I would point out to you that the brain is ever composed of atoms and cell units which vibrate to the energy of the ray which controls the physical body. This is a basic occult fact given out in a definite statement for the first time but ever deducible and implied when the student studies intelligently and has a real grasp of basic esoteric implications. Through the powerful aspiration of your first ray astral body (which is in fact transmuted desire) and its intelligent expression, and through the third ray power of your directing, awakening brain, soul contact is fairly easy of achievement for you at this particular point in your evolution. Your real problem is to free the results of this contact from distortion and glamour by the power of the illumined mind—an illumination achieved through conflict and discrimination and resulting (when the victory is gained) in the harmonising of soul and its form on earth.

I would like, therefore, to give some meditation exercises which will facilitate the achievement of this clear vision and a correct interpretation of emerging facts and relations.

I. Exercise prior to Meditation:
    1. Stand erect, facing your soul. Then say *audibly,* if possible:
        "I accept the responsibility of discipleship which my soul has placed upon me."
    2. Then pause a minute, endeavouring to realise the full significance of this undertaking. Then dismiss it.
    3. Again face your soul and say:
        "I accept with joy and with confidence and with a sense of comradeship, my share in the responsibility of making the spiritual work in the world successful."
    4. Pause again, trying to grasp the true implications of this pledge.

II. Meditation Work:
    1. Sit erect but relaxed. Withdraw the consciousness inward in successive stages, using the imagination in so doing. The imagination is a creative activity, producing definite inner change. Upon this you can depend because it is one of the forces influencing substance itself. Therefore,
        a. Withdraw from the physical brain, after definitely focussing your consciousness there. Withdraw to the astral plane.
        b. Withdraw from the astral body to the mental body. From that point recognise yourself as an integrated personality.
        c. Withdraw from the personality into the soul.
    2. As you do this work, try to see the thread of golden light which connects these three aspects of yourself. At the same time keep your consciousness steadily focussed in the head at the centre between the eyebrows, the ajna centre. This thread—dual in nature, like two golden cables intertwined—passes

from the heart and connects you, the personality, with the soul.

3. Having achieved this alignment and withdrawing, and having thus related the three aspects of the personality, quietly realise three facts:
    a. That you are now face to face with your own soul, standing before the Angel of the Presence.
    b. That you, this angelic Being, are essentially Reality, manifesting through three aspects.
    c. That therefore separation does not exist.

4. Then say with emphasis and understanding:
    "Having pervaded this world of the little manifested self with one fraction of my greater Self, I remain, greater, wider, inclusive and therefore overshadowing all my daily living."
    Ponder on this for five minutes.

5. Then add to the above the following statement:
    "I, the manifesting Self, through the magical power of my nature, redeem, reabsorb and revitalise this fraction, dwelling in my form."

6. Then sound the O M three times:
    a. Sound it mentally, breathing forth radiance on to the mental plane.
    b. Sound it next in a whisper, breathing forth the dispelling power of *Light* on to the astral plane.
    c. Then sound it audibly, breathing illumination on to the physical plane.

7. This is followed by a period of listening or what is called esoterically "egoic conversation."

I have, my brother, in this instruction given you much food for thought, also the basis for real encouragement and an indication of your needed line of approach to reality.

August 1942

1. The disciple has to learn a discrimination for which the discriminative personality has prepared him.
2. Gigantic thoughtforms dominate the sons of men, speak through a nation, focus through a group. Lean on your *Soul*.
3. Your field of service has been real, but older threads of service must later be re-grasped. Prepare.
4. Sensitivity to Those Who guide and know may indicate a mental interplay. You reach Their "forms of thought." Discriminate.
5. There is a triangle of force with which you should remain in closest touch—Myself, F.B., and A.A.B. Stay close.
6. Learn to use others in your work and train them so that they too may serve their fellowmen. This you can do. It is your Soul's behest, your personality's denial.

September 1943

My Brother:

I have seemed to you perhaps to have been silent and to have left you somewhat to yourself. Such is not, however, the case in reality. You have walked ever under my watchful eye, but there was little that I could do until you had somewhat broken the "intent to loneliness" with which your personality has so constantly met the advances of your soul. This personality reaction you are learning rapidly, as a conscious soul, to repudiate. Loneliness, isolation, a sense of being deserted and a separativeness (based on sensitivity in most cases) distinguish the first ray disciple, until he learns to preserve his divine sense of "unified identity" whilst merging, at the same time, with others. This again you are learning to do.

You have had by no means an easy time, my brother. You have tuned in on world distress and are discovering yourself doing so with increasing and oft distressing frequency. Thus are the sons of God trained and brought to the point of detached and spiritually oriented servers.

I would like to take this opportunity to express to you my appreciation (if such an inadequate word is aught but

meaningless!) of the constant and untiring service to the Plan
which you have so ceaselessly rendered. You have for years—
ever since you first returned to Spain, and later in the place
of your present abode—undeviatingly followed the path of
ceaseless, constant service. You have reached and have helped
many. I would have you know that we are not unmindful; I
would have you realise that the work which you do is planned
by us and that your task is to render yourself sensitive to our
"impression." This developed sensitivity is ever a difficult
task for the first ray person. They prefer to stand alone and
to generate within themselves the plans which they consider
fitted for the type of service which they seek to render. But
today disciples are learning that a fused and organised and
blended plan or scheme of world-wide service is required,
and that a master Plan of the Hierarchy must be carried out,
and that into this Plan all disciples, including you, must
endeavour to fit.

Have you studied with care the six statements I gave you
a year ago? I want today to call your attention to the third
statement; this set of words should condition your planning
for the future, particularly the sentence: "Older threads of
planning must later be re-grasped." You started work for us
in another country. Your major karmic destiny lies there,
even if you return not there physically or for any length of
time. The Plan must be served. I would ask you to prepare
to re-establish the work you started, once the war in Europe
is over. I would ask you to prepare to locate there again, if
necessary, and to begin by communicating with as many as
you can who earlier worked with you, seeking again to get in
touch with all of them and along the original spiritual lines.
I did not say along the original organised lines. I would ask
you to do so at first in a definitely personal manner, writing
friendly and personal letters and ascertaining the news and
the condition of those who earlier worked with you as members of the Arcane School. They will form the nucleus of the
spiritual work we seek to do and which you can aid greatly in
re-establishing.

The work of salvaging Europe, spiritually and psycho-
logically, which is our main preoccupation, must go on. It

must be entirely divorced from politics and partisanships, and I am asking all of you who are my pledged workers to move forward in this spiritual undertaking. Your link with the Master R. should help you much in taking adequate action in cooperation with A.A.B. and F.B. The triangle of force thus formed is strengthened by its link with my Brother, R. Where Spain is concerned, the picture is as follows:

$$\begin{aligned}
&*\qquad\quad\ldots\text{Master R.}\\
&*\qquad\quad\ldots\text{Master D.K.}\\
&\ *\qquad*\ldots\text{A.A.B., F.B.}\\
&\ *\qquad\quad\ldots\text{I.A.P.}
\end{aligned}$$

You will note here the direct line of spiritual force descending from the Master R., via D.K. to yourself, with F.B. and A.A.B. standing by as protecting agents on either side. They aid and sponsor all your efforts.

Much will be opening up rapidly now in the field of European assistance, and for this, in your place and sphere, you must begin to prepare. The spiritual demand of humanity is great and the need to be met is gigantic, but you have the equipment and enough surviving links in that ancient peninsula (where your work began) to salvage some remnants of the School and thus reconstitute a spiritual focal point in that land. Begin, therefore, to lay your plans. Write letters. Locate your students. Establish contact, and step by step, the way will open up before you and the work to be done will clarify. Count on your inner strength and rely on your inner spiritual contacts. Feel not futile or inadequate to the task, for in these days of urgent distress the aid given to—and consequently by—one disciple is greatly intensified and increased.

One suggestion I would here make to you personally. On receipt of this instruction, will you take a full month for the establishing of such a close contact with your own soul that love, enthusiasm, wisdom and certain fundamental spiritual recognitions (which must ever condition the life of an accepted disciple) will flood your whole being? Day by day link up with your soul; day by day pledge yourself to the work to be undertaken; day by day seek a deepened relation with me, with my Ashram, and with your group brothers; day by day investigate your service as rendered up to date in the searchlight of the soul, and then, my brother, with my aid and blessing go forward, recognised by us as one of our spiritual assets. Work to bring the light of love and of spiritual orientation to those whom you are called to serve—in the place where you now are, and increasingly in the future in the place of your earlier service. Again, I recall to you the closing words of the second statement: Lean on your soul.

I assign to you no particular meditation. I believe that the group meditation will give you all you need along this line, and the reflection upon emerging opportunity and the planning for the reopening work will suffice to provide due expression for thought, for holding the mind steady in the light, and for the required meditative concentration.

My instructions to you are occupied with the theme of work, are they not, my brother? But that, to you, is life. It is needless for me to tell you that the success of the coming reorganisation and the success of your spiritual effort will be largely dependent upon the depth of your individual spiritual focus, the closeness of your link with your own soul, and the recognition of your "attachment" (technically speaking) to my Ashram. These are the A B C of your relationship to me as an accepted disciple.

Until such time as your outer course of action appears clearer to you, and until the way opens up for a resumption of work, earlier started, you have two things therefore to do. I am but summarising.

1. Deepen the content of your own inner spiritual life by mature, profound daily reflection, carried forward on all levels of thought and in every interlude in your daily life of service and of work. Endeavour to sense the note or the vibration of the Ashram and to estab-

lish a much closer link with your group brothers. They value you and must also do their part.

2. Lay your plans for increased School activity, and concentrate also upon the work of the Triangles. Prepare definitely for the future, and seek also for those who can aid in your planned work.

The future ahead of my workers and the work to be done which will emanate from my Ashram is one of great activity. The plans are outlined and the work assigned is clearly proposed. I receive my instructions from a "joint committee" of the spiritual leaders behind the world scene; They are the senior members of the Hierarchy, working under the Christ. They arrive at Their decisions after due consultation with senior workers, such as myself—Masters and initiates above the third initiation. Thus the work becomes fused and blended, and the entire Hierarchy, at a time of crisis such as the present, is swung into one unified activity. From that point of focussed intention each then proceeds to carry out the Plan, via Their Ashram, and thus the work makes its impact upon the outer world.

I explain this to you as you are preparing to become an ever more intimate member in the "circle of the Ashram" which guards the heart of the hierarchical life.

With courage and with determination, my brother and my friend, move forward upon the Lighted Way.

November 1944

My Comrade and My Brother:

These are two appellations which are sincere and intended. You are at this time facing changes. The choice with which you are confronted is not so much where you will work, but whether you have arrived at a high water mark in your developed life of service and can therefore go no further, or whether there are still to be found in you those springs of interest and those inner urges which will enable you to reach outward and further into the life of the spirit.

Such is oft the choice with which the disciple is faced who reaches close to the three score years and ten of ordinary human enterprise, as you do today. The difficulty lies in the fact that, fundamentally, either decision is right. Few, however, face the choice consciously or intelligently or, having made it, abide by the decision made. From the standpoint of the ordinary aspirant, the choice is relatively unimportant because the time equation is of no great moment at this stage; a few years more or less are of no import in the eternity of soul reaction. Therefore, a decision to relax, to hold the point gained, but to refrain from further struggle, has in it no room for criticism. Remember this.

From the standpoint of the accepted disciple—such as you are—there may be more to the choice than at first appears. It might be of service to you, and to all who may later read these instructions, if I dwelt for a moment upon the inevitable problem of the working disciple, upon the problem of the man who reaches the age which you have reached. Shall he rest back upon his laurels (and you have laurels, my brother, as I pointed out in my last instruction to you) or shall he—to use a Biblical phrase—"gird his loins" anew and go forward with a fresh impetus and to a still higher summit of attainment? Shall he demonstrate the power of the seventh wave which will carry him forward much further upon the beach of life expression or will the strong undertow of ordinary human frailty pull him back from renewed effort?

The reasons why a disciple must at least endeavour not to relax unduly and should push on in spite of fatigue (the fatigue of years of living), in spite of the increasing "creaking" of the human apparatus and the inevitable tendency which comes from constant service and constant contact with others, might be enumerated as follows:

1. He must endeavour to carry the rhythm of service and of fruitful living with him when—free of the physical body—he stands upon the other side of the veil. There must be no gap in that service.
2. He must endeavour as far as in him lies to preserve the

continuity of his consciousness as a *working* disciple and should allow no gap to emerge between his present point of tension and that point of tension which supervenes after the death experience.

3. He must endeavour to close the episode of this life experience so that it is apparent that he *is* a member of an Ashram; he must permit no break in the established relationship, or any cessation to the flow of ashramic life through him to the world of men. This activity, on account of the natural and normal deterioration of the physical vehicle as it grows older, is not so easy a task; it requires a definite concentration of effort, thus increasing the tension in which a disciple ever lives.

4. For any disciple in my Ashram, the problem in this time of world crisis is peculiarly urgent, and this for the following reasons:

   a. My Ashram is the main affiliated Ashram with that of the Master K.H. To Him, my Master (as I am yours), is given the task, on a large scale, of world education along new lines. Through my Ashram, working under the inspiration of His, the newer, esoteric presentation of truth is to be given out. The work that I have already done—through my books and through all the teaching which you have attempted to embody—is to render the teaching of the other and older esoteric schools and groups entirely exoteric. There is little left to them that is new; they must now link up with the sources which I represent if their leaders are to present fresh and vital information to their students, or they must take what I have conveyed to the world, via A.A.B., and thus again reintegrate into the esoteric whole.

   b. Disciples in my Ashram have a dual responsibility to stand steady in a *preservation of realisation*—if I may use such a phrase. This steadiness must not be relaxed in any way as old age draws near, and it must not be permitted to disappear through the transition of death itself. It is through the unbroken conscious thinking of a welded group of disciples that the Master of an Ashram works. It is not so much the active outer service of a group of disciples which is of major importance (though it has necessarily a vital purpose) as the coherent, integrated group thought which is so potent in effecting changes in the human consciousness.

c. The peculiar problem of the present world crisis and the terrific readjustments in the human consciousness, incident to the inauguration of a new culture, civilisation and world religion, warrant my presenting the members of my Ashram (even affiliated groups, such as yours) with the opportunity to preserve intact and free from all deterioration their "state of mind" throughout the remaining years of this life, through the process of dissolution, and on into the freedom of the other side of the veil. This preservation of conscious integrity is no easy task; it requires understanding and most deliberate effort.

I call you, therefore, my brother, to exactly this effort. The consequences to you will be a much harder life of service from now on; the results will be the carrying out of your plans for work with greatly intensified effort.

You should now work in closer cooperation with A.A.B. and F.B. The task of carrying esoteric truth into Latin and Catholic America and southern Europe is no easy undertaking. It will be slow. Your foundation must be well and truly laid. The quality of those reached by you in the future is of more importance than the quantity. Bear this ever in mind. Relinquish not the various phases of the work you have so successfully launched, but proceed with them as heretofore— no matter where may be the place of your physical plane enterprise.

One of the many things which you need at this time to learn, and which you must initiate during the next few years, is how to gather people together and work through them. This, as you have been taught, is very difficult for a first ray disciple to master, particularly when the soul ray and the ray of the astral or emotional nature are both first ray. It is easy for the first ray disciple to withdraw into his soul consciousness, far easier than for any other ray types, and your problem (as it is also the problem of J.W.K-P.) is to give the second ray personality fuller sway, and thus balance the first ray ability to demonstrate detachment by the functioning of the opposite quality of attachment—so distinctive of the second ray nature. Ponder on this.

As I told J.W.K-P. some years ago, a "detached attachment" (paradoxical as it sounds) is the goal of the first ray working disciple. This is equally true of you. You and he have the same egoic, personality and mental rays. Hence the close link with him which you have ever realised. He is a disciple of the Master M., temporarily working in my Ashram. You have been admitted into the ranks of accepted disciples in my Ashram and by me, but you will eventually be transferred into the Ashram of the Master M. The free interplay thus established between my Ashram and that of the Master M. is due to the fact that He is the inner Head of all esoteric groups, and in the interest of the coming new world order, the teaching Ashrams are being strengthened by the inflow of first ray disciples. This should be a point of real interest to you.

What, my brother, shall be the type of meditation and interior work which you should be doing during the coming years? I would like to have you meditate upon the "three activities": Outward moving, persistent orientation, and interior withdrawing or abstraction. The *relation* of these three activities or three attitudes should form one aspect of your reflection upon these phrases; the relative activity involved in each attained position should constitute another; the effect produced by each of them in the three worlds, and also upon soul levels, demands careful and concentrated thought. What, for instance, is the nature of "outward moving" upon the astral plane? How would "persistent orientation" appear or express itself upon the mental plane? Or "abstraction and withdrawal" upon the physical level of consciousness? How can you, as a disciple, display these attitudes simultaneously? I think you will admit, my brother, that in these three concepts and in their working out in the daily life within the ring-pass-not of the three worlds and in the life of the soul upon its own plane, I have given you the theme for much thinking during the coming years. Take each of these phrases, therefore, and think each of them out in relation to each of the three planes in the three worlds, and to each other; carry the same directed thinking on to soul levels and shift the theme then into the three worlds of the Spiritual Triad, regarding the lower three worlds then as reflections of the higher, triadal three. Keep notes of all the thoughts of reality which come to you; watch the reactions produced in your vehicles of expression, and become increasingly aware of the changes which conscious, deliberate thinking will bring about in you. Think—if I may so express it—in your heart, and also in your mind, and endeavour to comprehend the distinction between these two modes of thought.

This reflective work should constitute your meditation work in the future; it will condition your interior development and will also inevitably make your outer work more dynamic.

One reason why I have emphasised the need for attachment in this instruction is that right attachment releases the love of the soul, and only love, consciously, intelligently and deliberately applied, can make for successful work, both in Europe and South America—your two recognised fields of service. Only your second ray personality will have the capacity to reawaken contact with your students in Spain or hold steady those already working in South America; it is through individually re-found, re-awakened and re-inspired realisation that the work, planned and intended by me, can be successfully carried forward. Such is your immediate task. Only your second ray personality can have the patience to cover the mass of detail needed and to persist in the face of *apparent* nonsuccess. Much skill in action will also be required. The Catholic Church is governed by the first ray as its soul ray, and by the third ray as its personality ray. Hence its love of politics and of temporal power; hence also its intensely commercial and financial preoccupations. The mental ray of this Church is sixth ray. Hence its narrow one-pointedness;

its emotional body is also sixth ray in quality, whilst the physical ray of the outer organisation is seventh. These are points which should interest you and which you need to bear in mind as you work. A realisation of this peculiar combination of rays will demand of you, and of all workers along esoteric lines, great skill in action.

With renewed endeavour, enlightened understanding and courage, go forth again, my brother, in the service of the light. I stand ever behind you. On that point, have no doubts. I shield and protect, but I leave you free to work.

August 1946

My Dear Brother:

This is a new way for me to address you, but you have endeared yourself to me by your patient persistence and your undeviating adherence to the service of the Hierarchy. For many years you have done our work in a most difficult sphere. I say this to you because I would not have you spend time (or should I say, waste time, my brother?) in wishing you had done the work better or differently, or in the unrewarding task of self-depreciation. I would tell you quite simply that we are not ungrateful and we are not dissatisfied. The Latin field—by that I mean the sphere in which the Latin race predominates, Italian, Spanish and Portuguese— is one of the most difficult in which to work. The narrowness of thought induced by Roman Catholic Church control, the crystallisation which comes from a very ancient development, and (in South America) the wide mixture of races, make the task of bringing spiritual liberation one of peculiar difficulty.

Do you realise, my brother, that you have been drawing the plough over the ground in preparation for the New Age teaching for the first time, and that that ground is very hard, very stony, and at present relatively unproductive?

So be of good cheer. Your work is more fruitful than you realise and in some life you will see the results of the apparently unrewarding toil of the years of your spiritual enterprise.

I have few instructions to give you. Proceed as heretofore, but deepen persistently your own inner life; give more time to quiet reflection and study than to the technicalities of the task; let others deal with the mechanics of the work whilst you seek to act as a spiritual reservoir from which they can draw strength and wisdom and understanding. The recognition of this phase of your work is perhaps the most important lesson you can learn at this time. You will experience a new power, the upwelling of new spiritual fervour, the joy of seeing others competently handling the mechanics of the work whilst you teach and aid them in their spiritual undertakings. Above all else, endeavour to reach and interest the young people. They are the hope of the future and are coming into incarnation subjectively aware of their predestined task of world reconstruction; you will find them acutely responsive to spiritual contacts, particularly if presented in nonreligious terms. Count, therefore, on this and try to reach them.

I am going to give you a somewhat brief meditation exercise to be done by you twice a day—on arising in the morning and the last thing at night, prior to going to sleep. It should not take you long to do, but—if done correctly and with as much of your first ray soul integrated into it as you can invoke—it will greatly aid you.

1. Sound the O M inaudibly three times.
2. Then, having achieved inner quiet and relaxed mental focussing, seek, with an alert consciousness, to contact:
   a. Your soul.
   b. My Ashram.
   c. Me, your Master.
   You thus, through the imagination, create a triangle of energy:

   Ashram.   *   * D.K.

               *   Yourself.

As familiarity with this meditation is developed, you should eventually arrive at a contact, at a registered sense of spiritual power (expressed through your second ray personality) and at such an increase of love and light that your sphere of service will recognise it, even if—at first—you do not.

3. Then, after quiet acceptance and a period of silent reflection, you will deliberately pour out the inflowing spiritual power into:
   a. Your immediate environment,
   b. The Arcane School, of which your work in South America is an integral part,
   c. The Goodwill Movement you have aided in starting in South America.

This type of meditation constitutes a definite act of service and should—when done in the morning—prove pronouncedly strenuous. It involves some practise in visualisation and (where I and the Ashram are concerned) the use of your confident, creative imagination.

4. Then say the Great Invocation, slowly and with much mental intention, pausing after each of the four stanzas for quiet thought and reflection.

5. Then again link up in thought with me, your Master. Sound the O M inaudibly again three times, and then proceed about your daily work.

My blessing continues to rest upon you.

November 1948

MY BROTHER OF LONG STANDING:

It had not been my intention to send you a communication, since the personal communications have been largely discontinued. I am, however, prompted to do so today because as I contacted you in my thought life this morning, I decided that a word from me and the touch of my hand (symbolically speaking) would give you strength and comfort.

There comes a time in the training of any disciple when he *must* stand alone and feel sometimes that he has been deserted by his Master and by the other members of the Ashram. It is the higher and occult correspondence of the mystical experience of the true mystic and to which he has given the name of "the dark night of the soul." All this is nevertheless only a part of the great illusion and has to be overcome and dissipated. When this victory has been achieved and there has been evidenced the willingness to work alone and apparently with no ashramic direction—except a general knowledge of the Plan—then the disciple has demonstrated that he can be trusted; he becomes available for a higher rating and more responsibility can be placed upon him—if not in this life then in the next.

You are not young, my brother, but you can have the rare joy of looking back (when the time comes to pass through the Portal into clearer light and life and *know*) to know that you have served and helped thousands, through the radio and through the translated material of the teaching I have tried to give; what you have sown has not fallen on sterile ground. This remains true, even if you do not register the fact. Since first you responded to my vibration, you have not turned back; this has been recorded and recognised by us.

Praise and commendation is an unusual line for me to take but a disciple has to learn to respond correctly to that as well as to correction. You have earned commendation and we withhold from no one their just due.

Go forward, my brother. These are troubled times, and steady centres of light in every land are sorely needed.

May the strength of your own soul and the knowledge that your place in the Ashram is secure enable you to complete the work which you have begun.

NOTE: *This disciple has persisted faithfully to serve as a steady centre of light, and in September, 1951, he passed into clearer light and life in the inner Ashram.*

To I. S. G-L.

August 1940

MY FRIEND AND BROTHER:

For several lives we have been associated, though this is only the second incarnation wherein you have been definitely regarded by me and by my Associates as a pledged disciple. I am pointing this out to you as it infers a consecration and a dedication which you have preserved inviolate and evokes a response which only increases as time goes on.

You are pledged as a disciple to further our plans and to occupy yourself with definite group work. Our disciples learn the processes of initiation in the fire and heat of the daily life battle in the world of the present. They grasp eventually the processes also of group work and the rules which govern group endeavour. These rules govern the Hierarchy. They recede increasingly into the background as the group grows in function, purpose and usefulness but this withdrawal into the silence of the Hierarchy is not based and never will be based upon any outwardly imposed silence by the initiate or disciple upon either himself or his group. The silence concerns himself, and is based upon a humble appreciation of the whole of which he is simply a part and is not based upon a silence and a technique which simply emphasises mystery. *The only true mysteries are those points of revelation for which the mechanism is inadequate* and which, therefore, find no response in the one whom the initiate or disciple contacts. Of these mysteries you, the teacher and leader, may be aware but the pupil remains unmoved when presented with them. He simply does not recognise them. The outer imposition of silence and mystery is focussed consequently around the teacher in the mind of the taught and only serves to distract his attention from the reality to an imposed glamour surrounding the teacher. I would have you ponder on this, my brother, for your service is needed, but is today—if you will permit me to say so—handicapped by the intensity of your devotion and the psychic pulsation of your solar plexus.

You will recognise the condition to which I here refer. It affects also at times the quality of your impact upon people and occasionally the fruitfulness of your service. The careful and considered following of the group meditation should do much to relieve the situation and so release you for fuller service.

You would find it useful also, once and for all, to face up to the complexities of your own nature and to do so joyfully. You could also try to simplify your own approach to truth, to me and to humanity. There lies your immediate problem —simplification. This involves the elimination of imaginative reactions, all hinted implications and a withdrawal from the centre of your group life (I refer here not to the group which I am here teaching) just in so far as you feel yourself a centre. It involves also the effort to become a potent living influence radiating from above and not from the centre and yet without any sense of being above.

I wonder, my brother, if I am making my meaning clear. It is not clear to A.A.B. who is taking down my words but it should be clear to you, for it concerns your established technique of service and your group activity. You have accomplished a good and fruitful life service. You have aided many towards the light and have demonstrated a physical plane selflessness which has been powerful in releasing others. You need now to demonstrate an equal selflessness upon the plane of aspiration and of devotion. There lies for you the battle ground, and victory must be yours prior to taking the initiation for which you are being prepared. Your capacity for suffering is abnormal; this must be ended through the cultivation of that divine indifference which changes or shifts the present almost too violent emotional reactions into that calm, understanding, compassionate wisdom which— through identification with the soul of those you seek to help —inevitably aids suffering personalities. I think you realise the significance of my remarks. Your intense desire to serve Us and your deep love for humanity must be preserved but not forgotten in the strenuous activity of your life.

You are as yet a comparatively young man. The crux of your whole problem is to be found in *the shift* which you are supposed to make this incarnation from the minor ray, the sixth Ray of Devotion, to a major ray, the second Ray of Love-Wisdom. When you have accomplished this, you will take initiation. The task is however a stupendous one because as an accepted disciple in the technical sense of the word, the characteristics of the sixth ray—owing to your having a sixth ray astral body—are very pronounced and dominant. This condition is aggravated (if I might so express it) by your having a first ray personality. When, as in your case, the polarisation is in the astral body and so the energy of power pours in, the situation becomes acute, which is to be expected. Fortunately, disciples are driven by intensity and devotion to take the needed steps which will bring release and a consequent moving forward, and the incarnation wherein they do this is always peculiarly circumstanced, subjectively at least, even if the exoteric life is of no major interest. This is not so with you. In your case the following conditions embody your problem and hence your opportunity:

1. The intense difficulty of shifting from one ray to another ray. The aspiration of your sixth ray astral body must be lifted on to the plane of knowledge. The power of sense realisation must become divine wisdom through surety. Vision must give place to intuitive focussed perception—a very different thing, my friend.

2. You were born in the sign Gemini which again presents its own peculiar problems. You vibrate between the pairs of opposites in a very pronounced and definite manner—as does A.A.B. The point of balance and of equilibrium is ever a difficult one for the disciple to achieve in this sign.

3. Your first ray personality works through a physical body which is on the same ray so that a triple first ray energy again complicates your life theme because all these forces are concentrated in the lower nature. This could lead (in the case of a pledged disciple) to a powerful and distracting spiritual ambition which in a group leader—such as you are—would be a detriment to the group. Where the astral body is on the sixth ray

and devotion is dominant, the glamour of devotion can veil the reality of any existent ambition.

4. The present world conflict enhances your problem and makes the whole life cycle one of the utmost pain yet one of prime importance.

There are, my brother, many lives of such a negligible nature that they warrant no comment. Then may come a life when the attention of the soul, of the Master and of the group upon the physical plane are focussed upon the struggling disciple, thus bringing intensification of his situation and forcing him to "struggle into the light of day," watched by those who understand and by those who do not understand. This causes much suffering to the sensitive worker. All this applies to you. You hate publicity and yet much that you do courts it. You are sensitively humble and yet can be trapped and misled sometimes by personality pride; you love deeply and sincerely but are apt to express this through devotion instead of through wise identification.

I have for you, however, no real concern. I tell you that you need haste in discarding impediments upon the Way but am assured, through study of your soul contact, that you will not be hindered.

I ask myself what I can do for you and so aid the process of transmutation and release through right meditation. I would suggest the following experiment in subjective attitudes. That, in the last analysis, is a definition of meditation. The end of all meditation is concerned with:

1. The attitude of the personality to the soul.
   This is self-control.
2. The attitude of integrated man to humanity.
   This is service.
3. The attitude of the disciple to the Hierarchy.
   This is intuitional sensitivity.
4. The attitude of the hierarchical worker to the Plan.
   This is selection of activity.

Ponder on these points, particularly the third which concerns aptly your sensitive reactions to Us. This reaction will be felt *in your soul* as a complete surrender in time and space; *in the personality* it will register either as a glamour or a purificatory process, and *in the group* as a force, having either a good or a bad effect, according to its colouring by the higher or the lower nature and the activity it will succeed in evoking when it impinges upon the personnel of the group.

The following exercise can be done four times and repeated three times each day:

1. Stand with your arms outspread in the symbol of the Cross.
2. Take six long slow breaths, thus establishing a rhythm.
3. Then take one long breath and gather up by the power of imagination the energy of the solar plexus. Then carry it along the spine and upward to the head, not to the heart as is usually the case.
4. Focus the dedicated aspiration and emotional energy in "the secret place" and then sound the O M. Breathe it down into the throat centre.

This can be regarded as an act of breathing in and breathing out and constitutes an activity carried forward on one breath with an interlude of conscious focussing. You will notice that, in combination with the group meditation, you will be working actively upon the solar plexus, the head, the heart and the throat. It will require careful watching of process, results in the centres and consequent activity.

Let me be ambitious for you, my brother of long standing. *That* I am. I have watched you with loving understanding for a very long cycle. My love ends not and my care of you is all-surrounding.

August 1942

1. One there has been. The second lies ahead—not far ahead. Prepare.
2. The simplicity of the soul opens the Way to Shamballa.

3. Be simple, clear as day and full of love.
4. A glamour settles down because a separating wall was built on false foundations. Destroy this wall and let the glory in.
5. Be not so troubled, brother. Close to my heart you stand and close to that of Morya. Talk to F.B., for you and he and I are close, and close to Morya.
6. Your field of service needs a certain note of quality. Learn to reject and thus discriminate the best.

September 1943

My Co-disciple:

My relation to you is slightly different to that which I face when approaching the bulk of the members of my Ashram; you belong, as does F.B., to the Ashram of the Master Morya. You have been assigned to my Ashram on account of the nature of the vibratory activity of your astral body, and because—owing to your own definite soul choice—you are shifting on to the second ray of love-wisdom. You might well ask, therefore, how it happens that your orientation has been towards the Master M. and that you have been affiliated with His Ashram. The reason is to be found in the fact that your personality, your mental nature and your physical body are all upon the first ray, and that consequently the power of your intelligent and focussed mind has driven you into the aura of the leading first ray Ashram, and has held you there. Closer participation was not possible, owing to your sixth ray soul, whose natural and predetermined destiny was to fuse its secondary energy with the energy of the second ray, thus opening the door for you into a second ray Ashram. It was felt, therefore, that I (through the medium of my Ashram) could provide those conditions which would facilitate this transition and at the same time prepare you for the next great spiritual expansion of consciousness—the initiation of which you know. This will mark the consummation of this major life cycle.

As you know, and as I have before pointed out, you have a profound task of balancing to carry out, owing to the ray energies which at this time condition your life. Three aspects of the first ray and two aspects of the sixth intensify each other. Were you not the advanced disciple which you are, they would be liable to produce a life and karmic expression of a fanatical self-will. To this difficult situation of balancing must be added the difficulties always entailed in a transitional life wherein a major transfer must be effected. To all this again must be added the present world condition, wherein the Shamballa force is abroad and potently affecting those natures which have a preponderance of first ray aptitudes. You have thus no easy time, my brother. This you realise, and I too know it, and stand by.

It was for this reason that I have urged you for some years to concentrate upon the book "The Way into Shamballa," knowing that an intelligent and loving consideration of the problem would do much to bring your first ray personality nature into line with the purposes of your second ray soul, and thus facilitate the transfer of your egoic consciousness off the sixth ray of devotion on to the second ray of love-wisdom. The first and the second rays work closely together; love and will are closely identified on the higher levels of consciousness and service; the two basic energies in reality constitute one great expression of divine planning and purpose.

It is in this connection too that your relation to F.B. and A.A.B. is no idle or temporary matter, but one of real import to all of you. This A.A.B. has recognised. Several forces—inherent in your own nature or engineered and manipulated by the ignorant or the less advanced upon the Path—have endeavoured to interfere and prevent the desired relationship. The matter is, however, entirely in your own hands and the amount of contact between the three of you is your personal matter, for there is no impediment upon the side of the other two. The three of you together could do potent work, and the need of the Ashram at this time for workers is great—workers who are, as H.P.B. has put it, "as the fingers on one hand."

I would remind you that the potency of disciples and initiates is out of all proportion greater than that of a similar number of aspirants. The interplay of loving understanding and of fused wills produces an exceedingly potent reservoir of energy. This is a point which all disciples should study and upon which they can count as they work together in united effort in any Ashram.

As I study you, my brother and my friend, and as I look ahead at your life of service and of right intention, one word stands out in my consciousness for you. To it, I referred in the six statements which I earlier gave you. That word is: *simplicity*. I stated in that earlier writing that the simplicity of the soul opens the way into Shamballa. That was and is an essential key statement for you. Those upon the second ray fall (as you know) into two groups, generally speaking; there are, naturally, numerous exceptions. Souls on the wisdom aspect of the second ray go to Shamballa and join the Great Council in some capacity or another. Such a one was the Buddha. Those on the love aspect of the second ray tread one or other of the various paths, primarily that of the World Saviours; They become the divine Psychologists and World Teachers. The Christ combined in Himself all these three great traits.

Those in this second group of souls upon the second ray likewise fall into two groups: They follow the way of specialised detail and of a comprehensive inclusiveness, and are the outstanding occultists; the other group is distinguished by pure love. Of the group which finds its way into Shamballa a developed simplicity will be found to govern all relations.

Simplicity and unity are related; simplicity is one-pointedness of outlook, free from glamour and the intricacies of the thoughtform-making mind; simplicity is clarity of purpose and steadfastness in intention and in effort, untrammelled by questioning and devious introspection; simplicity leads to simple loving, asking nothing in return; simplicity leads to silence—not silence as an escape mechanism, but as an "occult retention of speech."

For you, simplicity is a major essential practice in this next cycle of your life, but you will have to decide for yourself what it means for you, and I shall be interested to note your reaction to this word and practice and the changes it may make in your life and thinking. Simplicity connotes the blueprint which "substands" the outer structure of creation, of living, of loving and of service, and this is true of a solar system, a planet, humanity or the individual. It consequently has its immediate application to your own requirements and your mode of approach to life and to people. This loving simplicity—free from complicated thinking, from mystery and from selfish introspection—should provide the theme for your meditation work until I next communicate with you. To this I would add an increased concentration upon the preparation of the book which I seek to have you write and to complete.

You see, my brother, it is a book which will take much intuition and spiritual perception to write, and it can only be written by someone who has been trained in an Ashram. The theme of Shamballa is new, and little is yet known about it, its way of life and its governing laws. Only initiate-disciples can get a glimpse of some of the more exoteric significances, whilst the inner meaning must be drawn forth by you in deep and concentrated meditation and by the determined use of the will. There is no one who can aid you in preparing this book except some group brother or someone working consciously in an Ashram. You will look in vain for cooperation and help among those you seek to aid and among the orthodox and theological esotericist. Some key thoughts I can here give to you, and if you use them as the theme of your meditation, light upon the subject may break forth:

1. Shamballa is the place of purpose. It is a purpose which cannot be understood until the Plan is followed. Herein lies a clue.
2. Shamballa is not a Way, but a major centre of related states and a relatively static energy—energy held ready for creative purposes by the focussed intention of the Great Council, acting under the directing eye of the Lord of the World.

3. Shamballa is the major point of tension upon the planet. It is a tension that expresses loving intelligent will, free from all self-will or mental bias.

4. Shamballa is the major receptive agent upon the planet, from the angle of solar inflow, but at the same time it is the main distributing point of energy, from the angle of the kingdoms in nature, including the fifth kingdom. From the point of tension the life pattern of the planetary Logos and His will become embodied and finally matured through the processes of evolution.

5. Shamballa receives energy from various solar and extra-solar Entities or centres of emphatic and energetic life; i.e., from Venus, from the Central Spiritual Sun, from the current conditioning constellation through which our sun may be passing, from the Great Bear and other cosmic centres. Sirius, so important a factor in the spiritual life of the planet, brings its energies to bear direct upon the Hierarchy, and energy from Sirius does not normally enter our planetary life via Shamballa.

6. Shamballa is the head centre, speaking symbolically, of our planetary Life, focussing will, love and intelligence in one great and fundamental Intention and holding that focussed point throughout the entire life cycle of a planet. This great Intention embodies current purpose and expresses itself through the medium of the Plan.

These statements may be somewhat familiar to you, but they could provide the six seed thoughts for your meditative work during the coming year. Will you thus consider them? Out of the work which you will accomplish thus in meditation (using the heart centre as a balance for the head) you will greatly enrich the proposed book.

This coming period of deep reflection upon Shamballa, entailing as it will the entire problem of the Will (in its various aspects), of purpose as it works out in the planet, and of will as it conditions the human being, will bring to the fore in your consciousness the various relations existing between the differing aspects of the will: the relation of your individual self-will to the loving plan of the soul, of that will to the divine Will, of your spiritual will to the group will, of the group will to the Hierarchy, and of the hierarchical will to that of Shamballa. Such are some of the ideas which can govern your spiritual thinking, reflection and meditation until you again hear from me. You will find all these to be intensely practical considerations. The question of *motive* will immediately enter in, for motive underlies will in a most curious manner, and motive "substands" purpose. Therefore, your personality motives in life and service will have to come under review, and their relation to soul motive. The result of this entire process of thinking will be the subjugation of your motives to soul motive, and again, therefore, we shall have the *simplification of your life* and the opening up of a wider vision into Shamballa. Shamballa and simplicity, will and motive, will become the directing currents of thought which will sweep you on your way, closer to my Ashram, nearer to my heart (and here I am speaking both lovingly and technically), and nearer and closer to humanity.

November 1944

MY BROTHER AND MY FRIEND:

What I have to say to you today hinges upon one single question: Are you ready to pay the price which the taking of the next initiation entails? All accepted disciples are preparing for initiation. All are therefore under test. You know that you are preparing for initiation; you know which initiation it is. It is because of this preparatory period that the past three years have seen you seriously tested, and tested in every aspect of your nature. There is, nevertheless, little that I have been able to do for you because loneliness is one of the assets and also aspects of this work of preparation. Disciples ever take initiations alone, even when preparing for and taking group initiation. This is one of the paradoxes of the occult teaching which is not at all easily understood. It sounds entirely contradictory but is not so at all. It has not been easy to reach you either, because you have taken refuge from the tests in the work of your own group, rather than in the Ashram. In your own group you have sought forgetfulness and have not sought the protection and the love of your ashramic group. That is your privilege and your inalienable right. I would like, however, to point out to you that it is safer and wiser to take refuge in both the higher and the lower places of service, and to do this simultaneously. One place safeguards you as a soul and the other as a personality.

The call of Shamballa, the call of my Ashram, and the call of your own exoteric group (mark those words, my brother) have sounded forth in your ears and you have been bewildered; you have forgotten perhaps that if you stand at the midway point (which is my Ashram) you have immediate access to both "points of call." I have here given you an important hint and I want you to endeavour to grasp its significance.

You have been drastically tested in your physical vehicle, and that is hard, my brother, because it is difficult to preserve one's equanimity and one's balance under those circumstances. You need, however, to understand better than you do the "distortions" for which physical sickness is responsible, and thus learn more wisely to discount yourself and to pay less attention to the glamours of the lower self. This would simplify your life, and I told you earlier that *simplification was a needed attribute for you.* You have also been sorely tested in the emotional nature; surely, my beloved brother, you know by this time that when a definite transition is being made by the soul—as is the case where you are concerned—from one ray to another, that abnormal testing is automatically inevitable? This will be particularly the case when a disciple is moving on to the second ray, owing to its close relationship with the emotional-intuitive nature, and when also you have—as you know—three first ray controls in your personality equipment.

This necessarily engenders a serious problem. You have also been cruelly tested in your mental nature by the war and through your intense grasp of human pain, as well as by your understanding of psychological reactions. These have served to enhance your problem, and your entire emotional and mental reaction to war and its happenings has well-nigh crippled your essential (not your apparent) usefulness. You have, within yourself, questioned the foundations of all things, and life has been most complicated for you—physically, emotionally and mentally. Owing to the dominance of the first ray in your equipment, you have successfully withdrawn yourself from your group brothers; you have considered that they had naught to give you, and you realised that—feeling this way—you had naught for them. Detachment is the path of least resistance for a first ray nature, and (if you will permit me to say so and will accept this statement) indicates definitely the dominance at this time of personality reactions. Your second ray soul does not sanction detachment, and hence the conflict being waged within your consciousness.

Yet, my brother and my comrade, the deep and lasting love of two of your group brothers has steadily protected you during this time of trial and of difficulty, as has the love of A.A.B. She asks me not to tell you this, indeed she begs me not to do so, for she is sensitive interiorly to all that affects you. It is, however, right that you should know.

So, brother of mine, we come back to the question of the reason for all this harshness in life and to the initiation for which you are preparing. In connection with this I would say: Get back to the "midway point" and to the protecting love of the Ashram. Then the strength of Shamballa to which you so easily respond can *safely* pour in; then, too, will come the wisdom which will enable you to render better service to the world. See therefore how simple is the message which I have for you at this time, and remember that I told you last year that simplicity held for you the key to all success. You are not truly successful just at present. Simplicity does not rule.

Relinquish the thoughtforms which seem at this time to stand between you and the Ashram. You will know what these are if you will take three days of quiet retirement and during that time refuse to think about your work, about your groups, their personnel or about yourself and your past activities, as well as about your group brothers. Aim simply to achieve a point of orientation towards me and the Ashram; endeavour to respond consciously to hierarchical impression, shutting out (at least for those three days) every kind of reaction to human happenings. Aim at a point of tension from which new endeavour and new enterprise can become possible. Then rededicate yourself to the service of humanity; reconsecrate yourself to cooperation with the Hierarchy, and regain your early enthusiasm in relation to Us and Our work. Then again resume your world contacts. There will be three letters which you will find it necessary to write if these days are productive of renewed contact with hierarchical force. You will know to whom these letters should go and what they will state.

Take proper medical help, brother of mine. Take time to get the physical vehicle in better condition. The reflex action of the body upon the emotional nature and upon the mind is great. As a psychologist you know this, but fail to apply to yourself what you so helpfully apply to others. Have confidence in my belief and trust in you, and let the remaining years of your life be *triumphant in love;* let them be negative to criticism; all your group brothers are handling problems equal in difficulty to yours; proffer rich cooperation to them and to the Hierarchy. My love and blessing is ever yours, and this you know.

August 1946

My Beloved Brother:

I would like to start my communication to you with a clear and definite statement: You are in process of taking some of the final tests which precede the taking of the second initiation. For that reason, I feel the need of writing to you with clarity, of bringing you some measure of comfort and of strength, and of indicating certain steps which—if you will take them—may hasten the process.

Yet I feel very great difficulty in approaching you, though not for the usual reasons. Oft a Master cannot at some particular time reach a disciple because he is surrounded with too much activity, or with activities of the wrong kind; in some cases, the thought-life of the disciple has created so many thoughtforms that temporarily he cannot be reached;

or again, he is absorbed in some form of service which he deems essential and which looms larger in his consciousness than the work of the Ashram with which he is affiliated. These, however, are not the things which hinder an easy contact with you. What do hinder are the results in your consciousness, at this particular stage, of the tests of the initiation themselves. It is the emotional glamour which has engulfed you, and freedom from glamour has to be demonstrated at the second initiation; it is the intense awareness you experience, at this time, of yourself—the central factor. This again is a necessary but distressing prelude to this initiation. This glamour comes between you and me. The self-awareness comes also between you and the Ashram, as well as between you and the group which you have gathered around you upon the physical plane.

Having read this far, will you, brother of mine, continue? There is some probability that you will not. You may take the position (I say not you will) that you repudiate as false all relations to glamour. You may declare that it touches you not, which assertion itself would indicate that it does. Your deeply seated sense of spiritual superiority to your group (an attitude which is sadly affecting them) may prevent your listening to me, your friend and brother for many years—nay, lives. I would, however, ask you to read what I have to say; perchance I may throw light upon your problems and aid you to take the initiation which was your destined goal this life, but which you may yourself postpone until the next. For this postponement there is no need, if you grasp the significance of what is happening in your life at present.

The second initiation is a profoundly difficult one to take. For those upon the first or second rays of aspect it is probably the most difficult of them all. The astral nature is deeply self-centred, and this the inflow of soul energy in the initiatory period intensifies; it is endowed with acute emotionalism and swift response to glamour. Where there is so much first ray energy to be found (as in your case) there will be a strong conviction of destiny, a pronounced sense of power, and the feeling that you can see through people—from a superior position—so that their faults and failures and their little human failings loom large in your consciousness.

You are at this time in a state of intensely irritable sensitivity to all and sundry; you are overwhelmed by acute glamour. All that is in you of a first ray quality is drawn to the surface and conditioning all your contacts. Your soul ray of outgoing love is not much seen, and there is little love shown by you to your brothers in the Ashram or to the members of your own group.

You may here ask me at this point how I know this to be so and why I emphasise to you this knowledge. You have been taught by me that the Masters concern not Themselves with the personality details of a disciple's life expression; therefore, why do I concern myself with what is happening to you? Those are just questions and I will answer them.

I concern myself with your problems because you are taking the second initiation and—because of its intense difficulty—I have watched over you for the past four years with more than usual care. I *know* the inner turmoil, the self-recriminations and the self-rationalisings, the deep subjective discontent, the longing to be free, and the atmosphere of acute suffering in which you live. Your spiritual morale is not high because your solar plexus is wide open—responsive to every astral suggestion, disturbed by world pain as well as by your own, in a state of irritation and constant inner explosion over your brothers in the Ashram and over the members of your own group. Many of the latter are also of an emotional type, for forget not, my brother, we draw to ourselves those who respond to our major quality at any given time and—at this time—yours is emotional.

I would remind you that the emotion to which I refer in connection with you is not that of the ordinary person. *You are confronted with the emotion which the second initiation stirs up.* This is a very different matter. You should realise, therefore, that my rating of you is high. It is a spiritual rating and has nothing to do with the rating of yourself behind which you hide your hurt and suffering soul and which you seek to impose upon your students everywhere. My rating is true, and you will weather these stormy waters and arrive in the quiet land of realities, free from all emotion, yet at the same time, full of unimpeded love. This is the reward of perseverance throughout the tests and trials of the second initiation.

What I am seeking to do is to help, to indicate the nature of the tests and point out to you the reason why these tests and trials have overtaken you. Everything may seem to fail you—your knowledge of psychology, your groups of students, your friends and your brothers in the Ashram. Think not that this indicates the fourth initiation, the Crucifixion. That initiation has to be faced clear-eyed, free from glamour, with a heart full of love and a mind released from all criticism. For this, the second initiation prepares the disciple. Today, you know you are full of emotion and that it almost sweeps you off your feet at times; you know you are more prone to criticism than not; and you know that under the influence of glamour you oft wield the weapon of speech in a destructive manner and not constructively; you know that—deep within yourself—you are not satisfied with the work you do or the words you write.

The book you have lately published I have psychometrised and find it to be sixth ray in nature; it will prove most helpful to probationary disciples, and they need such help; it will not help disciples, for it deals with that which they know well. The call went out to you from the Ashram to write upon the theme of Shamballa, the centre where the will of God is known and from whence the love of God flows forth. This you rejected, owing to the emotional turmoil in which you found yourself. Yet I had a purpose and a reason in suggesting this theme. It was not just to have a book which would be of service to disciples, but because it was essential—as part of the pre-initiation tests for you—to bring in some of the Shamballa force to your consciousness. It was the impact of this Shamballa force (which you *can* touch and to which you *can* intelligently respond) which was the main factor in bringing to the surface all the latent emotion and all the glamour which are today enveloping you. As you considered the theme of Shamballa (and later rejected my suggestion to write upon it) you brought yourself in contact with the energy emanating from Shamballa. Yet, my brother, had you occupied yourself with my suggestion and dealt with the theme *The Way into Shamballa* much of that Shamballa force would have been transmuted along constructive lines and creative endeavour, and your condition would not be what it is today.

You may well ask here: If all this is so, what then shall I do? Have I failed in the tests for initiation? What do you suggest?

Most certainly you have not failed. You are at the climax or peak of the testing period. The only point to be determined is: Can you overcome in this life and free yourself from astral control, or will the tests be prolonged until next life?

These are questions which only you can answer. In order to answer them you should enter into a cycle of intense quiet and—if possible—of peaceful normality. Can you free yourself for two years, my brother, and at the end stand free? You would be well advised to do this; you should relinquish your groups and stand alone. At present you are not working along new age lines, for your work is along the old lines— of superior teachers, gathering their groups around *them,* of mystery where there is no mystery, because there is no mystery in esoteric teaching, and this is a lesson which you sorely need to learn, and of criticism (openly critical) of the student, which is sadly lacking in love. No new age teacher gathers a group around himself, exacting their loyalty and obedience, nor does he shut the door to other aspects of truth, as you have done. He offers the teaching, and regards himself as only a student.

So I would urge you to give up your group for two or three years (you can later resume it and with power) and study the handling of energy for yourself—free from emotion, desire for recognition, and in response to human need. I would also urge upon you a meditation, built around the words:

1. Occult Obedience.
2. Occult Meditation.

You would profit greatly. Seek to find me and walk with me in my Ashram, where your soul ray will be fostered into greater expression and your personality rays will retire into the background. If you have the strength to do this you will —at the close of the period of self-imposed discipline—enter into a cycle of very great usefulness. I foresaw this cycle of useful work when I first contacted you. There is still time for this emergence into wider world service. It need *not* be postponed until next life.

You have suffered much, my brother, and have few to whom you can go. My love and my blessing are around you always and I have held you specially close lately during these difficult post-war days. Disciples such as you react not only to their own tests and problems, but also to those of suffering humanity. You will find me near when you need me.

NOTE: *This disciple chose to withdraw from the Tibetan's group and, until the close of his life in 1953, carried on his own established line of service.*

To L. F. U.

August 1940

BROTHER OF MINE:

I scarce know what to say to you for the body is tired, the mind is bewildered, the emotional nature is striving to assert itself whilst the soul is pouring in a stimulating energy which is responsible for a very definite crisis in your life. It is of interest to me to know how many members of the group are now being tested—a thing which was foreseen by me but refused consideration by several of you. Several members of the group are undergoing the painful test of war, with its inevitable nervous effects upon the constitution, its strain upon the astral body as well as the physical, and the reactions to noise, suspense on behalf of others and the general psychic atmosphere in which they are forced to dwell. P.D.W., D.E.I., and L.D.O. are thus situated and the test is great.

You, my brother, and W.O.I. are likewise being tested in

the world of ideas, and you particularly are faced with an acute problem in discrimination.

Earlier—years ago—I gave you three words which were to be the keynotes of your life—Love, Fearlessness and Understanding. The first two have preoccupied you much. You have worked hard to express love and have materially sweetened and broadened your nature. As a result you are aware today, as never before, how lack of love betrayed you and brought untold suffering to three people in your life. This is known only to you. Fearlessness is now a glamour in your mind for your sixth ray brain and astral body have suddenly betrayed you. Your earlier freedom from glamour led to carelessness—and as you well know we are oft betrayed at the point where we judged ourselves the strongest. Nevertheless, *the past few years have seen real progress, pronounced liberation and true development.*

Have you, my brother, reached your high water mark for this life? Can you go further still along the Way? That is your problem. It will be solved and wisely determined and you will enter upon a new cycle of spiritual life if understanding and a search for meaning begins to parallel your reaction to love and fearlessness.

Your understanding is not deep enough. That which is academic and the result of reading, listening, and of your response to the work of the Arcane School is apt to take the place of true understanding. True understanding involves identification with humanity.

Your theories, your ideals, your fixed beliefs come between you and humanity as a whole, and the good of the form side of life looms unduly large in your attitude to service. You are, under the glamour of idealism, apt to sacrifice the spirit of love in order to preserve the form of your ideal. Ponder on this for it is basic in its teaching value for you if you grasp rightly the implications. May I ask you to reflect upon the esoteric significance of a truth which as yet seems to you most questionable: Ideals must go as they are now formulated because we are entering into a new age wherein all things will become new. They can safely be relinquished when their place is taken by a real soul love for humanity—

inclusive, sane and practical. Ideals are formulations by the human mind. The Hierarchy has no ideals. The Hierarchy is simply the channel for pure love and where love exists there is no danger of harshness, of cruelty, of misunderstanding, of evasion of facts or of harmfulness. Much also that many regard as harmless is definitely harmful in its general effects. Ideals, as usually held, feed pride, lead to stubbornness, and engender a separative superiority; they produce impractical attitudes and negative activities. The one who thus holds them frequently serves only in the limited field, conditioned by his chosen work and coloured by his idealism. He excludes the *Whole* and thinks in terms of the past and as he wants to think. There is no real understanding of an opposing idealism and often no real attempt to comprehend its basis. His emphasis upon his own ideals (in his own consciousness even when not imposed on others) prevents understanding, and he is so busy upholding them and defending them (oft again to himself) and being conditioned by them that the larger human issues escape his attention. He settles down within the limits of his own beliefs. This makes him immediately a theologian and his usefulness then rapidly evaporates, except in the intimate circle of his fellow idealists. As time goes on, crystallisation takes place. A "crystal barrier" is set up between the personality and the soul. The soul is seen but its influence is insulated. But—because there is a vision of the soul still persisting—the disciple is deeply dissatisfied. The crystallisation eventually affects all aspects of the nature. Emotions settle into "grooves of crystal"; the mind becomes set and brittle. The physical body crystallises also and gets old rapidly because there is no free flow of life.

One thing only will prevent this happening: Loving understanding and a consequent sacrifice of the life to humanity *as a whole*. The greatest good of the greatest number becomes his life theme and to this the whole man is subordinated.

Can you grasp this vision and let everything go? Only two types of ray energy are expressing themselves through your lower nature: intellect and idealism. Ponder a little on the effects of this unbalanced condition and consider what it will engender. Be not satisfied with your mental activity and your dedicated idealism. Reach beyond them to the soul whose nature is love and whose identification is with humanity and not with a school of thought or a group of ideals.

You stand at the parting of the ways, my brother. Will you come on to renewed service, to new ideals, and to a fresh cycle of creative living? Or will you settle down into a crystallised condition and to an ardent struggle to become creative and to express ideals which are perhaps already superseded in order to make room for higher and better ones. Thus you might stand still within the aura of that which is old and make no further progress, waking up later to the realisation that creative living is a spontaneous happening and that your ideals have been superseded by greater and more spiritual ones.

I give you no personal meditation. The one assigned to the group in the group instruction is peculiarly adapted to bring about in you the needed changes, provided you follow the meditation with regularity.

I would, however, ask you to take *two points of reflection* every day when it suits you best and for your reflective theme I would suggest "Understanding of the New Age Ideals," remembering that the new ideals concern the life and *not* the form.

My blessing rests ever on you for I have much for you to do. I would remind you that in your last instruction I asked you if you were strong enough to participate in the world distress with no barriers up. I asked this because I saw in you a glamour and a weakness (based on your true ideals) and a negativity which hid itself behind a fearless idealism. I pointed then—if you will recall—to the need for *"active* understanding." I reiterate again this call.

August 1942

1. From where you stand I see a point of light, a shimmering thread of gold. It passes from your heart to mine and strengthens day by day, each year. Pass onward on this bridge of light.

2. Ever to you my message has gone forth: Love and more love. Again I send it forth and with my love.
3. You restrict your field of service, brother of old. Expand again.
4. My brother, the need of your heart is the need of my heart and the need of your brothers. This fusing of need will call forth the sun and shadows will disappear.
5. Men climb a wall, the sage remarked, and sit athwart the top. Then they climb down. Ponder on this.
6. At the foot of the wall lies a well, added the sage. Love lies at the bottom of the well. It cannot be drowned, but men love not deep water.

September 1943

BROTHER OF OLD:

There are certain key points in all lives which are deciding and frequently releasing factors. A major one for all disciples occurs around the age of thirty-five, and still another at the age of forty-two. It was when you reached that age that I intensified my observation of you. You had, if I may so express it, wandered (unconsciously to yourself) to the very edge of the aura of my Ashram. Later, when you entered the Arcane School and became one of its workers, you penetrated deeper into the Ashram in response to a certain drawing power which I deliberately exerted. I had long registered your "seeking vibration."

Another key point comes ever at the age of fifty-six, and as you neared that age, the pressure exerted on you by the conflicting pull of the Ashram, of your own soul and your personality mental processes created a dominant test in your life. In consequence of the reaction of the personality, of the soul test thus drastically imposed, and of your response to circumstances, your life is today conditioned as it is. You will understand whereof I speak and there is no need for me to be more explicit. The age of sixty-three will see another and lesser crisis, and upon the decision then made by you (and it can be physical, emotional, mental or of soul origin) will depend the future of your life in this particular incarnation.

If your decisions—then and now—are made esoterically within my Ashram and where the focus of your life does persist, all will be well; if they are made through the use of the lower mind and under the influence of its rationalising influence, you are liable to make mistakes. Always in your life crises, you have been confronted by the way of love and by the way of mind, and usually your decisions have been the rational decisions of a somewhat aloof and self-focussed personality. Your last decision and chosen line of activity (which was of a definitely determining nature) was, for you, quite the most difficult, because you did not see as clearly as usual; your concrete lower mind did not apparently display its usual keen vision, and the "alternatives which love presents" —as one of the Masters has oft expressed it—blurred the usually clear *lower* vision but made decision on a higher level than heretofore possible. You underwent a period of much training and inner adjustment. Is this not so, my brother?

I watched with love and understanding, for that emotional disruption (well concealed from the outer world) was not concealed from me. I rejoiced, for it let in so much light that you have made more progress in the past three years than at any previous time in your life. You might ask me: Along what line? My reply would be: Along the line of an inclusive vision which sees the future of humanity more clearly in the light of the present than has ever before been possible to you. That is a great step onward.

For years I have emphasised to you the need for heart-love, and consistently and steadily you have tried to develop it through meditation, by theorising and by a conscious effort to love. Love, my brother, when present and of the right kind engenders a sense of personal responsibility. These are phases of responsibility which are based on love and not on work to be done, positions to be filled, people to be laboriously understood and the performance of your duties as a citizen, as an executive, or as an employee. Such phases have been curiously lacking in your life. You have evaded them, and this evasion has had its roots in an unrecognised fear of failure should responsibility (through love for others) be shouldered by you; you have reacted to a profound distrust of yourself and to a fear of the intrusion of others unduly (not altogether, but unduly) in your ordered, planned life.

Most things can be viewed as too late for changing if approached in terms of one incarnation, but the soul thinks in terms of life cycles. A full and rich life cycle will open up for you as a consequence of this present incarnation, if you will handle your remaining years in a spirit of selfless responsive love—asking nothing for the separated self.

I have no fears for you, my brother. I would recall to you that the disrupting of life processes and the upheaval of an ordered point of view and of a planned and reasoned approach to daily living is in a measure a great releasing—a releasing of hidden beauties, unsuspected and seeking the light of day. Have you not read that the bombing of London by high explosives produced great upheavals and that ancient layers of soil—hidden for centuries from the light of day—were brought to the surface? As a result, strange, rare, unknown and beautiful flowers have this summer appeared to excite interest and investigation and to hide the ruins with beauty and colour. Ponder on this, for so it can be with a human life. Beauty is beginning to flower in your life, bringing its own responsibilities, engendering its own magnetic field, bringing to you those who otherwise might not have ventured to come, and who will give you a love which may at first arouse questioning in your mind but which will greatly enrich your life. It will also evoke responsibility. This responsibility will definitely extend your field of service. Be willing, therefore, to descend into the deep water to which I made reference in the last of the six statements given to you last year. The higher the wall, brother of mine, from which you fall, the deeper into the water you will go, and that, paradoxically, will be your salvation—my beloved brother. Look for this development and welcome it.

In view of all the above remarks, I am going to ask you to write—during the coming year—three *short* papers. In the first will you give seven concise definitions of love—not of emotion or sentiment or feeling, but of soul or heart love.

Make three of these definitions practical and four of them abstract and esoteric. This will not be easy, and this distinction itself will increase your difficulty. Then write a short paper on love as it expresses itself through emotion. I mean the love of the soul as it defines itself astrally and uses the astral body as a medium of expression. Finally, write another paper on the mental expression of love. For this assignment of work much occult and psychological knowledge will be needed; you are however adequate to the task, and these distinctions and interpretations are badly needed by aspirants today and by disciples everywhere, struggling with the practical application of occult truths; you can help much by clear thinking upon this theme and consequent clear exposition. Ideas become individual possessions as you think them and write them down, and this is the way, par excellence, for you to learn, to absorb and to demonstrate.

Guard your physical health, my brother. Be not unduly concerned and cautious, but be reasonable whilst unafraid. There is work for you to do and your next unfoldment of work will come to you through the means of a breaking down of a wall of pride, and a conversation—and in that order.

The thread of gold which "passes from your heart to mine" is now an unshatterable chain of golden links, and there is work for you in my Ashram.

November 1944

MY BROTHER:

In my last instruction to you there occurs one sentence which could convey to you the key whereby you can unlock the door of the future. It is a sentence which has probably escaped your notice; I doubt if it ever registered itself adequately in your mind. I now recall it to you. I said: "If your decisions are made esoterically within my Ashram, all will be well."

Life, as you know theoretically, is one long series of presented opportunities—opportunities to make decisions. As a disciple is drawn closer into the focal point of his Master's sphere of influence, the Ashram, and as experience proceeds, these decisions become increasingly drastic, constantly more frequent and more crucial in their general trend; they lead, when made, to more eventful results. With a disciple at your stage of development, the lines of choice become clearer and better defined. The questions with which you are faced are simpler and yet more important: Is this presented activity the way my soul would have me go? Will such or such a decision lead to the fulfillment of my personality trends and bias? Herein lies much clarification plus increasing difficulty, because the decisions made are apt to affect many others besides yourself. Watch for the proof of the correctness of this last statement of mine. In all times of decision enumerate to yourself the number of lives apt to be affected by what you do, and remember that (as you travel the Way of the Disciple) your sphere of influence and the number of those affected by you steadily increases. With the average person who is kind, well-meaning and endowed with a normal sense of responsibility, decisions are made upon the basis of the effects which are liable to work out in the family, in the business office or within the radius of a relatively small circle of friends. In the case of a probationary disciple, decisions have oft a somewhat larger result. Where an accepted disciple is concerned, such choices affect many, for those related by united service are included with the other groups, and these can oft be unknown or include people who react to the aura of a disciple, plus his group of co-workers.

This whole question of spheres of influence is one upon which you need to ponder. It is closely related to the problem of the aura and its esoteric circumference; it concerns the "sound" of a disciple's life and the nature and quality of the radiations which emanate from the "place where he stands." It is tied to the whole theme of orientation and of spiritual location and to the magnetic effects of the at-one-ing of soul and personality. The problem of radiation and of magnetic influence is apt to be viewed from the one-sided point of view of the disciple who considers the results of his radiation and of his magnetism upon those he contacts. There is however another point of view; these qualities—inevitable and inescapable—lie behind the entire theme of karma. They draw to the disciple that which can hinder him as well as aid him; his aura—which is a combination of radiations, energies and arranged forces—can repel the good or attract the bad, and vice versa; it can determine—through the contacts made and the relationships set up—the trend of the disciple's life. It is one of the main factors in the presentation of choices, and I would have you think on this.

As I write this instruction I would call your attention to the subject of karma. There comes ever in the life of a disciple and in the soul's experience some one particular life wherein the Law of Cause and Effect assumes importance in the consciousness. From that life and that moment, the disciple begins to deal with karma, consciously and definitely. He learns to recognise it when events and happenings come which require understanding and which evoke questioning; he begins to study the quality of his radiation as a karmic agent, and therefore he becomes the maker and constructor, in a new and important sense, of his own destiny and future. His reactions to life and circumstances cease to be simply emotional in nature and become deliberately dictated by conscious observation; they then have in them a significant quality of preparation which is absent from the life of the average man. For the remainder of this life, therefore, I would ask you to carry the theme of karmic decision and of preparation for the future ever in your consciousness; I would ask you always to take action with as full an understanding of the probable following effects as you can manage to achieve, and to make a real effort to study the Law of Consequence and Compensation.

You are perhaps wondering at this time why I am thus emphasising a somewhat cold and difficult consideration. My reason is as follows: During your past life you have five times made certain definite decisions. By means of these decisions you have directed your energies in some one specific direction. You have thereby short-circuited these energies in another direction and you have brought by your action other lives than your own within your range of influence. I am going to suggest that you take each of these five points of crisis, if I may call them so, and (for your own aiding and help) analyse them, define accurately to yourself the conditioning motives which impelled you to action, measure the nature of the consequent results as they worked out in your life, and gauge these results in such a manner that you come to a realisation as to whether they were good enough to warrant the choice you made. I would ask you to see where causes for encouragement or regret may lie and thus, my brother, arrive at a clear comprehension of yourself as a *directing* agent.

I believe that it is essentially necessary that you discover —alone and by yourself—whether these five choices were made as a conscious result of soul or personality decision, and that you should understand the reasons why you think so. You have reached a point in your present incarnation where it is also essential that you undertake the summing up of the various conditioning factors in your life. If you can do this, you will be enabled to bring this particular incarnation to a finish on a high note of intelligent and useful living. When the time comes, therefore, for you to pass over to the other side, you will find that you can do so with a full realisation of what should be the theme of your next earthly experience. I would have you realise that this is no morbid or unwholesome line of thought. I would like to indicate to you the fact that in your next incarnation you will find that the theme of "conditioning motives and assumed responsibility" will be incessantly present with you from the moment of your birth.

In this life, your theme has been largely that of expediency and of expression to meet the expediency; these motives are in no sense basically wrong; they have enabled you to be soundly motivated; carefully implemented, these themes should carry you far. You have, however, definitely overemphasised creativity; you have made it a motive for your life, but you have forgotten that the expression of the creative faculty is radiation and magnetism. These bring to its possessor the material for creation and a magnetic capacity which arranges in due form and beauty that which radiation has evoked. Creativity is a consequence of a particular state of mind and a specific state of being; it signifies a point in evolution wherein the disciple is definitely radioactive. He can no more help creating in some form or another than he can help living. After all, my brother—returning to the original comments in this instruction—karma is ever the source of physical plane creation, happenings and events; it is the instrument of the soul in producing a personality.

We come now to the recognition that (where you are concerned) three words are of major importance, if you are to take what is for you your next spiritual step forward, *karmically* considered. These three words are: Karma, Radiation, Creation. For the remainder of this life you must earnestly aim at a closer relation to me and to my Ashram, for that is your karma. Fundamentally, nothing can interfere with this karma except the time equation, and you can therefore make this closer contact either with rapidity or slowness. It is the time factor which lies within the scope of your decision and it is in relation to time that you must do some careful thinking. That which will impel you to make a closer contact with your ashramic group will be an intensification of your radiation. A disciple is not drawn into a close rapport with the Ashram by the magnetic, radiatory power of the Ashram alone. Disciples need to grasp the fact that they, themselves, have to draw the Ashram to them, symbolically speaking, by the potency of their own magnetic radiation. It is necessary, therefore, that you intensify your radiation and that you carefully bear in mind that, as your karma carries you towards hierarchical contact, and as your radiation produces its individual effect upon the ashramic group, the consequent display of creativity must and will lie along the line of personality fulfilment and the meeting of deep-seated desire. Therefore, search your motives and the nature of your desires.

For years, my brother, I have sought to help you. You are in my Ashram, though you are not as yet in the inner circle; you belong to a group of brothers who—along with you—are struggling earnestly for spiritual fulfilment and who have been clearly told that their karma has brought them into the ranks of accepted discipleship and who are preparing for the next step ahead of them—the taking of an initiation. Each of you, in his own place, is facing this initiatory process. I might add that every member of the Hierarchy, from Christ down to the disciple who is preparing for the second initiation, is standing in the knowledge that initiation in some degree must be taken and may not be ignored or denied. Will you understand me, my brother, if I say to you: Take this consciousness into your thinking and let this idea or knowledge condition all your activities. Say to yourself each morning before you go forth to the duties of the day: "I am preparing to move forward upon the Path of Initiation." Let this affirmed realisation show itself forth in the quality of your daily activities.

Love more, my brother. You only deeply love two or three people; let that limited love be the seed which will produce the flowering forth of a loving spirit. Disciples need to remember that love brings all earthly karma to an end. Love induces that radiation which invokes and evokes not only the heart of God but the heart of humanity also. Love is the cause of all creation and the sustaining factor in all living.

Make your remaining years expressive of radiating love, which is not at all easy for you. Remember ever that my Ashram enfolds you, without cessation, in its radiation. Work steadily in cooperation with your group brothers. Even though the personality instructions come to an end, the group instructions will give you all the help you will need. But you must act upon these instructions and hold with steadfastness your relation to the life of the group. This is all I have to say to you, but if you measure up to these instructions, you will go far. My constant blessing rests upon you.

August 1946

MY BROTHER OF THE STEADFAST HEART:

I do not find as I approach you today that there is a great deal that I have to say to you. You are now accurately self-directing (like you not that phrase?) and your direction is right. The various suggestions which I have made to you, and which were of major importance, you have carefully followed, and I believe would testify to the good results attained. That occult obedience which signifies freedom, spiritual freedom, within a world of natural law, has garnered for you sound results. You have moved forward from the periphery of the Ashram to a position nearer the centre. See that you hold that position; it will give you a wider field of service, a greater spiritual influence and an understanding which grasps essentials and sees life in a truer perspective.

The disbanding of the outer Ashram need in no way disturb the rhythm you are achieving and many of your group brothers and fellow students will look to you for aid and comprehension. Say not always the nice or loving thing, but learn to say the hard things with unalterable love. This is not easy for you.

Being now the sannyasin and free, I would ask of you something practical and needed. The Arcane School stands at a point of real expansion; it is adequately staffed at its key points. I would ask you undeviatingly to stand by A.A.B. (as you do), and also by F.B., when need arises. The work in the world will grow in every land, and behind all the various activities stands the Arcane School. The Triangles and the Goodwill work will spread. But the Arcane School must continue as the heart of all the other activities. The staff is sound and can do much, but all of us need the cooperation, the co-inspiration and the use of a sustaining mind other than our own. Will you act in that capacity with them?

This will require on your part *extended vision,* for that has been somewhat lacking in your general attitude, as I think you would be the first to admit; you have prided yourself (and rightly) on being realistic and factual, but your realism must extend also to the inner realities and to the subjective, which are more important than the objective. You need to live more subjectively. It is this blended realism which I would ask you to cultivate, for it creates—when achieved—the understanding work with vision, a capacity for long-range planning, and yet withal the feet are truly planted on the earth.

I would suggest to you, my brother, a less intense consideration of the way you go and of the "demonstration" you make. That way is now established; you will not be deflected and you have wrought into the garment of your nature many new qualities and have rid yourself of many handicaps. Let that suffice, and for your remaining years be the worker, the guide, the serene watcher, and a strength to your co-workers —without fear, with confidence in the law, but—above all— with a much more inclusive vision than heretofore. Learn to think in wide terms and world planning, aiding F.B., when due time comes, in formulating the policies and the blueprints for the expansion of the work.

Make yourself accessible, my brother, and more and more people will seek you out. Your work in the future, as you well realise, lies with the Arcane School, and your field of service is unlimited.

As regards your meditation work, I would like it to centre more definitely on the Ashram and be less occupied with yourself and the formation of your own character or with your own development. As I said above, that is now stabilised.

Meditation on the Ashram—having dealt with the suggested theme as the soul, functioning through the mind—will deal practically with the effects of ashramic contact on the emotional nature and on the daily life on the physical plane. I give you the following themes, covering a year's work which, if diligently considered for several years, will produce a factual life of real value.

Themes for Meditation.
1. The *fact of the Ashram.* You like facts, brother of mine, so apply this factual consciousness of yours to this subject.
2. The Ashram as a centre of life. This will involve the use of the antahkarana.
3. The Ashram as a centre of love, wisely expressed.
4. The Ashram as a centre of perfected intelligence.
5. The Master of the Ashram.
6. The Ashram as a centre of living energy.

7. The relationship of the Ashram to world affairs.
8. The responsibilities shouldered by members of the Ashram.
9. The eventual externalisation of the Ashram and how it is achieved.
10. The qualities fostered by ashramic life.
11. The service rendered by the Ashram.
12. The Ashram and the Arcane School.

I am pleased with the progress you have made during the past few years. Failure has not deterred you and appreciation will not hurt you. My strength and understanding are ever at your service on just demand.

To I. B. S.

August 1940

MY BROTHER:

There is a question concerning the future and your responsibility which is at this time much disturbing your mind. It intrudes powerfully at times into your consciousness. Up till now—after a period of inner wrestling and consequent decision—you have evaded the full facing of the implications and the effect which action may have upon the future. The service of a disciple is frequently affected by his inner worries and defensive suppressions. The free flow of inspiration is halted in the astral body and there stagnates (if I may use so inappropriate a word). He is conscious of the inspiration but is puzzled at the small effect it appears to have upon other people. He wonders constantly where the difficulty lies. Often it lies in an unsolved problem which serves to bewilder the subconscious nature, as the psychologists call it; it may lie in a half-realised inability to work out right relations with people, fretting and gnawing at the lower layers of unformulated thought; it may be found in a state of inner rebellion against life, against people, against the disciple's own decisions, leading thus to a most definite orientation or focus of the entire personality.

When the personality ray is the same as the ray of the astral body (as in your case) a most difficult situation is apt to arise, handicapping the service until such time as right inner adjustments are made. In a curious way, you are isolated from many people by the power and focus of your third ray physical body—a thing which you are the last to desire but which is due to the dominance of the first ray element in your nature, for it conditions your soul quality and that expresses itself through the third ray physical nature. Intense focus is, therefore, the continuous theme of your life expression for—as you know—you have the first ray and the sixth ray continuously interrelated in your nature.

The offsetting factor is your mind which is governed by the fourth ray. This influence too is frequently found in this seed group, for ten of the group members have the mind as the battle ground of conflict—a conflict which is thus planned in order to produce an eventual harmony. Disciples such as yourselves, therefore, will not find release from conflict through the control of desire, or through evasion or through inhibition. They will find it through the right use of the thought processes and through the mind itself, for it can throw upon the problem the light which shines through it. This will bring right solution and correct understanding. You do wrestle with your problem, my brother, for your sincere desire is to follow the path of spiritual development but you make the astral body your battle ground whereas the whole problem should be elevated to mental levels. Think this out and then carry forward right action in two directions: on the mental plane for guidance and down to the physical plane for demonstration.

You will know to what problem or problems I refer. None of your group brothers will understand to what particular condition I now make allusion. It is a problem which you must handle in isolation and when handled, it will open for you a perfect floodgate of relationships and opportunities. Your aim should therefore be the intensification of the illumination of the mind so that the searchlight of the mind can be turned upon the fogs and difficulties of the astral body.

Of one thing we who are watching the disciples of the

world today are convinced, and that is that you are a sincere and intelligent devotee; intelligence and devotion go hand in hand in the accepted disciple, balancing each other and then producing a definite focus of power. For all of you this is an incarnation wherein the life focus becomes either irrevocably oriented toward the soul, as must be the case with newly accepted disciples, or powerfully expanded and inclusive as in the case of older disciples. In your case, the achievement of a definite focus is now essential. In the manifestation of souls in time and space, there come lives wherein—at times—a soul problem (as the personality embraces it) becomes a dominant theme and the whole incarnation (with definite points of intensive crisis) is given to the understanding of the problem and its solution. In the orientation of your life towards the soul, the keynote of renunciation is wisely clear but you need to see to it that even renunciation is not overemphasised and that its conditioning power is not applied to that for which there is no call, because such renunciation would constitute an error.

I am giving you, therefore, a personal meditation. I too must have this in mind, reminding you that renunciation itself can be a glamour and a sixth ray idealist is prone to over-express. I shall not give you what you would call a real meditation. That which will aid you the most at this time is a visualisation exercise on Light.

1. Sit quietly and relax. Deal not with problems but during the period of this exercise endeavour simply to be a point of focussed vision, with the eye of the mind directed towards the soul.

2. When your focus seems adequate then see (by the power of the creative imagination) a distant peak or pyramid and on its summit there shines a clear pure light of great intensity.

3. With that light you seek to identify yourself, to merge within and thus to avail yourself of its illumination in order that in it the lesser light may shine. You say, after some minutes of careful identification:

"Dim light am I and yet the pure light shines. Not distant is that light but daily, hourly drawing nearer.

The light that is my little self must disappear within the greater Light.

So with that Light, that all-pervading, all-consuming Light, I blend and merge.

I can no longer see the two—the greater Self, the little self, the pilgrim and the way, for only one is seen —the greater lighted Whole."

4. Picture the fusion of the light of the personality and the light of the Soul and see that light focussed in the personality upon the astral plane.

5. Then produce stabilisation of the light appropriated by the sounding of the O M.

Seek not to use the light directly for the clarification of problems, teaching or ideas. That will take place automatically once the light is focussed; it must inevitably bring release and knowledge. Seek simply to visualise the process, knowing that "as a man thinketh so is he." Then forget about the acquiring of the light and endeavour to manifest that which exists as the result of your own effort. Light is within you. Seek not for immediate instantaneous solution of your problems. Look not, my brother, for results. Remember ever that as you continue faithfully with the indicated exercise, the results are sure or I would not waste your time or mine in giving you this work to do. Regularly and without anxiety do as you are told. The results will in due time manifest.

August 1942

1. As the hours of service pass around the clock of time look for the sounding of *the* hour. What hour is that?

2. As the minutes tick away the passing hour, watch for the minute when My voice is heard. When will that be?

3. As the seconds note the passing of the minute hand upon the clock of time, expect the second when My face appears. Why has it not appeared?

4. When you think freedom lies within your grasp and when you think that you have done the utmost that you can, *Beware!* Obedience lies ahead, with freedom in its hand.

5. Within the Ashram you must work. Cycles of speech transmute themselves into periods of silence. Yet both must play their part.

6. You are passing on the Lighted Way, my brother. You have placed your hand in mine. I hold it firm.

September 1943

MY BROTHER:

You may have noted that there is a slight difference in the type of instructions which I am now giving to this group of disciples in my Ashram, of whom you are one. It is not that each of them is not definitely personal in their application or that they do not carry a meaning of very real import to the disciple for whom they are intended; this they do and should. It is now, however, my intention to convey certain principles and certain aspects of truth which have more of a group implication than a personal one. The previous two cycles of teaching to which you have all submitted yourselves were primarily concerned with the training of the threefold personality and with an effort to bring it into a closer relation with the soul, and therefore with the Ashram. This was peculiarly so in the work of the Groups of Nine, and in the first cycle of the New Seed Group work this was continued, though in a lessened degree and with a specific emphasis laid upon the required training for initiation. It was not so much the training of the personality which was under consideration. All this is a part of a definite plan, and the teaching which I intend now to give will have a clear group import, even though adapted to the disciple's personality and to the particular individual to whom the instruction is given. In spite of the individual usefulness, it will profit each member of the group also to read and study and apply the teaching *from the group angle.*

There are, of course, three basic principles governing all work in an Ashram. I refer not here to occult principles of life, but to governing principles in training. These three are: Occult Obedience. Group Integration. Right of Access. Let us consider each of them for a minute with a view to group instruction, but with an individual application which will be purely your own.

Occult Obedience. In the six statements given to you in the preceding instruction I used the words, "Obedience lies ahead with freedom in its hand." Upon these words I presume that you have pondered. The disciple so often gives obedience within limits. His personal sense of liberty (due largely to a rapidly developing mental grasp of life and living) prompts him to concede certain forms of obedience to the Master Who has him in training, but to refrain from a complete surrender through fear of losing his sense of free action, free thought and free choice of relationships. The older the disciple, the less is this the case, for the life of the Ashram and an increasing steady contact with the Master demonstrate to him the complete and utter freedom which governs the entire circle of ashramic life—both within the Ashram and within the field of its interior and exterior service. But the development of this discreet appreciation takes time, and the neophyte is always on guard against any intrusion into his organised field of determined self-government. Let me illustrate in a manner which I believe will convey to you a much needed suggestion.

The beginner and newcomer in the Ashram, new in his service (from the angle of his present life experience if not from the angle of the soul), new in his registering of a sense of power which relation to the Ashram always conveys, and new in his joyous reaction to the recognition given him by those to whom he seeks to give help, speaks increasingly of *"my* work, *my* group, *my* teaching, *my* people, *my* plans," and in so doing stabilises himself in his chosen field of service. This is a temporary phase, oft unrecognised by the disciple, though annoying to those who hear. As he proceeds in the spiritual life and intensifies his understanding of the Master, as he enters more deeply into the life of the Ashram and into the aura of his Master, and as his vision grows—revealing possibilities of service and the limitations of his equipment, plus a divine indifference—he drops the possessiveness of his approach to service and regards all that he does as his response to the life of the Ashram, as his contribution to the work of the Ashram, and thus eventually comes to the point where he himself fades out of his own picture and from the centre of his work, and only the need to be met and the power of the Ashram to meet that need remain.

This marks a definite step forward, and it is this attitude of selflessness and this capacity to be a channel for the power, the love, the knowledge and the life of the Ashram which constitute in the last analysis what is meant by occult obedience.

You, my brother, are now at a point where you need to fade more definitely out of your own picture of yourself as a worker. The first indication of this deepened approach to service will appear in your speech when in company of your group brothers and of other workers in the field of general human service. I stated in the last instruction to you that "cycles of speech transmute themselves into periods of silence." What does this mean? Something very simple, my beloved chela. Your service in the world and in your chosen and useful field could at present be characterised by the term "cycles of speech," could it not? Yet within the Ashram, if those cycles of speech are to be eloquent of truth, the quality which will distinguish you will be the balancing "periods of silence"; in order to acquire this quality of silence (ashramic silence) you will have to learn to practice silence within the ranks of your brothers and co-workers.

Speaking symbolically, and without enlarging upon the significances, it might be stated that an Ashram has three circles (I refer not here to grades or ranks):

a. The circle of those who talk and who stand close to the outer door. Their voices may not penetrate too far and thus disturb the Ashram.

b. The circle of those who know the law of silence, but find it hard. They stand within the central part and utter not a word. They know not yet the silence of the Ashram.

    c. The circle of those who live within the secret quiet
    place. They use not words and yet their sound goes
    forth and when they speak—and speak they do—men
    listen.

This triple presentation of the balancing potencies of speech
and of silence are the comprehended effects of occult obedience—in itself a voluntary response to the power of the life
of the Ashram, and to the mind and the love of the Master
of the Ashram. It is upon these potencies I would have you
reflect during the coming interlude between this instruction
and the next. Make the results of your reflection practical,
and thus learn to know when to speak and when to be silent,
remembering that the elimination of possessiveness and of
self-reference will reduce speech to its spiritual essentials.

Your next incarnation holds for you a peculiar form of
service, for which this life has been preparatory. It is related
to speech, to words, to the voice, and to the creative power of
sound; for the remainder of this life, the theme of much of
your thinking should be concerned with the occult meaning
of silence, of voiceless interludes and of the "spiritual retention of sound." This may, and probably will, manifest itself
in an increase of *voiced* teaching of those you seek to help,
but its quality will be different.

The teaching of the ones you seek to help will blot out
the picture of yourself, the teacher, and obliterate it from
your mind. This will happen automatically and not by
planned intent. Some years ago I could not have told you
this; you would not have accepted it. Today you will and will
profit thereby. Some years ago you would have wasted time
and strength in inner worry, in self-condemnation or in ref-
utation. Today you know better the meaning of occult
obedience and the acceptance of the statement and expressed
wish of your Master—and this because you know me better
and trust me more.

Let me give you a visualisation exercise to be followed by
you each Sunday morning, every Friday morning, and for the
five days which come at the time of the Full Moon each
month. In company of your group brothers, you have for

years visualised me standing by an open window, and you have thus sought contact with me. This trained facility forms the basis of the following suggested exercise, the procedure of which is as follows:

1. Picture to yourself a wood of pine trees, a purling brook, a winding, mounting path, and at the end a low built bungalow of undressed wood, in which I live. With you are walking your group brothers, and all of you are talking on the way.

2. You stand before the door, the outer door, and pass inside and hear a voice which says, "You stand within the circle of those who talk and, talking, cannot hear the Master's voice." Stand there. Listen. Reflect and cease from speech.

3. Picture a curtain, hanging across the space near to the place where you stand. Imagine yourself achieving, with effort, that complete silence which will enable you to hear a voice which says, "Move forward into the circle of those who know the Law of Silence. You now can hear my voice." Then imagine yourself obeying the summons and passing beyond the partitioning curtain into the central room within my place of retreat. There sit in quietude and contemplative reflection, and listen.

4. Then across the silence and breaking into the current of your quiet thought will come a voice, inviting you to enter the circle of those who live within the secret quiet place.

You will note, my brother, how I emphasise for you the need to listen. That must be the keynote of your inner life for the remainder of this incarnation. When you can thus listen, the two other principles to which I earlier referred as governing the life of the Ashram—*Group Integration* and *Right of Access*—will take on new and vital meanings to you. Within the circle of those who talk there is no group integration. Right of access comes to those who know the Law of Silence.

This exercise will deepen your life, increase your capacity to serve, make pregnant every word you speak to those you teach, and bring you to a point of group usefulness next life. Then you will carry out certain work that you and I together have already planned.

November 1944

MY BROTHER:

If you will reread the instructions which I gave you last year, I think you will realise that there is little that I need add to them. I gave you an instruction which through its directive injunction covered the remainder of your life events—as I foresaw them.

You have lived for years at the high point of tension. Fire has been the quality of your life. This fire was at first destructive, but in later years it has been warming and nurturing. I think you know that sound and fire are closely allied. I think you know also that disciples are gathered by the Masters into Their Ashrams when their sound has gone forth and when the fire that is in them has successfully burned away the intervening barriers between the soul and the personality. Then their sound can safely be added to the sound of the Ashram, enriching its volume, adding quality to its tone, and conveying the needed creative qualities.

The next few years will not be easy ones for you, my brother. Be not over-anxious over anything that may eventuate. Speaking symbolically, I might express your future thus: The nature of fire will be brought more clearly and essentially to your attention; fire will be the subject of your thinking. Do not infer from this that I am indicating to you the way of fire, of pain or of sorrow. Such is not my intention. I do not mean that the future holds for you any passing through the fires of purification. You have moved across the burning-ground—as have all your group brothers. The whole of mankind is passing en masse through the fires which precede the first initiation. Every disciple creates his own burning-ground; he then takes his stand within it, and eventually passes out of it to stand before the Angel of the Presence, at the very door of initiation. These are to you the platitudes of the Path and require from me no explanation.

There is one fire, however, with which you should now concern yourself. I would call it "the fire of comprehension." It is closely related to the blinding light of realisation, but ever precedes it because it destroys all the glamours which may hide or veil the immediate point of illumination for the disciple. You have approached this fire from the standpoint of the emotional nature and it has been associated in your mind with the waters of the astral plane, thus producing the symbols of mist and fog which are ever caused by the bringing together of fire and water. This concept has conditioned your thinking. I would have you now consider glamour in the light of the fires of comprehension. There comes a time in the disciple's life when he *must* assume that he knows; he must take the position that he comprehends, and must proceed to act upon the comprehended knowledge. That is definitely the point that you have now reached.

The results of this definite assumption, and of the activities which it initiates, are oft surprising and apt to be painful; that is why the symbol of fire is again appropriate at this point.

Act in the future "as if" there are for you no more glamours, and see, my brother, what will eventuate. Endeavour always to live within the Ashram, which is insulated from glamour, and act "as if" the consciousness of the Ashram was intrinsically your consciousness. Go forth to the service which you are rendering "as if" you remained immovable in the Ashram; live always "as if" the eyes of the entire Ashram were upon you. For the remainder of your life let the esoteric philosophical concept "as if" actuate all you do. It is this constant awareness which the two words "as if" embody that will produce in you a fresh use of the creative imagination.

Some time ago I told the group that *initiation was simplification*. Therefore, simplify your remaining years by ever acting "as if." Through this living process you will let loose the fires of comprehension. I wonder if I am making some idea of value clear to you? Govern yourself always "as if" your divine comprehension was perfected and the result in your daily life will be "as if" all concealed glamours and all hiding deceptive veils were nonexistent. The disciple acts "as if" he were initiate and then discovers that "as a man thinketh in his heart so is he," because the heart is the custodian of the power of the imagination. The imagination is released into creative activity when the disciple acts "as if" he were the soul in full expression, "as if" the Master were ever aware of the doings of His disciple, "as if" he walked in full liberation consciously. For you, these two words will bring release and happiness.

The trends of your life and service are established. Seek not to change them. The fund of knowledge which you have accumulated in this life is very real. Draw, however, what you need for your teaching work from the ancient reservoir of wisdom, and not so much from the pool of knowledge. Deepen your meditation and intensify the inner silence within which it is desirable that you should live. Think humbly, speak wisely and work ceaselessly. The opportunity today is great for all disciples everywhere, and the potencies at their disposal are more vital than ever before. Link up with me each day and count on my sustaining love.

August 1946

MY FRIEND OF MANY YEARS:

I know how greatly distressed you will be at the termination of our outer (not the inner) fellowship; forget not that the outer fellowship was only the sign of a strong, vital and unshatterable inner fellowship. The inner relation of the group to me and to the Ashram and towards each other is as strong as it has ever been; it is in no wise altered. Because of the very real progress you have made in freeing yourself from glamour, that fellowship can now become even more intimate. I can reach you more easily than in the past. I am telling you this because I know it will reassure you and because I know you will not take advantage of it. The further a disciple penetrates into the Ashram, the less need he finds for contact with the Master; he comes to realise the extent of the Master's responsibilities and arrives at a juster value of his own relative unimportance. He then submits himself to "the sustaining aura of the Ashram."

In my last two communications to you I left you with the impression that I had already given you as much teaching as would serve to carry you through this life. I urged on you a steadfast adherence to established spiritual habits. Enough emphasis is seldom put on the necessity for such a stabilisation of spiritual rhythm, and too much emphasis is frequently laid upon that which is new and on progress. Yet disciples have to learn to turn their spiritual habits into instinctual spiritual responsiveness; this is the higher correspondence to the instinctual animal reactions with which we are all familiar. When this has been achieved, the disciple can then depend upon himself automatically to do or say the right thing; more important still, the Master can count upon him, knowing that he can be depended upon. He is then "permitted to move throughout the Ashram without impediment, and all the Plan is safe with him." This is what I want you to aim at in your remaining years, so that you will (in your next life) from childhood, express the way of the disciple.

In my last instruction to you I gave you the injunction to act *as if* the ideal which you have set before yourself was an accomplished fact. This *as if* behaviour is one of the most occult of practices. It in reality presupposes the imposition of the highest grasped aspiration upon the normal personality in the form of changed behaviour. This injunction is not the same in meaning as the injunction "as a man thinketh in his heart, so is he." That injunction, if rightly followed, brings about the imposition of mental control upon the personality; it affects the brain, and therefore the two lower vehicles. The *as if* type of behaviour (for the disciple) brings in a still higher factor than that of thought; it involves the constant attempt to live *as if* the soul (not the mind but through the mind) is in constant control and the dominating aspect of expression.

This may involve close thinking about the soul and its relation to the personality, but it is a great deal more than just that. It necessitates, when correctly applied, the growing automatic control of the entire lower threefold man by the soul. I am going to give you six themes for meditation built around the *as if* idea. These will cover one year's work. I would like to see you take these themes and give them full consideration for three years. At the end of that time you will probably wish to go over all the work again, on a higher level and with a deeper intent.

1. Sound the O M inaudibly three times, as a physical person, as an emotional person, and as a mind.
   Then sound the O M as the soul.
2. Themes for meditative reflection:
   a. What, in your life, would happen if you really acted *as if* the soul were sounding the O M?
   b. If you are truly thinking *as if* the mind were the instrument of the soul, what lines of thought will you have to eliminate, cultivate or express?
   c. If you are realistically living *as if* the soul were visible in your daily life, what will happen to the astral body?
   d. Provided the *as if* theory were controlling your physical brain and consequently your daily activities, in what way would it alter your mode of living? (This is not the same as question a.)
   e. Do you understand clearly the difference between the "as a man thinketh . . . ," and the *as if* modes of procedure? How do they differ in application?
   f. What qualities would your particular mechanism or personality demonstrate if you acted *as if* you were anchored in the Ashram and not just on the periphery? Do not be vague in this reply, but be extremely personal in your analysis of the situation.
3. Then, *as if* you were consciously standing before your Master and definitely aware of my presence, dedicate yourself to the service of the Ashram for this life and the next.
4. Say the new Invocation, sounding the O M after each stanza.

5. Sound the O M at as high a point in consciousness as possible.

Then, my brother, go your way in peace, knowing the ferment of living energies within you will enable you to act *as if* you were the soul. This will be a growing, conscious experience. Know too that I, your Master and your friend, will also be aware of it. My love surrounds you and the link remains unbroken.

To R. V. B.

September 1943

It is, my brother, a source of satisfaction to me to have you functioning again as a recognised member of my group of chelas. You and I knew always that the link was indissoluble and that the interlude of interior work and the period wherein you worked out karma (engendered many years ago) was both needed and fruitful. It is of great value to the soul when the personality consciously recognises the activity of karma and adheres to the complete working out of the effects of earlier relationships so that to that relation the word "finis" can be written. Disciples should remember that when a karmic relation has been recognised upon the physical plane and the needed action has been taken, two possibilities are presented, according to whether the karma entailed was temporary or the relation enduring. One possibility is that spiritual identification takes place and the relation can then never be broken, or the transaction ends in an entirely correct manner by the cessation for all time of the relationship. These periods of decision and adjustment are most difficult, but curiously enough, when the disciple interiorly holds the right attitude (even if bewildered) the decision is seldom his. Life, circumstance, events or people take care of the situation and—holding on to his soul—the disciple stands steady until the problem or relationship disappears.

You stand now within my Ashram with clearer knowledge

and a more assured faith. Fuller service opens up before you —service which you can render in the place where you are and in spite of a physical vehicle which at times gives you much trouble and difficulty. Let not the physical limitation unduly control you, but pass courageously along the Lighted Way in spite of, as well as because of, the problems and difficulties. Forgive my twisting the old phraseology in this manner.

The link between you and A.A.B. grows closer each year and this you have yourself inwardly recognised. There is much that you can do to help her, for her confidence in you is great and she needs the kind of help which you can give. Her work grows heavier, her health is seriously impaired, and the needs of the world press heavier upon her than any of you—no matter how close—can ever guess. She values your cooperation and you can do much to interpret the work that emanates from my Ashram and thus aid seeking souls. To this work I call you afresh.

The meditation which I am going to ask you to do is in the nature of an act of service. It has little reference to yourself, but much to something that is close, very close, to my heart. I would ask you to take the new book, *Discipleship in the New Age,* and each day meditate upon its significance, its usefulness and its teaching value in this coming post-war period. Read it carefully, e'en when you know much of what is said; build a thoughtform of the book and see it going forth to the very ends of the Earth. This book, if rightly distributed, can act as a great magnet, drawing people from all over the planet into the Ashrams of the Masters, and thereby increasing the potency of the workers for humanity as well as increasing them numerically. This book should go forth upon the wings of meditation, and you can be a potent focal point upon the inner planes of such a meditation process, if you so desire. Will you join with me, my brother, in this launching of this book upon its career of service? I know that you will render this service to those who seek for the Light, and to me, for I am one of the distributors of the Light.

Increasingly must your life be filled with this kind of

service; it will lead to the establishing of lines of relationship; these, in later lives, will be less tenuous and will demonstrate to you as the nucleus of that group which every disciple begins to gather around him, preparatory to forming his own Ashram in a still later life. Thus the whole question of radiation and magnetism lies at the foundation of the hierarchical method of work. A disciple becomes spiritually magnetic; his radiation begins to make itself felt; this must inevitably be the case when head and heart are consciously related. Gradually that magnetism and that radiation make their presence felt in the disciple's environment and evoke response from others. Not only so, but the magnetic-radiatory vibration attracts the attention of the Master, and the disciple finds his way into the Ashram along the line or the beam of his own radiatory activity, which has been akin to that of the Ashram. There, the intensified training he receives makes him still more spiritually efficient and "esoterically attractive" in the world of men. He continues with his task of gathering to him those whom he can help and who recognise him as their chosen helper and guide. Thus is an Ashram formed—each on its ray vibration, and each taking much time and lives of choice and of radiation. Today sees many disciples—such as you—being trained to handle this phase of the hierarchical work among men. This might be stated to be the underlying motive and hierarchical purpose for the Arcane School. Each disciple in my Ashram should be aware of the intent that this life and the next should see him beginning to gather to himself his own. This new book is intended to aid in this process, and it is upon this aspect that I would ask your aid in meditation.

Let me now give you six statements which can form, if you so desire, six seed thoughts upon this particular theme during the coming year.

1. The Ashram pulsates with life. Its radiation penetrates the outer gloom and dark; waiting aspirants, one by one, and all alone, appear within the beam of light.
2. Along that beam the chela travels towards the central

point of light, the Master in His Ashram. The Master waits. He moves not forth but quietly radiates.

3. The chela enters through the door into the Ashram and stands before the Master of his life. He knows himself to be a soul. He knows that now his mind and all the lower natural forces must radiate the light he has attained.

4. As one by one the chelas find their way into the Ashram and to the central Light, the light therein intensifies. The radiation of the Ashram waxes to a great intensity. The tiny beam of light focussed within the chela's heart, directed by his eye, penetrates in turn the outer gloom and is seen by those who wait.

5. Within the Ashram I have taken my place. My little light is merged and blended with the greater light, for thus I best can serve. I face the Master and know His light and mine to be the same. I turn and send my light into the dark, to guide some wanderer home.

6. Grant me the light that I may shine. Let me throughout the world of time and space radiate light, create a light, transmit the light, and treading thus the Lighted Way (which is my Lighted Self), enter the light and so return the light to those who need, to Those likewise from whence it came.

Thus, my brother and my friend, travel life's way; work in my Ashram; aid your fellowmen, and know the joy of constant service and sacrifice.

November 1944

MY BROTHER AND FELLOW-WORKER:

Your spiritual life has deepened during this past year and your light within the Ashram shines brighter. I think that it is only fair to tell you this for your encouragement. The loneliness of your life warrants at times my endorsing any spiritual confidence of which you may be possessed. Disciples need to learn sometimes that their spiritual status is not always evocative of a life of violent outward activity. For such as you, with the handicap of a frail body and the limitations of karma, the place of triumph has to be exactly where you stand and within the circumference of a somewhat limited physical sphere. There—with no outer stimulation—the disciple himself, alone, becomes a focal point of power. His influence can then reach out to points unexpected and oft unknown to him. Frequently, prior to a definite step forward of a pronounced kind which is not due simply to a normal progress of a persistent aspirant, the soul of the disciple forces him into a quiet place where he has both the inclination and the time to deepen, to integrate more consciously into the Ashram, and to focus with definite intention upon work in mental matter, under clear, inner impression. Such is now your opportunity.

But, my brother, to make this duly effective and to get true and real benefit out of the opportunity, the disciple must accustom himself to a complete negation of concentration upon the physical vehicle and upon his physical surroundings. Note, I did not say neglect of concentration. It is his path and destiny in life to enter upon what has been called "the higher way"; he has to learn on those levels and to live constructively there, without reducing the effectiveness of normal, practical living upon the physical plane.

You might ask: To what specific end? You know that such a mode of daily life should not and must not last for several lives, because the goal thus expressed becomes increasingly active in its outer service and form. You will remember however, my brother, that there are times when the Master, speaking technically, goes into a state of consciousness which we call samadhi. This means that for a stated and qualified time, He quits His created threefold lower vehicle and "travels in consciousness" to those levels whereon the spirit aspect can commune with Him, wherein the force of the Spiritual Triad can restimulate and revitalise Him. On these levels, His vision is renewed and He draws from the force of Shamballa—according to His degree—the inspiration (again speaking technically) for a new cycle of service. This requires on His part absence or a state of withdrawal, for the space of several hours as we count them on Earth, from His body of manifestation. In the case of a disciple in training, true samadhi is not possible. The cycles of enforced quiet and of conscious withdrawal from the pressure of daily life out in the world of business and of men have to be of great length, though—as progress is made—these periods get shorter and shorter. On the lower turn of the spiral, the Ashram is to the disciple what the courts of Shamballa are to the Master. That is why, my brother, I gave you that special meditation last year upon the theme of the Ashram. I trust you have followed it with care.

The objective of this life of interlude and of a somewhat drastic, hampering experience, plus repeated frustration, is to fit you in a later life (next life, if you profit by the presented opportunity) for transfer into the Ashram of the Master K.H. As you know, one of the tasks I undertook in this time of world crisis was to relieve several of the Masters from the task of instructing and watching over Their junior disciples. The senior disciples and those that are called world disciples have retained their position in the older and more potent Ashrams. One of these senior disciples, A.A.B., as you well know, has aided me in this task. I also undertook to prepare certain disciples who had never been in the Ashram of either the Master K.H. or the Master M. so that they could transfer out of my Ashram into Theirs; among these you will find yourself. In your case you have here the chief reason for your present circumstances.

Another reason has been that you also brought about a great transfer of energy from the sacral centre to the throat centre, and here you have one of the causes of your present physical condition, but only one of them, my brother. A transfer and centralisation of the lower fires into a higher centre is oft the cause of trouble in the physical body; you can be thankful that it has worked out this way with you, for a centralisation in one of the subtler bodies is far more difficult to handle.

Thus you have presented to you a clear statement as to the goal ahead of you, and also the corroboration of many thoughts which have passed through your mind. You can now cease from all questioning as to the future, can you not? And in exactly the same place where you now are, you can use in a new and a fresh way the creative power of the mind and begin to use your pen in a more potent and dynamic fashion.

The above statement gives you, also, the incentive which you need for the remainder of your life; further detailed instruction from me will not be necessary—unless you make such important progress that I shall have to watch more closely over you. That also lies in your own hands. I would have you remember that I am not urging upon you a too intensive pushing forward, for I have due regard for your physical condition.

One thing, however, you will have to watch with care. As you know, and as I pointed out to you some years ago, you have an undue number of rays along one particular line; your equipment of energies is therefore somewhat unbalanced, and this will require the process of obtaining equilibrium before you can move on to the more potent Ashram of K.H. The potency of an Ashram is necessarily dependent upon the status, the degree and the experience of the Master at its centre or heart. The more advanced the Master, the more of the energy of Shamballa which will pour into the Ashram. The Master K.H., being a Chohan and one of the senior Masters (ranking next to the Christ Himself), can "walk into the courts of Shamballa" at will. Masters of my degree can only make contact with Shamballa at certain stated periods, and one of the goals of our training is to move steadily forward into a closer relationship with the Christ, and through Him with the Lord of the World. The Ashrams for which Masters of my degree are responsible are not, therefore, so potent.

It will be necessary for you to bring into your outer experience more force, and that of the first ray; it is necessary, also, that you should develop those conditions which will enable you to assume and work through a first ray personality when you next come into incarnation. To do this I would suggest that you study the instructions of I.S.G-L., given by me to him last year. There I gave him six statements anent this mysterious and holy centre which we call Shamballa. For this year's meditation, I would ask you to take the third statement and ponder it deeply, relating it to the sixth statement and endeavouring to arrive at an understanding of both of them. This you can do through the key which you will find in the first sentence of the meditation which I gave you in that same series. In these three statements and in their true comprehension you have the mode whereby you can put yourself en rapport with the Shamballa force. No disciple can do this without establishing a tenuous thread along which he can some day travel towards those sublime levels where the planetary Logos and His Council function. The first step is to respond to first ray energy; later you will come to use it consciously and constructively—not employing its destructive aspect—and thus learn to use first ray energy as a channel of approach; that, however, constitutes a much later stage.

The above three points for reflection will suffice for your meditation work for the coming year, and you should profit greatly by it. Every Sunday, however, I would have you take the meditation which I gave you last year and give thirty minutes to it, thus each week establishing a closer link with my Ashram and with me. My Ashram might be called the doorway to the Ashram of the Master K.H., and some day you will pass through to the higher and more potent centre.

August 1946

MY BROTHER:

You have profited much from the attention you paid to the last instruction I gave you; you have also done a good and creative task, aiding A.A.B. Even though it did not involve your own rays, I suggested your working temporarily along first ray lines because it would strengthen you greatly and bring the Will aspect more definitely into expression. You will have realised that it has been necessary for you to develop more will and fiery determination and powerful understanding, prior to transfer into the Ashram of K.H. This transfer will eventually take place, but you are not yet ready to stand the strong Shamballa pressure which is ever to be experienced in the Ashram of a Chohan. Mine, as you know, is an Ashram subsidiary to His.

Why, therefore, did I direct you towards the will aspect when both Ashrams are on the second ray and you are predominantly a second ray disciple? Because the subsidiary Ashrams deal with the ray *qualities* in action and in service, whilst the major or senior Ashrams concern in all cases the *will* in action through the ray qualities. This is possible because the major Ashrams are presided over by those who have achieved the sixth initiation; Ashrams such as mine are under the guidance of a Master or Initiate of the fifth degree.

You have needed much to study the nature of the will. A disciple's ideas on this subject are apt to be far removed from the reality; the understanding of the will is a progressive matter and disciples on all rays have to arrive at comprehension of Will activity as they move forward.

Perhaps some idea of what I am trying to convey anent the work done in the Ashram of a Master or that done in the Ashram of a Chohan would come to you if you meditated upon the two words: Goodwill and the Will-to-Good. The first is worked out as qualifying the life in all Ashrams under the care of a Master of the Wisdom; the Will-to-Good is developed and understood in the Ashrams of Those of still greater attainment. The first concerns the Plan whilst the second deals with Purpose. Again, in this same connection, you have: Vision and Illumination. I have here given all of you a vital hint as to the distinction between the work of the two types of Ashrams.

You can also, if you so choose, work out the same idea in the linking of the three periodical vehicles, finding a third word, allied and descriptive, to form a sequential educational picture:

1. Sight .... Vision .... Illumination.
2. Action .... Plan .... Purpose.
3. Self-will .... Goodwill .... Will-to-Good.

You would find the creation of similar combinations of spiritually explanatory words a valuable exercise.

I infer not here, my brother, that your will is weak. It is constantly oriented towards that which is good and towards the Hierarchy. But the use of the spiritual will as it can affect and direct the affairs of the personality is another thing altogether; it is here that you must seek to learn the direct action of the will of the soul as you face the opportunities and crises of life. I would therefore suggest to you the following type of meditation. You know enough of the meditation process to work it out through the years into your own reflective pattern of living, as it gradually takes effect and you see deeper into the subject of the will.

1. Sound the O M consciously as:
   a. The physical body, using the brain as the centre of dedication,
   b. The astral body, "lifting up the heart unto the Lord" thereby, in reality, ignoring the existence of the astral body,
   c. As the mind, orienting it with directness towards the soul.
2. Then sound the O M three times as the soul, flooding the triple instrument with light and love.
3. Then give some time to the expression of goodwill by the personality.
4. Centre the consciousness anew in the soul, orienting your soul-infused personality towards the Spiritual Triad. This will require the use of the imagination, until such time as it is factual.
5. Then take the following themes sequentially into meditative reflection, taking one each month and—when completed—resuming the sequence.
   a. From the centre where the Will of God is known.
   b. Let *purpose* rule the little wills of men.
   c. The purpose which the Masters *know*.
   d. The purpose which the Masters *serve*.
   e. Let Light restore the Plan on Earth.

    f. Let Love restore the Plan.

    g. Let Power restore the Plan on Earth.

    h. Let His Will be done on Earth as it is in Heaven.

    i. To the accomplishment of His Will, I dedicate my-
self from now until eternity.

  6. Sound the O M three times inaudibly.

Call on me when you *will,* but only at need. The words "when you will" have an occult significance. It is the use of the will which is needed when the attention of the Master is needed, in the case of a chela at your point of ashramic contact. Your link with me remains unbroken.

November 1948

MY FRIEND AND BROTHER:

There is relatively little that I have to say to you in this year's "touch of recognition" which I am giving to all who are actively affiliated with my Ashram. The circumstances of your life are such that you are eminently capable of handling its issues and dealing with its crises yourself; that ordains for you, therefore, a somewhat unusual state of affairs in the life of discipleship. You have been vouchsafed an interlude wherein you can perfect your work for individual souls; you have been provided full preparation. I would have you ponder deeply upon these conceptions.

You have not in this life functioned in any way as a member of your race, once you had reached due years of understanding; you have been held possessively by no binding family ties, though you have always been in touch with your relatives; you have had no difficulty in assimilating the Ageless Wisdom and you have served the Hierarchy consciously for many decades; you are giving real help to A.A.B. and she is, I know, going to ask for a deepening of the nature of that help though not necessarily for an increase in its quantity. . . . You have had the handicap of poor health which is not, in your case, a real handicap but a pronounced and definitely planned role whereby the disciple learns certain lessons of detachment and above all registers—as he learns—the relative unimportance of form. These things have happened to you and these lessons have been presented to you for assimilation; you are now faced with a greatly deepened esoteric service which you still perform in the place where you are.

So you see, my brother, your life is rich and full and free and promises to be even more so. Your need is to acquiesce in the limitations of the physical body, which need not necessarily increase until old age is upon you, and at the same time to refuse recognition of that body so that it in no way impinges *upon your* consciousness in such a manner that it curtails or hinders your pledged service.

You have progressed beyond the stages of set meditations and definite forms; your requirement at this time is to start each day of your life with a steadily deepening period of spiritual recognition. In that period, you do four things:

1. You render recognition to your own soul
   a. As one with the souls of men.
   b. As steadily fulfilling its life purpose.
2. You render recognition to the Ashram with which you are connected and to the group of co-workers with whom you are determined to cooperate.
3. You render recognition to me, your Master, D.K., by a flash of thought and of love.
4. You recognise your personality as a divine server.

If you follow this apparently very simple procedure in the morning and at night prior to sleeping, you will discover for yourself a renewed dedication and a very deep insight into another layer (if I may so call it) of esoteric truth and of the divine consciousness.

We are forever linked as workers in the one Hierarchy and under the leadership of the Christ and His Successor in a distant century. Count heavily on this, my brother, and go forward with my love and blessing.

To S. C. P.

August 1940

MY BROTHER:

It is often difficult to know just how to approach you on account of your exceeding sensitivity both to lack of love or understanding and also to criticism. Your first reaction is one of intense pain of being misunderstood—as you think—by me. This is caused by your complete identification of yourself on mental planes with your spiritual objective—an identification which is true, sincere and lasting. You are apt to think that you *now are* what you want to be. This is a thing impossible if the law of achieved progress is of any importance. Your resentment of criticism (which is sharp and glamour-producing) is not based on pride in fancied achievement but is more a fierce resentment over failure. You add your own criticism of yourself to my proffered suggestions and this creates a glamour. Forget not that contact with disciples older and more experienced than yourself will ever produce a stimulation. That stimulation will apply to any innate glamour as well as to your spiritual life.

Your second reaction is a silent acceptance of the criticism or suggestion, and a silent effort (once the emotional crisis is over) to change what is undesirable and to make the desired progress.

Can you, my brother, think of a single instance which did not (in the early stages after reading my instructions) produce a turmoil in your consciousness? I cannot, nor can I remember any time when you did not see the matter more clearly and profit by my words.

I make this preamble in the hope that this time you will waste no time in any futile reaction or self-defense and for the good of your group brothers, that you will see directly that which I—in love—seek to make clear to you.

Nothing matters these days (when the bulk of humanity is in such dire distress) except to aid in its liberation at any personal sacrifice. The temptation of many people these times is oft to evade the issue and find in the daily task and

karmic responsibilities as well as in a type of satisfaction
with their emotional reactions a way of escape from direct
and practical action on behalf of humanity. They employ a
forced preoccupation with their own concerns—in order not
to think, not to realise and subconsciously to evade doing
anything which adds to their present load. When I speak of
emotional reactions, I refer to the distress and sorrow and
anxiety engendered by having those for whom one cares in
the besieged or occupied countries. From that you, with thousands of others, naturally suffer and this is quite unavoidable
though it can be controlled. I refer to definitely constructive
interest and help upon the physical plane and I would ask
you:

What do you do of a practical nature to add your burden-
bearing capacity to the group of world workers everywhere
who are attempting to absorb the world's sorrow, who are
giving time and thought and effort to bring the war to an
end or to alleviate in some practical way what you can of
world distress and the physical plane needs of the unhappy?
Maybe you *are* doing something of a practical nature. I take
not the time to search into your daily activities. There is a
symbol which flashes out from the heart of all who serve their
fellowmen for which we look at times; when found, it indicates a world server. This symbol should flash with greater
frequency into my vision. You serve with fealty those you
love. I thank you myself and on behalf of K.H. for what you
have done for A.A.B. and ask you again to continue to stand
by her. But I would ask you again: What do you do of a
practical nature to bring your quota of effort to the present
world need? Because your creative enterprise deals with the
luxuries of life, you need to offset it with an equally potent
expression—again on the physical plane—of your service to
your fellowmen. That is the first question which I put to you.

The second question is to ask you if you feel that you are
freer from the ties of those who are regarded by Us as a
basically selfish and self-centred group—those who belong to
the so-called social set? I told you in my last instruction that
you were making definite progress in this respect and I believe that you yourself are becoming conscious of your own

reactions in this connection. Humanity, and not the group of so-called cultured people, should take your time and attention as well as your work along your chosen creative lines— those on which you are now engaged. Are you freer from the fear of what they would say and what they might think, or are you still guided by the massed self-interest of that group of men and women whose lives are preoccupied with possessions, with the social amenities and who regard doing Red Cross work as demonstrating adequately their usefulness? You, along with others, have refused to identify yourself and interests with any set except the one in which your destiny or your ambition placed you, and this proves an obstruction often to true spiritual growth. It is a problem and takes years to learn the lesson of *general* human interest. It is not easy to be a "fool for Christ's sake," and, my brother, the social set is one of the cruelest in the world. They need defying for their own sake and their own awakening.

Learn to stand free and unafraid, and as a soul include all with whom you are brought in contact within the dynamic vibration of your soul-directed personality. Seek to tune in on world need mentally and not emotionally; add to your service in meditation that which can practically help in this appalling world emergency. The problem of all disciples today is to achieve successful activity in their chosen task of competent citizenship and life occupation and yet, at the same time, to add to that *at any cost* a practical life of service. Such is not the duty or dharma of average man. It is sufficient for him to make good (as it is called) upon the physical plane, leaving to a later life cycle the development of a more dynamic and inclusive inner life. All disciples have both objectives, one outward and one inward, with also an ordained integrated expression. In your case, this situation is peculiarly ordained by the soul in order to bring about a needed bridging between your powerful astral nature and your definitely illumined intuition. This I pointed out to you some years ago.

The world of competitive business and the struggle with the financial situation calls for all the resources of your lower mind and this strengthens and brings your mind into practical effectiveness. The process is therefore one of a pronounced technique for the integration of soul and personality. The same process in the case of the average citizen produces an integration of the personality—what we might call an integration *downwards*. In the case of a disciple, such as yourself, it produces an integration *upwards,* leading to a definite reorientation of the life forces and the calling into creative activity the centre at the throat.

I will give you a short personal meditation which will aid in this development and increase your vision, effective service and usefulness. Do this meditation *prior* to the group meditation and do it with dynamic brevity.

1. A quick rising act of alignment.
2. A moment of poised attention.
3. Then sound the O M as the soul.
4. Arrest the downward flowing soul energy and effect its fusion with the uprising aspiration of the personality on mental levels. Hold the consciousness steady at that point.
5. Visualise then a golden band of light, extending from the soul—via the mind—to the physical brain. Attempt simultaneously to see a thin thread of light ascending upwards from the soul towards the Hierarchy, passing through the members of the group.
6. Then breathe out the O M again and see it going to the throat centre at the back of the neck.
7. Focus your consciousness there and at the same time hold it in the head. This activity corresponds to the dual life of the disciple to which I referred above.
8. Sound the O M six times as the soul, sending the energy
   a. To the mind, and there focus.
   b. To the brain or the highest head centre.
   c. To the throat centre and there focus.
   d. From that centre, imaginatively breathe out the O M throughout the personality.
   e. Then breathe it out over the group of your brothers.

f. From thence to humanity.

If you will do this simply as an exercise in the direction and right flow of energy, via the throat centre, you will find much instructive value emerging and increased usefulness and effectiveness in every aspect of your life, in the world and on spiritual levels as a disciple. You have learnt much, my brother, and I do not regret adding you to my group of accepted disciples.

NOTE: *This was the final instruction given to the disciple whose personal instructions are included in Vol. I. The footnote therein on page 341 still applies.*

To P. G. C.

August 1940

BROTHER OF OLD:

I wonder whether you have sufficiently realised that for you to bring through the love of your soul is the line of least resistance, owing to the fact that your personality ray is the seventh ray—the ray of consummation, the ray of expressing adequately on the physical plane the form through which the soul—whose nature is love—can express itself. This is particularly easy also in your case because the ray of your physical body is also the seventh. The line of descent, therefore, for the form building energy is direct. To this again you can add the fact that your personality vehicles are on the fifth, the sixth and the seventh rays; these follow each other in sequential order, producing again a direct channel. You should consequently (if you are truly to understand the mechanism through which your soul has to function) make a much closer study of the seventh ray. It is also the incoming ray for the next immediate cycle. A knowledge of the ray influences, techniques, mechanics and objectives will be ascertained by disciples in whom these rays are pronouncedly manifesting.

It is not possible for anyone under the degree of accepted

disciple to find out much. The type must be definitely pronounced and the investigator advanced enough to have reached the stage of a detached observer. This detachment you can frequently attain. Temperament and training have developed it in you. The second ray disciple has to learn detachment while at the same time he remains "attached and inclusive" esoterically, and this must be consciously achieved and the attitude preserved. The first ray disciple has to remain detached and at the same time to learn attachment and to admit entry into his aura of the entire world in a series of progressive attachments. This makes for difficulty for it involves that training in paradoxes which is the secret of occultism.

Your ray combination and the points of focus in your case explain your great interest in the centres, in their significance, vitalisation and conscious use. It is the unfoldment of an awakened consciousness which is the goal of all training for initiation and of this the training of children to develop an awakened conscience is a symbol. This awakening is brought about by:

1. Integration . . . . . the coordination of the mechanism.
2. Synthesis . . . . the fusion of personality and soul.
3. Appropriation . . the inflow of energy from the soul into the centres.
4. Awakening . . . . . the response of the centres to this inflow.

You will note the sequence, therefore, of this staged development in the way of white magic. Usually among the ignorant, the centres are first studied objectively, psychic exercises are undertaken in order really to produce *feeling* in the centres and so make the man conscious of their locality and quality. Later an effort is made through meditation to contact the soul. This order is wrong. Man should become aware of the centres as a final stage and this because his emphasis and identification is with the soul and not with the form aspect, of which the centres are a part. Be careful in all instruction that you may later give on these matters to make this point adequately clear. I would call to your attention another point. You may perhaps have noted that I have given some of you meditations which are concerned with certain of the centres and their relation. This I will increasingly do. Most of the meditations which I gave to the group members in the earlier stages of the forming of the groups, are in reality ray meditations and can be so adapted and reference to the centres later inserted; but—at this stage—only A.A.B. knows enough to make the adaptation and necessary insertions. I have instructed her to ask R.S.U. gradually to copy the entire file of meditations and you can then, during the coming months, cooperate with A.A.B. in their changing and assembling under the correct rays.

This service and this expansion of the teaching is of importance and should constitute the service of you and R.S.U. in collaboration with A.A.B. The assembled meditations and the knowledge gained will serve to provide some of *the practical* side of the teaching to be given by the Arcane School in the more advanced courses to be given in the future. After the war is over—provided that it terminates as desired by the Great White Lodge—many will provide evidence that they are ready for this advanced training and for this you, as a group, must be prepared.

You may wonder why I am dealing with this matter in my instruction to you personally. Simply, my brother, in order that you may aid in the preparation for the coming development of the race of men and because—owing to your training and the field of your daily work—you are equipped to provide that measure of technical knowledge which will guarantee the sanity and freedom from fanciful extravagances which is so needed in connection with teaching to be given on the centres and their development. It must always be borne in mind that evidence of the centres is to be found in the nervous and glandular systems and these three must ever be related if modern science is to appreciate and appropriate the new knowledge.

For yourself, my brother, I have but a word. Deepen your understanding and remember that owing to the fact that you have two rays upon the first line of outgoing energy, aloofness must be carefully avoided by you. It is the first step towards isolation. Disciples must ever remember that any overemphasis of the energies which govern the personality lays the foundation of the form nature in the next incarnation. In your case, for instance, an undue emphasis of your fifth and seventh lines of force in this life might produce a powerfully dangerous form nature in your next incarnation —one which would probably bring about a personality upon the first ray with a third ray mentality, the same sixth ray astral body and a fifth ray physical body. You can see the danger of this combination where a disciple is concerned and the problem with which he would be confronted. I have here given a hint as to the mode of unfoldment in connection with karmic responsibility for the future. Such a hint has not hitherto been made available to the public. In this paragraph I have given you much food for thought.

The objective of the personal meditation which I suggest that you should follow, is to bring into increasing activity the two head centres. It is a simple exercise but should only be done every other day because you are at the stage wherein you could unfold too rapidly, and so bring about needless difficulty. . . . It is a general preliminary exercise in facility and in the manipulation of the energies within the body.

August 1942

1. The stabilisation of your life along the line established is the next step. But, my brother, permit not crystallisation.
2. The secret of triplicity is yours. Work on it so the mind is clear.
3. Love more. Wisdom is yours, yet speed it out to others upon the wings of love.
4. Learn to transmute. Suppression is more easy but transmutation is more safe. Transmute.
5. The active double life of the disciple is your next goal. Your duty and your goal go hand in hand. You must walk with both at once. Thus can the rainbow bridge be built.
6. Go out among the sons of men and heal and lift, but balance keep and breadth of view. All ways are good.

September 1943

BROTHER OF MINE:

It seems to me that so oft I have to say this year to hard-pressed chelas: The way has been difficult. But so it is, and your way in life has been no exception. Great waves of kar-mic impact have beaten upon our Earth—that little ship adrift in time and space and sailing the great ocean of the cosmos. The Lords of Karma have looked towards our planet. Energy follows thought and that, my brother, is all that karma is—the impact of directed energy upon the Earth, upon the kingdoms in nature, upon man and upon the indi-vidual disciple. Much of this karma, especially now, is *not* individual in purpose, nor is it generated in any way by the individuals affected by it, be it an individual disciple, or an ordinary human being. It is largely incident at this time to the karma of the One in Whom we live and move and have our being. It is primarily also in the sphere of Shamballa, and has small relation in the first instance to humanity at all. This means but little to you, I realise. This karma working out in Shamballa has, however, led to the vitalising of the activities of certain "will-ful" men; they have loosed great evil upon the Earth. But this karma will also produce the stimulation of goodwill, and thus lasting good will offset temporary evil. This must not be forgotten.

The problems which have confronted you as an individ-ual, as a disciple and as a member of the New Group of World Servers have been difficult, but you are weathering the storm and your little ship will live through the gale. All is preparatory to an increased output in service—service which will develop normally without undue planning, and which will be accessory to your life task of meeting your home and your healing responsibilities.

This, as I hinted in your six seed thoughts last year, is summed up in the words there found: "Your duty and your goal go hand in hand." This condition is apt to present more difficulties than a definitely clear-cut distinction. Relation-ships have to be more carefully adjusted and the time equa-tion most carefully organised and planned. Your second ray nature makes the first possible, your first ray attributes aid in the second. Your major emphasis this year should be the establishing of the most loving "right relations" with all in your immediate environment.

What I am referring to, my brother, is *deepening,* and this deepening must be consciously carried forward. One of the things which I desire to see in all the members of this group in my Ashram is a process of deepening, carried forward through realisation, silence, loving understanding and inner synthesis. That is why it is essential that all of you read and study each other's papers and instructions, so as to arrive at this depth of insight, vision and source of activity. All the outer relations will then—both of the individual disciple and of the group—be implemented from this inner centre, and will therefore be lasting, sound and constructive.

Your particular work in my Ashram is (as well you know) connected with the Network of Light which must be created in the world, and with the furthering of the Triangles of Light. . . . I would ask three of you . . . to form the inner central triangle, and together and in constant consultation establish some uniformity and continuity of work. Continue with the work you are now doing and in the way you are doing it, but *deepen* (again that thought) the content of what *you* give to the people who read the notes you send out.

I feel no need to give you any set meditation. The group meditation, your own reflective work upon your task as a disciple (and this should be intensified), and your subjective meditation upon the Network of Light with your two Triangle members will provide you with adequate focal points for soul emphasis. Here I have given you a definition of meditation given by a Master to a group of disciples. He is not one of the Masters known to you or the outer world, for He only takes into His Ashram those who are in preparation for the third initiation, and then only those who are pledged to undertake certain definite activities for which He trains them. These "focal points of emphasis" are of many differing kinds and should distinguish your type of meditation throughout the coming year. Such focal points are brief, dynamic, potent and emphatic and are only possible when the antahkarana is in process of definite construction, as is the case with your work along this line.

I find little more to say to you, my brother. The reason for this is that we work in a peculiarly close manner at all times and you are very active in the work of my Ashram. You do not require, therefore, to hold lengthy discussions and to receive long instructions from me at various annual points. We talk at times throughout the year, and this again you know. Hence the brevity of this communication.

November 1944

MY FRIEND AND CO-WORKER:

Ever since my last communication to you, you have worked assiduously and earnestly at the task assigned and have laid a good foundation for future work. You have, I know, realised within yourself the value and the nature of what you have accomplished. I would ask you to read with care the instructions given as regards the work in connection with the Triangles; I need not, therefore, duplicate. The creative work of bringing these Networks of Light and of Goodwill into being is well upon its way. It might be said that the form (esoterically understood to be the vital body) is now strong enough to warrant an organised body upon the physical plane. I have consequently suggested that the emphasis of all your effort should now shift to the networks per se and away from a constant consideration of the quality aspect. You should now find it easier to promote the growth of the networks than to educate people in the nature of light and its uses, or even to bring them to an understanding of goodwill—though the latter is far easier than the former. The growth of a network (through organised enterprise) is something that the average man can understand.

The work has hitherto been complicated by the attitude of those who have sought to help but who have regarded it as a seriously difficult matter to form Triangles. What a man feels subconsciously conditions the success or the nonsuccess of his endeavour; this effort of mine started handicapped by the complexities which the concrete minds of my disciples wrought around it, by their failure to grasp its basic importance, and by much initial criticism. It is a very simple plan and can be "put over" (to use a familiar phrase) with simplicity. I hope to make this clear in a statement shortly to be written by me anent this work.

I would call your attention to the fact that statements emanating from any member of the Hierarchy, such as myself, have in them a potency which may not be arrested. This has oft been noted. Let me give you an illustration. The very first communication I gave to A.A.B., asking her to send it out to the public, was entitled *The New Group of World Servers*. This was followed by one called *The Next Three Years*. These were sent out exactly as dictated by me, without any deletions, with their occult implications intact, and with little or no editing. They immediately reached thousands of minds and were received with simplicity everywhere; their influence culminated in the highly successful campaign of 1936. The tendency to adapt such writings to what you and others conceive to be the capacity of the public mind detracts from the magnetism inherent in—if I may so express it—the unadulterated article. That, however, is the responsibility of all who seek to spread this phase of the Ageless Wisdom which I have been instrumental in revealing, and this A.A.B. has always understood. She has therefore been unresponsive to all suggestions to cut down or to simplify the writings. She will, I know, insist that the article or paper I propose writing goes out to the general public exactly as I dictate it, without Christianising it or rendering it innocuous by the deletion of all occult reference. I know that you also will cooperate. In the last analysis, the responsibility for the article is mine and that of A.A.B., and past history justifies the belief that the sensitive response of the public mind to esoteric truth is dependable.

Coming back from a consideration of the work to you yourself, my brother and my disciple, what can I bring to your attention that will give you strength and understanding? For those are two qualities which disciples need at this time above all else. You have an interesting combination of ray energies with the ray of order, permitting of the physical establishment of relationship between soul and form strongly controlling you. This dominant energy should render your outer work effective upon the physical plane, if you will remember that esoterically the form nature is the vital etheric body, and this automatically and easily conditions the physical organised vehicle. When your work is not effective, brother of mine, what is the reason? Note that this seventh ray potency is concentrated in your personality, and when your second ray soul energy sweeps into prominence, the initial effect is oft to negate the activity of the personality. This is oft forgotten and is most confusing to the neophyte in its earlier manifestations. Later, the disciple learns from experiment and experience that all the rays are subrays of the great second ray. This you know theoretically, but that is different from the wisdom which comes from understanding as the result of action. Once this fact is grasped, you can begin to use all the forces in your equipment as the implements of loving service. Here lies your major technical lesson. Your line of least resistance is that of establishing relationship with the end in view of building a form. This is also the line of pure magic and—as you know—it can be either black or white. There are two modes of creative work: One mode is that which is implemented by seventh ray potency. This builds and creates within matter and within the periphery of the three worlds; it is exceedingly forceful when it is wielded through the medium of a seventh ray personality and a seventh ray physical body, as is the case with you. The other mode is that of the second ray, which is applied from *without* the three worlds and from soul levels; it works through radiation, magnetic appeal and coherent energy. Ponder on these two modes.

Through your ray energies, you are in a position to use both methods under the inspiration of the Ashram. The result should be most effective service and the steady growth of any work you may undertake for me and for the Ashram. You would find it useful to make a study of the relation of the second ray to the seventh, for there is a close creative reaction or impulsive interplay between the two, and one which you need to employ consciously.

It is not for nothing that eleven of the particular group of disciples with which you are associated in my Ashram have the seventh ray as the controlling agent of the physical vehicle, whilst thirteen are upon the second ray or have the second ray powerfully present in their equipment. The entire group has, therefore, within its ring-pass-not all that is required to make it effectively creative; this divine creativity will express itself when all of you in the group begin to study your rays from the angle of group service, and not so much from the angle of your own individual conditioning. Which of you investigates his ray equipment of energy from this standpoint? Do not the majority of you regard the subject much along the following lines: This ray in my equipment enables me to be and do thus, and so this ray complicates my life; this ray needs stronger emphasis in my life; such and such a ray gives me this or that quality or capacity. Disciples must learn to study the group equipment as a whole, and discover where a potency of which they may be the custodian can enrich the group life, enhance its effort and round out its presentation as a serving unit in the world of men. The responsibility of wielding force is a fact to be emphasised in the consciousness of all disciples; it will lead to a more deeply conscious and intelligent use of ray energy.

It is needless for me to outline for you any set meditation work. All in this group (unless expressly forbidden by me) are in a position, as a result of years of teaching and of practice, to control and regulate their meditative thought and reflection. For you, certain phrases should condition such thinking, and I will give you four which can be revolutionary in their effect upon you and of major importance in the moulding processes of your life:

1. Loving relationship.
2. Conformity to the idea (not the ideal, my brother, for that is incidental).
3. Perception of reality.
4. Creative manipulation.

These four phrases have in them the seed of all right service and can be applied to your individual life theme in the home, in your business, in your work with the service of the Triangles, and in all your group undertakings. They govern, if you study them with care, the life of the Ashram—of all Ashrams. That life is one of inner and outer relationship, of sensitivity to the impression of the Hierarchy and the hierarchical idea at any given time, of correct perception of truth as it underlies relationship and impression, and of a true creative activity in the world of forces.

You are definitely penetrating closer to the heart of the Ashram and are now known there and recognised by the senior workers. This you have accomplished through the dynamic one-pointed energy of your emotional nature, which —fortunately for you—is balanced by your concrete mind. This is good and necessary, except when your mind wanders into the realm of criticism; this, however, happens far less than in years gone by. You have every cause for encouragement, my brother, and my blessing rests upon you. This thought of blessing has in it the idea of the transfer of spiritual energy.

August 1946

BROTHER OF MINE:

The past twelve months have been difficult for you in every aspect of your life but—what else can a disciple expect? The instructions I gave you last should have done much to carry you steadily forward, for an inner surety ever enables a disciple to surmount difficulties. The monotony of life itself, the cares of home and practice, the anxieties incident to the times and the constant sense of frustration have all contributed to what I might call your almost *grim* determination to stand steady in the light. Now comes the disbanding of the group, and a sense of failure which it naturally engenders.

I cannot too strongly urge upon you and upon all your group brothers the relative brevity of life. I say this not from the standpoint of the Christian ministry, which so frequently urges upon its members the remembrance of death, nor am I referring to the imminent passing away of any of you in the group. I refer simply to physical plane living from the angle of the soul, who sees in it but a fleeting experience, leaving a residue of learning. Some particular life in some particular cycle may indeed be momentous and of outstanding importance, dignified by a reorientation, a decisive moving forward, the initiation of some service, the taking of some major initiation; but such lives are rare until somewhat late in the soul's experience.

For you, this present life has two factors of prime importance: the working off and termination of karma in relation to some people, and secondly, the attainment of the control of your sixth ray astral body. You entered life as a disciple upon the verge of acceptance and upon the periphery of the Ashram, even though your consciousness registered it not; you will enter your next incarnation having advanced in discipleship, and will rapidly achieve consciousness of the fact. For the remainder of this life there is for you a beautifying of all experience, the conscious rendering of that service to others which obliterates karma, the widening of your point of view, particularly in the realm of healing, where you are as yet still somewhat controlled by your sixth ray idealism, and the increasing admission of your second ray energy so as to control your organising personality. Does this seem what you call a "tall order," my brother? Forgive my use of slang, but it is oft curiously descriptive. If you study carefully what I say you will see that you are already doing all these things and that all that I am asking is an intensification of present action.

I have therefore nothing spectacular or unusual to say to you today, and that in itself indicates much. You can be trusted to proceed as heretofore, but I would ask somewhat more.

I would ask you to undertake a special piece of work (of integrating work for me), and to do it in such a way that it does not become a formal service but a living process animated with purpose. I would ask you every Sunday to endeavor to contact the Ashram and myself (expecting no outer indication of success), and then—in my presence—name each of the people in the groups of nine and in the new seed group, as well as the three other people who have been in receipt of "the Ashram papers," the *Fourteen Rules for Disciples and Initiates.*

This will take some time, as there have been many. It will be like picking up a linking thread and tracing it to the Ashram, thereby definitely strengthening the inner link. Even those who have passed on should be mentioned, for they are still active in the service of the Ashram. I give you this task because of your trained persistence and because of your seventh ray ability to link the world of form with the world of spiritual reality.

I have no fears for you, my brother. You are a sound and self-directing disciple. My care and attention, when you need me, are always available. When need arises you can seek my aid—your Master, friend and teacher—remembering that it will take you at least seven days to reach me. Ask A.A.B. to tell you why. But reach me you can.

November 1948

My Friend and Brother:

I have registered and then recorded on your ashramic chart your strong and constant effort to fulfill requirements as I have presented them to you in my last two communications. Particularly have you—in this incarnation—mastered the lesson of occult obedience. Have you ever realised that occult obedience—correctly understood and applied—is the royal route through the astral plane, particularly in connection with glamour and with sixth ray tendencies, to the very heart of the Hierarchy? People are apt to regard obedience as the carrying out of rules and orders, imposed upon them by some authoritative source. This, as you well know, is not the case in any true hierarchical training. Obedience, for the disciple, is a quick spiritual reaction to the Plan as it emanates from the Hierarchy, rapid and correct sensitive registration of the quality of the Ashram with which he may be affiliated and a consequent and in time almost automatic undertaking (with speed) the required task. It is a task which the disciple assigns to himself and is *not* one ordered by the Master. The acceptance of the task is simply evidence that the disciple is an ashramic worker, pledged to the welfare of humanity.

You are, as I feel sure you know, in process of shifting your entire polarisation in preparation for your next incarnation. When that comes, you will renew your service with a first ray astral body, provided, of course, you have in this life reduced the usually obdurate sixth ray tendencies and are controlling them. This you are doing with real success and I have no question in my mind as to your ultimate success.

I seek to change your rhythm of work. I asked you—as you know—each Sunday to have in mind all the members of the personal group with whom I have worked with the aid of A.A.B. Did you realise, as you carried out my request, that I was seeking the aid of your one-pointed attitude to reality? Or that I needed the assistance of some of the disciples in my Ashram in producing a consolidation and integration within the Ashram itself? It is a new Ashram; there are only three as new as is this one. I realised that it needed a more closely knit relationship within the ashramic aura of some of its members; such a relation is brought about by the construction of the needed thoughtform. I would recall to you and to your group brothers that an Ashram is in reality a dynamic spiritual thoughtform, vitalised by the Master of the Ashram and by the initiates and disciples associated with it. The initial structure and consolidation is now concluded and I can assign other work to you.

Your work must now be more closely related to the Christ. I refer not here solely to the preparation work in which you must all be engaged; I refer specifically to the Christ Himself, as a living Individual, attentive to the reactions of disciples who possess sufficient strength of purpose, clarity of intention and dedication to enable them to touch the periphery of His aura (referred to in *The New Testament* as "the hem of His garment"). By this statement I do not mean the aura of the Hierarchy. You are all of you already sensitive to that to a greater or less degree, for His quality impregnated the entire aura of the Hierarchy. *I mean His individual aura.* A disciple has "the freedom of the Hierarchy" (as it is called) and can now make this attempt to reach within the individual aura of the Christ; success is entirely dependent upon the disciple's persistent but non-fanatic (or do I mean frantic, brother of mine?) and selfless effort. Make this attempt each morning for just five minutes, but not for a longer period. I can in this case give you no instructions; you will eventually find your way alone, as must all disciples. Those who are seeking to attain the degree of Master have—at some definite stage of their training—to make this attempt. A line of contact must eventually be built, and those of you who are now disciples in my Ashram can begin to make the needed effort. It will bring its own difficulties, such as over-stimulation and the arousing of glamour but—if you are watchful and alert—you can soon become aware of it.

This must suffice for today, my loyal friend and brother. There is much to do. Proceed with the work to be done, following the light which is in you and which will increasingly generate more light.

To J. W. K-P.

August 1940

MY BROTHER:

I have not much to say to you at this time and the reason thereof you know. Let not the pressure of work at this time and world strain overcome you in any way.

The task of world reconstruction still lies ahead but the disciples in the world and the dedicated groups can begin to take the needed steps of preparation. The reconstruction must begin in the place where the disciple at this time finds himself, and this will involve on a small and relatively unimportant scale the same processes, the same eliminations and changes, the same discriminative idealism and the same conformity to the new emerging pattern as will be required in world reconstruction. I would ask you to ponder on this, for

all disciples throughout the world can begin to prepare themselves for increased future activity.

There are three outstanding aspects of the new age pattern which must be borne in mind:

1. *The aspect of healing.* I would express it thus, for humanity will take much patient care before the shock and the
pain of the present has been transmuted into gained experience and understanding. Compassionate lovers of humanity
can do this healing work.

2. *The aspect of clarification.* The bewilderment of humanity as a whole requires recognition by the forces of reconstruction. Time and effort must be given to clear explanation
and to the pointing out of the law of cause and effect.
Trained interpreters are required.

3. *The aspect of reorganisation.* Rebuilding is needed
and this will require a dedicated, spiritual insight. The New
Age will not be ushered in and find true expression of its
latent energies through the medium of old and patched up
forms, or through the preservation of ancient techniques and
attitudes. It will come into being through entirely new forms
and by means of the intelligent discarding of old modes of
religion, government and economic and social idealisms. The
need for sensitive intermediaries who can sense the new
emerging realities and can take the needed constructive steps
is great. They must create the forms which these subjective
ideas must utilise. I make these few suggestions to aid you
and other workers in the task of reorganisation by indicating
the type of worker needed today in the world, and much
needed in the task you are seeking to do for humanity and
incidentally for Us.

Sound business methods must distinguish the physical
plane aspects of the revitalised organisations for which you
are responsible; a potent note of love and understanding
must express the desire and sensitive subjective aspects of
the active working group. Intelligent adaptability should be
the mental note. These things I think you already know and
I reiterate them not merely to emphasise them in your consciousness but also to weld the efforts of your group brothers

in the same united determination which will render them active cooperators in the plans laid down by Us for the helping of the world.

It is always difficult for the disciple who is working in the world of human affairs to strike the happy medium between sound physical plane techniques in expression and the measure of the vision which he sees; it is never easy to adapt and to relate the old to the new, thus producing that which the present requires. The task of the disciple, as you can see from the three words—old, new and present—is therefore primarily concerned with *Time*. This right comprehension of the time element requires the eye of vision, plus right interpretation of that which it sees. For this purpose I would give you a meditation based on sight and its suitability for your particular need will, I think, be immediately apparent. I make it very brief, for long meditations (reduced to form) are not adapted to your nature.

1. Sound the O M three times, withdrawing your consciousness as you do so to the ajna centre between the eyebrows. Hold it steadily there.
2. Then look forth imaginatively in three directions:
   a. *Upward* to the world of the soul, to the kingdom of God and to the Hierarchy. Seek as you do this to link up definitely with your own Master, of Whom I am, with His permission, at this time the chosen representative.
   b. *Inward* to the world of men, seeking to contact the subjective world of human thought and aspiration —the world of ideals and of human aspirational vision.
   c. *Outward* over the world of events, over the exoteric objective world of tangible happenings.
3. Still holding the consciousness in the ajna centre express to yourself in definitely formulated thought, the duty of the day in the light of this triple interrelation.
4. Then focussing the light that is in you, send out the dedicated energy of your personality into the sphere of your chosen work through the *medium of your left*

eye and the potent energy of your soul through *the right eye.* This will prove potent in effect.

5. Then—as a soul—draw from the realm of soul life a fresh supply of soul energy and concentrate it in *the head and heart,* holding it steadily there for use during the day's work.

6. Sound the O M three times inaudibly.

This should only take a few minutes but it must be done dynamically and with full control over thought and activity.

My blessing rests upon you.

August 1942

1. Hold in your hand the thread of all my outer work and hold it there for me.

2. The symbol of the hands and feet hold a secret that you need.

3. Your Master says this word to you and through my lips: You know the point achieved. Move on.

4. Three groups there are which you must aid and fuse them into one. And this upon the inner side.

5. Joy comes through pain and not alone through strength achieved or in the service wrought. It takes all three. These three you have.

6. The gift of play must come to you, my brother. Play upon the earth and play in the hidden place and sport yourself within the playground of the Gods.

September 1943

My Brother, Friend and Co-worker:

Have you lately read the statement which I gave you in my previous instruction? It carries for you your instructions for the future and gives you—as you now read it—far more of teaching value than it did a year ago. These instructions still hold good. You have had a most difficult year, my brother, and those of us who are working with all of you on the inner side are not unmindful of it. . . .

The work, planned and outlined by me during past years, has been largely at a standstill. But what did you expect, my brother? There is one point which you have perhaps failed to grasp, but which is to me a source of continual joy and satisfaction. The work of the Goodwill movement has been so eminently and essentially successful that today it demonstrates in the form of a myriad plans for post-war helpfulness, in the form of thousands of groups and of millions of well-intentioned people, forward-looking and kind, of all races and nationalities, who are preparing to do their share in salvaging humanity and in re-establishing (on sounder and better lines) the needed security and happiness. I refer not here to the work done by all of you since I published my first pamphlet, *The New Group of World Servers*, in 1932. That was only a part of the larger effort. I refer to the outpouring of the Christ consciousness and the spirit of love upon the world. This was initiated in 1825, and brought about the major welfare movements, led to the organisation of the groups which wrought for human betterment, aided in the founding of the labour movements which were founded on right motive, inspired educational processes, philanthropic enterprises and the great medical expansions, and which today is seeping into world government and beginning to condition all the plans for world peace and international relations. Success is assured, though movements may progress slowly. . . .

It is the massed endeavour which will release humanity in the coming cycle. You have worked better than you know or care; you are and can increasingly be a channel, for the simplicity of the first ray type of person is a terrific potency. Use it, my brother, free from isolation. It is ever easier for a first ray worker to proceed alone upon the way of his decision, but I would suggest that you work in closer cooperation with your fellow disciples. It is essential now that the projected work receive an intensification of vitality, that it should expand through the potency of its innate life, and that there should be a strengthening of the integral parts already built. It is of immediate importance that each co-operating server should be fired with a new and fresh enthusiasm, and should get the picture of the world-wide scope of the desired plan.

I suggest that the emphasis during the coming year be laid upon the objective aspect. The subjective quality has been presented, and this has been right because the subjective aspect of any form of expression must be living and expanding if the objective form is to take its place in world phenomena with power and usefulness. The potentialities of organised services for the spiritual strengthening of the world of men, the technique of their growth and the processes of their development—individual, group, and eventually a veritable network of interrelated groups—should now be elaborated. The more subjective work, emphasising the spiritual growth of humanity along the lines of the new approach to divinity has, as you can see, a definite relation to the new world religion and can eventually be focussed around the various full moons.

In the coming year let "joy be your strength." This is only possible when power, will and strength are blended with love, wisdom and skill in action and speech. My strength is yours, and the overshadowing care of your own Master rests ever on you.

August 1946

MY BROTHER:

(And I mean this in its fullest sense.) I start this instruction for you with two statements: First of all, in the discussion of the work which I undertook in 1919 and upon which I reported to the Hierarchy—the twenty years of work and the six years of that work during the war—your name necessarily came up as did that of your fellow disciples. The discussion was between the Master Morya (your Master), the Master K.H., and Master R. in whose hands lies the rehabilitation of Europe, and myself. The comment made by your Master was, "I am genuinely satisfied with him. A life of selflessness has fitted him for world-wide humanitarian work for the remainder of this life and the next."

The second statement I wish to make is that—given life

and health—you face a period of service unprecedented in your experience. I have watched your development during fifteen years since you passed into my Ashram to get the training which will enable you later to take a position in the Ashram of your own Master—a position similar to that of A.A.B. in the Ashram of K.H. You have learnt rapidly and moved fast, and it is only right and just that you should know it. You have certain difficulties to overcome in the use of first ray energy, and any mistakes you may have made in harsh judgments and in its physical expression in speech are simply incidental to the learning of the right use of soul energy. This is your immediate problem.

Every time that first ray energy pours through you it leads to a trifling or a true crisis in your relationships with others. You need to acquire a more general and genuine liking (as a means to understanding) of your fellowmen, particularly of those who are your co-workers in my work. When the time arrives this development will pay you good dividends if your fellow students *welcome* your leadership. They are prepared to do this but will miss the love and nonsense (frequently *teaching* nonsense) by means of which A.A.B. is apt to handle situations. Be not ruthless or dissatisfied with their efforts to make good. Many of them are in the preliminary stages of being trained so as to fit themselves to be on the periphery of some Ashram and there trained for discipleship.

You need, my brother, to be more appreciative of effort and less critical of accomplishment. With true failures you are ever kind and understanding and have demonstrated this often, but you are apt to despise (behind a kind manner) those who appear satisfied with what they have done. You need also to learn with wisdom to choose your workers when it is your task to do so. It is not easy for you or for any first ray disciple to get close enough, or want to get close enough, to a person to really know him. You may remember the episode when the Master M. was at one time asked to handle the pupils of the Master K.H. so as to release Him for some brief job, and found himself unable to understand them or to do anything with them. It lies in the natural isolation of the first ray type. Have this in mind.

Be sure to choose the workers (when the decision lies with you) who are on the second ray, or first ray people in whom the love element is highly developed, but not over-developed. You are apt to be suspicious of people's motives. Give them due credit for sincerity and for having something as yet to learn, and help them learn their lessons—by loving them and trusting them; confine your chief attempt to establishing a measure of intimacy with your workers—friendship and a working partnership; this will guarantee the success of your work.

Your mind and brain are full of the work to be done. You work as do all first ray workers and as the Master Morya. First ray workers provide the substance with which the second ray workers build and the other ray workers qualify and modify. You inspire substance with the energy and purpose and with the life necessary to render it responsive to the plan—the Plan of goodwill which the Masters are at present implementing and for which They seek workers. Write more, my brother; you have the vision and your meditation is sound. It has always been along first ray lines as taught in the Ashram of the Master Morya. This few people understand. Any other form of meditation would be false to you. Though you oft chide yourself for not acceding with exactitude to my demands, I judge your meditation nevertheless to be perhaps the most satisfactory of any in the group. I am, therefore, giving you a passage from the *Old Commentary* which has a direct reference to the work you are attempting to do.

"He stands in strength who sees the Will of God behind the Plan. The will-to-good substands all true goodwill. That will is he.

The Plan for this cycle of the sixth objective crisis is goodwill for all men, and through all men, goodwill. That Plan starts now.

The Plan, within our planet as a whole, is the changing of the energy discharging unit (the etheric subplanes —A.A.B.). The fourfold form must assume triangular relation. Ponder on this.

The objective of the Plan is to reproduce upon the plane of earth the inner kingdom of the soul. This has the Master of the Masters long foretold. Prepare the Way."

My blessing rests upon you for all the work which you have done. I—your friend, brother and teacher—ask and need your still continued help.

November 1948

BROTHER OF MINE:

Today in the ordinary course of events and as part of my final planning in relation to the work preparatory to the coming of the Christ, I have certain items of information to impart. The keynote of the next few years of your work is—as well you know—the making known and the steady and intelligent preparation of the human consciousness for His reappearance. With the subject of that reappearance I deal not here, but there is somewhat which I seek to say anent that which may be done by all of you upon whom I have kept a supervisory eye during the past few years.

There are five Masters and five Ashrams involved in this preparatory work. First of all, there is the Ashram of the Master K.H.; this is the presiding Ashram in this work owing to the fact that it is a second ray Ashram and, therefore, upon the same line of energy as that of the Christ Himself; another reason is that the Master K.H. will assume the role of World Teacher in the distant future when the Christ moves on to higher and more important work. Next comes the Ashram of the Master Morya; the reason for this is that the whole procedure is projected from Shamballa and the Ashram of the Master Morya is ever in close touch with that dynamic centre. The Master R.—as the Lord of Civilisation—is also closely involved; He is also—and this is of major importance —Regent of Europe.

I have also at times referred to the Master Who is responsible for the reorganisation of Labour; this work He began to do in the latter part of the nineteenth century but left it to carry forward on its own momentum when Russia entered the field and laid its emphasis upon the proletariat or the workers, to the exclusion of all other members of national groups. This produced what we might call the workers' revolution in the latter years of the first quarter of the twentieth century. I myself am the fifth Master concerned in this work and am—as it were—the liaison officer between those disciples who are working in the field of the world and Those Masters Who are directly responsible to the Christ for the needed work of preparation.

Certain picked disciples from all these five Ashrams have been or will be trained for the work of contacting the public. Many of them (perhaps the majority) are totally unknown to you. Some of them you know. I refer not here to A.A.B. whose exoteric work is known to you whilst her esoteric work is well known to Us. Her exoteric work is drawing to a close and this also is an idea to which you are well accustomed.

You, my brother, have ahead of you the consolidating of all the work which A.A.B. has started for Us. I refer specifically to the new teaching, embodied in the books which she has published, to the work of the Triangles and the work of Goodwill. I refer also to the counsel and help which you will give to the younger key people, as they endeavour to adapt the Arcane School to the pattern of the new teaching which I have given and which will eventually sweep the world (if the work is properly handled) and thus prepare the people for the new world religion. R.S.U. has also been designated for this work of preparation and—in my instruction to her—I shall indicate certain basic attitudes which she must develop and hold as she stands steadily with you and with the younger key people. I particularly want her to work with them because she is a true esotericist and the Arcane School is fundamentally an esoteric school. Another disciple, D.H.B., is also entrusted with a share in this special field of preparatory work; he is not, however, to be concerned with the Goodwill work, but in another field which I will indicate to him in his own instruction. I am not doing much more than mentioning W.W. because this is his first cycle as an accepted disciple; the service which he has to do is already recognised by him and will provide a serious and important life work. It is my intention to give him a word of encouragement and of advice. I am mentioning all these disciples to you as they should all work in the closest cooperation with you and that lays upon you much responsibility. R.S.U. has for years worked side by side with you; she has come through her test triumphantly, and in the task of serving as a channel for esoteric light and information she is competent and likewise humble in her attitude.

There is little else that I can say to you, brother of mine, save to tell you that you are trusted and that you will increasingly demonstrate the strength which comes to you from Shamballa, via your own Master. On that strength you may now draw. A.A.B. is quite correct when she says that your major hour of opportunity is now upon you as slowly she withdraws into that service which will (within the Ashram) enable K.H. to do more deeply spiritual work in collaboration with the Christ. It was to train her and thus enable her to do this that she undertook—*alone and without my help*—to found and organise the Arcane School; it gave her much needed training and experience and enabled her to demonstrate the quality of the teaching and that esoteric psychology which is the major task in each Ashram and particularly in the second ray Ashram.

You ask if there is aught that you can do. There is above everything else, the handling of the energy which is now streaming forth—*the energy of Love in its dynamic or electric form.* It is the *Will aspect of Love* which the Christ will of necessity use this time when He comes; when He earlier came He employed the teaching aspect of the second ray and not the Will aspect. First ray disciples are peculiarly susceptible to the *Will* aspect of Love, and for these reactions you must watch and endeavour always to lay your emphasis *not* upon the Will—of this latter quality you have (for this incarnation) an adequate and full supply. Let your fellow workers catch from you the radiance of Love. That, my brother, will release the financial supply so sorely needed; it will be the harmlessness which you and your fellow servers can demonstrate which will prove the needed agent. Proceed as usual, my tried and trusted brother.

This instruction may perhaps disappoint you. I asked A.A.B. what she believed conditioned my response to your question. She replied: "You trust in his understanding, self-discipline and consecration." She was right. I have no distrust in you at all. So, my brother, I can advise naught, for you need not my advice; I—your friend and companion—can only suggest that you proceed as usual upon your way, remembering always to keep a recognised and conscious link with your Master.

To R. S. U.

January 1940

You and I, my brother, have worked together for long years—longer perhaps than you know. There is little that I can say to you along the line of revealing to you the glamours which hold your personality in thrall. These you well know. Often I have told you what they are. In your case, it is not so much a particular glamour but the presence of several smaller ones. The more sensitive a person is the more responsive he is to others.

You have wisdom, beauty of purpose, devotion and sincerity—all characteristics of the advanced disciple. The glamour which holds you is inherited from other lives. You have immersed yourself in no new glamour in this life, and this is rare indeed and for this I commend you.

But certain ancient glamours—racial and personal—still hold you, and it is the overcoming of these that constitutes your life problem and your present failure to do so that keeps you where you are. If perhaps I define or indicate to you two glamours which intrude into your soul expression and prevent the entrance of the full light of the soul, and if I give to them names which are *not* usual you may, perhaps—by due pondering—arrive at the point where you will be able to dissipate them.

The glamour of "the flight into safety of the racial consciousness" is one of your dominant glamours, even if—in your own consciousness—you repudiate it. Every individual, without exception, is subject to this racial glamour and its potency is unbelievable. The subjective life of any nation, producing as it does racial psychology, national inclinations and traits and characteristics, lies behind every single individual and into it he can at any time throw himself, and into it he can retreat thus taking refuge in the past and emphasising certain racial attitudes. The overcoming of inherited traits and attitudes is, in your case, essential. You are really cosmopolitan. But in your life demonstration no one would know it. Disciples need to remember that it may only be in this life that they have been born into any particular race or nation and this *only* from the personality angle. Being, however, thus temporarily affiliated they may—if sensitive—become so identified with racial problems and relationships, with racial history and qualities that this ancient inheritance (which is racial and *not* personal and therefore not theirs) overwhelms them and constitutes a major conflict. So it is with you. In every race and nation there are those who—down the ages—have again and again incarnated in certain races and groups. There are also those who have incarnated in a particular race in order to acquire either certain valuable qualities with which a race or nation can endow a man, or to use that racial and national experience as a means whereby there can be the breaking of such bonds, a consequent release and a subsequent entering into the freedom of humanity itself. Ponder on this, my brother, and be not separative in your sensitivity and set as to your personality origins, to your so-called racial loyalties and characteristics, acquired through environing circumstance.

Is this too hard a lesson and a task, my brother? If so, determine within yourself if it is so or if it is not. Another life, the issue may be clear to you. It could be clear in this life if you accepted my suggestion.

Upon the second glamour I need not enlarge. We might call it the "glamour of continuous frustration." In your case and in the constant failure to achieve the fullest expression of your spiritual aims and goals, because of small and unimportant personality qualities (most of them tied up with your racial inheritance and your environing circumstances), you are constantly aware of lack of achievement and of failure to do what your soul has made quite adequately clear to you is possible. Here I cannot help you. The issue lies in your own hands. Do you realise, my brother, that *a week's perfected discipline* would carry you further than a year's aspiration, accompanied as it is (in your case) by a constant sense of failure? Go forward therefore, my beloved brother, and rest not content until liberation is yours.

August 1940

MY BROTHER:

Since my last instruction to you, you have attained to a certain measure of release and that means much and for that achievement I would indicate my pleasure and commend you. You are freeing yourself for service. All that I earlier said as to your problems still holds good and I would ask you to reread prayerfully and aspirationally what I said then. To the injunctions there given I would add some further suggestions. I seek further to clarify the issue in your mind. Once a disciple sees clearly, he can then take intelligent action.

You have not really liked my reference to racial limitations and yet, my brother and I can say my friend, why resent them? All national heritages lay their impress upon their peoples. A.A.B. is typically British in her personality attitudes and with her pride of race, heritage, ancient lineage and caste, with her stubborn persistence and dogged determination, with her sense of truth and her attitude of inner solitude. These qualities she has had to learn gradually to transmute into the dignity of soul consciousness, intelligent direction, clear expression of her sense of truth and a wide and general inclusiveness. This has not been easy though you, not possessing her particular problems and tendencies, may fail to realise that they are (or rather have been) as grave as yours. Some day I will give the group members a diagnosis of their racial colouring and consequent tendencies. Today I deal only with your peculiar difficulties because your battle ground lies right there and *it is mainly your racial faults which hinder you.*

I would add also to the above—which I rarely do—that you are likewise freer from the imposition of physical control than at any previous time in your life story, except once when you were much younger. Your second major limitation has been, as you know, a physical one and is incidentally also a part of the racial trouble, and of racial polarisation. Every disciple has to achieve complete freedom from racial limitations and to break down certain separative barriers; otherwise they remain and hinder, as I hinted elsewhere to S.C.P. This is however an attainable attitude for you. You have, secondly, also to release your personality from the control of that which is the most potent personality vehicle, owing to the focus of the thought and life being largely there. The visualisation of yourself as one who is unlimited in soul expression physically would aid you. It is usually only in the brain (not in the mind) that racial reactions and racial vibrations make their presence felt. The brain cells, the atomic lives of the brain organism, respond to the racial brain and thus condition physical plane activity. A conflict is then apt to take place between the mind and the brain as in your case, but brain-responsive *habits* are apt to remain powerful for a long time and hence the problem. I am explaining, my brother, as you can shift the emphasis if you so desire and become entirely unconscious of racial control and racial karma. At present you seldom forget it and it conditions you unduly. Will you please not misunderstand me here if I say that once you relinquish that emphasis, the integration of the personality will be complete and you will be ready for a major step onwards.

A Master watches His disciples long before they are aware of the inspection, for they themselves take the needed steps into His presence long before the brain registers the contact or the response of the Master. All in this group have been watched by me for many years and in three cases for several lives (so slow were they to register inner spiritual impression) before I communicated to them my intention to train them. This inner direction definitely precipitates situa-

tions and difficulties and engenders problems and none of
you are unaware of this. The lot of disciples in these days is
particularly hard owing to the fact that sensitivity and a conscious reaction to the impress of all the vehicles in the personality simultaneously is so rapid and direct. This is the result
of a measure of alignment and of conscious aspiration. But
the compensation is adequate if disciples would be more occupied with the inner realities and less engrossed with the
outer difficulties. But this, as you know, is most difficult of
achievement.

You ask me: What would I have you do in regard to your
own attitudes to the group and to the work with which you
are all engaged? It is not hard to answer your enquiry because for you the task is uncomplicated though not simple of
achievement. Be, my brother, on the outer plane, what you
are interiorly. You have much knowledge and wisdom. Use
it as much as possible because you have a sphere of usefulness in this connection right in front of you, . . . *Your destiny
is that of teacher. Begin, therefore, to fulfil it.* You have been
much occupied with organisational work—a choice of vocation made by your soul which was intended to offset the limitations with which I have sought to make you familiar. Such
a task was intended to provide scope for expression upon the
outer plane and this it has done. Now pour your energies
into the work of the groups with which you are affiliated.
Give to A.A.B. the aid which you are well fitted to give,
making yourself increasingly responsible for certain aspects
of the work which will make their appeal to you, and which
call for your conditioning. I am choosing my words with
care. Above all else give love with impersonality and true
understanding. It must not be the impersonality of a planned
and forced achievement but the impersonality of complete
self-forgetfulness. The task is so vital that you and all your
group brothers must lose sight of the little self in the need
and the opportunity of the moment. Oft have I told you this.
May I now see the result of this oft recommended truth?

As regards your personal meditation, I seek to give you
one which will intensify the activity of the ajna centre and
which will produce new vision and, above all, integration.

The ajna centre becomes active increasingly as alignment, leading to integration, is achieved. I would have you use this meditation twice a day, laying the emphasis upon the *exercise angle* or aspect of the work and paying no attention at all to the possible spiritual value. I would remind you here (and when I say this I am speaking to all the group members and not only to you) that work in connection with the centres is incidental to true spiritual development and is or should be purely mechanical and automatic. The centres are physical, being aspects of the etheric body and constructed of etheric matter, and their function is simply to express the energy which flows in from the astral body, or from the mind or from the soul (in three aspects). After the third initiation, they will register energy flowing in from the Monad—again through three types of force. If this can be grasped, disciples in training will not overemphasise the system of centres through which the expressive energy must come.

The object of this particular exercise is to centralise the consciousness (plus the energies of which it is aware *within* the physical body) in the centre between the eyebrows, the ajna centre. When this is done, you have a secondary form of integration made possible, i.e., the integration of forces coming from the outer world of impression, via the five senses and the synthesising sense, the mind. You have, therefore, energies seeking outlet and expression, via the etheric body as it conditions and renders active the dense physical body, and at the same time energies making known to the man the world of spiritual being. Of these two worlds of sense perception, the two eyes are the symbol, as you know.

1. Achieve quiet. Relax with as much rapidity as possible and with little mental activity. Then raise the consciousness to the ajna centre.
2. Sound the O M, visualising the integration of the personality with the soul. In doing this, link the pituitary centre with the head centre, above the pineal gland.
3. Then pause and after a mental grasp of what is to be done proceed as follows:

a. Take a long breath and draw the energy from the throat centre in so doing.

b. Repeat the breathing and draw the energy from the heart centre, holding these two withdrawn energies imaginatively in the ajna centre.

c. Repeat the process in connection with the solar plexus.

d. Repeat also in connection with the sacral centre.

e. Recognising then that four types of energy have been centred in the ajna centre, take another long breath and draw the energy of the muladhara centre to the ajna focus.

f. Then consciously endeavour to hold all the energies there.

4. At this point, dedicate the energies of the personality (which express themselves through these five centres and the ajna centre, making six centres in all) and breathe them back again—by an act of the will—into the centres to which they belong. Do not do this sequentially and piecemeal but as one dynamic outbreathing; see these energies travelling down the spine to their respective resting places, carrying new life, pure stimulation and dynamic will to each and every centre.

5. Then, as the soul *informing the body,* sound the O M and proceed with the group meditation.

This meditation should definitely aid in increasing the activity of the physical body along the lines you have for so long desired, and make the discipline for which you have striven, no longer a discipline but a life of unconscious, automatic spiritual expression.

August 1942

1. Your feet have onward marched. The Path stands clear revealed. You know the step ahead.

2. I would ask you *not* to backward look, my brother, but

tread with confidence the Lighted Way. It leads to Me. Your soul and I are One.

3. Yet I am always near thee—nearer than breeze, or breath or air. Your soul, your Master and yourself are truly one. Reflect.

4. Stand free. Let naught disturb your calm. Yet seek not peace. Keep poised upon a pinnacle of love.

5. I seek to have you come closer into the work. Seize upon opportunity when it may come.

6. Move forward in my Ashram; the middle Place within that Ashram is the outer Place within the centre of K.H. You know your place.

September 1943

My Friend and Helper:

It has been under discussion between K.H. and myself as to whether you should at this time move into His Ashram or whether you should still stay within my Ashram which—in the last analysis—is a part of His. I hinted at this fact to you in one of the six statements which I gave you in my last instruction. It has been decided between us (subject to the approval of your own soul) that the work in my Ashram calls for your cooperation and help, particularly as A.A.B. is now working at her own post within the Ashram of K.H. This decision was reached for certain definite reasons which it is only fair should be communicated to you:

First: It was felt that your present type of physical vehicle could not adequately take the heightened vibration which distinguishes the Ashram of a Chohan from that of a Master. It would require too much adjustment and consequent delay in the work to be done, especially in this time of world crisis wherein every disciple has to contribute all that is in him. You yourself know that consistently you have been told by me that your major hindrance was the physical body—a body equipped to render the service and complete certain karmic adjustments during this life. People seldom appreciate adequately the fact that the physical body is a definite channel of contact (and sometimes the only one as it expresses physical plane relationships of a karmic nature) between themselves and the people with whom they have to work out certain relationships. This has been pronouncedly so in your case; this is a fact which you will grasp with greater facility when no longer limited by that physical body, as are all who are in incarnation, particularly disciples at your stage of expression. Have you not realised that one of the lessons which every disciple has to learn is the lesson of limitations? Usually this lesson climaxes in some one incarnation wherein—again as in your case—there is full and free inner expression and at the same time definite physical limitations. If you were now transferred into the Ashram of K.H., it would necessitate too much expenditure of protective force on the part of K.H. in order to prevent the disruption of some of the atoms of your body, to offset a too rapid purification of the cells of the physical body, to stem a too direct stimulation of the centres in the etheric body, and a consequent arresting of the work you are doing—and doing so well. Your personal karma still demands that you stay where you are—and I still need your aid, my brother.

Second: This particular group of disciples in my Ashram, with which you are and will be affiliated, needs your help and service. That is another phase of karma (this time the karma of a pledged disciple) which you have assumed. The years have proved your staying power, your unswerving devotion and your stable love for your co-workers. All that is still needed and will be increasingly required. An understanding heart and a steady application to the work to be done are great attributes, and speaking esoterically, both I and your group brothers "know where to find you." The part that you have to play will slowly emerge and become clear to your mind and you, I know, will meet requirements as they arise.

Third: Your work must increasingly be that of the teacher, and you must learn more and more to bring through, for the use of the many, the knowledges stored up by your soul through many lives of training; this knowledge, rapidly being transmuted by you into wisdom, must be made available for your personality to use as it seeks to help and train other personalities to become soul conscious. If you were to move into the more advanced Ashram you might find that you could not do this, for you would not only be occupied in making certain needed adjustments, but would also have to apply yourself to fresh learning. It has been felt by Us, therefore, that for the remainder of this incarnation you should develop the facility to make full use of what you have acquired, so that the stream of outgoing teaching can become so direct that you will establish a teaching facility and technique for your next incarnation which will stand you in good stead when the work your soul has planned for you opens up in front of you.

You have, therefore, three things to do as the future unrolls:

1. Continue with the discipline and right control of the physical body so that it can increasingly become a better and more usable instrument.
2. Form a steady and stable focal point of loving attention to which your group brothers can turn in years to come.
3. Give out to others more and more of what you know. You have a good field of expression in the work for which A.A.B. tells me you are responsible. Use this increasingly—with firmness and judgment. Let not your heart always determine the issues at stake, but call in the balancing head increasingly. The so-called kind immediate thing or the thing which the student wants is not always the wise thing or that which will help him the most.

The remarks which I have made anent the two Ashrams will have awakened interest in your mind and you will be pondering upon the relation existing between the various Ashrams. Scattered throughout these personal instructions, as well as in the group teachings, will be found much that has hitherto not been given out or which is relatively new, and hence the value of reading with care the instructions of the individual group members. There was much of esoteric value in the various statements given last year to the group members, and the sixth sentence in yours embodies a new and interesting truth.

There are many Ashrams upon the various rays. My Ashram, being a second ray Ashram, is naturally closely related to that of K.H., which is the central or the most important Ashram upon the second ray line of energy as it penetrates the hierarchical centre. K.H. is at this time, under the Christ, the working Representative of the second ray in the Hierarchy. The Christ is the link between the second ray as it expresses itself in the Hierarchy and Shamballa. Initiates of high degree and Masters on all the rays have Their Own Ashrams, but not all are teaching centres; this is a point to be remembered, as well as the fact that all of them are not concerned primarily with the unfoldment of the human consciousness and with the needs of the human kingdom. There are other types of consciousness of deep and real importance in the great chain of Hierarchy, stretching from below to far above the human kingdom. This is a point apt to be forgotten.

I, as a Master upon the second ray, have an Ashram which is a branch, an affiliate, an outgrowth or a specialised part of the Ashram of K.H. It is because of this that the services of A.A.B. have been made available to me for two decades and more than two decades. Words here are limiting and confusing. In the statement of six sentences which was given to you last year, you were told to move forward in my Ashram. The meaning is that in the great interlocking directorate of the Hierarchy and in the basic relation between the Ashrams (as, for instance, all Ashrams upon the second ray) there arises a point where the circle of an Ashram overlaps or interpenetrates the circle of another Ashram, and at their point of contact and of overlapping an increased intercourse and interplay becomes possible. It is here that you have to find your place. It might be pictured somewhat like the diagram (page 610), as regards my Ashram and that of K.H.

At this Middle Point there is a coming and a going; there is relation and contact; there is increased opportunity and inspiration; there are focal points of transmutation, of transition and of transformation. It is towards this area of merging and of fusion that you are now asked to move. Reflect upon this and get the deep spiritual implications which this picture of relationship between the Ashrams can convey to you. By your effort, your determination and your understanding you can form part of the group which stands in this "Middle Chamber" (to use Masonic terminology) and can work from this point in the ashramic life. This important little diagram can be applied also to the relation between the Hierarchy and Humanity—the New Group of World Servers occupying this lower midway point.

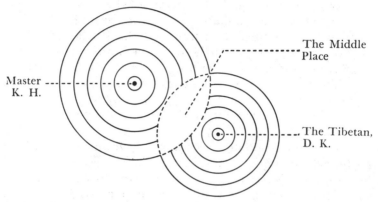

It will be obvious to you also how the symbolism of an eclipse will come into your mind, for when the merging is complete, humanity and the Hierarchy will be one; there will be no outer or inner and no middle chamber, but only complete unity. Later in our planetary history, this design will also depict the relation of Shamballa to the Hierarchy. It can also be applied most usefully to the relationship between soul and personality, wherein the "encroaching light of the soul obliterates the dim light of the personality, and within that lighted area the disciple learns to stand."

There is much more that could be said, my brother, but reflection and prolonged thought upon what has been said will enable you to add that much more.

I would suggest that you take these thoughts into your meditation, and that you also use this little diagram as the theme for reflection during the coming year. Draw up your own meditation form, embodying these concepts and preserving steadfastly in your consciousness the imperative command of your soul to "move forward." Look for indications of this moving forward in the growth of increased understanding, in a sense at times of a greatly heightened vibration, and also in a greatly increased facility in imparting knowledge. Learn to know yourself as the disciple, and be not so intensely preoccupied with yourself as the struggling aspiring personality. Personalities enter not into Ashrams—only souls.

There is no need for me to ask you to stand by A.A.B. The rhythm of years cannot be disturbed and you have always stood by her and you always will.

November 1944

MY BROTHER:

The past year has seen much change in your life, and for this I earlier sought to prepare you; it is change which is largely in the nature of release and of a freeing for more effective service. In reviewing what I said to you last year (and this I have carefully done in order to help you more effectively in the process of adjustment which faces you) I am impressed with the nature and scope of the information which I saw fit to impart to you. I wonder if the implications of what I said made due impression upon your mind? The following information was given you:

1. That the Master K.H. was aware of you and of your relation to Him.
2. That it had been decided, in view of A.A.B.'s recall for more definite work in His Ashram, that you would continue to work in my Ashram for the remainder of this life. A.A.B. had temporarily given up some of her work in the Ashram of K.H. in order to be of assistance to me in the specialised work I was attempting to do and which she was equipped to aid.
3. That the "middle point" between the auras or spheres of influence of the related Ashrams should form your

immediate objective and the goal of your endeavour. This would mean, in your case, that when you have achieved the "freedom of the middle point" you would be sensitive to impression from me and from my Ashram with which you are now affiliated, but you would also be sensitive to impressions from the Ashram of K.H., via A.A.B.

4. It was also indicated to you that the vehicle which you should seek to discipline and subject to refinement was the physical body. The density of your physical vehicle is both an asset and a liability; it is for you to discover the nature of both and offset the liabilities through discipline and employ the assets in active service.

These are four of the more important facts which I earlier gave you and I recall them to your attention, owing to their major significances in providing vision of possibility and of necessity.

The future holds much of true service and opportunity for you, and in the place where your heart lies. When you have successfully and rightly freed yourself from other claims, I would urge you to look forward with joyful anticipation to a fuller and a richer life. A great Law of Compensation comes into play in a peculiar manner and along special lines where accepted disciples are concerned. The emphasis laid upon discipline, upon purification, upon hard demanding work and upon relinquishing that which the personality holds dear, is a needed phase of occult development. This is generally and often sadly recognised. But — paralleling the period of pain and difficulty—is a compensatory activity of the soul which brings all life and circumstance into true perspective and changes attitudes so completely that the recognition of adequate reward supersedes the realisation of pain. The Law of Sacrifice and the Law of Compensation are closely allied, but the first to become active in the life and to become a recognised factor in daily living is sacrifice. Compensation comes later into recognition.

You have, my beloved brother, lived a full and rich life; you have been brought into contact with thousands of people of all degrees, religions and points of view; you have known a family life, oft of great pressures but also of frequent happiness; you have fulfilled your duties and adhered to your obligations. Along with all the many impacts upon your life and the many demands upon you, you have successfully endeavoured to live the dual life of the disciple, to serve me and participate, as far as you could see it, in the work of my Ashram. There have been failures, and of these I have not hesitated to tell you oft.

There still remains the conscious refining of the physical vehicle in order to enable you, in your next incarnation, to step into the ring-pass-not of the Ashram of the Chohan K.H. No one can do this for you. In your present circumstances it should be easy for you to apply that desired and recognised discipline—a discipline of such a practical nature that you need not that I should outline it for you. It is one that can and should be *gradually* applied; this method is more likely to be successful than a rigidly outlined and forcefully demanded procedure and life of physical sacrifice, which might succeed but which might, however, land you in another "field of failure."

Your place in relation to my work in the world is well recognised by you and I would have you remember that your major spiritual responsibility is essentially work that is close to my heart. Each soul you touch in the carrying out of these duties is placed in a particular and peculiar relation to you. Why, my brother? Because, as a member of my Ashram and as one who is approaching the more important Ashram of K.H., you can and do, by the fact of your relation to these aspirants and students, bring them en rapport with hierarchical force. This you should remember, and also bear in mind that the effects of implementing this relationship will be both good and bad. Contact with any disciple acts as a precipitating agency, evoking that which is good and bringing to the surface that which is undesirable and which needs revealing, in order to bring about its rejection. This force and responsibility you need to handle with more conscious understanding. Shrink not from the results, but see to it that reaction to contact with you and with your band of associates, *does* have definite results. To handle these reactions was something which A.A.B. had to learn both to understand and use; you must learn also, brother of mine.

I will be in touch with you increasingly as you bring the physical vehicle into a greater degree of purity and refinement. You are, in any case, sensitive to my impression. Move onward into light and find me ever there.

August 1946

MY BROTHER:

I would ask you at this time to reread the instructions which I gave you last, and to read them in the light of the present circumstances. This is a painful and rather dreadful testing time for you and—to date—the *immediate* issue is uncertain, though the final issue is not.

The problem with which you are faced falls, in your mind (if you would only think clearly), into two parts: the problem of your reaction to the minorities question, and the problem of your relation to D.R.S. The first problem you say does not exist; the second problem you consider entirely the fault of D.R.S., and therefore, my brother, you stand clear of all blame and responsibility on both scores. As you are still dwelling in a personality and have not yet taken the third initiation, such complete innocence is far from likely.

What really lies at the root of your reaction? Let me tell you. It is a latent, unsuspected and quite unconscious jealousy. This you will naturally deny, and this matters not if you will attempt to establish immediate contact with your second ray soul. Look back over your instructions. I have often told you, have I not, that you need to love more?

I have stated the above in order to help you to see and think clearly. Right down the years, my beloved brother, I have taught you that your major limitation is your physical body; that necessarily means that your physical *brain* is a centre of limitation. I have begged you for nearly fifteen years to discipline your body, to attempt to refine it and to endeavour to make it more sensitive to spiritual impression.

It is on the seventh ray, and therefore its task is to relate the inner to the outer. This it cannot yet do properly, as you have taken few steps to refine it and change its quality. Your brain, therefore, responds easily to your first ray mind, and very little as yet to your second ray soul. Had it done so, *truth* and *love* would have distinguished you during this testing time, and little of these were seen. Your handling of this dual problem should make clear to you your limitations.

It is not my habit to touch upon the relations on the physical plane of personalities; however, this attitude of yours has created an ashramic situation, because of your relation in the past to the Ashram of K.H. and to the work which it had been planned that you should do as liaison officer standing at the midway point. A.A.B. has a definite position in K.H.'s Ashram and would normally be the one to act in collaboration with you. The situation is, therefore, changed, and becomes something to be adjusted. It has to be adjusted from your side, and herein lies the difficulty.

This is enough on this distressing subject. It relates at present only to this life, but it has its roots in the past, and—unless *you* clear it up—will have to be dealt with again by you in a coming incarnation. Again I reiterate, this is largely due to your failure to refine the physical body.

You are an earnest disciple, my brother; you are oriented to and serve the Hierarchy; you are dedicated and have much, very much, to give. Fit yourself, therefore, for a richer giving. Drop self-pity and the sense of magnanimous superiority you have lately been cultivating, and just (how can I put it to you in such a way that I can help?)—just be sorry, truly sorry, for the trouble you have caused.

I am giving you no meditation outline. What you need at this time is a period of quiet reflection. I asked K.H. if He had any word for you, as He had sensed the situation, though He has no time for the details. He replied: "Tell R.S.U. to move to the periphery of your Ashram, away from the midway point, and *there* learn truly to love—and love the little ones."

I can leave you with no better thought at this time, my beloved brother. I am steadily standing by—as is A.A.B.

November 1948

MY BROTHER:

You are no longer in my Ashram. I wonder if you have realised this fact? Like A.A.B. you are back in the Ashram of K.H., understudying—to some extent—A.A.B. so as to free her for work definitely connected with the coming of the Christ. You know that it is the rule in all Ashrams that all senior disciples have those associated with them who can take up the work that they are doing if need arises. When A.A.B. expressed the wish that you train for her work (to be taken up by you in certain aspects though *not* her work in direct relation with K.H.) the transfer was made. Your present work in . . . provides a fine training ground for this future work, provided that you lay the constant emphasis upon the esoteric aspect of all the teaching which you must increasingly give, and learn yourself always to live in the world of meaning.

Last year you passed through a terrific test and it looked for a while as if the true significance of it all would escape you; the national thoughtform of any nation is necessarily a powerful entity. You can observe an instance of this in the thoughtform of the Jews which is the most powerful of all because they are *not* a nation in any true sense but an ancient religion; they have resurrected something which has been dead for many, many centuries and are now attempting to call it a nation. It is as if the ancient Incas and Aztecs suddenly announced themselves as nations in South America and sought to gain recognition; they were great nations and as civilised as were the Jews, possessing a great and beautiful religion. There is always trouble when that which should be passed and gone seeks recognition along ancient lines, and this is a lesson which the Zionists must perforce learn.

But you, my beloved brother, belong to no nation; disciples of your standing have no national allegiances but stand for the One Humanity; this was the basic lesson which confronted you last year. You learnt the lesson and earned the right to undertake advanced work. It is hard for disciples to realise what of beauty and opportunity lies ahead when confronted with a situation in which—at the time—they see no light and which involves the testing of their mental perception, their emotional reactions and their physical relationships. All these three were involved in last year's testing and it took some months for you to see with clarity the trend of events.

All that is past and over. Today you stand clear—a disciple who can pass back and forth into all second ray Ashrams, carrying benediction as you go. The parting of the ways has come for you this life as regards the family with which you have been associated through physical birth—with the exception of those few who are—perhaps as yet unconsciously to themselves—associated with my Ashram. The members of one's family upon the physical plane may or may not (in any particular incarnation) be also one's spiritual family. . . . This incarnation has for you one major lesson: the lesson of standing free from all environing limitations, whilst steadily giving love where association exists but doing so with complete detachment. That is the concept or idea behind the apparently peculiar episode in the life of the Christ where he repudiated His mother; it is a symbolic story and probably has no basis in fact but it nevertheless carries a lesson for all disciples.

The lines of your life have fallen for you now into those which your soul desires, for your brother travels with you and you are doing the needed work. Those who bear or have borne the same family name as yourself invoke your loving sense of responsibility and obligation but only temporarily and only for this life. Is this a hard saying for you? Think not about it unduly, brother of mine; your next incarnation is necessarily duly arranged, the needed relations retained and the unneeded discarded.

One of the great lessons to be mastered by all disciples and perhaps one of the hardest is that trained recognition which *recognises the spiritual family* to which one belongs and this is seldom the same as the earthly family. A.A.B. had to learn that none of her earthly family were related to her and it was not an easy lesson for her, particularly as she had to learn it while quite young. It is a lesson which I am now with deliberation bringing to your notice.

Your work lies in training the senior students and for this you are well equipped and need not to handicap yourself with self-depreciation as A.A.B. has done for years. It is, as she has learnt, a form of false humility and a desire to have people realise that you are not proud and so that they will then like you. Put it from you, brother of old, and move forward with confidence into fuller service both in this world and in the Ashram of K.H.

I indicate to you no meditation work. In the doing of the meditation work of the advanced group and your presentation of the problems, you bring to them both life and substance. That is the service which you can render and one that A.A.B. has quietly rendered for many years. Each group —through its meditation work—must have its focal point and its energising area and these you must attempt to provide. This is one of the most deeply esoteric arts. In the Groups of Nine and in the New Seed Group, it was the cause of much difficulty. I myself was the central focal point and the energising centre, and my vibratory quality was too potent for the majority; more than half of those chosen reacted in such a manner that they threw themselves out of the group. I may deal with this in greater detail when communicating with P.G.C. who has always been deeply interested and concerned with the causes of the various defections. A handful remain profoundly attached to the work and to the purpose. Another handful is still in receipt of the group instructions but lack dynamic. The rest have moved temporarily to the outer periphery of the Ashram awaiting another life.

This, my brother, is all that I have to say to you at this time. My love goes with you and you may call on me for strength when the pressures of life seem too heavy.

To W. D. S.

August 1940

BROTHER OF MINE:

A strenuous winter's work lies ahead of all disciples who are engaged in our service which is, as you have ever been told, pre-eminently the service of humanity. This service is intensively preoccupying us at this time and only in group formation can it be adequately handled. In spite of this, for some reason, my brother, you stand peculiarly alone. As I realise this, I find myself wondering in what manner I can bring you to a knowledge of this situation in your life, for you need to change conditions so that you can become an integral part of the group life. When I say *group,* I mean neither your immediate circle of co-workers nor the group of my disciples who are recipients of these instructions. I mean the *entire* group of serving disciples who are at work in the world and are the hope of the world at this time.

Of your desire to serve, of your inherent determination to serve and of the honesty of your dedication there is no possible doubt. Two factors which almost defy definition contribute to the fact that esoterically you stand alone, spiritually repulsing contact from the inner side of daily living (and consequently on the outer side also). It is not your willingness to cooperate, for that is proven; it is not your effort to understand, for that is evident; it is not intrinsically anything which you do which surrounds you as a wall, for that is really not the trouble. It is the fact that you yourself—as a personality—have for too long placed yourself in the very centre of your picture and also because your first ray personality militates against your identifying yourself with the world of relativity in which you find yourself. Your personality is always in your way. It is never forgotten and conditions everything you do and say. The realisation of this is not evident in your mind because all the time you yourself are the most real factor in the situation and yet—as you would yourself teach people—that personality attitude is the great deceiver and essentially illusion. This condition of personality emphasis gives to other people whom you contact a sense of insincerity and thus evokes from them a reaction that leaves you alone. This in its turn evokes a response from your personality which is in the nature of self-defense, plus an effort to force cooperation, a willingness to go the way that the majority go, to do the expedient thing and also to attempt to prove to yourself and to others that you *are* what you know yourself to be and that *they* are not right in their reaction to *you*. Having pointed this out to you, is anything really clearer in your consciousness? I doubt it, for words—requiring as they do right interpretation—can mislead as much as they can help. I might however put it this way. Your second ray soul and your second ray mind are stepped down in expression to such an extent that they are expressions of personality love and a loving manifestation (apparently, though not in fact) of a mental attitude. With these you delude yourself and make a wrong impression on others for there is no real expression of truth in any of this. There is also no soul strength in your expression of life but only the determination of the personality and this you misinterpret as strength. This shows itself in various ways, according to the type of person with you at any given time and does not demonstrate the steady force of the soul, centred in spiritual being and illumined by soul light, being dedicated to group work and not to personality aspiration and personality ambition.

What then can you do? I would remind you that one of the things which it is the task of the Master to demonstrate to His disciple is the particular "blind spot" in his life which it is the purpose of the soul to illumine and bring into the light of his consciousness, thus dispelling the darkness and the blindness. This is done by stimulation and suggestion. The stimulation you have been subjected to for years and it has had its dual effect in stimulating the personality to a measured (but inadequate) response to the soul and also by stimulating the personality tendencies to fuller expression. These tendencies, when evoked, registered and recognised for what they are and so handled rightly can then be eliminated. The task however becomes more difficult as progress on the Path is made, for the subtler qualities and weaknesses emerge and are not so easily detected as are the cruder forms of personality reaction. I would suggest, therefore, that you study the weaknesses of your position in connection with your fellow-workers and your group brothers and so discover the cause of your "aloneness" by registering daily your effect upon people. That means that you study them and not yourself. Do you evoke in your friends and associates a good and happy response or the reverse? Do they show a disposition to seek you out and spend much time in your company? Do they tell you their difficulties in happy discussion and seek your sympathy? How will you discover and be able to answer these questions? That is for you to find out. I can but indicate, for truths accepted on the statement of others are of no real service save as signposts on the way and are not often convincing. It is that which you know for yourself, which is self-ascertained and which is found out through pain, failure, suffering and hurt pride which will bring you to liberation and the end of your (as yet) largely unrealised loneliness.

Let the strength of your personality and of your emotional nature (which is today building around you an isolating barrier) be transmuted into that loving understanding which comes because its possessor is identified with others and not so much with himself. He does not take the attitude: "I am identified with others" and so watch to see if he is, being at the same time focussed on himself and his reactions and so seeking to achieve identification because he wants to end isolation because it is wrong, and he seeks to be happier in his work and so in his consciousness. He says to himself instead: "What is my brother feeling and thinking?" and he does this because he is more interested in the happiness of his brother than in his own feelings or thought and so forgets himself in ascertaining the situation in order to aid, stimulate and love with wisdom. These, my brother, are the platitudes of the spiritual experience and these are the platitudinous truths of which you need to make experimental use, thus turning them into the ascertained facts of your daily experience and expression. More I cannot say to you at this critical time. There is much that you can do in the work *if* you will face yourself by forgetting yourself; if you will be strong by rendering the personality weak; if you learn to love by not caring whether you evoke love or not. Such are the occult paradoxes which you must resolve and which—when resolved—will greatly increase your effectiveness in service.

If you care to talk to A.A.B. who is an older disciple than you are, you might find it suggestive and useful. But A.A.B. begs me not to suggest this and adds that she knows that a hint from me is worth more than a multitude of words from her or from anyone else. She will not speak of this matter to you or even make an opening for this discussion; but if you speak to her and seek light upon my words, she will do what she can.

One of your group brothers asked a rather lengthy question which I should like to answer here, for it has psychological implications which may be useful to you. His question was as follows:

"What precisely is the relation between thought and emotion? Can thought be best described as sublimated emotion? Do not our thoughts, however remotely, arise out of our feelings, past as well as present? As reflecting past emotional reactions, may not thoughts be described as 'fossil feelings'? In the connotation of the present, are not our thoughts but our finer feelings? Does not the mental grow out of the refinement of the emotional body?

"In this sense, the evolutionary, is not the emotional body itself but a sublimation of the etheric, as that in turn is but the sublimation of the inorganic chemical? As we progress on the Path of Return, do we not but successively 'gather up our bodies within us,' raising each into the Light of the next one above, and is not this the meaning of culture, education, refinement, purification? Is not that the personal work we should constantly be at, and is it not what is symbolised, in Roman Catholic Doctrine, by the Assumption by the Christ of the body of the Virgin Mary, His Mother, into Heaven?"

My reply to him is:

In the above enquiry, my brother, you have asked nine questions, all bearing on the same subject. Some of them would not have needed a reply had you had the time to study *A Treatise on Cosmic Fire*, for in that book much of your question is answered.

The difficulty in distinguishing between thought and emotion is due entirely to two things:

1. The point in evolution of the Observer, which determines very largely the field of his observation and the focus of his directed attention.
2. The present status of the human race. Most of humanity is not, at present, thinking but is actively feeling.

The quality of mind, which is primarily discrimination, is largely lacking in the bulk of mankind. The quality of emotion is however becoming understood as the mind develops. It is the result of a measure of discrimination which enables the Observer to realise that he is undergoing an emotion, or passing through an emotional crisis. This emotion is, in its turn, the result of sensory perception. There can be much feeling reaction without emotion. There can be no emotion, as a result of feeling, without some measure of mental unfoldment and of thought being present. Therefore, the relation between thought and feeling is called by us emotion. Your question is therefore answered by saying, in a large and general way, that feeling can be (and frequently is) present where there is no thought at all. But when thought enters in, then the result of the interplay between thought and feeling is the production of emotion.

We pass on then to your second question where you seek to describe thought as "sublimated emotion." Here you are putting the cart before the horse, as the saying is. Thought is the medium whereby emotion can be sublimated. It is feeling without thought which has produced the world of illusion, of glamour, and of delusion. It is thought, with its discriminating and analysing faculty which makes us aware of this maya in which we are ceaselessly walking. Thought throws a clear light into the fog and mists of the astral plane. Astral energy—the energy of sensitive feeling reaction—has for millions of ages been thrown into activity by all the forms of life in all the kingdoms of nature. This has produced the world illusion. Only in the human family, however, is it seen for what it is, and the power of thought and the white light of the mind begin to play upon the matter of that plane, producing emotion, but the emotion is an *astral condition recognised by the mind* and later seen to be one of the effects of the steadily growing mind power of the race.

This is the thought underlying the phrase found so often in the theosophical books, kama-manas—desire-mind—for all feeling-emotion inevitably evokes desire. If the emotion evoked by the mind's recognition of the feeling (registered in the astral body) is pleasurable, then desire is evoked for the continuance or the repetition of the experience. If it is not pleasurable, but painful, then the reaction is desire for the cessation of the experience and therefore liberation from it. This is the basic human desire, leading to desire for liberation (in the first and earliest instance) from the womb into life on the physical plane, on and up to that great and final desire which is for liberation into life itself. This thought leads us into the world of the most technical esoteric psychology.

It is very difficult for the beginner to grasp the basic differentiations which he has *welded into unities* through his innate capacity to identify himself sequentially with that which is revealed. Feeling and mind are, for the individual, the two basic differentiations in time and space. That which is registered in the interplay between the two is emotion and, later, thought. But thought is a later realisation and reveals emotion; it is not however emotion. It discovers feeling with which the soul has consistently identified itself for aeons, and—if I may so express it—it is the turning of the searchlight of the slowly developing mind into the world of feeling, of glamour and of illusion which reveals man's reaction to it all, and this we call *emotion*. In a deeply and truly esoteric sense, it is the intuition which is sublimated emotion, and not the mind.

Therefore, in answering your third question, I would say that thoughts do not arise out of our feelings, but that when the mind begins to be active, our feelings stand revealed and the result of that revelation we call emotion.

Thoughts, again, are not "fossilised feelings," but emotions which can be registered by the image-making faculty of the mind, and the thoughtforms thus created (embodying the mind's reaction to the world of feeling) can be so powerful that they can persist in the treasure-house of the memory and can be constantly revitalised by a recurring emotion. It is the mind's activity in relation to feeling or to the range of feelings which reveals emotion. In the present time when the average human being and the average aspirant cannot distinguish accurately between mind, emotion, feeling and the thoughtforms which memory guards, it is impossible for a clear line of demarcation to be drawn. But this is owing simply to the point of evolution of the race. Such lines and differentiations can be drawn clearly by the developed disciple and the initiate. He then discovers that thoughts are the product of the principle of intelligence, dealing with life and enabling a man to say: I am not my body. I am not my feeling apparatus. I am not that which is developed through the interplay between myself and my environment. I am something other than all this. *I am.*

In connection with the sixth part of your question, my brother, you have forgotten your technical occultism and the ancient teaching anent the involutionary arc, wherein the various bodies and forms are created by the descending, involving Spirit, and the consciousness appropriated in a great moment of crisis, when each kingdom in nature came into being. The mind exists and needs to be consciously used. Few are yet aware of that quality in matter which is called the mind. But, as on the involutionary arc Spirit created as it descended, and appropriates as it reascends, so each appropriation marks a new point upon the Path of Return and so the Eternal Pilgrim, the soul, does the same in a lesser way. On the path into physical manifestation, the bodies or forms are built. On the Path of Return, they are appropriated and used, and the consciousness of their use steadily grows. For the evolved human being, the goal is a clear and conscious appropriation of that which has been built and its use in the service of the Plan.

Forget not that all aspects or externalisations which the soul uses and through which it expresses itself are constituent parts of the vehicle of expression of the One in Whom we live and move and have our being. Therefore we appropriate that which we earlier "earmarked" (if I may use that ancient phrase in its deepest and truest occult significance) on the Path of Descent. We learn to use it consciously. We hear its note as we descend; we see it as we ascend. We identify ourselves with the form as its sound reaches us during the process of involution. We distinguish it on the evolutionary arc, and when the stage wherein we identify ourselves with form begins to die out, we then "see" it and enter the stage of duality.

Yes, my brother, we do indeed raise our bodies into heaven, but the raising takes place within the realm of conscious effort, for when the distinctions of the lower mind fade out, and the work—the necessary work—of discovery and of differentiation has played its part in teaching us the lesson of desirelessness, we find that the form and consciousness are *one*, the light is *one*, and the energy is *one*. But we find also that "one star differeth from another star in glory" because there is One Flame but many sparks of differing brightness within that Flame. Such is the glory of the great Eternal One. This realisation is the soul's aspiration and the goal of its great enlightenment. It is, as you rightly point out when viewing the subject from the angle of mother-matter, the assumption of the Virgin into Heaven, there to be glorified. Much of the mystery connected with "the three vestures of the Buddha" is related to this glorification of the three bodies. Much can be learnt by a careful study of the connection between the three bodies of a human being and the vestures or vehicles of the Lord Buddha. The whole story of Sublimation, of Purification, and of Transfiguration is hidden in this relationship. The correspondences remain, however, to be pointed out. It is a task that has not yet been done.

Let me now return to your own specific instructions. I am going to give you no set meditation form to follow. I am however going to give you something to do which, if successfully done, may bring you release.

Seek each day for ten minutes to get into touch spiritually, mentally and emotionally with one or other of your group brothers. Take each of them on successive days. Seek to establish a definite rapport and pour out love and help. Forget yourself in so doing and drive out of your consciousness the realisation that you are an emanating centre of force. Ponder upon the circumstances of their lives as you may know them; try to comprehend their problems of time, character and of aspiration. Write to them, if you care to do so, and try to get them to help you. Let them draw from you the very essence of spiritual service, which means that they will draw from your soul that which they need; in giving thus, you will be enriched yourself.

My blessing rests upon you, my brother.

August 1942

1. At the centre of a great tornado is a point of peace. Thus does the story go. It can be found. And thus it is with all the storms of life. They lead to peace if you are not a leaf.
2. Hold to your old established links and with your brothers walk. Walk as a group upon the Lighted Way. The chain of Hierarchy firmly stands.
3. The light that streams from out my Ashram is a part of the Lighted Way and on that thread of light you move and with you move your brothers.
4. Loneliness—such as you think you know—is but a glamour, brother of mine. You are not alone. But loneliness such as you can know is a light that lights the darkness. Seek that out.
5. Upon the pinnacle of loneliness is the sole peace where truth is known. Stand on that pinnacle.

6. And when the truth is clearly seen (blowing away the
cobwebs and the dust of lower life) then can your service
carry fresh truth to men.

September 1943

My Brother:

I have watched with interest as you have made many
drastic adjustments in your life during the past two years. I
have noted the increased strength of your spiritual links with
your own soul, with the Ashram and with me, your Master
and your constant friend. Of this you may not be constantly
or inspiringly aware, but you have done one surprising thing
—surprising because it is not usual. You have made these
drastic adjustments without losing temporarily any ground.
This is a thing rare indeed. Usually during these basic life
changes, and during periods wherein the pattern of a daily
life is altered, there is a temporary loss of time and of ground.
It is seldom permanent but it usually exists for a short time
until the new arrangements and adjustments have been regi-
mented into rhythm, and then the threads are picked up,
the old spiritual habits are reinstated, and the disciple again
proceeds upon his way. This has not, however, happened to
you. You seem to have gone steadily on, with no great or
vitally important spiritual experience but with a pronounced
stability. This should indicate to you something of importance. It means that you have reached that point upon the
Path of Discipleship where you need no longer ask yourself
if you are going to fail as far as a steady and undeviating
moving forward is concerned. You may and will fail on details, techniques and methods; you may err in understanding
or in prompt reaction to spiritual opportunity. That is inevitable, and the method whereby a disciple learns. But you will
not fail in going on; for you there will be no turning back
nor any real tendency to do so—only moments of unutterable
fatigue when temptation may appear, but to it you will pay
no attention.

I wonder if you can realise, my brother, what this means
to the Master who has a disciple under training and guid-

ance. It means that one possible danger can be definitely discounted and that along one line at least He can feel sure of His disciple. He need no longer question his staying power; He knows that it is good and that the disciple will take what is coming to him with steadfastness.

As you move forward you must, for the next twelve months, come to a clear understanding of my injunction to you, given earlier, to "seek the pinnacle of loneliness which is the sole place whereon truth can be known." This is an injunction to increase your capacity to withdraw into the focussed point in the illumined mind where no one else can accompany you, and there await the arrival of the truth—that particular truth which your personality demands from your soul and which you feel—at any given time—it is essential that you grasp if your service and your progress are to be properly furthered. This demand, based on a sensed need, will vary from year to year, but there will always be some truth, some aspect of understanding and some immediate revelation which you *know* (past all controversy and discussion) that you must grasp and know if you are to move forward as desired—by your soul and by your Master.

At this particular time what is that immediately needed truth, information and revelation which you must have? It is not for me to tell you, even though I know. It is in the formulating of that need and that requirement that your progress will be made. I would ask you, on receipt of this instruction, to determine in your mind, upon quiet reflection, what is your one immediate spiritual need. Then seek the pinnacle of truth within yourself and there await the revelation. It will inevitably come if you care enough and have adequate patience.

The past two years have been preparatory years for you, even if you do not yet know for what ends they are the preparation. They have taught you much. But here I would remind you that all the teaching, training and experience which you have undergone has now to be brought to a point of synthesis within the illumined mind; it then becomes a potent seed thought, capable of bringing much intuitive perception and later revelation.

Will you therefore do the following things and follow the procedure outlined below:

1. Summarise in your own consciousness, and in the light of your soul, the nature and purpose of the experiences and changes to which you have been subjected. Endeavour to see the big sweep of the intention and be not preoccupied with the detail. Formulate to yourself in clear concise sentences your conclusions, so that the lessons of the past can stand revealed to you.

2. Determine then within yourself what is the next needed truth, type of revelation or requirement which will enable you to move forward with increased potency, clearer vision and truer insight. This will not be as easy as it sounds, because this next truth must relate the past to the future of service, as you see that service.

3. Then with these two lines of thought held quietly and clearly in your mind, seek that "pinnacle of loneliness" which is to be found if due search is made. There the desired truth and revelation can be expected and awaited. Then wait.

4. When your intuition begins to move and your patient waiting, quiet reflection and steady mental poise bring their reward of clarified perception, then endeavour to apply the recognised truth and the germ of the revelation to the practical affairs of living. You will then find taking place a steady enrichment of your entire life.

This will constitute a richly rewarding exercise and—could you but grasp it—constitutes a definitely advanced form of meditation. You will find this meditation project a most interesting experiment.

Another thing, my brother. This war period will not last indefinitely. Already the end is in sight, and for its termination you must be prepared. This is not only worldly practical wisdom but also spiritual prevision. Your work in my Ashram must some day be more definitely an aspect of my work in the outer world than it now necessarily is; I would have you ponder upon what you can do. Disciples in all Ashrams (and mine is no exception) are pledged to the work of their Ashram, and this you have always known. E'en though it is true that all work is spiritual, given right motive and intention, yet disciples are definitely pledged to certain hierarchical forms of service which must take precedence in all life activities even whilst—at the same time—the disciple fulfils his other tasks in the outer world, based on his right obligations and responsibilities and upon his citizenship. Have this definitely in mind, and remember that I need the assistance of this entire group within my Ashram. I also need their individual cooperation and understanding of the problems to be met. It is permitted to me to give a general call and to state specific principles and lines of activity which should govern the work of my disciples. It is not permitted for me to say when or where that service must be rendered.

The group work and the four stages of reflection which I have outlined for you will suffice for your spiritual enterprise at this time. These and the work you are doing in your present field of labour present adequate opportunity for living and progress. My love and blessing are yours and upon that you can count.

November 1944

There is within your consciousness at this time, a major question. You have been taught by your soul to question; you have absorbed the injunction that a Master arrives at His goal through a process of questioning and of finding, alone and without any outer aid, the answer. With you, this is a fixed belief and understanding, and that is good. The question in your mind which still lacks an answer is evoked by my statement in the last instruction I gave you that the work of the Ashram is ever the prime obligation of the disciple.

Necessarily, this work varies according to the status of the disciple and his place within the Ashram. I have given you (in various group instructions) the stages of discipleship.

These were stages within the consciousness of the disciple and concerned his relation to the Master. They detailed his progress from a rare contact to a position close to the Master. It is of value now to add to these individual steps those which concern a disciple's position within the Ashram, and this from the angle of his ashramic duty and service. This is a different matter, and though related to the interplay between him and his Master, these stages are concerned with action and with the results of his expanding consciousness within the hierarchical awareness; they are related to his perception of truth as response to the Master's radiation evokes in him certain developments, stimulates certain qualities and new characteristics, and brings to his mind enlightenment.

These stages in service and in recognition of duty and obligation are related to status more than to soul growth and control, though this growth is one of the determining factors as regards his position in the Ashram. Let me enumerate them, leaving you to place yourself in the category of servers to which you belong, and leaving you also to demonstrate to the world the nature of your ashramic position. I will give you the esoteric names and symbols of this differentiation:

1. *The stage of the "awakening urge."* Of this stage, the half-opened eye is the symbol. The neophyte, just admitted into the Ashram, becomes (as the Book of Instructions for Neophytes expresses it) "the victim of a dual sight. With the right eye he sees a shaded way into the central Ashram; from point to point, from light to dark and dark to light as the pillars point the way, he sees a narrow corridor and at the end a room; within that room the passing figure of the Master appears and disappears. With the left eye, a world of mist and fog, of gloom and shadowy forms is seen—a land of woe and dire distress, with light and shadow moving back and forth. From within that gloomy land a cry comes forth: We need your aid. We cannot see. Come hither with the light." In these phrases is embodied the first reaction of the new disciple to the dual life to

which his admission to the Ashram has committed him—
the life of ashramic instruction and of steady approach
to the Master, plus the life of outer service which must
come as a response to need and not as a fulfillment of an
enjoined duty. He sees in neither direction with clarity.
Remember ever that approach and service must be self-
initiated and self-implemented. The only help which the
disciple gets at this stage comes from the stimulating effect
of the aura of the Ashram.

2. *The stage of "advance."* By this I do not refer to progress
in understanding. That is inevitable in time and incidental in space when the disciple is immovable in his
determination. I refer to the process of his moving forward (technically understood) along the pillared corridor,
simultaneously with his appearance in the outer world as
an ashramic worker. You have a phrase which is usually
employed in a derogatory sense of "social climber"; it refers to a person who—dissatisfied with his social position,
his social contacts and his social relationships—uses every
and any method to penetrate into those social milieus
which have seemed unattainable. It is a platitude to say
that all unworthy goals (because incorrectly motivated)
are the lower correspondence or symbolic expressions (e'en
though distorted) of higher aims and aspirations. This
thought should clarify your thinking. A disciple at this
stage is a man whose character and capacities have permitted him to enter the Ashram with the full consent of
its membership. He hovers, however, on the periphery of
its activities; he knows that here are action, contacts and
relationships—within the ashramic ring-pass-not—which
can be his some day. Yet he also knows that he has to
master the meaning of the paradoxical statement with
which his voiced aspiration was met: "Go out the door
and leave the Ashram as it was and as you are; seek for
another entrance; find what you seek by leaving it behind;
move forward through the art of moving back."

In the blazing light of the Ashram the disciple realises
that he has not yet earned the right to pass along the corridor to the Master's sanctum, but must needs go forth

into the world of men, of darkness and of pain; then he can return to the Ashram for strength to continue his work outside. What lies outside the door of the Ashram, symbolically speaking, becomes to him of greater moment than his own success in passing along the corridor. What has happened to him, as both his eyes "function in the dual light," is that his sense of values is adjusted and his own progressive satisfaction becomes of less importance to him than what he can do to ameliorate the pain and distress outside the door.

3. *The stage of "leaving each pillar behind its own shadow."* Is it only a truism to point out that as service proceeds, and the effectiveness of that service increases, the disciple when he enters the door of the Ashram, discovers he is no longer standing upon the inner side of the door but has already penetrated a definite distance along the corridor? Certain pillars are left behind. One of the Masters—using the word in its correct sense—has called these symbolic pillars the "pillars of propriety," meaning that each pillar passed indicates the attainment of certain aspects of appropriate conduct. When these aspects of behaviour are developed, the disciple can pass up and down the corridor at will, which symbolises to him the, as yet, undeveloped phase of ashramic conduct. These pillars embody the final phase of illusion—those illusions which bewilder the disciple but have no effect on anyone outside the Ashram. These you must discover for yourself. There are five more pillars which you must develop the ability to pass before you have the complete freedom of the Ashram. You have already learnt to pass seven of them and they, for you, are now nonexistent.

4. *The stage of the "withdrawing alcove."* I have to put these aspects of consciousness into material symbolic forms so as to bring pictorially to your attention the phases of approach which you and all disciples must follow. The pillars (again symbolically) no longer stand on either side of your way of approach. Though there for others, for you they constitute no longer any concern. The way stretches clear before you. The hope of free admittance into the

room where the Master works is a present possibility. But within the Ashram, protecting the seclusion of the Master, is the antechamber to the place where He works and in that antechamber His senior disciple presides. This disciple protects the Master from undue disturbance, is responsible for the care of His physical vehicle when He goes into "samadhi," has the right to interrupt Him in moments of emergency, and can be trusted to pass in and out of His study, whenever he deems it desirable. This arrangement requires the advancing disciple to recognise the senior disciple; it is this process of recognition which oft constitutes the final test, prior to being allowed through the inner door.

5. *The stage to which is given the name "the right of entry."* When this stage is reached, the disciple can come and go as his soul and the need of his service in the outer world may dictate. He has developed the sensitivity to know when, or when not, he may intrude into the presence of the Master. He finds, when he has arrived at this point, that all desire to contact the Master for his own satisfaction or help has left him. One thing only sends him on the wings of light along the corridor and strengthens his hand to open wide the door, and that is world need.

You will discover, my brother, under these symbols the lesson which I am seeking to convey to you. I enjoined you in my last instruction to realise the need of achieving a pinnacle of loneliness, for on that pinnacle lies for you that which you need. What that is, you must find out for yourself. Have you learnt something anent this lonely spot? If so, the next development for you may involve (I did not say "would") the lonely moments spent as you, from pillar to pillar, advance along the corridor, spurred by the needs of those you seek to serve. Then will come the moment when the senior disciple will symbolise for you the end of loneliness and greet you as a brother. What takes place later between you and the Master is your own individual secret, shared with Him.

One point I seek to emphasise to you at this time is the

need for you to recognise more definitely that *the way into the inner sanctum is the way of outer service.* This service must not be motivated by the exigencies of the period, or by financial considerations or the behests of the personality. It may or may not include the place where your outer work is being done; it may necessitate a change in your setting and circumstances, but the disciple—if true to his soul and the Ashram—serves his fellowmen *as an esotericist* as well as a humanitarian and a psychologist. This is a point which you must grasp. You must then fit the tasks assumed and undertaken into the symbolic picture which I have given you. I count upon your understanding because I am not speaking idle words; I count also upon your giving consideration and quiet reflection to my next statement.

There is some definite work planned by me which must be implemented by the members of my Ashram; it is work which you can undertake. It is related to the major task of goodwill which is so close to my heart; it will necessitate sacrifice upon your part and maybe a relinquishing of lesser goals. If recognised by you, it will mean that the "pillars which guard the approach to the sanctum" of your Master can be left behind; you will have reached the point where you can enter the "room of withdrawal." Again I speak to you in symbols. You are nearly sixty years old, my brother. The sixty-third year of your life, as in the life of all disciples, will be one of crisis and of supreme opportunity, and towards that point you should look and for it you should make preparation. The interim should be a time wherein you pass the pillars, wherein you go from point to point with your consciousness held steady within the Ashram and your personality activity adhering to the task imposed by your soul.

A basic decision will shortly confront you, and upon that decision will depend your right of entry, technically understood. I may not even indicate to you the nature of the coming crisis, nor may I give you any hint as to what your decision should be. I have, however, confidence in you, for you have learnt much in the past five years; you have gone from strength to strength and have passed from pillar to pillar, even if you did not realise it. You will discover the quality of your strength when the need for decision confronts you. I await you in the inner room.

August 1946

I have nothing to say to you today, my brother, of major moment. My last instruction to you was long and of vital importance; you have not yet absorbed its full significance. In that instruction there were two sentences which I seek again to emphasise in your consciousness. They are:

1. The way into the inner sanctum is the way of outer service.
2. The sixty-third year of your life—as in the life of all disciples—will be one of crisis and of supreme opportunity.

These two statements are closely related. Crises, my brother, can be objective or subjective; they can take place on the physical plane, and are then not of such great significance from the spiritual angle, even though they cause much suffering and pain to the personality; they can emerge into consciousness on the emotional or the mental planes, and they then present opportunity for action, but mostly for action connected with the personality; or they can be the result of soul intent, registered by the personality and recorded in the brain. They are then of supreme importance, but very frequently remain unrecognised unless the disciple is very alert and constantly aware of the cyclic flow of spiritual energy.

Such a crisis confronts you. Has your spiritual sensitivity increased during the past few years so that you can be sure that you can recognise the crisis for the opportunity it is, when confronted by it? Here are the points I would have you consider, for upon your recognitions and your decisions rests much of the usefulness of the rest of your life—that is, from the angle of the Ashram.

There is a peculiar difficulty connected with the realisation that there are relatively only a few years ahead for the majority of the group. Here are four of the difficulties which prevent the sensible and happy realisation of the future transition:

1. The tendency to settle down and take the position that one has done the best one can and that that is all one can be expected to do. This renders the few remaining years simply an expression of habit and of established character, and prevents the undertaking of any new spiritual adventure.

2. A recognition that one *has* reached one's high water mark for this life and nothing more can be expected. This may be true from the personality angle, but the soul remains eternally young and unsatisfied, knowing no static point.

3. A preoccupation, growing year by year, with the *processes* of growing old, with its liabilities, its physical symptoms and ugliness, and its required (?) withdrawals. This is a usual and ordinary way of approaching one's declining years and the regular procedure with the great majority. See that it is not yours as the next decade elapses.

4. The recognition that the soul, enjoying the full richness of life's garnered experience, is now free to serve. No new problems are tackled; no new disciplines are applied; but the disciple uses all that he has in the service of the Ashram, and that for the remainder of his life.

I am seeking to bring all these points to your consideration, for they embody choices which await you, and it is your right to know what they are. I will make no further comment beyond emphasising that there is a definite and conscious choice to be made, and leaving you free to think the matter through.

You have in the past done much to help the work I planned. You are today among those interested in discovering their spiritual enterprise. Discover it, my brother, and have an enterprise which will count in the realisation (I use not the word manifestation) of the Kingdom of God on Earth. Be interested anew and alertly in the hierarchical plans, and fit yourself into the time schedule of my ashramic purposes. Adjust your sense of values, which have shifted considerably lately (I say not whether for good or not, for that is your affair), and make your life count in the hour of humanity's need.

I have the following suggestions to make as regards your meditation work:

1. Orient yourself dynamically towards the Ashram and towards me, your Master, and ponder for a while upon your relationship with me and its various implications.
2. Orient yourself towards the spiritual enterprises (for there are several) which emanate from the Ashram, under my direction, and reflect upon your responsibility to them.
3. Orient yourself to your chosen daily work and consider where opportunity there arises which can be fitted into the spiritual vision which all disciples carry with them.
4. Orient yourself to your own soul and consider what are the duties and responsibilities and relations of that soul in all the three worlds of experience.
5. Then sound the O M three times in order to clarify the mind; quiet all emotional reaction and endeavour to make your brain receptive to the higher spiritual impression.
6. Then in your own words, and as the soul, speak to me and discuss with me your life and spiritual intention. I shall not respond, but (bear this in mind) record will be made of that which has the power to penetrate into the Ashram.
7. Say the New Invocation, sounding the O M after each stanza.
8. Close your meditation by saying—as the personality and with emphasis—"May I do my whole duty as I journey towards Thy sacred feet."

You have known me for many, many years now, my brother. I remain the same and unaltered; therefore my love, strength and understanding are factors upon which you can at all times assuredly count.

To E. E. S.

August 1940

BROTHER OF OLD AND CO-WORKER:

This year and in fact during the past three years, many problems have arisen in your life and these have been complicated by the fact that the physical vehicle is not functioning as it should. With that condition you must learn to live, treating it with due wisdom and at the same time ignoring it in the service of humanity and in ours. One attitude infers right physical care; the other attitude sets the note for the mental reaction. This I think you know and are working successfully towards this way of living. I mention it because one of the things all disciples have to achieve (prior to initiation) is a right mental attitude toward that aspect of the physical body which is *not* regarded as a principle and which is only the automaton of the inflowing forces and of the inner man. The energy which governs the physical body emanates from that aspect or integrated aspects where lies the focus of consciousness. Perfect health will come, therefore, when the focus of consciousness is permanently in the soul. This is not possible for any of you at present because of the point in evolution and because of the mass relation and the mass karma, superimposed upon the individual karma.

You are handling the situation adequately, my brother, and where there could be an imposed expression of soul life, you need not for me to tell you, for you are aware of your own limitations and of your own weaknesses. Your first ray physical body is of service to you in many ways. See to it that the tendency of the first ray to withdraw from contact to the isolated aloofness of the first ray does not unduly condition you upon the physical plane. You will know to what tendency

I refer. Your whole life goal at this time is to give *loving strength* to others through tapping the source of all love yourself. There are those you can aid. You will do so at this time through giving them increased loving understanding.

As regards certain problems of activity known to you, I would encourage you to persevere with much caution and wariness. The early stages of the work you are seeking to do are fraught with some danger, as again you know. These difficulties, if successfully surmounted, will lead to greatly minimising other risks later in your planned work. A.A.B. will talk with you about this matter if you so wish, and will convey to you my suggestions whenever you want them. I have spoken to her and made them known, hence the brevity of my communication to you at this time. You will comprehend.

I have however a meditation which I would ask you to follow and to do so dynamically. By that I mean: Become simply a point of concentration when doing it, with all personal problems and conditions temporarily obliterated from your consciousness. To produce this concentration, I will give you a breathing exercise with the meditation.

1. Relax and turn the eyeballs upward. The Hindu system of rolling up the eyeballs does aid in this matter, and the point where the quivering of the eyelids ceases or is forgotten indicates the point of relative physical poise.
2. Take seven long breaths, slowly and without strain and as you do so visualise yourself as mounting higher and higher with each breath. To do this the more easily, picture yourself as mounting seven steep steps.
3. Then, at your highest point, sound the O M, retaining its force in the head by an act of the will but without any strain or pressure. The retention of energy is *not* a physical matter but a mental process. This is a subject of importance.
4. Then, holding the consciousness as high in the head as possible, see how long you can achieve the position of *listening* without becoming negative or losing the

recollection of who you are or what you are doing. Never relinquish in this work the sense of personal identity. Until I give you permission, do not hold this listening attitude for more than three minutes.

5. Then breathe out the O M through the ajna centre, the centre between the eyebrows, and say:

I choose the way of the interpreter, and therefore ask for light.

I choose the way of loving guidance, and therefore ask for lifting power.

I choose the way of inspiration, and therefore ask for flowing life.

I choose the way of integrating, and therefore ask for the seal of silence.

6. Then sound the O M seven times and proceed with the group meditation.

These phrases have each three esoteric meanings. Take *one* of the above sentences each for one month and then repeat the process of reflection twice, thus covering a year's work. See if you can arrive at deeper significances than those which appear on the surface.

NOTE: *This final instruction to this disciple follows immediately upon the one which is concluded in Vol. I, page 649, and the footnote there still applies.*

To D. P. R.

January 1940

Life has been so difficult for you, brother of mine, that I hesitate (because I have an understanding of much that you are enduring) to lay upon you any further burden of self-discipline or more of the life of introspection. You have stood in the midst of your world and watched it come down, crashing around you; you have stood as a tower of strength to those who are tied to you in the closest links and have not

failed them; you have preserved your values clear whilst seeing the material values dissolve into thin air. That you still
have a few personal glamours and are still taken in by your
own high grade reactions to circumstance and people is of
course true but I question whether anything is to be gained
through your focussing your attention upon them at this
time.

Stand steady, therefore, and be not unduly distressed.
Avoid at least one glamour and that is the glamour that it is
your task to shoulder all responsibilities and make all final
decisions. Leave people, brother of old, the opportunity
which you yourself so much welcome, of learning the needed
lessons. Seek not unduly to lift and shield, for the shielding
mother-complex is in itself a glamour.

My love and strength is at your service.

August 1940

MY BROTHER:

One of the outstanding characteristics of the pledged
disciple is that he learns to stand steady and unmoving no
matter what may be happening to him or around him. Much
is happening to disciples these days for they bear the brunt of
the world's cataclysm. You may perhaps find this an astonish-
ing statement but I would ask you to remember that they
meet the prevalent conditions on all three planes simultaneously and are at the same time endeavouring to live as
souls. The accuracy of my statement is, therefore, apparent
if you will ponder for a few minutes on the implications.
There is appalling suffering everywhere. Physically and emotionally, people throughout the world are handling the maxi-
mum of pain. The accepted disciple, however, is suffering
also mentally and to this must be added his capacity to identify himself with the whole; his trained imagination also
presents special difficulty for he can include possibilities
which others may not envisage, and his sweep or grasp of
the plan is presumably greater; he is also endeavouring to
apply his knowledge of this plan to the immediate environing

situation and is strenuously attempting to understand and at the same time to interpret to others, no matter what he may be undergoing in his own personal life.

In many cases, such as yours, environing conditions and chosen associates tend to complicate matters and you are, therefore, today facing your major life crisis and, I would add, you are facing it satisfactorily.

There are many types of crisis in the lives of all aspirants, but in the case of those who are pledged disciples there are always two major crises in their lives: There is first of all *the crisis of opportunity* and its wise recognition. At some time, every disciple is faced with some determining choice which leads eventually to the distinctive nature of his life service. This usually takes place between the ages of twenty-five and forty, usually around the age of thirty-five. I refer not here to the choice which every able bodied and sane man has to take when he determines his life work, his place of living and his life associates. I refer to a free choice made when these other lesser choices have been made. Such a choice came to you in your earlier years. This crisis of opportunity relates ever to life service. This is true in spite of karma or environing conditions. It is not a choice of the personality, based upon expedient or earthly motives, necessity or anything else. It is a choice based upon the relation of the soul to the personality and *only confronts disciples*.

The second crisis is *the crisis of expression*. This usually comes towards the later years of a disciple's life. It concerns his stabilised life tendency and puts to the test all that he believes and for which he has stood and fought throughout his life experience. It is ever a hard and bitter test, going to the very roots of his life, and for those in preparation for initiation it is peculiarly acute. The conditions of the test may apparently seem no worse than the tests and difficulties which assault other people but, as I have pointed out above, they have to be met on all planes at once. Soul energy is ever involved thereby and this intensifies the response of each individual body in the lower man and also the personality as a whole, the integrated man. The stage of responsiveness which every disciple has achieved in relation to his environment, his associates and his service greatly aggravates his difficulties. I am explaining this somewhat in detail as I am anxious to have you comprehend the nature of your problem and so be able to handle it with increased poise, understanding and triumph. Behind you lies a crisis of opportunity; you met it well. Today you face your crisis of expression and you will come through; true triumph is dependent upon specific achievement upon the inner planes and upon wresting the true values out of any situation, and of these values based upon the physical plane are by far the least important.

If you will, all of you, study the instructions given by me to the individual members of the group and to the group itself, you will find that I am giving you definite instructions in the Way of Initiation. Your response and your search lies, however, in the field of esoteric recognition more than in the field of the reception of new facts. So much has been given out in the past few years and decades anent initiation; it has largely been made exoterically, and received exoterically, and the true import of the teaching has been veiled. My task with you is not so much the impartation of new facts, truths, points of view and interest, but the awakening into reality of that which your mind already has received as theory and hypothesis.

You stand today, my brother, at a major point of crisis and you stand alone. Those in your immediate environment are of no special service to you for they are not yet upon the path of discipleship. They are in the earliest stages of the path of probation and are unaware of it also. You have, therefore, only three sources of strength:

1. First and foremost, your contact with your own soul through meditation, reflection and joy.
2. Your contact with me, your Master, because through me some of the strength of the world of souls and of the Hierarchy can reach you.
3. Your group brothers in this new seed group.

I would like to point out that in these three contacts you have the three aspects of divine expression appearing—from the angle of stimulation and of vitalising power—and so three types of power are made available. Beginning with the lowest contact, your group brothers, you have the *intelligent activity* and consequent stimulation upon the physical plane of your contact with them; through your soul contact, the *love* aspect of divinity can be made manifest in you; and through your hierarchical contact, the *will* of God can pour into you. Thus all the three aspects of the divine nature can pour into you and meet with response from the three aspects of your lower manifested expression; thus you can become subservient to the divine. Ponder on this and seek to establish these contacts firmly and upon sound nonemotional lines.

You have a particularly interesting group of life forces or energies conditioning you, interesting because of the specific combination. The saving grace of your life expression has been your second ray astral body because the combination of a first ray soul, a fifth ray personality and a third ray physical expression might have resulted in a hard, concrete materialistic person. These rays are the ones which have produced what is called the Prussian type of mind. Incidentally, this ray combination produced your karmic relationships in this life. Fortunately for you, your past immediate incarnation as a personality was overwhelmingly second ray and of this you brought over a second ray astral nature and a fourth ray mental equipment. Hence the balancing in two directions and hence also the general trend of your life conditioning.

It was your first ray lines of force which placed you in the particular locality in which you live and brought your life partner to you. It was your second ray background and its effects in your present life expression which hastened your affiliation with myself and brought to you your particular group of brothers in the new seed group. This information may prove of use to you even if it only serves to strengthen your faith and to indicate to you the reasonableness of the situation which your circumstances are forcing you to meet.

Therefore, your major need is to strengthen and preserve the three contacts which form the background of your spiritual life: your soul, your relation with me and your connection with your group brothers. By so doing, the sense of universality and of an expanded consciousness will grow and deepen and enable you to achieve that sense of proportion which will reveal the little self as an integral part of the great Self or Whole. By this statement I refer not only to your relation between the soul and the personality but to your relation—as a living entity—to the greater whole of which Humanity and the Hierarchy are integral parts. I would suggest, therefore, a line of thought or of meditation which will deepen and strengthen these attitudes. To this end I am going to suggest five points of recollection for you each day:

1. On awakening in the morning, *before rising.*
2. At noon.
3. At sunset, whatever hour that may be.
4. On retiring at night.
5. At the time of the group meditation, whenever you may decide to do it.

Thus a living continuity of sensed relationship will be established in your consciousness.

1. On awakening, sound the O M inaudibly and say:
   "I am one with the light which shines through my soul, my brothers and my Master."
2. At noon, again sound the O M inaudibly and say with deep and slow reflection: "Naught separates me from my soul, my brothers and my Master. My life is theirs and theirs is mine."
3. At sunset again sound the O M and say:
   "Naught can dim the love which flows between my soul and me, the little self. Naught can come between my brothers and my self. Naught can stop the flow of strength between me and my soul, between my brothers and my soul, between the Master of my life and me, His pledged disciple."

4. On retiring, before you fall asleep, you again sound
the O M and say: "From darkness lead us to light. I
tread the way of life and light because I am a soul.
With me there walk my brothers and my Master.
Therefore within, without, and every side, there is
light and love and strength."

5. When doing the group meditation, begin to capitalise
on this growing consciousness and before doing the
work, link up with as much conscious realisation as
possible with your soul, your brothers and myself,
realising the indestructibility of the tie.

This work carried forward as a definite exercise will produce
in you a deepened available strength and poise. It will only
take a few seconds at each point or stated time, but those
seconds will serve as points of crisis and of inpouring
strength.

August 1942

1. I come to Thee, Lord of my Life, and from that point
achieved, close at Thy feet I work.

2. Between me and the outer world there appears a haze of
blue. That blue protects and hence I have no fear.
Through it, I may not pass.

3. And from this hour and henceforth upon the *Way*, I seek
to *Be*. I seek no more to know, because this life has taught
me how to know and with this knowledge gained, I now
can serve by *Being*.

4. Before me streams the Path of Light. I see the Way. Behind me lies the mountain path, with stones and cobbles
on the way. Around me are the thorns. My feet are tired.
But straight ahead stretches the Lighted Way and on that
Way I walk.

5. Pain comes from form-attachment. It takes two forms:
Attachment to the forms of earth, of men and place; attachment to the truth. They both bring pain and pain
must cease. Ask your soul *how?*

6. The threefold load, the blazing star, the path of light, the greater Star and through them all the throbbing of the heart of love, streaming from out the Ashram of D.K. enfolding all and thee.

September 1943

MY BELOVED BROTHER:

A.A.B. has just called my attention to the six statements which I gave you to reflect upon more than a year ago. Knowing all that you had been through in the interim and are now passing through, she realised how extremely apposite and suitable they had proved to be. Pain has engulfed you and yours; anxiety along many lines, and all of them severely testing, has been your lot. Had you not been "close to the feet of the Lord of your Life," you would have reached what might have been regarded as the valley of desperation.

Yet you have not been truly desperate because the "haze of blue" has protected you, your group brothers have stood as a shield around you, and the strength of my Ashram has been at your disposal. People often fail to realise the nature and the potency of that strength—a strength that comes from a deep impersonal love and from the realisation that, in the light of the eternal verities, all pain is but temporary, all trouble and struggle ephemeral, and that we have passed oft this way before upon the unhappy little planet of suffering which we call the Earth. *We come to know that we shall not pass this way so oft again.* Did you grasp the significance of that sentence, my brother?

Just as there are days in a year which seem to stand out because of their darkness and to be overcharged with blackness and agony, so there are lives which equally so stand out in a cycle of lives because of the varied experiences which they convey, the bitter piling up of pain and distress, and the handling of an accumulation of unhappy and oft agonising karma. But, my brother, all lives are not like this, and the fact that your present life has been for years so hard is the guarantee that you have worked off much karma, that you stand infinitely freer and are less handicapped. The fruits of all this suffering you will reap as you enter your next incarnation.

So be of good cheer, and look forward and out towards a future of service and of joy, and this because you have endeavoured to live selflessly and to carry your load bravely, and because your life and deeds and your entire career have helped so many.

I would remind you that pain, when it is lived out mentally for others, is the worst kind of pain. This you know. But I would remind you that the capacity so to do and so to identify yourself with pain that is not specifically your own is something that all disciples have to master, because it is one of the first steps towards shouldering world pain and the agony of the human family, thus becoming a participant in the "fellowship of Christ's sufferings" and a lifter of world burdens. We work and live on a planet of pain. Until a man is an initiate of high degree he cannot even begin to sense the reasons why this is so; he must perforce then take refuge in the trite platitudes that suffering humanity has evolved to account for things as they are. None of these in any way approximate the true reasons or give any real insight into the problem. Men must wait for understanding until they can no longer be hurt or limited by the pain of others. This follows when we have learnt to handle our own pain. Then and only then can they begin to lift the burden of humanity as a whole and do their responsible share in lightening it.

We come again here to those contradictory and beautiful words: Isolated Unity. When one is isolated from form attachments and when one is freed for identification with the life aspect, then one can know the true meaning of unity, then one is released from pain and one is free to release others also.

This you are learning, and it is the last great lesson for you this life. It takes some time to learn it, because it is one of the very few basic lessons, implicating principles which are inherent in the planetary life and requiring the implementing of the soul to arrive at true understanding. You have made much progress along this line during this life and have no cause for self-depreciation or regrets. I tell you this for your assurance, and would ask you to rest back upon my words.

Keep busy with my work, my brother, for there is naught left for the true disciple but the work of the Ashram, which is the work of the Hierarchy, which is work for humanity. Such is the outgoing sequence. For you now, it is not so much the eager, active, outer service, of which you have done so much in the past years, but it is the standing steady, and so becoming a channel and a link. Remember with care the words I gave you last year: "I now can serve by Being."

Do not strive so much, my brother. Accept life conditions as they are; acquiesce in the situation as it is; relax for the remainder of this incarnation, and exoterically rest from your labours and esoterically enter into light. Work not under such a sense of inner strain and effort. I refer not to the outer strains and stresses to which you are subjected for they exist and are hard and difficult. I refer to your own inner attitude of recognition and acquiescence, of Being and attainment.

Those are the four key thoughts for your personal reflection during the coming year. The year that is on its way will hold great changes for you but you are strong enough and experienced enough to carry through triumphantly. The coming months will hold for you revelation, and that revelation will enhance the light upon the Lighted Way which stretches out before you; they will hold opportunity for you also, if you learn the hard lesson of relinquishment, and when next year closes you may find yourself surprised at the distance you will find you have travelled, the enlightenment you may find you have gained, and the increased sphere of your subjective usefulness.

Remember—you are *not* alone. I stand by and carry you consciously within my aura.

November 1944

MY BELOVED FRIEND AND TRUSTED DISCIPLE:

My heart has gone out to you during the past year as you have struggled with fatigue, with loneliness, with foreboding and with anxieties of many kinds. You have stood with constant steadiness and you must know by now how highly steadiness is regarded by the Hierarchy. These culminating years of your life have been years of great difficulty and much pain—not only for yourself but for others. They have been years wherein everything has been wrested from you, leaving you upon that "pinnacle of loneliness" about which I spoke to your brother, W.D.S., in my instruction to him last year. I would have you regard that pinnacle as an exalted place from which the new vision can be seen. That pinnacle can be turned into a mount of initiation.

You have passed the three score years and ten of ordinary living and you are privileged to look back upon a life of great usefulness and of much inner spiritual progress. You have disposed of much karma and are far freer than when you entered into incarnation.

The crux of the lesson which you are now in process of learning is to refrain from expectation—from life, from people and from circumstances—except that expectation which concerns spiritual opportunity and your relation to my Ashram. Disciples need to regard the Ashram more definitely as a place of *spiritual enveloping*, if I may use so peculiar a phrase. They need to regard it as a circle of protection, remembering that if their consciousness can escape into the Ashram, they are in a place of complete security where naught can reach or hurt them. Neither pain nor anxiety can overwhelm the man who dwells in the consciousness of eternity; this sense of the eternal, coupled with the realisation of essential unity, marks all dwellers in an Ashram.

Herein lies your safety in the vicissitudes of your life. I am not speaking idly or symbolically, nor am I referring to the usual platitudes expressed in the injunction "dwell in the eternal." I refer definitely to the place of a disciple within an Ashram of one of the Masters, and in particular to your place within my Ashram. This place is a reality and not a dream or a figment of wishful thinking; it is a sphere of focussed awareness where the minds, the love, the aspiration and the spiritual consciousness of many meet, and meet in truth. Of this meeting you can—as many have and do—

become conscious. Avoid vagueness as you think of the Ashram with which you are affiliated. Oft I warn and urge disciples to concentrate upon their service and upon their outer contacts, and thus avoid concentration upon the Ashram and upon me, the Master of the Ashram. Knowing your circumstances and seeing into your future, I reverse the injunction in your case and urge you to make the Ashram a reality in your life and to count with greater definiteness and surety upon my presence there and my understanding welcome. Your natural diffidence and humility will permit this and protect me and the Ashram from any undue pressure on your part, even if—in the stress of circumstances—you were prompted to make it.

I would outline for you a meditation which will suffice for your needs for a long time to come. I am not putting it in the ordinary form, for all of you in this group should now have reached the point at which you can formulate your own meditation and reflective approach. I only indicate to you the setting for certain seed thoughts.

I suggest that you think, first of all, of the Ashram, my Ashram, as a great centre of energy with which you (in your place and in your own way) are privileged to establish contact. See the Ashram as a sphere of radiant, magnetic light; then see me, as you know me, at the centre of that sphere, both emitting and receiving light, via the Christ and via the Ashram of which I was at one time a part—the Ashram of the Master K.H. See yourself also as a soul in contact with first ray energy, and thus contributing some of this energy, reaching you via the Ashram of the Master M., to the light and power of my Ashram. Having thus served and been served, and having taken your group brothers into your consciousness and recognised them as within the ashramic light, you can proceed to take three ideas or symbolic sentences as your theme for reflection, during the next few years. They *will suffice* to meet your need and to evoke in you the necessary spiritual attitudes.

I. The Cross, erected high, reaches from the pinnacle

upon which I stand into the place of light, where dwells my Master. Against that Cross there rests a ladder. The golden Cross and the ladder of pure light are one, and by their means I rise. Upward I look and see an outstretched hand. Downward I look and see the many hands demanding aid. With gladness and with hope, I recognise the purpose of the two hands I possess. I climb the ladder, hard as it may seem, with both my hands outstretched—the one above my head to find it clasped with strength, the other down below to find it full of power to lift.

II. A burning sea of flame. Beyond, a radiant sun. Behind, a world of darkness, gloom and heavy rain—a rain of tears. There, in the centre of a fire I stand, my eyes upon the sun. The vortex of the fire, the flaming rays of heat cast outward by the sun, blend with my fire and lo! it disappears. The greater fire blends with and consumes the little one. I turn and pass back—out of the light and warmth—into the world of gloom and mist and, as I turn, I hear a voice crying aloud: "Well done. Pass through the gloom; enter the mist; dry up the rain and tears and find yourself upon the other side, and near my heart."

III. A garden full of flowers, of bees and glowing light and sun. I see a wall which separates the garden from the world of men. Beyond its gates I see the forms of those who long to enter. Into my heart there come the words, spoken I know not when: "The key is in your hands; open the gates and let the crowd in. This you can do, for the garden now is yours and yet is theirs, though you have entered first. Open the gate and welcome with a smile and words of love and cheer the sad, unwelcome, miserable crowd. The garden stands between the outer world and the inner sacred place you call my Ashram. Within the garden take your stand. There rest. Move forward to the gate at need, returning ever to the place of rest. Open the door when called upon,

but retain the key. The surging crowd will touch
you not nor hurt the garden in its loveliness."

Behind these three symbolic stanzas, if I may so call them,
are veiled three needed lessons which you must learn and
master. I am not telling you what these lessons are, for the
joy of discovery must be yours.

I do not need to tell you either that I send you with constancy thoughts of strength and sustaining understanding.
Long years have taught you that my strength goes out to you
when your own inner strength is called into play and is used
by you consciously and rightly. I give not what you yourself
can provide, but I can and do supplement your strength
when need demands. Rest, therefore, brother of mine; be
not unduly concerned at the plight of those you love. Trust
their own souls and know that they, alone, must learn the
needed lessons. Rest in peace.

August 1946

MY TRIED AND LOVED DISCIPLE:

The last few years have been years of agony and distress
for you, both physically and mentally. You have endured almost to the limit—in pain of body, in agony of anxiety,
through financial stringency and its wearing uncertainty, and
in the distress which comes from watching others suffer. You
have stood steady, and in your steadiness, serenity and
staunchness you have brought joy to my heart and strength
to the Ashram. I would have you know this.

You have worked off much karma, and whilst so working
you have served. In you I now have a disciple upon whom—
in your next life cycle—I can depend and lay responsibility,
and whose service therefore can be great. Disciples are apt to
forget that when they reach a point of complete dependabil-
ity (because the lower self has been obliterated and no longer
obstructs the vision) they lift a load off the Master's shoulders.

It is your due to tell you this, for your sufferings, unself-
ishly endured, have earned you the right of recognition. The

Lighted Way stretches ahead in still greater brightness, and you can enter into the brightness with confidence and surety.

This is the sumtotal of my brief word to you today; it will, I know, suffice. Take what I have said exactly as I say it and for what the words exactly mean, and know that I, your Master and your friend of many lives, am satisfied.

NOTE: *Seventeen months later, this disciple entered "into the brightness" of the inner Ashram.*

To D. H. B.

January 1940

This has been for you a hard year, my brother, and (as with your brother, D.P.R.) I seek not to add any fresh complications or considerations to the load which you already carry. You are, likewise, a clear-sighted disciple and there is small need for me to indicate the glamour which at this time disturbs your service. One thought, however, I would give you for careful pondering. The personality with its aims and ambitions, its intelligence and experience, in itself constitutes a glamour and one with a most potent effect upon you. When—as in your case—the personality is of a relatively high order and well integrated, the problem is then very real. This you realise, but in moments of service you are apt to fall into personality glamour without being aware of it, and those around you, serving with you, help you not.

Walk in the light, my brother. Let the light and radiance of the soul illumine your service and let your intellect not prove to be the dominating factor. Let spontaneous love and not a cultivated kindness condition your relations with your fellowmen. Be not glamoured by your own grasp of spiritual realities and by your spiritual knowledge. You have much to do in this life, and particularly in the next when this life's lessons have been learnt and assimilated. For this you must consciously prepare by the development of clear-sighted vision. I should perhaps point out to you that illusion more than glamour is your major difficulty for you are mentally polarised.

August 1940

MY BROTHER AND MY FRIEND:

So much have I said to you anent glamour that in this instruction I shall not deal with it. If you have not developed an instinctual reaction to it at this time, then there is little that I can say. This instinctual recognition of a fault, a quality, a tendency and, eventually, of a revelation is one of the first steps that the disciple takes towards the transcendence of the astral plane. I would point out to all of you (for glamour is general as well as particular) that *the dissipation of glamour brings revelation.*

For you, this is a time of interlude in service on a large scale and it is not easy for you to accept it. The conflict of the nations has brought about an exoteric interlude in spiritual action on earth. It is also causing (and this must not be forgotten) a deepening inner growth and a subjective spiritual reorganisation which—when the war is over—will bear much fruit. It is a period of preparation for disciples and is an opportunity for greatly increased inner, spiritual relation which later will produce that outer synthesis for which all men wait.

My message to you at this time is to retreat inward and achieve a deepening which will, in its turn, produce wisdom and truth. I do not urge you to cease any of your exoteric activities, but I urge you to carry them forward in a spiritual *silence.* Pursue your physical plane activities and your spiritual dharma but live within yourself an intense life of aspiration, of questioning and (if I might so express it) of questing. Become, brother of mine, spiritually dissatisfied for this will produce in you an intensification of the major qualities which I suggested you cultivate many years ago. There comes a time in the life of the disciple when he goes through a process of detaching himself esoterically (though not necessarily exoterically) from his chosen and designated task and from all past achievements and thereby learns his next step upon the Path of Liberation. This detachment, based on a phase of spiritual dissatisfaction engenders also humility of heart— a quality you much need to cultivate. Humility of head is

largely theoretical and imposed; humility of heart is practical and inherently spontaneous. I would have you ponder
on these distinctions for you will learn much thereby.

Consecrate therefore the period until the war ends to
the cultivation of *depth,* of detachment, of humility. This
process you will never regret, and in the coming period of
reconstruction you will then bring to the task much that you
cannot now give. As you know, it is the heart quality in
you which needs intensifying and purifying. Your first ray
astral body and mind produce too much of the will nature in
all your activities. You need to bear this in mind particularly
in connection with the astral body, for it is through that
body that the love energy of the soul must pour on its way to
the heart centre. It is, therefore, the second ray quality which
must—in connection with your first ray astral body—be imposed and that means two things in relation to you:

1. That your soul contact must be intensified.
2. That your life problem today involves primarily three
   factors:
      a. The soul .... second ray.
      b. The personality .... sixth ray.
      c. The astral body .... first ray.

This constitutes an interesting and somewhat unbalanced
triangle of energy, for the sixth ray personality is quick to
respond to soul energy but the effects work out in a fanatically oriented and powerful astral body. The consequent interplay produces much of the glamour which besets you and
which it is the task of your first ray mind to dissipate.

You are perhaps surprised at my use of the word "fanatical" in connection with you for you in no way regard yourself as a "fanatical devotee." Nor do I so regard you. The
fanaticism which you display is in respect to your own judgment where other people are concerned and it involves also
an almost proud dependence upon the wisdom which you
have undoubtedly developed during many lives. This tends
to give you a surety of opinion, in relation to others, which
conditions and your decision do not always warrant; it pro-

duces also a willingness to impose your own ideas and your judgment upon others when, my brother, it may be neither your duty nor your right so to do. This quality (oft found in disciples who are learning the nature of true spiritual humility) is esoterically called "the fanatic opposition of the wise person to the facts." This statement is most paradoxical but it is one which it would profit you much to consider and study.

Disciples like yourself (and they are fairly numerous and constitute some of the most promising material for training that we possess) are apt to be hard and unyielding—both to themselves and others. They have learnt much and surmounted much in the crucible of suffering and nothing has prevented them from a steadfast pursuit of reality. This capacity leads them to judge with harshness those who do not, apparently, achieve results or possess their own staying power. When such a disciple is naturally upon the teaching line as you are, he then handles opportunity on the basis of his truly enlightened personality but his methods are nevertheless personality ones and when—as in your case—the personality is on the sixth ray, one is apt to have a disciple fanatically identified with his own way of approach and one who expects others to go his way; he will be wedded to his own methods and anxious to impose them upon others. He is convinced that the techniques he employs are the best for all. All disciples have to learn to recognise the many ways, the many methods and the widely differently developed techniques. Their attitude (when they have learnt this lesson) is ever the fostering, the interpreting and the strengthening of the ways and the methods which suit those with whom they are associated and working, or those whom they are endeavoring to help. Remember this, my brother, and aim at decentralisation without diffusion. Think about this statement and seek to understand it and make it practical. If you can learn this lesson, there will open for you a wider field of opportunity. Decentralisation in mind from yourself and identification with the self in all should be your steady and practical objective.

To aid you in this, I suggest the following short meditation exercise which should be done each day at the close of your group practice. Its objective is the increase of the flow of energy to the heart centre, remembering always that the heart centre is a twelve-petalled lotus.

1. Visualisation exercise.
    a. Achieve alignment as rapidly as possible.
    b. Hold in the mind, imaginatively, the straight line of the spinal column, the head centre, the sutratma and the antahkarana—thus linking the centres in the body with the soul.
    c. Then carry the line which your imagination has constructed, from the centre at the base of the spine to the closed lotus bud in the centre of the twelve petalled egoic lotus.
2. Having done this, recognise your identity with all souls who constitute—in their entirety—the One Soul.
3. Then sound the O M as a soul, as far as in you lies, breathing it out from soul levels with no fixed objective in your mind. Do this six times.
4. Then sound the O M again after a pause (thus making seven in all) sending it out into the ajna centre and from there carry it down to the heart centre and *hold it there for later use.* Do this as a soul whose nature is love.
5. Then, bearing in mind that the heart centre is the repository of twelve forces or energies, seek to develop them by pondering upon the virtues through which these energies express themselves, taking one each month for a year.
    a. Group love, embracing individuals.
    b. Humility, signifying your personality attitude.
    c. Service, indicating your soul's preoccupation.
    d. Patience, signifying the embryonic immortality and persistence which is a soul characteristic.
    e. Life, or expressed activity which is the manifestation of love because it is essential dualism.
    f. Tolerance, which is the first expression of buddhic understanding.
    g. Identification with others, which is embryonic

fusion, carried eventually to synthesis when the head centre is developed.

h. Compassion, which is essentially the right use of the pairs of opposites.

i. Sympathy, which is the consequence of knowledge and of the unfoldment of the knowledge petals. Such energy then is in touch with the heart centre.

j. Wisdom, which is the fruit of love and indicates the awakening of the love petals of the egoic lotus.

k. Sacrifice, which is the giving of the heart's blood or life for others.

6. After a quiet meditation on one of these qualities of soul expression as they manifest upon the *physical* plane, sound the O M three times.

I would remind you that these soul qualities, which express themselves through the heart centre, must be interpreted esoterically and in terms of relation. Bear this in mind and as you meditate, seek ever the inner significance and not just the assembling of thought upon these qualities. Most of the thoughts and ideas which will come to you in this connection will be well known and so purely exoteric. There are, however, secondary meanings which are of real significance to the disciple though almost unknown to the average man. Endeavour to find these.

I would ask you, my brother, as a service to the group, each month to write a short paper on these twelve qualities as expressions of soul energies, thus giving your brothers the fruit of your month's meditation. Be of good courage and let not physical liability hinder your inner life and joy. Seek closer contact with me, your Master, and look for response.

August 1942

1. The call to some disciples is to live the triple life: to serve without surcease, to suffer on the plane of outer things and always dream. This is the call for you.

2. Ponder the distinction between the dream, the vision and the plan. They form the world of meaning.

3. To understand impels the heart detached. And with that understanding there awakes the will to dissipate the pain of those who tread the darker ways of earth. On these you do not walk, yet know and see.

4. The pen, when dipped in love and understanding, must be used by you for several years as your major mode of service. I tell you therefore, *Write*.

5. Search for the younger members of my group whom yet you do not know. Recognise them when you meet them on the way of life, and from your point of garnered wisdom and your trained experience give them a helping hand. Three await your service.

6. Stand by A.A.B. and aid her in the service of the Plan. The link is close between the Ashram of K.H. and mine. The lines of interplay must closer be.

September 1943

BROTHER OF MINE:

The call has now gone forth from your soul and from my Ashram to develop and evolve your own definitely planned service, and therefore to begin the task of finding those whom you can help—not only in this life but primarily in the next. I start with this statement because I seek to say something which will arrest your attention and give incentive to the next few years of your life.

The sixfold statement which I gave you last year was, if you have not ascertained this for yourself, full of information, indicative of your soul's desire or plan for you, and full also of esoteric symbolism. It is a symbolism which holds for you the key to the future. I would like to take these six sentences in this instruction and give you a deeper insight into them. They hold for you the blueprint of your future, and particularly are they the blueprint for your next incarnation. Study them afresh from that angle.

What, my brother, has been the keynote of your present life? I refer here to the obvious personality keynote. Is it not

perhaps and above aught else *frustration?* Plans which have
not materialised; dreams which have not come true; friends
who have consistently failed to understand; lack of appreciation from those who should justly have given it to you;
apparently no situation in which your deep knowledge and
understanding could be made available. Learning and esoteric knowledge have both apparently (I said apparently, my
brother) failed you. A home life which has not measured up
to your earlier dreams and a physical body which limits all
you have sought to do. You likewise see the years slipping
away, and from the angle of the personality there seems little
to show for it all. Such is one side of the picture, is it not?

But what about the other side, my friend and co-worker?
This, it is easy to overlook, because from the angle of personality appraisement it appears so nebulous and evasive and
dependent for verification upon those rare moments when
you contact consciously your soul, and then suddenly *know.*
But this happens none too often. Let me tell you in words
what that other side appears to us, knowing that you will believe me and that what I say may give you a fresh and living
grip on life and enough confidence to enable you to make the
coming years increasingly fruitful.

This has been for you an incarnation wherein certain
major happenings have taken place. Your soul has, for one
thing, taken possession of your personality and gripped your
mind (a major determining factor in all processes connected
with reincarnation), and has done this in such a way that you
will return to incarnation when the time comes with a sense
of convinced awareness. Secondly, you have stepped upon
the Path of Accepted Discipleship and are definitely in preparation for initiation—which initiation it is for you to discover. A hint lies for you in the fact that frustration has been
the keynote of your personality life, and that *divine indifference* is your quality objective. Do you realise the importance
of those two major happenings? Again, you have learnt the
meaning of pain, and again divine indifference is your goal.
You have made many contacts and helped many more than
you know, and you have thus established links—for what
purpose, my brother? May it not be that each life that you

have touched with helping and with strength indicates to you those who may form the nucleus of your own group in a later life experience?

One of the things which I shall have to indicate to the senior members of this particular group of chelas in my Ashram (as their teaching is carried forward after the preparatory personal processes have been duly taught) is the Technique of Magnetism, which is the clue to the manifestation of all Ashrams. It is through spiritual magnetism and through pure love, impersonally applied, that an Ashram is assembled. It is a technique which you must learn and are beginning to learn, but the motive for so learning is now presented to you. You have made many friends and evoked much love, and that is a lasting process entailing responsibility which may not be ignored. You are learning to know me and you have ever the staunch love and confidence of A.A.B., who has a peculiarly deep appreciation of you based on ancient work together in past lives. You have also gained a little knowledge as to the intent of my Ashram, as far as you are concerned. You have worked off much karma (far more than you think) and stand much freer than was deemed possible when you entered into incarnation this life. From the angle of your soul your life has been triumphant. From the angle of your personality it has been frustrated. Which matters, my brother? Perhaps neither matters from the angle of the initiate vision and the attitude of the trained disciple.

"In neither pain nor joy is liberation found.
In neither dark nor light will the spiritual sun appear.
The pairs of opposites distract the eyes of men.
Only the single eye directs the steps
Of the initiate upon the Way."

Will you ponder my presentation of these two contrasting aspects of your life, and then pass on to fuller light and service?

I told you in my last instruction that you were called to live the triple life of ceaseless serving, of constant pain, and of endless dreaming. I started off in that statement with the enunciation of that which is factual in your life. Let us see which are the other statements of fact pointed out by me, for in their sumtotal your future integration, development and service lie hidden. Let me, therefore, enumerate:

1. Service and pain and dreaming are your present lot.
2. You do not walk as yet the darker ways of earth. For that hard task you are in preparation, for some must serve this way and only the strong and tried can thus be trusted. Regard all that has happened to you as special training, what might be called "basic training," in order that your future initiate service may be carried out according to plan. That service is the choice of your soul. It is not imposed upon you by me or by the will of the Ashram or by any other factor save your soul.
3. The use of the pen in writing is at present your major mode of service. Find your own people, and write that which will inspire and help. Let love speed your fingers and light travel between you and those you seek to serve. Therefore, my brother, write. You have the gift and the time and a wide open door for impersonal service.
4. Search for those who are not yet in my Ashram, who are still probationers, and lead them on. Prepare them for the transition which they face when they step off the Probationary Path onto the Path of Discipleship. Have you found and recognised the three who await your guidance and your help?
5. Continue, as ever, to stand by A.A.B. The reason for this is that my Ashram is an affiliate of the Ashram of K.H. I would ask you to study what I say to R.S.U., for it applies also to you.

I have here clearly given you certain instructions which will only prove their effectiveness in your development and their ability to open doors for you when accepted and obeyed. I can but indicate and suggest from my standpoint of greater knowledge, but it is for you to recognise the usefulness of the suggestions and to move forward in line with them.

I have a most interesting theme for your thought on the distinction between "the dream, the vision and the Plan." There are many ways in which these distinctions can be approached, and the interpretations will be dependent upon the status of the thinker. For you, a disciple in preparation for initiation, as are all in my group—accepted disciples in training—I will suggest the following lines of approach.

To you, *the dream* is the reaction of a high grade imparted knowledge and world need for service. The personality dreams of using that knowledge and meeting that need, and as he thinks of serving he thus becomes a server and a teacher. *The vision* is the realisation of the goal (embodied by the particular initiation for which you are being prepared); according to the status of the initiate, so will be the vision. It is the sensing of the united purpose and the spiritual intention of those who have already taken the initiation for which the disciple is being prepared. I cannot express this more clearly, as it is not permitted, but once you are clear in your own mind for which initiation you are being prepared, you can then ascertain for yourself (and will, perforce, have to ascertain) the objective, secret scope and field of service, plus the esoteric quality of those who have passed through a certain door and undergone a certain expansion of consciousness. Remember that initiation does not simply enhance and deepen the soul quality; it does not simply enable the personality to express soul powers, and thus emphasise and draw out the best that is in the disciple and his service, but it makes available to him, progressively, forces and energies of which he has had no previous knowledge and which he must learn to use as an initiate of a certain degree upon the Lighted Way. It reveals to him worlds of being hitherto unsuspected and unrecognised, with which he must learn to cooperate, and it integrates him more definitely into the "lighted area" of our planetary life, bringing fresh revelation and vision but making the unlighted area dark indeed.

The Plan is as much of the hierarchical intent (as an entire and whole picture) as the initiate can grasp, plus an understanding of the part which he, as an individual server, must play. There is more to it than that, but I fear to complicate certain simple truths which I seek to have you grasp. The clarity of the vision and the grasp of the Plan, it might be added, are dependent upon the conscious and intelligent construction of the antahkarana. You will see, therefore, why I have asked this group within my Ashram to study the antahkarana instructions as given in the papers of the advanced section of the Arcane School. All of you have already begun to build this bridge; I seek to have you comprehend how and why.

So, my brother, see your life pattern more clearly. See the underlying purpose of all happenings in the past, and endeavour then to grasp the picture of the future, and thus make your dreams come true, because you see the vision and are cooperating with the Plan; thus materialise the vision and work at intelligent understanding of the Plan. Let naught—fatigue, frustration, people or circumstance—deflect you from your purpose. Carry all forward in silence and with love.

Take the four words: Dream, Vision, Plan, Realisation, and make them the theme for your meditation work during the four quarters of the coming year. If you will, write during this year four papers on these four words, but only write after three months' quiet reflection upon each word, and from the angle of the personality—illumined by the Spiritual Triad. I would have you note the wording of this request with especial care. This will tend to bring in more than just soul wisdom, for the angle of the spiritual will and of spiritual love (of which both soul will and soul love are only the reflection) will begin to enter in.

Go forward with joyful expectation. Get ready for your future service in this life and in the next; seek to fulfil instructions and learn to come and go between my Ashram and that of K.H., for in the one your service will appear, and in the other your love will be deepened and your heart become more understanding.

November 1944

MY FRIEND AND CO-DISCIPLE:

I would have you note this mode of address. That we are friends you have known for many years. That we are co-disciples may be, as yet, a somewhat new idea. As a wide generalisation, the theory is accepted that all in or affiliated with the Hierarchy are disciples, and therefore in a close relation to each other. I am here, however, using these words in a new sense—new, I mean, to you.

There are within the ranks of disciples certain of them who have been singled out for a peculiar and particular relation to the Christ. Such a one is the Master K.H., Who is slated (is that not the word I should use?) to fill higher office when the Christ moves on to other work than that of the World Teacher. I myself hold a similar position to the Master K.H. Through K.H. and through myself and through two other Masters, a number of disciples of high standing, and some neophytes or disciples of lesser rating, are upon the line of this contact or designated service. By the training given, these disciples of high or low degree (yet all accepted in the technical sense) are rendered singularly sensitive to the Christ force. Curiously enough, these particular disciples are selected to take this training because of their interest in esoteric values, and not because they possess a particularly loving nature, as might have been expected. They are usually on the wisdom aspect of the second ray and not on the love aspect.

The work which it is planned for them later to undertake will eventually prove so difficult that it is essential that they start with a strong bias towards *wisdom*. Contact with the "Ashrams of loving intent" (as certain Ashrams close to the aura or periphery of Shamballa are called) suffices later to evoke the love aspect in greater fullness, enabling the disciples, therefore, to present a balanced instrument to the Divine Organiser of their future work. Just what this work will be is not for me to say. It is connected with the training to be given neophytes and aspirants in the next race, where the average aspirant to discipleship will be expected to be as intuitive and motivated by pure reason as the aspirant today has to be mental. Technically speaking, that means that the buddhic plane will be the focus or place of growth, and those who train disciples will work from the plane of atma or pure spiritual will, just as today they work from the plane of buddhi or of rational unity. Ponder on that last phrase.

The relation of the Christ to the entire Hierarchy is that of Supreme Master. His group of disciples includes all initiates over the third initiation. But through these initiates and certain of the Masters, and at their suggestion, He is slowly selecting a band of lesser disciples who can be trained for special work during the next two or three lives. Of these, you can be one. The first phase of the training given is to impose at least one life of most drastic discipline and difficult circumstances, not karmically ordained but of an educational and disciplinary nature. You have had two such lives and have consequently built up and established a persistent endurance and a trained response to events which is a guarantee to the watching Master that your stability is assured and immovable.

Much further training necessarily is demanded, but there is little that you can add to that already given during this life. The next life will see a continuance of the teaching. You can, however, develop within yourself a more conscious comprehension of the nature of "wise love." This is love free from emotion or devotion; it is love aware of the objects of love as they essentially *are* and a love which is able to see in character and temperament the working out of karma. It is difficult for even an advanced disciple at this time to comprehend the nature of man when he has dropped all *physical* conflict out of his conscious life experience and when the urge to combat (upon the *physical* plane) has faded completely out of the human consciousness. The field of battle then shifts to other realms of awareness, and the effect of this —within humanity as a whole—is the cause of the choosing of this special group through whom the problems emerging out of the changed conditions can be solved and handled.

Men will have to be trained for a state of discipleship even newer and different to the type which I have presented at this time and which intrinsically differs from that previously given.

One of the major needs in your nature is the evocation of a new and fiery incentive. For this reason, I have (as I seldom do) indicated the future ahead of you. You and F.C.D. are both numbered among the "friends of Christ," as this special group is called, and are upon a peculiar path of training. Step by step, the nature of this Path will be revealed to you, and, little by little, you will perceive the quality of the unfoldments which presented opportunity can give you.

Be not mistaken, my brother. This does not mean that in this present vehicle and with your present equipment you can contact the Master of all the Masters; nor does it mean that your advancement is ahead of that of your group brothers. There are those in this group and in my Ashram who are ahead of you, if such inexact terms can be used. The Christ, through your own Master and in no other way, knows you. Not yet can you know Him. You can, however, ponder upon the significance of what I have said; you can learn to distinguish within yourself the dual aspects of your soul ray energy, love and wisdom; you can record when either of these two forces is functioning, and which one it is. A closer study of your five rays (literally only four) will aid you to do this, particularly as your seventh ray physical vehicle will greatly facilitate the process. This seventh ray is a ray of a dual activity, because through its means the energy of the soul and of the personality can be brought consciously into relation, and this more easily than on the other rays, once the disciple is freed from glamour. Thus there can be built a true expression of the life content—from the angle of a long soul experience. This may sound to you somewhat ambiguous, but the statement is by no means as vague as it appears. It should provide you with ideas for reflection.

For the remainder of your life twelve seed phrases can provide the theme of your recurrent meditation—either for a year of twelve months or for twelve years. The longer and the more earnestly you reflect upon them, the richer will be your life expression, and that I know is what you yourself desire.

1. Relation to the inner Ashram.
2. The friendship of the Christ.
3. The way of the intuition.
4. The source of your life expression.
5. Wisdom, blended with love.
6. Reaction to the consciousness of the Hierarchy.
7. The "Ashram of Loving Intent."
8. An out-going consciousness, esoterically understood.
9. The "Lighted Way of the Buddha and the Christ."
10. The pinnacle whereon the thorny crown is won.
11. The *moment* of perceptive understanding.
12. The quality of the perceptive race of men.
   (This refers to the future race.)

These phrases have a significance which is not immediately apparent; they are what I might be permitted to call "sparking" concepts, and they can be revolutionary in their effect, if you reflect upon them correctly and persistently. They are intended to make you responsive to the different currents of energy to which those who are to undergo a special training to fit them to form the special group of the "friends of Christ" must submit themselves. This right you have earned. It is my present task to aid you on this way of peculiar training.

Have you ever thought, my brother, that just as there is a discipline of pain and of sorrow, there may also be a discipline of joy and of achievement? This is a thought worthy of attention. Men need these days to learn this new truth, and its perception will greatly change human consciousness. That which is bliss *is* today here or on its way, and the disciples and aspirants of this present time must be taught how to recognise and implement it. Again—this is a right which you have definitely earned.

I shall be in touch with you, my brother. This instruction

is not long, but—coupled with that last given to you—it gives you a prospect of a possibility which should cheer you on your way. You can regard what I have told you as the reward of a life of patient endurance, of overcoming and of acceptance. It should also enable you to bring a fuller tide of loving understanding. You will thus enhance your usefulness.

August 1946

MY BROTHER:

I approach you today with such complete understanding that I believe you will immediately recognise its reality. My last instruction to you is distant and remote in its implications, and you are today wondering if I meant all that I said there and if your spiritual status is as I stated. It most certainly is, and on that statement I would have you take your stand. Will you understand me if I say that one of the guarantees to you of the truth of the past instruction is that this instruction will be relatively short? The last instruction was the important one. In that instruction I emphasised two things:

1. That you were at the point in evolution where a definite rapport with the Christ was possible.
2. That you were in process of preparation for taking a certain important initiation (as, my brother, are several of this group).

Your reaction to this was normal—as far as your human nature was concerned—but distinctly undesirable. It evoked in you a realisation that was false in many ways, but you have often been susceptible to glamour; you felt that your status was ahead of the majority of your brothers and that (because of this) you had specialised work to do for me. You took the position that, in the eventuality of A.A.B.'s passing over, you were slated to take her place as far as this group is concerned. You gave that impression to some of the group members you met last year and you gave that impression to A.A.B. She was deeply concerned over this, for she has for you a very deep love and understanding as well as a clear perception of your status as a disciple.

Since that time you have yourself been inwardly disturbed, because you are fundamentally sound and correct in your reactions; for this reason I would ask you to forget all this past history and any past reactions to glamour, and to regard the present as the only factor of importance.

The new seed group is discontinued. My contact with you and with some other members of the group is *exoterically* not disturbed, and therefore (as long as A.A.B. is alive in the physical sense) you may, at intervals, hear from me. Subjectively, you are ever in touch, as is F.B. and three or four others in the group. The rest of the group members are linked with the Ashram, and therefore with myself, and because time is of no account esoterically, their relation remains unimpaired and is preserved intact over whatever years are necessary to *re-establish* their occult obedience or their true interest.

You need to bear in mind, my brother, that your second ray emphasis is that of wisdom and not of love. Therefore the love quality is not so potent, and this presents difficulties to you of which you are curiously unaware. It is your task—at any cost—to develop the love quality. The wisdom attitude makes you hard, and you have not yet balanced it—in intensity—by the love quality. This hardness you *must* transmute on a large and general scale. You can transmute for individuals you love or for whom you feel a sense of responsibility. It is this quality of love which you must develop before you see the Christ—not simply as an initiate taking an initiation, but as a disciple warranting His attention. You see now the purpose of my remarks in an earlier instruction? Today, few disciples realise that the Christ has two relationships to them: that of initiation, and another—far rarer—that of One Whom they may consult in connection with their work. This permission to approach is only accorded when love and wisdom are balanced and equal. This is not so in your case as yet, and I would have you bear this point in mind. Your personality ray is a serious handicap to you, not because of its developed aspect but because of its crystallised assurance aspect. A sixth ray personality is ever sure of his recognition of truth, and is consequently very easily glamoured, and when this is coupled (as in your case) with a first ray astral body, the difficulty which confronts you as a disciple is very great.

Therefore, brother of mine, your immediate problem is one of glamour, plus a feeling of distress because you know that A.A.B. and I have recognised this glamour. We have, but may I assure you that it makes no difference in our understanding, love and appreciation of you. It may be a long time since I, personally, was overcome by glamour, and it may be a short time since A.A.B. succumbed, but neither of us has forgotten the difficulties encountered or lost our horror of glamour; we are therefore *not* critical, and upon that fact rest back.

May I recall to you an instruction I gave you in 1938 upon indifference? Ponder upon it again.

Go ahead, brother of mine, in our service. Every contact has its unrealised importance; give of yourself, therefore, and not only through others. You can induce others to work, but *give of yourself* and see (as far as is possible and common-sense dictates) everyone who seeks to contact you, and this with love and willing understanding. This is hard for you, but it is essential for the development of that loving understanding which is the complement of wisdom. F.C.D. needs to develop wisdom as the complement of love.

As regards your meditation during future years, build up its structure yourself, laying emphasis upon three points: the Christ, the need for the balancing factor of love, and *outgoing* service. I give you no outline. You have outgrown that technique and are capable—as a soul—of formulating your own.

Above all else, curb your critical mind and cease all harsh judgments. When in difficulty, go or write to A.A.B. She knows from wide experience, and she understands.

You will again hear from me, either through A.A.B. or through the medium of your own soul.

November 1948

MY BROTHER AND MY FELLOW WORKER:

I am deeply concerned in this communication to say something which will be of real service to you at this crisis in your life of discipleship. Disciples of all degrees are now being tested and tried out in preparation for the work they should do, prior to the reappearance of the Christ. Your whole life has been in reality a preparation for the work which it is hoped that you will do. This life has been for you what we call in the Hierarchy "a life of dual possibilities." When that is the case, a most difficult setting upon the physical plane is presented to the disciple and he faces two possible lines of activity:

1. He can decide to adjust himself to the circumstances and give his whole attention to their surmounting (which in this case means changing them) and he, therefore, submits to the wear and tear of life, and to the constant consideration of karmic unfoldments within his personality scope. He has no time for outstanding service but regards the period of incarnation as an interlude wherein karma is worked off.

2. Or—he accepts the seemingly impossible situation and determines that nothing in his personality or his circumstances shall deter him from the active service of humanity. He, therefore, handles both the situations and opportunity from an inner point of enlightenment and from a sustained peaceful position within the Ashram.

In what I am here saying, I am considering only an accepted disciple such as yourself.

You chose and have faithfully followed the second method of handling this present incarnation. With a frail and seriously injured physical body and a partner who is ever the cause of constant concern (though withal you owe her much), you have gone ahead with the task of a working disciple; you have done much good and have helped our work greatly and —as the Master said—the Hierarchy is never ungrateful, for gratitude is the hallmark of an enlightened soul and a basic releasing agent from an occult and scientific angle. I am not ungrateful to you, my brother; I hope to move you on into a closer relation to myself provided you succeed in handling a somewhat difficult situation with which you are now confronted and dominate an aspect of your nature which *must* be controlled before the move I contemplate in connection with you can be consummated.

At this time I have the responsibility of deciding whether you will accept what I say and then set in to change certain attitudes or whether you will refuse to recognise their existence and go your own way. That would make it impossible for me to offer you an esoteric possibility which will next life orient you in such a manner that, when you face the Initiation of Decision, the Path which you must follow will clearly appear to you.

I wonder whether you have ever studied the reasons why the various members of the groups of nine stopped their work with me and are not (for this short period) participants in the work of my Ashram. Please note that I do not use the phrase "participants in spiritual work." Many of them are still just as spiritually motivated. An Ashram exists for work and not primarily for training disciples. That training is necessarily given, but *the prime object of an Ashram is to accomplish a particular phase of work.* This is a sentence which I would beg you here to pause and reflect upon. It is of prime importance to you at this time.

The work of the Hierarchy is an integrated whole; each Ashram within the Hierarchy is dedicated to that whole and to that particular aspect of it which can be best carried out through its members of all degrees—the disciples in training for some initiation or another. To insure that the work goes forward as desired, necessarily (as I said) the individual disciple or initiate receives training, injunctions as to character development and personality attitudes. A close study of *Discipleship in the New Age* (Vol. I) will disclose to you that it was on this point of personality correction—if I may use so

harsh a word for the hints and suggestions I gave—that de-
fection occurred. In spite of sincerity, dedication and wide
knowledge, and even a subjective recognition of the accuracy
of what I said, they would not accept it; rebellion set in; self-
justification through rationalisation took place and temporarily—very temporarily—they became inactive, though
still disciples on the periphery of my Ashram.

If I now address to you certain comments upon your attitude the past three years, towards the work which has its
spiritual focal point in New York, do I risk losing you after
all these years? Will you, for the remainder of your life, go
your own way? I am going to believe that such will not be the
case.

As you well know, my work in the outer world has taken
the form of three major activities. . . . You have done much
to help with this work and the door of opportunity stands
wide open to you, provided the work is held true to the
original picture, given prior to World War II. There are,
however, one or two things you are apt to forget.

1. The centre from whence the Goodwill work goes out
   and the source of its spiritual potency is located in
   New York at this time, though later—if deemed wise
   —it may be moved to London. This I mentioned several years ago and I would remind you also that both
   these cities are among the five focal points of spiritual
   energy through which hierarchical activities can be set
   in motion. Your city is not.
2. The major task of the Goodwill work is threefold:
   a. It must mobilise *world goodwill*.
   b. It is responsible for the distribution of the message
      The Reappearance of the Christ and for a great
      deal of the work preparatory to His coming.
   c. It must aid in drawing the attention of the masses
      —as far as may be—to *the problems of humanity*, and
      thus help create the thoughtform of solution.

This F.B. and A.A.B. have already realised and are laying
plans in line with the above. All over the world before long

(and already in different countries) *much* is being accomplished by students and others, always under instruction from New York, so that their work fits in with the general picture and the plans of the New York workers.

3. There are, my beloved brother, three things in connection with your relation to the work which I would like to call to your attention:

a. You have a strong feeling that all the Goodwill work should be completely divorced from what you choose to call occultism. Do you mean from the spiritual centre, the Hierarchy? If this is done, in what way will the goodwill work you propose to do differ from the thousands of goodwill movements so ardently and actively working in the world today?

This A.A.B. told you, since which time you have never spoken to her, bade her farewell even by phone or written her a letter. These personality details matter not to her and are of no importance except as they indicate a strong reaction on your part of almost violent disagreement. F.B. and A.A.B. have done what they could to "absorb" you into the work of the new cycle, but hitherto quite unsuccessfully.

b. You tend to emasculate the work and rob it of all potency by a drastic elimination of any word or phrase or paragraph which could be considered to have an occult meaning or implication. Yet, my brother, in the years 1932-1936 the goodwill literature went out practically as dictated by me and it met with enormous and overwhelming success. It had the spirit and the rhythm of the Hierarchy behind it. Today the demand for things esoteric and occult and of the new era is greater still, and the unique thing which the Goodwill work has to offer is the *Plan* for humanity which the Hierarchy is seeking to implement.

c. Then, my co-disciple, you have lately succumbed to

two personality faults or weaknesses which seriously hinder your work for me, and in the Ashram, and for humanity.

You are again intensely critical of all who do not see things your way and—when their ideas do not coincide with your conception as to how the work should be done—you refuse to cooperate. I would remind you that the Members of the Hierarchy are highly individual even though relatively free from personality reactions. Each Ashram has its part to play in materialising the Plan and some project to carry through connected with that Plan. Sometimes this will require the joint cooperation of two or three Ashrams. All the senior workers called in to help may not see eye to eye with the Master responsible for a certain aspect of the Plan, but (when united in a cooperative task) they work under the direction of the Master Who is responsible. Here lies a great deal of your difficulty.

You want to work your own way many thousand miles away from Headquarters where I have established my work, instead of working out the plans as proposed to you.

We come, therefore, not only to the field of criticism in which you find yourself stranded but we come to that latent ambition which, you have oft admitted over the years, is perhaps your deepest rooted failing. . . . You are anxious to see the new seed group members take control of the organisational situation should anything happen to A.A.B., forgetting that the work of that group is mainly to create a subjective channel of spiritual love, light and power—a point to which few of the members pay any attention at all. You would like to run the work with your own chosen group of workers. You are not working with love and in cooperation with the workers at Headquarters; you are forgetting, are you not, that unless such a plan as the Goodwill work is founded and engineered by a group of disciples who are working *in the closest rapport* with each other and (in the case of *world goodwill)* with the Hierarchy (via my Ashram and the Ashrams of the Masters M., K.H., and R.), the work cannot go forward as desired.

My brother, your choice is clear and one of two paths is open to you. You can work with loving cooperation with F.B. and the other goodwill workers so that there is unity of approach and uniformity of technique, or else—you can create, engineer and run your own goodwill movement, which may turn out to be a big thing numerically but a poor little thing specifically because you are not in your place and doing your work in my Ashram as had been your soul's decision. This latter choice is *not* what I seek to see happen but at present you stand isolated and relatively useless between these two alternatives.

The new cycle is upon us, brother of mine; there is no time now for personality plans, for criticisms and for disagreements. I have asked you to cooperate with those who have been asked by me to undertake the task of bringing the Goodwill movement to the world.

An era of frustration has swept the world, due to certain planetary influences; the work that I have sought to do has consequently suffered. This period will not last. I need you in the new cycle and in the new expanding work. There is no place today for personal ambition, personal criticisms, hard feelings or self-pity.

Deepen your spiritual life, my brother. Much that interests you is not constructive. Also the cleaning up of your country by ardent search for undesirable citizens can well be carried on by others than yourself. Your work is and must be for the Hierarchy and the furthering of its plans. Take again your place as an outpost of my consciousness in the activities of my organisations. Be humble. F.B. needs you but he knows that the Goodwill work is *not* an American movement but an international one; he has travelled much and seen the need. This you cannot really know as your life circumstances and your karma have confined you largely to one single and distant locality. Broaden your horizon and bring in Europe, Australia and distant Asia and—as your vision quickens—you will arrive at understanding. Contribute your ideas and suggestions to the reservoir of plans at Headquarters and learn to consider and take part in other people's plans besides your own.

What more can I say to you, my brother? We are ancient co-workers and those with whom you are associated in New York are your true co-workers, far more than those well-intentioned aspirants you seek to dominate in your environment. Work closely with your co-disciples and with the Ashram members. They all love you and want your cooperation. A.A.B. wants to see certain things accomplished in the relatively brief interlude which is left to her. Will you help? F.B. is going to need you and many like you as the work expands in the new cycle. Will you stand by him, by my work, and by me?

My love goes out to you. Much in your present situation and spiritual dilemma reminds me of myself when I was in preparation for the third initiation; therefore, I understand and with this thought I leave you and will not fail you.

To D. I. J.

January 1940

For you, my brother, I have somewhat the same message as I gave to S.C.P. Free yourself from the glamour of inherited ideas and national concepts and prejudices. The world picture is clearer and more beautiful than you know, seeing it as you do today through the windows of prejudice, pain and limitation. If I sound harsh in so speaking, it is simply because I, the Master D.K., value what you will be able to do and be when you have released yourself from the glamour of prejudice. You have made real progress in this condition but there is much still to be done and this your heart of love can accomplish once you see clearly and with understanding the true nature of your glamour. There are many points of view, coming from the many types of men, the many races and the many nations and grades of human beings. Who, my brother, are you to determine what is right and which point of view is correct? The Hierarchy sees the beauty in them all. Ponder on this and seek to see it too.

August 1940

MY BROTHER:

A.A.B. has told me of your comment on the quality of my communications with the group, that you felt the need of a greater expression of love. There was no need for her to tell me as I had "listened in" on the group (as you call it in radio language) and I saw your thought, but she wanted to ask me to deal with this matter as it will be of service to the group; she also sensed your sincere desire.

I wonder, my brother, if you realise that the basis of your feeling lies in your reaction to the short instruction I gave you earlier in the year? This you did not like, nor did you truly agree with what I said, nor have you really freed yourself from the prejudices to which I referred and for two reasons:

1. Your judgment is clouded by your resentment to what you, perhaps naturally, regarded as a criticism.
2. Your sensitivity and your reaction to glamour tunes you in very frequently on a certain section of public opinion and when this happens (as it is happening today) you are no longer a free agent.

My underlying thought when giving you that instruction was to awaken you to the fact that your feelings and loyalties are based on a class idea and on class resentment and not on clear thinking through to the facts which should condition all loyalties and partisanships. It is not the objectives or the decisions of those loyalties with which I am dealing. Those are entirely your own affair and are of no real importance in the light of eternity, but I am endeavouring to awaken you to the condition of your emotional reactions and to the quality which motivated you—not clear thinking and then decision, but prejudice, resentment and fear.

But today I shall not deal with this. You know enough to deal with it yourself or at least to realise the truth of my criticism of your *attitude* but not of your decision. That which works out into expression upon the physical plane is not the concern of the members of the Hierarchy. They concern themselves with motives and predispositions and it was with these that I was dealing.

Brother of old, we have worked together for some time—for some years. I have chosen you for instruction and to be part of my group of disciples and this choice, being accepted and responded to by you, indicates relationship, activity, and an allegiance which will confront you for many lives. Have I ever, since the time that our relationship started in this life, failed to meet your need when that need was of a spiritual nature, determining character and conditioning the future? Is not such a response on my part an expression of true love? Love is not making the object of the love feel comfortable superficially. If I induced that reaction in you, I would not merit your confidence and trust and in the long run I would not thus hold your respect. Love is far-seeing wisdom which seeks to keep alive in the object of that love those sensitivities which will guarantee safe progress. Love is, therefore, guarding, stimulating and protective. But it is not a personal matter. It is a positive protection, but does not lead to a negative attitude of being cared for on the part of the one who is the recipient of the love and protection. It is the stimulating power of divine love which I seek to pour out upon you and upon all whom I serve as Master and Teacher. This will lead you wisely to protect yourself from glamour, illusion and personality reactions, also from error and prejudice in order the better to serve both Humanity and the Hierarchy. Ponder on this.

These are days of terrific stress and strain, far greater and more far reaching than you can guess or grasp. We who work on the inner side of life and who deal with the mass movements and reactions of humanity, and who have kept the light shining with radiance no matter how dark the night of human affairs may be, have ourselves to rest back on the understanding selflessness of our disciples. We have not the time or the inclination (in the light of greater need) to waste in useless gestures or loving phrases, of teaching so tactfully worded that much of its import might be lost, and in making our disciples aware of their *personal* relation to us. There *is* a personal relation or you would not be in my group, but it is of secondary importance to your group interrelation and activity. There is no need for me thus to explain but it seemed advisable once and for all to make clear that my failure (should I call it that, my brother?) to express love in words to any of you and also my expressed intention to waste no time in indicating weaknesses in character and areas of failure in performance must not be and should not be interpreted by you as harshness, failure to understand or a detachment so cold that my very impersonality would defeat its own ends. What all of you need to grasp with greater clarity, both as individuals and as a group, is the present need of humanity and the law of cycles. The urgency of the time and the uniqueness of the opportunity seem little understood by most of you.

Again, my brother, have you realised that if I evoked from you a personality devotion I should be hindering you and in no way demonstrating to you that soul love which actuates all my reactions to each and all of you. Your sixth ray personality would respond to such an attitude on my part and then—what would that feed and develop in you? Just self-satisfaction and a settling back upon the fact of relationship and not upon the fact of the soul. It would produce an increase of the glamour to which you are prone. In past lives, your progress has been from one devotion to another, from one position of pledged fealty to another. In this life, you are faced with the opportunity to free yourself from such personality reactions and relations and become stabilised in soul behaviour. It is to this end that I help you. Disciples would do well to appreciate somewhat the problem of the Master. He has to watch the effect of all the energy which flows from Him to His disciples and to guard against its stimulating unduly their personalities, and thus tend to the evocation of personality reactions.

Will you therefore rest back on facts and lived experience and waste not time in wishing and in emotional reactions? You have made much progress in this life, my brother. You are not young but that, in your case, need not deter you from further search for liberation, based on a planned relinquishing. Sixth ray aspirants have a particularly hard task at the close of this Piscean age, due to the sixth ray expression of the Christian era. Today the energies are concretising and working through that which is old and honoured, that which is "conditioned by gold" (as the saying is) and that which belongs to a passing age—an age which should pass. This affects also your sixth ray personality and, consequently, from many angles your allegiances and your loyalties are motivated by the sixth ray and based on personality decisions and not on the illumined vision of the soul. The fact, however, that you have broken with orthodoxy where theology is concerned indicates (to us who watch) a great measure of emancipation and of emerging soul control. You will find, if your intuition gets more dynamic and your first ray astral body (the ray of government and politics) does not unduly affect you, that an increasing measure of thought release will be yours.

In this connection and in order to enlarge your perspective, I would add that Christian Science is a fifth ray expression of thought and was one of the effects of the incoming fifth ray life. A very large number of Christian Scientists are either fifth or sixth ray egos, for this particular school of thought was one of the means whereby the fanatical emotional idealism (engendered by the potency of the sixth ray influence dominant for so many centuries) could be offset, and the mental grasp of truth and of life carefully fostered. Under its influence, the stage was set on which many mystics could begin to organise their mental bodies and discover that they had minds which could be used, and thus be prepared for the occult way. It is therefore a masculine or positive influence in its general effect, but its positivity is in relation to the personality—the mind as the factor dominating the human expression. It can, and eventually will, be negative to the soul, revealing the higher mind. It is interesting whilst considering the pairs of opposites (the negative and positive factors) to study the following groupings:

	Spirit	Positive
I.	Soul	Balancing
	Personality	Negative

	Higher mind	Positive
II.	Soul	The point of balance
	Lower mind	Negative

	Lower mind	Positive
III.	Emotional nature	Field for balancing
	Brain	Negative

You have, in the above groupings, three great fields of reflection. These groupings can also be worked out in many ways. It must be borne in mind that (as H.P.B. points out) any such groupings, such as the seven principles, will vary according to the point in evolution of the investigator.

I will give you now a personal meditation which will serve, I hope, to lift the life of the astral body out of the solar plexus into the heart centre, thus breaking down some of the limitations which will disappear when the astral body and the sixth ray astral force are transmuted and love of the whole takes the place of love of the part.

1. Take up the position mentally of the Observer. Your fourth ray mind should enable you to observe with detachment the conflict between the personality and the soul.

2. Then, noting the dim light of the personality and the bright radiance of the soul, observe then another duality, i.e., the bright and powerful light or influence of the solar plexus and the wavering, fluctuating light of the heart centre.

3. Then, through the power of the imagination, focus your consciousness in the radiant soul and hold it there steadily, linking the soul and the head centre, again by the power of thought.

4. Then sound the O M three times, breathing out the energy of the soul into the threefold personality and bringing that energy to rest (as in a reservoir of force) in the ajna centre. There hold it, enhancing the light of the personality with the radiance of the soul.

5. Next say:
    "The light of the soul puts out the dim light of the personality as the sun puts out the flame of a small fire. Soul radiance takes the place of personality light. The sun is substituted for the moon."

6. Then, definitely throw the light and energy of the soul into the heart centre and believe—through the power of the creative imagination—that it evokes such a powerful, vibratory activity that it acts like a magnet in relation to the solar plexus. The energy of the solar plexus is lifted up or drawn up into the heart centre and is there transmuted into soul love.

7. Then still as the Observer, see the reversal of the earlier process. The solar plexus is dimmed. The radiance of the heart is substituted. The light of the soul remains unchanged but the light of the personality is greatly brightened.

8. Then again as the soul, united with the personality, sound the O M seven times, breathing it out into your environment.

This, my brother, is more of a visualisation exercise than a meditation, but its efficacy is dependent upon your ability as a spiritual observer to preserve mental continuity as you do it. Energy follows *thought* and this is the basis of all occult practice and is of prime significance in this exercise. You will discover that if you do this exercise with regularity and with no biassed idea as to results, that changes will be wrought in your consciousness of a lasting nature and the light of the group will also be stronger.

August 1942

1. Much you have learnt, my brother on the Way, and closer to the centre of all life you stand. Let knowledge now be shewn as lighted wisdom and gentle loving poise.
2. Let tenderness emerge like a stream of healing strength. Ponder the relationship of tenderness and strength when devoid of selfish interest and unrestrained devotion.
3. Guard well the servant of the soul, the bodily frame, and shorten not the term of service. There is much for you to do.
4. Prepare for changes and welcome each departure from the normal way. Cultivate a fluidness of living when demand arises.
5. Two there are upon the inward way whom you must carry in your heart and seek to reach. C.D.P. is one; the other is more easily attained.
6. Each Thursday night, when sleep descends upon your eyes, seek Me and know that I am there.

September 1943

BROTHER OF MINE:

The years slip away, do they not? And each year sees and should see changes. In my last set of injunctions, if I may call them so, which I gave you a year ago, I asked you to prepare for changes. I have an idea, my brother, that you interpreted that to mean physical changes in your life—the changes which environment and circumstance impose upon a person, which cannot be avoided. But it was not to this kind of change that I referred. Let me see if I can make what I intended to convey to you somewhat clearer.

There are certain changes which disciples must themselves initiate; these may not touch environing outer conditions, but concern inner developments, attitudes and mental processes. These self-initiated decisions can and do lead to basic inner unsettlements (is there such a word?), and these inner disturbances are necessary to and preparatory to great inner crises. These inner crises lead to points of tension, as well you know, and from a point of tension the merging soul-personality can then move onward into greater light and a more surely realised Love.

With devotion and steadfastness you have stood, down the years. Of this I am aware, and for all that you have accomplished I am happy. The question I now ask you, my brother, and am wording in a current phrase in order to arrest your attention is this: Where do you go from here? What is your next step? Can you take another step this life? Can you put your finger on something in your consciousness —subtle perhaps and unseen by others except by those with a truly perceptive attention—which, if altered or developed, discarded or intensified, would bring about a great and surprising unfoldment—an unfoldment much to be desired, prior to entering upon another incarnation.

You are probably now assuming that I am referring to faults, handicaps or limitations. Perhaps I am. I might, however, be indicating the need to foster some divine quality, to move some latent spiritual attribute into a more prominent position in your life, or suggesting that you intensify some spiritual contribution that you are or could be making. That is for you to discover in the secret place of your own heart. At any rate, my brother and my tried friend, you know that until the final initiation is taken, all progress is a series of releases, and that from stage to stage of liberation we pass onward into light.

You are not young. You have a somewhat frail body. You take with pain and distaste the impacts of life, and you seek ever to measure up in truth and sincerity to the presented opportunity. You are prone to think that life must be for you now largely a process of waiting; that there is little that you can further do; in this you are wrong. You can most definitely love more—with less devotion to the few and with a greatly increased inclusiveness and depth for the many; you can free yourself from certain thoughtforms which condition much of your thinking; you can learn more easily the lesson that to be a true disciple means desiring what *is* best for all humanity, and not what you think is best in terms of some group, some school of thought, or some historical, or political sequence. You must learn to think in larger terms than those of some national group or group of nations. That means an intensified study upon the Plan and this means quiet reflection within yourself, not reading books or subjecting yourself to deep meditation; it means the breaking down of ancient prejudices and preconceived ideas, so that that which is new and totally different to what you have surmised or thought can enter into your thinking and condition your future.

Unless you can do this (and it is not easy for you to break loose from tradition and background) crystallisation is apt to set in, and that is something which I know you fear and which need not happen. The great preventive to any growing hardness or rigidity of perception is Love, and the great lesson for all disciples is *to love more and more until the Day be with us.*

I am not being very definite and specific with you, my brother. You need it not, for you are an experienced and tried soldier and you are singularly free from glamour, though susceptible to established and powerful thoughtforms. These latter can always be dissipated by love—developed and consciously expressed—but it is not so with glamour. That is a much harder task, as you know well, having watched the struggles of L.T.S-K. for so many years with sympathy and comprehension. You have given him more of that than almost anyone else in the group and in his immediate circle of co-disciples. It is because glamour has no lure for you.

As to your meditation, I am only going to give you certain words which you can incorporate into the general meditation at any point which you may deem appropriate. I would ask you to give five minutes at least to a dynamic concentration upon these words. Study them—as far as you can—from the angle of the world of meaning and in relation to your attitude to humanity as a whole. Do not consider them from the angle of your personal relationships or your personal environing circumstances. All that I have said indicates your need to relate these ideas to universal concepts; that is for you the next practical step. I give you six words or phrases, and during the coming year you can therefore deal with them twice:

1st month . . . Humanity. The framework of Experience.
2nd month . . Fluidity. Reaction to new Impression.
3rd month . . The Ashram. The centre of radiating Love.
4th month . . Money. The medium of loving Distribution.
5th month . . Recognition. The mode of divine Relationship.
6th month . . Identification. The key to Understanding.

These words are probably not what you might anticipate, but they will open up to you a group and mental approach to realisation, and that is the way for you to proceed. Your keen analytical mind will know what to do with these matters. I would suggest, for the process to be employed, that you approach each phrase each month with three questions. Let me illustrate for you what I mean by taking two words out of the six:

Humanity . . . . What does humanity mean to me in reality?
What new development faces the human family?
Can I contribute by my thinking to this new unfoldment?

Recognition . . What does recognition mean to me?
What new recognitions confront all disciples?
How can I develop the power to recognise the new, the divine, and the reality which is already here?

From these suggestions you can adapt three questions to each of the remaining words.

It will be apparent to you, my beloved brother, that what I am really doing is training you for a special piece of service —the service of thoughtform building in the New Age. This you can do if you will free yourself from prejudices and from criticism of certain individuals. This service you can do in the quiet of your home and without undue effort, and you will learn to do this because you love and will love increasingly.

I enfold you within my aura and with security, and from that point of safety I ask you to go forth upon the work of the Ashram.

November 1944

MY BROTHER AND MY FRIEND:

I would like to start this instruction with a word of commendation. The entering stream of love is much more potent now than it was. Years ago and even months ago this was not so. Today, the second ray strains (if I may call them so) in your equipment are far more dominant than heretofore. Had you realised how over-potent was your first ray astral body? It conditioned you unduly and it hindered you from seeing all around the picture of your relation to humanity. It forced you almost fanatically to adhere to certain ideas and concepts which were emotionally aroused and which were related principally to the people and the relatives with whom you associated. You frequently failed to see life from the angle of the ordinary man and from the effect which karma produced in the life of the average citizen. You thought in terms of one group. This you are learning to negate and the loneliness of your present life has greatly aided your withdrawal from this astral concentration upon a group thoughtform.

I have earlier told you that you are being trained to work with thoughtform creating processes. Hence, another reason for the long hours by yourself which characterise your life at this time and which will be expressive of your days for the remainder of your life. To this desire of your soul you must happily reconcile yourself. Because of this planned training —planned with the consent of your soul and of me, your Master—you are already peculiarly susceptible to group thoughtforms; you must learn increasingly to work under the influence of the Law of Abstraction.

This is a law which is ever present in the world in relation to the processes of death. The aspect of its importance in connection with physical death is deemed of slight importance in comparison to its emphasis in connection with the world of thought. The training given to a disciple when he enters the periphery of an Ashram lays an emphatic emphasis upon the need of abstracting one's consciousness from phase after phase of thought. The lesson of *detachment* in relation to one's possible emotional *attachments* is hard to learn, but a disciple must have mastered much of it, prior to entering the Ashram. When he does this, the inference is that detachment is now one of his established processes. However, the process of abstracting one's mind from all imposed thoughtforms—imposed by one's background, one's tradition and one's social group—is a very difficult and subtle undertaking. It must definitely be learned, prior to mastering the science of thoughtform building. The disciple has to stand free from mental impression and mental concepts before he can successfully create under direction of the Ashram.

When the Law of Abstraction is wielded consciously by you from within the Ashram, you will discover that it has (as it might have been expected) various meanings and policies which will function on the different planes of consciousness, such as:

1. Death or the effect of the Law of Abstraction upon the physical plane. This can refer to the abstraction of the life principle from the physical body in response to soul command; it can refer to the death of an old physical plane relationship; it can also refer to a cycle of physical plane conditioning or circumstance, to the termination of a relation to a physical plane group, or to the abstraction of an interest regarded hitherto as basic.

2. The termination of an outgoing affection towards a person or a group of persons upon the astral plane. This can precipitate a definite emotional crisis which brings about the withdrawal of devotion to people or causes. This statement covers the intensity of the emo-

tion, expressed in many and varied directions. Emotional abstraction is the hardest lesson which a disciple has to master.

3. The severing of connection with specific lines of thought. This may refer to the preconceived need which may dawn increasingly upon the disciple as he draws closer to the Ashram to which he is assigned; it may and will lead him to sever connection with schools of thought and with social, political, religious and circumstantial thoughtforms (using the word "circumstantial" to mean the mental conditioning brought about by circumstance), prior to being immersed in any ashramic thoughtform.

These specific abstractions are being rapidly learned by you; you should therefore enter your next life infinitely more liberated than you now are, and should function freer for service. Your present life condition is very favourable to your progress along these lines, and this I think you know, even if it displeases you to recognise the truth.

The entire process is one of abstraction, involving pain. There is a close relation between pain and the law with which I am dealing. It is the Law of Abstraction which lifts a disciple out of the three worlds of human endeavour; it is this same law which brings about the upward drive which all units of life express and the search of all of them for identification with the ONE; it is with this law that you—along with all disciples—must learn to work.

I would give you the following words for meditative reflection:

1. Abstraction   5. Renunciation
2. Detachment   6. Withdrawal
3. Liberation   7. Negation
4. Relinquishment   8. Rejection
     9. The O M

All these words embody certain major preparatory lessons. You will note how increasingly, as this particular group develops, I have ceased to give stanzas and symbolic phrases and have endeavoured to centre your attention *upon words.* I would have you deal with these words from the purely physical angle, from the quality angle, and from the purpose angle, as well as that of divine identification. Please use the process outlined for disciples in *The Yoga Sutras of Patanjali.** In these words you have adequate work for the remainder of your life. Approach them with consideration from the angle of personality detachment, from the angle of soul detachment, particularly when the antahkarana can be consciously used. In this way, great divine potencies can be used, and as one abstraction after another is mastered an increasing liberation will be sensed by you. Keep full notes and in a year's time (if you care to do so) bring these monthly notes all together and write a paper upon the Law of Abstraction as it makes its presence felt in the mind of a typical disciple. This will be of service to you and also to your group brothers.

Strive to cultivate a happy spirit. Let not life, loneliness or any circumstances unduly depress you. Dwell not too much upon world horror, but aim—in meditation—at conveying strength and wisdom to the world leaders as they seek (as they do) to bring order out of chaos. I would like to see you resume your work in the teaching group. You have the time, my brother, and a definite service which you needs must render would be good for you. Your help is needed.

You can, if you so desire, move forward into a clearer and closer relation to me and to my Ashram. You must, however, bear in mind that every step forward into the light and into a closer relation to the Hierarchy is made under the influence of the Law of Abstraction. Be strong, therefore, and know that the powerful qualities of your second ray soul relate you to D.H.B. and J.S.P. Take them into your daily meditation upon the plane of the soul, and remember that you three form an inner triangle which has certain spiritual activities for an esoteric objective for which this present incarnation is only preparatory.

My thought is yours, my brother, and I am *not* abstract-

*See: *The Light of the Soul,* Book I:17.

ing or withdrawing my love or my attentive care of your interests.

August 1946

MY BROTHER AND LOVED FRIEND:

In publishing the book *Discipleship in the New Age,* your friend and teacher, A.A.B. made the remark at the end of your instructions that you "still persist in your endeavour to work in the Tibetan's Ashram and remain steadfast and sure." A.A.B. knew what she was saying, but I wonder if you yourself realise the esoteric values of steadfastness and surety? The rarest compliment was knowingly made to you by A.A.B., but you probably did not understand its significance. A stable vibration is the keynote of the universe; surety is the sign of the Knower. These are two qualities of which you are in possession to the point of expression; I would have you realise it and count upon their registration in the Ashram you so much love.

In your hours of loneliness, and when you realise that life for you is mainly a waiting process, you are apt to forget these two facts which I have brought to your attention. Fight not against disability or against what the world calls "old age." This is a thing you are very apt to do, and it is a normal reaction. Why not welcome Transition? Learn to glory in experience, which is the gift of wise old age, and look forward to the Great Adventure which confronts you. You know well — in your highest moments — that that Transition means realisation without any physical plane limitations.

My brother, the ray of your astral body is the first; the failure, weakness or sin of the astral body is delusion. In your case, it is the delusion of pride—social pride—and of this you must rid yourself. It is not a mental quality, for if it were, sound thinking would soon show the futility of social pride. In the eyes of the Masters of the Wisdom, there are only human beings at various stages of unfoldment, of developing selfishness or of unfolding service. There are no classes such as the world recognises, neither is there any age, except the age of the soul; that need cause you no concern; your soul is old in its expression on the physical plane, and you know this to be so.

Pay not undue attention to the physical vehicle. Its preservation is of no moment and can—as in your case—become of too prominent importance. The time of your liberation is set by karmic law; this ever determines the demise of the real man within the body, but if the physical body is unduly nurtured, and if it becomes the recipient of undue care, it can hold that real man in prison in defiance of karmic law. That is a sorry spectacle to watch, for it means that the physical elemental is assuming power. Be careful in this connection, for the ray of your physical body would easily produce this situation.

Not so long ago—two years ago, I believe—I gave you nine words for your mature consideration. Today, I will give you twelve seed thoughts which (for the remainder of your life) should govern your morning reflection, following a definite process of linking with me and with my Ashram. Here are the seed thoughts:

1. Looking forward.
2. Hope.
3. Immortality.
4. Radiation.
5. Freedom from partisanship.
6. Anticipation.
7. Life purpose, persistent ever.
8. Friendship.
9. The triangle: yourself, D.H.B., J.S.P.
10. Eternal persistence.
11. Quality.
12. Future Mastership.

These ideas are suggestive and would prove fruitful and lead to much expansive thinking.

You are in my Ashram and for ever have naught to fear.

To L. U. T.

August 1942

1. The path of the pledged disciple is one of constant rending. The disciple does the rending. You have not yet

achieved the beauty of acceptance—the acceptance that releases.

2. Project your values to a higher sphere and know that nothing matters connected with the earthly role of life, save learning understanding. To that attain.

3. There are three souls who can in differing ways lead to achievement of your liberation: one, close to you, because she needs a guiding, loving understanding heart; one you will meet and needs must save; the other is Myself. For three lives now I have sought to serve your need. Respond in love to all these three.

4. Break through the double cloud which has so long erased the vision from your heart. You have the vision but it is ever on ahead. When will it pierce the cloud and settle in your heart?

5. Health, strength and opportunity confront your steps. A new departure can today open the door to greater, fuller life. Move on.

6. Let the ray of your soul dominate the man of everyday and become a radiant centre of saving force.

November 1944

MY WARRIOR (OR SHOULD I SAY "WARRING"?) BROTHER:

I call you this, for never do you cease fighting and struggling, sometimes under the urge of your soul and oft under the influence of a restless and unhappy personality emphasis. Can you not begin to cease from strife and struggle, and thus give opportunity for the evolution of that loving spirit which your first ray isolated personality seeks to hide, and often quite successfully? There is an aspect of the relationship between the first and second rays which is very apt to be overlooked. The second ray is outgoing, inclusive, friendly and prone to attachment; the first ray is isolated, exclusive, antagonistic and prone to detachment. It is the conflict between these two energies—brought together in one incarnation—which has brought about the distorted and unhappy life conditions which have characterised you, which you recognise, and which cause you so much real distress. It is time that this clashing of the two forces should end, and the conflict can only be determined *by the subjugation of your first ray personality by your second ray soul.* That is a clear statement of fact and indicates your immediate and essential endeavour. Your focus of identification has been the personality, but so strong is your soul quality that it leaves your personality constantly disturbed. Your aim, therefore, should be to cultivate all the characteristics which are the most distasteful to your lower nature—contact with other people, particularly with your group brothers, friendliness to and interest in all you meet, inclusiveness and the development of an outgoing spirit of goodwill to strangers and to friends. I have instructed D.I.J. to learn to work with the Law of Abstraction; I tell you to practice a reverse attitude to all life circumstances and contacts and to lose yourself in the interests of your associates and of humanity. Can you do this, my brother? At least you can try.

How can I help you to bring in the power of your loving, intelligent soul so that it can release your personality from its fever and bring about an ordered quiet in your life? There is so little that I can tell you that you do not already know; you have been under my instruction for many years, and you still are. One of the major linking and blending processes is the creative work of music. I would suggest to you that you bring music into your life far more than you have hitherto done, *particularly orchestral music.* In these days of radio programmes this is easily accomplished, and the effect of blended instruments and broad sound productions upon your personality will be to break down the opposition which it presents to soul contact and impose a different note and key upon your life.

Does this injunction surprise you, brother of old? You are on the verge of release from the struggle of the past and can enter upon a more constructive and happier phase of living *if* you permit music to play a major part in your life rhythm; choose only the best music, such as that played by the great symphony orchestras. God created by the power of sound, and the "music of the spheres" holds all life in being (note that phrase). The soul on its tiny scale can create "the new man" by the power also of sound, and a musical rhythm can usefully be imposed upon the personality life by the disciple.

This is what you need—music in your life, literally and figuratively. I have here given you a most important hint. Let the great music of the masters of sound enter (in a new and powerful way) into your consciousness. If you take this advice, in three years, if you insist on subjecting yourself to the musical impact, I suggest great and significant changes will be brought about in your life. Once you get away from self-pity and irritation, there is little that is wrong with your thinking. That, my brother, can be said of few.

I would like to see you enter within the inner place of the Ashram, yet you persist in remaining on the periphery of its sphere of influence. Let love and light and music enter more definitely into your daily life. Spurn not this practical suggestion, but give your mind the opportunity, through the massed sound of music, to break down the personality-imposed barriers between the free flow of soul life and you.

There is little else that I can say. This is a short instruction. I stand unchangingly ready to welcome you to a greater ashramic intimacy, but the moving forward into this closer relation must be accomplished by you—alone and unaided, except by my suggestions. There is naught more that I can do but to stand behind you with love and understanding.

August 1946

MY BROTHER:

There is little I can say to you. For the remainder of your life you have only one thing to do: to prepare yourself for successful spiritual enterprise when again you return to incarnation. Surely you would like to re-enter physical plane existence with a different and more adequate desire nature— a desire nature which has ever conditioned your physical body and militated against higher conditionings? Desire has ever driven you; at the same time, high aspiration has goaded you, and between the two your life has been one of misery and frustration, and frequently of despair.

In spite of the profoundly unsatisfactory demonstration which you register in your consciousness and of which I am also aware, you are still hovering on the periphery of my Ashram; you are still linked to your group brothers and to me, even if you ignore them and me and go your own way, following your inclinations at any cost. It is always hard when two major rays govern both the personality and the soul. It indicates past achievement of a high order, for the transfer from a minor ray is involved, and this is ever indicative of preparation—at some future date—for initiation. It indicates also great struggle, particularly when the first ray personality is strongly linked to the desire nature.

All this you know, for there is nothing wrong with your intelligence, my brother. What is wrong is that—in the face of knowledge—you will not use the will to force the spiritual issue and to emerge once and for all into the clear light of the soul. Nevertheless, it should not be hard for you to use the will, once contact can be more firmly established with the soul, for you are a first ray personality, and therefore the will aspect can be more easily contacted and comprehended by you than by those on the other rays.

R.S.W. helps you not, much as she has attempted to do so. She does not accept or recognise you for what you are—a man whose lower nature dominates most of the time, but whose basic intent is identification with the higher nature; she sees you differently and her surety along this line is no help to you.

I, your friend and teacher, know you as you are, and I understand; that understanding forces me to stand by you (with steadfastness) behind the scenes ready, at any moment, to make my presence felt when the higher triumphs and the lower is negated. You might ask me why this is so? I would answer that in the distant past—a past which lies behind all of us—you made, at a terrific cost, a sacrifice which permitted entry of the soul as a thread of radiant light. By that sacrifice much good came to me, and we, the Masters of the Wisdom, lay much emphasis upon gratitude. It — with service — is deeply scientific in nature and closely related to the Law of Karma. Gratitude is something about which you need to learn, or the steady friendship of F.B. and A.A.B., as well as that of your group brothers, would evoke from you some recognition. Their friendship is soundly founded on the mental plane, and there is little that they can do to help in current conditions.

What, then, my brother, shall we do? What shall I say to you in this my last instruction? First, let me say that I am hoping to see, in the next few years of your life, a complete reversal of the past. I look to see you apply, with *will and spiritual insight*, those physical disciplines which will feed your aspiration and negate and render futile all desire. I look to see you strengthen the tie between yourself and me, your Master.

Do you realise what is the task that confronts me where you are concerned? It is the task of aiding you to transmute your personality nature into such an instrument that your soul can remove you out of my Ashram into that of the Master K.H. Such is my task with several of you in this group; you and they do not essentially belong in my Ashram but stay and work there until the spiritual laws control, the vision is firmly established, and the soul is in control. Will you, with constancy, bear this in mind, and for the remaining years of your life wrestle with the lower nature until it is purified, disciplined, enlightened and integrated?

I give you no set meditation. I enjoin upon you the prime necessity of linking up with your soul, with the Ashram and with me three times a day. I would ask you to do this with a definite act of the will. This triple exercise, carried forward in the morning, at noon, and when you retire at night, will be more potent in transmutative effect than anything else that you can do. Forget not that by means of this exercise you train the will, and you likewise bring spiritual energy into your personality in order to help you with the task, the spiritual task, ahead of you.

On my cooperation you can ever count, but this is dependent upon your ability to "get through" to me.

To D. E. I.

August 1942

1. As a chela in my Ashram you move through life with all the power which flows out from that centre. Forget it not.
2. The future opens up with much that must be done. Let not the doing intervene between the loving.
3. Love all, as love all chelas, and let *pity* rule your acts.
4. The noise and turmoil of the way of life is great and you respond with undue pain. Others escape in many ways and build a wall. For you, compassion is the way. Face facts and have compassion.
5. Lift up the weak for you are strong, and strength from many comes to you. Attract that strength, then forward move with power to love and lift.
6. Question not the staunchness of the strength and love which comes to you from three: Myself, your brother A.A.B., and one other, little guessed by you as yet.

September 1943

MY BROTHER AND MY FRIEND:

Since you entered the cycle beginning with your forty-second year, life has held for you constant change, many and drastic adjustments and much responsibility. To this must be added the turmoil and the chaos of the war. This has made great demands upon your strength and your judgment. You have responded well. You have helped many and have grown in wisdom. You have shouldered responsibility for some phase of the work initiated in my Ashram or by my co-disciple, A.A.B. She is not a member of my Ashram. You have my understanding and her unfailing support.

Inevitably, my brother, this situation which you have had to handle in relation to the work for which you are responsible, in relation to your personal and family life and to the future which lies open before you, has entailed much strain. To these factors must be added another one which is that you are essentially alone. This basic loneliness is due to several things: First, that you are in training for leadership, and leaders have to learn to stand alone, and can ever do so if they love enough. Secondly, the force of circumstance and the need to work off certain karmic relations has increased your daily contacts, and at the same time has left you far more alone than you were six years ago. Thirdly, because the greater can always include the less is a lesson which all leaders in training have to grasp; the reverse, my brother, is not true, and the result is loneliness. Ponder on all this and accept it; stand free and move forward on your chosen path, refusing to be limited by those who cannot go your pace. This again means loneliness. And finally, a need for a more loving understanding at times isolates you from your fellow-men, particularly from your co-workers, and you need to beware of a growing critical spirit.

The lessons of leadership are hard to learn, and with these lessons you will be confronted as the years slip away—if you so wish and can face the music. The music is there and will emerge in full tonal quality once you have resolved the discords and established the theme and the rhythm.

What are the lessons which all true leaders have to learn? It might be of service to you if I put one or two before you —very briefly, so that you can (if truly in earnest to serve your fellowmen, as I believe you are) begin to master them, to understand their need and to apply them to yourself with a view to fuller and more useful service.

The first lesson is the *lesson of vision*. What are your goals? What is the spiritual incentive which will be and is strong enough to hold you steady to the purpose and true to the objective? No one can formulate the vision for you; it is your own personality problem, and upon the strength of the vision and the beauty of the picture which you paint with your imagination will depend much that you do and become.

The second lesson is the *development of a right sense of proportion*. This, when truly developed and correctly applied, will enable you to walk humbly on the Way. No true leader can be anything but humble, for he realises the magnitude of his task; he appreciates the limitations of his contribution (in the light of the vision) and the need for constant self-development and the cultivation of the spirit of steady inner spiritual learning, if he is ever to make his proper contribution. Therefore, keep learning; keep dissatisfied with yourself and your attainment, not in any morbid sense, but so that the principle of growth and of pushing forward and onward may be fostered in you. We help others through our own effort to attain; this means clear thinking, humility and constant adjustment.

The third lesson is the *development of the spirit of synthesis*. This enables you to include all within the range of your influence and also to be included within the range of influence of those greater than yourself. Thus is the chain of Hierarchy established. You still hold a somewhat isolated position, and this with the best intent in the world; but you need to love more deeply and more understandingly. The hindrance here lies in your personality, which is more wise than loving. Let your soul control your first ray personality more, and many of your present difficulties would disappear.

Another lesson which in reality grows out of the above is the *avoidance of the spirit of criticism*, for criticism leads to barriers and loss of time. Learn to distinguish the spirit of criticism from the ability to analyse and make practical application of the analysis. Learn to analyse life, circumstances and people from the angle of the work, and not from the angle of your personality point of view; analyse also from the angle of the Ashram, and not from the angle of the executive or the schoolmaster upon the physical plane.

In the six statements which I gave you a year ago were three sentences to which I would call your further and close attention. They are:

1. "Let not the doing intervene between the loving."
   This has much to do with the distribution of time.
   Study the value of the heart at leisure from itself and
     its problems.
2. "Lift up the weak, for you are strong, and strength
     from many comes to you."
   This has to do with recognition. Be not entirely occu-
     pied with helping, but be willing to be helped.

Study the value of the imagination in this connection.

3. "You move through life with all the power which comes from out my Ashram."

This has to do with the handling of energy—and with energy of great potency which will not only invoke the best that is in you but will also evoke the latent seeds of difficulty, which must perforce be removed. Study the task of living ever consciously in the Ashram and working from that point of power and peace—going without, yet ever staying within.

I am speaking thus directly to you, my co-worker, because the future holds much of useful service for you, if you *continue to be a learner*. It takes time, humility and certain recognitions, within yourself, of place and position in the chain of Hierarchy. I cannot too strongly emphasise that to you. Let not the pressures of family life (and no family life is devoid of pressures) and the exigencies of the work, plus the activities of an active mind, interfere with the inner learning process which is so essential to all teaching-leaders. That, my brother, is what you can be.

A.A.B. has spoken to me of you from the standpoint of your place in the work of the School. She has not touched upon the personality angles or the need for special developments and growth, for no trained disciple, such as she is, ever interferes with the relation between a Master and His chela. She knows that your relation to me is that. But she has spoken to me about you from the angle of the future. I asked her what she felt was your major need and one that you must meet as you prepare for a larger field of service when she passes over. She made an unexpected reply. She said: "The need for a more fertile imagination." She is entirely right.

The imagination is a creative faculty. Wherein are you thus creative? Can you picture to yourself by any flight of imagination the task ahead of the Arcane School, for instance, in the post-war world, and your approach to the problem from the angle of what you would like to change or see altered? Changes mean nothing unless they are the result of new vision, for if they emerge out of a criticism of the past and of what has been done, they will prove useless from the angle of the spiritual life, no matter how useful they may be from the angle of the organisation.

Have you the perception to realise what an esoteric school essentially has to be? It is not an organised method of meeting world problems, of organising new orders and ways of living, or of underwriting the efforts of the men and women of goodwill. It goes far deeper than that. All the above are only effects of the esoteric life. Can you imagine your position when—from the teaching angle, the esoteric angle—you may have to be a source of inspiration, and not A.A.B.? From whence will you draw inspiration, and how will you make the world of meaning and the spiritual realities real and provocative to the neophyte?

Can your imagination picture to you your reaction when —because you are the leader—you have to shoulder all the blame for any failure, even when not personally responsible; you have to accept without retaliation the attacks of those you are trying to help, who expect too much from you and who force you to live in the blaze of public opinion; what will you do when your chosen workers fail to understand or prove disloyal or criticise without warrant or pit their ambitions against you, and wilfully refuse to see your point of view, and talk about you among other people and whip up resentments against you—resentments which are probably without foundation? These are not the kind of things that your personality easily accepts, and your creative imagination had better begin dealing with these problems so that the emerging principles of conduct may stand clear before you. Have you the inner grace of heart to admit error and weakness or to say that you made a mistake in technique or method or approach, in judgment or in speech, should need arise to heal a breach and in the interests of the work? That has never come easily to you either, my brother. It is a thing you seldom do.

And having said all this, let me point out your assets and the valuable gifts which you can bring to the work and have for years contributed; they are the qualities which make A.A.B. your loyal friend and ambitious for your progress.

You have a recognition of principles which is vital and somewhat rare, and on principles all true work is securely founded. You have a gift of impersonality, as a general rule, which is a great safeguard; and in those times when your personality impulses have controlled, the phase has not been lasting. You have a gift of teaching, clear insight and executive ability and a loving heart when it is sparked into compassion. You have a steadfastness of purpose and an unswerving adherence to duty and dharma and a capacity to shoulder responsibility which has, in the past, and will in the future, prove invaluable to the work required. You have the gift of the written word and an increasing ability to speak, and these are valuable assets indeed when wielded by the soul on behalf of others. You are impulsive, and this at times creates temporary difficulties, but the general trend and tendency of your impulses is right and truly oriented. This is a major asset in your life. You are a pledged and accepted disciple, with the power of your Master's Ashram behind you and the love of your co-disciples with you.

You have the understanding and loyal affection of A.A.B., and will—from life to life. Against her wishes, I ask you to give her in some small measure what she has so largely given you. At times you fail to grasp the strength of her belief in you. Her health is precarious and she counts much on you. Fail her not, and seek to understand the problems with which she is faced.

You have also my belief and trust, my confidence that you will carry on—learning and living and loving—and again I repeat, on the strength coming from my Ashram you can count, but it reaches you through your soul, and therefore a closer soul contact is increasingly needed by you as the work grows and develops.

November 1944

MY FRIEND AND CO-WORKER:

I intend to be in touch with you with constancy, and you must train yourself to an increased sensitivity to my presence and to the contact of my mind. Contact with me will affect your heart centre; contact with my mind will bring about changes in your head centre—probably (at this stage of your development) in the ajna centre. Sensitivity is one of your major needs. That involves a freer use of the imaginative faculty, as I told you in my last instruction. You need badly to develop sensitivity not only to me, your Master (for that you yourself desire), but a greatly increased sensitivity to your co-disciples. Above everything else, you must develop a much more sensitive response to all you contact in your life of service. That is primarily what you lack; it is based upon a definite lack of true love in your nature. You earnestly, and usually successfully, do your duty to all you meet, with certain exceptions where your personality is almost violently antagonistic; but more than this is needed in a leader upon the second ray line of teaching.

You are one of the people (relatively few) who have a sound and beautiful *group* effect, but your individual contacts are not so constructive, and it is along this line that you must work. You must learn to set up a helpful and an understanding relation with all who come your way—high and low, rich and poor, the socially important and the under classes, the likable and unlikable. The need to develop this was one of the reasons, plus incorporation in national karma, which has *temporarily* removed you from an active participation in the work you have done so well for years. You are being given an interlude wherein you can enrich your life, add something needed to your equipment, and then return to your previous work and service with far more to give than heretofore. This I know would be your own desire; I have here given you the clue to its fulfilment.

One of the ways in which you can arrive at this deeper comprehension of humanity lies in the unfoldment of the creative imagination; this will enable you to tune in upon the background and the consciousness of people contacted. You are a man of strong likes and dislikes; you have also prided yourself upon the fact that no matter how much you might dislike a person, you would endeavour to do right by him and you usually succeed in so doing, with the exception of three people—dislike of whom renders you unreasonable and often unkind. Who they are you well know, and it is not my intention to mention their names, as this relationship is entirely your own affair.

But, my brother, a working disciple entrusted with a definite task by his Master, and working from within the Ashram (as you do), must work not only from a sense of duty and deep intense devotion, not only from a sense of karmic responsibility and a knowledge that the task undertaken is, by reason of soul injunction, obediently followed, but he must work also under the inspiration of true Love. You have a second ray soul, and when it is in control, your attitude is all that could possibly be desired; you have (which is unusual) a second ray mental nature. This enables you to realise *theoretically* what should be your attitude and to know exactly when and where love does not control. Your first ray personality and astral vehicle provide barriers to the free flow of love and impede a constant contact with the soul, imposing themselves between the soul and the three lower vehicles. They also come between the soul and the physical body, stopping or hindering the downflow of the energy of love into the vital or etheric body, from whence it would automatically control and actuate the physical life expression.

The existence and the possibilities inherent in the concentration of these two first ray energies in your personality should have the effect of adding strength and potency to the inflow of the love factor, and they should enable you to isolate the energy of love with facility and apply it one-pointedly. I tell you this for your encouragement.

One other thing I would point out. It should be recognised by you that your entire ray equipment is so well balanced that your capacity to serve the Ashram and humanity is very great, provided that you unify all these forces into one intelligent, serving and constructive unity. You are singularly well equipped; you have a dual capacity to use second ray energy to enhance and implement the use of the teaching ability; you have also a third ray contact with the physical plane which should enable you to focus and utilise all this inherent capacity upon the physical plane in outer effective human service. You have made great strides in so doing.

and it is only when your first ray isolationism, implemented by your personality and emotional natures, obliterates for a moment (in relation to other human beings) your second ray qualities that your physical plane output is affected, and it is sometimes affected quite seriously. Unless you consider this matter and remove the impediments to the free play of your love nature, you will always be a trusted server, but your field of service will be needlessly circumscribed and you will not be able to serve as generously and successfully as you otherwise might. Always you will serve; always you will have the freedom of the Ashram, and always you will have access to me, earning my confidence, and always you will persist. *But I seek greater things for you, and so does A.A.B.*

The work of the Arcane School holds in it much of promise—far more than at present appears. Workers will emerge who will be entrusted with wide responsibility, and A.A.B. will give them a free hand as she has ever given you *within the limits of the School's principles and objectives.* The leadership of the Arcane School must be that of a group, when A.A.B. is not with you and has passed on to other and more important inner work; this group will necessarily be under the general direction of F.B., but certain of you will have much responsibility and power, provided there is potent and correct motivation, and that you work with self-effacement; love ever produces the retirement into the background of the personality and its attitudes.

I would thank you, my brother, for all that you have done, your influence has been good and useful to many, and I am well aware of it; A.A.B. has also expressed her appreciation to you on several occasions.

The interlude of work upon which you are now engaged should give you the time for much inner reflection; it should deepen your power to live the dual life of a disciple. Get ready, therefore, for a resumption of my work when the right time comes, returning to it with a wider understanding, a more expressive love, and a more enthusiastic dedication to the principle of service. A.A.B. (if I may again point this out) has a deep appreciation of you and love for you, both personality and egoic in origin, and you can do much to lift burdens off her shoulders, if you so desire. She never troubles about the inevitable and unimportant mistakes that her workers make. She has made them herself and knows their relative unimportance. She troubles greatly when there is a misinterpretation of principles, a side-tracking of major issues, or a general inertia. Stand by her. With the unfailing love of F.B. and the developed understanding of yourself, of R.S.U. and F.C.D., she can round out this life cycle with satisfaction to her Master—which is all that she cares about. She has earned this from all of you. She has, I may add, refused to take down this last sentence (as she thinks not in terms of reward or recompense), but has done so when I enjoined upon her the need for impersonality.

The three Arcane School centres, New York (the major centre), London and in Switzerland, must become more potent and should constitute three major points of light in the world. At the centre of each should work a disciple. Later, I shall suggest that the work in Australia be extended, and that in Sydney another centre or power station should be opened.

Your meditation during the coming year should be focussed around the effort to bring through second ray energy—the energy of your soul and of your mind—into the physical brain, via the etheric body. You must do this through the power of the creative imagination; you must act "as if"; you must see this energy pouring in, literally, to the head centre and from thence to the brain. You must work out your own way of doing this, for that will be for you the best way. Two suggestions only will I make: See this energy of love as a great descending stream of light substance, pouring down from the soul into your threefold lower equipment, and from thence out into the Arcane School, enveloping its membership. Secondly—and here you must endeavour to understand my meaning without any elaboration from me— you must take the people you do not like, particularly the three who so painfully disturb you, *into your heart*, thinking of them (as far as in you lies) in their own terms and from their own point of view and *not* from yours.

The way into the Ashram stands ever open to you and I

am ever accessible to those who, like you, have worked and served in difficulty and distress and under the drastic circumstances imposed by this world war. You have served without any deviation from the path of duty. Forget this not, and avail yourself of "the privilege of entrance." You will ever find me at the inner point.

To H. S. D.

September 1943

MY BROTHER:

This year has seen certain liberating processes taking place in your life. You stand much freer from entanglements than heretofore; you face fresh opportunity for service and for growth. My problem is how to help you to capitalise on the past, thus enabling you to make the future a more fruitful period than ever before. You have been connected with my Ashram for some time now and have been readmitted into the new seed group. The reason that I mention this is because I want to emphasise to you the word "seed." It is the germ, and only the germ, of the spiritual life with which you have to deal, and I want you to withdraw your thinking and your emphasis from the concept of the flowering of your life in the coming years to the concept of nurturing and fostering the seed or germ of the new life which is just beginning to emerge. The *Old Commentary* says:

> "The seed develops five flowers and five only. One flower long precedes the others. The second flower is hard to grow, the third is harder still. The fourth flower dies and, dying, gives forth light and in that light the fifth flower blooms."

I leave you to interpret this for yourself.

The future which lies ahead of you—be it long or short —must be approached by you now in a different manner to the past. You stand alone. You stand, however, with your brothers in the Ashram, and are therefore not alone. What lies ahead for you? How can the coming years be constructive, organised and creative? These three words—Constructive, Organised, Creative—have been chosen by me with care and I would ask you to reflect upon them. What is the constructive contribution which you can now make to the work that your chosen co-workers are doing? How can you organise your life so that there is a definite result and something to show for any activity instituted? How can the intense activity of your mind be slowed down and channelled so that something creative and worthwhile may emerge? These are the problems which must be faced, and these are the points where I can be of service to you, my brother, if you will accept my suggestions and carry them through.

It is the carrying through of any one settled project which has always been the major weakness with your group service. You work a little bit in some department of the group activity, and then you turn to something else; your basic purpose is steadfast and true and your steadiness in adhering to my work in some phase or another is unbreakable and real, but the surface effort is unstable, and from the angle of time, never persists long enough to show results. Why is this?

The answer lies in two directions: Your overactive mind flits from this to that and back again, and over-organises everything it touches. Secondly, the physical body under this intense mental tension and constant movement is necessarily very nervous and constantly depleted, for seldom is anything carried through, and the carrying through of a project and adherence to a plan bring through energy on to the physical plane and consequently into the physical body. Your vital body feels the constant pull upwards of mental force, but that mental force is not expressed through activities which are carried through to concluded expression upon the physical plane. Your mind is like a whirling humming-top which is constantly toppling over and has to be set in motion again, accomplishing nothing of value.

This, brother of mine, is *not* your intent or desire. What then is wrong? Let me tell you simply what the fault is.

There is a constant overstimulation of the mind, of such a potent nature that there is no time or energy left for physical plane expression. What is the cure and what shall we do to prevent this overstimulation and slow things down so that there will be time for accomplishments? My answer is: Complete cessation from all meditation work for a year at least, or until I again give you permission to resume. You are constantly withdrawing and escaping into the meditation process, and you do it so successfully that the result is that all the energies you contact become focussed in the mind. You do not need to do this. You need now to garner the results of past meditation work through active service, chosen with deliberation and carried through steadily without any meditation at all but on the strength of the stored-up knowledge you have, and which you have never used.

I am asking you, therefore, to stop all meditation, even the group meditation. You can give fifteen minutes to dedication, consecration and contact with your soul and with me every Sunday morning and at the full moon period. You can participate in the group meditation at the School, but see to it that the group meditations are regarded by you as acts of service and not as means whereby your own nature is stimulated and refreshed. You can take part in the group held by A.A.B. on Friday evenings, for there is much that you can there learn. But I do not want you otherwise giving any time whatsoever to meditation—particularly in connection with any work you may be doing. I want your active cooperation on the physical plane along some particular line connected with my activities, and I want that work adhered to at any cost so that a *finished* something emerges. What that work shall be, what phase of the undertaking you can do, and what responsibility you can shoulder should be, I feel, talked over with A.A.B., but only if you so desire.

If you will follow out these instructions, you will be surprised to discover how much easier life will be for you. Your mind will gradually become your instrument and not your master, as it is at present; your etheric body will stabilise and your general health will improve; your interests will grow and your usefulness increase, and that I know, my brother, is what you yourself desire. I am only attempting to help you to measure up to your own idea.

One other exercise I will permit. I give you below certain sentences or statements, one for each month of the coming year. Every morning before you rise out of a recumbent position say the one for that particular month aloud—just once —thus striking your keynote for the day. But do not proceed to meditate, ponder or reflect upon the sentences.

1st month . . . In quietness and in confidence shall be my strength as I walk today the ways of earth.

2nd month . . I descend in thought unto the plains whereon men walk, and there I work.

3rd month . . In spiritual being I stand upon the Way. It is the way of men. I am. I neither think nor dream, but work.

4th month . . . With my brothers I dwell within the Ashram. I issue forth and carry out the Plan as best I can.

5th month . . . Let love stream out today—from out my eyes, my hands, my feet, because my heart beats with the love of God.

6th month . . . Within my hand I hold the keys of life. I unlock the door for others and they pass through—yet see me not.

7th month . . . As I am strength and power and love and understanding, I bring these gifts into the haven of my work. Thus strength goes forth to others and love to all I meet, and to these gifts I add an understanding heart.

8th month . . . The cry goes out for workers. I answer, Master of my Life, and stand within the ranks of those who serve. What shall I do? The answer comes: The thing before thine eyes.

9th month . . . I climb the mountain top with others and watch the sun. I descend into the valley

with my fellowmen and therein walk. The
dark is great, but I am with my fellowmen.

10th month . . . I think no thought, I speak no word, I do
no deed that hurts another. This means I
use a guarded brain against myself—the
little personal self.

11th month . . . The chain of Hierarchy reaches from
heaven to earth and in that chain I am a
part. Above me stand the Ones I seek to
serve; below me stand brothers demanding help.

12th month . . . The cross is mine. The sword of love is
mine. The word of Power is mine because
I love—my Master and my brothers on
the upward Way and on the lesser way,
my fellowmen.

This change is not going to be easy for you, brother of
mine. It will appear to disrupt and to disturb the rhythm of
your life, but it will net you good results and you will never
regret acceding to my request. The best lies ahead for you.
You are needed, and there is service you can render along
with your group brothers and with me.

November 1944

BROTHER OF OLD:

This is the last specific and individual instruction I shall
give you. It is not my intention to continue repeating what
I seek you—and all of you—to be, to become or to do. You
have had much given to you over the years which still needs
to be worked out in practical effectiveness. I wonder if you
have noticed how frequently, in this series of group and individual instructions, I have used the word "effective"? This
has been deliberate upon my part, for the word conveys
something which I would see each of you express. True effectiveness is the result of a merging of soul energy with personality force, and through this etheric merging, the physical

demonstration becomes adequate to the demand and commensurate with the forces blended. Each of you who have been admitted in the Ashram has already established a measure of definite contact. The way into the inner circle of the Ashram is through a still closer rapport with the soul, and upon this rapport you must definitely concentrate.

You are making a real effort to cooperate and to carry out my instructions; this has not been easy for you. It has taken you a long time to get down to work since receiving the last instruction I gave you; it has taken you long to arrive at a point of focus upon some definite activity, as I enjoined you some time ago. This again is the result of your over-rationalising mind which in dealing with all life circumstances is—in your case—prone to make complicated and intricate the simplest of physical plane matters. You are apt to make important, things which are not of the slightest importance whatsoever.

Your goal for the remainder of your life should be simplicity in all affairs and in all relationships. To this simplicity I would have you add a greater sense of personal dignity—a dignity which will work out as a physical reticence; of this, you as yet know little, but it will reveal itself to you as you reflect upon the word. To these two necessities of your physical plane expression I would have you add understanding—an understanding based upon love and not upon any mental process. This will be hard for you, for it involves being guided by your heart, unprompted by your versatile and fluid mind. If you will develop these qualities—*simplicity* from the mental angle, *understanding* from the emotional and astral angle, and *dignity* from the physical angle—and will work at these qualities during the rest of this incarnation, you will start your next life equipped for fuller service and with a more reliable physical instrument.

A.A.B. tells me that it distresses you that you are what you call "behind" the others in the new seed group, as far as the reception of the series of group instructions is concerned. She asks me what she should do, as she would not withhold them from you if it is my wish for you to (using your own words) "catch up." Catch up with what and whom, my brother? A reception of the written instructions is no indication of capacity or status, for in the spiritual life and in all life free from physical brain awareness (as you understand it) such a "catching up" is non-existent. From the angle of esotericism, which is concerned with the soul aspect of life, time is simply a sequence of states of consciousness as registered by the physical brain. It does not in reality affect the inner spiritual man. Could you but know it—and this is a point which all disciples need to grasp—you, the true Being, need no instructions. The task of any Master is only to bring to the attention of the man, working through the medium of a physical brain, that phase of the Ageless Wisdom which his own soul is seeking to have him register. In reality, you have had the instructions at closer and more rapid intervals than have your group brothers, because of your importunity and the grasping demand of your agile, unsatisfied mind. But you have by no means mastered what has been imparted, nor have you done the needed meditation; you will therefore only receive the current group instructions after the sun has moved northward, and I will intimate to A.A.B. the right time.

As regards your meditation work, you may now begin to follow the meditation outline given in the last series, but you must do it with no undue pressure; you must do it without any eager expectancy, but simply as a demanded duty. I would have you watch yourself with extreme care and I would ask you to refrain from using the Sacred Word, except when in group meditation, when the aura of the group will absorb the incoming energies and you will not then be unduly stimulated. The mind, when awake and active, is the great transmitter of the energies loosed by the Sacred Word. When sounded by the emotional type, it fortunately proves ineffectual in the majority of cases, and no energy is drawn into the mechanism of the personality. But when the mind is active and en rapport with the soul at certain points of evolution, it can and does draw out soul energy, and relates it rapidly and immediately to the brain. Hence much of the difficulties connected with overstimulation of which you are the victim. Adhere strictly to this injunction.

One of the factors in ashramic relations which you need to find and express is the assured peace and inner confidence which characterise its vibration. There is too much fever in your life. You ascribe it to a delicate body, my brother, but this is not so. It is due to a feverish mind; until calm and peace and tranquility distinguish your mental processes, it will not be wise for you to penetrate any further into the Ashram than the point where now you find yourself. So endeavour to keep the mind quiet. The physical vehicle is far stronger than you think, and a much larger measure of real health will be yours if your mind can be better regulated.

An Ashram is a place of quietly confident, regulated effort. The plan and the immediate service-activity are known, and disciples and initiates—each aware of his task and equipment—proceed to carry out the phase of the One Work which is theirs. Each senses its relationship to the phases of the work undertaken by his group brothers; it is in learning to see the picture whole (as the Master ever sees it) that confidence and security are developed.

In the place of your Sunday morning dedication, I want to give you four pictures upon which to reflect, seeking to read behind their symbolism the message of your soul to you, the personality.

I. A quiet sea of midnight blue. Above, the shining, round-faced moon. Across the sea, a path of light, and moving *slowly* down that path a little boat and —smiling, with the oars in hand—H.S.D. is seen.

II. A pillared cloister, dappled with the sun and broken by the shade cast by the pillars. A garden spreads on either side, redolent with the smell of many flowers and noisy with the hum of many bees and gay with butterflies. Ten times a bell rings out. Its tone is deep and clear and musical. But the one who sits and writes and thinks beneath the cloister's shade moves not. He writes, and measures to the task assigned.

III. A room in shadow, full of peace and calm, of books and enterprise. And at the desk, the Master sits and works and thinks, projecting thought, working within, above and all around, whilst through the room pass many. It is their right to pass.

IV. A golden door, wide open to the sun. Before the door lie rocks and bits of stone. A path winds towards that door, and o'er its lintel are the words: Enter with calm; speak low and only if a need is there. Enter the stream behind the door and wash away the stains of travel. Then face the Master, but only when the quiet of evening light shines forth and all is still within.

Take these pictures—one each Sunday in the month—and work creatively with them. At the close of a year, send in to A.A.B. (for the helping of the group) your interpretation of these symbols. Speak truth through them and fear not criticism.

You are making progress, my brother, and can—if you so will—be of service to your fellowmen. Forget not that at the centre of the Ashram I can be found at all times, but only when you can penetrate there with simplicity, understanding and dignity.

August 1946

MY BROTHER:

In my last instruction to you I stated that it was the last which I would give you. At that time, I had no intention of closing the outer ashramic affiliation. Today it is closed, and I give you, therefore, a parting word of practical import upon the physical plane, along with those of your brothers.

I approach you with much concern because your physical plane life is now as fluidic as your mind has been, and you know, brother of old, that that restless, grasping, unsatisfied mind has given both you and me much trouble over our years of association. Let us look at your situation clearly, and I would like to indicate to you the wise procedure for the future.

You are a dedicated disciple and have proven yourself so to be; you are a member of my Ashram, but your mental fluidity has militated against your passing into any closer relation within the Ashram. You still remain upon the periphery, whereas you should have advanced to within the first circle of working disciples, at least. This, however, has been impossible and will remain so until you have brought quietness and rhythm into your physical plane life. It was the realisation of this which prompted A.A.B. to beg you, not long ago, to settle down. She could not give ashramic reasons, for she intrudes not into that which I perforce must do, but she earnestly sought to help.

My brother, no matter where you are, a settled place of abode is needed for all disciples, and this for several reasons. Over the months or years, where a true disciple is concerned, this settled abode becomes a shrine, something is built which becomes magnetic and responsive to the Ashram, and occultly speaking, "the sensitive receiver of the disciple's physical brain can be located and found to be at peace." I trust you understand, and I would have you ponder on these words and reflect upon my suggestion. I would have you seek (and you will find) a place of suitable residence which will be of *prolonged* usefulness to you and from which you will not move, except in response to the normal procedures of life. Because of the instability with which you have come into incarnation and which constitutes your major life problem, you know that you need the steady rhythm and the heartbeat of the Headquarters in New York, through which I work; this should condition your choice of a place in which to settle and, my brother, I emphasise and re-emphasise to you the word "settle."

This is for you a spiritual necessity, and will eventually mean for you health and peace and a stable settled personal rhythm. This again will signify a step towards liberation. Your restlessness and instability have been accepted by you as conditioning factors in your life, and herein lies a major mistake which you have always made. Both are a serious detriment to your spiritual progress and usefulness and one reason why you are not as useful as you should be to those around you.

For whatever time lies ahead of you, my brother, let this constant movement *end*. Endeavour to *be* where you can be found; gather around you what you need for peaceful, quiet and useful living, and *there abide. I cannot too strongly urge this on you.* Fill your life with interests related to my work (a work which has evoked your sincere dedication), but give not time to meditation. It is this constant urge to meditation which is responsible for much of your difficulty, because meditation overstimulates your fluidic and active mind; this, in due course, results in a restless, constantly changing physical plane life. Talk this over with A.A.B., who has watched you with loving concern for many years and is peculiarly disturbed over you at this time.

There is much that you can do, *if* you are willing to do the little things. You have given generously of your means and have made much of my work possible; for this I am grateful, and for this I tender to you the thanks of those of us in the Hierarchy who stand behind the work for which A.A.B. and F.B. are responsible. We shall always be grateful for that help, as are the two who work with us; we shall be grateful for your continued help along this line if your soul so prompts you, provided you ever retain that which is needed for your quiet, gracious, restful living in a suitable abiding place, close to the centre of our work.

We are endeavouring to prolong the life of A.A.B., which should have ended this year; we are doing so, much against her wishes, in order that the work in Europe can be stabilised and the books completed. I put these two things in the order of their importance. Help her all you can. She asks me not to write this, but has my instructions so to do. Her life is harder than you know, and but for F.B. she would not be here at all.

Every morning, at noon, and each night before retiring to sleep, align yourself with your soul, with the Ashram and with me, and say very quietly and with no tension:

"I stand a point of peace, and through the point

which I can thus provide, love and true light can flow.

I stand in restful poise, and through that poise I can attract the gifts which I must give—an understanding heart, a quiet mind, myself.

I never am alone, for round me gather those I seek to serve, my brothers in the Ashram, souls that demand my help, e'en though I see them not, and those in distant places who seek the Master of my life, my brother, the Tibetan."

That is all the meditation I would have you do *for the remainder of your life,* except the meditations in group formation at the Headquarters of our work. You will find that these affirmations, affirmed by you three times a day, will suffice to calm your mind and turn the place where you *abide* into a shrine.

This communication may be somewhat surprising to you. Seldom do I deal with physical plane matters, and I deal with this matter of a "centre of peaceful abode" for you only because its lack and your refusal (an interior refusal) to seek a *suitable* place to live are indications of a mental condition which should be brought to an end by you. This restlessness affects the quality of your vibration, and this in turn, to a slight (a very slight) degree, affects your ashramic group of brothers.

A future of service opens wide for you if, I repeat, you are willing to do the little things and finish what you begin.

My blessing and my love for you—the love of a Master for his disciple, distant and close, remote yet near—is ever yours.

To L-T. S. K.

September 1943

BROTHER OF MINE:

Our association together has existed for many years. It also began many lives ago. You should have advanced to a more intimate stage of discipleship had it not been for your always ready and still persistent response to the unreal, the unnecessary, and to that which comes in between you and the clear, steady enlightened progress upon the Path which should be yours. You will note that I use not the word glamour here. The reason is that it is apparently an entirely meaningless word to you, and I felt that I should emphasise the fact that glamour (as far as you are concerned) means that which sidesteps you from the desired service, that which engrosses your attention and prevents you from concentrating on the realities of life and circumstance, that which places you always at the centre of some big scheme as the master-mind making some discovery, as the architect of some building which is intended to house humanity, and that which comes between you and the simple duty of a pledged disciple—for *that* you unchangeably are.

You have, my brother, a good illustration of what I mean in the two plans which you have evolved during the past six months for world salvage and unity. One of them was supposed to be in response to my request for a paper, but another paper which I asked you to write is still unwritten and that paper was more important than the other. These plans were drawn; time was taken in submitting them to various people, and to what end? There was in them nothing new. The minds and some of the best minds in every country in the world are formulating them. Your plans were simply compilations of familiar suggestions which have already been presented in better form to the public. What end, therefore, did they serve? Only to sidetrack you from the simple duty of today; only to feed that inclination on your part to do something great; only to prevent you from a true and practical cooperation in my plans which you know well and which the disciples in my Ashram are pledged to materialise. It is their group duty, *not* from the angle of authoritative demand, or in a spirit of blind obedience but because from free choice and identity of purpose (as far as they can realise it) they are in my Ashram; they have willingly responded to my planned intentions and in a spirit of dedication to the good of humanity.

All this indicates to me that you are still prone to slip into the thraldom of the vague vision, the grandiose formulations of something and are negatively responsive to the collective ideas of forward-thinking men, for you do no positive or original thinking of your own. Glamour still holds you.

You might well ask, my brother: Why then keep me in your group? Why not wait until I have learnt better and have dropped this tendency? Because you need the protection of the Ashram and you need—from the centre of protection —to learn then to accept the duty of obedience to the ashramic intent and to work under the direction of the loving intentions of Those Whom you do recognise as more experienced disciples than yourself. You are in my Ashram also from old association and because you earned the reward of this recognition and opportunity by being the first to appreciate the significance of my books and the teaching that they convey, and to aid the effort of A.A.B. For that reason you earned the right to my appreciation and hers, and have had them both. That was the one clear bit of spiritual thinking you have done in this incarnation. Therefore, the Ashram protects you, and your brothers stand around you, and for this brief incarnation you are a liability—but a liability which can, with your cooperation, be changed in your next incarnation into a group asset.

There is consequently no need for the slightest discouragement and I say that with definite purpose and truth. There is only room for the acceptance of facts. What facts, brother of mine? Let me (with my usual frankness) tell you. Let me point out to you what I feel and those who know you best feel should be your attitude for the remainder of this life. If you accept these ideas and cooperate willingly, you will do much to free yourself; if you refuse to see the light, you will but delay the process and continue to exact the protecting care of the Ashram for a longer period. Let me first highlight your career of glamour so as to prove to you, intelligently, the points I seek to make.

I shall not deal with your life, prior to the recognition period which enabled you to render me and the world outstanding service. Your recognition and aid of the work I was doing has released certain energies which will have much to do with the changing of the consciousness of humanity. Remember that the Hierarchy has this service of yours in mind.

There was the glamour of the wonderful discovery you were going to make, covering several years of experimentation and leading nowhere. Why? Because you had neither the training nor the capacity to do the work. It will be better done and in other ways and by better minds than yours. Your equipment was not adequate.

There was the glamour of spiritual power which led some of your group brothers astray for months. There has always been a glamourous response to personalities who have misled and glamoured you in the business world and led you into devious and difficult situations, and which forced you, eventually, to recognise that they were not the least what you had thought. What is this but the glamour of personalities? Until you have learnt to see people as they truly are, you cannot do the exoteric work of a disciple.

Then came an interlude. I asked for your resignation from the group, and the door of the inner Ashram closed upon you. That was very good for you and you endeavoured in that period to attend to the business of life, watching yourself with care. Then the door of the Ashram reopened and you were readmitted to the group life. For a year all seemed well, but the dual stimulation of the Ashram and the active work in my group proved too much, and glamour again enveloped you.

You started by formulating large schemes for world regeneration and for a super-organisation, and yet all that time the work that I wanted done and the outlines of the work as indicated by me, and to which your group brothers and my Ashram are pledged, played no part in your planning. You have been unhappy and bewildered because of the lack of sympathy, yet what would you have your brothers do? Would you have them aid me in helping you to free yourself from wild schemes and planning, or would you have them back you up and strengthen the hold that glamour has upon you?

Here are my suggestions, brother of mine, given in all

love and understanding, and with a real appreciation of your sincerity of devotion, your great and beautiful staying-power, your essential humility and your very real need for protection.

1. Accept the fact that you need protection, and be grateful.
2. Accept the fact that in this life you have neither the mental equipment nor the clear vision to enable you to be a leader, an organiser or a drawer of blueprints for the Hierarchy.
3. Accept the fact that you are not young enough to make many basic personality changes, for the sixth ray crystallises too rapidly.
4. Accept the fact that in the performance of your home and business duties and in the effort to bring happiness to those in your environment lies for you the immediate solution of your problem. A simple, humble life of service and of self-forgetfulness will do more to free you than any violent endeavour to understand and combat glamour. You do not yet even comprehend what it is; it can only be overcome by the illumined mind, and there is therefore, for you, nothing else to be done but to strengthen your soul contact by practical spiritual living upon the physical plane, and by a complete refraining from all thought anent the future world, future scientific discoveries, future world orders, and the manner whereby they can be instituted.

The moment your mind becomes preoccupied with the universal aspects of life it is thrown into confusion; its thought-form-making proclivities become violent, and the illumination of the soul is then unable to penetrate. You need to learn to *bring that illumination into your personality daily life upon the physical plane.* What measure of it you have received has been retained upon the mental plane and dedicated to matters far too big for you in this incarnation and with your present equipment. This has led to a chronic state of glamour. Live practically, sweetly, humbly and lovingly for the remainder of this life, and demonstrate beauty in personality relations. You will thus release your mind from pressures too great for it, and so begin to tread the way of liberation.

Can you do this, my brother? Can you bring spirituality into business and live in the business world as a disciple? If you cannot do this, you will have to learn to do it, because discipleship leaves no aspect of life unlived, and business is an aspect of human living. Can you bring naught but peace, happiness and confidence into your home and into your association at the Headquarters of my work in the world? Can you begin to be one to whom the enquirer can turn for help, knowing that he will get enough practical assistance to enable him to see the next step ahead? You can do and be all these things, my brother. Your task is to demonstrate discipleship in the daily life, and not to duplicate the discipleship of those more advanced than yourself.

Do the group work and meditation as indicated. I assign you no special work. I seek to see you more closely integrated into the group in my Ashram of which you *are* a part. Have no doubts and questionings. You are a part of my Ashram, and that brings the needed protection, as well as certain risks of overstimulation. The love and understanding and gratitude of your group brothers stands with warmth around you. I have no need to assure you of my protecting care and constant interest. The years must have proved it to you.

November 1944

My Brother and Friend of Olden Time:

There is absolutely no need for the profound depression and for the process of self-accusation in which you so constantly live. Years ago, your dream was to serve the Master, to be known by Him and to be a part of His group or Ashram. You longed for the status, technically understood, of an accepted disciple. You have served the Master and rendered us, as I told you, notable service; you are known by me, and it is perhaps the fact of this knowledge and its implications which disturbs you so deeply; you are an integral part of a group, affiliated with my Ashram; you are an accepted disciple. You have, therefore, every reason to feel encouraged.

You are, however, aware of weaknesses and of failure. So be it. But the fact remains that the major trend and purpose of your life has brought you into the Ashram. So be it again, my brother. All within the Ashram, except those of higher initiate status, fall short at times.

One of the things which I said at my last word with you was that your age was such that it was well-nigh impossible for you to change. Yet you have changed quite definitely during the past year, and by your refusal to cultivate the glamourous thinking which characterised you in past years and so oft proved your undoing, you have made real progress—more real progress than at any previous time. This has almost surprised me. When I raised the point with a member of my Ashram (known to none of you in this group which I am instructing), he remarked: "The soul is after all a Master, and when the force of masterhood is released, bringing quiescence and acquiescence, it is difficult to predict the happenings possible." Your quiescence, demonstrated upon the physical plane, largely as depression and fatigue, produced a negativity which made it difficult for any positive glamour to show itself; this greatly helped, weakening through attrition the hold which it has had upon your astral body. See that it gains no strength again. But be not depressed; simply be negative to all the suggestions of glamour and be encouraged at my words, for I speak not lightly or untruly. No spectacular progress will be made by you in this life. Accept that as factual and be happy at the quiet of the coming period before you pass over to the other side. Make full use of the time and read, study and think.

You have for long asked me to tell you the rays upon which your three personality bodies are to be found. I do so now, for you can profit from the information.

You have, as you know, a third ray soul and a sixth ray personality. Your task as regards the latter is to transit on to the first ray, so that next life you will come into incarnation with the difficult combination of three and one. For this the training, discipline and discoveries of the present incarnation should have prepared you, and you can therefore face the future with caution but with surety.

Your *mental body* is on the fifth ray and hence your interest in things scientific; but the calibre of your mind is not yet of such a nature that you can profit from this, and this is a fact which you must accept.

Your *astral body* is first ray in nature and hence the potent hold which glamour has had on you—a glamour inherited from three previous lives and rendered one-pointed and powerful in this life through your first ray astral nature. You *willed* to deal with glamour; you ran, last life, a great risk of wandering on to the path of black magic. Your recognition of me and my work and your instantaneous cooperation, completely negated that possibility, but the tendency to glamour remained and still does.

Your *physical body* is third ray in type, and this has intensified the worst aspects of that ray, because soul energy (undirected by an illumined mind) at times stimulates it and the glamour can take effect in physical plane activity.

If you can develop mental perception to a fuller degree, and if you can achieve in this life and the next a measure of real illumination, all the difficulties now troubling you will be resolved. In your next incarnation, you should endeavour to work through a second ray astral body, for there is a real lack of second ray force in your most difficult equipment. There are too many energies in your present equipment along the line of the first ray, and your ultimate goal must be a second ray personality, following upon the coming first ray personality of your next life. Love and light are greatly needed by you, and their reception by you in your lower fourfold nature would produce great transforming results. These must be brought about by you through keen interest in and love of others, and by stern mental control and unfoldment.

August 1946

BROTHER OF OLD:

This is but a parting word to you as regards your physical plane affiliation with my Ashram. I will start by assuring you that the inner link remains unbroken and will persist, though even I have no idea when freedom will distinguish you or when you can advance with surety into the Ashram itself. Any progress that you could have made this life, as a result of my corrective teaching and aid, has been largely negated by your supine acceptance of failure, by your profound and lasting "conviction of sin" (if I may use so old-fashioned a phrase), and by your constant inner dwelling on your group relations. You did fail, my brother. But why stay overwhelmed by failure for year after year and remain with your eyes concentrated on the lower self that failed? All have failed and will again along some line. E'en the Masters fail at times to pass through one or other of the highest initiations at their first attempt and—from the hierarchical angle —that connotes failure. But the failure is scarce recognised; the effort is made to register what caused the failure and the inability to stand before the One Initiator, for all effects emanate from some *ascertainable* cause. So should it be on all levels of advancement, even such a relatively unimportant effort (from the point of view of hierarchical work) as your attempt to gain the right of entry into my Ashram or what is called "ashramic penetration," and then on and up through many graded failures, until you meet the well-known failure of the Buddha to attain His goal.

I have therefore for you a message based on the words of the initiate, Paul: "Forgetting the things which are behind, press forward." Dwell no longer on the past but make the relatively few years which are left you of this life, years of usefulness and of purpose in my work. This will require the acquisition and the recognition of a spirit which is unembarrassed by ambition but which is pledged to *the perfecting of each day's relationships*. Preoccupation with the beautifying and the spiritualising of the day's affairs will give you no time for any reaction to glamour; your mind and desire (your kama-manasic nature) will be—with definite purpose —physically oriented; your demonstration of right living upon the physical plane will be to you the factor of major importance.

Your spiritual focus will remain unaltered, and it is this tenacity (which you have ever demonstrated) which has preserved untouched your relationship with me and with your brothers; you need therefore have no concern in relation to your spiritual expression on its own plane. It is your physical expression which has been at fault. Reflect with assiduity on these words of mine. A focussing of your spiritual attitude and nature upon the physical plane will result in a more dynamic life, instead of the basically negative life you at present demonstrate; you will be surprised at the results which may eventuate.

I am giving you no meditation. I seek to see the flow of your spiritual life *downward* into daily life, and I seek not to see you raising your human soul towards a soul contact you seldom achieve, consciously at least, this life. Your problem has been due to the fact that in the past you at one time achieved a most definite soul contact, but knew not how to handle the force engendered. In this incarnation, this force flowed into the astral body to a very great extent and evoked the glamour and the deception which have coloured your life. But—you have a vast stored reservoir of spiritual potency on higher levels than the astral, and can perhaps draw upon its source of love and light *if* your major concentration and preoccupation is the perfecting of your daily living in the place where you are and in the environment and the circumstances for which you are responsible.

You need have no fear that I shall withdraw from you the attention and the careful thought which I have given you all these years. I earnestly desire to see you achieve success; I have been sorry when you failed. I seek to have you *within* the Ashram, which is *not* as yet the case. A move forward can, however, be made this life if—in your closing years—you obey instructions. Go forward in confidence, my brother; the group has never left you or deserted you, and you need no assurance from me that I hold you in my thought.

To R. S. W.

January 1940

Your glamour is, as you know, that of psychic sensitivity. Like S.C.P. you function on the astral-buddhic line; but, having a trained mind from the educational angle (for you passed through college, did you not, my brother?) you have a somewhat different problem. Your task is to use your mind for the unfoldment of the intuition and for the control of the lower psychic nature. This psychic glamour does *not* unduly distort your point of view but its very presence constitutes a disturbing element to you. You neither like nor desire this psychic sensitivity or the knowledge which it brings, but it constitutes an environment in which you have to learn to walk with freedom and with grace. It is not some situation from which you must aim at escaping for it is part of manifestation and you must learn to work with it and function in it but with complete detachment from it—just as you do not identify yourself with physical phenomena such as rain or storm. Glamour exists. It is. The higher glamours are goals towards which the lower psychics must work and your work may lie along the line of helping them in the midst of the glamour and by this remark I may aid in reorienting your thought and dissipating some of your concern.

A person, for instance, who has been astrally and psychically controlled by the glamour of selfish desire and material aims will have made a real step forward when he escapes into the glamour of devotion to a teacher—a glamour which, for you, would be a thing lying behind in your experience and no longer of controlling importance.

Ponder on this and, if you care to do so, list the higher and lower glamours and indicate how the lower can be transmuted into the higher powers, leading to a later liberation. In this problem of the glamour of psychic sensitivity, you can do much to solve it by the right handling of the time equation (for time in reception of contacts, as it is called at times, has a real relationship to the growth of glamours) and in the elimination of nonessentials. Go forward, therefore, in service with joy and with confidence. The glamours hold you not in truth but you need more understanding of their nature.

August 1940

BROTHER OF MINE:

I would ask you whether the implications as to the relationship between your soul and personality rays to the rays of your astral and physical vehicles interests you in any way? The two lower rays are the same as the two higher and in between stands the ray which is, par excellence, that which provides the battleground for the disciple in training. Twelve of the group members have the fourth Ray of Harmony through Conflict controlling the mental body, hence consequent conflict and proffered opportunity, plus an expressed ambition for the achievement of psychic harmony between the soul of form and the soul itself. It is through the conflict between these two that harmony becomes possible. This is the ray of testing, the energy which brings about trial. People struggle with ideas, with attaining the goal of their current idealism and are driven by longing to find peace, joy and divine assurance. After the cycle of lives in which the mental ray varies from life to life, there arrives an incarnation wherein the ray of harmony through conflict dominates; then the disciple is specifically put to the proof and is tested and tried in order to demonstrate to him the gain or the nongain of the past cycle of living experience. Such a proposition faces many in this group today as it, in its turn, faces humanity, one of whose controlling rays is the fourth.

You can, therefore, expect to have to face up to a life of testing and of change. This is not to posit that the testing and change and battle will be of a physical nature or on the physical plane or will involve physical plane decisions. This ray produces the "harmonising" strain and stress on any of the planes (using these words technically) and for the majority of you it is pre-eminently active upon the astral plane.

There the tests will come, with repercussions—if I may use such a phrase—upon the buddhic or intuitional plane.

You are facing changes in your life. I would here point out to you that changes in the life of a pledged disciple can be due to two main causes: the working out of karma which is unavoidable but which presents opportunity, or it can be due to the free choice and free decision, involving direct initiating activity on the part of the disciple; these decisions can be carried out or avoided according to his own planning. This line of activity has, therefore, little to do with precipitating karma but is concerned with intelligent initiating of new karma which will, in its turn, produce its inevitable effects later. I call this to your attention, my brother, because you are reaching the point in your career as a soul where you can consciously engineer situations and conditions which are *not* effects or results but are the commencement of new cycles. It is a momentous time in the soul's progress when conscious decisions can be made with due appreciation of consequences.

I am also referring to this because you are meditating steps (are you not, my brother?) which will produce effective change. I seek to have you ponder upon the responsibility involved and know with clarity your motive. Lives of indecision come wherein the man balances back and forth between decision and indecision, arriving apparently at no action. They are lives of apparent futility but nevertheless of great value. Needless to point out that such incarnations are frequently lived under the sun-sign of Libra or have Libra as the rising sign. Prior to that particular life, the man has had little difficulty. He is conditioned by precipitating karma and at the same time experiences little difficulty in arriving at decisions, because his choices and aims will be motivated by the personality and determined by the lower self. Later, after a life or lives of balancing, the die is cast and the period of inactivity and of indecision ends and the soul begins to determine action; karma then comes under the processes of conscious transmutation. Motives become purified and objectives shift from those of personality ambition to the spiritual goals of humanity.

Such a life is upon you now, my brother, and I am therefore seeking to make the issues clear to you. Personality decisions are not for you; and for you, likewise, the period of indecision *must* end and it will end when you see soul purpose more clearly. You might here ask: In what way can I know? How can I arrive at right decision? First of all by eliminating selfishness and arriving at that unconcern as to the happiness or the experience of the personality; secondly, by refusing to move hurriedly. The disciple has to learn that when he has arrived at right—and therefore for him irrevocable decision—that this very motive and decision starts energy working along the indicated lines and that, having decided, he now moves slowly in the wake of that energy. There are deep significances in what I am here telling you and I beg you to strive to understand my meaning.

I would ask you (in order to help you to see clearly and so be of greater service to others) to make a study this winter of the Law of Karma. Read the books upon the subject but take not too seriously their deductions. Gather out of that which I have written all the information you can find concerning this theme. And, my brother, having done so, you will then arrange that material in its right and spiritual order and significance, and at the same time reduce your ideas to written form for your own clarification and the helping of your brothers. This teaching has a group significance.

I am not referring more clearly to your life decisions and plans. They are your own concern. I have sought to widen the "spread" of your consciousness so that you can bring to any planned life of service a reasoned judgment and a seasoned experience. These two phrases should express the personality quality of the trained disciple. For your personal meditation I suggest the following:

Take ten minutes twice a day for deep reflection on one of the themes listed below, viewing them in two ways: the individual interpretation and, secondly, that interpretation which concerns humanity as a whole. If you will do this regularly, you will build the bridge between the part and the whole.

    a. The dharma of the individual in the home.
    b. The duty of the individual in the group.
    c. The obligation of the individual to humanity.
    d. The responsibility of the individual to life.
    e. The reaction of the individual to karma, personal and human.
    f. The relation of the individual to the Hierarchy.

You have there six months' work in meditation. It will involve the practical relation of man to karma, individual life to the mass life as its flows through him, and life also as it actuates the group to life and as it expresses itself through nations and through humanity as a whole.

The blessing of the soul rests upon you, my brother— your soul, my soul and the soul of all.

August 1942

1. Shift your consciousness into the lighted mind, for lit it is, and look not down but up; be not so conscious of the outer form.
2. For two years study, read and serve within the circle wherein your soul has placed your feet. Then look for greater scope, perhaps within that selfsame circle or perhaps within another. But relinquish not the first.
3. Develop joy in self-forgetfulness and serve your brothers in my Ashram. Two of them need you much.
4. Ponder the usefulness of *shock*, applied by you in love and yet with full detachment and clarity of speech.
5. You need to learn the art of reverence, my chela. The chain of Hierarchy is a fit subject for reflection.
6. Upon that chain you have your place. Some move ahead of you. Some move along with you. Others again move on with hands out-stretched to you. True occult reverence holds the key. This means recognition, not obedience, not stooping down or looking up.

September 1943

MY BELOVED BROTHER:

I have been concerned about you. The strain under which you work and live is not good, and has a definite physical effect which is not desirable. I foresaw this risk, and it was for that reason that the first of the six statements I gave you enjoined you to:

1. Shift your consciousness into the lighted mind.
2. Look up, not down.
3. Be not so conscious of the outer form.

In these words I sought to have you turn your eyes away from the form aspect of the present world catastrophe, because your sensitivity led you to assume too close an identification with it. Such identification is a handicap and not a help. It feeds the life of the solar plexus, because the solar plexus centre of humanity as a whole is in a condition of appalling riot—if I may use so peculiar a phrase.

The next statement sought to swing you into the circle of your service in relation to your group brothers and the senior group within the Arcane School. Circumstances, however, moved you from my Headquarters, and this became difficult of fulfilment.

The need for you at this time is to *study* deeply and to do work which is practically entirely along occult lines. The study of psychology which interests you so much and for which you are in so many other ways so eminently fitted, tunes you in at this time too rapidly on world distress and you should avoid it. The duties of the home, the bringing of joy to those you daily meet, and the keeping of the mind upon things occult will do much to offset the astral sensitivity which is one of your major assets in helpful service, but which under the pressure of the world events has become almost too strong for you to handle. The "chain of Hierarchy" is a good subject for your constant reflection, and I want you to pay close attention to my recommendation that this concept form the background of your daily thinking. As you keep that chain in mind, it tunes in on the Ashram, and therefore on the Hierarchy, for you are a disciple of some standing. This will offset the astral sensitivity, for the energy of the Ashram stimulates the head and heart centres and draws up the astral forces from the solar plexus.

I set no meditation of a special kind for you. The group meditation will suffice. I ask you to do much occult study and much teaching and helping of occult students. Your work for another year should be primarily with the senior students, and you should endeavour to have a larger and more organised output of work in that connection; it will serve to focus the consciousness more firmly in the head. If it were possible at some time in the near future, I would suggest that you go and talk to A.A.B. She had your problem in a worse degree, but had more experience to offset it and less time in which to succumb. I have told her certain things anent you which I do not wish to write, and she will give you all the time you need, if you will come to where she is.

It is for this reason I write no more today. Also, my brother, I give you at this time much attention in the Ashram, and my strength surrounds you. There is no cause for anxiety, for the future is assured, but seek during the coming year to take advantage of my suggestions.

November 1944

MY BROTHER:

Last year my instructions to you were very brief, but they were full of suggestion and potent to bring you release, had you followed them with exactitude. There are certain forms of pride from which every one suffers more or less, though the degree and quality may differ according to ray or type. Yours is a determination, or I might call it predilection, to use your mind at times when the simple acquiescence of a loving heart is what you need. L.F.U. has a form of pride also and makes a fetish of his personal liberty, consequently putting himself in bondage to the concept of freedom; he needs to learn that no one is really free, a disciple least of all.

You, my brother and disciple, love the activity of the mind, and you enter—with your eyes open—into situations in order to learn and experience the delight which comes from analysis, reflection and mental activity, followed by some decision.

I am speaking thus frankly to you, my tried and loved disciple, because I see more effective service to be rendered by you if you can master a difficult lesson at this time. You are exceedingly well equipped to serve. Your second ray energy, coupled with your seventh ray force, makes for almost unique and unusual service; however—and here lies a hindrance—your fourth ray mind, constantly presenting fields of conflict which you must conquer, deflects the energy which, pouring through your soul, could lead to a planned and organised activity upon the physical plane. But it does not. The descending soul energy and the ascending personality aspiration meet upon the mental plane, and there both of them are arrested by your over-analytical mind. You need not infer from this that you are not of service to people; but it is an individual here and there that you assist, and there is no rhythm or organisation in your service, owing to the constant mental conflict.

From the very first time you were admitted into my Ashram, I have tried to aid you to centralise all your forces upon the physical plane. When a disciple does this, and when he is one-pointed in his activity, there is much that he can do. When to these tendencies of inflow and of concentration there is added a trained and illumined mind, then the disciple becomes a focal point of spiritual attraction. He can reach many, yet ever remain polarised at his own centre; his life then has an ordered rhythm, and there is a steadfast adherence to a plan which is carried through at all costs. He takes also his rightful position as a representative of an Ashram.

Forget not that the Masters choose Their disciples, not only from karmic relation (if such a relation exists), not only because the disciple demands light and has a powerful aspiration towards spiritual things, but because the disciple is equipped to render some definite service which fits into the ashramic intention of the moment. You are thus well equipped; your health is good, even if you think it not, and will be better still when rhythm enters into your life. You have a free mind and much, very much, intuition. You have (could you but realise it) what many people dream of possessing—time and leisure. You do not believe this, but that is because your daily life is full of the nonessentials—nonessential in view of world emergency. You are magnetic and attractive and can reach people through the expression of your potent love nature. Yet at the close of each year you realise that you have not accomplished very much. You may have helped a person here or there and your general influence is good. But I look for more than that from those in training and in preparation for initiation. You are in your forty-seventh year. By the time a disciple reaches the age of forty-nine his pathway of life service should be clearly defined. Yours is not. You have, however, two years left in which to bring through on to the physical plane all the energies with which you are endowed and to produce that ordered rhythm and arranged living which are required to make a definite impact upon the minds of those around you.

You play around with ideas all the time; you experiment all the time, but that should now be past history. I ask you now, for the sake of a needy world, and because I seek to see you fill your rightful place in my Ashram, to readjust your living conditions in order to serve more adequately. I would call your attention to the words, "your rightful place in my Ashram." Do you know what that place is? I would have you find out.

An Ashram is ever in a state of constant flux and movement. Disciples are passing out of it to form their own Ashrams or to take up a specific place in another Ashram as they meet the requirements of more advanced stages. They are shifting from one degree to another; they are moving forward steadily from the periphery to the centre, from the outer ring-pass-not to the lighted dynamic centre. As they move forward, preserving ever the close inner unity, place is made for new disciples—to be admitted and trained for service.

Part of the service rendered by members of an Ashram is

to make way for new aspirants. This they do by hastening their own progress and moving forward. When disciples take one of the final initiations, or when they are admitted to a higher and more potent Ashram, vacancies occur which are always promptly filled. The occult law which governs all progress in an Ashram is sometimes called the Law of Fulfilment. By this is meant the full compliance of a disciple with the service demands upon the outer plane. When his service is as full and as effective as he can render it, then— under a condition which is in the nature of a group occult paradox—his outer effectiveness produces an inner effectiveness. You have all been taught (though theoretically for the most part) that inner effectiveness produces illumined and potent service. Now learn the reverse side of this truth. I will elucidate no further, for your own thinking should suffice.

You have, my brother, three things to do:

First of all, you must so think, reflect and meditate that your brain will be the recipient of your planned thinking, and not simply a sensitive registering instrument. Through right meditation, the energy from your soul and mind must be focussed, via the head centre. Speaking in symbols which you easily understand, "the lighted triangle of soul and mind and head will awaken the centre between the eyes and bring into activity the eye of direction"; this is at present closed, and only occasionally opened. You have been greatly concerned for years over the direction of your thoughts and the trend of your thinking; shift now your attention to directed service. Undertake a task for me and bring it to accomplishment.

The second thing you have to do is to assess your equipment and ascertain—from within yourself—where lies your field of service—one field, my brother, not many. A disciple of your standing serves a group and not just a person here and there, and frequently persons of no spiritual importance whose destiny can be well left to their own souls or some teacher not of discipleship grade. I do not choose to be more explicit. Your field of service is clear, could you but see it, but of no use to you unless you enter it voluntarily, freely and with understanding.

The final thing which calls for your attention is to grasp in a new and dynamic manner the dual life of discipleship. Your field of service and your field of karmic obligation must never rule each other out, but you must learn to function efficiently in both careers. Your time for learning, technically understood, must now give place to the use of what you have acquired of understanding and wisdom.

I suggest for your helping, the following meditation. You must bear in mind that it is only of service to you if followed steadily and with continuity. It is largely in the nature of a visualisation exercise.

1. Rapid alignment and the sounding of the O M three times.
2. Focussing the consciousness in the soul with a corresponding concentration in the head at as high a point as possible.
3. Then sound the O M four times. This is followed by a pause.
4. The following visualisation exercise is carried forward from the point of concentration attained. If your attention wanders, sound the O M again. This is sometimes called the "recalling O M."
   a. See in the mind's eye a sea of light.
   b. Then see yourself standing and awaiting direction upon the physical plane. Hold these two thoughts quietly for a little time or picture them simultaneously.
   c. Then you—the disciple upon the physical plane— sound the O M inaudibly, dynamically and clearly, and as you do so, see a movement or current in the sea of lighted energy, converging towards you.
   d. See it take form as a stream of down-flowing energy —the energy of love, of strength and of understanding.
   e. Imagine next that divine flow sweeping through your mind and your astral body and settling into your etheric vehicle, awaiting a Word of Power.
   f. Then again sound the O M and feel the impact of

the tidal wave (if I may so call it) of spiritual energy, entering into your head centre, passing from
thence to the ajna centre, and involving in its flow
the centre in the medulla oblongata—the alta major
centre.

g. Then, at the exact moment of this realised dispersion, say, "This source of power is all I am and
have; I send it forth to serve my fellowmen; I thus
prepare the way into the Ashram, thus drawing men
toward the source of power and strength."

5. Having completed this exercise, then meditate for
ten minutes upon the service you are asked to render;
see it motivated and implemented by the energy just
received, and let your creative imagination build for
you a structure for your service.

I have spoken to you with directness, my brother. I am,
as I have told several of your group brothers, ambitious that
all of you in my Ashram may become creative and constructive workers within and for the Hierarchy. I am exceedingly anxious also to see you expressing in fuller measure
all that you are, and thus end this time of "flighty service"
(forgive me for this word, but I speak to arrest your con
sciousness) and enter into that full demonstration of the will-
to-good which brings always joy and effectiveness.

We have walked the path of life in relation to each other
for years now. I have held you safe from harm whilst you
got your bearings and tested out your strength, but that
time should now be past. I stand by you at all times, but you
must now come forth into steadfast ordered work, shouldering responsibility and "growing up" spiritually. The time of
spiritual adolescence is past for you. Will you realise that
and now *work?*

August 1946

MY DISCIPLE:

You are of those in this group who are *within* the Ashram, and that fact carries with it a definite obligation and

responsibility. In my last instruction to you (given two years ago) I dwelt much on this, and I would like to tell you that you have made progress, that you have eliminated much non-essential living, and are finding more time for real service. You are becoming—as an occult phrase puts it—"grounded in your place"; that was for you an essential step. Now must come the mastering of the technique or method whereby (from that place) you move forward in any *needed* direction —along the line of service.

In this connection, no one can help you; you have to find the ways and means, alone and unaided. This effort on your part, this groping here and there for a rightful field of service, is largely responsible for your exceeding sensitivity; you move in one direction and react to a needed opposition; this proves upsetting and may lead to a psychic crisis. You move in another direction and are immediately assailed by that which is to you a phantom of fear; you move elsewhere but the opportunity for service proffered measures not up to your capacity, and this you register and again withdraw, conscious always of psychic atmospheres and conditions. What then to do?

A great experiment is being attempted in the Arcane School. It is an endeavour to lift off the shoulders of the Masters the training of aspirants for discipleship and thus to prepare them to take their stand upon the periphery of an Ashram—in this case mine. I am thus lifting much along this line off the shoulders of other Masters. Masters such as K.H. and M. deal only at this time with trained disciples— such are the exigencies of world work. In the advanced section of the Arcane School this experiment is going on, though as yet only in an embryonic manner; more difficult and specific training should be given to the few who are reacting correctly to the "call of the Hierarchy." I have spoken to A.A.B. upon this matter, and along the line pointed out to her I ask your help and your time; I would ask you also to permit A.A.B. to train you more specifically for this work, and to do so with confidence, as the link between you two is strong and you have ever permitted her to speak to you with frankness.

You need to learn to protect yourself from people, in a psychic sense. This protection can be applied in several ways. I could myself put around you a protecting shield; I choose not to do so, for you would learn naught thereby. The work must be done by you yourself, and basically involves the transmutation of the sacral centre (not the solar plexus, as you might naturally think) to the throat. In the sacral centre lie the ancient racial fears and deep-seated personal desires. Ponder not upon the sacral centre, for that would bring these ancient inheritances to the surface, but let your work be related to the creative throat centre. Then perform the following exercise:

1. Sound the O M within the throat centre, as the soul focussed in the ajna centre.
2. See (with the creative imagination) the throat centre as a radiant, vibrant, brilliant reservoir and *know* it to be so.
3. Then send forth from that centre a broad and vital stream of energy, down the spine to the sacral centre in the spine, preserving the stream intact in your consciousness so that no part of it is deflected to the physical counterparts of the sacral centre, the gonads.
4. Then see the sacral centre (in the spine) as a radiant reservoir of energy, but as energy deflected from physical creative activity to the destruction of ancient racial fears in the world. Then project that energy out into the world of men, to aid in the destruction of fear.
5. Next, reaffirming your consciousness positively in the ajna centre, withdraw your attention from the sacral centre and the throat centre and sound the O M—as the directing disciple—seven times, slowly and inaudibly.

Use this exercise as often as needed, but just now and for six months use it every day. You will be surprised what it will do for you.

The meditation I last gave you will serve you for the rest of your life, so I give you no meditation now.

To you, as to others in the group, I say: Go forward with

confidence and with joy; establish a closer contact with me, your friend and teacher.

November 1948

MY BROTHER:

I start today with a word of real commendation to you. Since my last communication to you, you have succeeded in doing two things: stabilised the "grounding in your place" in my Ashram (to which I referred in my last communication to you) and you have also paralleled that by a very definite shifting of your astral polarisation on to higher astral levels —a task that is occupying the attention of a very large number of disciples at this time. The reason for this is that a very great part of the work of the returning Christ will affect greatly the astral plane. Disciples are therefore needed who can absorb, transmute and transfer light. For this task you are peculiarly equipped and hence the psychic difficulties which have for some years confronted you and caused you difficulty. This trouble will greatly lessen from now on, particularly if you proceed to labour at your task . . . preparatory to the reappearance of the Christ.

Those disciples who work today in the world and do so *consciously* in order to aid the Christ and His mission, come within the protecting aura with which the Head of the Hierarchy at all times surrounds certain work undertaken by the Hierarchy in connection with our planet. This work of preparation for His coming is curiously fraught with danger because of the immense and constant antagonism it arouses (and is arousing increasingly) in the opposing forces of evil. The main attack of these forces is upon disciples and particularly those in a position and at the point in evolution where they can act with potency and greatly help in the task of reaching others. This you can do, and *along with all disciples* are, therefore, marked "for protection," as it is esoterically called. This does not mean that you will be free from attack and—because you are a disciple—attack on all three bodies simultaneously, but it means that such attack will arouse in you no fear. Remember always, brother of mine, that it is fear that permits the entry of wrong potencies, and that such an attack may not be aimed at your weakest point but preferably at your strongest; it is there where disciples are often caught unawares and thus suffer a temporary setback.

The astral plane is in a great state of turmoil today—but that is a theme upon which I will dwell in my next communication to this group of disciples. It is nevertheless something to bear in mind. This turmoil is caused by an increasing descent of the Christ energy from the buddhic plane into the astral plane—a necessary aggregation of spiritual forces of a strength sufficient to create a reservoir of this energy of which the Hierarchy can avail itself as it proceeds towards externalisation. Of that force (which is astral-buddhic in nature) disciples such as yourself can take advantage. It carries the qualities of "embodied light," sensitivity to the new incoming vibration, and protective *pliancy*—I know not what other word to use. It can only be used by working disciples; therefore *work,* my brother, and let that penetrating energy find a channel through you.

I have told you these things in order to reassure you, for you have been in the past somewhat prone to psychic fear, though a very great improvement in this respect can be noticed. Those who work in this coming cycle must cast off fear and refuse to register in their consciousness—by an act of the spiritual will—the very existence of that which causes the reaction of fear. It is not the "little wills of men" which must here be used, but the bringing in of the higher spiritual will, via the antahkarana. It was with this in view that I gave out the teaching upon the antahkarana before proclaiming the reappearance of the Christ.

In the reorganisation of the Arcane School, I would ask you to take your full share and to concentrate your major effort upon the work of the senior students. Have in mind always that it is *spiritual* esotericism that is required; teaching the students to create a line of light between themselves and all circumstances and problems. This is possible because every problem is in reality a vital thoughtform, effective for good or evil. The line of established light can dispel the evil or act as a transmitter of the energy of the will-to-good. In the above few sentences I have given you a potent hint and one which should be taught to all true aspirants.

There is little more that I have to say to you. You might find it of true helpfulness if you gathered together and read at one sitting, slowly and carefully, all which I have given to you in your personal instructions since this group was organised. This will give you (as nothing else can) a synthetic view of the general pattern of your spiritual growth and advancement.

Go forward with a sense of strength, knowing that the power of your soul, the solidarity of the Ashram, and the protective aura which surrounds the work of the Christ can ever be relied upon.

To D. L. R.

January 1940

BROTHER OF MINE:

I find it most difficult to give a name to the glamour which holds back the full expression of your soul. I might perhaps call it the "glamour of continued circumstance." This leads to an almost unavoidable construction of a wall of small and unimportant events, of negligible contacts, of monotonously regulated and determined duties, carried forward year after year because they constitute your duty and life function and also provide the wherewithal whereby the needs of life can be met. These provide a slow moving glamour, behind which you conscientiously and laboriously stand and daily work. Such a state of affairs leads to a static situation and to a constant conditioning of your life expression. To this, your soul at times takes exception and will do so increasingly. For this you must be prepared. You must be ready for a certain feeling of nausea and of frustration as your life goes on and on along its predetermined lines. And for this nausea, you will find no real understanding in your environment. For this also you must be prepared and to accept it without criticism of those who fail to render you right comprehension.

Hitherto, you have regarded such moments of nausea as rebellion to be immediately suppressed; you have thrust from you all aspiration towards change, regarding it as a hindering glamour and seeking always to believe that your choice of the stable, the safe and the familiar is entirely right. Such choice has indeed been right at times, but it has not always been so in spite of the determination evidenced in your environment to hold you to the tried and the familiar.

Seek, my brother, at any cost, to be alive and eager for the future. Hide never behind the thought of past achievement or of achievement in some future life; learn to recognise opportunity when it stands before your thought and be ready to change the stable rhythms of a high grade and adequate personality for the eager forward looking attitude of a world disciple. Changes will then come because your inner attitude has prepared the way.

Sometimes, my brother, I wonder if you will recognise them, knowing them for what they are? Will you see the open door, leading to a fuller and a richer life? I call you to preparedness, and for freedom from the glamours of the familiar, of the family and of your surroundings.

August 1940

There are within you at this time, my brother, stirrings of revolution and rebellion which have in them the seeds of liberation. Does this astonish you? Of their depth and purpose you have as yet but little understanding. You must remember that rebellion may be based on purely selfish desire for a way of life which your personality may demand. But it can also be soul-produced, and such is the case with you. One of the first things which a disciple has to learn is the real nature of that which is directing him and conditioning him. With many it is some aspect of the personality or of the personality as a whole; in a few, it is the soul. With still others, the promptings may come from a sense of inferiority and its consequent reaction of a carefully considered defence mechanism; with still others, it may be circumstance, or the race mind or popular opinion or the people with whom they are associated through ancient ties, karmic liabilities or self-chosen responsibility. I will tell you here certain things which may aid you towards a fuller life and a deepened soul expression.

Your link with your soul is real and it was not achieved in this life. It is therefore one of the stable factors in your life. Your mind is of a high quality and is easily responsive to the intuition and illumination; you have your emotional or astral body well under control. On the inner planes of the personality, your life demonstration is good and you lead a faithful and progressive spiritual life—so much so that your vibration reaches *upward* so intensively at times as to sound within the periphery of the hierarchical sphere of influence. This is somewhat rare. But *outward* and *downward* (these inadequate expressions make the teaching hard to communicate) this is not the case. Your outgoing energy seems short circuited and your radiation is inadequate to your inner spiritual life. You will recall that I gave you the word "radiation" some years ago as your desired keynote. For years I have watched the intensification of your spiritual life upon the inner planes only to see it arrested on the eve of expression upon the plane of daily life. I refer not here to character expression or to being what people ordinarily call good. I refer to *effective radiation*.

What causes this, my brother? I would say: Outer circumstances, and two people in particular, plus an acutely sensitive receptivity to the mental and emotional life of others. Ponder on this. This sensitivity causes an arresting of physical expression, plus a mistaken interpretation of duty at times. Know you not, my brother, that those who are at the stage of accepted discipleship (as you are) should be radiating centres of light on a relatively large scale. With you this potency of radiation is present but is rendered ineffective by your reaction to the outer details of physical plane living and to the reactions of those less developed than you are. Is this a hard saying? Study it with the detachment you have so ably developed and you will find in due time that I am correct in my diagnosis.

Re-apply and re-interpret this virtue of detachment and much will be revealed to you. I shall not be more explicit. My function is to indicate direction, but it is for you to understand rightly and then react. Your initial interpretation given to my words may not be the right one in all cases. Usually the integration of the spiritual life and of the personality proceeds as follows:

1. The astral body integrates with the physical brain, via the etheric body and the solar plexus.
2. These two then integrate with the mental body and thus complete the personality expression.
3. This is followed after much struggle and time by the definite integration of personality and soul.

You have, however, carried the integration from the astral body to the mental body and from thence to the soul but have not yet succeeded in integrating these three with the physical man, dominating the brain and producing a vibrant expression of the inner man outwardly. This is somewhat rare a condition. Could you see yourself as you essentially are, you would make the acquaintance of a vibrant, radiant, wise disciple. But you hide all that behind a wall which has been built through your conditioning supersensitive nature and circumstances, and also by the influence of several people. Come out from behind that obstructing wall, my brother, and—for the sake of those whom you can serve—*be what you are.*

That this emergence on your part may bring its own problems is probably true, but with the results of right action (carried wisely and not fanatically forward) you have naught to do.

A brief visualisation exercise and meditation may aid in this process of emergence. It is well to bear in mind that the dramatisation of the spiritual life leads to creative appearance, strengthening the will-to-do, directing the desire nature in the right direction and producing effectiveness in physical plane expression. You will see, therefore, that when humanity can begin en masse to work in this manner, they will enter upon a cycle wherein evil karma will no longer be engendered and past karma will work out in experienced, spiritual living.

This meditation exercise should be carefully thought out before practising so that you can know just what you are attempting to do and can then do it with adequate results. I would ask you to do it twice daily, when convenient. I set no regular time. A year's steady practice (with belief, plus skill in action) may cause almost dramatic changes in your life.

1. Bring about focus in the soul of the potencies of the lower man by the power of the imagination and careful visualisation. This can be done by rapid, right alignment.

2. See the soul as a radiant sun within you (the personality hiding behind its rays). You, the real spiritual man, produce the veiling of the lower man.

3. See the rays of the sun extending first to the *mind* bringing illumination.

     Pause here and focus your consciousness in the mind. The work is done by projecting yourself along the ray of your personality and along your mental ray which is the fifth ray of concrete knowledge or science. This should be relatively easy for you.

4. Then see the rays of the soul (the sun of your life) extending and embracing your *astral* nature and irradiating the astral plane with which you are in contact, thus bringing an outpouring of love. This again should be relatively easy of accomplishment as your astral ray is the sixth ray of devotion and idealism.

5. Carry the radiation of the sun to the vital body and see it bringing (on the beam of the seventh ray of your physical nature) such a dynamic energising that you will have the power, figuratively speaking, to break through the wall which prevents the inner radiation extending into the outer physical world.

6. Then sound the O M softly seven times, concentrating upon the picture of this sun (which is you and your solar quality), thus irradiating the outer life.

This process should be fairly easy as all your rays tend to facilitate it. The process is also highly scientific for it is in reality the manipulation of radiant solar energy straight from "the heart of the sun," technically speaking. Work patiently along these lines and take with patience and courage the effects produced. For these you will be eternally grateful.

August 1942

1. Be not afraid of loneliness. The soul that cannot stand alone has naught to give.
2. Cut deep into the roots of all thy life. Seek freedom from the past. Yet move not from the plane where life has placed you in a part to play.
3. The rhythm of all life pulsates in time and space and in that rhythm you must find a note that liberates.
4. Ponder on the work of the Destroyer, why comes destruction and why the loss of beauty that has been. Your task in life should make that knowledge possible. Then build.
5. Be a sannyasin—free, alone with God, your soul and Me. Then work and love.
6. Your major life theme in this coming year is: Search freedom. Ponder on this. It is the goal for all.

September 1943

MY BROTHER:

As a Master studies His chelas year by year, He arrives at certain definite knowledges anent them which are very different to those arrived at by even the dearest or closest earthly friends. The latter are apt to fail in grasping life essentials, because the detail and the minute aspects of the daily expression attract attention and the surface is confounded with the depth. It is *the depth* which the Master sees; *the essential quality* which He grasps, and *the major need* which emerges.

What, my brother, lies at the very depth of your personality in this life? I refer not here to the deeps of the soul, but to the particular hidden thing which is and has been struggling for expression throughout this entire incarnation. What is your essential quality? Here I refer to the outstanding quality which, given due process of experience, will radiate from your life and thus constitute your major working asset. What is your predominant need this life? Reduce all this to the requirements for initiation (for which you are being prepared) and you come to three fundamental things which must be manifested, prior to that tremendous step forward upon the Path. You will note that I am not preoccupied with your mistakes or failures. These are inevitable and are relatively unimportant, because a disciple at your point of development is ever aware of them and can be trusted to take the needed steps toward adjustment.

For years I have watched you. You have made steady progress in all directions but have reached a point which it is necessary that all disciples reach, where a supreme effort, based on clear perception and insight, is essential. To aid you in making this supreme life effort, I would like to touch upon these three points. I must touch upon them in such a way that only you will comprehend the implications. There is no need for your group brothers, or any one else who may come across and read your papers, to grasp my meaning. Two factors of interest emerge here. In veiling (from the point of definite personal application) the truths I seek to have you grasp, I present to you a compromise between the Eastern method of hinting and the Western method of plain speaking! I am, at the same time, endeavouring to convey to you the attitude of all disciples in training for initiation. This attitude is one of extreme personal reticence and of withdrawing from those verbal contacts which reveal too much of individual soul growth. This is one of the first lessons in the silence which initiation entails. It is also one of the first steps towards comprehension of that "isolated unity" which is distinctive of the Master. In the Hierarchy there is complete unity, based upon a recognised isolation of spirit from matter. This thought should provide you with a theme for much profound thinking.

What, therefore, brother of mine, should be the unique realisation which this particular incarnation should help you to express? What lies at the depths of your being, seeking revelation? What is the essential quality which you should radiate? What is your outstanding need? I will tell you the truth as I see it, reminding you however that it is the truth as *you* see it which changes and conditions your life. You must therefore regard my suggestions as valuable, but regard them primarily as the subject of a defined spiritual investigation—to be carried forward with an open mind and a willingness to recognise them as correct and just when your own conclusions and your intuitive response justify your agreeing. Here are my conclusions:

1. *The hidden beauty* seeking expression in your life is the power to use words to arrest others and to put them, as a consequence, upon the Path of Return. This will undoubtedly surprise you, but your apparent inability to write, for instance, a fluent letter or an eloquent appeal, or to evoke the words of arresting power which you feel seething within you, are only indicative of a pronounced *personality* inhibition which you *can* overcome, if you so wish. Words are the expression of the soul, when rightly employed. You do not use those words. You can, if you determine to do so. The art of spiritual letter writing will release this inner beauty and enhance your service.

2. *The essential quality* which you should radiate is an understanding holding of those for whom you are responsible. I said "holding," brother of mine. A.A.B. has called my attention to the interesting fact that it is the rarest thing for you to lose a student out of your secretarial group, yet at the same time you write less and (apparently) upon the outer plane, do less, than the other secretaries. Why is this so? It is indicative of the quality which you radiate. This quality is in the

nature of a potency. It is the power to hold others steady by the nature of your understanding; this they feel, even if you do not consciously express it. It remains still basically subjective. A quality such as this —binding, forceful and enduring—carries its limitations as well as its benedictions. People can be held too closely to you for their own good, and it is ever the weaker who are thus held and the less advanced. People in this way can become dependent upon the one who holds, and thus fail to express themselves, and thus again their weaknesses are developed and a tendency to negativity. You can develop this theme yourself. But the beneficent aspect of this radiation is predominant in you and must be increased and this deliberately.

3. *Your major need* (and this you know) is freedom, is liberation. I do not mean freedom from incarnation or liberation from the pressures of life, but the freedom which the sannyasin knows as he roams free in the three worlds—unsupervised or unintruded upon by aught but his own soul. It is the freedom which gives mental help, emotional response and physical time as and when the disciple chooses. These are not evoked by habit or by the demand of others, but are the free contribution of the soul to a current need. Your response is not always to *need,* is it, my brother? Ponder on this.

In the six seed thoughts which I gave you a year ago, this theme of liberation, of a desirable divine loneliness, and of a search for a note that could bring freedom was a dominant one. They still should be the major subject of all your meditation work. I would suggest that for the coming year you take them as the seed thoughts for your definitely planned morning meditation. I am leaving you to do the planning, but would make one suggestion. These six thoughts will need to be taken one each month for six months, and then repeated for another six. For the first six months reflect upon them from the angle of your subjective realisation as a soul;

for the second six months study them from the angle of practical expression in your daily life.

I am anxious for you to make the grade this life, my brother, and here I am speaking technically. I am anxious for you to take the initiation planned by your own soul, and to take it this life, so that you can enter into your next incarnation with the initiate consciousness (of the grade desired), and thus start with greatly increased assets for service. I would remind you that initiation is taken alone; hence my emphasis to you during the past few years upon the need for you to travel alone—spiritually and mentally speaking. From other angles you travel *not* alone. The spiritual life is full of paradoxes. We set out to develop a sense of unity and of oneness with all beings, yet at times we must learn the lessons of loneliness and of isolation. A great "aloneness" is the supreme test of the fourth initiation. Remember this. Yet never, my brother, will you be alone, and this too you must have in mind. It is, in the last analysis, a question of recognitions. Let me assure you: I recognise you and, my brother and close friend on the inner side, I know you and love you.

November 1944

BROTHER OF MINE:

In what sense do I call you this? For this appellation conveys no idle statement but is of deep significance. It is particularly so in your case and in reference to your individual relation to me. My last instruction should have indicated to you how deep is my comprehension of you and your nature, and how well I understand your problems, your limitations and your assets. Every Master needs to have such an understanding and to know infallibly what is in a disciple's heart and mind; He must understand what motivates his action. When also there is a karmic tie as well as a spiritual one, when there is a recognition of unity of purpose, plus a past history of close relationship when the Master was also only a disciple and the disciple was only an aspirant, then the words "Brother of mine" take on a deeper meaning. They might indicate a steady moving forward, side by side, of a younger and an older brother, resulting in a consequent close relationship, easy contact and a deep comprehension. In this sense, therefore, my mode of addressing some of you is not simply significant of an occult truth but of an existent fact in the three worlds. There are four of you in this group who have such a relationship to me. It is—between us—an old story. Others in this group, as you know, are temporarily under my instruction until such time as they have fitted themselves to fill vacancies in other Ashrams; still others are, for the first time, making contact with me in my Ashram, having had no previous contact with any Ashram. I bring these points to your attention because I would have you utilise a possibility which remains as yet a hoped-for event in your case—the possibility of a realised, easy contact with me. It has always been possible for you to contact me with facility but you have seldom realised it. I want you now to realise it and to develop into outer expression what has always interiorly existed.

How, brother of mine, can you do this? One definite means of intensifying this inner recognition would be to avail yourself more fully of the period of the Full Moon approach. For years you have all been utilising this monthly opportunity but with relatively little results; this has somewhat surprised me for, on the side of the Ashram, there has been a great readiness for such an approach and an eagerness to stimulate "the process of absorption," as it is called. This is a process which serves to integrate the disciple regularly and cyclically into the consciousness of the Ashram, with subsequent and consequent results to the disciple.

I would ask you, therefore, each month and for the rest of your life to follow for three days a definite procedure. . . . I ask this because I believe you have that persistent staying power which is characteristic of all those whose personalities are on the ray which is yours. The procedure will involve putting yourself en rapport with my Ashram and to register it in your physical brain consciousness. You may not and probably will not succeed in this endeavour immediately, but in due course of time and with persistent effort you inevitably will. Think of me as you know me to be; let not your sixth ray devotional nature play any part in this process or contact. Bear in mind that first ray disciples are in my Ashram, and that there are aspects of my nature which are of first ray origin, but when you remember this, bear also in mind that the aspect to which I refer is Triadal.

The Masters have no personalities as you understand personality. Their conditioning factors are the three aspects of the Spiritual Triad, and these aspects, being creative, build the phenomenal apparatus or mechanism by means of which a Master makes contact with the three worlds. This means, consequently, that disciples will need to study with greater attention the teaching on the antahkarana, for it is via the antahkarana that they make contact with the Ashram and with the Master. Forget not that I have assured you that such a contact is relatively easy for you; the implications of this statement are clear. Let your reflection be upon the *purpose* of such a contact. Realise also that the intention of this work is to facilitate a great possibility which confronts you, that the urgency of the time demands "accomplished servers" and wise disciples, and that this urgency warrants an intensified training given disciples such as you. The contact with the Ashram will serve to emphasise in your mind the concept of yourself as the serving disciple. You are strong and able to take what the process requires; you can rest back on your own strength when it is implemented by an increasing clarity of vision. You see people and life more truly than you did when you were first affiliated with my group, and the last two years have brought about much change in this connection. Count on yourself and on your soul with greater confidence; move forward with surety towards the consummation of this life's effort.

I would call to your attention that in the instructions I gave you last year and in this one, you have a complete unit of teaching which can suffice you for the remainder of this life. Read both these instructions over once every month regularly, thus renewing your interest and your enthusiasm. It is interesting to observe that initiation is often taken (I might say it is usually taken) after passing the milestone of half a century. The reason is that if the disciple can produce the needed staying power and the required enthusiasm—by which I mean dynamic purpose—he can then be trusted to handle the powers conferred with wisdom, to display the needed poise, and to proceed upon his outward way with humility and caution.

I have told you much in these last two instructions; they consummate the teaching which I have given you since 1933. Ponder on them. Act upon them and then strengthen the Ashram and present to the Masters a wise server and a trained companion on the Way.

August 1946

My Disciple:

I would have you note the change in the manner in which I am addressing you. It has significance and my word to you in this instruction is simply this: Give to the years ahead a deep study in order to ascertain the implications and the opportunities that this word—given you at this particular time—implies; study the consequent effectiveness in contact (upward, inward, and outward, if one may use such inadequate terms!) that will result.

Occultly speaking, you stand alone; you lead a lonely life, for there is no single person in your environment who shares with you the same quality or grade of spiritual perception. This you may deny, for your life is very full. Life has its constant points of revelation, some of which we recognise, and others pass by unnoted. The revelation of a certain type of spiritual loneliness is one through which all disciples have to pass; it is a test of that occult detachment which every disciple has to master.

This solitariness has to be faced and understood, and it results in two realisations: first of all, a realisation of your exact point on the ladder of evolution, or on the Path; and secondly, an intuitive perception of the point in evolution of those we contact along the way of life. For quite a long time every disciple refuses to do either of these two things. A false humility, which in reality borders on a lack of truthfulness, keeps him from clear-eyed recognition of status—a recognition which necessarily involves more intelligence and sounds out no call to pride. Few too dare trust themselves to see their fellowmen as they really are, for fear of a critical spirit —so hard it is to develop the true practice of loving understanding which leads to the seeing of all people in truth, with their faults and their virtues, their pettiness and their grandeurs, and still to love them as before and even more.

This occult solitariness must be consciously developed by you, and not left to circumstances. It is a solitariness which rests on soul attainment and upon no spirit of separateness; it is a solitariness which boasts of many friends and many interruptions, but of these many, few—if any—are admitted to the point of sacred peace; it is a solitariness that shuts none out, but which withholds the secrets of the Ashram from those who seek to penetrate. It is, finally, a solitariness which opens wide the door into the Ashram.

This is the factor you need the most to cultivate at this time. It will necessitate a conscious and definite withdrawal of yourself, and at the same time will lead to a still warmer expression of love upon the outer plane of life.

The closing of this outer group may enable you the more easily to do this, and may deepen your inner life immeasurably. Welcome, therefore, this opportunity. As regards the outer group, I would ask you to keep in close touch, however, through correspondence, with J.S.P.; she is a group brother who sorely needs your strength and knowledge. She has suffered far more than any of you and sorely needs lifting into a sense of security and peace. I commend her to you, and she will be good for you as you for her.

As for your meditation work, my brother, I would have you adhere to the Full Moon procedure outlined earlier by me, and I would ask you to keep this practice up for the remainder of your life. I would have you add to this monthly work a daily practice, founded upon the theme of a chosen solitariness. Note the word "chosen." It is wiser to cultivate the quality of spiritual solitude than to have it forced upon you—as so often happens to so many. I will suggest only the themes for your meditation, leaving you to work out the form or procedure to suit yourself, or to do without any form if it seems better to you.

Themes For Meditation. One for each month, to be reviewed year by year.

1. The nature of solitude.
2. The difference between solitude, loneliness, separateness and isolation. I would refer you to Patanjali* who speaks of "isolated unity."
3. Solitude and the daily life.
4. Solitude and the soul.
5. Solitude as a quality of the interior life of an Ashram.
6. The solitude of spiritual perception.
7. The solitude necessitated by the service of the Plan.
8. Solitude as the background of a radiant life.
9. Solitude and contact with the Master.
10. The rewards of solitude.
11. The voices heard in the silence of solitude.
12. The silence of the Spheres.

In this solitude there is no morbidness, there is no harsh withdrawing, and there is no aspect of separateness. There is only the "place where the disciple stands, detached and unafraid, and in that place of utter quiet the Master comes and solitude is not."

---

*The Light of the Soul, Book III:50.

THE MYSTERIES

THE MYSTERIES

Great is the mystery of godliness!

The word went forth to all the sons of men, the Sons of God: Shew forth the signature of God. Leave this High Place and, in the outer realm of darkness, toil and serve; bring forth the Real; unveil the hidden depths of light. Reveal divinity.

Great is the mystery of thought!

The word went forth to all the sons of men, the Sons of God: Think on the past, the future, and on that which is today. Learn that through thought the *Way* into the innermost can stand revealed. God thought, and all the worlds emerged and ran their courses. Man, in his distant radiant past, before his life on earth, the past that was before all time and space, evolved a thought. Forth into the light of day he came and ran his course. He runs until today.

Great is the mystery of pain!

The word went forth to all the sons of men, the Sons of God: Learn through the struggle of earth life to choose the way that is the better—then the best. Evade not pain. Seek not the easiest way, which is not to be found. Tread then the *Way* which leads through sorrow, pain and dire distress to that High Place from which you came—the Place where God walks with the sons of men, who are the Sons of God. Before the august Presence, all pain shall disappear; sorrow shall fade away, and death shall triumph not. Beauty and goodness and the strength of God irradiate the face of men.

Great is the mystery of those who blaze the trail back to the Father's Home!

The word goes forth to all the sons of men, the Sons of God: Those who have reached the Portal of the Final Way must prove themselves and in their proving teach and lift those who would follow in their steps.

Thus down the ages have the sons of men, who are the Sons of God, embodied in themselves the Light which shines, the Strength which lifts and serves, the Love that evermore endures. They walked the *Way* of purity, the *Way* into the innermost. We follow after. They served their time. We seek to do the same.

Training for new age
discipleship is provided
by the *Arcane School.*
The principles of the
Ageless Wisdom are
presented through esoteric
meditation, study and
service as a *way of life.*

*Write to the publishers
for information.*

INDEX

A

Abode, settled place, need of disciple for, 722, 723, 724
Abstraction—
types, 268, 453, 454–455, 505, 693–694
See also Withdrawal.
Adepts—
evolutionary development, 252
See also Great White Lodge; Hierarchy; Masters.
Adeptship, initiation conferring, 467
Affirmation of a Disciple, use, 174–175
Affirmations with alignment, 723–724
After-death activities of New Seed Group members, 33–34
Age, significances, 644, 696–697, 742, 761–762
Ageless Wisdom, teaching, next stage, unfoldment, 314
Air, vital, 262, 266
Aligning, procedure, vision of, 399
Alignment—
acme, production, 129
at third initiation, 399–400
between personality and Spiritual Triad, 364
complete, of initiate, 399–400
cosmic, planetary and individual, exercise, 187
creative, of instinct, intellect, and intuition, 198
ease in, 143
group, 129, 198, 206–207, 267
in meditation. *See* Meditation, alignment.
in relation to antahkarana, 248
in telepathy, 154
individual, group, and planetary, production, 198
key to spiritual events, 349
need for, 128, 254
of—
concrete mind, Son of Mind, and abstract Mind, result, 399
disciple's centres, 128, 152–153, 198
eyes, 349
heart, mind, and will, 183

three planetary centres, 198
processes, 131, 152–153
relation to meditation, 198
results, 603, 604
with soul, results, 258, 364
Aloneness, great, test of fourth initiation, 759
Analysis, distinction from criticism, 705
Angel—
of the Presence, 13, 14, 32, 174, 431–433, 496, 554
Solar, relation to lunar forces, 55
Anima mundi, light of, 436
Antahkarana—
agency in alignment, 248
anchorage, 267
Ashrams upon, 416, 417
building, 59, 64, 180, 194, 198, 254, 270, 408, 416
channel for energies of Triad, 269, 378, 433
channel of spiritual will, 378, 749–750
completion by disciple, 193
connection between personality and Triad, 364
conscious construction, 236
constructed, brain registration, 348
creator of, 195
definitions, 193, 194, 195, 196
dual nature, 321
group, 8, 19, 73, 79, 267, 345
higher, creation, 106
human, development, 408
importance, 761
in meditation. *See* Meditation.
means of contact with Ashram and Master, 761
planetary, 189, 204
purpose, 194, 364
reference to in Formula One, 262, 266
reflection upon, 130
results, 46, 64, 128, 193, 236, 260, 378, 433
source, 195
symbols, 128, 193
teaching on, 195
understanding conveyed by, 341
use, 19, 144, 269, 274, 281, 399, 406, 414
with sun and black, 321

Consideration, stage in meditation, 139–140

Contact—
and approach, mechanism, 72
impression, and relationship, capacity, increase, 486–487
impression, and relationship, meditation on, 489–491

Contacts and development of resultant mechanism, 484

Contemplation—
attainment, 213, 401
concentrated, static point, 419
of significances, 420
results, 213

Continuity of consciousness. *See* Consciousness, continuity.

Conversion, true, "blinding Light" accompanying, 327

Cooperation—
blended, of seventh Ray energies, 426
in externalisation of Master D.K.'s Ashram, 141
of disciple with Plan, 138
of Lord of the World and Council, 427
with D.K., 138

Cosmic
astral plane, entrance, 292
astral plane, work from, 189
centres, energy from, receiving station, 520
etheric body, energies permeating, 403
etheric levels, lowest, 405
levels, penetration and revelations, 435
mental levels, work of planetary Logos, 385

Council—
at Shamballa, communication with, 104
Chamber at Shamballa—
aid to, 202
contact with Extra-Planetary Beings, 197
Lords of, creative meditation, 209
understanding, 172
work, 147
Chamber of Sanat Kumara, relation with, 137
Great, of Shamballa, recruits, 518
of planetary Logos, functioning, 565

Courage, need for, 42–43

Creation—
by meditation, 182–183, 198, 200, 207–239
by initiate, 313
duality, 467
meditative, process, diagram, 213–214
needed, in field of divine activity, 432
of his own cross by disciple, 189
processes, 224
star of, 377
techniques, 346
under direction of Ashram, 693

Creative—
activity, planned, 347
activity, relation to acting "as if", 554–555, 556–558
Aspect, universal, Formulas from, 365
faculty, expression, 539
imagination. *See* Imagination, creative.
living, 532
meditation. *See* Meditation, creative.
process, 306–307, 311, 345
work, 177, 218–224, 344, 363, 461–463, 582

Creativity—
centres concerned, 122
for Master, 348
in meditation, 200–203, 207–224, 235–236
revelation, 323, 367
significance, 539–540

Creator, Voice, blending of planetary meditation with, 224

Crises—
bringing about fitness to take initiation, 70
handling by disciple, 13–14
in life, 533–534, 689
of initiation, 351
of planetary Logos, 70
types, 428, 430, 636, 637–638

Crisis—
of expression, 644–645
of opportunity, 644
points, 22–23, 247, 293, 538–539
present world (November, 1944), peculiar problem, 504

Criticism—
effect on telepathic interplay, 20
spirit, avoidance, 705

Cross—
creation by disciple, 189
seven stations, 472

Intuitional—Continued
  meditative focus, 220
  perception of soul, 252
  plane, 370
  sensitivity, definition, 514
Intuitive—
  appeal for will-to-good, 160
  focussed perception displacing
    vision, 512
  ideas. *See* Ideas, intuitive.
  insight, 175, 366
  instinct, 267
  perception, 47, 105, 106, 176,
    312, 364, 415, 762
  recognition, results of reflection
    upon formulas, 263–264
Invocation—
  and evocation, 210–211, 216–218,
    322, 424
  distribution, 150–151
  Great, 148–150, 157–176, 179,
    187–189
  of—
    Christ, 426
    intuition by hints, 413
    light, love, and will-to-good, 160
    revelation by group, 355
    Sanat Kumara by "seeds of
      life", 287
    Shamballa, 217
    soul, 479
    Spiritual Triad, 59
  results, 170
  "sons of men are one", 117, 146–
    147
  invocative appeal, oldest in world,
    304–305
  potency, seed of, 400
Irritation, intense, emotional, cause,
  526

J

J.W.K-P, letters to, 588–599
Japanese, knowledge of thought
  power, 62
Jesus, Master, cooperation with
  Christ, 406
Jewel in the Lotus—
  awakening, 249
  revelation, 250
  See also Lotus.

K

K.H. *See* Koot Hoomi, Master.
Karma—
  agent, 538
  cessation, 340, 558
  creation and precipitation, 322
  dealing with, 538, 558

definitions, 540, 578
effect of love, 541
in life of disciple, 736
in service, 492–493
liberation from, 340
misconception regarding, 189
nature of, 365
no longer engendered, 349, 754
obliteration, 340
of disciple, 189, 480–481, 538,
  601–602, 607
of relation to D.K.'s Ashram, 540
planetary, 350
relation to creation, 540
revelation regarding, prophecy,
  323
theme, qualities behind, 538
working out in Shamballa, 578
See also Law of Cause and Effect;
  Law of Karma.
Karmic—
  Law, function of Nirmanakayas,
    206
  obligation, field of functioning in,
    744
  relation never broken, 558
Keynotes, daily, for twelve months,
  716–717
Kingdom of God—
  definition, 407–408
  door into, symbol, 52
  on Earth, 184, 406–408, 432
Kingdoms in nature—
  four, relation of initiate to, 438
  lower, effects of humanity, 217,
    224, 327
Knowledge—
  acquisition, 393–394
  and wisdom, 279, 403
  concern and recovery, 279
  contrast with wisdom, 279
  of initiate, 279, 282, 307
  origin, 396
  petals. *See* Lotus, egoic, knowl-
    edge petals.
  simplification in hint, 414–416
  soul, 394
  transformation, 394–395
  transmutation, 248
Koot Hoomi (K.H.), Master—
  approach, 613
  Ashram—
    attacks, repercussions, 177
    entrance, 565
    freedom of Shamballa, 564
    work, 596, 609
  assistance by Master D.K., 563
  discussion with, 470, 606
  impressions from, 612

M